Slapstick: An Interdisciplinary Companion

Slapstick: An Interdisciplinary Companion

Edited by
Ervin Malakaj and Alena E. Lyons

DE GRUYTER

ISBN 978-3-11-125544-6
e-ISBN (PDF) 978-3-11-057198-1
e-ISBN (EPUB) 978-3-11-057097-7

Library of Congress Control Number: 2021938530

Bibliographic information published by the Deutsche Nationalbibliothek
The Deutsche Nationalbibliothek lists this publication in the Deutsche Nationalbibliografie;
detailed bibliographic data are available on the Internet at http://dnb.dnb.de.

© 2023 Walter de Gruyter GmbH, Berlin/Boston
This volume is text- and page-identical with the hardback published in 2021.
Cover image: Luiza Folegatti and Cleo Wächter
Typesetting: Integra Software Services Pvt. Ltd.
Printing and binding: CPI books GmbH, Leck

www.degruyter.com

Acknowledgements

This project began as a random exchange among colleagues about the striking commonality of some texts of the German-language late classical, romantic, and the Biedermeier period: "slapstick" seemed to us at that moment the most obvious description for the sometimes comic, sometimes tragic excesses in works by, among others, Heinrich von Kleist (1777–1811), E.T.A. Hoffmann (1776–1823), or Annette von Droste-Hülshoff (1797–1848), which usually only relate loosely to each other. It was this fortuitous find that brought us in conversation with excellent scholars across fields and at different stages of their careers.

We are deeply saddened by the untimely death of Laura Isakov in 2020, who was a PhD Student at the University of British Columbia and served as research assistant, as well as translator from German into English for a number of the contributions in this volume. Portions of this project would not be in the shape they are were it not for Laura's dedication to the work. We write with gratitude and will cherish our memories of working with Laura on this project.

We are grateful for a number of institutions, which in various ways supported the research, writing, and editorial work of this project. First, we would like to thank the Department of Central, Eastern, and Northern European Studies at the University of British Columbia (UBC). In particular, we would like to express gratitude for the UBC Scholarly Publication Fund, which helped offset publication costs for the volume. We would like to thank the UBC Faculty of Arts for providing additional funding for research assistantships.

Next, we would like to thank our colleagues at De Gruyter: Myrto Aspioti, Marcus Böhm, Stella Diedrich, Anja-Simone Michalski, and Antonia Mittelbach. They have supported our project at various stations over the course of four years. Their review, recommendations, and the organization of an anonymous peer review of the volume all improved the book exponentially. Here we would also like to thank Luiza Folegatti and Cleo Wächter for the cover image.

Maggie Hennefeld's chapter in our volume, titled "Slapstick Comediennes in Silent Cinema: Women's Laughter and the Feminist Politics of Gender in Motion," was initially published as Chapter 13 of *The Routledge Companion to Cinema and Gender*, edited by Kristin Lené Hole, Dijana Jelača, E. Ann Kaplan, and Patrice Petro. We would like to thank the editors of the Routledge volume, as well as Routledge/Taylor & Francis Group for permission to reprint the chapter in our volume.

Our special thanks go to the contributors to this volume who have shared their perspectives, research, and ideas with great openness to collaborative and interdisciplinary work. Through their diverse scholarly backgrounds, they have facilitated the coming together of literary studies, film history, theology, musicology, queer, Jewish, and disability studies, and the visual arts. We thank them all for their contributions, as well as the good, intensive collaboration and for their patience.

Ervin Malakaj would like to express his gratitude to Siham Bouamer, Katia Bowers, Kyle Frackman, and Ilinca Iurascu for their ongoing support. Their friendship and expert guidance were invaluable in navigating the work that went into this volume. Most importantly, Ervin would like to thank his partner, Gary Kujawinski, whose unyielding support made the work on this volume possible. Finally, Darlene has been an inimitable research companion and, as such, deserves to be recognized.

Alena E. Lyons's gratitude goes to those dear friends and colleagues who have accompanied the progress of this project with exciting conversations, good wine, unabated interest, and a large portion of positive energy, especially Anne Brannys, Katrin Gellrich, Ingrid Oehm, Arno Schmittel, Michel op den Platz, Maik-Sören Hanicz, Daniela Reich, and Markus J. Roick. She is deeply indebted to Luiza Folegatti for allowing her extensive insights into her projects, her ideas, and thoughts over the years. Folegatti was patiently available for short questions as well as long conversations and generously provided a number of her photographs to be reproduced in this volume. Finally, she would like to thank those people who, in truth, cannot be thanked, and who know what a slapstick life is: her mother Edeltraud Lyons and her sister Wiebke Lyons, without whose extensive support, great kindness, and above all love and humor, neither the work on this project would have been possible nor the ideas that have been incorporated here.

Contents

Acknowledgements —— V

Ervin Malakaj & Alena E. Lyons
Introduction: Interdisciplinary Approaches to Slapstick —— 1

Part I: History of Slapstick

Alena E. Lyons & Ervin Malakaj
Introduction —— 11

Paul Michael Babiak
The Descent of Slapstick —— 15

Peter Edwards
Ideology, Performance, and Ironic Distance in Musical Slapstick —— 37

Carolin Struwe-Rohr
Sinking and Falling Bodies: The Beginnings of Literary Slapstick in the Pre-Modern Era —— 53

Part II: Instruments of Slapstick

Alena E. Lyons & Ervin Malakaj
Introduction —— 73

Sebastian Hauck
The Broken Mirror: From *Commedia All'Improvviso* to Slapstick Comedy —— 79

Courtney Andree
Harold Lloyd and the Reappearing Hand: Disability, Embodiment, and Slapstick —— 101

Addie Tsai
Wardrobe Malfunction and Slapstick Humiliation in The Lonely Island's
Popstar: Never Stop Never Stopping —— 121

Alena E. Lyons
Gazing at Slapstick with Luiza Folegatti's Drag King Series *O Deleite da Mulher Barbada* —— 139

Part III: Narrative Structures of Slapstick

Alena E. Lyons & Ervin Malakaj
Introduction —— 161

Alexander Kling
Telling and Showing: Slapstick in Stephan Schütze's Comic Theory and Heinrich von Kleist's *Der zerbrochne Krug* —— 165

Claudia Sassen & Stefan Schroeder
A Constraint-Based Approach to the Slapstick Seriality in Larry Semon Comedies, 1918–1920 —— 187

Claudia Sassen
The Anonymized Randomness of Vicco von B.: On Chaos and Order in Loriot's Agfa Advertisements —— 215

Part IV: Bodies of Slapstick

Ervin Malakaj & Alena E. Lyons
Introduction —— 245

Caroline Frank
The Tragicomic Body: On the Relation between Tragicomedies and Slapstick —— 249

Irina Hron
'Or Words to That Effect': The Antimetaphysics of Slapstick —— 269

Valerie Weinstein
Gender and Jewish Difference in Early German Slapstick —— 293

Part V: Politics of Slapstick

Ervin Malakaj & Alena E. Lyons
Introduction —— 311

Maggie Hennefeld
Slapstick Comediennes in Silent Cinema: Women's Laughter and the Feminist Politics of Gender in Motion —— 315

Ervin Malakaj
Lubitsch's Queer Slapstick Aesthetics —— 333

Ignacio M. Sánchez Prado
The Slapstick of Greater Mexico: The Poetics and Politics of Eugenio Derbez —— 351

Jiří Hoblík
Interpersonal and Social Sensibility in Slapstick from the Perspective of Religious History —— 367

Part VI: Sticking to the Slap: The Contact Points of Slapstick

Alena E. Lyons & Ervin Malakaj
Closing Remarks: Creating Openings —— 389

Anne Brannys
Each One, Who Falls – A Conversation —— 391

Contributors —— 407

Index —— 411

Ervin Malakaj & Alena E. Lyons
Introduction: Interdisciplinary Approaches to Slapstick

Commedia dell'arte, a variety of sixteenth-century improvisational Italian theater (see Chaffee and Crick 2015, 1–4), frequently forms a point of departure for scholarship on slapstick comedy. The *battacio*, "a slapstick made of two short slender pieces of wood bound at the handle" (Preeshl 2017, 262), was a *commedia* prop an actor could use to exaggerate for audiences the effect of hitting another actor. With little force, an actor could simulate physical violence on stage, which was followed by a hyperbolic performance of pain. The climax of the scene, which is conditioned by a steadily intensifying situation, is additionally characterized by the moment of shock: the sound accompanying the slap enhances the moment of performed pain and produces a rupture in the narrative. At first, this rupture jolts spectators into astonishment; however, audiences immediately find repose in the realization that all is well on stage, that the pain was performed and exaggerated, and that the characters are able to endure and overcome it (see Peacock 2013). Collectively, the scene stimulates laughter.

We, too, see the *commedia* as an important starting point for a framing of the undertaking in this project. Its emphasis on the material conditions of humor (see Henke 2015), the politics of the performance of pain (see Peacock 2014, 129–131), and the investment in narrative rupture inform the lines of inquiry taken up by the contributors to this volume in some fashion. More importantly, a link to the *commedia* in scholarship on slapstick served as the inspiration for the volume at hand in a very specific way. In their now classic comparative study *The Triumph of Pierrot: The Commedia dell'Arte and the Modern Imagination* (1986), Martin Green and John Swan examined the many influences between the *commedia* and modern forms of performance including slapstick cinema, on the one hand, and then the cross-influence between modern slapstick performers and other cultural practitioners (e.g., dramaturgs, stage actors, and dancers), on the other. For them, these complex paths of influence and cross-influence constitute "much traffic" that is worthy of scholarly attention (Green and Swan 1993, 119). It is this "traffic" in ideas that inspires the various approaches to slapstick collected here in this volume.

Slapstick, as understood by the editors of and contributors to this volume, can be found in many places and in many forms. For one, it can be found in familiar places and forms, i.e., the physical film comedies popular in the 1910s and 1920s. Take, for instance, the iconic motorcycle chase from Buster Keaton's (1895–1966) *Sherlock Jr.* (1924). The film's protagonist, a projectionist and janitor played by Keaton, falls asleep on the job and imagines himself in the role of the detective Sherlock Jr. On the run and pursued by a gangster, Sherlock Jr. is stopped by a police officer. The film's protagonist is in luck. The officer turns out to be his assistant Gillette (Ford West) in disguise. Sherlock Jr. jumps on the steering wheel and the two escape together. Shortly thereafter, Gillette falls off the bike without Sherlock Jr. noticing. In fact, Sherlock Jr. remains on the steering wheel, driving full speed ahead. In this sequence, shot after shot brings new adventures in which Sherlock Jr. comes very close but always evades a fatal end (see Knopf 1999, 73–74). He speeds by cars without hitting them, crosses an intersection without getting into a car accident (although he nearly causes accidents for others), crosses the train tracks in just the right moment so as not to get hit by the train. When the motorcycle collides against a pile of wood, Sherlock Jr. is catapulted off the bike, through the window, and into a house. As he lands on the table, his feet jolt the villain holding a hostage out of the house and incapacitate him. Sherlock Jr. saves the hostage and miraculously avoids any harm in an otherwise quite dangerous set of circumstances. At each station, his excessive luck – augmented by Keaton's flailing hands and expressive facial gestures – stimulates laughter.

The contributors to the volume who study this familiar type of slapstick comedy seek to activate it for current scholarly discourse in crucial ways. In this vein, some contributors to this volume ask, What feminist or queer potential lies at the core of classical slapstick cinema? What insights can disability studies yield when used as a main approach to classical slapstick cinematic performance? What role did print culture play in shaping classical slapstick comedy cultures?

Slapstick can also be found in the long tradition of slapstick performance that emerged in the aftermath of the early film comedies. Take, for instance, the 1976 television sketch "Zimmerverwüstung" ["Room Devastation"] by German comedian Loriot (also known as Vicco von Bülow, 1923–2011). It shows a chain reaction of unfortunate events set off by the protagonist's attempt to fix a crooked picture, leaving the room devastated by the end of the three-minute sketch (see Kling 2018). The protagonist's accidents that set off and stimulate a chain of failure to navigate the physical setting of the room delight in exaggeration: from one breaking object to the next one falling, the ridiculousness of the situation intensifies, and the scene ultimately stimulates laughter. In this regard, the contributors to this volume consider materiality and embodiment as crucial qualities of a recognizable slapstick-like aesthetic that can be traced across media and across cultural history.

Slapstick also lives beyond visual culture. For example, Kurt Vonnegut (1922–2007) found inspiration for his 1976 novel *Slapstick* (also known by the title *Lonesome No More!*) in the comedy of Stan Laurel (1890–1965) and Oliver Hardy (1892–1957). Vonnegut noted that Laurel and Hardy's commitment to the affective force produced and stimulated by slapstick scenarios helped him capture the grotesque, unpredictable pain characterizing modern life, on the one hand; on the other, slapstick helped him convey the insistent regularity by which characters condemned to fail at the world are able to get back up and move on, using humor as a strategy to overcome hardship (see Klinkowitz 2004, 112–113). That is, Vonnegut is not explicitly committed to the physical comedy familiar from slapstick cinema, but is inspired to deploy the reverberations characteristic of slapstick gags – i.e., the force emanating from the effect of one actor's use of the slapstick on another actor – as a model for scenarios in which characters are at the mercy of life's forces.

In this vein, contributors to the volume ask, What effects do slapstick-like gags and ruptures yield in literature? What function does slapstick serve in musical performance? What valence does it have for new media? Such a broadening of the scope of slapstick – i.e., both in terms of methodologies to approach classical slapstick film comedies and slapstick features in cultural production broadly – stimulates approaches that collectively produce insights about slapstick's many lives and purposes. This volume indeed celebrates slapstick's malleability and plurality. To do so, it studies slapstick from an interdisciplinary perspective.

In this context, the necessity of an interdisciplinary investigation pertains to the subject matter itself. Consider, for instance, approaches to slapstick as a film genre. Film in and of itself is a highly complex medium whose scholarly study had to be interdisciplinary from the beginning. Thus, the institutionalization of film studies in the 1960s (see Grieveson and Wasson 2008) drew insights and methods from various disciplines (in this case, theater and performance studies, sociology, psychology, literary studies, and philosophy, among others). According to Heinz Heckhausen's conceptualizations of interdisciplinarity, film studies can be understood as "unifying interdisciplinarity" (qtd. in Jungert 2013, 6). With this concept, Heckhausen aims to describe the convergence of disciplinary methods and theories in such a way that a clear disciplinary separation among them can no longer be ascertained. Out of this process, a new discipline emerges.

If the film genre of slapstick is first and foremost a subject of study for an interdisciplinary discipline such as film studies (but, beyond this, also performance studies, musicology, etc.), then slapstick is an object of study that can only be comprehensively examined by means of diverse scholarly methods and theories. This is especially true for those aspects of slapstick that reach beyond its expression in film, such as slapstick's pre-film origins in various theater traditions. This is also the case for studies that examine the socio-culturally specific qualities enacted in slapstick in particular moments of cultural history, as well as developments triggered by slapstick but deployed in other cultural and media contexts. Finally, this is also especially true for elements of slapstick, which in turn connect it to other cultural products, such as studies that examine various expressions of humor and the comic across cultural history. It is this immense complexity of slapstick that necessitates interdisciplinary approaches, which enable methods that can grasp its wide terrain.

We understand this volume, on the one hand, as an example of the interdisciplinarity that Heckhausen theorizes, insofar as diverse disciplines, methods, etc. are brought together to study slapstick. The main aim here is to demonstrate how certain limitations afforded by one method are complemented with tools and concerns qualifying approaches as defined by another. For instance, insights from theology and religious history help shed light on concerns about humility as articulated in the experience of the slapstick protagonist in ways previously understudied by scholars solely approaching the subject from the perspective of established approaches to slapstick. On the other hand, we understand this volume as an example of "supplementary interdisciplinarity" (qtd. in Jungert 2013, 6), insofar as a large part of the research areas applied here are already strongly interdisciplinarily constituted (e.g., queer theory, Jewish studies, and disability studies).

Thus, on the one hand, our interdisciplinary approach arises from the research object of slapstick itself, and on the other hand, it is the approach of interdisciplinarity decidedly applied to slapstick that enables new insights into slapstick, but also into the backgrounds, and contexts in which slapstick had not been located before.

Approaches to slapstick present in this volume view slapstick both as a genre of situational physical comedy and as a mode of communicating an affective situation as captured in various cultural products across various periods in cultural history. Contributors to the volume examine cinematic, literary, dramatic, musical, new media, and photographic texts and performances. From medieval chivalric romance, to the nineteenth-century theater, to contemporary photography, the contributors study the treatment of slapstick across media, periods, and geographic locations. The aim of adopting such a broad perspective is to illustrate as many approaches to slapstick as possible. In fact, we see these various approaches to slapstick as rehearsed in individual chapters of the volume as starting points for additional scholarship. They are invitations to future slapstick scholars to think with contributors about the various lives that slapstick lived and continues to live across cultural history.

We are particularly indebted to the work of Donald Crafton. His discussion of gags in slapstick cinema has shown how gags stand in a contentious relationship to the narrative that houses them (Crafton 1995). In fact, Crafton suggests that that gags indeed can stand on their own and produce laughter without the narrative that seeks to explain them. As such, gags lay claim to a semi-autonomous status that can follow a logic sometimes at odds with the logic of the narrative to which it belongs. For us, this capacity of slapstick's constitutive components to serve a function that is out of line of the narrative logic in which it is embedded creates interpretive openings. It prompts us to embrace slapstick's playfulness and daring willfulness as driving forces for studying slapstick across time and place and to deploy insights about slapstick to cultural histories where some might not have thought it productive to do so.

The volume is divided into six sections: "History of Slapstick," "Instruments of Slapstick," "Narrative Structures of Slapstick," "Bodies of Slapstick," "Politics of Slapstick," and a concluding section featuring a creative contribution reflecting on the range of interdisciplinary approaches to slapstick captured in the volume. Each section will be prefaced by a short introduction by the editors, who outline its most central aims and offer brief summaries of each chapter. For us, these sections represent the broad components for an interdisciplinary approach to slapstick studies. Each offers case studies that are intended as heuristics for ongoing scholarship on the topic.

In the first section, "History of Slapstick," the contributors are preoccupied with slapstick's complex relation to cultural history. Slapstick's history is far from straightforward, even if some trans-historical continuities can be established (e.g., the link between the *commedia dell'arte* and slapstick cinema of the teens and 1920s). In this regard, the contributors to the section collectively suggest that slapstick has many histories. From the print cultures that shaped slapstick discourse in American slapstick cinema of the teens and 1920s, to the extensive history of slapstick in musical theater and opera, to slapstick's functions in pre-modern literature, the section offers a rich exploration of select slapstick histories.

The section, "Instruments of Slapstick" turns to individual constitutive components of slapstick such as mirrors, prosthetic devices, masks, and theatrical props to investigate the centrality of objects to the slapstick operation in drama, film, new media, and photography. Objects have been central features of slapstick's humor economy. As such, they can be vital focus points for interdisciplinary approaches to slapstick that consider a plethora of effects that slapstick objects set into motion. In this section, contributors examine how slapstick objects help us make sense of disorientation, disability, humiliation, and empowerment in slapstick across different media. They ask us to consider the vitality of objects to animate scenarios in which characters confront their deepest existential and social anxieties.

In "Narrative Structures of Slapstick," the contributors examine various constitutive components of slapstick narrative. They consider the tension between slapstick's narrative structure and the function of gags along the lines of Crafton's insistence that gags can live lives without a need to be subsumed under the auspices of narrative. In this regard, the chapters that comprise this section focus on telling and showing, seriality, and randomness as key features for an analysis of slapstick narrative in drama, cinema, and comic advertisements.

In "Bodies of Slapstick," the contributors study the physicality and politics of embodiment at the core of slapstick comedy. The slapstick subject's body is a site at which the vagaries of life are negotiated. This body is simultaneously a locus of suffering and resistant to violence (i.e., by the logic of the genre, slapstick bodies are resistant to the harms that befall its characters). This agility in the face of violent force offers a means to tackle various burdens humans face living in a world of commodities. The contributors to this section study the slapstick body's capacity to give voice to tragedy and comedy at once, its generic predisposition to be deployed in narrative situations in which it questions the limits of physicality, and reflect on its status as a site in which cultural difference registers. These contributions analyze stage plays and cinematic texts, examining the medial specificities of each in deploying the slapstick body to different ends.

In "Politics of Slapstick," a series of studies considers the political valence at the core of slapstick. Women's laughter, queer aesthetics, transnational humor, and religious qualities of key slapstick figures are at the core of these studies. In particular, the contributors to this section consider slapstick's predisposition to excess as a key means by which politics can come into view or through which they can be constituted. Extreme situations, vulgarity, and hyperbolic acting, among other related features, are starting points for commentaries about the political. The contributors do not address the politics related to governing populations. Instead, their chapters reflect quotidian relations among people and the type of politics that shape them.

The final section provides an artistic reflection on the many approaches to slapstick in this volume. We hope that this reflection, as well as the contributions by scholars from various fields, will stimulate ongoing inquiries into the many lives of slapstick.

Bibliography

Chaffee, Judith, and Olly Crick. Eds. *The Routledge Companion to Commedia dell'Arte*. New York: Routledge, 2015.

Crafton, Donald. "Pie and Chase: Gag, Spectacle and Narrative in Slapstick." *Classical Hollywood Comedy*. Eds. Kristine Brunovska Karnick and Henry Jenkins. New York: Routledge, 1995. 106–119.

Green, Martin, and John Swan. *The Triumph of Pierrot: The Commedia dell'Arte and the Modern Imagination*. University Park: Pennsylvania State University Press, 1993.

Grieveson, Lee, and Haidee Wasson. "The Academy and Motion Pictures." *Inventing Film Studies*. Eds. Lee Grieveson and Haidee Wasson. Durham: Duke University Press, 2008. xi–xxix.

Henke, Robert. "Form and Freedom: Between Scenario and Stage." *The Routledge Companion to Commedia dell'Arte*. Eds. Judith Chaffee and Olly Crick. New York: Routledge, 2015. 21–29.

Jungert, Michael. "Was zwischen wem und warum eigentlich? Grundsätzliche Fragen der Interdisziplinarität." *Interdisziplinarität: Theorie, Praxis, Probleme*. Eds. Michael Jungert, Elsa Romfeld, Thomas Sukopp, and Uwe Voigt. Darmstadt: Wissenschaftliche Buchgesellschaft, 2013. 1–12.

Klinkowitz, Jerome. *The Vonnegut Effect*. Columbia: The University of South Carolina Press, 2004.

Kling, Alexander. "Aus dem Rahmen fallen: Dingtheorie, Narratologie und das Komische (Platon, Vischer, Loriot)." *Das Verhältnis von res und verba*. Eds. Martina Wernli and Alexander Kling. Freiburg: rombach litterae, 2018. 309–332.

Knopf, Robert. *The Theater and Cinema of Buster Keaton*. Princeton: Princeton University Press, 1999.

Peacock, Louise. "Conflict and Slapstick in *Commedia dell'Arte*: The Double Act of Pantalone and Arlecchino." *Comedy Studies* 4 (2013): 59–69.

Peacock, Louise. *Slapstick and Comic Performance: Comedy and Pain*. New York: Palgrave, 2014.

Preeshl, Artemis. *Shakespeare and Commedia dell'Arte*. New York: Routledge, 2017.

Part I: **History of Slapstick**

Alena E. Lyons & Ervin Malakaj
Introduction

Slapstick's sometimes crude material devised to reach broad audiences could be read as universally appealing. On the one hand, such universality suggests that slapstick's gags, for instance, are legible as humorous and elicit laughter in any cultural setting across time; on the other, claims to universality assert that, for example, the humbling frailness of the slapstick protagonist purports to share the spectators' profound anxieties about modern life. However, such totalizing assumptions overlook slapstick's historicity. In so doing, they risk obstructing attempts to locate expressions of slapstick in concrete socio-cultural contexts, as the following example illustrates.

From July 2013 to February 2014, the Kunstmuseum Wolfsburg [Wolfsburg Art Museum] presented the exhibition *Slapstick! Alÿs, Bock, Chaplin, Hein, Laurel & Hardy, Keaton, Matta-Clark u.a.* [Slapstick! Alÿs, Bock, Chaplin, Hein, Laurel & Hardy, Keaton, Matta-Clark et al.], curated by Uta Ruhkamp. This exhibition aimed to bring iconic scenes from slapstick films from the silent film era in dialogue with contemporary art. In each exhibit, a scene from a slapstick film was juxtaposed with a work of art that in some way or other took up elements of the scene and transformed them. For example, Steve McQueen's (*1969) video installation "Deadpan" (1997) was shown together with Buster Keaton's (1895–1966) hurricane scene from *Steamboat Bill, Jr.* (1928, Dir. Charles F. Reisner), to which McQueen's approximately four-minute video explicitly refers. Starting with a clear definition of slapstick as a primarily US-American comedic film genre from the 1910s and 1920s, the Kunstmuseum Wolfsburg made it possible for exhibition visitors to recontextualize classic slapstick films by seeing them in dialogue with individual works of contemporary art, which in turn encouraged audiences to take on new perspectives on the 'original' slapstick as well as its legacy today.

In a 2013 clip advertising the exhibition to the public, art historian and then director of the museum Markus Brüderlin (1958–2014) simultaneously gestures toward but also flattens what otherwise was a sophisticated, trans-historically situated exhibition. By means of an anecdote he invites the audience to reflect on the peculiarly unpredictable interrelationship between laughter and slapstick films:

> [T]he filmmaker and theatre man, Robert Wilson, once did an experiment [. . .]: he confronted young people from an African tribe [. . .] with these slapstick films – and they cried. And then he confronted them with the mountains of corpses in concentration camps – and they laughed. Maybe it's a very good example that allows us to think about laughter. (form-art.tv 2013, TC 00:01:50–00:02:31, translated by Alena E. Lyons)

Regardless of which work of the US-American dramatist and video artist Robert Wilson (*1941) Brüderlin references, Brüderlin appears committed to differentiate among comedy, laughter, humor, and slapstick. His description suggests that slapstick is, in fact, not universal; its non-Western reception is radically different from what Western viewers would expect. But the framing of his claims is highly problematic. The example he uses overtly adopts a colonial-racist perspective: channeling Wilson, Brüderlin evokes an exotic image of faraway Africa at some indeterminate point in history, and of young Africans whose reactions to Western images are the opposite of what is seemingly intended. Furthermore, the example posits that American slapstick and the piles of dead bodies in German concentration camps are extreme poles of what human beings can produce and to which human beings can react as human beings. Presented as extremely different from Western reactions, the reactions of the young people in Wilson's experiment bring these separate and incompatible poles together in a way that for Brüderlin helps to shape a new perspective on what slapstick can or cannot do in terms of laughter. But even if this example illustrates that slapstick is more complex than we thought (i.e., different audiences respond to it differently), it does so using extreme examples in a totalizing fashion without attending to the complex social and cultural histories behind them.

The last decade has seen a rise in the scholarship on slapstick that explores the historical and cultural conditions that shaped different slapstick traditions. Tom Paulus's and Rob King's anthology *Slapstick Comedy* (2010), for example, presents a sophisticated overview of the genre's history with contributions studying a broad variety of elements relating to US slapstick cinema and link these to the cultural context of early-twentieth-century modernization. King's monograph *Hokum!* (2017) likewise focuses on early twentieth-century slapstick, with a specific interest in the 1920s. King studies the technological and historical conditions that informed the emerging sound film against the backdrop of the Great Depression. Both studies are interested in, among other ideas, the growing technologization of modern life and slapstick's investment in reflecting its constitutive elements. A few more recent publications are increasingly concerned with the role of neglected groups of people involved in slapstick, such as women (see e.g., Ellenbürger 2015; Massa 2017; Hennefeld 2018). In addition, scholars such as Louise Peacock (2014 & 2019), Bryony Dixon (2010) or Jeffrey Richards (2015), consider the prehistory of slapstick. Their research concerns the relation between slapstick and European theatrical or other performance traditions, in particular those of the nineteenth century, like British music halls, and those of the sixteenth century, like Punch-and-Judy shows or the *commedia dell'arte*.

Slapstick is highly complex in its make-up. How one traces its historical trajectory depends on which of its many – e.g., thematic, linguistic, visual, sound etc. – elements one considers essential for its definition. Because of this, the historiography of slapstick is far from being exhaustive. Indeed, the future of slapstick historiography will likely bring studies that break down slapstick's diverse elements and trace the historical tradition(s). In this sense, slapstick does not look back on one history, but on numerous histories. And this applies not only to its prehistory and early beginnings, but also to its more recent iterations. William Solomon's *Slapstick Modernism* (2016) is a good example of a historically nuanced approach to slapstick and goes beyond the boundaries of film to explore the intertwining of slapstick as a stylistic or expressive mode with modernism – i.e., slapstick's themes, its demands, its techniques, and its representatives.

With this section we want to make such questioning about and also with slapstick possible. On the one hand, the contributions trace the historical beginnings and developments of slapstick. On the other hand, since this is also a project invested in a holistic approach to slapstick research, the contributors provide examples of what an interdisciplinary historiography of slapstick across media can look like. Paul Michael Babiak's chapter studies the emergence of the term 'slapstick' and its use by drawing on the discourse on the term proliferated in print culture. According to this research, slapstick is first and foremost a clearly identifiable stylistic feature of US-American cinema of the early twentieth century. In this respect, this form of comedy is deeply embedded in a specific social context. The expectations about the technical execution of slapstick performances as well as of the comic and entertainment factors of slapstick films emerge from this context, and eventually became a defining element of slapstick. Whereas Babiak offers a contextual history of slapstick, the next two chapters in the section offer approaches to the history of transmedial and intertextual history of slapstick.

Peter Edward's contribution demonstrates how productive an interdisciplinary and transmedial approach to slapstick research can be. With the exception of William Solomon, few studies on the history of slapstick have focused on slapstick beyond film and theatre studies. In fact, the notion that slapstick may also be present in literature, music or other art forms, and that these appearances may have even contributed to its development in the course of its broad history, has not been sufficiently researched. In this light, Edwards investigates the question of whether elements of slapstick can also be found in classical music and how they are formed. In music theatre and opera, where classical music has a special relationship to the performative, Edwards traces a history of musical slapstick. In this way, slapstick is activated as a rich object of study for further research in, for instance, the field of sound studies.

In her contribution on early modern prose literature, Carolin Struwe-Rohr demonstrates an approach to a literary study of slapstick. Using selected examples, some from the narrative genre of the Arthurian saga, she shows how slapstick can be applied as an innovative means of reading early modern literature. By identifying elements in narrative patterns that are constitutive for slapstick (e.g., the comical framing of pain and humiliation), Struwe-Rohr establishes slapstick as an analytical category for literary analysis. In so doing, she shows that *slapstick as an analytical category* can be applied to texts that at first glance might appear to be outside of the purview of approaches to *slapstick as a genre*. By differentiating her approach to slapstick studies in such a way, Struwe-Rohr acknowledges that slapstick is not universal across time. In fact, in the chapter slapstick serves as a key to examine literary prose on the threshold from the late middle ages to the early modern period, which cultural specificities are not distorted in the process. As a side effect of this approach, Struwe-Rohr shows that the emergence of slapstick is much more complex, i.e., it does not only have its origin in the realm of performance and theater, but also necessarily has to be sought beyond these fields.

Works cited

Dixon, Bryony. "The Good Thieves: On the Origins of Situation Comedy in the British Music Hall." *Slapstick Comedy*. Eds. Tom Paulus and Rob King. New York: Routledge, 2010. 21–36.

Ellenbürger, Judith. "Frauen in der Filmkomödie, oder: Wie Slapstick mit Samthandschuhen funktioniert." *Die Körper des Kinos. Für eine fröhliche Filmwissenschaft*. Eds. Christian Hüls, Natalie Lettenewitsch, and Anke Zechner. Frankfurt am Main: Stroemfeld, 2015. 215–226.

Hennefeld, Maggie. *Specters of Slapstick & Silent Film Comediennes*. New York: Columbia University Press, 2018.

King, Rob. *Hokum! The Early Sound Slapstick Short and Depression-Era Mass Culture*. Berkeley: University of California Press, 2017.

Massa, Steve. *Slapstick Divas: The Women of Silent Comedy*. Albany: BearManor Media, 2017.

Peacock, Louise. *Slapstick and Comic Performance: Comedy and Pain*. New York: Palgrave, 2014.

Peacock, Louise. "Conflict and slapstick in Commedia dell'Arte – The double act of Pantalone and Arlecchino (4:1)." *The Routledge Comedy Studies Reader*. Ed. Ian Wilkie. New York: Routledge, 2020. 49–58.

Paulus, Tom, and King, Rob. *Slapstick Comedy*. New York: Routledge, 2010.

Richards, Jeffrey. *The Golden Age of Pantomime: Slapstick, Spectacle and Subversion in Victorian England*. London: I.B. Tauris, 2015.

Solomon, William. *Slapstick Modernism: Chaplin to Kerouac to Iggy Pop*. Chicago: University of Illinois Press, 2016.

Kunstmuseum Wolfsburg. "Slapstick! Alÿs, Bock, Chaplin, Hein, Laurel & Hardy, Keaton, Matta-Clark u.a." https://www.kunstmuseum-wolfsburg.de/kunstmuseum/fotos-and-videos/slapstick/ (accessed 17 May 2020).

Museum of Modern Art. "Steve McQueen." https://www.moma.org/collection/works/98724 (accessed 17 May 2020).

Paul Michael Babiak
The Descent of Slapstick

In an interview published in the *Washington Times* in September 1915, Mack Sennett (1880–1960) issues what may well strike the contemporary reader as a startling denial. In "Sennett Objects to 'Slapstick' as a Term to Define Film Comedy," the legendary "father of slapstick" explicitly denies that, as a critical term, the word 'slapstick' has any meaning at all.

> I have been heralded as the originator of the so-called "slap-stick comedy," [. . .] As a matter of fact, there is no such thing as "slap-stick" comedy. There are two recognized types of comedy, the low comedies of the early stage days and the light comedies. The former were very popular in the old days of the stage, and with some improvements, have enjoyed immense popularity in motion pictures. [. . .] Who ever heard of the old-time low comedies spoken of as slap-stick? No legitimate actor ever knew of such an expression. It is essentially a modern term. (*Washington Times* 1915, 11)

This claim is surprising to those of us whose appreciation of slapstick has been shaped by the assumption that the silent-movie slapstick genre was the product of the more or less straightforward adaptation of a pre-existing theatrical genre to the circumstances of the fledgling cinema. It suggests instead that the slapstick comedy was a new departure, its specific difference not deriving from an inherited textuality – in the form of certain sorts of story or even of a loose repertoire of specific gags – but rather from the combination of a revamped stage technique with a number of medium-specific stylistic elements (such as undercranking or stop-motion). In this chapter I shall argue that the distinguishing quality of the slapstick genre resides not in the comedic representation of 'low,' and especially violent, physical tropes (since doing so tends to make 'slapstick' a synonym for all "low comedy" or "violent physical comedy" and thus elides its historicity), nor in the specific conditions of the early classical cinema (since non-cinematic slapsticks are possible and their existence acknowledged), but the combination of a period-specific performance style with a cinematic style unique to the slapstick comedy's historical moment. As the quote from Sennett suggests, to do so is therefore to interrogate what we mean by 'slapstick' itself.[1]

For most of us, genres are typically named after some part of their content: a boxing film is a film that contains scenes of boxing, a Western is a film containing

---

[1] Since my argument depends on our carefully maintaining the distinction between the *word* 'slapstick' and its possible referent(s), in the following I shall place all occurrences of the word for which purely verbal supposition is intended within single quotation marks.

scenes set in the American West, and so on. So a slapstick film should be a film containing slapstick. But virtually no lead comedian in a silent comedy is ever seen actually using a slapstick. So if we ask what specific element comprises this 'slapstick' in the film, the answer will typically make reference to some particular action – usually a violent one – that the sound of a slapstick might be taken to emblematize. But not all violent activity qualifies as slapstick – only that which provokes our laughter. We are then forced to modify our claim: it is the fact that the action is being performed *for laughs* that makes it slapstick. So 'slapstick' must refer, not to all violent representations, but only to *comic* violence; and the critical emphasis shifts from the genre's typical content onto its typical form. However, there is much performed violence that is comic, that would fail to qualify as slapstick: the macabre, but comic, violence of the *Grand guignol*, for example, Kathakali body comedy, or the mudhead clowns of the Hopi and the Yaqui Chapayekam tribesmen (see Schechner 1995).

Conversely, not all slapstick comedy relies on physical violence – the tropes of getting stuck on flypaper or of the "composite body," for example, are not inherently violent at all. So the term has to be primarily associated with a wider, but more or less specific repertoire of actions belonging to a particular historical period: falling on a banana peel, being sprayed with soda water, or one character flinging a coconut-cream pie into another's face. All of these actions can be (and frequently are) performed in films for serious effects – effects that we would never dream of calling 'slapstick.' Some scholars therefore, holding to the conviction that the quiddity of the slapstick genre must reside in some aspect of its textuality, but specifying its difference as formal, have concluded that slapstick must be a *mode* of comic production, like parody or satire (cf. Neale and Krutnik 1990). But textual modes are ahistorical – so to treat it as one is likewise to elide the historical specificity of slapstick, which, as Sennett insists, did not exist as such prior to the early 1910s. The presence or absence of slapstick therefore would seem to rely primarily not on a production's textual features but on a particular *way* in which its comic actions are selected and rendered – one that implies less a specific repertoire of activities than a set of conventions governing their being performed and received so as to produce a specific quality of laughter. I shall argue, therefore, that the distinguishing characteristic of slapstick is a function of its quiddity as a type of (comic) performance. This implies in turn that slapstick performance presupposes a specific *audience* to whom it is addressed in a specific way. But as audience tastes are continually evolving, so slapstick too must therefore be the product of a historical evolution, which it will be the major task of this chapter to outline.

The slapstick itself, in the form of Harlequin's *batocio*, appears on the scene late in the history of physical comedy – not until about the sixteenth century.

Although the *word* 'slapstick' had been in the English lexicon since a little before 1800 – David Garrick is credited with having invented the English counterpart of the continental tool on March 21, 1755 (*The Washington Herald*, March 21, 1912, 6) – the word remains in infrequent use until the first decade of the twentieth century. At this point it becomes one of a number of *pejorative* synonyms (including "rough-house" and "horse-play") for low physical comedy usually performed on variety and music hall stages (cf. Gilbert 1940, 47). But throughout the years from 1850 through 1910 'slapstick' is *never* employed as a descriptor for a narrative genre, or, indeed, for any genre of performance whatever. You will search in vain through show-business trade papers such as the London *Era*, the *Illustrated Sporting and Dramatic News*, the *Figaro*, the *New York Clipper*, *Billboard*, *Variety* or the *New York Dramatic Mirror* at any time between the years 1850 and 1910 for any mention of a slapstick duo, trio, or quartette, a slapstick song and dance, a slapstick sketch, a slapstick play, or a slapstick ballet. No such article existed. It is not until early 1911, when the term is first used in an ad to describe two films released by Carl Laemmle's (1867–1939) Independent Moving Pictures Co. of America, that "slap-stick comedy" becomes a formal descriptor for a genre with acknowledged characteristics – and at the same time becomes a term not of opprobrium, but of high praise:

> You have been begging us to produce some high-class slap-stick comedy on split reels. Very well! We give you a corking good dose of it in "The Mix-Up," released Thursday, Feb. 2, and "An Imaginary Elopement" on the same reel. The picture shown herewith is a climax in one of the funniest chains of silly horse-play you ever saw and we'll guarantee it will bring down your house with roars of delight.
>
> (*Moving Picture World*, Jan. 21, 1911, 168)

It is only in 1914 that 'slapstick' becomes the preferred identifier for a clearly demarcated corpus of comedy films; and it is not until 1921 that 'slapstick' has come to include what *Moving Picture World* calls the "High Art in Low Comedy" of Charlie Chaplin (1889–1977) and Buster Keaton's (1895–1966) shorts (cf. *Moving Picture World*, Mar. 26, 1921, 412; Oct. 1, 1921, 574). In the years before the emergence of the silent-slapstick film, when contemporary commentators use the word in any sense more specific than as a mere term of opprobrium, they use it to characterize a sort of "method" or technique (of producing laughter); that is, the practical basis of a style.

If the quiddity of slapstick resides in a unique physical technique, then, this technique must be what distinguishes it as a performance style. In that case the genre of "slapstick comedy" will most likely be named not primarily for the tropes that it includes (most of which, like falling on one's bum or the glass of wine *lazzo*, are common to the repertoires of other periods and available for treatment in other styles) and not for the textual mode under which it can be subsumed (like parody and satire), but for the unique *style* in which it is performed, like "bel canto opera," and "pointillist painting." That, in turn, involves distinguishing slapstick as a subtype of "physical comedy" or "body comedy" (Austin 2006).

1 The quiddity of slapstick

But what kind of style was the slapstick style? I would argue that the slapstick style of physical comedy is to be distinguished by four major hallmarks: i) "Lowness"; ii) modernism; iii) naturalism; and iv) "rationalization."

i) *"Lowness."* As Sennett observes in 1915, slapstick was acknowledged to be a "low" style – though, as we have already seen, it was on the verge of a dramatic revaluation:

> The lower type of comedies have been criticized in certain quarters as being somewhat of a jar to the more refined sensibilities, but that they are popular is proved by the enormous demand for them from all sections of the world. The demand for them in Europe is even greater than in this country. I might add, however, that the lower comedy is fast becoming merged with the lighter type, and that the so-called "slap-stick" laughs of today are a vast improvement over the lower comedies of twenty years ago [. . .].
>
> (*Washington Times*, Sept. 21, 1915, 11)

The "low" styles of the late nineteenth century position themselves against a repertoire of available "high" styles – for example, the elegant style of the comedy of manners, or the erudite style of Shavian comedy – each of which was grounded in a particular physical technique: the former on the maintenance of an erect but relaxed posture and graceful movement, the latter on a virtuoso vocal technique sustained in tandem with a naturalistic gestural style. The entire system of a continuum of movement styles ranging from low to high, and corresponding with a system of social types similarly ranged, is therefore imbricated, and legible, within the spectrum of movement techniques of the nineteenth century theater. It should consequently be no surprise if we find these "higher" styles frequently alluded to within the low-comic productions of the period (as we later do in the villains' performances in many slapstick movies – for example, those of Eric Campbell an [1880–1917] in Chaplin's Essanay films), and often within the lead comics' performances themselves (as, for example, Chaplin often enters a scene in the guise of a "walking gentleman" of the Victorian popular stage). A self-consciously "low" style defines itself by contrast with a corresponding "high" style.

ii) *Modernism*. As Roberta Pearson (1992) has shown, the emergence of the classical from the preclassical cinema depended on the development of a uniquely cinematic performance style that involved replacing what Pearson has termed the "histrionic" style, derived from the theater, to a more "verisimilar" style appropriate to film. Indeed, according to Pearson, the invention of a distinctive acting style adapted to the circumstances of the screen was integral to D.W. Griffith's (1875–1948) innovations in the production of the screen melodrama – the same innovations that Sennett had appropriated for the screen comedy during his apprenticeship under Griffith at the Biograph Studios (Sennett and Shipp 1954). The development of cinematic performance is therefore situated within the larger cultural transition from nineteenth-century romanticism to twentieth-century modernism. Within the spectrum of "low" styles, therefore, slapstick is also a distinctly modernist style, though it displayed both residual (romantic) and emergent (modernist) tendencies. By the conclusion of WWII, however, the Victorian continuum of styles had lost its meaning – perhaps as a result of the disappearance of the social order that had supported it. Even in the sound slapstick shorts of the 1930s, the sense of the gestural "excess" of the lead comedian usually depends no longer on the shared notion of an "ideal" (and implicitly aristocratic) character type, but instead relies on an evolving psychologistic notion of a "normal" character type, so that the audience's judgement tends to operate outside of the polarity of "high" and "low."

iii) *Naturalism*. If slapstick is a modernist style (Hansen 2012), then it is also a *naturalist* style. This might seem to be a paradox, since some (though not most) slapstick gags seem to rely on either the violation of "natural laws" (for example, by cinematic properties such as undercranking or stop-motion photography) or on "exaggerated" and "unrealistic" behaviors. But the slapstick "genre contract" always brings with it the *expectation* that events will, or ought to, follow the same order of probability that they do in other films, which are presumed to be the same as those of "real life" – rather than as in, say, a Bible story or a Grimm's fairy tale. If the film's engagement with naturalism is disrupted too completely, the audience will become unable to laugh. The same is true, though it may seem equally paradoxical, at the level of performance: as I argued above, the slapstick comedian acts in a verisimilar mode, with a goal, a psychological motivation, and a chance of succeeding that can engage the audience's sympathies; once these are lost, the spectator's capacity for laughter will be lost as well. Due to the centrality of the gag as the defining aspect of narrative in slapstick, his or her behaviors must inevitably seem excessive or deficient in such a way as to derive incongruities from the audience's expectations. But, once again, the extent to which the comedian can do so without forfeiting the spectator's engagement with the character as an agent whose acts are ultimately intelligible is a mark of the quality of his or her skill in slapstick comedy. This is perhaps why the fiction that the comedian's behavioral excesses can be written off to "theatricality" has been so useful. Nonetheless, the "theatricality" of slapstick is simply another measure of its "lowness." Different slapsticks are "broad" in different degrees. And some, like that of several of Harold Lloyd's (1893–1971) later features, are not particularly "broad" at all. But as in the case of the slapstick film's "un-" or "anti-realism," "theatrical" and "broad" are simply negative value judgments that performers in a slapstick style work to provoke in their audiences in order to provide an appropriate sense of "lowness." The representational mode in which they are working remains one of naturalism.

As a modernist, verisimilar style, slapstick also reflects the *habitus* of its period through a defining difference of most body comedy and another gauge of its "lowness" – its violence. Above and beyond the requirement of all (contemporary) comedy that portrayals of serious harm must be, in Noël Carroll's words, "bracketed" in order not to disrupt the comic frame, it has to be acknowledged that the violence of slapstick is considerably qualified (Carroll 1999, 145–160). In slapstick comedy, representations of such serious physical calamities as decapitation, penetrations of the body, or any manifestation of the Kristevan abject (see Kristeva 1982) in the form of bleeding or mangling of limbs, are limited to threats or illusions of one kind or another. Though the slapstick film teems with runaway motor vehicles, explosives, toppling buildings, gun violence, allusions to police brutality, the aggressiveness of modern urban life, and the equipage of twentieth-century warfare, its references to real-world violence are invariably allusive, and obliquely so. In the "lower" slapsticks, like the comedy of the Three Stooges, the intrapersonal violence is likewise more sadistic, and can include eye-gougings, attacks on the (male) genitals, and so on. In the "higher" slapsticks, personal violence is most frequently displaced onto the possessions of the disputants (especially their clothes and living spaces). Slapstick violence is thus additionally qualified by the parameters of acceptability in laughable re-presentations for early twentieth-century working- and middle-class audiences.

So, if the technology of the slapstick cinema makes it possible to confront the comic protagonist with a greater variety of more harrowing catastrophes than any dramatic medium ever had before, its conventions simultaneously reduce those catastrophes to the status of *threats* that the slapstick comedian invariably escapes "just in the nick of time." Slapstick violence, therefore, represents two conditions unique to the early twentieth century: a suddenly and dramatically expanded capacity for violent incident through new technologies such as planes, trains and automobiles; and a simultaneously lowered "threshold of repugnance" at violence – that is, the expectation of a progressively *decreasing* presence of violence in everyday life. This expectation may be viewed as the complement of a steadily *increasing* expectation of civility in the public sphere. While on the one hand both the type and degree of violence *threatened* by slapstick comedy reflect twentieth-century technologies and social conditions, the types of behaviors considered as violent and the degrees of them eligible either for direct or displaced representation (in a verisimilar mode) reflect twentieth-century tastes and twentieth-century expectations of the public sphere. They reflect an expectation of an environment that is "civilized" and hence pacified. In this environment, each individual has a right to dignity and propriety; and these rights can be both asserted and transgressed against in comparatively trivial ways.

iv) *Rationalization*. The final distinguishing difference of the slapstick style is the omnipresence within it of *rationalization*. Rationalization refers to the regularity of the succession of gags out of which a story emerges. Since the earliest days, slapstick laughs had been measured and sold by the foot in the film exchanges: Chaplin reports how in 1915 Essanay's price for rentals of his films jumped from thirteen to twenty-five cents a foot on the strength of his increasing popularity (1964, 176). The "laugh-a-minute" formula is carried to its logical extreme in the taxonomy of laughs described by James Agee (1909–1955) and supplied with industrial efficiency by Hollywood's slapstick "fun factories" (1974, 438). Central to this Fordist mass-production of laughter is the narrative structure peculiar to slapstick: the punctuation of the story by a regular succession of gags – particularly, during the silent era, the sight gag, which, as Noël Carroll points out (1998, 156), comes to dominate film comedy throughout the latter half of the 1910s.

In citing the gag as an example of rationalization, I am not referring here to its content, but rather to its function as a regular and, indeed, rhythmic unit by which the quantum of humor in slapstick product might be measured and meted out. The gag as a defining aspect of the slapstick comedy has been the focus of much of the literature (Carroll 1998; Carroll 2007; Gunning 2010; and Crafton 1995). It has itself a compound structure, consisting at a bare minimum of a set-up that has to be succeeded by a payoff in a more or less specific amount of time (Carroll 1999, 147); in cinematic slapstick, this rhythmic structure is elaborated by the interplay of editing, character movement and/or speech, and sound. The complexity of the slapstick gag therefore calls for a high degree of redundancy in its presentation: and the extent to which this narrative redundancy makes the comedy obvious is another mark of the "lowness" of slapstick comedy; one which links the comparative "lowness" of diverse slapsticks to the industrial contexts from which they emerge. The more predictable the comedy, the less respectable the demographic at which it is targeted.

The rationalization of movement in slapstick is ultimately a function of this same need for redundancy. It is true that early projectionists found that a gratuitous comic effect could be produced by projecting film comedies at a higher frame rate than usual, and that, during the silent period, slapstick filmmakers habitually undercranked while shooting to produce the same effects once projectors had been mechanized at standard frame rates. Certainly the quantization of movement by numbers of frames per second represents a form of rationalization that has usefully illustrated Henri Bergson's (1859–1941) claim that the comic consists in the "encrustation of the mechanical upon the human" (2019, 11b). It is equally true that numerous silent comedians' styles of physical movement anticipated this effect by selectively either eliminating or exaggerating the windups to and recoils from their movements.

These four characteristics of the slapstick style – "lowness," modernism, naturalism, and rationalization – both distinguish slapstick from other styles of physical comedy belonging to other periods and help to connect it back meaningfully to what Raymond Williams has theorized as the "structure of feeling" (1992, 29) qualifying the decades during which slapstick emerged.

2 The emergence of the slapstick comedy

If we consider the germ of the slapstick comedy as residing in a unique *physical* performance style, we can place this emergence within the larger context of the major trends in the evolution of physical performance during this time, including: i) the renaissance in athleticism that begins during the 1830s; ii) the separation of theatrical pastimes from sporting ones throughout the latter half of the nineteenth century; iii) the development of twentieth-century entertainment industries; and iv) the progressive mediatization of the human body in popular entertainments from the early 1890s on. But it further becomes possible to trace in broad outline the emergence of the cinematic genre in the years between 1912 and 1914. As scholars of early cinema have shown (see Keil 2001), the emergence of the various genres within the classical Hollywood system was predicated on the development of specifically cinematic stylistic features that were themselves determined by the technological and industrial realities of their day: we can therefore also trace the incorporation of the *physical* style within a distinctive *cinematic* stylistic context. In tracing the descent of slapstick, therefore, we need to begin by surveying the repertoire offered by the various forms of nineteenth-century low comedy. We can then examine the industrial circumstances surrounding the selection of a preferred model and its incorporation into the Sennett style of filmmaking. Finally, we can then take note of the proliferation of variant forms of slapstick that followed upon Sennett and Chaplin's astonishing successes in the years 1912–1915.

Nineteenth-century low comedy. The cultural status of the human body – and actual people's consciousness of themselves as bodily beings – had undergone both a thorough debunking and a renaissance in the first half of the nineteenth century. Perhaps the most traumatic phase of the process was the worldwide dissemination of Darwinian theory, with its suggestion that the abstract perfections of the human body were actually the products of contingent environmental adaptations. But at the same time, doctrines of physical fitness and the benefits of exercise were promoting a new awareness of the relationship between physical and mental well-being. This period saw the organization and regulation of traditional athletic pastimes into the forbears of modern sports and the establishment of international sporting administrative associations. At the same time a host of mechanical devices were being invented to extend the capacity of the human body for motion through space, resulting in new modes of theatrical performance: the introduction of roller skates in 1743; the creation of the velocipede in 1817 by Karl Drais (1785–1851), and its variations that appeared throughout the nineteenth century; the invention of the flying trapeze by Jules Léotard (1838–1870) in 1859 and the rapid development of a wide variety of forms of aerial performance, especially the popularization of the tightrope by Pablo Fanque (1796–1871), Charles Blondin (1824–1897), and Henri L'Estrange (ca. 1842–ca.1894). As athletics and theatrics began to develop along independent routes, a profusion of new clowning styles appeared. John Towsen (1976) reminds us how, by the late eighteenth century, the remnants of the *commedia dell'arte* had evolved into the harlequinades of British pantomime – specifically in "transformation scenes" in which the characters of the modern stories (Puss in Boots, Dick Whittington, the Babes in the Wood, etc.) metamorphosed into stock types derived from *commedia* (Harlequin, Columbine, Pantaloon) in scenes culminating in reckless acrobatic chases through trap doors, revolving scenery, and other theatrical devices.

By the early nineteenth century the increasingly acrobatic and balletic Harlequin had acquired an oafish nemesis in Pantaloon's servant, Clown, the character popularized most famously by Joseph Grimaldi (1778–1837), who anticipated Chaplin's "transformation humour" in many of the specialties he devised. Secondly, following the success in 1825 of Edmond Rochefort's (1790–1871) *Jocko ou le singe du Brésil*, a rage developed for man-monkeys – acrobats playing the part of gorillas, orangutans, and chimpanzees – that lasted throughout the century and included some of the most prominent pantomimists of the century, including Charles-François Mazurier (1793–1828), Étienne-Hughes Laurençon (1800–1883), Edward Klischnigg (1813–1877), and Paul Martinetti (1852–1925). A related trend was the development of contortionism as a performance genre. Forward-bending contortionists became known as *klischniggs* and a combination of contortion, acrobatics and tumbling coalesced into the performance style of the French *grotesques*, the most prominent among whom was Jean-Baptiste Auriol (1806–1881). During the latter half of the nineteenth century *grotesquérie* became a dominant stylistic trend among English and American comedians likewise in the form of "grotesque song and dance," practised, among others, by the Vokes family (active ca. 1860–1894), the Majiltons (active ca. 1868–1890s), the Girards (active ca. 1875–1897), and the Phoites (active ca. 1875–1898).

Theatrical low comedy had a variety of exponents as well: there were, to begin with, the dramatic "low comedians" such as Richard Yates (1706–1796), who had been in Garrick's company; Joseph Munden (1758–1832), John Liston (1776–1846), and John Lawrence Toole (1832–1906). Indeed, for Oscar Brockett, the nineteenth century was "the era of the low comedian" (1990, 407). These performers qualified as "low" rather because they presented socially marginal types than because of the disreputability of their actions. Low comedians typically played ethnic, aged, or physically challenged characters. These were largely rendered in dialects, and performances featured grotesque postures and exaggerated movements. Male low comics would improvise before a closed curtain to cover for scene changes taking place backstage, the performance consisting largely in a flirtation with the female low comedian in the role of a chambermaid. Though their repertoires included physical comedy, theatrical low comedians' performances were predominantly verbal; they were especially notorious for their exploitation (and overuse) of the "catch phrase"; for example, "Who does not remember Mr. L(awrence) Brough's 'Put it in the bag,' or Mr. H(arry) Paulton's 'You'll be sorry for this?'" ("Low Comedy Gagging," 1880, 8). Theatrical low comedians, male and female, were ubiquitous in straight drama, melodrama, and pantomime as well as comedy.

At the same time there were the theatrical *farceurs*, whose technique covered a wide range. At one extreme might be the relatively sedate bourgeois types of *Slasher and Crasher* (John Maddison Morton, 1852) whose movement across the farcical action might become highly frenetic without ever crossing the line into athletics. At the opposite extreme were acrobatic *farceurs* such as the Hanlon-Lees or the Byrne Brothers (*Variety*, March 21, 1908, 16), who practised a highly athletic form of farce elaborating on the transformation scenes of pantomime, exemplified by the Hanlon-Lees' legendary *Voyage en Suisse*, which premiered in Paris in 1879, and eventually toured the world (Cosdon 2009). The helter-skelter acrobatics of *Le voyage en Suisse* established a tradition of vaudevillian farce that was taken up in the early 1900s by such groups as Joe Boganny's Troupe of Lunatic Bakers (*Variety*, Oct. 17, 1908, 12), Fred Ginnett's English Company (*Variety*, Dec. 25, 1909, 21; *New York Clipper*, Nov. 20, 1909, 1033), the Spissel

Brothers (*Variety* Oct. 2, 1909, 16; *New York Dramatic Mirror*, Oct. 9, 1909, 23), and Fred Karno's (1866–1941) London Comedy Co. (*New York Dramatic Mirror*, Mar. 26, 1910, 21; *Variety*, March 19, 1910, 14).

But the defining style of physical low comedy in English and American popular culture from the mid-nineteenth century until the beginning of WWI was unquestionably what was known as knockabout comedy. In knockabout we find aplenty in nineteenth-century show-business annals that we search in vain for references to slapstick: a highly developed genre of performance with its own distinctive technique, repertoire and conventions; with a variety of subgenres, including knockabout circus clowning, knockabout sketches, knockabout song and dance, knockabout plays, and even knockabout ballets. Knockabout performance featured a variety of sub-forms: there was "Ethiopian" knockabout, Irish or "Hibernian" knockabout, and "Dutch" (i.e., German) knockabout (both also often conventionally performed in blackface). There were knockabouts who employed some relics of the pantomime tradition, others that foregrounded contemporary acrobatics, and knockabout specialties such as those of the "Silence and Fun" men. Advertisements from managers in British trade papers like the London *Era* or *The Stage* repeatedly solicit for circus, music hall and variety knockabout performers; and performers differentiate their services by reference to the generic identifier. Many of the defining tropes of what came to be known as 'slapstick' are evidently borrowings from the knockabout repertoire: for example, the conventional twinning of a tall, thin man with a short, fat one.

Knockabout performance emerges from three distinct matrices (cf. Towsen 1976; and Dissher 1925): the circus, the blackface minstrel show, and the music halls. Until the mid-1850s, circuses were small, and circus clowning was a predominantly verbal affair (Bratton and Featherstone 2006). However, after the advent of the three-ring circus, knockabout and acrobatic clowning became the dominant styles (*The New York Clipper* Jan. 25, 1890, 759). The earliest ad for a knockabout performer of any kind is one for a knockabout clown for Pinder's Circus in England (*The Era*, Dec. 11, 1864, 16). But by 1870, minstrel knockabouts have already begun to appear in show-business journalism (*Era* Sun. June 12, 1870, 7). Indeed, since the appearance of the minstrel show in the United States in the early 1840s, it had been customary to conclude an evening with a rowdy sketch, often improvised around a single, physically violent, gag (Price 1911, 27). These playlets, called "Ethiopian sketches," were printed for performance by amateur companies, and widely disseminated from the mid-1870s through the early 1900s. Their stage directions constitute a repository of the tradition of "hokum stuff" (Jolson 1915, 5) that later came to be regarded as the source of many of the major tropes of slapstick.

In the music halls, the major form taken by knockabout was that of the two-man team, which typically featured a tall, slender man (who administered the violence), and a short, heavily padded, fat man (who absorbed it). The staple of a music hall act was the "knockabout song and dance," in which violent actions were inserted into four-bar "breaks" between phrases of song (or dance). The "knockabout song and dance" was evidently a variation on the "acrobatic song and dance" introduced during the 1870s by such American minstrel teams as Welby and Pearl (*New York Clipper*, Feb. 23, 1878, 379) and Crumley and DeForest (*The New York Clipper*, Dec. 6, 1879, 294).

The technical basis of acrobatic song and dance was evidently fundamental to the technique of knockabout song and dance. Its two basic premises included i) the return, before, and after the execution of each movement, to a "root position" (Bruce 1935, 8); and ii) the avoidance of "double-time" (i.e., the suppression of both preparation and recoil in the execution of a movement) (24). These techniques give the body either a quasi-mechanical or else a 'dancelike' quality; and it is remarkable how closely they anticipate the effect of overcranking by silent-cinema projectionists. More than any other, then, it is the knockabout style that defined physical low comedy for the popular culture of the late nineteenth and early twentieth centuries.

By the mid-1890s, knockabout had developed in several different directions. There were the knockabout clowns of the circus; there were the knockabout teams that accompanied the athletic combinations on their tours; there were the bone-crunching knockabouts of the burlesque theaters; and there were the knockabout sketch artists and song-and-dance men of the variety theaters. As the first decade of the twentieth century wore on, the affinities between knockabout farce and the acrobatic farce style of the Hanlon-Lees and their ilk were developed in vaudeville, while the "lower-class" musical comedy and burlesque theaters catered to an increasingly less sophisticated (and more violent) taste in physical comedy.

The Establishment of the Sennett Style. In 1912 therefore, when Mack Sennett turned his hand to the task of appropriating for cinematic comedy D.W. Griffith's innovations in melodrama, he had a wide selection of stylistic models from the popular theater on which to draw. All of them, however, reflected both a debunking of the early nineteenth-century sense of humanity's physical place within the universe and the technology-based compensation for it. The human body was no longer the repository of a transcendent set of spiritual values that compensated it for its bodily vulnerability to the forces of nature; it was an object within a world of objects.

Sennett also had a variety of formal options. The new cinematic genre was still in an experimental phase, and critics in the trade papers were still groping for means of understanding and evaluating it. The earliest movies, from 1894 to 1907, had been brief and told none but the most rudimentary stories. Amongst these were the "trick" films and the "prank" films, and, after the introduction of editing in 1903–1904, the earliest "chase" films. Although producers initially sought to promote them as "comedies," these brief "views" were thought of by analogy primarily not with theater pieces, but with the sequences of humorous pictures in the newspapers – in honor of which by 1900 they were named "comics." After 1907, however, as the length of films begins to increase and rudimentary forms of cinematic storytelling begin to appear, the paradigm based on the analogy with the funny papers begins to yield to one based on traditional narrative models – especially theatrical ones. During this period, "comic" and "comedy" are no longer synonymous (as they may be thought to be before 1904), but actually reflect *competing* visions of what film humor is and what it should set out to do (see *New York Dramatic Mirror* Feb. 6, 1909, 16). The consensus among critics is that the business of film is to tell stories, not to provide moments of outrageous spectacle. During the period from 1907 through 1911, the average length of a film expands to a full reel (about ten or eleven minutes) and then, between 1912 and 1914, to twice that. In the meantime, the critical consensus about the medium of film is that what elevates the cinema above the stage is its heightened "realism" (by virtue of its photographic authenticity) (*Moving Picture World*, May 14, 1910, 775) and thus its increased capacity for moral uplift (*Moving Picture World*, May 28 1910, 887).

The element of moral uplift – and with it, the refined comedy – was essential to the agenda of the film industry in the early 1910s as increasing popularity and influence brought with them increasing opposition from traditional institutions, including the churches ("Maligners of the Moving Picture" 1908, 444). Among theirs are the first voices of concern that mass media may exercise a deleterious influence over young people: they resulted in widespread calls for a censorship ("Moving Pictures and Narrow-Minded Prejudice" 1911, 8). Numerous polemics in the trade papers advert to this opposition, maintaining the motion picture as a superior moral influence on audiences ("The Church and the Moving Picture" 1910, 250–251). The critics repeatedly call for comedies that have "an interesting story as a basis, and (appeal) more to the milder sense of the humorous than to the boisterous" (*New York Dramatic Mirror*, June 28, 1911, 28). In consequence, the "refined" or "polite comedy" makes its appearance at about the same time as the slapstick comedy begins to emerge. Among these may be included the first comedy series featuring bourgeois comic types such as Edison's Jones and Bumptious in 1910 (both played by John R. Cumpson, 1886–1913), and, beginning in 1912, the highly successful Vitagraph comedies featuring John Bunny (1863–1915) and Flora Finch (1867–1940).

The political climate was complicated by the industrial situation. Throughout the first decade of the twentieth century, the Edison Company, which claimed patent rights over cinema technology, had attempted to establish monopoly control of the industry by means of a series of patent infringement lawsuits over its first wave of competitors: American Mutoscope and Biograph, Lubin, George Kleine & Co., Selig Polyscope, Kalem, Vitagraph and Essanay. In 1908, these disputes came to an end with the establishment of the Motion Picture Patents Company and its distributing arm, the General Film Company. In exchange for uncontested use of Edison's patents, these companies were permitted to participate in oligopolistic control of the film industry in the United States. A Supreme Court action was undertaken against non-participating producers ("Independents"), who were thus to be driven out of business. In pursuit of its unofficial goal of hegemonizing the entertainment industry (articulated obliquely through its industry organ, *Moving Picture World*), the "Trust," as it was called, followed a policy that had been successful in the establishment of the Keith-Albee combine's dominance over vaudeville – the espousal of high moral standards, a policy of "clean" productions, and the rigorous suppression of material potentially offensive to middle-class audiences.

The Trust's domination of the industry was soon contested, however, by the establishment in 1910 of a federation of independent producers led by Carl Laemmle, and distributing (at first) through the Motion Picture Distributing and Sales Company. The Independents launched a series of counter-suits against the MPPC and undertook an aggressive campaign to win exhibitors away from the General Film Co. to do exclusive business with the Sales Co. They lured foreign producers such as Great Northern, Lux, and Itala, to join them. Comedy films, not surprisingly, became a major weapon in the war between the Trust and the Independents. A slew of small independent producers – Solax, American, Éclair, Nestor, Reliance, and Powers – began producing comedies as part of their regular output, many of them roughhouse comedies.

In numerous ads like that of Imp from 1911 (see Figure 1), quoted above, the Independents address populist tastes in comedy while simultaneously courting bourgeois preferences for "high-class" comedy catered to by the MPPC signatories. In 1912, Laemmle established Universal Pictures, and one of his first moves was to acquire the popular series of "Snakeville" low comedies featuring Alkali Ike (Augustus Carney, 1870–1920) away from Essanay.

The consequence was a crisis in film comedies. In the periodical press from late 1910 until 1912 numerous authors bemoan the problem of a "dearth of comedy" ("The Dearth of Comedy" 1911, 3). A *Billboard* editorial of late 1910 reflects that the instability in the industry has produced "a state of pseudo-panic that holds down the orders of the exchanges, limits the out-put of the manufacturers, and . . . throws a wet blanket on the whole business" ("No Cause for Panic," 1910, 3). In spite of the proliferation of producers, the comedy market in the United States was conspicuously under-supplied: "Just think," writes one

Figure 1: 1911 *Moving Picture World* advertisement for Independent Moving Pictures (Imp).

exhibitor in December, 1910, "we have twelve short comedies out of fifty-seven subjects put on the market this week!" ("Another Cry for Comedy" 1911, 37). A *Moving Picture World* editorial of June 10, 1911, estimates that "(i)n moving pictures the tragedy outnumbers the comedy at a ratio something like 16 to 1" ("The Dearth of Comedy" 1911, 1293). The "drought of comedy" was still being felt as late as mid-1912:

> Never before in the history of motion pictures has the supply of good comics been scanter than now . . . many of the manufacturers who formerly could be counted on for one or two comic pictures every week have given up the plan of regular "comedy" releases and bring out comic pictures whenever the spirit moves them. Some weeks there is an oversupply and then again a total absence of comedies. ("Éclair Notes" 1912, 18)

The problem would seem to have been as much qualitative as quantitative: while genteel comedy production failed to satisfy demand, reviewers tirelessly decried roughhouse comedy as outworn and boring: "The public today fairly loathe the old 'china-smashing' and 'chase' variety of 'comic' pictures and demand something which is original" (18). Like most, this writer blames the current situation entirely on the formative influence of the low comedy of the early cinema: "The present dearth of comics is . . . a natural reaction from the low, cheap 'comedy' which characterized the early motion picture. People are so thoroughly sick and tired of this ancient variety that they will prefer any other picture" (18). Throughout this discourse, the words 'slapstick' and 'slapstick comedy' are reiterated endlessly as expressions for the "badness" of the old "comics" and the tiredness of their repetitive tropes.

At the same time, the trade journals call for a new kind of specialist comedy producer:

> It has been suggested time and again that if some film manufacturing company were to make a specialty of comedy and comedy only, it would in time establish a reputation as a comedy house to which all exhibitors would turn in their time of need . . . .
> ("The Dearth of Comedy" 1911, 1293)

In hindsight, the problem was evidently simply a question of style. Until 1912, the style of comic films such as the "Bumptious" series retained the characteristics of the stylistically elementary "comics": they consisted of series of tableaux within which "funny" actions were placed, with relatively little effort to construct a consistent diegesis. These tableaux were staged much as their counterparts were in the popular theaters, and presented largely in long shot, so that they resembled nothing so much as "canned theater." In the meantime, D.W. Griffith, working at the Biograph Studios largely in the genre of melodrama, had established the rudiments of the classical Hollywood style, constructing by means of eyeline matches, matches on action, and meticulous use of screen direction a stable diegetic space within which the dramatic action could then be placed, giving the impression of a direct experience of reality.

The critics of roughhouse comedies during this period find themselves caught in a dilemma: while they endlessly attempt to write off the old chase-, trick- and prank-forms as passé, the demand for them continues to increase in proportion as the refined comedies fail to satisfy the ongoing demand. These critics seem to be groping for a new vocabulary with which to define the problems with the old methods and prescribe new forms more suitable to the screen. They borrow some terms from theater (e.g., "farce," "travesty," "clown comedy," "burlesque," *Motion Picture World*, Aug. 10, 1912, 545; *Moving Picture World*, Feb. 4, 1911, 249). They try to invent others (e.g., "photofarce," "chase farce," "crockery-smashing farce," "prank pictures," "trick pictures"); and combine them with terms of theatrical provenance (e.g., "split-" or "one-reel farce-comedy"). Their theorizing, as it tacitly acknowledges the comparative failure of the refined comedy, aims at discovering what *combination* of these elements is appropriate for a comic style proper to the evolving new medium, rather than imagining what new stylistic context would give these old tropes new meaning.

It should be no surprise, in view of our understanding of the contemporary industry, that when Sennett and Keystone made their appearance in September 1912, they appeared from among the ranks of the independents. Sennett's success was immediate thanks in part to his lead comedians Fred Mace (1878–1917) and Mabel Normand (1892–1930). But as contemporary reviewers emphasize, it was largely a function of style, particularly an accelerated sense of tempo, combined with a highly rhythmic editing style full of ellipses, that distinguished Keystone product, and gave a new lease on life to the motion picture comedy (*New York Dramatic Mirror* March 5, 1913, 33; *New York Dramatic Mirror* April 16, 1913, 33).

Sennett's eccentric editing style relentlessly parodied Griffith's key techniques: he used eyeline matches and matches on action to construct impossible juxtapositions of place and to extend actions over improbable distances and varieties of locale. In general, he tried to burlesque his spectators' own expectations of the "realism" of the cinema. In effect, he turned Griffith's technique inside out: instead of constructing a stable diegesis and then inserting a plausible action into it, he began with the most extravagant actions and constructed on the fly conspicuously ramshackle diegeses around them. As to its generic affinities, contemporary reviewers are quite unanimous in dubbing the Keystone genre of comedy as a recombination of farce and burlesque: the farce-burlesque (*New York Dramatic Mirror*, Dec. 25, 1912 30). Instead of minimizing the "badness" of his product, Sennett adopted a style that emphasized it; and the very disreputability of Sennett's style of films proclaimed the dissent of slapstick from the values espoused by the polite comedies of the MPPC. The cinema's potential to enhance the violence of body comedy by shifting it from the stage to the "real world" while at the same time, through closer shot scales and rhythmic editing, making it more intimate, was finally being realized.

It should be no surprise either, that the Keystone performance style drew most heavily on the model of the bone-crunching style of knockabout that had evolved in the burlesque theaters, modified to fit a more verisimilar acting style that parodied the one that Griffith had pioneered. But as his business prospered, Sennett's comedies increasingly represented a recombination of this burlesque-style knockabout comedy with the fast-paced acrobatics of vaudevillian farce. It is due to Sennett that the emergence of the slapstick comedy thus accompanies the coalescence of a variety of low-comic procedures into a *relatively* – by comparison with the much broader histrionics of circus and vaudevillian knockabouts – "verisimilar" performance style. This new style necessarily retained its difference from the more "serious" styles of other genres by retaining an "excessive" quality that read as theatrical but that in fact represented a rationalization of the need for the performer to "telegraph" his/her intentions for the purposes of milking the visual gag. This "excessive" quality simultaneously functioned to provide a "comic frame" capable of de-realizing any violence that might have threatened to disrupt its innocence (in the literal sense, i.e., its "harmlessness") for early twentieth-century audiences.

A Proliferation of Slapsticks. So successful indeed was the Keystone formula that Sennett was immediately plagued by a host of defections. By June 1913, Fred Mace had accepted an offer to take the Keystone style to the Majestic studios; in 1914 his successor, Ford Sterling (1883–1939) left to headline in Sterling Films; and in 1915, Keystone director Henry Lehrman (1881–1946) left to establish his own company, L-Ko Studios, for the production of a hyper-violent variation on Keystone slapstick featuring himself and comedian Billie Ritchie (1878–1921). By 1915, when Chaplin was lured away from Keystone to Essanay, most of the Independents and all the major MPPC producers had established comedy companies producing variants on Keystone slapstick, featuring comedians drawn from various live-theater provenances. By 1917, slapstick comedy was firmly entrenched as a genre with at least three dominant strains. The "Photoplay Editor" of the Philadelphia *Evening Public Ledger* provides a taxonomy:

> There are only four schools of comedy regnant today – the episodic anecdote that Sidney Drew does well, the quasi-realistic burlesque invented by Sennett, the Chaplin mixtures of violenec (sic) and funny dumb show, and the Fairbanks-Loos-Emerson comedy of satire plus beauty and action. (1917, 9)

From here on, the descent of slapstick follows, in broad outline, the life-cycle of cinematic genres as famously described by Thomas Schatz (1981). By 1917, the experimental phase of the slapstick comedy is effectively over. Kalton Lahue describes in detail how the proliferation of studios dedicated to slapstick filmmaking continues through a classical period in which the two-reel comedy evolves into, on the one hand, the great slapstick features of Chaplin, Keaton, Harold Lloyd and, on the other, the extravagant two-reelers of Larry Semon, Lloyd Hamilton, Laurel and Hardy, and many others (1966). Rob King has suggested that a third phase arrives during the period after the transition to sound, when studios such as Educational Pictures and Columbia produced consciously archaic two-reeler slapstick comedies in the same spirit of pastiche that had initially motivated the development of the Sennett style (2017, 157–160).

By the end of WWII, however, the slapstick style is no longer vital and the film genre is effectively obsolete. The Victorian system of values in the context of which slapstick performance read as "low" (as opposed to "high") had crumbled by this time; and the Western world's entire *habitus* with regard to violence had inevitably changed in the wake of the Holocaust and the bombings of Hiroshima and Nagasaki. During the 1950s the worldwide dissemination of television technology established a new standard of "verisimilar" performance. In the meantime, the function of adapting to a culture of industrialization that the "rationalized" stylistics of slapstick subserved had largely been accomplished. Through the 1950s and 1960s we see in the comedy of Jerry Lewis, Lucille Ball, and especially the Monty Python troupe, a new style of physical comedy emerge – one dominated by a physical *grotesquérie* out of key with the stylistics of slapstick.

3 Conclusion

If we view the quiddity of slapstick as residing essentially in a performance technique specific to its period, and extended by analogy to a cinematic style suited to it, we begin to be able to preserve the specificity of 'slapstick' as a critical term with a determinate meaning. Though the descent of slapstick through Victorian low comedy culminated in the slapstick comedy's emergence through the twentieth-century medium of film, however, there is no need to restrict our use of the *word* to specifically cinematic contexts. In theory there is no objection to the idea of extending slapstick's stylistic quiddity by analogy to performances in other media by means of other technologies, including those of the live theater. On the contrary, to do so enables us to view slapstick as a phenomenon unique to a particular historical moment, while leaving us free to speculate on its similarities to and differences from practices unique to other moments, and other technologies.

Bibliography

Agee, James. "Comedy's Greatest Era." *Film Theory and Criticism: Introductory Readings*. Eds. Gerald Mast and Marshall Cohen. New York: Oxford University Press, 1974: 438–457.

Anderson, Gilbert M., dir. "Alkali Ike's Auto." The Essanay Film Manufacturing Company, 1911.

Austin, Guy. "Body Comedy and French Cinema: Notes on *Les visiteurs*." *Studies in French Cinema* 6:1 (2006): 43–52.

Bergson, Henri. *Laughter: An Essay on the Meaning of the Comic*. Trans. Cloudesley Brereton and Fred Rothwell. http://www.gutenberg.org/ebooks/4352.mobile (accessed February 20, 2019).

Bratton, Jacky, and Ann Featherstone. *The Victorian Clown*. Cambridge: Cambridge University Press, 2006.

Brockett, Oscar. *History of the Theatre*. Toronto: Allyn and Bacon, 1990.

Bruce, Bruce R. *Acrobatic Dancing and Tumbling*. Chicago: Baigen & Company, 1935.

Capra, Frank, dir. *It's a Wonderful Life*. Liberty Films, 1946, dist. RKO Radio Films.

Carroll, Noël. *Comedy Incarnate: Buster Keaton, Physical Humor, and Bodily Coping*. Oxford: Wiley-Blackwell, 2007.

Carroll, Noël. "Horror and Humor." *The Journal of Aesthetics and Art Criticism*. 57.2 (1999): 145–160.

Carroll, Noël. *Interpreting the Moving Image*. Cambridge: Cambridge University Press, 1998.

Chaplin, Charles. *My Autobiography*. New York: Simon and Shuster, 1964.

Chaplin, Charles, perf. "Sunnyside." First National Pictures Co., 1919.

Clopper, Lawrence M. *Drama, Play and Game: English Festive Culture in the Medieval and Early Modern Period*. Chicago: University of Chicago Press, 2001.

Cosdon, Mark. *The Hanlon Brothers: From Daredevil Acrobatics to Spectacle Pantomime, 1833–1931*. Carbondale: Southern Illinois University Press, 2009.

Crafton, Donald. "Pie and Chase: Gag, Spectacle and Narrative in Slapstick Comedy." *Classical Hollywood Comedy*. Eds. Kristine Brunovska Karnick and Henry Jenkins. New York: Routledge, 1995. 106–119.

Dissher, M. Wilson. *Clowns and Pantomimes*. London: Constable & Co. Ltd., 1925.

Fairbanks, Douglas, perf. "Down to Earth." Douglas Fairbanks Pictures, 1917. Dist. Artcraft Pictures Corp.

Fairbanks, Douglas, perf. "Wild and Woolly." Douglas Fairbanks Pictures, 1917. Dist. Artcraft Pictures Corp.

Gilbert, Douglas. *American Vaudeville: Its Life and Times*. New York: McGraw-Hill, 1940.

Gunning, Tom. "Mechanisms of Laughter: The Devices of Slapstick." *Slapstick Comedy*. Ed. Tom Paulus and Rob King. New York: Routledge, 2010. 137–151.

Hansen, Miriam Bratu. *Cinema and Experience: Siegfried Kracauer, Walter Benjamin, and Theodor W. Adorno*. Berkeley: University of California Press, 2012.

Keaton, Buster, perf. *Our Hospitality*. Joseph M. Schenk Productions, 1923. Dist. Metro Pictures Corp.

Keaton, Buster, perf. *Sherlock Jr.*, Buster Keaton Productions. 1924. Dist. Metro Pictures Corp.

Keil, Charlie. *Early America Cinema In Transition: Story, Style, and Filmmaking, 1907–1913*. Madison: University of Wisconsin Press, 2001.

King, Rob. *Hokum! The Early Sound Slapstick Short and Depression-Era Mass Culture*. Berkeley: University of California Press, 2017.

Kristeva, Julia. *Powers of Horror: An Essay on Abjection*, trans. Leon S. Rudiez. New York: Columbia University Press, 1982.
Lahue, Kalton C. *World of Laughter: The Motion Picture Comedy Short, 1910–1930*. Norman: Oklahoma University Press, 1966.
Lloyd, Harold, perf. *Safety Last*. Hal Roach Studios, 1923. Dist. Pathé Exchange.
Morton, John Maddison. *Slasher and Crasher: A Farce in One Act*. London: Duncombe and Moon, 1852(?).
Neale, Steve and Frank Krutnik. *Popular Film and Television Comedy*. New York: Routledge, 1990.
Pearson, Roberta. *Eloquent Gestures: The Transformation of Performance Style in the Griffith Biograph Films*. Berkeley: University of California Press, 1992.
Rabelais, François. *Five Books of the Lives, Heroic Deeds and Sayings of Gargantua and His Son Pantagruel*, trans. Sir Thomas Urquhart of Cromarty and Peter Antony Motteux. Chicago: Encyclopedia Britannica, Inc., 1952.
Schatz, Thomas. *Hollywood Genres: Formulas, Filmmaking, and the Studio System*. New York: Random House, 1981.
Schechner, Richard. *The Future of Ritual*. New York: Routledge, 1995.
Sennett, Mack and Cameron Shipp. *King of Comedy*. Garden City: Doubleday & Company, Inc., 1954.
Towsen, John. *Clowns*. New York: Hawthorn Books, 1976.

Periodicals

"A Talk With A Clown," *New Haven Evening Register*, Vol. XLI Issue 100, April 29 1882, 4.
"Al Jolson's 'Hokum Stuff'," *Evening Public Ledger*, Philadelphia, Pa., February 13 1915, 5.
"Another Cry for Comedy," *Moving Picture World*, January 7, 1911, 37.
"The Church and the Moving Picture – Which is the Most Moral Place of the Two?" *Moving Picture World*, July 30 1910, 250–251.
"The Dearth of Comedy," *Moving Picture World*, June 10, 1911, 1293.
"Éclair Notes," *Moving Picture News*, August 24, 1912, 18.
The Era (London), December 11, 1864.
The Era (London), June 12, 1870.
Evening Capital Journal (Salem, Or.), January 14, 1893.
Evening Public Ledger (Philadelphia, Pa.), August 22, 1917.
Evening Star (Washington, D.C.), October 4, 1898.
"Low Comedy Gagging," *The Stage*, November 11, 1880, 8.
"Maligners of the Moving Picture," *Moving Picture World*, Vol. 3., No. 23, (December 3, 1908), 444.
"The Moving Picture as an Uplifter; How it Reaches the Multitudes," *Moving Picture World*, May 28, 1910, 887.
Moving Picture World, January 21, 1911.
Moving Picture World, July 20, 1912.
Moving Picture World, March 26, 1921.
"Moving Pictures and Narrow-Minded Prejudice," *Moving Picture News*, September 2, 1911, 6; September 9, 1911, 8.

Music Hall and Theatre Review, April 8, 1904.
New York Clipper, February 23, 1878.
The New York Clipper, December 6, 1879.
New York Clipper, November 20, 1909.
New York Clipper, January 25, 1890,
New York Dramatic Mirror, February 6, 1909.
New York Dramatic Mirror, March 26, 1910.
"No Cause for Panic," *Billboard*, October 15, 1910, 3.
Price, Arthur L. "In Vaude-Village: Its People and Its Vernacular," *San Francisco Call*, July 9, 1911, 27.
"Realism in Moving Pictures," *Moving Picture World*, May 14, 1910, 775.
"Reviews of Mutual Films," *New York Dramatic Mirror*, January 1, 1913, 33.
"Reviews of Mutual Films," *New York Dramatic Mirror*, March 5, 1913, 33.
"Reviews of Mutual Films," *New York Dramatic Mirror*, April 16, 1913, 33.
"Reviews of Supply Co. Films," *New York Dramatic Mirror*, December 25, 1912 30.
"Sennett Objects to 'Slapstick' as a Term to Define Film Comedy," *Washington Times*, September 21, 1915, 11.
Variety, March 21, 1908.
Variety, October 17, 1908.
Variety, October 2, 1909.
Variety, December 25, 1909.
Variety, March 19, 1910.
The Washington Herald, March 21, 1912.
Wood, Frank. "Spectator's Comments," *New York Dramatic Mirror*, June 28, 1911, 28.

Peter Edwards
Ideology, Performance, and Ironic Distance in Musical Slapstick

From the plays of the ancient Greeks to the court jesters of the Middle Ages, from Wolfgang Amadeus Mozart's (1756–1791) *Così fan tutte* (1790) to music hall of the nineteenth and early twentieth centuries, and from the music theatre of the avant-garde to emergent forms of comedy in new media, slapstick has always played an important part in music drama and musical comedy. This chapter will draw on a range of examples in an attempt to offer insight into the distinctive character of musical slapstick. Little has been written on the theme of musical slapstick specifically, and there are challenges to be overcome in attempts to define any comic genre, given the continually evolving nature of comedy. Comedy thrives on subverting fixed definitions and stable meaning; the resistance it offers to perceived norms of representation and signification is key in achieving a desired comic effect. Comedy challenges normative thought, and, as such, it possesses much potential as an instigator of social and political critique and change. It is often regarded as a medium through which to channel critique of the establishment and dominant socio-political currents, without the negative consequences this sometimes entails in more formal settings. Even under the most totalitarian of regimes, comedy is one of few domains in life that cannot be subjected to total control. It provides an at times subterfugeous, or often an explicit means of critiquing societal conventions, preconceptions, stereotypes, and ideologies and is commonly expressed through forms such as satire, farce, irony, and parody.[1] Situated somewhere in this broad landscape, musical slapstick is an effective tool for eliciting laughter. It is a lucid lens through which to understand physical comedy, the conditions under which it operates and the diachronic development of comedy. Moreover, musical slapstick sheds new light on musical expression and performance and expands concepts of slapstick humor and laughter in the context of the wider field of musical comedy.

Musical humor has received an increasing amount of scholarly attention in recent years. Yet, as Asbjørn Øfsthus Eriksen has noted, studies of humor in musical works often focus on musical content without convincingly connecting their findings to general theories of humor (2016, 251–252). Eriksen proposes a

---

[1] For a wide-ranging historical survey on the power of humor in framing social protest and as a vehicle for expressing critical thought on policy, see Hart and Bos 2008.

https://doi.org/10.1515/9783110571981-004

taxonomy of humor in instrumental music to address this gap. Examples from the Western musical canon provide the basis for this taxonomy, which demonstrates how humor in music may be accounted for through the theories of Henri Bergson (1859–1941), Sigmund Freud (1856–1939), John Morreall (*1947), Victor Raskin (*1944), Thomas C. Veatch, and others. Eriksen's analyses result in the identification of the following five categories:

> A). Imitations of phenomena in the outside world, especially nonmusical sounds (onomatopoeia); B). Quotations: excerpts from well-known pieces placed in a new stylistic context; C). Departures from stylistic norms (inter-stylistic humor); D. Excessive repetitions (of melodic or stylistic clichés); E. Incongruities in relation to the premises of the musical piece (discrepant musical characters or musical syntax) [. . .]. (251–252.)

Eriksen's study indicates that, even in "abstract" instrumental music, the nature of humor broadly resembles humor as experienced in other domains, dispelling any assumption that underlying representational logic is required in order to induce laughter. In this current chapter, my intention is not to pursue further taxonomies in the domain of musical slapstick, but to say something of the multifaceted aesthetic character of musical slapstick, and the nature of its resistance to representational logic. My hope is that by focusing not on categories, but on the patterns or manner by which musical slapstick runs contrary to perceived norms of expression, I might offer some insight into how musical slapstick has developed through history, and how it can be understood across various musical styles and genres.

Bergson's theorization of laughter lies at the core of Eriksen's study and has proved hugely influential in the scholarly study of humor during the course of the past century. Bergson highlights three conditions in particular as prerequisite for laughter to be elicited: a main character demonstrating unsocial behavior (2007, 65); a callous disposition on the part of the audience (59–60, 65); and a situation characterized by a degree of automation or repetition (65). For Bergson, laughter provides a social corrective for human behavior. We might even read into Bergson an understanding that laughter is not only an expression of joy, but a manifestation of suppressed fear to which it is thereby correlative (cf. Edwards 2017, 109; Zenck 1979, 158–159). The underlying implication of Bergson's theory, it might be argued, is that laughter is a form of release, a spontaneous letting go, through which reality is repressed, creating an ironic distance from what might ultimately be considered a deep-seated angst or fear. Slapstick corresponds well with this interpretation of Bergson's theory, while at the same time it accentuates a level of physicality – the exaggerated forms, and absurdity of which, only enhance the sense of ironic distance experienced by the audience from the actions and events onstage.

Louise Peacock draws on Bergson's theory in her study of slapstick and comic performance, while a focus on comic pain and violence lies at the heart of her analyses of slapstick. Through a number of examples from *Jackass* and reality TV, Peacock illustrates that *Schadenfreude* and the respondency of audiences to comic pain are very much alive in the twenty-first century (2014, 171). While the origins of slapstick seem to build on this kind of delight at the physical misfortune of others, a vernacular understanding of slapstick is arguably more broadly conceived. And while pain and violence are often used in the context of musical slapstick, a direct corporeal enactment of pain is not necessarily prerequisite for a physical, music comedy moment to be understood as slapstick.

Pain or violence in itself – and representations of, or associations to this alone – are not funny; it is the exaggerated means by which the pain is inflicted that is comical in musical slapstick on the stage. Moreover, slapstick is commonly understood as the exaggerated movements of jester-like buffoonery, which similarly does not necessarily entail the infliction of pain. Certain forms of exaggerated movement often suffice in upholding a sense of ironic distance from what might otherwise seem like normal actions, which become funny for their seemingly pointless physical overexertion. Music can enhance or even instigate an audience's sense of this ironic distance; through the exaggeration of musical norms and by others means, it can transform how we perceive physical actions, as will be illustrated. The subversion of a signifying moment creates ironic distance, in a similar fashion to how, in parody, we recognize a significant gap between the meaning we attach to a signifier and its appearance in an unfamiliar context or form. Musical exaggeration, expressive incongruence, mechanization and repetition, and challenges to the physical and technical abilities of a performer, are all common features of musical slapstick, as is the permutation of perceived musical norms. These qualities of musical slapstick will be revisited throughout this chapter.

1 Slapstick: from the Greek stage to the opera house

Slapstick would appear to have roots in the sounds and acoustically enhanced effects of early forms of theatre and can be traced back to the use of sticks on the comic stage of ancient Greece. Comments on the manuscript for Aristophanes's (ca. 446 B.C.–ca. 386 B.C.) play Νεφέλαι [*Clouds*, 423 B.C.], most likely made during a period he spent revising the play (though it is not certain that the comments are his), offer rare insight into the mise-en-scène of the play, and describe among other things an old man beating his neighbor in order to hide feeble jokes (Griffith 2015, 530). Conventions of the time indicate that stage directions always had to correspond closely with the dialogue in the play, anything else was not permitted; and while not much evidence is given by Aristophanes regarding such directions, his plays often feature one character, often a master, beating another, often a slave, with a stick (531). Notably, these sticks may have been fashioned in ways that intensified the sound of the blows and caused much less pain than sound. In Greek theatres, with their carefully designed acoustic attributes, artificial sound effects were an important feature in plays (532). R. Drew Griffith suggests that these sticks may have their origins in the cobbler's workshops of the time and a device used to hold leather while cutting it – two meter-long slats of wood, fastened together like giant tweezers and covered with leather. In principle, such a tool may have been used much like a clapper. The onomatopoeic names applied to similar instruments of the time in Turkish would suggest that the noise was indeed distinctive (532–533).

There is good reason to believe that the revival of Greek style dramas in the sixteenth century brought with it a revisiting of the tools and techniques used in the mise-en-scène of earlier times. The *batocio* or "slapstick" used by Harlequin, a stock character in *commedia dell'arte*, may well have served as the modern counterpart of the kind of stick referred to by Aristophanes. The connection between cobblers and *commedia dell'arte*, with its origins in sixteenth-century Italy, is well-documented – the masks used in the plays were crafted by cobblers (Griffith 2015, 533).

The improvised theatre forms of *commedia dell'arte* also proved a significant influence on opera, seemingly perpetuating the influence of early slapstick from Greek style dramas into a new domain. The characters and comedy set pieces of *commedia dell'arte* provided stereotypes and comedy action, and a means by which to satirize real-life situations on the operatic stage. The Da Ponte-Mozart operas, for instance – operas such as *Le nozze di Figaro* [*The Marriage of Figaro*, 1786], *Il dissoluto punito, ossia il Don Giovanni* [*Don Giovanni*, 1787], and *Così fan tutte, ossia La scuola degli amanti* [*Thus Do They All, or The School for Lovers,* 1790] – elaborate on and satirize contemporaneous social behavior and feature roles that recall the masked character types of Harlequin (Figaro and Don Giovanni), Pantalone (Doctor Bartolo), and Columbina (Zerlina, Susanna and Despina). *Così fan tutte* in particular is famous for its hyperbole, overblown stereotypes, and narrative of fiancé swapping, challenging socially-accepted norms and affording a great deal of potential for physical comedy and slapstick in productions. As opera scholar Burton D. Fisher writes, it is an exaggeration for effect that is not meant to be taken seriously. In Da Ponte's hands, it most assuredly has undertones – and overtones – of Enlightenment conflicts, ideology, and contradictions: those historic prejudices against women, their lack of power, the gender divide and the hypocrisies inherent in male attitudes to women. In the end, *Così fan tutte* may simpl[y] be a sceptical questioning of the Enlightenment, and in a certain sense, a bridge to nineteenth-century Romanticism, and eventually, to twentieth-century feminism.   (2005, 21)

While on the surface an unassuming comedy of light-hearted confusion, the underlying themes of emotional dysfunctionality and sexual oppression are nevertheless formative for most productions. The greater the level of outrageous satire and slapstick behavior that we are presented with, the further suppressed – yet conversely apparent – are the cruel social norms of reality. The distance between laughter and misery can be short; the opera provides a measure of the norms against which it defines itself and is as relevant today – and offers as much opportunity for satire in new productions – as it was when first composed. The recent revival of Jonathan Miller's production, by Henry Fehn at the Seattle Opera, is testimony to this, with its mix of exaggerated physical and sexual onstage antics, slapstick innuendo, and contemporaneous celebrity stereotypes as if taken from *The Kardashians*, with mobile phones in hand. As such, the production performs a counterpoint to darker issues recently addressed by #*metoo* and anti-harassment movements.[2]

Music is often used as a vehicle through which to articulate and animate physical gestures, imitating or enhancing these. In *Così* the counterpoint of the melodic lines flows in such a way – with exaggerated musical gestures and rhythmic changes – as to accommodate or motivate physical movements and dramatic interaction between the characters. Nowhere is this more apparent than in the Sextet in Act 1, "Alla bella Despinetta" ["Meet the pretty Despinetta"]. The spiraling imitation, repetition and parody between the melodic lines invites overstated physical interaction between the characters in productions, challenging audience expectations and perceived conventions of performance practice in the operatic tradition. Jesusa Rodríguez's (*1955) 1995 lip-synced film version, set in a Mexican holiday resort, rates among the most satirical and obscure of productions, with no shortage of sexual innuendo, the Sextet culminating in a stylized *Lucha libre* (freestyle wrestling) match.[3]

At other moments in the opera the music is explicitly motivated by the possibilities of exaggerated physical actions: Wolfgang Amadeus Mozart purportedly composed into the parodistic soprano aria "Come scoglio" ["Like a rock"]

---

[2] See excerpts on the Seattle Opera website: https://seattleopera.org/on-stage/cosi-fan-tutte/. Accessed 23 September 2018.
[3] See https://www.youtube.com/watch?v=txtFZC0Cio0. Accessed 23 September 2018.

in *Così* absurd extreme leaps in register, not only to melodic effect but also to visual effect (see Marek 2016, 46; Mann 1982, 542): Adriana Ferrarese del Bene (c.1755–c.1804) was Da Ponte's mistress at the time of the premiere and performed the role of Fiordiligi. She was renowned for her remarkable range and had the habit of lowering her head for low notes and throwing her head back for high notes (Marek 2016, 46; and Mann 1982, 542). Wolfgang Amadeus Mozart, nurturing his dislike for Ferrarese and poking fun at her, apparently composed the angular intervallic leaps in order that she appear as undignified as she sounded, with her head nodding back and forth repeatedly (Marek 2016, 46; and Mann 1982, 542). The music, then, not only articulates physical comedic action for Wolfgang Amadeus Mozart, but actuates it.

2 From music hall to the silver screen

While the musical slapstick of *commedia dell'arte* proved influential for Wolfgang Amadeus Mozart, as it did for a number of operatic genres, from *Comédie-Italienne* to *opera buffa*, its influence would later extend into any number of popular genres of music theatre, music hall traditions in Britain and Vaudeville in the United States, and of course musical cinema and comedy films. In these comic genres, music was an effective means by which to create ironic distance from graver contemporaneous issues. This was very much the case in the film *Let George Do It* (1940) (a.k.a. *To Hell with Hitler* in the US), starring British music hall and film icon George Formby (1904–1961) in the role of George Hepplewhite (Figure 1). In the film, a banjulele player from a British dance band performing in Bergen, Norway, before German occupation, is found dead in his hotel room. The banjulele player, it turns out, was a British agent sent to monitor the bandleader who was suspected of passing information to the Germans. British intelligence dispatches another agent to take the place of the Banjulele player, but due to a case of mistaken identity, Hepplewhite, also a banjulele player and on his way to Liverpool to play a gig with a band called the Dinkie Doos, is mistakenly shipped to Bergen in the place of the new agent. The unassuming Hepplewhite auditions for the band with what was to become one of Formby's most popular songs, "Mr. Wu's a Window Cleaner Now," and begins his tenure with the band. He raises the bandleader's suspicions and, having being administered a truth serum in an attempt to persuade him to confess his part in counterespionage, he begins to hallucinate. In his dream, Hepplewhite envisions himself in an airship which carries him to Berlin. Floating above a Nazi rally, he climbs down and enters into a dispute with Hitler on the podium. With the words "you're my last territorial demand in Europe" (*Let George Do It*, 1940,

00:59:34–00:59:37), Hepplewhite promptly plants a right hook on Hitler's face. Hepplewhite awakens, beating his pillow. The performative value of slapstick is key to the propaganda conveyed in the scene, with the dance hall star, Formby, placed on the frontline in a direct confrontation with Hitler. He is simultaneously the unassuming comedian with whom his audience could identify, playing himself on the silver screen, and the hero who takes on Hitler singlehandedly.

This example illustrates how the public personae of a performer can contribute added value in musical slapstick. The effectiveness of the slapstick moment is closely connected to the audience's understanding of the performative role of the musician. Formby is able to engage with grave issues in a light-hearted manner, his character constructed in the mold of a natural, unassuming entertainer: if he can punch Hitler, anyone can. Formby's character displays similarities with the unassuming buffoonery of the Harlequin type, and is typical of his performances which combine musical prowess with slapstick physical comedy. In *Let George Do It*, music is core to the narrative plot and slapstick comedy situations, and is integral in establishing ironic distance from the underlying theme. At the same time, the music and complex performative levels in

Figure 1: Movie poster for the US release of "Let George Do It." Image courtesy of Everett Collection/Mary Evans Picture Library.

Formby's role invited an audience in and served to bolster morale around a common understanding of the dark realities of the time.

3 Ideological undercurrents: from the tragic to the comic

The grave events of the twentieth century also provided the backdrop for the early career of Danish-born musical comedian of Jewish heritage, Victor Borge (1909–2000), who fled the Third Reich for the United States age 32 in 1940 (Henty 2016, 1). Borge's unique combination of pianistic virtuosity and comic aptitude owed much to Vaudeville, and was as effective on stage as on screen. His ironic take on the Western classical musical canon and his slapstick performances, navigating masterfully between the highbrow and lowbrow, attracted huge audiences and installed him as a household name. His slapstick physical gestures and frowns, and exaggeration of and interruptions to the works he performed, became all the more effective set against his genuine, virtuosic talents at the piano. Few comedians have traversed the divide between serious performance practice and facile comic wit with such elegance.

In some of his best-loved sketches, music and physical comedy are seamlessly interwoven. Appearing on the Dean Martin show in 1969 (Borge 2003, 00:42:50–00:48:00), Borge – following a brief comic rendition of Ludwig van Beethoven's (1770–1827) *Mondscheinsonate* [*Moonlight Sonata*, 1801] – launches into Gioachino Rossini's (1792–1868) *Guillaume Tell* [*William Tell*, 1829] overture. But the notes of the version he begins to perform are inverted, as the page is upside down. He stops, turns the page up the right way, and starts again, this time with the correct pitches, to much laughter from the audience. A version of *An der schönen blauen Donau* ["The Blue Danube," 1866] then ensues, with Borge slamming the piano lid in time with the music during the introduction, before adding an ascending glissando during the theme, which sends his right hand off the end of the keyboard and Borge off the piano stool and on to the floor. He gets up and continues where he left off, increasingly exaggerating the strides in his left arm until he raises his arm so high as to knock himself on the nose. The tessitura of the melody also expands, until with no keys left at the top end of the piano he strikes the piano frame beyond with his right hand. He stops, gets up and pushes the piano to the right in order to resolve the problem, then continues. Reaching the climax, he again encounters the same problem. This time he tears away and disposes of the right-hand-side of the music page onto the floor and continues once more, only to then end up repeating the same phrase over and over like a broken record – the lack of further musical notation preventing him from continuing. Looking to the floor he eventually picks up a fragment of paper, licks it and slaps it onto the music stand and begins to play; however, the reverse side of the page he plays from contains Felix Mendelssohn's (1809–1847) *Hochzeitsmarsch* ["Wedding March," 1842]. Interrupting the performance once more, he looks again to the floor for the correct piece of music. Retrieving this he tears off a fragment, sticks it to the piano and plays a resounding perfect cadence, rounding off the sketch.

Borge's dry humor, combined with musical virtuosity and physical comedy, crosses effortlessly between serious and popular entertainment. Poking fun at the conventions of the classical art music tradition, he is still no less an insider, as his mastery of the piano confers. The subtlety of his unassuming frowns and physical comic gestures are all the more effective against his credibility as a "serious" performer. In making light of the serious, the gravity of that which is labelled trivial paradoxically becomes more apparent (Henty 2016, 79).

Speaking in a candid interview on the television show, *Day at Night* with James Day (1918–2008) in 1973,[4] Borge comments:

> the funny thing about humor [. . .] is that it is very serious [. . .]. Humor itself is not funny, it is the seriousness that makes humor. A very serious situation – a person falls on a banana peel for instance – that is darned serious, isn't it? But you can't help laughing if you see it on the stage if somebody does it. If somebody does something terribly serious then it is hilariously funny.   (1973, 00:09:44–00:10:39)

Borge continues to explain that such serious things happen in reality. Pianists have been known to fall off the piano bench. In the concert hall, the reaction is one of shock. But when Borge does it, it is hilarious. "The more serious, the more humor there is to be found in it" (00:11:57–00:12:00). Day and Borge speak of Borge's time in occupied Denmark. Borge was a reputed comedian in Denmark before he fled, and made fun of the Nazis, who of course represented a serious threat. Borge follows up, saying:

> You cannot fight a situation like that with words. You must have more than just words, because you cannot do it scientifically. You have to have something that goes deeper than words. And that is, I think, humor. Humor is one of the things that can create things in a man or a woman, in a person that nothing else . . . it's like tickling somebody.
> (00:18:27–00:18:57)

---

4 Day at Night, "Day at Night: Victor Borge, Danish Comedian, Conductor, and Pianist" interview with James Day, 1973. Accessed 19 February 2018, https://www.youtube.com/watch?v=_RmOHm3owG4.

As Hanako Henty aptly puts it, "his work contains a deeper message: that music and humor are powerful forms of expression, capable of reaffirming human connections as well as redefining what it means to be human in the face of adversity" (2016, 79). The interview revolves around the mutual dependence of seriousness, or even the gravest of circumstances, and humor. As Borge indicates, the distance between the two can be very short, and physical comedy cuts quickly to the essence, articulating in the most perfunctory of gestures a satirical take on convention or even a cutting response to contemporaneous societal challenges.

4 Parody and musical slapstick in Kagel and Ligeti

While slapstick often inflicts violence or misfortune, this is not necessarily prerequisite in vernacular conceptions of slapstick. The musical slapstick of Borge attests to this. Other more outrageous forms of physical overexertion display any number of means by which to poke fun at convention or norms of social behavior. Nowhere is this more evident than in Monty Python. With sketches such as "The Ministry of Silly Walks" (*Monty Python's Flying Circus*, season 2, episode 1, 1970), movements exaggerated to the extreme for no apparent reason satirize the very action of walking. Yet, even the act of walking contains within it associations to different activities, such as the sport of walking represented at the Olympics or the marching of Nazi soldiers. With seemingly innocuous and meaningless gestures, more complex issues can potentially be awoken in the collective (sub)consciousness, which extend beyond visual representation and representationality. The issues at stake are much greater than can be explicated in any straightforward way in the signification of actions. The meaninglessness of the actions represented are in part responsible for making them funny. Rather, it is the way in which slapstick comedy manages to undercut such representational logic in a counterproductive and outrageous way that renders it meaningful in new ways. Slapstick is characterized by the *manner* in which it transgresses the norms of behavior, and as such cannot be defined normatively. Slapstick shares in this way certain affinities with other subversive forms of expression, such as those associated with parody.

Parody and outrageous, seemingly inadvertent movements, provide much of the creative impetus in the works of German-Argentine composer Mauricio Kagel (1931–2008), noted for his experimental approach to music theatre. In *Staatstheater* (1970), the apotheosis of absurdist theatrical performance, we witness not a coherent narrative or consistent musical form, but fragmented sounds and actions. Dubbed an anti-opera, the conventions of the opera house are inverted or negated and performers are themselves required to piece together the parodic scenes. Actions normally considered extraneous or secondary in a theatrical or operatic context – for example, the movement of a singer on the stage from one place to another – are constitutive of the form and material for Kagel (see Edwards 2017, 130; Heile 2006, 58). The apparatus and machinery normally relegated to the wings is brought into full view in tandem with the fragmented parodic references to opera history. Metronomes and other items normally confined to the practice room or hidden behind the scenes are brought to the fore. Performances engage with the media through which music and opera is performed. There is no plot to accompany the obscure choreography of the performers and the objects with which they interact. In a performance by Das Kölner Ensemble für Neue Musik of the hour-long movement entitled "Repertoire," the opening scene features a man in speedos and painted green, with diving goggles on his face and scuba diving fins on his feet. He appears from behind a wall, strides slowly across the stage striking a mounted tuning fork intermittently, until he disappears off the stage again. The one-hundred scenes of the movement that ensue are a display of absurdist physical interaction with various props, parodying operatic tradition, fragmenting and exaggerating norms of performance convention.

György Ligeti's (1923–2006) magnum opus, the opera *Le Grand Macabre* (1974–1977, revised 1996), one of the most successful operas composed in recent decades, extends the tradition of absurdist music theatre in a new direction. This "anti-anti opera" (Ligeti 1983, 68 and 111) – the double negative resulting in a positive – is an opera between and beyond Kagel's anti-opera, and an absurdist avant-garde diagnosis of the human condition. The opera tells the tale of the gluttonous, hedonistic people of Breughelland and their tribulations when faced with the threat of imminent destruction. The expressive heterogeneity of the opera corresponds with the full scale of emotional responses to this impending fate, from neurotic anxiety and deep-seated fear of death (embodied in the character Gepopo) to the suppression of this fear expressed through satire, parody, and comedy (embodied in the Harlequin-like character Piet the Pot). In the end, the forewarned apocalypse is averted and the people of Breughelland are spared and left to continue as before, while the lack of closure leaves the audience wondering whether these events occur every night (Sewell 2006, 40).

The opera finds its creative point of departure in the subversion of norms and resistance to musical conventions. The music displays exaggeration, parody and juxtaposition at almost every juncture. This lends the opera its grotesque character, while slapstick plays a significant part in assimilating the comedy with the music. The suppression of the fear of death is core in the narrative, and is very much in correspondence with notions of laughter as correlative to the suppression of fear.

Moments of musical slapstick effectively enhance a sense of ironic distance from the underlying theme, inducing laughter. Ligeti describes similar sentiments in relation to his music, succinctly summarizing this as "fear from the wrong side of the telescope" (1983, 81). Moreover, "the comic elements, fear, buffa and seria are not only inextricably mixed up in it, they merge and become one and the same thing. What is serious is at the same time comical and the comical is terrifying" (81). Musical slapstick in the opera is frequently accompanied by musical parody and quotation, heightening the sense of ironic distance. As Ligeti describes, "pseudo-quotations are always intended for the comic moments" (120). Nowhere is this more apparent than in the opening of the second scene of the opera, in which the Court Astronomer, Astradamors, is subject to a violent pursuit by his sexually oppressive wife, Mescalina. Their "grotesque, shameless dance" (Ligeti 2003, 94) is a veritable sadomasochistic romp, during the course of which Astradamors is subject to varying levels of violence, written into the stage directions, including whiplashes, injections with a spit, a karate chop, and a stick, accompanied by the appropriate percussion cracks in the orchestra, before a spider is introduced into the escapade. The sight of it sends Astradamors into a frenzied "mad, Baroque aria" (90). The scene is accompanied by a frenetic orchestra, performing percussive interjections and exaggerated rhythmic patterns somewhat akin to Igor Stravinsky's (1882–1971) "Danse sacrale (L'Élue)" ["Sacricial Dance (the Chosen One)"] from *Le sacre du printemps. Tableaux de la Russie païenne en deux parties* [*The Rite of Spring*, 1913, revised 1922 and 1943]. A distorted rendition of the 'Infernal Galop' from Jacques Offenbach's (1819–1880) *Orphée aux enfers* [*Orpheus in the Underworld*, 1858] is interjected into the scene, marking something of a tumultuous climax, while Robert Schumann's (1810–1856) "Fröhlicher Landmann, von der Arbeit zurückkehrend. Frisch und munter" ["The Merry Peasant," 1848] and a distorted fragment of Franz Liszt's (1811–1886) "Grand galop chromatique" ["The Grand Chromatic Gallop," 1838] appear juxtaposed with other references often submersed in the chaotic textures (Edwards 2017, 54–56).

The fragmented and distorted musical quotations provide a disorientating accompaniment to the physical acts of abuse and violence onstage. The parodied material, removed from its usual context and twisted into new and fragmentary states, corresponds with the exaggerated, ridiculousness of the actions, granting an audience the opportunity to maintain a level of ironic distance from events onstage and the prerogative to suppress recognition of the uncomfortable truths at the heart of the narrative acted out by the characters.

Yet another episode of physical comedy and violence occurs between two characters at the start of the third scene of the opera, as the Black and the White Minister of Breughelland exchange insults in the Royal Palace. The seriousness of the predicament facing Breughelland is forgotten as the two become increasingly embroiled in ludicrous political posturing. They proceed to reel off a new obscenity for each letter of the alphabet, abusing one another physically in the process: "Arse-licker, arse-kisser! Blackmailer, bloodsucker! Charleton, clodhopper!" (Ligeti 2003, 140–147), and so on, all punctuated by interjections in the orchestra. The language becomes increasingly abusive and is interrupted, as marked in the stage directions, by slapstick-style gestures as the ministers take turns to box each other on the ears. Frustrated by their quarrelling, the Prince of Breughelland, Prince Go-Go, threatens to resign, only to be set straight by the politicians, who thrust him onto a rocking horse for riding lessons and then force a crown onto his head for posture exercises. Different stagings of the opera adapt the political jibes in the libretto in accordance with local and national colloquialisms and in response to the political circumstances where the production is staged. The La Fura Dels Baus production of the opera alledgedly caused some commotion at its Italian premiere in Rome in 2009, when individuals in the audience joined in with the exchange of insults between the ministers, apparently as an expression of their disapproval of the performance.

Such comical moments engage an audience yet maintain a certain distance in the co-presence of the spectator and the performer. We are struck by the violence and precariousness of the situation in the underlying plot, yet exaggeration and irony prove a powerful means by which to allow the audience to suppress and even laugh at the peril of the people of Breughelland. Slapstick makes apparent the unreality of the situation, allowing an audience to build a callous disposition to the characters onstage. Yet, as is the case in *Le Grand Macabre*, laughter conceals underlying issues connected with ideology and convention. Critical engagement with prejudices and preconceptions is a creative point of departure for the opera. And slapstick plays counterpoint to normative thought, normal behavior, conventions and ideology. Perhaps it might even be said that the more effective and hysterical we find the slapstick subversion of antisocial behavior on display, the more thoroughly cognizant we actually are of the normative function of that to which slapstick provides relief. As such, slapstick might be considered a significant marker of norms of behavior or ideology in society, drawing attention to challenging circumstances that it is more desirable to distance oneself from than to address. Ligeti was himself deeply affected by the events of WWII and lost family members in the Holocaust. This nurtured in him a deep aversion to any ideology that, left unchecked, could lead to disastrous consequences. These views carried over into his creative and compositional poetics and provided the foundation for his compositional approach to challenging convention, stable meaning and closed conceptions of knowledge (Edwards 2017, 136). Musical humor and slapstick are effective means to this end.

The greater our laughter at the performers in their overexertion, misfortune, suffering or pain, the more we acknowledge and simultaneously suppress the undercurrents, ideologies, stereotypes and conventions that define our reality. As such, slapstick contributes a greater understanding of contingency and critical thought. When laughter subsides, we might do well to reflect over the deeper significance of the conditions that provide the sustenance for slapstick to exist.

5 Slapstick and new media

More recent strains of musical slapstick have emerged in wake of the digital revolution. Continuing in a similar vein to the absurdist slapstick of Kagel's music theatre, engagement with technology and the apparatus involved in how we experience music is key in the comedy of new media. For instance, Beyoncé's (*1981) exaggerated dance moves in the music video for "Single Ladies (Put a Ring on It)" (2008) are inimitable but nonetheless consistent with the genre to which the song belongs and accepted as such. But in the viral YouTube mashup video entitled "Beyoncé the Tank Engine," in which the sound is replaced by the theme for Thomas the Tank Engine, the video becomes a comical, slapstick parody of the original.[5] The synchronised, exaggerated dance moves are perceived as incongruous, on many levels, when accompanied by the simplistic *oompah* of the children's television theme.

Similar incongruities prevail in countless YouTube "shredding videos." Santeri Ojala, a Finnish media artist who goes under the name of StSanders, soon found fame with his juxtaposition of videos by famous guitarists such as Eddie Van Halen, Santana and Slash with rerecorded guitar parts and ambient noises. The intensity of the gestures, concentration and gratified expressions of the artists are incongruous with the random notes and sounds performed on inferior rigs with a poor room acoustic, all superimposed with the noises of an appreciating audience.[6]

Perhaps the most hysterical example of these new media slapstick parodies of recent years is the overdubbed version of the video for David Bowie (1947–2016) and Mick Jagger's (*1943) cover of "Dancing in the Street" (1964; 1985) by sound designer Mario Wienerroither, one of several films in a series of what he terms "musicless music videos."[7] The wild dancing and gestures of Bowie and Jagger become

---

[5] See https://www.youtube.com/watch?v=w8qaGcq8Ruk. Accessed 22 September 2018.
[6] See https://www.youtube.com/user/StSandersMisc/videos. Accessed 22 September 2018.
[7] See https://www.youtube.com/user/digitalofen/videos. Accessed 22 September 2018.

bizarre and outrageous accompanied by a soundtrack of shuffling feet, whispering, strained voices, shouting, a Mick Jagger burp and ambient night-time sound effects. In Wienerroither's videos, the energy invested in the flamboyant gestures by the artists, consistent with their expressions and the visual representations of the genres with which they are normally associated, become ridiculous. The absurdity of Bowie's and Jagger's actions is reminiscent of works such as *Staatstheater* by Mauricio Kagel, and in particular the sudden appearance of a leg or an arm from behind a wall, as in "Repertoire."[8] The videos draw attention to the movements of the performers in new ways, the soundtrack accentuating the elements of performance, the scratches and bumps, normally concealed and considered undesirable. It is these sounds, combined with the exaggerated movements, that form the comic meaning, negating normative expectations to the genre with which the performance was originally associated.

Music has the capacity to transform the meaning of visual, physical actions. In the case of the abovementioned YouTube films, expectations and perceived norms are transgressed, the music, or even lack thereof, drawing attention to physical excesses and absurd qualities in the performances that might otherwise be perceived as broadly generic in their normal context. In the case of Formby, the role and public personae of the musician in itself provides a vital premise for understanding the conditions under which slapstick operates. By contrast, Wolfgang Amadeus Mozart satirizes social behavior in his operas, which is enhanced in productions through the enactment of slapstick comedy set pieces. At the same time, music could generate exaggerated physical actions for Wolfgang Amadeus Mozart and challenge the abilities of his singers in a comic fashion. Borge's personae and virtuosic talent is also formative of a particular brand of musical slapstick, challenging convention with his physical wit, and demonstrating that the distance between oppressive ideologies and humor can be very short.

Musical slapstick is a powerful and direct strain of comedy, expressing with apparent ease a response to potentially complex circumstances and underlying ideologies. Through parody, quotation, exaggeration and fragmentation, music creates ironic distance while simultaneously nurturing critical engagement with challenging issues. Music is by nature a physical activity, and the full force of its performative influence is clearly palpable in musical slapstick. Musical slapstick challenges preconceptions and resists stable meaning, highlighting instead the shift in meaning as exaggerated, incongruous musical expressions and physical actions infuse in the familiar something new.

---

8 See Das Kölner Ensemble für Neue Musik's performance from 0:28:48–0:29.50: https://youtu.be/IuM8sYuZPp8. Accessed 22 September 2018.

Bibliography

Bergson, Henri. *Laughter: An Essay on the Meaning of the Comic.* Trans. by Cloudesley Brereton and Fred Rothwell. Gloucester: Dodo Press, 2007.

"Beyoncé the Tank Engine." https://www.youtube.com/watch?v=w8qaGcq8Ruk (accessed 22 September 2018).

Borge, Victor. *The Best of the Dean Martin Variety Show* [DVD], Vol. 6., Palm Desert: Guthy-Renker Entertainment, 2003.

Day at Night, "Day At Night: Victor Borge, Danish Comedian, Conductor, and Pianist," interview with James Day, 1973, https://www.youtube.com/watch?v=_Rm0Hm3owG4 (accessed 19 February 19, 2018).

Edwards, Peter. *György Ligeti's Le Grand Macabre: Postmodernism, Musico-Dramatic Form and the Grotesque.* Abingdon and New York: Routledge, 2017.

Eriksen, Asbjørn Øfsthus. "A Taxonomy of Humour in Instrumental Music." *Journal of Musicological Research* 5 (2016): 233–263.

Fischer, Burton D. Ed. *Così fan tutte.* Boca Raton, FL: Opera Journeys Publishing, 2005.

Griffith, R. Drew. "The Aristophanic Slapstick." *The Classical Quarterly* 65.2 (2015): 530–533.

Hart, Marjolen 't, and Dennis Bos. Eds. *Humour and Social Protest.* Cambridge: Cambridge University Press, 2008.

Heile, Björn. *The Music of Mauricio Kagel.* Farnham: Ashgate, 2006.

Henty, Hanako S. *A Fine Line Between Art and Entertainment: Music and Humor in the Performances of Victor Borge.* MM diss., University of Miami, 2016.

Kagel, Mauricio. "Repertoire" from *Staatstheater.* Das Kölner Ensemble für Neue Musik: https://youtu.be/IuM8sYuZPp8 (accessed 22 September 2018).

"Let George Do It", *George Formby Collection* [DVD]. London: StudioCanal, 2007.

Ligeti, György. *György Ligeti in Conversation with Péter Várnai, Josef Häusler, Claude Samuel and Himself.* Trans. by Gabor J. Schabert et al. London: Eulenburg Books, 1983.

Ligeti, György. *Le Grand Macabre* 1974–77, revised 1996 [score ED8522] (Mainz: Schott, 2003).

Mann, William. *The Operas of Mozart.* New York: Oxford University Press, 1982.

Marek, Dan H. *Alto: The Voice of Bel Canto.* London: Rowman & Littlefield Publishers, 2016.

Monty Python's Flying Circus, "The Ministry of Silly Walks", season 2, episode 1, 1970.

Mozart, Wolfgang A. *Così fan tutte.* Jonathan Miller's production, by Henry Fehn at the Seattle Opera: https://seattleopera.org/on-stage/cosi-fan-tutte/ (accessed 23 September 2018).

Mozart, Wolfgang A. *Così fan tutte.* Production by Jesusa Rodríguez: https://www.youtube.com/watch?v=txtFZC0Cio0 (accessed 23 September 2018).

Peacock, Louise. *Slapstick and Comic Performance: Comedy and Pain.* New York: Palgrave, 2014.

Sewell, Amanda Jo. *Blending the Sublime and the Ridiculous: A Study of Parody in György Ligeti's Le Grand Macabre.* MM diss., Graduate College of Bowling Green, 2006.

StSanders. YouTube channel. https://www.youtube.com/user/StSandersMisc/videos (accessed 22 September 2018).

Wienerroither, Mario. YouTube channel. https://www.youtube.com/user/digitalofen/videos (accessed 22 September 2018).

Zenck, Martin. "Auswirkungen einer 'musique informelle' auf die neue Musik: Zu Theodor W. Adornos Formvorstellung." *International Review of the Aesthetics and Sociology of Music* 10. 2 (1979): 137–165.

Carolin Struwe-Rohr
Sinking and Falling Bodies: The Beginnings of Literary Slapstick in the Pre-Modern Era

1 Early modern literature and slapstick

It is funny and absurd when Charlie Chaplin (1889–1977) gets pied by a robot, a feeding machine again and again (*Modern Times*. Dir. Charlie Chaplin, 1936. TC 00:13:10–00:13:28) or when Buster Keaton (1895–1966) on the run manages to get rid of his persecutors through a series of coincidences, but is then, through another series of coincidences, running straight into the arms of the law enforcement (*Cops*. Dirs. Edward F. Cline & Buster Keaton, 1922. TC 00:13:03–00:17:50). Or, in general, when heroes lose the power over their bodies, start to stumble and fall. Research has defined such scenes as *slapstick*, a term which was established in the sixteenth century within the *commedia dell'arte*.[1] However, with regard to narratives of former periods, there are already narrative scenes in the late Middle Ages as well as in the early modern period, which significantly resemble the cinematographic scenes mentioned above. Take, for instance, when in Hartmann's (presumably died between 1210 and 1220) *Iwein* (ca. 1200) Keie, a respected knight of King Arthur, falls off his horse like a sack of potatoes during a fight,[2] or when the protagonist of *Prosa-Lancelot* [*Prose-Lancelot*, ca. middle of the thirteenth century], a German adaption of the French *Lancelot en prose* (1215–1230), forgets about his hand that holds a weapon and almost kills Queen Ginover.[3] Other examples include *Die Wiener Meerfahrt* [The Viennese Sea Journey, thirteenth century], in which a man is thrown out of a pub window, because he has supposedly disturbed a so-called pilgrim's journey of drunken visitors. In "Der fünfmal getötete Pfarrer" ["The Pastor Who was Killed Five Times," late fifteenth century], a dead pastor is accidently 'killed' over and over again.

---

[1] In this generic context, slapstick had a literal meaning: "a stage prop constructed of two wooden paddles, joined at one end, used by circus clowns to hit each other, thereby producing a slapping sound" (Crafton 1995, 108).
[2] "[D]â mite wart ouch er gesant / ûz dem satel als ein sac" ["At the same time he was beaten so hard, that he fell off his horse like a sack of potatoes"] (Hartmann 2008, 459). Unless otherwise indicated, all translations throughout the chapter are my own.
[3] "[D]er hant [vergaß] da er die glen inne hette" ["forgot the hand as he was holding the lance"] (Lancelot 2005, 622).

In the following, I will focus on these premodern scenes as examples of a particular kind of narrative mode abiding by its own narrative logic. To expound this narrative mode, I will use the concept of *slapstick* as a starting point and means to analyse and describe it.[4] Considering only the logic of action, research on medieval literature has pointed out that these scenes or texts should evoke laughter among the readers and that they are set between the poles of nonsense and violence (Keller 1999, 94). Yet other research has shown that they present some kind of social and systemic disturbance (Müller 2007; Philipowski 2002), or that they simply just have no meaning at all (Haug 1993; Grubmüller 1993). However, these comedy scenes are by no means pointless. Through the application of the concept of slapstick on these texts – or, rather, text passages – it is possible to connect different angles from which we can better understand such textual moments. In this regard, I will refer to Lisa Trahair's and Alex Clayton's definition of slapstick. Slapstick "reduces narrative to the barest components of time, space, events, and consequence so that coincidence and arbitrariness become the instigators of history and fate" (Trahair 2007, 44). This can be observed in tales as well as in scenes that digress from the main text (*digressio*) and thereby establish new or other spatial or chronological settings and logics that compete with the already existing ones. The cause of the events portrayed in the texts is either an absurd coincidence or some kind of interference, a situation which is ambiguous for the characters and causes incongruent chains of action. With this accentuation of causality, slapstick can be understood "as a jesting mode, a playful treatment of the relations between cause and effect" (48). It enables various perspectives on the topic of causality and unsettles the readers' opinions about established causal relationships. This playful handling with causality is often combined with a focus on the presentation of physicality and materiality of the protagonist's body: "Narrative comedy thus evacuates the significance of the identity of the protagonists and the determination of their existence as the embodiment of fundamental states of being" (44).

---

[4] In this manner, one could use the concept also for the analysis of narrative texts. With this in mind, I do not state a difference between narrative and slapstick as Trahair does (she speaks of a "duel between slapstick and narrative, where the former is bent on exploring the multifarious possibilities of the anarchy of pure pleasure and the latter is determined to rein in that impulse, limiting it by subordinating it to the desire for meaning" [2007, 36]), but I think of literary slapstick as a form of explorative and sometimes even anarchic form of narrative mode. With this understanding literary narrative slapstick can be not only a form of "exemplifying the conditions of the restricted economy" (9), as Trahair assumes, but also exemplifying "those of general economy" (9).

In sum, slapstick is "a declaration of the physicality of its objects and people" (Clayton 2007, 11). Hence, slapstick moments can be created where judgement is overridden by the actions of the body, such as in any situation "that calls our attention to the physicality in a person" (Bergson 1980, 93). Frequently, this focus on the body is accompanied by the distinction between the body and the mind: "The prevalence in slapstick comedy of matters of activity and passivity, of control of the body and the loss of control over it, may derive from a fundamental incongruence of human existence" (Clayton 2007, 205). This can also lead to uncertainty regarding the interpretation of bodies, gestures, and actions, which points to "the capacity of the body to mislead us in our reading of characters' status of mind" (42), which can happen to characters of the fictional world as well as to the reader. These two dimensions – playing with causality and presentation of corporeality – create narrative forms of slapstick, which are either in harmony with or in opposition to each other. In this way, slapstick can tell us about the outrageous or about something which is not meant to be, while really explaining it. Slapstick can be a part of exploring the possibilities of narration as well as the limits of it.

In the following, I will apply these conceptual considerations on two texts of the premodern period: a late courtly epic and a short epic. To begin with, I will take a closer look at an episode of the *Prose-Lancelot*. In the next step, I will analyse the tale of "The Pastor Who was Killed Five Times" by Hans Rosenplüt. On the basis of these texts I will outline how slapstick ideals function in premodern literature.

2 Sinking bodies

The *Prose-Lancelot* contains more than 40,000 lines, was probably compiled around the middle of the thirteenth century, and tells the story of Lancelot, his parents, and his son. It also outlines the legend of King Arthur and the Knights of the Round Table, from its flowering stage until its ending, and all adventures and quests related to the Holy Grail.[5] In particular, the novel describes the illegitimate love between Lancelot and Queen Ginover, the wife of King Arthur. On the one hand, Lancelot's knighthood is driven and strengthened by this love. On the other hand, he is weakened by it, because it also causes paralysis and inaction in him. For instance, when Lancelot hears the voice of Ginover or sees her face, he is totally lost in thoughts. Within the text, this phenomenon is

---

5 For information about transmission, writers, and a summary of the text see Ruberg (1985).

called *gedencken*. It describes those moments in which Lancelot is absent-minded and cannot react according to the situation he is facing. In fact, he becomes a stranger to his own physical existence. As Judith Klinger has shown,

> Lancelot's passive *gedencken* is marked as a loss of self-control and temperance of affect, as a passion caused by the violence of courtly love, which is expressed in the involuntary physical gesture and forms the flipside of his chivalrous public activities. (2001, 196)

The characters within the fictional world describe such scenes as "wunderliches [Verhalten]" ["strange (behaviour)"] (Lancelot 2005, 620). As the hero is refusing to act according to social and chivalrous rules and is momentarily not interested in any kind of interaction, the inactivity is seen as a form of disruption of the courtly social system (Klinger 2001, 193). Moreover, Lancelot obscures insights into his inner thoughts and feelings in that he presents an external appearance resistant to the analysis and mindreading of the other characters. In this manner, he breaks the fundamental rule of the courtly world, which Harald Haferland describes as a metonymic relationship between body and mind (1989, 225). The text is dealing with this scandalous "differentiation of action and thinking by means of a not directly accessible 'inner space' of a person" (Klinger 2001, 192),[6] using a specific form of narration in *digressiones*, in which the narrative logic of slapstick plays an important role. Thus, the text not only outlines the destructive force of the relationship between Lancelot and Ginover with regard to the courtly system, but also explores boundaries of the narration in epic texts.

In the following, I will focus on a scene of the *Prose-Lancelot* in which the phenomenon of *gedencken* features prominently. Here, *gedencken* not only emerges through Lancelot's inactivity (as in Lancelot 2005, 240 & 634), but rather through a kind of comedic performance by the protagonist. When Lancelot meets Ginover in search of another knight, her sight and her voice generate *gedencken*, leading to a physical incongruity of chivalric action, which is recognisable for the bystanders within the fictional world, as well as for the reader: "The Queen said: 'Go now!' Therefore, Lancelot spurred his steed into full gallop. The horse ran where it wanted to, because Lancelot was only looking back, only paying attention to Queen Ginover" (Lancelot 2005, 616).[7] The queen's order and the absolute supremacy of her words "Rytent bald!" ["Go now!"] trigger a chivalric but aimless activity. Lancelot races his steed into full gallop but

---

6 Katharina-Silke Philipowski notes on the topic of this rule: "The nobleman has neither psychological nor religious depth – he IS his conspicuous appearance" (2002, 75).
7 "Da die koniginn sprach: 'Rytent bald!', da nam er das roß mit den sporen und reit so er baldest mocht. Das roß lieff war es wolt, wann er endeth anders nit dann das er hinder sich geyn der konigin sah."

simultaneously looks back at Ginover, who captivates his attention. Here, looking backwards to apprehend his love while riding forwards to carry out the command of Ginover are at odds. Lancelot serves as an Arthurian knight and therefore has to obey all orders by King Arthur and Queen Ginover, but he also secretly relies on the love to Ginover.[8] The problem is that this love is an illegitimate one and its consequences lead to a hostile attitude towards Arthur's Court (Remakel 1995, 38).

> One side or the other can only be forgotten temporarily over and over again. In trying to positivize Lancelot's passion for the queen and yet hold on to her social integration, narration reaches a limit. The radical individualization seems neither livable nor narratable.
> (Müller 2007, 467)

We find a paradoxical situation which occurs regularly in the text but for which no solution is offered. In this scene the intensity of the *courtly love* of Lancelot is almost equally confronted with another form of intensity, which is moving away from it. It could therefore be interpreted as a kind of eruption of this tension within the text – and this eruption is shown by the logic of slapstick.

The focus of the scene, however, lies on presenting the disintegration of body and mind. It shows the moment of the *gedencken* in which Lancelot becomes a stranger to himself by changing the narration's point of view. It does not show what Lancelot is thinking or feeling, but what his horse is feeling. By courtesy of an internal focus, the reader is only presented the cause of the following events – the existential need of the horse to drink:

> The horse thirsted for water and ran towards the river and jumped right into it. The river was deep and wide, but he [Lancelot] turned his eyes only to the Queen. The river was great and it reached the wall nearby, on which the Queen was standing. But when the horse swam cross the river and reached the wall, it could not climb the wall; and it turned back, it swam until it was tired. The steed drowned, and the knight stayed on it till the water reached his shoulders. He did not strive to get out and let the steed do as it wanted to, and remained sitting still. As the Queen saw that the knight was so deep in the water, and she thought he wanted to drown now, she began to scream: "Help, Saint Mary, a knight is drowning here!"[9]
> (Lancelot 2005, 616–618)

---

8 As Jan-Dirk Müller states, in Arthurian epics "*courtly love* and chivalry cannot exist without each other" (Müller 2007, 468; emphasis in original).
9 "Das roß durst und lieff zu dem waßer und sprang darinn. Das waßer was tieff und breit, und sin augen waren allweg off der koniginn. Das waßer was groß und ging an die muren von den loien da die koniginn off was. Da das roß uber geswamm biß an die muren, da enmocht es daruber nit und kerte wiedder umb, es schwamm so lang biß das es müde wart. Das roß ging under das waßer, und der ritter bleib daroff siczen, biß im das waßer an die schultern ging. Er múte sich nit wie er uß keme, und ließ das roß gewerden wies wolt, und saß er allschone. Da die koniginn sah das der ritter so tieff in dem waßer was, und das sie ducht das er yczunt

Ackermann-Arlt has already pointed out that the horse and the rider have to be seen as parts of a metonymic relationship:

> The thirst of the horse corresponds to Lancelot's boundless courtly desire, they are two corresponding powers. [. . .] The irrational animal is in its existence at the mercy of the potential support of the rider, who himself, however, appears as a subjected one.
>
> (1990, 177)

The horse represents the physical dimension of affects which have to be reined by the knight's *ratio* (Friedrich 2008, 233) as a kind of corporeality which got out of control due to Lancelot's desire. This corporeality initiates an unstoppable chain of cause and effect: the thirst leads the horse to the water and to a jump into the water; when the horse is no longer able to swim further it gets tired and finally starts to sink with the knight on its back. This narrative style reveals how Lancelot only seems to be inactive from the outside, but from the inside his *gedencken* is presented as a kind of somersaulting activity, which Lancelot seems not able to control.

This scene shows the incongruity of Lancelot's body and mind during the *gedencken* in the most drastic way: "Man is incongruent within himself. Human existence is an on-going balancing act between *being* a body and *having* a body. [. . .] [I]t is also possible that the sense of humor repeatedly perceives the in-built incongruence of being human" (Berger 1997, 209). This is also displayed by the horse's jump into the water: "In this way the author, who endeavors to establish realistic causal links, certainly spans the range of behavioral psychological probability" (Ackermann-Arlt 1990, 176). Nevertheless, I understand this as an intended moment of irritation by the text, in which the activity of the mind and the inaction of the body, both caused by *gedencken*, are confronted and played off against each other. "A dynamic deployment of the body (the body that he *has*), [is] thwarted because of the momentum, weight or physical placement of the body (the body that he *is*)" (Clayton 2007, 206; emphasis in original). The horse that jumps into the water, driven by its thirst, could therefore be seen as an imaginary fulfilment of Lancelot's desire for Ginover. Yet, the text shows this fulfilment as an overmodulated activity, which runs and runs until it is confronted with the reality of an inactive, sluggish body. If a knight forgets the ethic of chivalry and the knight's *ratio*, the chivalric body and his chivalric horse become a sluggish, heavy mass, which is drowning because of physical conditions. When body and mind are not in sync, a gap between having a body and being a body appears. The text shows the scandal of a chivalric

---

ertrincken wolt, da begunde sie zu ruofen: 'Helffent, frauw Sancta Maria, hie ertrincket yczunt ein ritter!'"

body without *ratio* as an endangerment of the courtly body, which leads to isolation or even the (social) death of the knight. Compared to other epic texts, like *Erec* (ca. 1180–1190), *Iwein*, *Parzival* (ca. between 1210–1220), or *Tristan* (ca. 1210), one can also observe a changed relation between the hero and his environment which arises "as not merely a social milieu or situational locale, but as a physical arena, wherein the body's immediate relation to surrounding topographical features constitutes the primary relation between self and world" (Clayton 2007, 61). This arena is no longer just a venue for chivalric fights, in which courtly bodies are just moving and interacting with each other, but the environment itself turns out to be an enemy of the knight's corporeality.

Moreover, the knight's body becomes available for other people: "Sir Ywain took the steed's bridle and lead it forcibly out of the water. The knight's [Lancelot] weapons and body were completely wet"[10] (Lancelot 2005, 619). Shortly after Ywain, a knight of King Arthur's Round Table, saves Lancelot's body from drowning Lancelot is captured without resistance by a fool called Dagenot:

> After a while of riding he encountered Dagenot, the fool, who asked him where he wants to go. Lancelot sat there and thought and did not say a word to him. Dagenot took the bridle and said he would be captivated; he took him [Lancelot] with him, and the other one did not object.[11] (620)

When, however, the best knight can be captivated by a fool without a fight and therefore becomes the worst knight, the courtly system, that insists on the stability of hierarchies, is brought to falter. In this vein, Lancelot's almost-drowning does not only metaphorically depict the consequences of his and Ginover's love for Lancelot's individual chivalry, but it also figures this love's threat for the whole chivalric system. Considering this explosive force of illegitimate love, the end of the slapstick *digressio* should be understood in a different manner than before. When Dagenot takes the defenceless Lancelot in front of queen Ginover the text shows another disintegration of the knight's body – Lancelot has no control over his hand:

> The knight [Lancelot] held his lance beside him. As he heard the Queen talking, he raised his head at once and, at the same time, forgot his hand in which he was holding the lance, and he dropped the lance and pierced the iron through the Queen's coat. She

---

10 "Myn her Ywan nam das roß mit dem zaum und furts uß mit gewalt. Dem ritter waren die wapen naß und der lip überal."
11 "Da er unferre gereit, da begegent im Dagenot der schnúdel und fragt war er hien wolt. Er saß und gedacht und antwurt ym ein wuort nit. Dagenot ergreif yn mit dem zúgel und sprach, er were gefangen; er fuort yn mit in mit im, und der ander endet keyn were darwiedder."

> looked at the knight and whispered to Sir Ywain to her the knight seemed to have lost his mind.[12] (622)

The excessive activity, which was caused by erotic desire, is now directed against the mistress. In contrast to Klinger, who understands the scene as an expression of erotic aggression (2001, 269), I read this kind of disintegration as an expression of endangering the domination of king and queen caused by the illegitimate love. The hand which tries to kill Ginover could therefore be interpreted as an attempt of the knight to get rid of this threat. Of course, this can actually not be done explicitly but can only be implied.

In sum, slapstick should not only be seen as a "physical assault on, or collapse of, the hero's dignity" (Dale 2000, 3). Rather, there seems to be more to this text of the late Medieval Ages which describes the downfall of the Arthurian Court. In my reading, the text deals with the tension and the special problem of the chivalric epic. In this genre, courtly characters have to *have* a body to fight and gain honour, as well as to represent the domination of King Arthur, but should actually not *be* a body because of its savage, trivial and non-courtly state.

At the same time, the text evokes a new kind of experience for readers: they can in some ways participate in Lancelot's experience. Through the slapstick scene, the reader can get an impression of what is going on within the protagonist, even though Lancelot himself cannot tell or verbalize it. Klinger speaks here of a "representational strategy for authenticity" and "involuntary suffering" (2001, 196). The slapstick scene shows that *gedencken* is not only about passivity but rather about a desire which causes disintegration of the body and a state between activity and passivity. And it can tell about love and a desire which lead to self-abandonment, which cannot be understood nor tolerated within the narrated world. Slapstick, however, can show this absolute monstrosity without explaining or answering any questions that may arise on the side of the reader.

---

[12] "Der ritter hielt syn glen neben im. Da er die konigin hort reden, da hub er zuhant syn heubt off und vergaß der hant da er die glen inne hette, und entfiel im die glene, und schoß das ysen durch der kóniginn mantel. Sie sah den ritter an und rúmde mym herrn Ywan das sie der ritter nit wol sinnig ducht."

3 Falling bodies

Compared to the *Prose-Lancelot* where the disintegration of body and mind came about through a digression in the text that gave rise to a narrative logic interfering with a courtly one, in the tale "The Pastor Who was Killed Five Times" slapstick is now used to establish an even more drastic logical pattern. In this narration, the body is not only configured clearly as "a merely corporeal" (Haug 2004, 86), but is also an "object of injury" (Grubmüller 2005, 122). In this tale, a secular logic is established which competes with the Christian one. Slapstick is not only apparent in a *digression,* it is incorporated into the main theme of the tale.

At the beginning of the tale, a pastor prepares a trip to a dying man in order to give him the last sacraments. While he is getting ready, he discovers a cut in the sole of his boot. Because he wants to avoid the dirt and manure on the street, and following the advice of his housekeeper, he goes to a shoemaker. Since the pastor is in a hurry, the shoemaker fixes the boot directly on his foot. The shoemaker accidentally pierces a wire through the pastor's foot, so that he bleeds to death. To salvage the precarious situation, and following the advice of his wife, the shoemaker puts the dead pastor back on his horse and takes him into a field of oats. When the owner of the field sees the pastor on his field, he angrily wants to know what is going on and protests, but the dead pastor does not respond. Because of this insulting impudence, the farmer gets furious and throws a stone at him. The dead body falls on the ground and the farmer believes he murdered the pastor. By night, the farmer leans the dead body against the garden door of his neighbor to get rid of the dead body (again). And again, the neighbor is wondering what the pastor is doing on his property, protests and, when the pastor neither responds nor leaves, he forcefully pushes the garden door open. Again, the pastor falls to the ground and the neighbor believes that he has become a murderer. Along with his wife he devises a plan. They drag the dead body into the house of the sacristan, set him down in front of a baking trough and stuff the pastor's mouth with the batter, so that it appears that the pastor has eaten too much and finally suffocated. In the early morning, the sacristan and his wife find the pastor. He dresses the dead pastor with the chasuble and leans him against the altar in the church. During early mass, an old woman is pulling on the robe of the pastor to give it a kiss as a humble gesture – the dead body falls again to the ground and strikes the pious woman dead.

Right from the beginning of the tale, one characteristic slapstick-like element emerges: the concentration on the action and chronology in which the text deals with the death of the pastor. The pastor's death is shown as the outcome of an absurd chain of actions (Grubmüller 2006, 199), an interference of partly independent events and coincidences which lead to a fatal consequence because of their chronological compression (the pastor needs to get to a dying man quickly): a cut in the sole, dirt on the street, the advice of the housekeeper to see a shoemaker, the hurried stitching directly on the foot and the prick of a needle are needed to get the 'effect' of death. His death contrasts his good intention to give the last sacraments to a dying man from the beginning of the tale. Research assumes that the pastor's death can be understood as a punishment for the sinful behavior and mentality of the religious man: he fails to give the last sacraments to a dying man because of his selfishness and arrogance, and therefore he must die (Keller 1999, 97–101; cf. Glier 1987, 147 and Schumacher 2014, 150). But to me it seems that death itself is in fact the crucial point of the text, not the aspect of punishment or sin.

Obviously, the text illustrates a failed attempt to give death a Christian meaning; by letting the sinless soul get rid of the body (after the last sacraments) and rise to heaven, the text focuses on the dead body in this world. As Alan Dale puts it:

> My point is just that one of the central elements of the theology – the debasing effect of the body on the soul – enables Christians to overcome this discord only by denying and finally getting rid of the body, whereas slapstick achieves accord here on earth by a comic concession to the body at its most traitorous. [. . .] Christianity seeks eternal triumph over physicality after life [. . .]; slapstick seeks a temporal acceptance of physicality by a cathartic exaggeration of its very limitations.
> (2000, 14)

Accordingly, the tale does not provide a moral valuation of the pastor's death, but instead focuses on the dimension of immanence since it provides only a short description of the events that lead to the death. However, the heterodiegetic narrator does not explain much and refuses to offer a context for the actions described, but rather pretends not to know what exactly has happened:

> I don't know how he could pierce so badly
> that he hit a vein in the foot.
> Down to the ground sank the pastor
> and there bled himself to death.
> That got the shoemaker into trouble [. . .].[13]
> (Rosenplüt 2008, 900)

---

[13] "[I]ch waiß nit, wie er so leppisch stach, / das er am fuß ein adern traff. / hin zu der erden sank der pfaff / und plutet sich aldo zu tot. / davon der schuster kam in not [. . .]."

The narrator only presents the absurd improbability of the events and their situational context. He does not provide an interpretation of the death nor does he tell if the pastor was punished for his sins, but rather raises these unanswerable questions. Within the narrated world, the shoemaker accordingly tries to get rid of the scandalous dead body. At first, this seems to be easy, because the body becomes a passive object which can be moved and used by others. In the unfolding plot, the pastor's body is staged as a kind of mass, which otherwise would not be thinkable nor tellable because of the pastor's dignity.

The second part of the tale contains three episodes in which different characters try to get rid of the dead body. Whereas the first part concentrated on demonstrating the priest's death as an effect of a savage kind of contingency, the death is now put into perspective through the presented staging of the body and its 'deaths.' The trick itself to get rid of the dead body, which is used again and again, is simple. But, at the same time, it is inscrutable for the people of the fictional world. The dead body is staged as if it were still alive and serves in this manner as a social disturbance that must be resolved. The previously shown cause-effect relation (action/death) is therefore playfully reversed (death/action): the dead body demands a cause for its death again and again. In particular, the pastor is put on his horse and pushed into an oat field where the horse automatically begins to eat. The appearance of the speechless and inactive pastor causes the resulting action. Angered by the missing reaction of the pastor, the farmer throws a stone against the pastor's chest whereby the pastor falls to the ground. The farmer believes he has murdered the religious man. The fall of the body is part of the trick of the shoemaker and his wife, but at the same time surprising and funny for the readers because of its drop mechanism (cf. Dale 2000, 13). The farmer and his wife are trying to get rid of the body in a similar way. They lean the dead body against the garden door of their farming neighbor, as if the pastor is trying to intrude their privacy, also provoking an action of the second farmer. Here, too, the trick works perfectly. As the pastor is not answering any questions of the second farmer and remains silent, the farmer gets angry: "The gate he pushed open forcefully. / He made the pastor fell down, / so that he laid there in front of him" (Rosenplüt 2008, 906).[14] The dead body falls to the ground again. The farmer believes that he killed the religious man. In sum, the episodes refer to the repetitive murder of the priest and deliberately question the first act of killing. Therefore, the falling body stands for the successful tricks of the couples. But at the same time, the characters in the fictional world cannot get rid of the body, it

---

14 "[D]en gattern stieß er auf mit gewalt. / den pfaffen er dernider fallt, / das er vor im gestrecket lag."

can only be passed on. The body itself as a heavy mass remains in its immediateness and leads to the questions of why and what over and over again. This is also reproduced by and in the characters' questions within the fictional world. The first farmer asks the (dead) priest: "herr, warumb tut ir das?" ["Sir, why are you doing this?"] (900), the second farmer wants to know: "was tut ir do?" ["What are you doing here?"] (904). However, major questions – e.g., What happens to the pastor and why is his (dead) body? – still remain unanswered. The general lack of responses and explanations is literally embodied by the silent priest, practiced by the apparently uninformed narrator as well as symbolized by the physical drop mechanism of the body. The pastor cannot explain anything anymore – he has become sluggish mass.

What stands out, apart from this mechanism, is the reaction of the farmers, who try to justify their violence and the murder of the priest as a reasonable Christian punishment. Because the priest did not show charity to all and transgressed God's commandments, he had to be punished:

> Why did the fool walk around here?
> Didn't want to consider, this dunce,
> what he was preaching to us every day,
> that nobody should harm his neighbor.
> As he didn't want to take care,
> I don't want to mourn for him.[15]
> (Rosenplüt 2008, 904–906)

Therefore, the farmers try to disguise their murder as a just Christian punishment. But this 'punishment' and its implementation are as "stiff" as the dead body itself and cannot be applied on the situation, for the priest cannot be judged and punished because he is dead and has no intention to transgress norms. In this light, he also cannot commit a sin. By revealing the regularity of transgression and penalties as a "stiff" mechanism – in showing that there can be a punishment even without committing a crime – this Christian regularity becomes absurd. The text questions these mechanisms of social and moral condemnation and punishment in showing the mechanism of a body that can only fall.

In its episodic repetition, the text further illustrates the problem of the pastor's 'first death' as a possible punishment handed down by God. Of course, the staging of the priest could be understood as a staging of his committed sins during his life – priests in pre-modern tales are frequently not very pious. But this

---

15 "[W]es gieng der narr dann do umb mausen. / wolt nit selbs bedenken der tor, / was er uns alltag predigt vor, / da keiner seim nechstn schaden solt. / do er sich selb nit hüten wolt, / woll ich in zwar nimmer klagen."

symbolic dimension is duplicated by episodic repetition and therefore interpretation is difficult. Of course, every unlikely coincidence might be interpreted as a sign of fortune and God's activity. But to understand an accidental event as God's will and therefore as a punishment, there must be a clear, sinful attitude first. However, there is no mention of such an attitude or intention in the text. Instead, the priest's 'sins' are only staged by characters within the fictional world. At the same time, the possibility of God's activity is involved in an immanent context of events. Within this context, the repetition of a physical as well as a social mechanical regularity that develops a life of its own is emphasized. One could call this an independent regularity of the course of the world, a wonderful world of gravity, which acts as a counterpart to normative directions and of alleged claims of a transcendental power. Admittedly, this can only be deciphered by the recipient who understands the claims of meaning and attribution of meaning by the characters as parts of this immanent course of the world. Therefore, the tale does not merely show meaninglessness or failure of order, but rather the confrontation of an order which is justified by transcendence with an immanent counterpart. Or, in other words, the tale portrays two competing logics. In the second staging of the priest's body, the farmers have brought the dead body into the house of the sacristan, set him down in front of a baking trough, and have stuffed the pastor's mouth with batter so that it appears that the pastor has eaten too much and finally suffocated. Through this staging, the established drop mechanism is shortly interrupted. The focus of this staging lies not only on the sin of gluttony, but on the sluggishness and the weight of the body: "Then they took the heavy pastor/and put him into the sacristan's room" (Rosenplüt 2008, 908).[16] The emphasis on the heaviness of the priest's body therefore is the basis for the climax of the tale. In the final part of the text, the priest's body is carried back to his original domain, the church, and leaned against the altar. The sacristan knows that visitors of the church will think that the silent priest is praying:[17]

> When the people will come by,
> and see, that he [the priest] doesn't move himself,
> they will think he is beatific,
> in great devotion, in which he is.[18]
>
> (912)

---

[16] "[D]o namen sie den pfarrer schwer/ und dunsen in des meßners gemach."
[17] Rosenplüt added this scene. It was not included in the Old French fabliaux (see also Grubmüller 1996, 1309–1310).
[18] "[S]o dann die leut herzu werden gan, / und sehen, das er sich nit verrückt, / so wöllen sie wänen, er sei verzückt, / in grosser andacht, die er hab."

Through the adjective 'verzückt' ['beatific'] the text refers to the state of religious ecstasy, "[t]he sensation of being imbued with a different, higher or further reality, and this as a testimony of the divine action in human life" (Wißmann 1982, 489). By using this religious term, the tale introduces the subject of transcendence as well as the hope for a connection with god and for divine truth. But this hope will be dashed in an extreme way using slapstick elements again. An old woman who visits the early mass approaches the priest and touches his robe to participate in the salvation of god, but instead she is crushed by the heavy body of the priest falling to the ground:

> [S]he grabbed the tunicle.
> And as it was in her hand,
> she moved it to the mouth
> and wanted to kiss it according to peasant custom
> and even pulled it that much to one side,
> that he fell down on her/and struck her dead with his heavy fall.
> Then arose wailing and misery.[19]
>
> (Rosenplüt 2008, 912–914)

Ralph Tanner (2005, 493) has already pointed out that this scene resembles another one in the Bible, where a woman is breaking through the crowd to touch the robe of Jesus to be healed through his participation in divine salvation (Mk 5, 25–34). In the present tale, this scene is parodied: instead of participating in salvation, the old woman is confronted with the remorseless immanence, with banal corporeality, the priest's heavy body, and her own mortality. The dead body kills the old woman and thus claims another life – with a slap, as it were – in a slapstick-like way: this "violent aural effect, the slap, may be thought of as having the same kind of disruptive impact on the audience as its visual equivalent in the silent cinema, the pie in the face" (Crafton 1995, 108; cf. Keller 1999, 104).[20]

---

[19] "[S]ie ergriff das meßgewand. / und do es ir ward in die hand, / do fur sie gen dem mund damit / und wolt das küssen nach peurischem sit / und rückt in auf ein seiten gar, / das er viel auf sie nider dar / und schlug sie schweres falls zu tot. / do hub sich jamer und auch not."

[20] The end truly puzzled researchers. Whereas some literary scholars are speaking of an "omnipresence of evil" (Schumacher 2014, 145) or state the "absurdity of the course of the world" (Grubmüller 1993, 53), others try to grasp the meaning of the text by reading it as a criticism regarding cunning women (cf. Keller 1999, 108) or as "exposure of misunderstood, typically female practice of piety" (Schnell 2004, 376). In contrast, Katrin Schumacher pointed out: "This interpretation does not take into account the serious difference in the depiction of the wives, who are hostile to the priest, on the one hand, and the pious old woman on the other" (2014, 156).

The text shows no salvation, but only a mechanism, the falling of a body, which functions as an "intervention of the physical in the realm of the spiritual" (Clayton 2007, 130).

To conclude: The epic of *Prose-Lancelot* uses slapstick-like elements in *digressiones* in which the disintegration of body and mind, and the scandal of *being* a body poses a threat to the courtly order. At the same time, slapstick as a narrative form makes the reader to participate in the experience of Lancelot and enabled the recipient to carefully explore the boundaries of narration in epic texts. Compared to this, "The Pastor Who was Killed Five Times" already uses the narrative form of slapstick to establish a narrative logic which presents the independent regularity of the course of the world as a counterpart of normative directions and of alleged claims of a transcendental power. Both texts can therefore be interpreted as evidences of imaginable disturbances, or even as attempts to destroy orders (within the narrated world as well as orders of narrative forms). And they must be read as early evidences of the productive potential of this new kind of narration – early literary slapstick.

Bibliography

Ackermann-Arlt, Beate. *Das Pferd und seine epische Funktion im mittelhochdeutschen 'Prosa-Lancelot.'* Berlin: De Gruyter, 1990.

Berger, Peter L. *Redeeming Laughter: The Comic Dimension of Human Experience*. Berlin: De Gruyter, 1997.

Bergson, Henri. "Laughter." In: *Comedy*. Ed. Wylie Sypher. Baltimore: Johns Hopkins University Press, 1980. S. 61–190.

Clayton, Alex. *The Body in Hollywood Slapstick*. Jefferson: McFarland, 2007.

Crafton, Donald. "Pie and Chase: Gag, Spectacle and Narrative in Slapstick Comedy." *Classical Hollywood Comedy*. Eds. Kristine Brunovska Karnick and Henry Jenkins. New York: Routledge, 1995. 106–119.

Dale, Alan. *Comedy Is A Man in Trouble: Slapstick in American Movies*. Minneapolis: University of Minnesota Press, 2000.

Friedrich, Udo. *Menschentier und Tiermensch: Diskurse der Grenzziehung und Grenzüberschreitung im Mittelalter*. Göttingen: Vandenhoeck & Ruprecht, 2008.

Glier, Ingeborg. "Hans Rosenplüt als Märendichter." *Kleinere Erzählformen im Mittelalter*. Eds. Klaus Grubmüller, Peter Johnson, and Hans-Hugo Steinhoff. Paderborn: Schöningh, 1988. 137–149.

Grubmüller, Klaus. "Einleitung und Kommentar." *Novellistik des Mittelalters: Märendichtung*. Ed. Klaus Grubmüller. Frankfurt am Main: Deutscher Klassiker Verlag, 1996. 1005–1384.

Grubmüller, Klaus. *Die Ordnung, der Witz und das Chaos: eine Geschichte der europäischen Novellistik im Mittelalter: Fabliau – Märe – Novelle*. Tübingen: Niemeyer, 2006.

Grubmüller, Klaus. "Wer lacht im Märe – und wozu?" *Lachgemeinschaften: Kulturelle Inszenierungen und soziale Wirkungen von Gelächter im Mittelalter und der Frühen Neuzeit*. Eds. Werner Röcke and Hans-Rudolf Velten. Berlin: De Gruyter, 2005. 111–124.

Grubmüller, Klaus. "Das Groteske im Märe als Element seiner Geschichte: Skizzen zu einer historischen Gattungspoetik." *Kleinere Erzählformen des 15. und 16. Jahrhunderts*. Eds. Walter Haug and Burghart Wachinger. Tübingen: Niemeyer, 1993. 37–54.

Haferland, Harald. *Höfische Interaktion: Interpretationen zur höfischen Epik und Didaktik um 1200*. Munich: Wilhelm Fink, 1989.

Hartmann von Aue. "Iwein." *Gregorius – Der arme Heinrich – Iwein*. Ed. Volker Mertens. Frankfurt am Main: Deutscher Klassiker Verlag, 2008. 317–767.

Haug, Walter. "Entwurf zu einer Theorie der mittelalterlichen Kurzerzählung." *Kleinere Erzählformen des 15. und 16. Jahrhunderts*. Eds. Walter Haug and Burghart Wachinger. Niemeyer: Tübingen, 1993. 1–35.

Jenkins, Henry and Karnick, Kristine Brunovska. "Introduction: Acting funny." *Classical Hollywood Comedy*. Eds. Kristine Brunovska Karnick and Henry Jenkins. Routledge: New York, 1995. 149–167.

Keller, Johannes. "Norm – Lachen – Gewalt: Komik des mehrfachen Todes in einer Erzählung Hans Rosenplüts." *Grenzen und Übergänge*. Eds. Thomas Hunkeler et al. Bern u.a.: Peter Lang, 1999. Zugleich: *variations. Literaturzeitschrift der Universität Zürich* 3 (1999). 93–108.

Klinger, Judith. *Der mißratene Ritter: Konzeptionen von Identität im Prosa-Lancelot*. Munich: Wilhelm Fink, 2001.

Lancelot und Ginover I und II. Prosalancelot I und II. Nach der Heidelberger Handschrift Cod. Pal. germ. 147, hg. von Reinhold Kluge, ergänzt durch die Handschrift Ms. allem. 8017–8020 der Bibliothèque de l'Arsenal Paris. Translated, commented and ed. Hans-Hugo Steinhoff. 2 Volumes. Frankfurt am Main: Inselverlag, 2005.

Müller, Jan-Dirk. *Höfische Kompromisse: acht Kapitel zur höfischen Epik*. Tübingen: Niemeyer, 2007.

Philipowski, Katharina-Silke. *Minne und Kiusche im deutschen Prosa-Lancelot*. Frankfurt am Main: Peter Lang, 2002.

Remakel, Michèle. *Rittertum zwischen Minne und Gral: Untersuchungen zum mittelhochdeutschen 'Prosa-Lancelot.'* Frankfurt am Main: Peter Lang, 1995.

Ruberg, Uwe. "Lancelot (Lancelot-Gral-Prosaroman)." *Verfasserlexikon – Die deutsche Literatur des Mittelalters*. Eds. Kurt Ruh et al. Volume 5 of 14. Berlin: De Gruyter, 1985. 530–546.

Rosenplüt, Hans. "Der fünfmal getötete Pfarrer." *Novellistik des Mittelalters: Märendichtung*. Ed. Klaus Grubmüller. Frankfurt am Main: Deutscher Klassiker Verlag, 1996. 898–915.

Schnell, Rüdiger. "Erzählstrategie, Intertextualität und 'Erfahrungswissen.'" *Wolfram-Studien* 18 (2004): 367–404.

Schumacher, Katrin. *Von lebenden Toten und anderen Grenzgängern: Ordnungsdiskurs und Liminalität in höfischen, exemplarischen und grotesken Mären, in der Binnenerzählung III,8 des 'Decameron' und im Fastnachtspiel 'Der Bauer im Fegefeuer'*. PhD Diss. University of Bremen, 2014.

Tanner, Ralph. *Sex, Sünde, Seelenheil: Die Figur des Pfaffen in der Märenliteratur und ihr historischer Hintergrund (1200–1600)*. Würzburg: Königshausen & Neumann, 2005.

Trahair, Lisa. *The Comedy of Philosophy: Sense and Nonsense in Early Cinematic Slapstick.* Albany: State University of New York Press, 2007.

Wagner, Silvan. "Die Lust an erzählter Gewalt: Virtuelle Gewaltgemeinschaften in der Wiener Meerfahrt." *Gewaltgenuss, Zorn und Gelächter: Die emotionale Seite der Gewalt in Literatur und Historiographie des Mittelalters und der Frühen Neuzeit.* Eds. Claudia Ansorge, Cora Dietl, and Titus Knäpper. Göttingen: V&R unipress, 2015. 31–44.

Wißmann, Hans. "Ekstase." *Theologische Realenzyklopädie.* Vol. 9. Eds. Gerhard Krause and Gerhard Müller. Berlin: De Gruyter, 1982. 488–491.

Part II: **Instruments of Slapstick**

Alena E. Lyons & Ervin Malakaj
Introduction

Given its iconic status, it seems appropriate to open the section of this volume on the instruments of slapstick with one of its most popular tropes. The gag in question revolves around the slapstick protagonist slipping on a banana peel. In the course of film history, the slip on the banana peel has indeed become a staple of film comedy: initiated in Charlie Chaplin's (1889–1977) short film *By the Sea* (Dir. Charlie Chaplin, 1915), the gag was taken up and developed further by Harold Lloyd (1893–1971) (*The Flirt*. Dir. Billy Gilbert, 1917), and a decade later figures prominently in the iconic pie fight with Stan Laurel (1890–1965) and Oliver Hardy (1892–1957) (*The Battle of the Century*. Dir. Clyde Bruckmann, 1927).

Along with other, similar devices, the slip on the banana peel points to slapstick's inherent commitment to body comedy while also drawing attention to material objects that give rise to it. The slapstick protagonist's encounter of the material world frequently takes place, as Andrew Scott notes, through the objects that constitute its gags:

> Slapstick is [. . .] where the body meets the world of things, and hence it is suitably fascinated with objects. By examining the identity and utility of things and playing with the spaces they occupy, their dimensions, properties, and cultural significance, the body's relationship to the external world is made strange. (Scott 2014, 74)

Drawing on the work of Henri Bergson (1859–1941), Scott's reflections on slapstick's body politics are also a means by which to highlight slapstick's investment in the mechanical, which scholars like Rob King have attributed to corresponding social developments, i.e. "the formation of mass culture and its relation to turn-of-the-century technological advance" (2010, 116; see also King 2008; Solomon 2016). In the same vein, Tom Gunning points to the apparent life of their own that machine objects can develop in slapstick gags: "Besides actual machines or involuntary bodily reactions, recalcitrant objects can block or defeat purposes unexpectedly. With their seemingly intentional resistance to human purposes, such demonic objects often resemble crazy machines, as their resistance becomes sustained and seemingly purposeful" (2010, 139).

The slip on the banana peel, like other physical gags, has a long history. Its predecessor is the trope of "the laughable fall," which is featured in various texts throughout cultural history. Take, for instance, "Die Geschichte von Hanns Guck-in-die-Luft" ["The Story of Johnny Look-In-The-Air"] by Heinrich Hoffmann (1809–1894). It was published in the collection *Der Struwwelpeter oder lustige Geschichten und drollige Bilder* [*The Struwwelpeter, or, Pretty Stories and Funny Pictures*, 1845], which contains a lot of comedic scenarios deployed in the service of violent pedagogy. In the story, a child constantly looks up into the air while walking and trips – first over a dog, later into a river. The river scene features fish that evade the protagonist's fall in time only to comment on it:

> And the fishes, one, two, three,
> Are come back again, you see,
> Up they came the moment after,
> To enjoy the fun and laughter.
> Each popp'd out its little head,
> And, to tease poor Johnny [. . .].[1]
> (Hoffmann 1909, 23)

The protagonist in this tale is one of the few to survive and is among the few non-injured characters of *Struwwelpeter*. His only pain is humiliation. The passage cited here is accompanied by an illustration showing the protagonist not looking upwards towards the sky; he instead looks for the first time down into the water, from where the fish laugh at him and thus usher in his shame. The failed encounter with the material world and the subsequent shame about this failure, which is brought about by laughter, is his punishment and is intended to secure his future good behavior.

The child's luck to survive misbehavior is dubious, for the laughter engenders shame and thus channels the affective register of the scene away from pure enjoyment into pedagogy. The dubious role of laughter (as violent source for humiliation) accompanying the trope of "the laughable fall" is already present in an example from antiquity. The trope of a person walking, stumbling, and producing laughter without sustaining much or any physical harm has a predecessor in the story of Thales of Miletus (ca. 624/623 BC–548/544 BC). Socrates (ca. 469 BC–399 BC) relays the story in Plato's (ca. 428/423 BC–348/347 BC) Θεαίτητος [*Theaetetus*, ca. 369 BC] as follows: "While [Thales] was studying the stars and looking upwards, he fell into a pit, and a neat, witty Thracian servant girl jeered at him, they say, because he was so eager to know the things in the sky that he could not see what was there before him at his very feet" (1921, 174a). At first glance, Thales's fall precipitates the laughter of the Thracian woman, who according to the hierarchical understanding of society in ancient Greece takes the absolutely opposite position to Thales's social standing. For this reason, her laughter is

---

[1] "Doch die Fischlein alle drei, / Schwimmen hurtig gleich herbei: / Strecken's Köpflein aus der Flut, / Lachen, daß / man's hören tut, / Lachen fort noch lange Zeit [. . .]" (Hoffmann 1876, 23).

all the more humiliating. But what has been the very point of interest here is that the fall – anticipatorily – embodies the social meaning of the laughter. Insofar as the fall and the laughter relate to each other causally, they also metaphorically reflect each other, which is the most important aspect of this anecdote, shaping Socrates's as well as later philosophers' discussion of it. Over the course of Socrates's dialogue, this social imbalance is corrected through his insistence to consider the perspective in the scenario: philosophers are able to think and know (no matter the conditions within which this thinking and knowing emerges); it is thus the laughter at the philosophers that is ridiculous (174a–175b). But Socrates's restoration of Thales from humiliation was lost over the course of the story's long reception history, which primarily remembers his humiliation alone.[2]

In 1900, the predecessor of the banana peel gag appears in Henri Bergson's "Le Rire: Essai sur la signification du comique" ["Laughter: An Essay on the Meaning of the Comic"] in two versions. In the first, Bergson connotes it pejoratively in that he describes its comic qualities through the external, i.e., physical mechanical stiffness of a person falling. He frames the second variant of the gag as ameliorative by drawing a parallel between Plato's anecdote of Thales and the literary figure of Don Quixote. Bergson illustrates the comical, which can be traced back to absent-mindedness: the presence of the falling person in their imagined world that causes their mental absence in reality (Bergson 2011, 17–25). Despite his fondness of those who stumble (i.e., Thales or Don Quixote), Bergson, like Hoffmann, foregrounds the humiliating laughter of others in his description. Neither Bergson's figure of the first variant nor Hoffmann's Hanns Guck-in-die-Luft have a valid cause for their mishaps outside of neglect, which justifies the laughter that accompanies the scenes.

These abbreviated versions of the Thales anecdote thus become part of a schema that Chaplin takes up in 1915 in his banana peel gag. This gag generates a link between the body and its environment in a way that, on the one hand, harms the body and, on the other, provokes laughter, as it suggests a reversal of the subject-object relation. This section centers around the instruments that set this process in motion.

Sebastian Hauck's chapter in this section concerns the so-called mirror scene, a scenario structured by the prop of a mirror frame (without mirror glass). Through

---

[2] The reception of the Thales anecdote by the German philosopher Hans Blumenberg (1920–1996) is worthy of special mention here. He read this as a foundational scene for theory and developed his reflection on it into a leitmotif of his writing and thought (see Blumenberg 1976; Blumenberg 1987). Alexander Kling (2018) also draws on the Thales anecdote when theorizing the comedy of things.

comparative analyses of well-known variants of this sketch routine, he traces its history from the Italian *commedia all'improvviso* of the sixteenth and seventeenth centuries to the era of silent film. On the one hand, Hauck's examination of theater and film history proves that and to what extent the beginnings of slapstick can be traced back to the repertoire of *commedia all'improvviso*. On the other hand, it is also shown to what extent the 'multiplication' brought about by this prop entails the duplication of fundamental worlds of human experience in slapstick: with the broken mirror in the center, this scene is not only highly virtuosic and entertaining, but at the same time revolves on several levels around the themes of identity and, linked to it, existence. Hauck shows how the drawing of boundaries and their concurrent erasure in this scenario attend to vital concerns about the distinctions between mask and actor, the mirrored and the mirroring, illusion and reality.

Courtney Andree draws on disability studies to examine Harold Lloyd's (1893–1971) filmic slapstick performances. In particular, Andree examines the consequences of extreme slapstick performances, which left Lloyd permanently disabled, and which in various narrative strategies over the course of his career came to be part of his gag repertoire. Through this example, Andree brings into focus the function of props in the shaping of illusion and reality in slapstick films with consideration of the disabled body. This research shows that beyond the actor's material body, actors have to cover up, mask, extend, or supplement their actual, physical pains, injuries, and sensitivities. In this reading, the limits and failures of the body come to be vital considerations for slapstick as physical comedy.

In a chapter about *Popstar: Never Stop Never Stopping* (2016), a feature film by the comedy group The Lonely Island's, Addie Tsai takes up two considerations introduced by Hauck and Andree. On the one hand, the chapter examines the slapstick-value of various moments of multiplication. These are staged in the film through wardrobe changes in the context of a music show as well as enacted in the form of digital reproduction of the performance through smartphones by the intradiegetic audience. Both forms of multiplication generate as well as thematize illusion. On the other hand, the chapter analyzes the white cis-male body of a pop star figure who, at the moment of failure conditioned by the appearance of lacking genitalia during a wardrobe change, faces extreme humiliation. By focusing on the critical-subversive moment with regard to gender normativity, Tsai links the two strands from the previous contributions and shows how slapstick is used as a stylistic device to address the physicality of human life and at the same time the valence of showing the loss of dignity in a project dedicated to critique white, cis, heteronormative masculinity.

Alena E. Lyons's contribution on a series of portraits by the photographer and video artist Luiza Folegatti (*1988) studies the function of disguise and make-up in order to show how slapstick is constituted in the medium of photography. The chapter traces the interplay among masquerade, body politics, and subversion – which were already addressed in detail by Tsai – in the images of the drag king figure Barba Luluxo. For Lyons, slapstick elements in photography that captures the theatrical niche form of kinging are first and foremost articulated through make-up and disguise. The chapter shows how Folegatti's photographs thereby problematize the physical as well as the social vulnerability of its subjects. Such unsettling through make-up and disguise transforms the audience's gaze. In Lyons's reading, it indeed generates a communion between audience and performers.

Works cited

Bergson, Henri. *Das Lachen. Ein Essay über die Bedeutung des Komischen*. Transl. by Roswitha Plancherel-Walter. Hamburg: Felix Meiner, 2011.

Blumenberg, Hans. *Das Lachen der Thrakerin. Eine Urgeschichte der Theorie*. Frankfurt am Main: Suhrkamp, 1987.

Blumenberg, Hans. "Der Sturz des Protophilosophen – Zur Komik der reinen Theorie, anhand einer Rezeptionsgeschichte der Thales-Anekdote." *Das Komische*. Eds. Wolfgang Preisendanz and Rainer Warning. Munich: Fink, 1976. 11–64.

Gunning, Tom. "Mechanisms of Laughter. The Devices of Slapstick." *Slapstick Comedy*. Eds. Tom Paulus and Rob King. New York: Routledge, 2010. 137–151.

Hoffmann, Heinrich. *Der Struwwelpeter oder lustige Geschichten und drollige Bilder für Kinder von 3–6 Jahren*. Frankfurt am Main: Literarische Anstalt Rütten & Loening, 1917.

Hoffmann, Heinrich. *The English Struwwelpeter, or, Pretty Stories and Funny Pictures*. Transl. unknown. London: Routledge, 1909.

King, Rob. *The Fun Factory: The Keystone Film Company and the Emergence of Mass Culture*. Berkeley: University of California Press, 2008.

King, Rob. "'Uproarious Inventions': The Keystone Film Company, Modernity, and the Art of the Motor." *Slapstick Comedy*. Eds. Tom Paulus and Rob King. New York: Routledge, 2010. 114–136.

Kling, Alexander. "Aus dem Rahmen fallen. Dingtheorie, Narratologie und das Komische (Platon, Vischer, Loriot)." *Das Verhältnis von* res *und* verba. *Zu den Narrativen der Dinge*. Eds. Martina Wernli and Alexander Kling. Freiburg (Breisgau), Berlin, and Vienna: Rombach, 2018. 309–332.

Plato. "Theaetetus." *Plato in Twelve Volumes*. Plato. Vol. 12. Transl. by Harold N. Fowler. London: William Heinemann Ltd., 1921.

Scott, Andrew. *Comedy*. London and New York: Routledge, 2014.

Solomon, William. *Slapstick Modernism: Chaplin to Kerouac to Iggy Pop*. Springfield: University of Illinois Press, 2016.

Sebastian Hauck
The Broken Mirror: From *Commedia All'Improvviso* to Slapstick Comedy

1 Slapstick and *commedia all'improvviso*

Without *commedia all'improvviso* slapstick would not exist. Slapstick did not only get its name from *commedia all'improvviso*. Parts of its repertoire, its routines (*lazzi*), and scenes are also derived from this theatre tradition of professional actors. Originally, slapstick denominated a musical instrument, which was also called "clappers" or "whip." "The whip consists of two pieces of wood [. . .] hinged at one end and [was] provided with straps or handles; the player slaps the two surfaces together. A variant known as a Slapstick incorporates a spring and requires only one hand to operate" (Blades and Holland 2001, 336). This musical instrument became an important component of Harlequin's – Arlecchino's, Arlequin's – mask and was part of his theatre dress since Tristano Martinelli (1557–1630) created the stage figure in 1584 (see Figure 1).

From the illustrations of the *Recueil Fossard* [Fossard Collection, ca. 1584], a rare collection of engravings concerning *commedia all'improvviso* in Paris, as well as Martinelli's *Compositions de Rhétorique* [Compositions of Rhetoric, 1600], a parodistic treatise on rhetoric, mostly consisting of empty pages, Siro Ferrone derived the following constituents of Arlecchino's dress: a close-fitting overall with a myriad of colorful patches – later changing to a geometric rhomb pattern – which emphasizes the athletic body and draws attention to the movements of the muscles, "light dance shoes," "the black animal mask," similar to a cat, "the wild beard," "the pouch," and, finally, "the stick attached to the belt" (Ferrone 2006, 78).[1] As late as 1841, according to Philipp Jacob Düringer and Heinrich Ludwig Barthels in their theatrical dictionary, the "wooden stick" is part of Arlecchino's "theatre dress" (Düringer and Barthels 1841, 645). This wooden stick refers to the "slapstick," whose function on stage is to create as much noise as possible during the obligatory beating scenes without hurting the other actors (see N. N. 1977, 718). Thus, slapstick is associated with Arlequin in two ways. Its name originates from a constitutive part of his theatre dress, but also parts of the repertoire de-

---

1 Unless otherwise noted, translations are mine.

https://doi.org/10.1515/9783110571981-007

Figure 1: Nicolas Bonnart: Arlequin with his slapstick (Domenico Biancolelli?).

rive – at least in this case – from Domenico Biancolelli (1636–1688), the famous Parisian Arlequin.[2]

In this chapter, I will demonstrate this relation to the repertoire of professional actors, who appeared centuries before the great silent movie stars, by means of a concrete example: a scene or comic routine called *The Broken Mirror*. Its narrative essence consists of a simple constellation: on either side of a broken mirror are two actors, one of whom seems to be unaware of the situation.

---

2 The actors of the *commedia all'improvviso* are closely connected to the masks (*maschere*) they present. Even though actors could change between several masks in the course of their lives, they only played one at a time. Therefore, the well-known actors are always mentioned in connection with their masks: Francesco Andreini-Capitano Spavento, Orsola Posmoni-Flaminia or Carlo Cantù called (*detto*) Buffetto. Tristano Martinelli even signed his letters as Arlecchino.

The other has to keep the illusion of an intact mirror while attempting to imitate the gestures and movements of the first actor. The framework for these scenic sequences may vary: a supplier or servant accidentally breaks the mirror (Schwarz Brothers, *Der zerbrochene Spiegel*, 1911), pretends to be a ghost (*Early Morning Reflections*, 1911), unmasks a disguised spy (Marx Brothers, *Duck Soup*, 1933), or fools the audience when the scenic illusion is emphasized and both actors reveal themselves as twins (Lyman Twins, *A Merry Chase*, 1899).

In order to measure the significance, not only quantitative, of the broken mirror in this context, it is necessary first to give some examples from popular culture that illustrate the popularity and persistence with which this comic routine has maintained itself on the stage and in film and television – including some absurd court cases that have been conducted around the alleged copyright (e.g., Carl and Camillo Schwarz against Max Linder). For more than 300 years, this scene has evidenced an astonishing continuity and persistence of the repertoire, which lasted from the *commedia all'improvviso*, more precisely the Parisian *Comédie Italienne*, to the London pantomime, vaudeville acts and circus, to the origins of cinema – the silent films of Max Linder (1883–1925) and Charlie Chaplin (1889–1977) as well as to Groucho (1890–1977) and Chico (1887–1961) Marx – and, finally, to the present. Slapstick (as an '*acting* routine') is not an invention of cinema and early silent films, but originates from the acting techniques of the Italian *comici*, dating back centuries and generations of *commedia all'improvviso* actors, English pantomimes, clowns, and music hall artists. This, however, is a continuity that refuses simple analogies among and across techniques, for instance a simplistic equivocation between *Harlequin's stick* and *Charlie's Cane* (Madden 1968). From 1674 on, when Italian *comico* Domenico Biancolelli as Arlequin first introduced the "mirror act" (Gambelli 1993, vol. ii, 646) to his Paris audience in *A fourbe, fourbe et demy* [The fox knows much, but more he that catches him], it has never disappeared from the stages, arenas, and screens in Europe and the United States, and is still keeping audiences fascinated today as it did 350 years ago.

2 The mirror act in theatre, variety, and circus

There exist many examples of *The Broken Mirror*, and almost as many theories and assumptions, how and from which play or archetype this scene was adopted. Moreover, there are just as many actors, who claimed the 'invention' of this scene for themselves. In this regard, Tony Staveacre refers to a major representative of English pantomime in the early twentieth century, Jack Melville. At the end of each year, Melville compiled his repertoire in an "index of 'gags'" (Staveacre 1987, 5) – comparable, perhaps, to the *zibaldone* (a kind of notebook) of Italian professional actors of the early modern period. Such archive of gags has stimulated what Staveacre describes as "the accumulation of comic routines and 'business' that are fundamentals of the slapstick tradition. Handed down from one generation to the next, sometimes hijacked, endlessly recycled, they are none the worse for having been aired a hundred times before" (5). In 1911, Melville mentions the comic routines *Jumping on Hat* and *Matrimonial Bliss* as well as *Broken Mirror*. "The premise is simple: servant has broken master's mirror and, to prevent him finding out, impersonates his reflection in the frame" (5). Having carried out some "detective work" to shed light on the scene's origins, Staveacre mentions the Hanlon Brothers, six Irish brothers who performed at Niblo's Gardens in New York in 1860, and who "also claimed to have invented it" (5). During the 1910s, the mirror act was still part of their *Just Phor-Phun* show (cf. McKinven 1998, 66). As Anthony Balducci has shown, "this version of the routine centered on a ham actor getting dressed in his hotel room and a member of the hotel staff pretending to be the man's reflection" (2013, n.p.). Lupino Lane (1892–1959), born into a British theatre family, and a famous Harlequin, attributes the invention of the scene to his grandfather George Hook Lupino (1820–1902), "who had originated it for a Harlequinade at Drury Lane" (Staveacre 1987, 5). In 1899, when American twins Howard (1877–1923) and Herbert Lyman (1877–1953) staged their first musical comedy, entitled *A Merry Chase*, the "broken mirror illusion" (Collier 2015, 8) marked the climax and grand finale:

> The illusion pitted the Lyman twins facing one another in a large, door-sized frame, that appeared to be a mirror. As one of the twins walked in front of the 'mirror,' the other did so, too. The synchronized movements of the twins made it appear as if only one performer were one stage, and that the audience was simply seeing his reflection. The gag revealed itself when the twins purposely went out of sync. Then the audience knew that they had been tricked, and had been looking at twins for the duration of the scene. (9)

In addition to vaudeville and pantomime, especially at the beginning of the twentieth century, *The Broken Mirror* is also an integral part of the repertoire of numerous clowns. Kenneth Little points out that the clown duo *The Chickys* (featuring Bruno Stutz as Whiteface and Eugen Altenburger as August) "insist on performing the 'broken mirror' entrée because they say it's part of an established repertoire of entrée sketches that circus clown artists now use to define the uniqueness of their performance tradition" (1993, 124). Even if they were mistaken about the uniqueness of this scene, the entrée can also be defined as an integral part of the clown repertoire. The compilation *Ce rire qui vient du cirque*

[This laughter from the circus], published in 1969 by the librarian and circus historiographer Paul Henwood, mentions two *Entrées clownesques* [Clown Scenes] that resemble each other: *La poupée mécanique* [The Mechanical Doll] and *Le miroir brisé* [The Broken Mirror]. The introduction of the printed mirror act is arranged in a similar way. Monsieur Clown orders August to take care of his robot and to touch him by no means. Needless to say, as soon as the clown has turned his back on him, August switches on the robot and prompts it to walk a few steps, but in such a way that eventually breaks the robot. He cries bitterly but has a great idea. In order to disguise the mishap, he stands in for the robot and imitates its movements when the clown returns (Adrian 1969, 62). *Le miroir brisé* deals with a mirror that August breaks, and thus he has to emulate the movements and gestures of the clown standing on the other side of the mirror (62).

The Broken Mirror describes the entrée as a part of characteristic circus performances. It is preserved in a recording of Pipo Sosman (1901–1970) and Achille "Rhum" Zavatta (1915–1993) for French television from 1966. The scene starts with a servant breaking his master's mirror by accident, the master being an actor who needs the mirror to rehearse a new sequence. The servant now dons a similar costume and imitates his master's gestures and movements in front of the mirror. The actor appears to be drunk, making it plausible that he cannot easily unmask his servant. Thereafter, the interplay of movement and improvised, delayed imitation, as is characteristic of the mirror scene, unfolds, and the audience's laughter results from August's distress and the mistakes he makes. This is also evident in the moment the clown lights a cigarette:

> The Clown [Pipo] reaches in his pocket and takes out a cigarette case. August [= Rhum] feels around in his pocket – he has no case. The Clown turns, opens his case, and, with a large gesture, takes out a cigarette. August jumps through the mirror, takes a cigarette from the case, which is lying open, returns to his chair, and sits down. The Clown lights his cigarette. August comes back and lights his cigarette from the same match. The Clown regards himself in the mirror, draws on his cigarette, and blows smoke in August's face, who does the same. The Clown swallows smoke and coughs. August also coughs.
>
> CLOWN: There's an echo!
> AUGUST: Yes, there's an echo!
>
> The Clown holds his cigarette in his right hand. August does the same. The images do not agree. The Clown is uneasy and takes his cigarette in his left hand; August does the same. Finally, August catches on and transfers the cigarette to his right hand while the clown has his in his left. The Clown laughs out loud; August also laughs.[3] (Rémy 1997, 210–211)

---

3 "Pipo fouille dans sa poche et en sort un étui à cigarettes. Rhum palpe ses poches, mais n'a pas d'étui. Pipo se tourne, ouvre son étui et, le geste large, en tire une cigarette. Rhum enjambe alors la psyché, prend une cigarette dans l'étui que Pipo a laissé ouvert, et regagne sa place.

3 Who invented it? The Max Linder-Schwarz Brothers-lawsuit

The examples cited above, to which one could certainly add many others, reveal at least one thing: in effect, not one artist, actor, playwright etc. could claim the copyright for *The Broken Mirror*. All the more astonishing then are the legal proceedings taken by the two vaudeville artists Carl Schwarz and his brother Camillo. The brothers are mentioned by Max Bauer in the 1914 edition of Karl Friedrich Flögel's (1729–1788) *Geschichte des Grotesk-Komischen* [History of the Grotesque-Comical, 1778] and are described as "grotesque parodists of music hall performances" (Flögel 1914, 412) of some international repute. "Carl und Camillo Schwarz are real children of the theatre. [. . .] Their burlesque one act play 'The Broken Mirror' is a turning point in the Varieté grotesque comedy" (Flögel 1914, 412–413). That *The Broken Mirror* routine was the Schwarz Brothers' masterpiece is indicated by a small booklet, anonymously compiled and entitled *Der Zerbrochene Spiegel im Siegeszug durch die Welt* [The Broken Mirror Conquers the World, (n.d.)]. Twenty-seven pages relay their guest performances across Europe and even in South Africa (see Figure 2).

Variety magazine critic Bayard described the scene in detail on the occasion of their performance at the London Hippodrome in 1911.

> The story is that in the course of the struggle between a maid servant and a manservant a large mirror is knocked over, and the glass smashed to atoms. The master of the house, who is an actor, is suffering from the effects of a late night. When he goes to look at himself in the mirror, he sees what he thinks is a reflection of himself, but which is actually his manservant. The movements of the two are identical, the only appreciable difference being that the manservant is by no means so good looking as his master. Finally, the master tries to kiss the maid and the manservant in his jealousy knocks the mirror over, leaving the impression that it has been newly broken. It is a dialog piece, but the best thing in it is the pantomime between master and man. (Bayard 1911, 17)

Pipo allume sa cigarette en se regardant dans la glace. Rhum s'approche et prend du feu à la même allumette. Pipo tire sur sa cigarette, envoie la fumée dans la figure de Rhum qui en fait autant. Pipo avale la fumée et tousse. Rhum tousse lui aussi.
Pipo: C'est l'écho!
Rhum: Oui, c'est l'écho!
Pipo tient sa cigarette de la main droite. Rhum de même. Mais les images ne se superposent plus. Pipo, intrigué, change sa cigarette de main. Mais Rhum aussi, tant et si bien que l'inversion se reproduit. Rhum comprend enfin et prend sa cigarette de la main gauche, alors que Pipo la tient de la main droite. Pipo rit bruyamment. Rhum de même" (Rémy 2017, 189–190).

Figure 2: The Broken Mirror Conquers the World.

In the same article, Bayard indirectly refers to the popularity and enhancement of *The Broken Mirror*, mentioning three other variants that were staged simultaneously: one at the Hippodrome, one at the Orpheum Circuit in the United States, and a third as the "copy act *Early Morning Reflections*" (17) at the Palace. It is this Palace version, whose star was Lauri Wylie (1880–1951), brother of the mime-impresario Julian Wylie (1869–1934), against which the Schwarz brothers sued for copyright infringement on 8 December 1911. David Devant (1868–1941), an owner of Maskelyne's Theater of Mystery, emphasized for the defense the differences between the two versions. In *Early Morning Reflections*, a ghost who eventually turns into Mephistopheles, appears in front of a man and foretells him the woman he would marry. A point mentioned by the defense was the fact that the scene had already been recorded in print: the play *My friend from India* (1894) by Henry A. Du Souchet (1852–1922) had existed for almost two decades prior to trial.

As a result, the judges decided against Carl and Camillo Schwarz; however, shortly after the Schwarz brothers filed another lawsuit against silent films star Max Linder. This time they succeeded to some extent. In 1912–13, Linder had toured Europe, and in December 1912 he gave a guest performance at the *Wintergarten* in Berlin (Spears 1965, 277). Even the German emperor and the crown prince visited the performances, which combined film sequences with Linder's personal appearance in front of the audience. The ten-minute sketch *Pédicure par Amour* [Pedicure by Love, 1911], which Linder later adopted in the film *Max pédicure* [Max as Pedicure, 1914], proved to hold a special appeal for Berlin audiences. During its time in Berlin, the *Wintergarten*'s program also included performances by Carl and Camillo Schwarz. This is probably the reason why Linder adapted their *Broken Mirror* in his film *Le duel de Max* [Max's Duel], which premiered simultaneously in Berlin and Paris on 25 July 1913. In cinemas it played in two different versions:

> Since Linder seems to have been so much impressed with "The Broken Mirror"-Sketch [. . .] that he decided to include it in this film, despite the fact that the Schwarz duo claimed, and already had gotten copyright protection, confirmed by the courts. Therefore, countries like France, Spain and Germany had to settle for a shortened version of 970m (45 min.), whereas in countries like the United Kingdom, the Netherlands, Australia and Brazil, where Carl and Camillo Schwarz couldn't enforce their claims, the complete version with a length of 1300m (60 min.), was released. (Renken 2018)

During his next stay in Hollywood from 1920 to 1923, Linder utilized the scene a second time, probably because of the distance to Europe and the legal disputes there. For United Artists, he produced *Seven Years Bad Luck* (1921). As the title insinuates, the film also contains *The Broken Mirror*. In the film, a butler is trying to kiss the maid and they fall against an expensive full-length mirror and break it. Max, hungover, is awakened by the noise and the butler, fearful of losing his job over the broken mirror, persuades the cook, who greatly resembles Max, to stand behind the frame and pretend to be Linder's reflection (Spears 1965, 285).

4 *The Broken Mirror* in cinema and television productions: a genealogy

Max Linder was the first silent film star to introduce the mirror scene. As a result of his great success, everyone followed his example: Charlie Chaplin in *The Floorwalker* (1916), Harold Lloyd (1893–1971) in *The Marathon* (1919), Charley Chase (1893–1940) in *Sitting Pretty* (1924) and, of course, the Marx Brothers in *Duck Soup* (1933). In addition to a scene with a nut seller, who is harassed by Harpo and Chico Marx in several routines or *lazzi*, the mirror scene becomes the film's highlight. Embedded in a diplomatic intrigue, which deals with war plans of the fictional state Freedonia, the spies Pinky (Harpo) and Chicolini (Chico) as well as the president or dictator Rufus T. Firefly (Groucho Marx) stay in the house of the immensely wealthy Gloria Teasdale (Margaret Dumont). Intent on stealing the war plans, the spies encounter the president in the living room, after having him already met in the lady's bedroom, made up as Firefly's doubles. Everyone wears a nightdress and a nightcap, Groucho's painted-on beard, beetle brows, and glasses. Finally, Firefly and Chicolini face each other in a doorway arch, in which a mirror was installed, previously broken by a running Chico. Now they act out their version of the mirror scene that is (clearly) reminiscent of Domenico Biancolelli.

> In a longer shot, FIREFLY walks slowly to the centre and does a wild charleston, facing the mirror; PINKY does likewise, grinning. FIREFLY spins round; PINKY doesn't, but strikes the right pose when FIREFLY ends up facing him again. FIREFLY moves to the edge of the alcove, fluttering his hands like part of a Negro hallelujah chorus; PINKY disappears around the corner doing the same. FIREFLY has another idea and goes off. Back to the previous shot as FIREFLY enters slowly with a panama hat behind his back; PINKY does likewise, but we see that he has his black top hat. Convinced that he's caught him out this time, FIREFLY laughs and steps up to the 'mirror'; so does PINKY. They circle through the mirror, reversing their positions. FIREFLY spots the black hat and heaves with silent laughter – now he's got him – and PINKY does the same. They circle back through the 'mirror,' and suddenly FIREFLY puts on his hat. Seen in a closer shot, PINKY does likewise – producing a panama hat he has been hiding. FIREFLY points – 'Haha, I caught you'; PINKY mirrors him – 'Haha, I caught you.'
>
> PINKY is so pleased with himself that he points out of turn, then pulls a face as he realizes.
>
> Back to the scene as they both take off their hats and bow. PINKY drops his and FIREFLY hands it back to him. PINKY grins thank you. FIREFLY slowly puts his hat on and takes it off again; PINKY does likewise, but getting more and more out of phase.
>
> A closer shot as FIREFLY, mirrored by PINKY, turns away and ponders. At that moment, CHICOLINI enters on PINKY's side of the 'mirror.' PINKY gazes in horror at his nightshirted figure and hurriedly pushes him out of sight. He just recovers his pose as FIREFLY turns

towards him again. CHICOLINI wanders on again and PINKY runs off, while FIREFLY grabs CHICOLINI by the tail of his nightshirt and holds him fast.

(The Marx Brothers 1993, 139–140, emphasis in original)

Since then, *The Broken Mirror* lives on in popular culture, cinema, and television: Bob Hope (1903–2003), Errol Flynn (1909–1959), Bugs Bunny and Elmer Fudd, Bud Abbott (1895–1974) and Lou Costello (1906–1959) in *The Naughty Nineties* (1945), Lucille Ball (1911–1989) and Harpo Marx in *I Love Lucy*, David Niven (1910–1983) and Robert Wagner (*1930) as two gorillas in *The Pink Panther* (1964), Woody Allen (*1935) in *Sleeper* (1973), Benny Hill (1924–1992) in a television sketch, Bette Midler (*1945) and Lily Tomlin (*1939) in *Big Business* (1988), Roberto Benigni (*1952) in *Johnny Stecchino* (1991), Garfield in *Tale of Two Kitties* (2006), Otto Waalkes (*1948) and Olli Dittrich (*1956) in *Otto's Eleven* (2010), Kermit and his lookalike in *Muppets Most Wanted* (2014), episodes of *Gilligan's Island* (1964–1967), *Scooby-Doo* (1969–1976), *The X-Files* (1993–2002) (David Duchovny [*1960] and Michael McKean [*1947] including Groucho's "classic butt-wiggle" [Balducci 2012, 167]), *Family Guy* (1999–; Stewie and a cartoon-Hitler) and *The Simpsons* (1989–; Moe and a *Wizard of Oz*-monkey). Certainly, a lot more examples can be found.

Vaudeville, circus, music hall performances, pantomime, cinema, television, theatre – one question still remains: "And who really started it?"[4] Paul Bouissac is skeptical about finding the initiator: "It is, of course, impossible to retrace with any certainty the genealogy of a particular clown act" (2015, 115). Anthony Balducci hopes to "find evidence of a 15th century version of the mirror routine [one day]" (2013, n.p.). He has not succeeded. However, there is evidence that the Italian professional actor Domenico Biancolelli invented the routine in the seventeenth century.

---

4 Staveacre himself gives the following answer: "The smart money's on the anonymous author of a seventeenth-century Spanish play, *The Rogueries of Pablillos*." He refers to the seventeenth-century Spanish *Entremes del Espejo, y burla de Pablillos* (N. N. 1723, 130–141), a scenic interlude mentioned several times in connection with the mirror scene. "Pablillos" refers to the jester and actor Pablo de Valladolid (1587–1648), painted by Diego Velázquez: "From 1632 he was among the many dwarfs, jesters, and hombres de placer (entertainers) on the court payroll. Since his presence at the court was probably because of his comic and theatrical ability, he appears in this painting (which was known for a long time as *The Actor*) in a declamatory pose. His legs are extended, and he gestures with his hand at some verbal allusion" (Portús Pérez 2003, 453). The contents of the interlude, which in the French translation is entitled *Le miroir et la fourberie de Pablillos*, could not serve as a model for *The Broken Mirror*. A dialogue between an old man and Pablillos reveals that the latter assumes his mistress's mirror to be a window, and thus her reflection to be a real human being. As he has promised his master to keep his wife away from other men, he lashes out at the mirror and knocks it into a thousand pieces. There is no scenic aspect, in which one actor emulates the reflection of another.

As stated in the beginning, in addition to its name, the repertoire and the scenes, sketches or gags, and comic routines of slapstick derive from the *commedia all'improvviso*. Stefan Hulfeld refers more precisely to the the *lazzi*-routines, which form a fundamental narrative element of this theatre: "In the Commedia, *lazzi* are the comedic-artistic numbers of the improvisation actors; they correspond to what today is mostly called slapstick"[5] (Meister and Hulfeld 2016, 93). According to Hulfeld, between approximately 1580 and 1630, while professional theatre, i.e., the *commedia all'improvviso*, was emerging in Italy, individually performing actors united in *compagnie* [troupes], and the *lazzi* became part of more or less coherent narratives. However, Hulfeld does not consider this relation between slapstick and story in a pejorative way by assessing positively the renunciation of slapstick "numbers" and the turn to larger narrative contexts, but emphasizes the progression of "sequential narration and narrative momentum" as "a fundamental condition for the theatrical deployment of their own, special world-view"[6] (93). The *lazzo* as a *pezzo chiuso* [closed piece], as a self-contained and independent, bodily narrative scenic element, Hulfeld continues, creates a dynamic correlation with the story. This may be the reason why, on European and American stages, *The Broken Mirror*-routine persisted for more than 350 years: the autonomy, which is not necessarily connected to a specific story or context, but at least – referring to Hulfeld's definition of the *lazzo* – picks out existential and elementary experiences as a central theme.

I will highlight this viewpoint by using the example of Domenico Biancolelli who, besides Tristano Martinelli, was the second important Arlecchino (Arlequin) in the history of *commedia all'improvviso* and who invented *The Broken Mirror* as a comic routine. The latter half of the seventeenth century saw Biancolelli as an outstanding actor and the star of the *Comédie Italienne* in Paris. Many *comédies* that he performed are well documented – both in collections of scenarios by Evaristo Gherardi (1663–1700), his successor as Parisian Arlequin, and in a manuscript translated into French by Thomas-Simon Gueullette. In it, Biancolelli collected particular scenes, *burle* [jokes], *lazzi* [comic routines], which he performed on stage, comparable to a *zibaldone* [miscellany], i.e., a notebook with a collection of prologues, dialogues, fragments, scenarios, *canovacci* [canvas], owned by every actor or *capocomico* [head of the theatre troupe] (see Ojeda Calvo 2007). Biancolelli's *zibaldone*

---

5 "Als *lazzi* werden in der Commedia die komödiantisch-artistischen Nummern der Improvisationsakteure bezeichnet; sie entsprechen damit dem, was heute mehrheitlich Slapstick genannt wird."
6 "sequenzieller Narration und narrativem Momentum" . . . "eine Grundbedingung für die theatrale Entfaltung der komödiantischen Weltsicht."

also includes *The Broken Mirror* or, in his own words, "cette scene, qui est celle du miroir" ["this scene which is the one with the mirror"] (Gambelli 1993, vol. ii, 646).

5 *The Broken Mirror* for the first time: 1674

The scene in question was part of a scenario entitled *A fourbe, fourbe et demy*, presented to Paris audiences for the first time on 20 October 1674. It combines two aspects that mark *The Broken Mirror* as the first known instance of this scene. Biancolelli performed with virtuosity in the style of the *commedia all'improvviso*: through "moltiplicità di personaggi," the duplication of the personas or figures he acted (Münz 1979, 146). Secondly, he picked basic questions about human existence and fears, as well as questions concerning the constitution of the subject as the central theme. In view of Biancolelli, who performed *The Broken Mirror* several centuries before the great stars of slapstick comedy, a historical perspective also opens up for the understanding of slapstick. It is simply not enough to define slapstick as a certain kind of physical comedy based on grotesquely exaggerated gesticulations. At best, slapstick is always more, expanding to include a general human dimension that addresses basic problems and fundamental questions of human existence and confronts them with laughter – not argumentatively or with raised forefinger, like Chaplin does as hungry tramp eating up his shoe in *The Gold Rush* (1925), to name another example besides *The Broken Mirror*.

The interdependency between "sequential narration" and "narrative momentum," which Hulfeld characterized as distinctive for the first *commedia all'improvviso compagnie*, also plays a decisive role in *A fourbe, fourbe et demy* and *The Broken Mirror*. The scenario as a whole is determined by the "moltiplicità di personaggi," the *travestimenti* [transformations] of the Zanni, Scaramouche and Arlequin, representing the constitutive element of the intrigue. The point of departure is typical for a *commedia all'improvviso* scenario. The two male lovers lost their hearts to the daughters of Dottore (the Doctor). In order to get the men inside or the women outside, Capitano Spezzaferro (Captain Steelbreaker, another famous *commedia* mask) needs the help of Arlequin and Scaramouche, who appear in numerous disguises: Scaramouche (the actor Tiberio Fiorilli) as (stereotyped) moor, Turk, pious Spaniard, lemon tree, peasant, a peddler selling Venetian mirrors, and Arlequin (Domenico Biancolelli) as moor, gazetteer, giant, orange tree, Dottore and Diamantine, captain and pharmacist. These disguises bestir a multitude of "fourberies," which intend to enable the wedding of the *innamorati* [lovers].

Finally, Capitano Spezzaferro and Scaramouche hide Arlequin in a mirror. Scaramouche, as a peddler, sells the huge fake mirror to the Doctor, in whose house Arlequin is finally carried. The scenario of *A fourbe, fourbe et demy* describes the scene as follows:

> XIV
> Scaramouche, Arlequin, Doctor
>
> Arlequin in the mirror, on one side dressed as a Doctor and on the other as a daughter of the Doctor, who opens the curtain and sees himself in it. He notices the deception, "but," he says, "I will catch her, for I am having a daughter come."
>
> XV
> [Scaramouche, Arlequin, Doctor, a daughter]
>
> She enters and Arlequin turns around. The Doctor is amazed and after several lazzi they [Arlequin and Scaramouche, SH] are discovered and exit.[7]   (Colajanni 1970, 359)

The fictional sphere plays with the expectations of the Doctor, who wants to expose the fraudsters. The factual sphere, in turn, plays with the expectations of the audience, which wants the dizziness to be immediately revealed; however, the 'performance' continues regardless as a result of the second disguise of Arlequin as the daughter's reflection. Biancolelli-Arlequin, who acts simultaneously as Doctor and his daughter, performs once again with virtuosity. The performance of the other *comici* [comedians] must also be regarded as virtuoso, because Arlequin has to create the illusion of a true reflection in coordination with his colleagues on stage – "the best thing in it is the pantomime," as Bayard had written about the Schwarz Brothers (Bayard 1911, 17). This becomes apparent in Biancolelli's more detailed description:

> In this scene – which is that of the mirror – I am dressed as a doctor on the front, and as a Diamantine on the back. Scaramouche opens the curtain that covers the frame of the mirror, you don't see anything and it seems to be just a canvas that represents the glass of a mirror, and you only see that; then I stand in the frame with the side where I am dressed as a doctor. The Doctor notices me, takes off his hat, I take it off too, he lifts one foot, I do the same, the curtain closes. He calls Diamantine; then a scene between the two, the curtain opens; I show myself in the mirror from the side where I am dressed like Diamantine; she dances, I dance too; she makes bows, I make some too, finally I imitate her completely. One

---

7 XIV / Scaramouche, Arlequin, le Docteur / Arlequin dans le miroir, habillé en Docteur d'un côté et de l'autre comme une des filles du Docteur qui ouvre le rideau, se voit dedans, il s'apperçoit pourtant de la fourberie, "mais," dit-il, "je vais les attraper, car je vais faire venir une fille."
XV / [Scaramouche, Arlequin, le Docteur, une fille] / Elle vient et Arlequin se tourne. Le Docteur demeure tout étonné et après plusieurs lazi, ils sont découverts et s'en vont.

closes the curtain again, Diamantine withdraws, the Doctor opens the curtain again, I reappear as a Doctor in the mirror, he raises an arm, I raise it too, he pretends to make an attack, I do the same; he sneezes / I sneeze too; he takes off his hat several times and puts it back on again, I do the same; he quickly takes it off and puts it back on again, I take mine off too and put it on again; when he wants to put his hat back on, he drops it to the ground, so I get out of the frame to pick it up, I hold it out to him and want to return to the frame of the mirror; because the Doctor notices the villainy there, he beats me up, I escape, he chases me, and we finish the second act.[8]

(Gambelli 1993, vol. ii, 646)

Some of these elements can also be found in the Marx Brothers' scene (taking off the hat, dancing) or in the *Entrée clownesque* (sneezing). The mirror sequence in *Duck Soup* also has in common with Biancolelli the last element or scene, in which the mirror image picks up the hat of Dottore. Whereas in *A fourbe, fourbe et demy* the sequence closes with a beating scene – which Arlequin probably structured acoustically with the rhythmic use of his 'Slapstick' – and with the exposure of Isabella, and Arlequin as the wrong Doctor, the Marx Brothers go one step further. The illusion of the mirror's reflection is not spoiled by the hat picked up by Harpo, but by a second brother, who is also disguised as a Firefly double.

6 *Comödien-Stil* and slapstick

As already mentioned, for this scene Domenico Biancolelli utilized – in contrast to slapstick – a special acting technique, for which the term "moltiplicità di personaggi" has been coined on the occasion of the Venetian guest performance or

---

8 "Dans cette scene, qui est celle du miroir, je suis habillé par devant en Docteur, et par derrière je suis vestu comme Diamantine. Scaramouche ouvre le rideau qui cache la bordure du miroir, on ne voit rien et il ne paroist qu'une toille qui represente la glace d'un miroir, et l'on ne voit rien que cela; ensuitte je me mets dans la bordure du costé où je suis habillé en Docteur. Le Docteur m'apperçoit, il oste son chapeau, je l'oste aussy, il leve un pied, je fais de mesme, on ferme le rideau. Il appelle Diamantine; apres une scene entre eux, on ouvre le rideau; je me presente dans le miroir du costé où je suis vestu comme Diamantine; elle danse, je danse aussy; elle fait des reverences, j'en fais aussy, enfin je l'imitte en tout. On referme le rideau, Diamantine se retire, le Docteur ouvre encore le rideau, je reparois en Docteur dans le miroir, il leve un bras, je le leve aussy, il fait comme s'il poussoit une botte, je fais de mesme; il esternue / j'esternue aussy; il oste et remet plusieurs fois son chapeau, je fais la mesme chose; il l'oste et le remet prestement, j'oste et je remets aussy le mien; en voulant remettre son chapeau, il le laisse tomber par terre, alors je sors de la bordure pour le ramasser, je le luy presente et je veux retourner dans la bordure du miroir; le Docteur, s'apperçevant alors de la fourberie, me rosse, je me sauve, il me poursuit, et nous finissons le second acte."

"adventure" of the Viennese actor and impresario Johann Joseph Felix von Kurz (1717–1784) in 1763/64. During Carnival, he performed at the famous and renovated opera theatre of San Cassiano, and intended to revitalize the Venetian opera prior to the reform of Apostolo Zeno (1668–1750) and Pietro Metastasio (1698–1782). Kurz's aims were to merge his theatre and his acting with the *commedia* or *Comédie* in Biancolelli's tradition. Like Biancolelli as Arlequin, Kurz appeared as Bernardon, in many disguises and numerous dresses. In *Die drey und dreyssig Schelmereyen des BERNARDONS* [The Thirty-three Rogueries of Bernardon], he acted in eleven different disguises, namely as "Wälscher Cervelade-Würst-Händler" [outlandish sausage seller], "armer Bub" [poor boy], "ein Engländischer Laquey" [English flunky], "eine flüchtige Dame" [a fugitive lady], "Croatel" [Croatian], "Husar" [hussar], "recommandirte[r] Kutscher" [recommended coachman], "Persianischer Sclaven-Handler" [Persian slave trader], "holländischer Bauer" [Dutch peasant], and finally, "Americanische[r] Menschenfresser" [American man-eater] (Müller-Kampel 2003, 205–212).

In these transformations that constitute a basic technique of the *Comödien-Stil*, the figure/*Kunstfigur* or mask/*maschera* (Bernardon, Arlequin) as the body or the mask that encompasses the whole actor body performs constantly conjoined with the actor (Kurz, Biancolelli). More precisely, the actor Domenico Biancolelli uses the *Kunstfigur/maschera* of Arlequin and its special abilities to create these transformations. The *maschera* of Arlequin shows that Arlequin always remained recognizable to the audience during the transformations (see Baumbach 2012, 216–229). The close relationship between the actor and his *Kunstfigur* or *maschera* as "narrator, and basic principle of multiplying"[9] (231) becomes apparent in the fact that today we speak of Kurz-Bernardon, Isabella Andreini-Isabella, and Biancolelli-Arlequin. This *Kunstfigur* (*maschera*) and its provenance (the *strutturale personaggio*) (see Avalle 1989) enable the transformations into a variety of social roles, gender roles, gods, spirits, animals, other *maschere* and even into objects (see Baumbach 2012, 251). This is clearly the case in *A fourbe, fourbe et demy*.

Biancolelli's *The Broken Mirror* is not the only scene in which he performed these transformations with virtuosity. Eight years later, a scene without a mirror shows once again that Arlequin is simultaneously transformed into two figures – in this case social roles: *Scene de la lingere et du limonadier* [Scene of the linen maid and the lemonade seller], which was first staged on 4 October 1682 at the Hôtel de Bourgogne. The way Biancolelli made use of the "moltiplicità" reminds of slapstick comedy and is described as follows: "Arlequin, dressed half as a

---

9 "Erzähler und Grundlage der Vervielfachung [moltiplicità; SH]."

woman and half as a man, appears against the background of a lingerie shop bordering on the shop of a lemonade seller"[10] (Gherardi 1969, vol. i, 61). Furthermore, the scene is shown on the engraving that illustrates the *comédie*: the picture showing Arlequin is divided in the middle. Situated on the left is the booth of a linen maid, on the right the one of a lemonade seller. Arlequin plays both – recognizable by his black face mask – with the linen maid on his right side, the lemonade seller on his left. In the scene, he talks to an ignorant Pasquariello (a Neapolitan mask played by Geronimo Cey), who wants to buy new underwear, alternating between speaking as a woman and as a man, from their respective booths. The actor Domenico Biancolelli alternates between the different spheres – fictional and real – and the various transformations into Arlequin and linen maid/lemonade seller, a 'playing' which not only exasperates Pasquariello, but also astonishes the audience. The scene ends in a quarrel between the two vendors, in which Arlequin acts out on his own body the dispute between the two:

> ARLEQUIN as linen maid.
> I will show you how long my yardstick is. *He takes the yardstick and, pretending to give the lemonade seller a punch, he beats Pasquariello.*
> PASQUARIELLO.
> Oh, upon my soul, this is too much.
> ARLEQUIN as lemonade seller.
> Yes! Oh, I will teach you to raise your hand to a man like me. *He takes a ceramic pot and, pretending to throw it at the lingerie saleswoman, he throws it at Pasquariello. Then two or three repetitions of the same lazzo, Arlequin goes off as a lemonade salesman; & as if he wanted to jump on the lingerie saleswoman, he turns sometimes on one side, sometimes on the other: so that Pasquariello, who sees the man from one side and the woman from the other [. . .], tries to separate them & gets several blows. After which Arlequin laughingly withdraws [. . .].*[11] (Gherardi 1969, vol. i, 65–66, emphasis in original)

---

10 "Arlequin habillé moitié en femme & moitié en homme, paroît dans le fond d'une boutique de lingere, contigue à celle d'un limonadier."

11 "ARLEQUIN en lingere. / Je te vais montrer que mon aune est de mesure. *Il prend l'aune, & feignant d'en donner un coup au limonadier, il frappe Pasquariel.*
PASQUARIEL.
Oh, par ma foi, c'en est trop.
ARLEQUIN en limonadier.
Oui! Oh je t'apprendrai à lever la main sur un homme comme moi. *Il prend un pot de fayence, & feignant de le jetter à la lingere, il le jette à la tête de Pasquariel. Après deux ou trois répétitions du même lazzi, Arlequin sort en limonadier; & comme s'il vouloit sauter sur la lingere, il se tourne tantôt d'un côté & tantôt de l'autre: ensorte que Pasquariel qui le voit homme d'un côté & femme de l'autre [. . .], s'empresse à les separer, & reçoit plusieurs coups. Après quoi Arlequin se retire en riant [. . .].*"

If Biancolelli's *The Broken Mirror* is classified as a *lazzo* – or as scene which consists of a sequence of several *lazzi* – then, according to Hulfeld, we can define it – and slapstick as well – as "scenic processes that debate the issues of existential experiences, wishes, desires, and fears" (2014, 93). Thus, the focus is not on generating any meaning or significance. It is on theatrically debating those emotional experiences, but not through a theatre that is based on the *lógos* and capitalizes on it. Actors like Biancolelli communicated and performed non-verbally, bodily, enabled by the *maschere* – in this case Arlequin. One element of this performance was the more or less direct communication with the audience: to tear down the theatre's fourth wall, and thus achieving a different kind of attention and participation within the audience. In fact, the 'real' spectators – and the same is true for silent films, which, however, lack the actors' bodily presence – are directly involved in the fictional events. *The Broken Mirror* – *commedia* or slapstick – is based on the fact that the audience is as excited as Dottore – or Rufus Firefly or one of the Schwarz brothers – when the (perfect) illusion of the mirror reflection is unmasked. Certainly, the new ruse, the new trick of how to give Arlequin access to Dottore's house, was prepared in detail and revealed to the spectators of *A fourbe, fourbe et demy*. After Scaramouche has sold the mirror to the Docteur, and the mirror has been brought into the house, the charm of the *lazzo* consists not only of the perfect illusion of an intact mirror between the real Doctor and Biancolelli-Arlequin *as* Doctor, but also in the procrastination of the moment when he blows the whistle on Arlequin. The fraud is made obvious to the audience because Arlequin is clearly recognizable by his theatre dress and his black face mask. The spectators' amazement is not only provoked by the timing – Dottore and the disguised Arlequin simultaneously take off their hats, or sneeze, for example – but is enhanced by the fact that when the daughter is summoned, the fraudulent Arlequin is actually prepared for this, and now imitates her dance and movements she enacts in front of the mirror. The Marx Brothers develop this effect further by not ending the scene as Biancolelli does, when the one 'in the mirror' picks up the other's hat. Flabbergasted, the spectators observe Groucho and Chico putting on their hats without destroying the mirror illusion. In *The Broken Mirror*, the spectators, who face the climax and wonder if and when the one who imitates the mirror reflections will be exposed – and if he will get a beating in punishment of his escapades – become accomplices in the scenic illusion.

The practice of "moltiplicità di personaggi" allows the actor to alternate between the different levels of actor (Domenico Biancolelli), mask/*maschera* (Arlequin) and 'disguise' or transformation (Doctor and Diamantine), and in this way allows him to jolt the predefined world view and its accompanying idea of humanity. Thus, Arlequin transforms into almost anything: humans and animals, social roles, machines, objects, etc. Using these transformations and the alternation between the levels, the *comici* jolt the determination of the human being derived from the humanist ideal, which sought to define the human being as a second god to distinguish them from animals. Via "moltiplicità," certain conditions of being human emerge that should be excluded according to the traditional and approved ideas of humanism. For example, the disjunction of subject and object is suspended. This discrepancy and uncertainty that are also expressed in *The Broken Mirror* can be traced back to the fact that the Doctor seems to regard his mirror reflection as another, a second person. He takes off his hat, seemingly to 'test' the mirror, which then launches a culmination of ever new imitations and impersonations. In this way, the boundaries between subject and object, between the Docteur and his reflection (of Arlequin disguised as Docteur) dissolve – not only on the fictional level, which leads the Docteur to doubt his own existence, but also for the spectator, for whom the mirror image and the *maschera* in front of the mirror must progressively merge. In the scenario the Docteur says, "je vais les attraper" ["I will catch them"] (Colajanni 1970, 370) to let the audience know that he is aware of the deception, but the uncertainty must increase with each gesture and every new trick done by Arlequin. The illusion of a clearly defined individual is challenged and begins to dissipate – casting doubt on its own perception. This doubt and uncertainty are highlighted by the various grotesque movements and gestures the Docteur displays, who is only (back) on firm ground when Arlequin puts on the hat and spoils the illusion.

Thus, the *Broken Mirror* routine in *commedia all'improvviso* and slapstick – according to Hulfeld's definition of a *lazzo* – broaches issues of existential experience, desires, and fears. The *commedia all'improvviso*, at least when superficially regarded, consistently presented its spectators with the same vain acts: how to gain access to a house using virtuoso ideas and amazing inventions, for example. In truth, their *lazzi* and actions enabled the *commedia* actors to pick human existence out as a central theme – but from the seventeenth century onward, *commedia all'improvviso* was reformed or disappeared completely. Of course, there were also representatives like Vsevolod Meyerhold (1874–1940) or Dario Fo (1926–2016) and Franca Rame (1929–2013), who grappled with the *Comödien-Stil*, but they all did from a historical perspective, because *commedia all'improvviso* no longer existed. *The Broken Mirror* shows how its 'spirit,' that is to say certain *lazzi* or scenes, have survived over the centuries – from Domenico Biancolelli to the Simpsons. Specific *commedia all'improvviso* routines and techniques continued to exist in other forms of theatre, vaudeville, music hall, pantomime, circus, slapstick comedy and then film and television, so they are known and popular to this day. The Schwarz Brothers, for example, referred no longer to Biancolelli, especially since they claimed to have invented *The Broken Mirror* themselves. But they must have taken the scene from someone else, just like Max Linder did for his *Le duel de Max*, taken from Carl and Camillo Schwarz, and then Chaplin probably did from Linder, the Marx Brothers from vaudeville shows, Roberto Benigni from the Marx Brothers, and so on. The result is a long-standing tradition, and in many ways a diminution that reaches to this day, and is probably not finished yet.

Bibliography

Adrian [Henwood, Paul]. *Ce rire qui vient du cirque: L'art, la vie, l'histoire, les blagues des clowns, Augustes, excentriques et de leurs "faire-valoir."* Bourg-la-Reine: Collection »L'Encyclopédie du Cirque«, 1969.

Avalle, D'Arco Silvio. *Le maschere di Guglielmino: Strutture e motivi etnici nella cultura medievale.* Milan: Riccardo Ricciardi, 1989.

Balducci, Anthony. *The Funny Parts: A History of Film Comedy Routines and Gags.* London: McFarland & Company, 2012.

Balducci, Anthony. *The Pirates of the Palace: The Troubled Stage History of the Mirror Routine.* 2013. http://anthonybalducci.blogspot.com/2013/08/the-pirates-of-palace-troubled-stage.html (accessed 12 August 2018).

Baumbach, Gerda. *Schauspieler: Historische Anthropologie des Akteurs. Band 1: Schauspielstile.* Leipzig: Universitätsverlag, 2012.

Bayard. "Schwartz Brothers (3). 'The Broken Mirror.' 15 mins. Hippodrome, London." *Variety* 24.9 (1911), 17.

Blades, James, and Robert Anderson. "Clappers." *The New Grove Dictionary of Music and Musicians. Second Edition. Volume 5: Canon to Classic Rock.* Ed. Stanley Sadie. London: Macmillan, 2001. 891–893.

Blades, James, and James Holland. "Whip [clappers, slapstick]." *The New Grove Dictionary of Music and Musicians. Second Edition. Volume 27: Wagon to Żywny.* Ed. Stanley Sadie. London: Macmillan, 2001. 336.

Bouissac, Paul. *The Semiotics of Clowns and Clowning: Rituals of Transgression and the Theory of Laughter.* London: Bloomsbury, 2015.

Colajanni, Giuliana. *Les Scénarios Franco-Italiens du Ms. 9329 de la B.N.* Rome: Edizioni di Storia e Letteratura, 1970.

Collier, Kevin Scott. *Grand Haven's Lyman Twins: A Vaudeville Memoir featuring News, Reviews and Rare Photographs.* Grand Haven: Book Patch Publishing, 2015.

Duchartre, Pierre-Louis. *The Italian Comedy: The Improvisation Scenarios Lives Attributes Portraits and Masks of the Illustrious Characters of the Commedia dell'Arte.* Transl. Randolph T. Weaver. New York: Dover, 1966.

Düringer, Philipp Jacob, and Heinrich Ludwig Barthels. *Theater-Lexicon: Theoretisch-practisches Handbuch für Vorstände, Mitglieder und Freunde des deutschen Theaters.* Leipzig: Wigand, 1841.

Ferrone, Siro. *Arlecchino: Vita e avventure di Tristano Martinelli attore*. Rome: Bulzoni, 2006.
Flögel, Karl Friedrich. *Geschichte des Grotesk-Komischen: Ein Beitrag zur Geschichte der Menschheit*. Vol. 2. Munich: Georg Müller, 1914.
Gambelli, Delia. *Arlecchino a Parigi: Lo scenario di Domenico Biancolelli*. Rome: Bulzoni, 1993.
Gherardi, Evaristo. *Le Théâtre Italien ou le Recueil général de toutes les Comédies et Scènes françaises jouées par les Comédiens Italiens du Roi*. Vol. 3. Genève: Slatkine, 1969.
Hulfeld, Stefan. "Einführung in die Lektüre der *Scenari più scelti d'istrioni*." *Scenari più scelti d'istrioni. Italienisch-Deutsche Edition der einhundert Commedia all'improvviso-Szenarien aus der Sammlung Corsiniana*. Vol. 1. Ed. Stefan Hulfeld in collaboration with Demis Quadri, Sebastian Hauck, and Stefano Mengarelli. Göttingen: V&R Vienna University Press, 2014. 9–112.
Little, Kenneth. "Masochism, Spectacle, and the 'Broken Mirror' Clown Entrée: A Note on the Anthropology of Performance in Postmodern Culture." *Cultural Anthropology* 8.1 (1993): 117–129.
Madden, Charles. *Harlequin's Stick – Charlie's Cane: A Comparative Study of Commedia dell'Arte and Silent Slapstick Comedy*. Bowling Green: University Popular Press, 1968.
The Marx Brothers. *Monkey Business, Duck Soup and A Day at the Races*. With an introduction by Karl French. London and Boston: faber and faber, 1993.
McKinven, John A. *The Hanlon Brothers: Their Amazing Acrobatics, Pantomimes and Stage Spectacles*. Glenwood: David Meyer Magic Books, 1998.
Meister, Monika, and Stefan Hulfeld. "Slapstick und Story: Über das Wechselspiel von sequenzieller Narration und narrativem Momentum." *Bruch und Ende im seriellen Erzählen: Vom Feuilletonroman zur Fernsehserie*. Ed. Birgit Wagner. Göttingen: V&R Vienna University Press, 2016. 93–108.
Müller-Kampel, Beatrix. *Hanswurst, Bernardon, Kasperl: Spaßtheater im 18. Jahrhundert*. Paderborn: Schöningh, 2003.
Münz, Rudolf. *Das 'andere' Theater: Studien zu einem deutschsprachigen teatro dell'Arte der Lessingzeit*. Berlin: Henschel, 1979.
N. N. *Arcadia de entremeses*. Madrid: Imp. de Ángel Pasqual Rubio, 1723.
N. N. "Slapstick". *Buchers Enzyklopädie des Films*. Vol. 2. Eds. Liz-Anne Bawden and Wolfram Tichy. Munich: Bucher, 1977. 718–719.
Ojeda Calvo, Maria del Valle. *Stefanelo Botarga e Zan Ganassa: Scenari e zibaldoni di comici italiani nella Spagna del Cinquecento*. Rome: Bulzoni, 2007.
Portús Pérez, Javier. "Diego Rodríguez de Silva y Velázquez. The Jester Pablo de Valladolid." *Manet – Velázquez: The French Taste for Spanish Painting*. New York: Metropolitan Museum of Art, 2003. 452–453.
Rémy, Tristan. *Clown Scenes*. Transl. Bernard Sahlins. Chicago: Ivan R. Dee, 1997.
Rémy, Tristan. *Entrées clownesques*. Paris: L'Arche Éditeur, 2017.
Renken, Georg. *Max Linder Filmografie. Le duel de Max*. http://www.maxlinder.de/dueldemax.htm (accessed 17 March 2018).
Spears, Jack. "Max Linder Was the Motion Picture's First Truly International Star." *Films in Review* 15 (1965): 272–291.

Staveacre, Tony. *Slapstick! The Illustrated Story of Knockabout Comedy*. North Ryde and London: Angus & Robertson, 1987.
Taviani, Ferdinando, and Mirella Schino. *Il segreto della Commedia dell'Arte. La memoria delle compagnie italiane del XVI, XVII e XVIII secolo*. Florence: la casa Usher, 2007.
Towsen, John H. *Clowns*. New York: Hawthorn Books, 1976.

Courtney Andree
Harold Lloyd and the Reappearing Hand: Disability, Embodiment, and Slapstick

On 24 August 1919, slapstick star Harold Lloyd (1893–1971) was posing for a set of publicity stills when he was instructed to light a cigarette from one of the papier-mâché bombs in a prop box at his feet. Unbeknownst to him, a real explosive had been slipped into the batch. The blast tore a hole in the photography studio's sixteen-foot ceiling, severely burnt the skin on Lloyd's face, reduced him to temporary blindness and partial deafness, and tore away two fingers on his right hand, as well as a sizeable portion of his palm. The actor would speak openly in industry publications about his brush with death and his fears that he would be "blind for life" and "so disabled that [he] would never be able to work again," yet he would never publicly acknowledge the permanent disability that resulted, and set about restoring his broken hand to visual "wholeness" with the aid of a prosthesis and the collaboration of friends and studio colleagues (Hall 1930, 90).

In spite of the fact that slapstick comedy so frequently relied upon marked physical difference for comedic effect and even as tens of thousands of wounded and permanently disabled U.S. soldiers returned from the battlefields of WWI, Lloyd sought to reconstruct his biography and public image along the lines of conspicuous health and normality. The actor's efforts to "mask" and at times "reveal" his disability, the recurrent references to the accident that appear at the margins of his films, and the accommodations that he would make in the years to come all point to the centrality of the body in slapstick narrative and performance – a body that has been sidestepped and largely forgotten in scholarly discussions of the genre. As I argue in this chapter, slapstick performance is grounded in an understanding of the vicissitudes of the body, its failures, accidents, and capabilities. Taking Lloyd's accident and subsequent career as my focal points, I consider the place of disability and the body within slapstick narrative, performance, and promotional frameworks and ground the discussion in disability theory and history.

At the time of the accident, Lloyd had only begun to refine his "glasses character." Designed to be ordinary and relatable in the extreme, this new comic persona offered a marked departure from the physically exaggerated and frequently outlandish figures that typified slapstick cinema of the 1910s and 1920s – such as Charlie Chaplin's (1889–1977) waddling and ill-attired Little Tramp and its many imitators, the cross-eyed Ben Turpin (1869–1940), oversized "Fatty" Arbuckle (1887–1933), or Sammy Brooks (1891–1951), who measured four feet, six-inches tall and appeared alongside Lloyd in 127 early shorts (D'Agostino Lloyd 2004, 41). In his autobiography, *An American Comedy* (1928), Lloyd outlined his intentions for the character, noting that "The glasses would serve as my trademark and at the same time suggest the character – quiet, normal, boyish, clean, sympathetic" (Lloyd 1971, 59). Developing a conspicuously "normal" and "average" character, a character unmarked by any physical difference or aberration (but for his spectacles), Lloyd attempted to set his comic persona apart from the fray. Importantly, his glasses character would give him greater license to develop complex narratives, three-dimensional characterization, and romantic plots, which were all major innovations in the genre of slapstick. Believing that he would no longer be "tied to low-comedy coat tails," Lloyd saw his glasses character as a path to respectability and box office success (Lloyd 1971, 59).

To better introduce the new character to the world, his distributor Pathé requested some new publicity images of Lloyd's new character, "The Boy," for lobby displays and promotional purposes (Lloyd 1971, 74). Donning his trademark horn-rimmed glasses without lenses and a checkered suit, Lloyd took a break from the filming of his two-reeler *Haunted Spooks* (1920) for a sitting at Witzel Studio in downtown Los Angeles. After taking a few formal shots (some of which were developed and used for publicity purposes in spite of the accident, see Figure 1), the photographer turned to Lloyd and asked if they could bring in some props. Director and gag man Frank Terry (1870–1948), who had accompanied Lloyd to the studio, casually picked up what he thought to be a prop bomb, lit it, and passed it to the comic. Unbeknownst to them both, it carried a live charge and had been made for a prank weeks earlier; after an identical bomb shattered a thick table at Bear Lake the stunt was called off and the bomb somehow made its way back to the studio's prop room and in turn to the photo shoot at Witzel's (Lloyd 1971, 74).

In his autobiography, Lloyd describes the scene in terse sentences and in dramatic terms, omitting any mention of the injuries he sustained to his right hand:

> Had I not lowered my hand at that instant I should have been killed instantly, my head probably blown off. The force of the blast was principally upward [. . .]. The photographer fainted dead away. Blinded, bloody, and stunned, I staggered outside [. . .]. The pain by now was excruciating. (1971, 75)

After he was taken to Los Angeles's Methodist Hospital, Lloyd was given ether for the pain and his wounds were tended to by a team of doctors. Fearing that the burns on his face would turn gangrenous and that the actor would lose sight in one or both of his eyes, the hospital kept him under observation for the next month. Believing himself to be potentially blind and badly scarred, and

Figure 1: *Pathé* publicity still of Lloyd, taken at Witzel's studio in Los Angeles on the day of the accident in 1919.

with two fingers severed, Lloyd feared that his career was over – just as he was primed for greatness: "At twenty-six, after six years of incessant hard work and little money, I had stood on the threshold of, to me, breathless possibilities, only to be cut down [. . .]. I was scarred and torn beyond all thought, of course, [of] ever acting again before a camera" (75). He painstakingly details his slow healing process and notes that his face resembled "raw meat" as it developed "a maddening rash and an outbreak of boils" (76), but never references his permanent losses – the two missing fingers that he would mask with a cosmetic prosthesis for the remainder of his life and the lingering pain that would accompany the injury, as muscles, nerves, and tendon were torn away from bone.

Even as Lloyd was barely conscious in his hospital bed and contemplating the certain end of his career as a slapstick star, film trade journals and daily newspapers light-heartedly reported on his injuries and his certain return to the silver screen. On 25 August 1919, the day following the accident, *The Los Angeles Evening Herald* published two pieces that reference the explosion – one, a two-sentence item on the circumstances of the explosion and the second, a rhyming jingle that appeared on the front page:

> Our slugging fleet sails for the north: a movie star was hit –
> A bomb has injured Harold Lloyd: it nearly wrecked his mitt. (1919, 6)

The newspaper makes light of the actor's injuries and adopts comic form in order to make the announcement. *The Los Angeles Times* would likewise quip that "Reel Bomb is a Real One," in their headline from the same date (1919, 1).

Other outlets would take a more somber and balanced course. *The Los Angeles Examiner* devoted several column inches to the events of 24 August, making it their lead story on the day following the blast. Interviewing both Frank Terry and Lloyd's father, James "Foxy" Lloyd, the paper suggests that the actor's immediate concern at the time of the blast was not for life or limb, but instead his future career prospects. A still conscious Lloyd reportedly "writhed on the floor, crying, 'My career is ruined'" before being rushed to the hospital (*LA Examiner* 1919, 1). Foxy Lloyd reiterates that "Lloyd's greatest suffering is over the effect the accident may have on his career" (1919, 5). Industry publication *Wid's Film Daily* published a lengthy piece on Lloyd's ordeal in their 27 August edition, acknowledging that "the thumb and forefinger of his right hand were amputated. His condition is now very good except that it is impossible to determine the extent of the injury to his eyes" (1919, 1). *Variety* likewise reported on the loss of "finger and thumb," and reminded exhibitors that film "releases will not be affected by his absence from work" until the new year (1919, 65).

Film industry publications and Hollywood dailies were far from the only outlets to disseminate news of Lloyd's permanent disabilities in the weeks following the accident. A week after the explosion, the *Omaha Bee* reported that while "the thumb and forefinger of his right hand had to be amputated," the actor "is expected to be able to continue his career" (1919, 1). By September another update on Lloyd's condition had gone out over the wire (presumably disseminated by producer Hal Roach [1892–1992] or distributor Pathé), and the piece would be picked up by outlets across the nation, including *The Great Falls Daily Tribune* (MT) and *The Washington Times*. Optimistic and slightly jocular in tone, the news item stated that while the actor was "mending nicely and the surgeons now assure him of restoration to his brilliant career," (*Omaha Bee* 1919, 1) "at last reports Lloyd was said to be two fingers shy after the accident" (3).

As Lloyd remained in recovery and was presumably unable to manage his public persona from his hospital bed, news of his physical losses was openly communicated. Studio heads and his distributor were firmly of the opinion that he could continue in screen comedy after the accident, but it is evident that the actor felt that his future was in peril and that his disabilities undercut the conspicuous normality of his glasses character. Tellingly, the comedian repeatedly referenced the story of a stage comedian by the name of Toto (1889–1938) in interviews and autobiographical writings. As he writes, Toto "had a minor cast in one eye. It was so inconsequential that no one noticed it until the first close-up. Close-ups distort any [. . .] variation from the normal" (Lloyd 1971, 63). Unfortunately, since "close-ups are essential" (63) for a career in film, he held that the comedian could not sustain a career because of this minor physical imperfection.

Toto's disqualification is somewhat surprising, given the fact that comedies of the era showcased a diverse array of body types; if anything, corporeal difference was the rule rather than the exception in early slapstick film. As Lloyd admitted, "in that period we all sought to have an identifying symbol or something. You had to have either a moustache, or a chin piece, or sideburns, or crossed eyes, or be fat or skinny or something that identified you" (Cohen 1971, 127–128). The character that he originated was intended to break with this tradition, and while he would continue to tangentially present disability and bodily variation in his films, physical and psychological ordinariness was his aim: "My character didn't look unusual as a rule [. . .]. As a whole, my character's appearance was almost what we call 'straight'" (Cahn 1964, 101). First and foremost, "everything about him was normal – his shoes, his clothes, the way he walked and talked" (99). In a sea of comic grotesques, Lloyd constructed himself as healthy, wholesome, and relatable. And as he returned to the screen in the months following the accident, this drive toward "normality" and typicality was further bolstered. Admitting that "the accident speeded up the evolution of the character to a completely straight role," the silent comedian worked to obscure his new disabilities and adapt to the requirements of his physically demanding roles (Lloyd 1971, 81).

1 Empathy, disability, and the slapstick body

Prior to the explosion, Lloyd had a reputation as one of the most daring and agile comedians of the silent screen and his exploits were much discussed in the trade and popular press. His earlier tramp character, Lonesome Luke, had been branded as the "Human Rubber Ball" in Pathé ad campaigns (see Figure 2, "Nothing Succeeds Like Success" 1915, 93) and appreciative audiences would take note. Following suit, a reviewer for *Moving Picture World* suggested that he "must be made of India rubber. The way he suffers himself to be kicked all over the map, hit on the head with a mallet and fall down a dizzy flight of stairs is

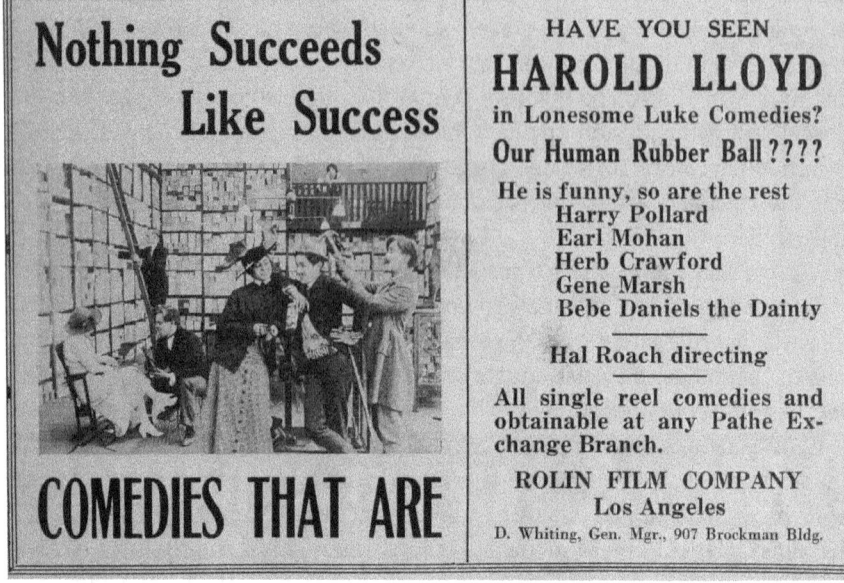

Figure 2: Harold Lloyd's early Lonesome Luke character was branded as the "human rubber ball" in Pathé display ads for the series, which appeared in a range of industry publications from 1915 to 1917.

marvelous" ("Pathe's 'Lonesome Luke' Comedies Unique" 1916, 963). It is evident that it is Lloyd's apparent imperviousness to lasting injury that set him apart; like the "rubber ball" he is compared to in ad campaigns, he is required to bounce back in short order. *The Detroit Free Press* would also applaud Lloyd's physical prowess in a 16 July 1917 column:

> Screen comedy [. . .] demands unusual athletic ability. Mr. Lloyd possesses this to a marked degree, being an excellent rider, swimmer, fencer, and boxer. He also excels as a tumbler, and it is this accomplishment which enables him to do stunts in his comedies which do not seem humanly possible.
> (1917, 6)

His "glasses character" would also be recognized for its derring-do. In June 1919, just two months before the accident, *Motion Picture Magazine* profiled Lloyd and discussed the changes facing the field of comedy as pratfalls and pies were being replaced with more sophisticated narratives. Nevertheless, the physical risks remain significant: "Mr. Lloyd spends many a day in his home nursing the bruises and sprains he has received the previous day [. . .] He said once that every laugh he gave the fans was at the cost of great pain to himself" (Granger 1919, 92). As Lloyd suggests, laughter and pain are irrevocably linked in slapstick cinema; the business of being funny often results in covert pain and injuries that must be tended to in the privacy of the actor's home.

It is interesting that both before and after the explosion at Witzel Studio, the comedian felt comfortable discussing his on-set injuries – particularly injuries that were sustained in dramatic fashion and soon healed. In some cases, these stories of near catastrophe became significant parts of the publicity apparatus for his films, as was the case with an incident that took place during the filming of *Girl Shy* (1924), five years after his accident. The press book for the film claims that "A fractious fire nozzle got away from Lloyd, striking him with trip hammer force across the forehead and knocking him off the fire engine" (D'Agostino Lloyd 2004, 95). After this spill, "other members of the Lloyd company who witnessed the accident thought he had suffered a fractured skull" (95). While Lloyd's injuries would require six stitches to the forehead, "it was soon apparent that, while painful, the injury would not prove really serious" (95).

While the actor did many of his own stunts before and after the explosion (with some notable exceptions, as will be discussed in greater detail later in this chapter), he was far from the only comedian to be broken and bloodied by his craft. One of the most infamous cases was Buster Keaton's (1896–1966) neck fracture – an injury that was not discovered until years later. During the filming of *Sherlock Jr.* (1924), Keaton fell from the top of a freight car to the rails below, striking his neck on iron, and would get up, dust himself off, and finish the scene (Sweeney 2007, 60–61). Even a decade earlier, screen comedians' physical injuries and exploits were already popular fodder for the funny pages. In a 1916 cartoon from the *Topeka State Journal* (see Figure 3) a genteel couple, with lapdog in tow, gossip about the screen comedian they encounter at their vacation spot: "'Who is that poor cripple with his arm in a sling and his head all bandaged up?'" The retort: "'He's a moving picture comedian on his vacation'" (1916, n.p.).

"Tell alls," interviews, and studio press materials emphasized the *real* risks faced by screen comedians and itemized the injuries sustained and overcome on set, but it remains notable that the slapstick body was always resilient and almost always intact. Muriel Andrin suggests that this coupling of violence and cruelty with lasting "physical integrity" is a unique feature of the genre:

> The near total absence of injury on the slapstick body is indeed quite striking; burlesque characters do not bruise, bleed, or die. Pain and suffering exist, yet they are portrayed in an excessive, unrealistic manner [. . .]. While injuries were everyday fare on a knockabout set (as Buster Keaton testifies in his autobiography), wounds or broken limbs are nowhere to be seen on screen. (2010, 231)

Figure 3: This playful cartoon appeared in newspapers from Topeka, Kansas to Richmond, Virginia in 1916, poking fun at the dangers underlying screen comedy.

Slapstick bodies deliver and deal out violence, yet they almost always recover in time for the final credits. In *Slapstick and Comic Performance: Comedy and Pain* (2014), Louise Peacock similarly suggests that the genre is characterized by the performer's seemingly superhuman strength and agility and an ability to recover: "put simply [. . .] an ability to do things with their bodies that the watching audience could never conceive of doing with their own [. . .] bodies that appear capable of physical feats beyond the ability of ordinary, everyday people" (2014, 33).

But, even as slapstick required extraordinary athletic prowess from its lead comics, the genre also relied upon real *and* performed pain. And, it often traded in *schadenfreude* and called upon disability in the service of comedy. If we are to take joy in another's pain or laugh at physical difference, empathy must be constrained. Walter Kerr suggests that this is a feature of slapstick, as it necessarily "suspended our obligation to feel [. . .] we were freed to stare at sights we might, but shouldn't, enjoy without penalty" (1975, 27). With empathy suspended, we do not only fail to understand the pain experienced by slapstick bodies, we feel empowered to laugh at it. The laughter that results can be seen as what Anca Parvulescu has deemed "a form of self-applause," which "in relation to others [. . .] often borders on cruelty" (2010, 37). Unsurprisingly, early theories of laughter frequently focused on bodily infirmity and difference. Whereas Aristotle (384–322 BC) held that "laughter is a reaction to something ugly or improper" (Qtd. in Parvulescu 2010, 4), Thomas Hobbes (1588–1679) offered a more complex definition: "Laughter is nothing else but a sudden glory arising from some sudden conception of some eminency in ourselves, by comparison with the infirmity of others" (34).

Lloyd would reflect upon the uneasy relationship between empathy and screen comedy in a 1926 piece for *Ladies' Home Journal*, noting that

> It is, of course, a trite observation that one man's tragedy is another man's comedy, but we must constantly have it in mind. The humor must be human enough to be understandable, but it must be sufficiently remote so that the suffering of the character will not arouse too much pity or sympathy in the audience. (1926, 234)

Seeking to elicit human interest without an excess of pity or sympathy, Lloyd was faced with the choice of presenting his changed body to the world after the accident – a body seeming to demand explanation. In *Harold Lloyd: Master Comedian* (2002), Lloyd's granddaughter Susan Lloyd and film historian Jeffrey Vance suggest that the actor "never publicly discussed the loss of his right thumb and index finger" because "he did not want audiences to be distracted by, or view him with, pity or curiosity" (2002, 41). Walter Kerr similarly speculates that Lloyd "did not want this information to linger with the audience as it watched him stunting: that would create *too* much apprehension, too much sympathy, for comedy" (1975, 116). Not wishing to disrupt the comic narrative, Lloyd made the decision to never appear on screen without his prosthesis. And, aside from a couple of accidental exposures of his right hand late in his career, the comedian would remain incognito.

In *Staring*, disability theorist Rosemarie Garland-Thomson observes that "when bodies begin to malfunction or look unexpected, we become aware of them" (2009, 37). They remind us of the contingency of our own existence: "the truth of our body's vulnerability to the randomness of fate" (19). The appearance of disability provokes uneasy identification and empathy in onlookers:

> Sick, disabled or pained bodies both experience and invoke [. . .] 'dysappearance,' meaning that their differences from acquiescent bodies make them appear to us and others. Extraordinary-looking bodies demand attention. The sight of an unexpected body – that

is to say, a body that does not conform to our expectations for an ordinary body – is compelling because it disorders expectations. (37)

Importantly, these are bodies that demand a narrative, bodies that seemingly demand an explanation.

Prior to 24 August 1919, Harold Lloyd could comfortably be classed amongst the omnipresent and archetypal "norm" that Erving Goffman defines in his landmark study, *Stigma: Notes on the Management of Spoiled Identity* (1963), occupying a body that did not demand explanation. As a young, white, Protestant, heterosexual male with excellent career prospects, a pleasant appearance, and an athletic bent, Lloyd was notable for his apparently "untainted" normality and all-Americanness. The explosion would not only jeopardize the comedian's career and financial security, but also his identity and his conception of self. Rather than run the risk that the unadorned appearance of his hand would be off-putting or jarring to audiences, Lloyd scrambled to rewrite the story of his accident in the months – and years – that followed and soon developed an ingenious prosthetic device for his return to the screen. As Garland-Thomson notes, the "intended purpose" of prosthetic devices such as Lloyd's was "to rescue stareable people from stigma" (131). In brief, a cosmetic prosthesis "answers the needs of its starer," and does not necessarily improve function for the person wearing it (129). The device that Lloyd wore for filming and public appearances served as a defensive strategy: masking physical difference and keeping his "ordinary" and "average" comic persona intact. It also rescued viewers from excess empathy and made it easier for audiences to forget that Lloyd's accident had ever occurred.

In early cinema, disability was most commonly deployed in the genres of comedy and melodrama. Disability studies scholars Sharon Snyder and David Mitchell recognize that disability most frequently appears in "body genres" like melodrama and slapstick and that "disabled bodies have been constructed cinematically and socially to function as delivery vehicles in our transfer of extreme sensation to audiences" (2010, 186). Martin Norden suggests that people with disabilities "tended to be portrayed as either the butt of practical jokes or as helpless dependents whose disabilities were the source of considerable misery" (1990, 222). Admittedly, films of the era freely exploited physically disabled characters for comedic and dramatic effect, but it is notable that film censors and critics treated documentary, medical, and eugenics films (i.e., films that presented real people with disabilities) much less charitably. As Martin Pernick acknowledges in *The Black Stork* (1996), "Especially in the transitional years from 1915 to 1920, critics and censors sometimes distinguished between the exhibition of 'real' disease victims and the use of 'normal' actors to simulate illnesses or disabilities" (1996, 124–125). "Real" disabilities were rarely tolerated on screen (with some notable exceptions, particularly during the years of WWI), while simulated ones were genre staples.

This de facto policy of limiting the representation of people with disabilities in film is unsurprising in light of the legal status of disability in the early twentieth century. As the eugenics movement gained ground and increasing numbers of people with disabilities faced institutionalization, the spectacle of disability came to be tolerated less and less in public life, including the realm of entertainment and the spaces of the cinema, peep show, circus, and carnival. In fact, as Susan Schweik traces in *The Ugly Laws: Disability in Public* (2009), public disability was codified as a punishable offense in scores of American cities around the turn of the century, as was the case with the first such law, the Chicago City Code of 1881. The ordinance begins with the following stipulation:

> Any person who is diseased, maimed, mutilated, or in any way deformed, so as to be an unsightly or disgusting object, or an improper person to be allowed in or on the streets, highways, thoroughfares, or public places in this city, shall not therein or thereon expose himself to public view, under the penalty of a fine of $1 [. . .]. (Qtd. in Schweik 2009, 1)

Although most of the "ugly laws" adopted over the late-nineteenth and early-twentieth centuries sought to target the urban poor and the beggar, they also served to control the aesthetics of the modern city and codify which bodies did and did not belong in the public sphere. This standard would, of course, be shaken by WWI, as thousands of U.S. soldiers returned home with permanent (and often catastrophic) injuries. Nonetheless, it is easy to understand why a newly disabled individual might opt to mask their deformities in this climate.

2 Masquerade and slapstick

In "Disability as Masquerade" (2004), Tobin Siebers considers the strategies that people with disabilities have developed in order to conceal, and at strategic moments, showcase bodily difference. Adapting the epistemology of the closet – a closet theorized with gay and lesbian identities in mind – for disability studies, he argues that "passing is possible not only because people have sufficient genius to disguise their identity but also because society has a general tendency to repress the embodiment of difference" (2004, 3). In turn, the "more visible the disability, the greater the chance that the disabled person will be repressed from public view and forgotten" (6). Masquerade emerges as a means of communication, offering people with disabilities the opportunity to reveal an identity that is otherwise hidden from view or repressed: "Voluntary slips and disclosures always involve self-presentation" and alternately serve to inform the able-bodied public and other people with disabilities that "a disabled person is in their midst" (9).

Even as Lloyd made the decision to "pass" as able-bodied and unmarked by the accident, the actor's disability remained an open-secret in Hollywood and a known fact for some of his fans. Moreover, many of the films that he made after August 1919 contained covert allusions to his accident and technical "slips" that made his prosthetic interventions visible to audiences. And, later in life, his philanthropic work on behalf of the Shriners Hospitals for Crippled Children would bring his private life and public persona into alignment.

Besides news of his loss of thumb, forefinger, and palm circulating in the trade and popular press in the weeks following the accident, the facts of Lloyd's disabilities circulated to friends and industry insiders as he sought help in devising his prosthesis. He and producer Hal Roach finally turned to Samuel Goldwyn (1879–1974), who had begun his career as a glove salesman. As Roach recounts in an interview for *Harold Lloyd: The Third Genius*, a 1989 documentary, "I figured in some way, there could be a glove [. . .] to cover up for the thumb and finger that he lost. And when I thought of gloves, I thought of Sam Goldwyn who was a glove salesman to start." After taking a rubber mold of Lloyd's intact left hand, they reversed it and cut away the portion that corresponded to the missing area of the actor's right hand. Goldwyn worked with a firm to develop a thin, tight fitting, flesh-toned leather glove that fit over the prosthesis and Lloyd's remaining fingers (D'Agostino Lloyd 2004, 34–35). With the index and middle fingers of the glove sewn together at the knuckles, Lloyd was able to move his prosthetic index finger, while his thumb remained immobile. A rubber garter system was attached to Lloyd's upper arm, which held the device in place for even the actor's more difficult stunts. While Lloyd would often wear a plain leather glove or place his right hand in his pocket on social occasions, it is notable that he only wore the prosthetic device for filming and occasional public appearances – as was the case with his 1927 appearance at Grauman's Chinese Theatre (Vance and Lloyd 2002, 41). The fifth inductee into the theater's sidewalk gallery of handprints, Lloyd pressed hands, feet, and glasses into the cement.

This device would serve Lloyd well throughout the 1920s and into the 1930s, but further adaptations would need to be made as he ventured into "thrill pictures," and depending upon the narrative arc of his films. In March 1920, his production team sought to tackle the problem of water. Hal Roach reached out to Tom Dowling of the *New York Evening Journal* for assistance, asking

> Will you be good enough to look around New York and see if you can find a rubber glove, the kind used by Physicians and Nurses in hospitals, that is flesh color. I need these for Lloyd for water scenes [. . .]. If you can find a glove like this will you mail me three or four. (Qtd. in D'Agostino Lloyd 2004, 35)

In the months following the accident, it was not uncommon for industry insiders from coast to coast (even individuals Lloyd was not personally acquainted with) to intervene on his behalf – a practice that would unofficially continue for the rest of his career. While Goldwyn made use of his prior contacts in the glove manufacturing world as he sought just the right firm to manufacture Lloyd's prosthetic device, Dowling was asked to scour New York City for the requisite rubber gloves, and Roach made discreet inquiries in his attempts to keep the cameras rolling.

There was also the problem of the close-up; while Lloyd's prosthetic hand did not draw undue attention in medium and long-shots, close-ups revealed the fact that he was wearing a glove and prosthetic device – a fact that some audience members picked up on, as revealed by fan magazines and gossip columns of the time. Readers of *The Evening Star* (Washington, D.C.) wrote in to the paper's "Questions" columnist on several occasions to inquire about Lloyd's hand. In 1923, one reader probed, "Is it true that Harold Lloyd the movie actor, has an artificial arm or hand?" (*The Evening Star* 1923, 6) and in 1927 another individual asked if it is "a fact that Harold Lloyd's right hand, or any of the fingers on that hand is artificial?" (*The Evening Star* 1927, 8). "Billie," an inquisitive *Picture Play* reader of 1930, would likewise ask the editors of the "Information, Please" column what had happened to Lloyd's hand (1930, 119). And, when W.S.H. from Arkansas wrote into *Photoplay* to ask about Lloyd's fingers in April 1922, the "Questions and Answers" columnist would confirm Lloyd's permanent injuries and offer the assurance that, "Lloyd is one of the finest chaps I know" (1922, 121). These brief and factually correct confirmations of Lloyd's disabilities quite curiously contradict coverage published in late 1919 and early 1920.

After Lloyd's release from the hospital, he worked diligently to relaunch his career and granted a number of interviews to fan magazines and mainstream newspapers – interviews that tended to gloss over (or fully misrepresent) the explosion, as was the case with a curious piece in *The New York Tribune*. Published in November 1919, the headline reads "Harold Lloyd Enjoys Vacation Thrust on Him By [sic] Turning of a Bomb." Misreporting on both the circumstances of the explosion and the outcomes, reporter Harriette Underhill claims that

> In one of his comedies Lloyd – you always feel like calling him Harold after knowing him for a half hour – had to use a bomb [. . .]. The bomb needs to be timed; the custard pie doesn't. Lloyd had too great a confidence in the one which he was about to hurl, and it turned on him.
>
> (1919, 10)

The comedy set replaces Witzel Studio in this retelling and the bomb is transformed from an apparently harmless, yet deadly prop, into a tool of slapstick comedy. At the same time, Lloyd's recovery process, working through of trauma, and relaunch of his career are passed over as Underhill repeatedly emphasizes that Lloyd is taking a "vacation" from the serious cares of comedy filmmaking. His injuries are referenced in such an oblique fashion that a casual reader is likely to forget that the comedian had ever been injured. The lone reference to Lloyd's physical state comes mid-remark: "'However,' he said cheerfully, as he steadied his grapefruit with his right elbow and jabbed at it with a spoon held in his left hand, 'This cloud had a particularly fine lining [. . .]. I had a chance to come to New York on a vacation'" (*The New York Tribune* 1919, 10). While the reporter clearly sees Lloyd's bandaged hand and witnesses the actor's struggles to feed himself and adapt to the new demands of his body, she glosses over these facts, favoring a lighthearted narrative of restoration.

Photoplay's January 1920 issue offers a more palpable reminder of Lloyd's very real physical trauma, even as it seeks to downplay its gravity. A full-page photograph of Lloyd appears, with the actor casually leaning against the side of a convertible, with his right hand swathed in thick white bandages and his still-healing eyes hidden under sunglasses (see Figure 4). Lloyd smiles in spite of all that has befallen him, yet it remains evident that the physical and psychological turmoil of the explosion have not seamlessly resolved in a matter of weeks. A cheery, and patently false, caption announces that this is "Mr. Lloyd's newest picture, taken on the day he emerged from the hospital after the disastrous bomb explosion that threatened – but fortunately didn't bring – disfigurement for life" (Leigh 1920, 68). The remainder of the article does not mention or engage with the accident.

Once Lloyd returned to the set in the first months of 1920, he and the production team adapted the way they staged and shot his films. The reasons were twofold, as they coped with the decreased strength and functionality of his right hand *and* sought to minimize audiences' recognition of his disabilities. The comedian revealed that when a scene called for a close-up of his hands, they would frequently shoot using his left hand and a mirror (D'Agostino Lloyd 2004, 255). At other times, particularly when a view of both hands was required,

Figure 4: A bandaged and bespectacled Lloyd smiles at *Photoplay*'s photographers in this image taken just a few months after the explosion.

they would make use of a double.[1] At times the deception was hard to keep up, as was the case with *Never Weaken,* a 1921 thrill comedy. Lloyd's "glasses character" enlists the services of a local acrobat (played by Mark Jones [1889–1965]) to simulate disability, disease, and cure in order to drum up business for the doctor's office his girlfriend (Mildred Davis [1901–1969]) works at. The plot revolves around the public spectacle of disability; as the acrobat takes falls (particularly in front of throngs of aged and infirm people on the city sidewalks), Lloyd's character, Harold, painstakingly "fixes" his patient. After witnessing one such miracle cure, a man in a bath chair and a man on crutches rush in excitement to the doctor's office nearby to seek the same restoration.

---

[1] It was not uncommon for Lloyd to make use of a double, particularly for dangerous and physically demanding stunts, though he was reluctant to discuss this practice. See Cahn's *Harold Lloyd's World of Comedy* for more details on the comedian's stunts.

This overt – and largely comic – representation of disability is presented in conjunction with more covert reminders of Lloyd's own physical losses. After misunderstanding an exchange between his lover and another man, a distraught Lloyd returns home, pours himself a glass of poison, and sets about writing his suicide note. While the scene's multiple high-angle, close-up shots show Lloyd writing with an intact and ungloved right hand, midway through the scene he gets up to consult a dictionary and we return to a medium shot of him grasping his pencil in his *left* hand – a continuity error that is repeated moments later, when Lloyd walks into the bathroom and approaches the medicine cabinet. A tightly framed medium-close-up reveals a shaving brush, a clearly labeled bottle of poison, and other toiletries, and a lone, ungloved right hand snakes into the frame, retrieving a dish of baking soda. Cutting to medium shot of Lloyd back at his desk, the dish has somehow (and instantaneously) been transferred to a gloved left hand. One might even read these back-to-back continuity errors as a witting slip of the mask – as a potential means of revealing disability.

In spite of the best efforts of the production team, makeup artists, and perhaps even Lloyd himself, the comedian's right hand remained a constant consideration and cinematic presence over the 1920s and 1930s, "resurfacing" in the many continuity and visual errors contained in films made after the accident and in the many gags and refused gags that referenced the explosion. In "Mechanisms of Laughter: The Devices of Slapstick" (2010), Tom Gunning discusses a sequence from Lloyd's 1920 film, *Get Out and Get Under* that best exemplifies what he terms a "refused gag" (2010, 146). Audiences are shown the possibilities of a gag and setup to expect it, but it never happens. Here, Lloyd offers viewers a variation on the tried-and-true explosion gag, as he irresponsibly dangles a lit match over a car's gas tank. Unlike the fateful day at Witzel Studio, the explosion never comes; Lloyd seems to explore and enact an alternative reality wherein no losses are sustained, no lives are irrevocably altered.

In *Welcome Danger* (1929), Lloyd's first sound film, he engages more directly with past trauma in a memorable scene with Roman candles. After traveling into the heart of San Francisco's Chinatown in search of the "Dragon" (Charles B. Middleton [1874–1949]), an opium smuggler and king of the city's underworld, goofy botanist-turned-detective Harold Bledsoe (Lloyd) unwittingly wanders into the gang's lair as they are poised to execute Dr. Gow (James Wang [1863–1935]). Incidentally, Harold feels a pressing need to rescue the doctor since he is presently working to "cure" the physically disabled younger brother of Lloyd's love interest. As in many of Lloyd's films, overt representations of physical disability (i.e., the simulated or performed disability of secondary characters) are presented alongside covert reminders of Lloyd's real bodily trauma. After gingerly stepping into the basement beneath the flower shop, Harold strikes a match on the bottom of his shoe and we cut to a close-up of a partially illuminated crate of Roman candles. Lloyd's left hand grasps the match and initially obscures the word "Roman" on the label; a visual cue that sets up the gag. We cut immediately to a three-quarter shot of Lloyd holding the lit firework in his already-exploded right hand, the clearly labeled crate visible on screen right. As the Roman candle begins smoke and pop, Lloyd jumps and contorts his body while keeping the explosive at arm's length. Eventually, after what seems like an eternity, he violently tosses it to the ground and it unloads its charge with a flash of light. While he is left unscathed by this cinematic stunt and releases the firework in the nick of time, it seems significant that Lloyd comes so close to reenacting his trauma, fuse, charge, and all.

Lloyd's performance in this film and others reminds viewers of the fact that slapstick is predominantly a physical genre – a genre that is intimately tied to the body and showcases unexpected stores of strength, bodily variation, and often physical precarity and real and simulated pain. While early slapstick cinema was predicated on the comedian's ability to seamlessly recover and "bounce back" from his or her exploits, Lloyd's story reveals that full restoration was not always a given. Slapstick performers were placed in a position where they had to constantly negotiate the risks and choose whether to put their bodies on the line. Whereas most other screen comedians of the era crafted exaggerated comic personae and relied upon grotesque physical trademarks, Harold Lloyd sought to elevate his comedies and developed a conspicuously "ordinary" and "normal" character in the months before the accident. For Lloyd, relatability was the end goal, and excessive empathy was a liability for a comedian who prided himself on his physically daring exploits. Fearing that audiences would pity him in the aftermath of the accident or experience undue anxiety as they saw a disabled comedian stunting, Lloyd made the decision to control the image that he presented to the public and recast himself as able-bodied and untouched by the events of 24 August 1919. Nonetheless, the comedian would continue to work through and reenact the traumatic events leading up to the explosion in his screen performances, and his disability would resurface in the visual gags, refused gags, and continuity errors contained in his comedies – covert disclosures of a disability identity that Lloyd never claimed in his everyday life.

Bibliography

"Actor's Hand Shattered by Film Bomb." *Los Angeles Examiner*, 25 August 1919: 1, 5.
Andrin, Muriel. "Back to the 'Slap': Slapstick's Hyperbolic Gesture and the Rhetoric of Violence." *Slapstick Comedy*. Eds. Tom Paulus and Rob King. New York: Routledge, 2010. 226–235.
Haskin, Frederic J. "Answers to Questions." *The Evening Star* (D.C.), 19 November 1923, 6.
Haskin, Frederick J. "Answers to Questions." *The Evening Star* (D.C.), 21 February 1927, 8.
Cahn, William. *Harold Lloyd's World of Comedy*. New York: Duell, Sloan and Pearce, 1964.
Cohen, Hurbert. "The Serious Business of Being Funny: an Interview with Harold Lloyd." *An American Comedy*. Harold Lloyd. New York: B. Blom, 1971.
"Comedy Star Badly Injured When Movie Bomb Explodes." *Omaha Bee*, 31 August 1919, 1.
D'Agostino Lloyd, Annette M. *The Harold Lloyd Encyclopedia*. Jefferson, NC: McFarland, 2004.
Garland-Thomson, Rosemarie. *Staring: How We Look*. Oxford: Oxford University Press, 2009.
Goffman, Erving. *Stigma: Notes on the Management of Spoiled Identity*. Englewood Cliffs, NJ: Prentice-Hall, 1963.
Granger, Frank. "Five Hundred a Laugh." *Motion Picture Magazine* (June 1919): 48–49, 92.
Gunning, Tom. "Mechanisms of Laughter: The Devices of Slapstick." *Slapstick Comedy*. Eds. Tom Paulus and Rob King. New York: Routledge, 2010. 137–151.
Hall, Gladys. "Discoveries About Myself." *Motion Picture Magazine* (October 1930): 90.
"Harold Lloyd's Accident." *Variety*, 27 August 1919: 65.
Harold Lloyd: The Third Genius. Dir. Kevin Brownlow. PBS, 1989.
"Information Please." *Picture Play* (May 1930): 119.
"Jingles from the News Jungles." *Los Angeles Evening Herald*, 25 August 1919: 6.
Kerr, Walter. *The Silent Clowns*. New York: Knopf, 1975.
Leigh, Anabel. "Specs without Glass." *Photoplay* (January 1920): 68.
"Lloyd Badly Hurt." *Wid's Film Daily*, 27 August 1919: 1.
Lloyd, Harold. *An American Comedy*. New York: B. Blom, 1971.
Lloyd, Harold. "The Hardships of Fun Making." *The Ladies Home Journal* 93 (May 1926): 32, 50, 234.
"Lloyd Improving." *Great Falls Daily Tribune*, 28 September 1919: 3.
McRuer, Robert. *Crip Theory: Cultural Signs of Queerness and Disability*. New York: New York University Press, 2006.
"Movie Actor Hurt in 'Bomb' Explosion." *Los Angeles Evening Herald*, 25 August 1919: n.p.
Never Weaken. Dir. Fred Newmeyer. Rolin Films, 1921.
Norden, Martin. "Victims, Villains, Saints, and Heroes: Movie Portrayals of People with Physical Disabilities." *Beyond the Stars: Stock Characters in American Popular Film*. Eds. Paul Loukides and Linda Fuller. Bowling Green: Bowling Green State University Press, 1990. 222–233.
"Nothing Succeeds Like Success." *Motion Picture News*, 13 November 1915, 93.
Parvulescu, Anca. *Laughter: Notes on a Passion*. Cambridge, MA: MIT Press, 2010.
"Pathe's 'Lonesome Luke' Comedies Unique. *Moving Picture World*, 12 February 1916, 963.
Peacock, Louise. *Slapstick and Comic Performance: Comedy and Pain*. New York: Palgrave Macmillan, 2014.
Pernick, Martin. *The Black Stork: Eugenics and the Death of "Defective" Babies in American Medicine and Motion Pictures Since 1915*. Oxford: Oxford University Press, 1996.

"Questions and Answers." *PhotoPlay* (April 1922): 121.
"Reel Bomb is a 'Real' One." *Los Angeles Times*, 25 August 1919: 1.
"The Reel Players." *Detroit Free Press*, 16 July 1917: 6.
"Resting." *The Topeka State Journal*, 13 May 1916: n.p.
Schweik, Susan. *The Ugly Laws: Disability in Public*. New York: NYU Press, 2009.
Siebers, Tobin. "Disability as Masquerade." *Literature and Medicine* 23:1 (2004): 1–22.
Snyder, Sharon L., and David T. Mitchell. "Body Genres: An Anatomy of Disability in Film." *The Problem Body: Projecting Disability in Film*. Eds. Sally Chivers and Nicole Markotić. Columbus: Ohio State University Press, 2010. 179–204.
Sweeney, Kevin. *Buster Keaton: Interviews*. Jackson: University Press of Mississippi, 2007.
Underhill, Harriette. "Harold Lloyd Enjoys Vacation Thrust on Him By Turning of Bomb." *New York Tribune*, 23 November 1919, 10.
Vance, Jeffrey, and Suzanne Lloyd. *Harold Lloyd: Master Comedian*. New York: Harry N. Abrams, 2002.
Welcome Danger. Dir. Clyde Bruckman. Paramount Pictures, 1929.

Addie Tsai
Wardrobe Malfunction and Slapstick Humiliation in The Lonely Island's *Popstar: Never Stop Never Stopping*

Starting in the early-to-mid 2000s, the cult popularity and pioneering achievements in past and present contemporary American popular culture of the all-male comedian trio known as the Lonely Island has reached legendary status. The Lonely Island's biggest claim to fame, albeit an unprovable one, is that the ensemble was solely responsible for the creation and popularity of the viral YouTube video as one of the first artists known to ever post their work solely on a digital platform during YouTube's early days. Since that beginning, largely due to pioneering the *Saturday Night Live* digital short and five comedy feature-length films, the Lonely Island has created a reputation among American popular culture for their use of slapstick, physical humor, and musical comedy. The aim of the Lonely Island's humor: to parody other American popular cultural figures and texts, which ultimately served as an incendiary critique on the limitations of heteronormative white masculinity, or, to use R. W. Connell's foundational term, hegemonic masculinity.[1]

The Lonely Island's most recent film, *Popstar: Never Stop Never Stopping* (2016), is a feature-length mockumentary satirizing the musical industry and many of its well-known figures, such as Justin Bieber (*1994), Justin Timberlake (*1981), 'N Sync, and Macklemore (*1983). This chapter will focus on the slapstick employment of wardrobe malfunction in *Popstar: Never Stop Never Stopping*, in which the main character, the fictional pop star Conner4Real, inevitably exposes himself on the concert stage during a costume change gone wrong. Writing about humiliation in slapstick, Alan Dale asserts, "that's the appeal of the slapstick outlook, even in life – we have to laugh at the loss of our dignity, which is what makes the constant recurrence of such losses bearable" (2000, 11). The Lonely Island performs this very gesture toward humility through its crass slapstick moments.

---

[1] Australian scholar R. W. Connell's foundational concept of hegemonic masculinity, "the configuration of gender practice which embodies the currently accepted answer to the problem of the legitimacy of patriarchy, which guarantees (or is taken to guarantee) the dominant position of men and the subordination of women" (2005, 77), serves as a central tenet for how men are expected to behave in contemporary, mainstream society. Even more to the point is Connell's assertion that hegemonic masculinity is constructed in relation to women and subordinated masculinities (1987, 61) qualified by Blackness or homosexuality.

This chapter will argue that *Popstar*, much in conversation with the Lonely Island's previous work, such as the digital shorts featured on the vaudeville-inspired television show *Saturday Night Live* (1975–2019) and film *Hot Rod* (2007), employs slapstick to speak not only to the physicality of human life, but also to slapstick's inherent link to the loss of dignity, which comments upon the central crisis in the expression of hegemonic masculinity as imagined in the film. Dignity is, as seen here, an independent concept but one often utilized to mark a cis man as performing appropriately within the strictures of hegemonic masculinity. In the case of *Popstar*, the laughter at this failed costume change comes not only from the audience watching the film, but also the audience within the film narrative watching that particular live performance. Laughter also comes from Conner's own supporting team (including his nemesis and opening act, the hip hop artist Hunter the Hunted), as well as from the eyes of the global world witnessing the act yet again via mainstream media once the video has been shared virally, which occurs, for comedic effect, just moments after its real time occurrence.

1 The Lonely Island and the creation of a new evolution

As Derek Yates and Jessie Price explain in *Communication Design: Insights from the Creative Industries,*

> the development of desktop filmmaking tools during the early 1990s provided an outlet for a new generation of filmmakers, who were able to bypass what up until this point had been a long apprenticeship into filmmaking [. . .]. At this time, new freedoms and economic prosperity had led to the establishment of a global youth culture, and the launch of TV stations like MTV provided an insatiable demand for short-form, visually led films that could accompany the pop music that formed this audience's staple diet. (2015, 42)

By championing the short-form of the music video, the cable television network MTV offered a venue for white male filmmakers, such as Spike Jonze (*1969), Michel Gondry (*1963), David Fincher (*1962), and Chris Cunningham (*1970) to experiment with a hybridized format that illustrated the technological transition of the time. Oscillating between film and video, these filmmakers collaged old and new technologies in order to reflect the simulated reality of contemporary American life. Because the music video's primary purpose was to promote the song for which the video was created, it lent itself to a visualization of a musical text. The music video's format thus allowed for more abstract narratives told utilizing moving images and non-traditional cinematic narratives. In other words, this era of the short-form video, combined with technologies made more readily available and accessible to the average consumer (e.g., through the camcorder and editing software on personal computers), resulted in fans of the network attempting to make videos on their own. It is this conglomeration of forces that produced one of the most influential voices in digital music video parody: the Lonely Island.

The men that comprise the Lonely Island, founded by Akiva Schaffer (*1977), Andy Samberg (*1978), and Jorma Taccone (*1977) in 2001, first met in junior high school in the early 1990s. Considered members of the MTV Generation in that they came of age during the network's height in popularity, they are representative of the young men who dominated the network's ratings (Business Wire 2013). Although the trio experimented with making short videos at home since early on in their personal friendship, the Lonely Island has taken seriously their efforts in making short comic videos, often set to music, since the late 1990s. The Lonely Island's first big break came with *Saturday Night Live*, which hired the Lonely Island to create what the group referred to as "Digital Shorts," pioneering a new type of format for the live television variety and sketch comedy show, which first aired in 1975 on NBC (Saturday Night Live 1975–2018). According to James Andrew Miller and Tom Shales in their oral history titled *Live From New York: The Complete, Uncensored History of Saturday Night Live as Told by Its Stars, Writers, and Guests,* the Lonely Island exposed the mediated quality of its sketches

> because, they would later explain, the production quality was so crappy, so much lower than SNL's big-time network standard, that they felt they had to distinguish it up front, in the labeling. But Lonely Island proved that filmmaking could now be done – segments conceived, shot, edited, scored, and polished – on the family PC or Mac. (2015, 547)

The Lonely Island was able to capitalize on their own hybridized journey by making home videos in response to their own fandom of *Saturday Night Live* and MTV; however, they formalized their practice when Andy Samberg attended New York University and the University of California, Santa Cruz in Film, which intersected with the shifting technological moment of the late 1990s/early 2000s (Miller and Shales 2015). In other words, the Lonely Island's success came directly out of an important cultural shift with regards to film and digital production – in addition to being able to more easily purchase handheld recording devices, editing tools also became more readily available with the rise of personal computers. What that meant was that, in a certain sense, anyone could become a filmmaker. This cultural shift then intersected with the accessibility of digital media through wide dissemination via the Internet. It was this conglomeration of forces that the Lonely Island utilized to their advantage, which enabled the Lonely Island's quick rise to fame and visibility.

The Lonely Island also came to popularity during an important cultural and technological moment with regards to the developing Internet age. The group is largely credited with being the pioneers of the first viral video. According to Jesse David Fox, "Comedy is all about timing. YouTube officially launched on December 15, 2005. The Lonely Island premiered their second SNL digital short, 'Lazy Sunday,' two days later. The site and the group have been irrevocably linked ever since" (2016, n.p.). An unknown fan of the video, which was a gangsta-rap parody celebrating the trio's day off, posted it on YouTube at the end of the same weekend that the video aired on *Saturday Night Live*. By the end of that following week, the YouTube video had more than 2 million views (Fox 2016).

Over their fifteen-year career, the Lonely Island has been awarded an Emmy and a Peabody, three Grammy nominations, and produced two top-ten albums and two platinum singles (Fox 2016). Their videos have racked up 1.7 billion views on YouTube (Fox 2016). The trio has released two feature films. Throughout that time, the Lonely Island has been foundational in the contribution of a new kind of comedic voice, one that largely uses the music, narrative film, and short video format in order to comment on, and at times, directly indict, contemporary American (straight) white masculinity.

It would be nearly impossible to include at-length discussions of all the pertinent texts in which the Lonely Island has employed comedy in order to interrogate the dangers of toxic masculinity, a legacy through which *Popstar* is likely viewed by its audience members. Instead, I will briefly mention three of the Lonely Island's most important contributions preceding the film's release and will outline how they use audiovisual texts to challenge the ideology of (straight) white masculinity. Most pointedly, the examples that follow will illustrate how the Lonely Island employs slapstick as a recurring device to further unveil and ridicule (straight) white hegemonic masculinity.

The Digital Short "Dick in a Box" (*Saturday Night Live* 2006) was performed to a song the Lonely Island also wrote and produced. The song, "Dick in a Box," which received an Emmy in 2007, was an R&B parody mocking (straight) white men's misogynistic entitlement, particularly as it pertained to white male perceptions of personal sexual prowess. The short video, which incorporates movement and gestures associated with R&B, also offered a mockery of (straight) white men's appropriation of Black music genres like R&B and hip hop, especially in their featuring of Justin Timberlake, a white male pop star who is influenced by and appropriates both the performance and styles of Black music genres such as soul and hip hop.

As AV Club's Chris Mincher describes,

> The setup: Samberg and Timberlake, two indoor-sunglasses-wearing crooners riding indefinitely on the coattails of Color Me Badd, are sharing special moments in yuletide tableaux with their girlfriends (Maya Rudolph and Kristen Wiig), who are similarly trapped in an early '90s time capsule. The atmosphere having been appropriately set, the duo breaks out a little serenade to accompany their Christmas gifts. "So just sit back," Samberg instructs, "and *listen*."
>
> With that seductive command, an instantly catchy, throwback, horns-punctuated midtempo jam begins to soundtrack a rapidly unfolding nightmare. Wrongly approximating how to combine romance with class, Samberg and Timberlake aggressively rub roses and feathers in their girlfriends' faces and gently caress their jawlines. Furnishing their ladies a full feast for the eyes, the two posture and pose and stroke their goatees.
>
> The presents themselves are based on a premise borrowed from *Diner*'s infamous penis-in-popcorn scene, yet still so absurd (and unexpectedly raunchy) that few watching it live could see it coming. But the humor of a dick in a box (with wrapping paper and a bow, of course) isn't just that it's gross and silly, or that guys seem perpetually obsessed with their own sex organs. Rather, it's a pinnacle of terrible gifting that globally implicates all kinds of masculine holiday mistakes. (2015, n.p.)

In addition to what Mincher describes regarding the implied metaphor of two straight white cis men ridiculously gifting their girlfriends their genitalia for Christmas (i.e., that men are terrible at gift giving, cheap, and in love with their own phalluses and thus egos), the metaphor extends past the narrative itself in regards to the movement as well as the overall parody of the video. Given that the video is constructed as a 1990s R&B parody video, complete with Timberlake's backup falsetto, the Lonely Island also mocks straight white music groups (like Color Me Badd) appropriating Black musical genres such as R&B. Movement wise, Samberg and Timberlake nod their heads and employ hand movements that accompany the kind of cross-racial appropriation found in similarly styled 1990s R&B groups this video parodies. Finally, their exceedingly simple choreography of step-together-touch, combined with their pelvic thrusts further the notion that (straight) white men believe so much in their own prowess that they do not need to do much in order to be fawned over, completely clueless as to how their actions are actually being received by the women to whom they sing in the video.

The following year, the Lonely Island released their first feature comedy film, *Hot Rod*, starring Andy Samberg. The film, which similarly commented on (straight) white masculinity, depicted the amateur stuntman Rod. In the film, his abusive stepfather Frank constantly derides and mocks his position within hegemonic masculinity, largely because Rod is unable to successfully beat him in a fight, a classic symbol of hegemonic masculinity. For example, in the beginning of the film, Rod creeps up on his stepfather while he is working out on a mat on the floor of the basement. Frank sweeps Rod's leg, immediately commanding Rod to get to his feet and challenging Rod to a fight by providing both men with a Rhodesian fighting stick. Between attacks, Frank baits Rod verbally, calling him "pathetic" (5:01) or stating "Play the victim and you will be the victim" (5:14). The battle closes with a comedic verbal sparring about Rod's fake mustache – Frank threatens: "I'm gonna knock that ridiculous mustache off your face," to which Rod responds, "All great men have mustaches." Frank then provokes Rod by saying, "Yeah, but real men actually grow them." In a comedic turnabout, Rod responds defensively, "You know I have a hormone disorder!" (5: 25–5:37) – just before Rod's vow (while Frank has Rod pinned to the ground) of how he will finally affirm his manhood: "You'll see, Frank! One day I'll punch you right in the face and you'll respect me" (5:43–5:48). The fight between them ends with Frank quipping, "I'll believe it when I see it, Muchacho," (5:48–5:50) ripping Rod's fake mustache from above his lip and re-attaching it above his eyebrows, before telling Rod to take out the garbage.

While this fight proceeds between the two in the basement, the mother sits in the living room upstairs, reading while listening to classical music. The audience can hear the pounding just below the classical music, where the mother (comically) seems either not to notice the noise of her husband and her son fighting, or does not find it out of the ordinary to interfere. Additionally, the difference in Rod and Frank's attire comically addresses how the over-prepared is the less masculine: Rod is dressed simply in a T-shirt and gym shorts, while Rod wears protection on his upper body and his crotch that seems more fitting for a wrestling match (and then some). Finally, after Frank leaves the basement, the audience witnesses Rod weeping in his bedroom, gazing mournfully at a photo of his father, an anonymous stuntman who died during a stunt.

This early scene sets up a precedent for the Lonely Island's utilization of slapstick in the film (and in their career generally regarding slapstick and masculinity) in order to speak to the pressures of hegemonic masculinity on young men. Later in the film, Rod comes home, wearing a blue jumpsuit and a yellow cape with the words Rod painted on it in big red capital letters, upset that Frank has missed the performance of his latest failed jump (although Rod claims he "landed it" [10:89–10:91]) across the community swimming pool. Rod comes home, wet and deflated, to discover that Frank needs a heart transplant, one impossible for the family to afford. Rod races to Frank's side and comically does not want Frank to die, not because it would mean the end of Frank's life, but because he still needs to beat him to prove to himself and to Frank that he's a man – "How can I do that if you're dead?" (11:43–11:45) Immobile on the couch, Frank still taunts him: "I guess I'll die still champion" (11:47–11:49). Rod tries to fight him in that moment, afraid he will have lost his chance, as he whips a night stick out of his pocket and extends it towards Frank's face. Frank only continues to bait Rod to threaten his masculinity and emasculate him further: "Well maybe you shoulda thought of that, before you sucked at being a man all your life. [. . .] Let's face it. You're a kid. You live at home, you've got no job, all you're good for is goofin around with your friends on your moped" (12:33–12:53). Rod lashes out verbally in a kind of comic take on toxic masculinity: "You're wrong, Frank. I'm not a kid. I'm a man. I am gonna get you better. And then I'm gonna beat you to death" (12:53–12:58). Frank, as always, gets the last word, even on his sick bed: "You couldn't beat a drum" (12:59–13:01). Rod lunges towards Frank with his night stick, but is unable to attack Frank, breaking the lamp instead next to Frank's head. Seemingly unable to perform in accordance with masculine expectations, Rod chooses to flee to "his quiet place" (13:03–13:05) instead where he fight-dances by himself in the forest.

Rod's fight-dance is an explicit parody of a similar scene from the 1984 dance film *Footloose* (1984), in which Kevin Bacon's (*1958) character angrily dances to the same song used in *Hot Rod*. The scene, which depicts Andy Samberg's character performing many similar movements evoked in *Footloose*, parodies the obvious use of the stunt double in highly choreographed scenes in cinema. Additionally, the Lonely Island appropriates the gymnastics-styled scene of the original in the forest by turning a felled tree into a pommel horse. However, the real comic thrust of the scene occurs at the end, when the film shifts suddenly from the extended dance sequence of the obvious stunt double back to what is assumed to be Andy Samberg performing as Rod. After performing a series of unrealistically virtuosic flips (especially given the inadequacy of Rod's physical coordination thus far in the film), the audience witnesses Rod trip over a log and fall for an absurd amount of time (approximately a minute of film time) down a cliff, pointing to the gap between the unrealistic hyperphysical expectations of a (straight) white male and the reality of a man who dances in the hazardous environs of a forest. Further, this scene uses the slapstick fall in order to highlight the fragility of the physical body as opposed to the artificial staging of virtuosic movement often employed in cinematic film. Instead of using the stunt double to demonstrate embodied virtuosity, such as in *Footloose*, the Lonely Island instead turns the use of the double on its head when the fall is obviously performed by a stunt dummy. Further, while Rod is falling, the film cuts to stock imagery of the beauty of the forest contrasted against Rod's cries heard softly in the background. As Rod comes out of his fall, grimacing and crying in pain, he stands up to see before him a billboard ad for skydiving, which states: "Do you have what it takes to make one big jump?" This leads Rod to decide to perform his most elaborate stunt – an absurd jump over an accumulated length of fifteen school buses – in order to raise money for his stepfather's operation. The comic thrust, of course, lies in the audience's knowledge that Rod's efforts to save Frank are only so that he can beat him physically to be affirmed within the pressures and gains of hegemonic masculinity. As can be seen previously, slapstick features prominently in the scene. This scene ironically highlights the impulsivity and fragility of threatened masculinity. The fall itself, as a slapstick device, unveils the true fragility of the body, set against the unrealistic expectations of toxic masculinity, in which the abled body is meant to perform and labor flawlessly in service of masculine affirmation.

The Lonely Island explores further this wide gap between how a (straight) white male feels obligated to overperform masculine bravado and the more realistic image of (straight) white male behavior in the *Saturday Night Live* digital short titled *Like a Boss* (2009). A hip hop parody of the first official single from Slim Thug's (*1980) first album, *Already Platinum* (2005), identically named *Like a Boss*, the sketch opens with a corporate superior, performed by Seth Rogen (*1982) asking his employee, played by Andy Samberg, to describe a typical workday. The hip hop parody is composed of Samberg performing his various impressive boss duties in vernacular rap and the associated gestures, which are celebrated with the hook, "Like a boss." At the beginning of his rap-rant, he brags about tasks such as "talk to corporate," "lead a workshop," "direct workflow," "micromanage," and "promote synergy." However, as the song continues, the Lonely Island's lyrics reveal the seedy underbelly of masculinity. First, the lyrics describe how Samberg "hit[s] on Debra, get[s] rejected, swallow[s] sadness." Second, Samberg performs oral sex on another man in a garage, "cries deeply" on a sex line, receives a "harassment lawsuit," fails to commit suicide by gun, loses his promotion, and tries to perform oral sex on himself. At the end of the sketch, Rogen tries to question Samberg further on his homoeroticism, and in a kind of mockery of homophobic (straight) white men who repress homoerotic desires or even seem to sexually desire themselves vis-à-vis masturbation, Samberg refuses admission: "Nope. Naw, that ain't me" (1:38–1:42). The sketch uses the short digital format to comment on a similar type of failing bravado of corporate white masculinity. "Like a Boss" furthers a similar type of satire popularized on the American version of the television show *The Office* (2005–2013), which first aired four years prior to this sketch on the same television network.

From the beginning of its inception, the Lonely Island has formed a substantial brand in its use of the digital short and the feature film to largely parody the relationship of white masculinity to the music industry, particular within genres associated with Blackness as well as to challenge the notion of the hypermasculine physical expectations against the interior expression of emotional vulnerability. The Lonely Island uses elements of comedy such as slapstick in order to comment upon the fragility of the position of white masculinity, not only in what is expected of young white men, but also what is often lying beneath that performance.

2 Slapstick humiliation and viral exposure: *Popstar: Never Stop Never Stopping*

The Lonely Island's most recent feature-length film, *Popstar: Never Stop Never Stopping*, which stars all the members of the troupe in front of the camera and is directed by the Lonely Island's Akiva Schaffer, offers an extensive music parody of (straight) white masculinity. The entire film is primarily shot as a mockumentary but also periodically incorporates narrative film format. The film concerns the rising solo career of fictional music legend Conner4Real as he attempts to continue his solo career after breaking away from his best friends in the hip hop group the Style Boyz. The film spoofs many real pop music and rap music artists in its construction and reception of Conner, such as Justin Bieber, Justin Timberlake, 'N Sync, The Beastie Boys, and Macklemore. However, this section will be particularly concerned with how the Lonely Island employs the slapstick device of the wardrobe malfunction in the film.

Before the wardrobe malfunction itself occurs, the audience witnesses Conner and his team preparing logistically for Conner's costume quick changes that occur in the middle of his musical set on stage: two members of Conner's crew pull up a circular silver screen around Conner as he instantaneously changes into different wardrobe ensembles. During rehearsal, his genitalia get trapped in the garments. Conner plans for this by tucking his genitalia back between his legs. Hours before the concert, Conner then posts a video of himself promoting the publicity gimmick on Snapchat – *new trick tonight* – in order to entice potential audience members to attend the concert.

This moment in rehearsal where Conner's genitalia get trapped in the garments constitute a wardrobe change that calibrates slapstick to address masculinity and the loss of dignity. The slapstick device is further employed in this moment when Conner decides to tuck his genitalia between his legs in order to prevent this from happening in the live show. The tuck sets up a risk of further emasculation, given that now the audience might not only see him naked, but will also see him metaphorically castrated for the purposes of a showy trick.

At the live performance, the first two quick changes go off without a hitch. However, the third quick change to a tuxedo backfires, and he shouts to the audience, "Top of the World!" before he realizes he has exposed himself on stage completely naked, with his shaved genitalia tucked between his legs. It is only when he notices the crowd's reaction, with hundreds of camera phones flashing at him, that he looks down to realize what has happened. This wardrobe malfunction is purposefully heavily gendered as it is the lack of pubic hair and genitalia that desexualizes and emasculates Conner in this case, rather than the way in which the appearance of a nipple would expose a female body (I examine this further below in relation to Janet Jackson's famous exposure). Knowing how this must look to his fans watching and the possible backlash to the absence of his genitalia and pubic hair, Conner immediately rushes to explain: "Oh, shit. No. Uh, no. It's tucked. I shaved for the trick! Don't post those pics! It's an illusion! It's tucked. I tuck it back! Don't post those. It's a tuck it back . . . . I don't know what to do right now. I want to show ya'll my dick but I can't show you my dick! It's a great conundrum! It's a great conundrum!" (37:27–37:51) In this regard, part of the humor lies not only in the lack of genitalia seen in his accidental exposure, but also what the film audience knows of how Conner himself contributed to this further loss of dignity in shaving and tucking his genitalia between his legs to hopefully prevent his malfunction in the first place.

The scene cuts to Conner and the team backstage, where Conner angrily and hysterically tries to determine who is at fault for the malfunction. A bemused Hunter, a Black hip hop artist who functions in the film as Conner's nemesis and opening act whose popularity he must rely on due to low album sales, grills him: "Where the fuck was your dick, dawg?" (37:55–37:56) Harry, Conner's manager, tries to calm Conner down by insisting that the audience did not see anything, to which Conner retorts: "I wish they had seen something! Now there's 10,000 people who think I got no dick! Wait. You guys know I have a dick, right?" (38: 01–38:09) After Hunter stops laughing endlessly, he questions Conner further, by reiterating his former question: "But, like, where was it though? Because that motherfucker was gone," to which Conner responds, "We've gone over this! You know that I've got to tuck my shit back so that it doesn't get tangled in the garments!" (38:14–38:22)

When Hunter thanks him for the hilarity that ensued from the failed publicity stunt, Conner responds angrily, "Well, I'm so glad I could entertain you, Hunter" (38:40–38:42). The rest of the scene backstage focuses on Hunter's provocation of Conner, in which he claims to have been responsible for the prank, and then denies it repeatedly in an obviously comical manner. The scene concludes with Harry cutting off Hunter, stating that it is not news, and at that point, the news on the television set behind them depicts the latest trending story as an image of the malfunction, with the headline: "CONNER4REAL HAS NO D**K?" The final moment in the scene is a spoof of the celebrity news/tabloid online media outlet/

television show TMZ, referenced throughout *Popstar* as CMZ, in which the staff of CMZ are watching the same developing story of Conner on the news, while laughing uproariously. (37:01–39:47, 39:26–39:47)

Before assessing how the Lonely Island employs slapstick as humiliation in the wardrobe malfunction scene in *Popstar: Never Stop Never Stopping*, I would like to offer both Lisa Traihair and Alan Dale's theories of slapstick, specifically how their work can be reconfigured for contemporary cinema. According to Lisa Trahair's *The Comedy of Philosophy: Sense and Nonsense in Early Cinematic Slapstick* (2008), slapstick was first named after an object, rather than meant to denote a comedic style. Trahair notes how the term "originally referred to a stage prop constructed of two wooden paddles, joined at one end, used by circus clowns to hit each other, thereby producing a slapping sound" (2008, 47). Engaging with the work of Don B. Wilmeth, Trahair remarks that slapstick eventually grew to refer to "'physical or broad comedy'" (47). Moreover, as Trahair cites Larry Langman: "Slapstick [. . .] 'implies both the use of physical gags aimed against someone for laughs and a sense of unreality as a result of the broad gags and the improbability of the stunts'" (47). In other words, according to Langman and Trahair slapstick is an instrument used *against someone for laughs* as well as that which communicates an *improbability*. In the case of the wardrobe malfunction in *Popstar*, the Lonely Island does employ Conner's exposure as "used against someone for laughs," but in *Popstar*'s case, the exposure is reconfigured to be a probability, given that it is the practicality of the tuck combined with the exposure that leads to Conner's downfall.

Alan Dale's ideas about slapstick in his *Comedy is a Man in Trouble: Slapstick in American Movies* (2000) offer yet another way to articulate slapstick's function in *Popstar's* wardrobe malfunction:

> M. Willson Disher claimed that there are only six kinds of jokes – falls, blows, surprise, knavery, mimicry, stupidity. They all play a part, but for comedy to register as slapstick, you need only the fall and its flip side, the blow. (The importance of the blow is evidence in the adoption of the term "slapstick," since that's what a slapstick was for.) In their iconic form, the fall is caused by a banana peel, and the blow is translated into a pie in the face. Thus the essence of a slapstick gag is a physical assault on, or collapse of, the hero's dignity; as a corollary, the loss of dignity itself can result in our identifying with the victim. The mishap can be heightened by the plot – it's worse if the hero's late for his wedding than if he's just out strolling – but that's a difference of degree, not of kind [. . .]. Because slapstick plays on our fears of physical and social maladjustment, many of the typical gags slide into nightmare territory. Disproportion itself can be eerie, but often the hero acts out classic nightmares; for example, being caught onstage unprepared [. . .] or losing your pants at a party. (2000, 3–5)

The wardrobe malfunction's employment of slapstick, as witnessed through this contemporary context, offers a number of ways through which to read Conner as a humiliated hero as well as an emasculated figure. As addressed by Dale, the slapstick of the failed trick removes Conner's dignity, which has not only consequences for his depiction as a hero, but also financial consequences. It is from Conner's exposure (and the loss of manhood and dignity) that Conner's tour (and album) begins to tank. He attempts to change the perception of him created by this failed stunt with yet another publicity stunt, that of proposing to his girlfriend with a pack of wolves and a performance by the musician Seal (*1963). The music causes the wolves to become so agitated that they break free of their restraints, attacking the private guests as well as Seal, who eventually sues him in retribution for his injuries. Yet again, the humor lies not only in the slapstick outcome, but also in the lack of forethought that Conner gives to the probability that his stunts will work without issue or obstacle. The publicity stunt Conner orchestrates in order to rectify the damage to his public image caused by yet another publicity stunt also fails and causes his career to tank. In essence, the wardrobe malfunction does result in a "loss of dignity," as Dale states; however, I would argue that in this parody the malfunction causes the audience of the film itself to, as Dale states, identify with the victim while the audience within the film, aka Conner's fandom, to simultaneously disidentify with Conner.

Another way in which to read the slapstick mode of the wardrobe malfunction is through the particular way that the nature of the malfunction comments on the fragility of masculinity. Just before the scene occurs in the film, the audience witnesses one of the first videos for Conner's new album, titled "Equal Rights" (featuring P*nk). A spoof on Macklemore and Ryan Lewis's "One Love," the video seems to be promoting equal rights for homosexuality. The comic thrust of the song is not only that Conner reiterates that he's "not gay," no less than twenty times throughout the duration of the song, often parenthetically. Conner also inserts symbols of masculinity randomly to further affirm his heteromasculinity with such words as "titties," "sports," "sweat pants," "beer," "beef jerky," and "Lynyrd Skynyrd," to name a few examples. Through this video and other details throughout the first half of the film, the film sets up the fragile masculinity of our hero. As gender studies scholar C. J. Pascoe asserts in her ethnography *Dude, You're a Fag: Masculinity and Sexuality in High School*, the "'fag' position is an 'abject' position and, as such, is a 'threatening specter'" (2007, 14–15). Pascoe further explains in her text that high school boys referred to one another as fags not to necessarily label themselves as homosexual, but rather to indict one another as being unmasculine (2007). It is through this masculinist context that we can read not only the video and lyrics for "Equal Rights," but also how to view the damage caused by the audience being unable to see his male genitalia.

This malfunction also succeeds in castrating him in front of his sexual partner, his fans. Earlier in the film, in the use of the voiceover, Conner states, "My fans and me, we're in love. My songs are love letters, and the arena is our bedroom. The stage . . . the stage is where we fuck" (3:54–4:08). One of the last concert scenes that takes place before the tour is cancelled, the audience can see one of his crewmates, Owen, playing a game on his iPhone in which you have to try to pin a penis on the image of Conner on stage exposed with his penis tucked behind his legs. As Owen uses his finger to try to place the penis on Conner's crotch, the game continues to tell the player that it is "Blocked!" If the stage is where Conner has sex with his fans, and he is rendered without male genitalia, then the malfunction itself has created a scenario in which his masculinity is obliterated and there is no ability for the fans to merge with him.

3 The fall and the blow: the wardrobe malfunction as racial indictment

In some ways, the film in its entirety (and the wardrobe malfunction scene in particular) speaks to how white masculinity appropriates Blackness within the musical tradition and perhaps offers a corrective lens through which to read this problematized dynamic. For example, the number of Black musical artists who are interviewed to (comically) sing their praises of the musical genius of the Style Boyz include Nas (*1973), Usher (*1978), 50 cent (*1975), Questlove (*1971), and A$ap Rocky (*1988). Conner's debut solo album is parodically titled *Thriller, Also*, which races to the top of the charts. Their manager Harry, played by Tim Meadows (*1961), represents both the Style Boyz and Conner, and was once, fictionally, a member of the 1990s R&B group, Tony! Toni! Toné! And finally, when Conner's album and tour sales begin to decline, he brings on hip hop artist Hunter the Hungry (performed by Chris Redd [*1985]) as the tour's opening act. Hunter plays a crucial role in the wardrobe malfunction scene. These are just a few ways that the film sets up the dynamic that has been suggested in the Lonely Island's shorts throughout its career with regards to interrogating white masculinity as it particularly takes form in white pop stars' appropriation (and profiting) of Blackness.

With the aim of assessing how the wardrobe malfunction scene in *Popstar* offers a kind of corrective lens through which to indict white masculinity and in particular its appropriation of Blackness through musical performance, let us first take a look at the wardrobe malfunction. The Lonely Island spoofs this malfunction in *Popstar*, which occurred in the Super Bowl XXXVIII halftime show in 2004, featuring Justin Timberlake and Janet Jackson (*1966).

In order to situate pop singer Justin Timberlake's particular brand of white negritude, it is important to locate Timberlake in a regional tradition of the same, i.e., Elvis Presley (1935–1977). Justin Timberlake was born in 1981 in Memphis, Tennessee, close to Elvis's mansion in Graceland, where Presley lived out his last days. Elvis's contribution to both music and musical performance revolves around his ability to merge signifiers of Black and white culture – the hip rotations he would perform during his songs, and the fusion of country music and R&B. According to Minstrelsy scholar Eric Lott's work on Elvis impersonation,

> the problem is how to represent this crossing into 'blackness' without blackface, and it is here that Elvis impersonation comes to the rescue. It is as though such performance were a sort of second-order blackface, in which, blackface having for the most part overtly disappeared, the figure of Elvis himself is now the apparently still necessary signifier of white ventures into black culture – a signifier to be adopted bodily if one is to have success in achieving the intimacy with 'blackness' that is crucial to the adequate reproduction of Presley's show. (1997, 204)

Not only is Presley's contribution to white negritude incredibly influential in the history of white musical performers but Presley's formative position within the region that Timberlake first began his musical career can offer a lens through which to understand Timberlake's own white negritude.

Justin Timberlake's solo and dance career is frequently compared to that of Michael Jackson (1958–2009), who also offers a complex merging of both white and Black signifiers. As cultural critic Jamilah King states, "he was the white boy with the bleached blonde face and vague hip-hop swagger who could really sing the black music he unabashedly recorded. Image-wise, he chose and performed suave and often provocative black masculinities embodied by the likes of James Brown, Michael Jackson, and Prince" (2013, n.p.). It is worth noting that in terms of this issue of appropriation, Timberlake is most often associated with Black pop musicians who are known to have substantial white fan bases due to their ability to merge musical traditions associated with both white and Black markets. However, as King further discusses in her article, Timberlake is able to pick and choose when to benefit from Blackness and when to benefit from whiteness. One example is his refusal to be held accountable for the Super Bowl scandal largely known as "Nipplegate," when a wardrobe malfunction caused his co-performer and Michael Jackson's sister, Janet Jackson, to be inappropriately exposed on live television: "And that's what becomes tricky with

Justin, that his whiteness acts as both an entryway into popular culture and a buffer against its criticisms. Janet's career, on the other hand, stagnated" (King 2013, n.p.).

This "stagnation" was re-visited, or perhaps it is more apt to say was re-ignited, October 2017 when Justin Timberlake accepted an invitation to perform at the halftime show during Super Bowl LII in 2018. Michelle Ruiz addresses the consequences that Janet Jackson's career suffered as a result of "Nipplegate":

> It was Jackson, not Timberlake, who was reportedly pressured to "bow out gracefully" from the 2004 Grammys shortly after the Super Bowl saga; in fact, Timberlake not only went but won two awards [. . .]. Though Jackson was the halftime show headliner back in 2004 and Timberlake was her surprise guest, he was the one who, post-incident, was to have a smash solo artist career, while, as *Rolling Stone* reported, Jackson was blacklisted by CBS's parent company, Viacom, which reportedly kept "her music videos off [its] properties MTV, VH1, and radio stations under [its] umbrella." Over time, "the blacklist spreads to include non-Viacom media entities as well." (2017, n.p.)

Racially speaking, this accidental exposure speaks volumes given how much Timberlake is indebted to the Jackson family specifically for the creation of his own brand of soul-infused pop music. Not only does Timberlake suffer no consequences for the exposure that he himself causes, but also Janet Jackson becomes the hypersexualized Black female to be blacklisted as a result of his actual actions.

Recast in *Popstar*, however, the scene speaks volumes with regards to the crossracial exchange and identities in the film. Conner, a white pop star who has formed his career as a hip hop-infused pop artist, must rely on Hunter in order to make his tour successful. Later in the film, a standoff occurs between Conner and Hunter when Hunter begins to play a longer and longer set, angering Conner. Conner responds by coming on stage before Hunter exits, which causes the two to try to perform over the other. Neither of them budges, but as Conner begins to argue with Hunter on stage, Hunter admits that it was Hunter in fact who was responsible for the wardrobe malfunction. In the light of the racial dynamics that play out in "Nipplegate," this dynamic is corrective in comparison. In this case, Hunter, a Black male hip hop artist who is responsible for keeping afloat Conner's live tour, is the one in fact who is responsible for the slapstick "blow" to Conner's "fall." As a kind of assault on Conner presumably for his position of privilege, it is Hunter who gets one over on the white co-opter. It is Hunter, a Black cis man, who exposes Conner, the straight white cis man, a racial turnabout from the historical incident that the Lonely Island parodies in the wardrobe malfunction scene. However, instead of Jackson's sexual body exposed,[2] in this case of *Popstar* it is the lack of male-signified sexual organs that makes the exposure so symbolic for Conner. In *Popstar*, there is no scapegoat for the trick itself, for it is Conner who was exposed, and Conner whose career suffers as a result. Although Conner does redeem himself at the end of the film, it is not done so on the backs of Black entertainers. The slapstick mechanics of this scene enact a layered commentary on the history of white and Black stage entertainment. When Conner retorts to Hunter backstage that he is so glad that he can entertain Hunter, the comment speaks to the heart of this satiric symbolism, given that Black performers have served as mere entertainment for white audiences since the age of slavery and Minstrel Theater.

The Lonely Island offers a way to view the slapstick instrument as both a narrative and satirical device, in which the slapstick moment is significant not only in how it addresses the imperfection of human life, but also how straight white men respond to the limits of the body once the moment strikes. In *Popstar*, the Lonely Island updates its use of the slapstick mode by placing it within a contemporary context, in which the moment of humiliation multiplies through the immediate power of the Internet and social media. As Henri Bergson (1859–1941) states in his canonical essay "Le rire. Essai sure la signification du comique" ["Laughter: An Essay on the Meaning of the Comic," 1900], "the comic does not exist outside the pale of what is strictly human" (1956, 62).[3] For even pop stars like Conner4Real must live within bodies and it is this breakage between the unrealistic expectation of the twenty-first-century music fan and the unrealistic pressure of the twenty-first-century white male performer to which slapstick humiliation can speak most cogently.

Bibliography

Bergson, Henri. "Laughter." *Comedy*. Ed. Wylie Sipher. Baltimore: Johns Hopkins University Press, 1956. 61–190.

Brown, Sherronda. "It Has Nothing To Do With Clothing – Black Women's Bodies Are Hypersexualized No Matter What We Wear." *Afropunk*, 15 November 2017, https://afropunk.com/2017/11/nothing-clothing-black-womens-bodies-hypersexualized-no-matter-wear/ (accessed 12 January 2018).

Connell, Robert W. *Masculinities: Second Edition*. Berkeley: University of California Press, 2005.

---

[2] For a discussion of how Black women's bodies are hypersexualized in contemporary American culture and media, see Brown 2017.

[3] "Il n'y a pas de comique en dehors de ce qui est proprement humain."

Dale, Alan. *Comedy Is a Man in Trouble: Slapstick in American Movies*. Minneapolis: University of Minnesota, 2000.

Footloose . Dir. Herbert Ross. Paramount Pictures, 1984.

Fox, Jesse David. "How the Lonely Island Changed the Internet, Comedy, and Especially Internet Comedy." *Vulture*, 1 June 2016, http://www.vulture.com/2016/05/lonely-island-changed-the-internet-comedy.html (accessed 12 January 2018).

Hot Rod. Dir. Akiva Schaffer. Paramount Pictures, 2007.

King, Jamilah. "The Trouble With Justin Timberlake's Appropriation of Black Music." *Colorlines*, 22 Mar 2013, https://www.colorlines.com/articles/trouble-justin-timberlakes-appropriation-black-music (accessed 1 January 2018).

Lott, Eric. "All the King's Men: Elvis Impersonators and White Working-Class Masculinity." *Race and the Subject of Masculinities*. Eds. Michael Uebel and Harry Stecopoulos, Durham: Duke University, 1997. 192–230.

Miller, James Andrew and Tom Shales. *Live From New York: The Complete, Uncensored History of Saturday Night Live as Told by Its Stars, Writers, and Guests*. New York: Back Bay, 2015.

Pascoe, C. J. *Dude, You're a Fag: Masculinity and Sexuality in High School*. Berkeley: University of California Press, 2007.

Popstar: Never Stop Never Stopping. Dir. Akiva Schaffer and Jorma Taccone. Universal Pictures, 2016.

Ruiz, Michelle. "Justin Timberlake Will Perform at the Super Bowl Halftime Show – But What About Janet Jackson?" *Vogue*, 23 October 2017, https://www.vogue.com/article/justin-timberlake-super-bowl-halftime-show-2018-janet-jackson (accessed 25 January 2018).

Video, *Saturday Night Live (SNL Digital Short: Dick in a Box)*. 2006. Dir. Lorne Michaels, http://www.nbc.com/saturday-night-live/video/snl-digital-short-d-in-a-box/3505985?snl=1, (accessed 5 January 2018).

Video, *Saturday Night Live (SNL Digital Short: Like a Boss)*. 2009. Dir. Lorne Michaels, http://www.nbc.com/saturday-night-live/video/digital-short-like-a-boss/n12470, (accessed 5 January 2018).

Trahair, Lisa. *The Comedy of Philosophy: Sense and Nonsense in Early Cinematic Slapstick*. Albany: State University of New York Press, 2007.

Yates, Derek, and Jessie Price. *Communication Design: Insights from the Creative Industries*. London: Bloomsbury, 2015.

Alena E. Lyons
Gazing at Slapstick with Luiza Folegatti's Drag King Series *O Deleite da Mulher Barbada*

In the multi-part photo series *O Deleite da Mulher Barbada* [*The Bearded Woman's Delight*] by Brazilian photographer and video artist Luiza Folegatti (*1988) we encounter the photographer taking on the role of the drag king Barba Luluxo. This chapter uses the example of this unfinished photo series of mainly self-portraits to examine slapstick in photography. The aim will be to bring together three components: slapstick, the medium of photography, and kinging. The reason for this approach is to offer a productive re-reading of slapstick by considering how one of its constitutive features – the slapstick subject's relationship to pain – helps theorize the interplay between the slapstick figures captured and the spectators looking onto these figures, a dialectic which actively shifts from engendering a precarious attachment to the protagonists affiliated with *Schadenfreude* on the one hand and empathy on the other (see Trahair 2007).

Since the characteristics of Folegatti's works play an important role in the approach to slapstick proposed here, I will first introduce them, and then discuss the respective aspects underlying the parallelism of kinging with slapstick in particular. Next, based on examples from *O Deleite da Mulher Barbada*, I will show how, in the particular case of Folegatti's pictures, slapstick and kinging overlap. By exploring the use of disguise and makeup in Folegatti's works, I will trace how they shape the physical as well as the social vulnerability of their slapstick and drag king subjects, and how these practices ultimately transform the audience's gaze: audience and performers enter into community through these photographs, a process that renders them a social space for empathy and therefore potentially politically-charged solidarity.

1 Introducing Luiza Folegatti

Luiza Folegatti is a Brazilian photographer and video artist who moved her work and life from São Paulo to Berlin in 2016. She completed her Master's degree in Visual and Media Anthropology at the Freie Universität in 2018. Her academic education plays a role in her artistic work, in which she applies anthropological methods. Such academic interest informs the highly differentiated depictions of body and gender in her work. Entwining scholarship and artistic praxis, Folegatti establishes her own media anthropology through which she questions the manifold relationships among the individual, society, media, media practice, and culture. As I will show later, this explicitly research-based approach can be seen clearly in the development of the long-term project *O Deleite da Mulher Barbada*, where she stages not only her artistic character Barba Luluxo, but also features her own person in her reflections.

Folegatti's work appeared for the first time in 2013 in an exhibition. This was followed by exhibitions in Brazil and Germany, most recently in 2019 at the Internationale Photoszene Köln [International Photography Exhibit Cologne]. Folegatti developed the video and stage design for three performance collaborations with Grupo VÃO, a Brazilian dance collective that has been experimenting with contemporary dance forms since 2009 ("Bando" ["Walk," 2012/2013]; "Corpo Projeção" ["Body Projection," 2015]; and "MOVE COVER," 2016). In addition to various other inter- or multimedia, often collaborative projects, film documentary is playing an increasingly important role in her work. For example, her 15-minute documentary *King ON, Brasil!* (2018) portrays six Brazilian drag kings and their activities in the context of social media. The long-term photo series discussed here also has an accompanying documentary film, which Folegatti directed herself.

Body, gender, and, as of recently, migration are the major themes of her photography and video art. Among this work, *O Deleite da Mulher Barbada* occupies a special place due to its unfinished nature and its scope. The series also draws on elements she explored in her previous projects. I will use the photo essay *Sequências* [*Sequences*, 2012], which consists of twelve photographs, to frame my discussion of *O Deleite da Mulher Barbada*.

Sequências features two people in six pictures each. The two sequences display a transformation. As Folegatti notes in her description of the project, "Inside a daily context two people's expressions are transformed, by changing clothing, props and gestures as a way to think gender as a spectrum" (Folegatti 2012, n.p.). Capturing the fluidity of gender, the two six-picture sequences of the two people show their transformations from male-presenting to female-presenting, and female-presenting to male-presenting in full-body portraits set against a neutral, white studio background (see Figure 1). For the exhibition space, the two sequences of people are juxtaposed, whereby the starting point and the end point (male-presenting to female-presenting and vice versa) are also positioned sequentially facing one another (Folegatti 2012, n.p.). Despite the dynamic variation from picture to picture, each full-body portrait is composed in the same way: a young adult is positioned standing or sitting in the center of the picture and in all but two of the photographs directly gazes into the camera and thus at the viewers.

From picture to picture, clothing, hairstyle, make-up, posture, gestures, and facial expressions change gradually. In both sequences, these rather small, quite simple changes are staged in a very restrained manner. On the one hand, this contributes to a kind of flipbook impression. On the other, this tempers emotional as well as socio-cultural classifications. In this light, nothing can be said about the characters' feelings or states of mind. For example, the smile of the figure who stands before us as female-presenting in the beginning can reflect a positive feeling – perhaps even with regard to the gender expression staged in the image. The smile could also be part of the facial expressions that stage and establish gender, for example in the sense of a female conditioned 'desire to please' through facial expressions. Such smiles are supposed to fulfill a wide range of communicative signals, which eventually serve to demonstratively display a consent or even identification with the social role of being female. They are intended to prevent social conflict and reproduce and affirm the patriarchal hierarchy of heteronormativity.

Figure 1: One sequence of *Sequências* by L. Folegatti; for the purpose of illustration, the pictures have been merged into one.

Among other things, this methodic ambiguation ultimately makes it impossible to determine the gender of the respective figures, which in all probability will instinctively come up as an issue for some viewers. In fact, this question, and especially the refusal to answer it, is decisive for the reception of the photo essay: even those viewers for whom this question does not arise will be aware that *Sequências* is concerned with it. Without a provocative note, without exaggeration, Folegatti works with elements that belong to the main semiotic instruments in the social production and attribution of gender identity. In doing so, she not only adopts the means in and of themselves, but also their use, i.e., what they are supposed to mean. This is of course the performative constitution of gender as captured by Judith Butler (see 1990, 136). For this reason, *Sequências* is structured by gender binarity at first glance. But the same instruments of gender performativity are those of the theatrical, of the performative art, whereby the trick of the photo essay consists in its specific self-referentiality: by means of the performative, the performative is thematized within the framework of the performative. In this sense, Folegatti's *Sequências* realizes Butler's dictum that "gender is a kind of imitation of which there is no original" (1993, 313) by using performative means of norm and normality to – only in the context of these photographs and their compilation – suspend the normativity of gender binary.

By always showing the same person in a sequence, whose supposed gender identity changes primarily through clothing, and by the fact that there is no temporal sequence in the sense of a before-and-after momentum, i.e. in the sense of an original 'starting point' (for each sequence can be read in both directions), the sequences stage withdrawal or refusal. The socially internalized automatism of ascribing a gender identity cannot be performed by the viewer. The social process is brought to its limits and – with regard to the photo essay – loses its otherwise powerful reach. This can be described as subversive in that, beyond the disturbed mechanism of gender attribution, the very same processes are exposed to the viewers in all simplicity. For as one looks on, one sees nothing except clothing, facial expressions, and gestures – and a human being who behaves in and through them. *Sequências* also goes beyond undermining performative habits, insofar as here – framed between the binary beginning and end photographs – each individual photograph illustrates a self-contained possibility, an individual variation of gender outside the female-presenting/male-presenting binary. Thus, two parallel readings unfold, which can only emerge through the chosen genre of the portrait. On the one hand, the viewers see a sequence of photographic moments that represent a movement or a process. This was described above as 'flipbook impression' and brings Folegatti's photo essay close to the mode of film. On the other hand, viewers see a sequence of portraits, i.e., self-contained photographs that stand on their own and can be related to each other in other ways than by temporal or spatial causality.

2 The *O Deleite da Mulher Barbada* projects

In *O Deleite da Mulher Barbada*, Luiza Folegatti further develops the technique of the mode of portraiture she used in *Sequências*. Strictly speaking, this project consists of four individual works, some of which are closely and some loosely connected to each other, some of which were created simultaneously and some of which are consecutive. Common to all four *O Deleite da Mulher Barbada* projects is that none of them has been completed; according to Folegatti, it is a work in progress. This work now extends over several years, has no declared goal or end point in sight, and is defined by its extensive process and diversity of ideas informing it. Here, I will focus on the initial project, which was launched in 2015 in São Paulo.

In an interview I conducted with Folegatti November 12, 2019, she noted the following about the project:

> For a long time, I was interested in gender and how to talk about gender through art. I completed a lot of works on other people like interviewing them, photographing them and in in doing so I realized that I also had to question myself. What are my problems? What are the things that I'm facing? What are the things I want to change? How can I express them? (Lyons 2019, n.p)

As different as the photographs of *O Deleite da Mulher Barbada* are, they always follow the same setting: Folegatti makes portraits of herself as drag king Barba Luluxo. All the photographs in this series were and are taken in a studio environment. Similar to *Sequências*, Barba Luluxo stands in the center of the picture together with the few objects he uses – i.e., the background environment varies slightly, but is kept simple, usually bright. And similar to *Sequências*, Barba Luluxo changes gestures, facial expressions, posture, props, costumes, hairstyle, and make-up from photo to photo. In contrast to the strictly symmetrically composed photo essay, these changes are more varied, colorful, and expressive.

There is no further recognizable concept of composition or style exceeding this: in some cases there are smaller, self-contained photo series or groups of photos, which are arranged differently to one another depending on the exhibition or publication context (see Figures 2–4). Otherwise, most of the portraits are not in a superordinate compositional context. Folegatti varies some portraits a few years later through remaking. Public accessibility also fluctuates greatly: only a few excerpts from the extensive project can be found on her homepage, which is also subject to change from time to time. A remake from the group of photographs examined here was published as a single picture in an art journal (see And She Was Like BÄM! 2020), and there are also various exhibitions in which only parts are shown. Although one of the main reasons for this exclusivity is certainly the precarious conditions under which artists often work and publish, another reason, which should not be underestimated, is the semi-private setting and the fundamental lack of completion characterizing this work. Folegatti started this project as an attempt that is primarily conceived assuming that she herself would be the sole audience for it – that is, she initially focused more on private production and less on concrete publication and exhibition options. According to her own statement, the photos of this sub-project are ultimately made for the Internet (Lyons 2019, n.p.), which opens up a rather striking parallel to kinging. Drag king shows or competitions take place in small, urban, rather exclusive subcultural scenes. But drag kings also use social media platforms for international networking and exchange as well as the development and staging of drag king personas.

In 2018, *O Deleite da Mulher Barbada II* started, a project in which Folegatti changed the previously decisive structures: The portraits of Barba Luluxo are now photographed in analogue and black and white. They are not only taken outside the studio, in public space, but also in natural surroundings. Among the photographs, some of which appear abstract, there are some in which Barba Luluxo does not appear at all, but still provides the contextualizing framework for reading these 'portraits,' which exclusively show nature. At the same time, Luiza Folegatti carries her drag king into public space in a different way. As Barba Luluxo, she roams through the Westend district of Berlin, where Luiza Folegatti lives, and its surroundings, trying to enter into conversation with passersby. For each encounter, a Polaroid image is produced showing Barba Luluxo with the person involved. The focus is on the encounter and the interaction with the dialogue partner, so that gestures, facial expressions, posture, and the like are not specifically composed in these pictures. A short text is mounted on the lower white edge of each picture, which explains in a note-like manner the encounter captured in the snapshot. These montages of image and text are accessible on her homepage under the title *Bearded Talks: Polaroids* (Folegatti 2018). Here, as in *O Deleite da Mulher Barbada I & II*, each individual Polaroid image forms a self-contained unit; beyond the encounter, no background or context of the performance becomes apparent that could order the individual works in their entirety.

Folegatti simultaneously filmed the same performance. It was partly captured in the quasi-documentary Polaroid montages, which ultimately results in two types of documentation of the same material. This secondary documenting is provisionally titled *Bearded Talks*. While the focus of the Polaroids is still on the interaction of individual encounters, the film document captures the interaction of Barba Luluxo with the urban environment in the sense of social geography. The project is thus concerned with the question, How does the drag king Barba Luluxo "function" in the cosmopolitan, diverse Berlin Westend? And, in turn, How does this city quarter, its society "function" in being confronted with and by Barba Luluxo?

3 Kinging: "performing nonperformativity"

It is precisely this example that underlines a clear difference between Folegatti's concept of kinging and what is commonly subsumed under it. Barba Luluxo does not imitate or clearly parody forms of masculinity. Passing, with which LW Hasten (1999) describes the non-theatrical kinging in everyday life in which drag kings try to imitate masculinity in such a way that they can enter spaces of social life as men and the social privileges that go with it, is just as little the aim and effect of Folegatti's performance as those type variants of stage kinging that Halberstam describes in *Female Masculinity* (1998, 246–255). One reason for this is the concern underlying Folegatti's drag king:

> What is this project about? It's about the reason of doing drag king. [. . .] I'm doing drag king, because [. . .] for me as a woman to experiment with this is a way of trying to find a masculinity, a representation of masculinity that I'm okay with [. . .]. (W)hen I do drag king I'm confronted with patterns of masculinity [. . .] that I don't like and at the same time I feel like there is the possibility of changing that to something that I would like.
> (Lyons 2019, n.p.)

Thus, when Barba Luluxo in the *Bearded Talks* performance wanders the streets of Berlin, he deliberately makes himself and the variety of masculinity he literally 'embodies' the object of observation for the others walking by (and often enough also the victim of fierce hostility and sexualized, verbal violence [Lyons 2019, n.p.]); however, brought about by the two documentary procedures described above, the passersby are the ones who capture the spectator's gaze. In contrast to an audience in a drag king show, for example, it does not matter whether the performance as a performance pleases or displeases, convinces or does not convince the spectators. Rather, what is of interest is whether and how they react, accept, and adopt such new, different patterns of masculinity and, if necessary, accordingly adapt and restructure their perception of it, their own behavior towards it and, finally, their public space, at least for the moment of the encounter, which would otherwise not be possible. Seen in this way, the framework of photography and film potentiates the act of gazing and the directions of gazing for the photographs. The photographs thereby realize something different than the cinematic documentation of their creation.

The chosen format of the Polaroid creates an atmosphere of an idyll. As an outdated technique, it offers a low-resolution, rather blurred look and special coloring for today's eye. Given the popularity and wide distribution of instant cameras in the 1960s through the early 1990s, such instant images are strongly associated with the amateur as well as the area of private photography, evoking a pleasing retro effect by today's standards. The stereotypical Polaroid is the medium for spontaneously and easily capturing memorable, albeit smaller, moments such as the birthday party or family trip. Folegatti's Polaroid photographs, too, present themselves in this way, clearly working with these cultural-technical references: Barba Luluxo is always shown smiling into the camera, obviously on the streets of Berlin, together with a different person in each photograph. Although the short texts provide some details about the "talks," the images show less the conversational situation than the end of it – the conversations are over, all possible tensions and inconsistencies have dissolved, happily, perhaps even amicably, people now stand next to each other and smile into the lens. These are the privately staged memories of Barba Luluxo and his spontaneous acquaintance, seemingly captured in the picture only for the two people shown in it. Thus, those who look at the picture are pushed into the role of private viewers, made into people who are in relation to the photographed and thus part of the community shown, which is why they also look at their own memory. Both individually and collectively, a past is constructed, a moment to be remembered, which also has the function of rewriting the actual past, in which to this day a drag king would precisely have no visible, recognized place, taking away its effectiveness in the present.

In contrast, the filmic documentation contextualizes the constructed harmony of the Polaroids by recording entire performances, including the nonoccurrence of conversations, the near-failure of such performance expeditions. While Barba Luluxo occupies an equal place in the socioverse of the Polaroids, the filmic recordings problematize this and in this way produce a critical view of the acceptance of the harmony shown in the Polaroids: their coming into being is unmasked as discursive-social work, sometimes even threatened by violence, and the need for it is exposed as tragic in the sense of a socially caused deficit. As a result, the object and subject of gazing are brought into a complex and precarious balance, so that the hierarchical structures and problematics that often accompany this relation do not come into play.

The reciprocal economy of gazing that Folegatti produces stands and falls with Barba Luluxo, who in many respects breaks with well-known models of kinging, but at the same time can be identified as a drag king. So, the question arises: How does Barba Luluxo work? In order to answer it, one must reconsider the extent to which this figure differs from other drag kings and their practices.

What Folegatti herself calls "doing drag king," I call and categorize as "kinging" based on Jack Halberstam's definition. Halberstam understands this to mean the performative practice that one carries out as a drag king and – in reverse – which identifies one as a drag king: "A drag king is a female (usually) who dresses up in recognizably male costume and performs theatrically in that costume" (Halberstam 1998, 232). Halberstam takes up the term "kinging" common in the English-speaking subculture to describe performances of masculinity by drag kings. This is also an important aspect in identifying possible intersections between slapstick and kinging, since Halberstam points to "mainstream definitions of male masculinity as nonperformative. Indeed, current representations of masculinity in white men unfailingly depend on a relatively stable notion of the realness and the naturalness of both the male body and its signifying effects" (234). According to this, the performance of masculinity is hardly possible, especially in the case of white masculinity, because that which "'just is'" (234) can hardly or only with difficulty be transferred into masquerade, i.e., into the performative (234–235). Thus, kinging is always and fundamentally in danger of failing (234). The performative act of kinging is vulnerable in that the failure of "performing nonperformativity" (259) simply means the non-transforming, i.e., non-parodic representation of masculinities, which is therefore first of all an artistic failure of the individual drag king. At the same time, the drag king is exposed to embody masculinity in an affirming, restorative way, which humiliates him of all people, as well as – if one has the subcultural scene in mind – large parts of his audience in those social mechanisms and structures to which he and the audience are exposed anyway.

Slapstick is confronted with a comparable problem, namely to transform the banal, non-comical (i.e., objects and routines of everyday life), and at the same time powerfully painful (i.e., the threat of injury or death caused by such objects and routines) into comedy and intactness. If something goes wrong, the gag fails artistically because it is simply not funny, and the protagonist actually sustains physical harm. This process of transformation as well as its risky side of slapstick is the very reason why pain seems to be what both slapstick, as a cinematic genre, and slapstick, as a style adopted outside the medium of film, have in common (cf. Peacock 2014). More precisely, the characteristics that justify the identification of slapstick as a stylistic device beyond the medium of film and even beyond the comic – as is the case with Folegatti's *O Deleite da Mulher Barbada* – are derived from the pain the protagonist is poised to experience in cinematic slapstick comedies (see especially the section "Bodies of Slapstick" in this volume). However, the slapstick protagonist obviously does not suffer severe physical pain and is not always the subject of humiliation, but the issue of pain and/or humiliation are constantly raised by the many life endangering ways in which the protagonist stumbles through the world. As Alan Dale puts it, the slapstick protagonist is "a man in trouble" (2001).

Moreover, the troubled human being is the metaphorical definition of slapstick's comic, which seems contradictory and raises the question of the relation between the actually non-comical and its comical transformation within slapstick, for what is so funny about everyday life or the perils of everyday life? As noted above, one important answer to this is in fact the notion of *Schadenfreude*, which characterizes the relationship between the laughing audience and the stumbling slapstick anti-heroic figure. But, as scholars like Tom Gunning, Maggie Hennefeld, and Rob King have shown, one must take a closer look at the occasions, the objects, or simply the world that put the slapstick protagonist in distress. These often reflect working environments and technical or media developments that the audience not only simply knows from their own lives, but which decisively shape their living conditions, sometimes downright determining them (cf. Gunning 2010; King 2010; Hennefeld 2018). In this respect, the collisions of the slapstick protagonists with their mostly material environment are understood as a shared experience, which, however, becomes visible in the slapstick context precisely through the means of excess. This reinterprets the audience's laughter, for it is directed less humiliatingly against the slapstick protagonist than self-empoweringly against those objects and conditions of life and work determined by objects whose non-naturalness, even nonsense is, as it were, exposed. However, this laughter has a price, because it works against the background of the knowledge of the vulnerability of the body that is exposed to these objects that endanger it.

For kinging, this problem of vulnerability results in completely different necessities for theatrical strategies and instruments. As Halberstam notes,

> Within the theater of mainstream gender roles, femininity is often presented as simply costume whereas masculinity manifests as realism or as body. [. . .] (D)rag kings produce a plausible masculinity using suits, crotch stuffers, facial hair, and greased hair. In general, however, the theatrical performance of masculinity demands a paring down of affect and a reduction in the use of props. (258)

"Understatement, hyperbole and layering" (259) are therefore three seemingly paradoxical yet necessary procedures of kinging.

4 Barba Luluxo and kinging in *O Deleite da Mulher Barbada*

In fact, Barba Luluxo can be considered a drag king because he uses these three methods. Nevertheless, Barba Luluxo does not produce a plausible or convincing masculinity, as would be usual especially in the context of a drag king show or competition. As is customary in the drag king scene, Folegatti develops an artificial character who, as the above quote makes clear, may be understood in this as an alter ego. This is an element that drag king culture has in common with slapstick: historical precursors of slapstick, such as the *commedia dell'arte* are type comedies: they are based on a fixed, traditional compendium of characters that are composed of a few character traits and characteristics – i.e., that are types (see Chaffee and Crick 2015, 1–4). In the performance history of the *commedia*, actors often specialized in portraying one or a few types, so that they were strongly associated with their standard roles (see McGehee 2015, 9–20). This comedic theatrical tradition is also continued in slapstick films – probably best known is and remains Charlie Chaplin's (1889–1977) tramp. A similar statement can be made about modern forms of comedy, when comedians develop one or a series of different characters, which usually do not have a complex personality, but are based on a few distinctive characteristics that are therefore masterly enacted. Striking examples of this are the character personnel from the Britcom *Little Britain* or the casting bits in Anke Engelke's (*1965) *Ladykracher* ["Lady Stunner"], a German TV sketch comedy series.

But Folegatti's drag king does not originate from the stage context. Barba Luluxo was created especially for and through the photo series *O Deleite da Mulher Barbada*. He therefore does not represent a type of person who, for a performance in a competition or show act, has to parodically represent masculinity in a coherent way, possibly within the framework of a stringent plot, and who therefore has to refer back to existing forms of masculinity (as stereotypes). The show act is replaced by the portrait or a group of portraits, so that Barba Luluxo is a complex figure in that he presents himself very differently from photograph to photograph (see Figures 2 and 3), sometimes being conspicuous by his absence (see Figure 4).

The relationship of drag kings to private and public space and thus to different audiences is quite complicated. Those drag kings who, in the sense of the above-mentioned passing, do not act on stage, but move in non-theatrical spaces, have no audience at all for it would be contrary to the intentions of passing. Those drag kings, who perform off-stage, can hardly be grasped in the diversity of their motivation, their practices, the contexts they appear, etc. The only thing that is certain is that their kinging is also related to a changing audience. Those drag kings who act on-stage have a no less complex relationship to their audience. In principle, the theatrical space is the public space and the theatrical practice is one that works in the consciousness of this public. In fact, the bars, theatres, etc. where competitions and shows take place are open to the public. At the same time, these places are largely subcultural places and thus open spaces as well as shelters for social minorities and marginalized groups, which are quasi removed from public life, and which are characterized by various modes of exclusivity. Consequently, the theatrical setting in which on-stage kinging takes place and the audience located within it can only be described with the categories of public and private to a limited extent.

Through the medium of photography and publication on the internet, Folegatti transfers the kinging to a broad public, insofar as these media, together with film and television, belong to the mass media and thus also to those of pop culture. But the first and, from the initial conception of the project, only spectator

Figure 2: From *O Deleite da Mulher Barbada* by L. Folegatti.

envisaged by Barba Luluxo is Luiza Folegatti herself. Seen from a European feminist perspective, one is easily tempted to compare the conceptual setting of a specific creative work process, which is only possible by retreating to a closed space (studio), excluding an instance of spectatorship modeled by what Virgina Woolf (1882–1941) imagined with "A Room of One's Own" (1929). But this view fails to recognize that Folegatti, with this form of creative work, is in the tradition of Latin American women artists who, since the 1960s, have often thematized their own body, their own face, as the body (of the woman, the Indigenous person, etc.) suppressed by heteronormativity, patriarchal, and dictatorial regimes in non-public spaces such as their own apartments or studios, and have incorporated it into their visual art (see Giunta 2017). This context undermines the private approach of *O Deleite da Mulher Barbada* declared by Folegatti and politicizes the project despite Folegatti's purported interest in the private. At the same time, it underscores the significance of the working process without other

Figure 3: From *O Deleite da Mulher Barbada* by L. Folegatti.

participants, in a closed, non-public space. It is a self-protection or withdrawal that makes the transformation of the body at the core of her work (i.e., the body of Barba Luluxo) possible and quite comparable to the drag king community about which Halberstam writes.

Another politicization that Barba Luluxo undergoes is the chosen genre of the portrait, which in the history of visual arts initially was a mode of expression for people in power. Originally it was intended exclusively for representative purposes, for the display of one's sovereignty. In this respect, the artistic self-portrait is already a subversive act – a body/face presents itself in the gesture of sovereign representation. Self-portraits go past the thematization of one's own person and/or body, because they recur to the functions and effects of the portrait. As a framing genre, the portrait imposes semantics of power and empowerment onto who (or rather what) is shown. Barba Luluxo would probably find it difficult to be recognized or acknowledged as such in a drag king competition, but as a figure in a self-portrait he is a drag king, since he appears in the performative framework of masculinity (the portrait is 'drag,' and as the genre of the prince, even the 'king's drag'). The rediscovery and transformation of the (self)portrait in the iconography of Latin American women artists of the twenty-first century

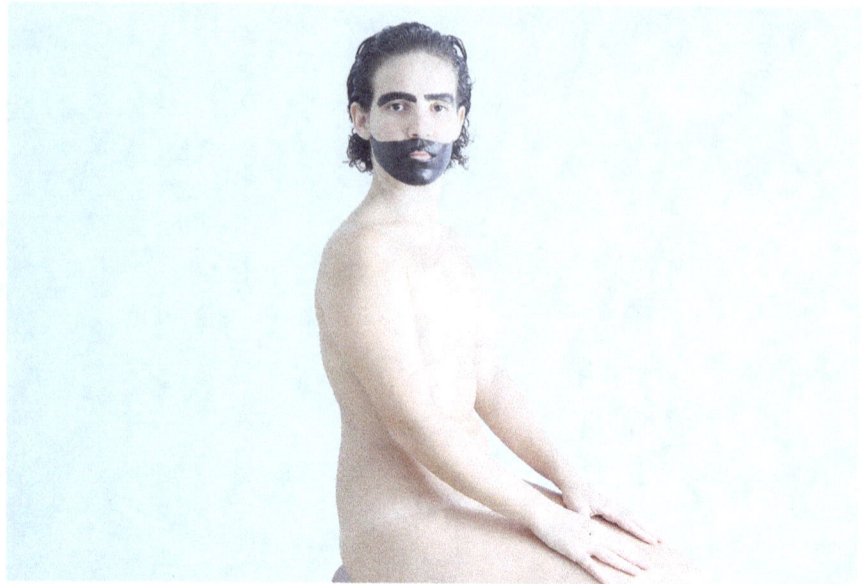

Figure 4: From *O Deleite da Mulher Barbada* by L. Folegatti.

provides the cultural knowledge of violence for which portraiture stands. Not only the portrait genre, but also this young, very diverse artistic development denotes Barba Luluxo's body as one that is representative of the 'new' bodies of Latin American women artists, namely as one that can defend itself, but also needs to defend itself:

> The self-portrait and the portrait put forth questions, subjectivities, paradoxes formulated by female subjects rising up against canonical representations of the female face throughout art history.
>
> The portrait was also the form of representation used to address the violence of the region's dictatorships: the faces of the disappeared (Roser Bru, Luz Donoso); the faces of one's own children as a way to measure the time of dictatorship (Paz Errázuriz, Julia Toro); the faces and bodies of the tortured (Olga Blinder, Sonia Gutiérrez). In some works the portrait is also associated with the violence waged against Native American peoples, whether exterminated (Nelbia Romero) or rendered exotic. (Giunta 2017, 31.)

This proximity to the historical and ongoing experience of the body, which is actually or potentially massively affected by systematic violence, pushes the problem of the fragility of kinging to the extreme. In a figurative sense, the Latin American female body already brings into play an infirmity that Barba Luluxo's kinging exposes to a particular degree.

In this way, the difference on the one hand, and on the other hand, the only fragmentary stringency or typecasting with which Barba Luluxo presents himself, seem to be due to the specific layering Folegatti uses. Formulated in reference to Halberstam (1998, 260), Barba Luluxo's diversity (or brittleness) is layered on top of the diversity (or brittleness) of the underlying, representative body, and thereby exposes the violence that the social mechanisms of masculinity or gender roles signify. Each portrait shows a different Barba Luluxo, shows a different damaged body from which he draws his performance.

The only connecting element between the portraits is on the one hand the mostly blatantly made-up body hair, which varies in form, color, and position, and on the other hand reduced clothing or complete nudity (see Figure 4). In most of the pictures Barba Luluxo wears a made-up beard (see Figures 2 and 4). With this Folegatti refers to common practices in drag king art, in which above all the artificial beard as a sign of masculinity is one of the most important props (see LW Hasten 1999). However, Folegatti does not adopt the practice of working with artificial hair that looks as realistic as possible, but rather hints at it by exposing her painted beards as clearly artificial. In this way, she not only marks the artificiality or made-upness of Barba Luluxo, but also the artificiality or made-upness of what is supposed to identify him as masculine – in this case the beard. For Folegatti, the beard or body hair in general not only stands in for masculinity, but is also an occasion to regulate female bodies: bearded women, unshaved women, women who deviate from certain norms with regard to the hair (e.g., cut too short, bald, etc.) are women who are subjected to humiliation, to whom these elements are denied as not being their entitlement (see Folegatti 2019). Barba Luluxo's beards unmask the performative instruments of kinging as equally constructed and perhaps also problematic as masculinity itself and transfer them – almost in the transforming gesture of reconquest, as it is also apparent in the self-portrait – back to the body, to the gender role, from which this beard was literally 'taken.'

The use of the highlighted artificial body hair, as well as the effects and implications it carries, corresponds with the use of the body in slapstick as a genre. Here, the protagonists' bodies form the interface with their material as well as social environment (see Scott 2014, 74). The body also marks the tipping point between exaggeration and trivialization that is crucial for slapstick (cf. Peacock 2013), which is reflected in the derivation of the slapstick term from the *battacio*, that stick prop of the *commedia dell'arte* that causes much noise and no pain (cf. Preeshl 2017, 262). The protagonist's body has two dimensions here. On the one hand, the body is the problem of the protagonist, who fails to encounter their surroundings with their body, which hinders them from taking a place in the world in terms of the material realities of the world/their body, but also in terms of the social realities this materiality indexes (see also Alexander Kling's contribution in this volume). Viewed in this light, the protagonist is less at the mercy of the viciousness, dangers, and imponderables of their environment than the protagonist is at the mercy of their own body. Conversely, the body is at the same time the solution to the same problem, because – this is also an essential element of slapstick – it remains fundamentally and against all logics of realism intact. Its property of surviving absolutely unharmed levels the extreme of threat and brutality emanating from the fictional world in question. However, the illustration or thematization of precisely this threat and brutality would not be possible if the protagonist did not constantly survive it unscathed, i.e., if the protagonist did not live through it completely and in excess for the viewers.

Finally, this structure is contextualized by the knowledge, the experiences, as well as the expectations of the spectators: only against this background can the body of the protagonist be developed both in its subjectivity and objectivity. Because the spectators know about the highly improbable nature of the respective slapstick actions, the intactness of the slapstick body is shown to be artificial. Folegatti resorts to exactly this strategy and even multiplies it by bringing two physicalities into play. She separates the beard, which is ultimately a body part, from the very body and allows both elements to reflexively interact with each other. Just as the mere body of the slapstick protagonist is both problem and solution, the beard is both problem and solution for Barba Luluxo. Here, the beard is the interface for the drag king to his social framework, which is also that of the viewers. As explained earlier, the beard is an element that indicates and thus produces the masculine body as such, that regulates and thus produces the feminine body, and that indicates and thus produces Barba Luluxo's masculinity. In this sense, the beard becomes both an embodiment of the problematic, violent framework of a heteronormative society to which Barba Luluxo (and his body) is exposed, as well as a symbol of surviving it unscathed and designing a body that is actually not allowed to be in such structures. The beard is the element to which Barba Luluxo is virtually at the mercy of as an object. But its clearly demonstrated artificiality and visual playfulness can no longer be assigned to that outside world or social reality, but can signify its use as an instrument for the production by himself of the physicality of the drag king that breaks the boundaries of heteronormativity. It is his body part, his make-up.

Indeed, the reflective play and variation with the instruments of kinging is in fact typical of Barba Luluxo. In the photographs, in which he is not to be seen, but his props are (see Figure 3), he literally disappears behind the objects, behind his instruments. This is the special wit and humor of *O Deleite da Mulher Barbada*: the performance of the non-performative consists here in non-performing. And the joy of the bearded woman arises from the adoption of the orphaned props, costumes, and scenery, which takes place in the performance and through the performance.

5 Conclusion: the bearded woman gazes at slapstick

Parallels between kinging and slapstick can be identified due to slapstick's and kinging's proximity to theatrical and comedic forms: the typecasting or de-individualization of the protagonists on the one hand, and the particular susceptibility to failure of the performative on the other, which would entail various possibilities of wounding. In both areas, the latter results from the problem that what is to be staged in a way that is bearable for both protagonist and audience can hardly be transformed into a performance.

With *O Deleite da Mulher Barbada*, Folegatti develops a drag king that is only defined by and within the chosen medium of photography and is, therefore, an example of photographic kinging. It is above all through the technique of the portrait as well as the original production context that her work stands in as a highly politicized art practice. Her focus is on the negotiation of the body of those who represent forms of non-masculinity or of non-white masculinity, produced or impaired by masculinities and their political, social and ideological consequences. Thus Folegatti's photo project thematizes the damaged corporeality of all non-masculinity and makes it visible by two means: by the striking display of all artificiality of these momentous masculinities and by the adoption, the playful and pleasurable new use of those artificial and performative means that otherwise contribute to the construction of masculinity.

The adoption of methods of theatrical kinging and their intertwining with visual arts techniques causes or potentiates those aspects of kinging that are close to slapstick: play, joy, liberation vs. pain, violation, and humiliation. It is impossible to laugh at the bearded woman in the photographs or otherwise humiliate her. The gaze that precedes such a possible approach eludes itself, because the complex portrait structure virtually forces the spectator to take a different view. A recognizably female body is exposed, whose representative deformity is fed by this attribution as well as by the corresponding cultural context. The drag king does not remove this woundedness, but removes it from an objectifying, diminishing gaze, which implies either pity or mischief, by taking up elements, mainly representational elements of masculinity, playfully varying, understating, exaggerating, and thus clearly emphasizing their performativity. The concentration on a few individual props in the respective pictures and the absence of a story or plot nearly remove Barba Luluxo, although he is the main protagonist of these pictures, and make him seem barely comprehensible. This culminates in pictures in which Barba Luluxo is not to be seen, but only the objects with which he was equipped. In this way, a reverse structure emerges, which is typical of most of Folegatti's works. In emphasizing their performativity and at the same time their significance in the production of masculinity, Barba Luluxo deprives the objects of the damaging moment of harm, so that these instruments – in the pattern of their performativity – can be incorporated for new performatives. Thus, in the context of the photographs, a community is created between the role and its variants and the performing body or bodies that carry it. Only the willingness to accept the gaze, as *O Deleite da Mulher Barbada* suggests to the viewer, makes it possible to participate in Barba Luluxo's play.

The intersections between *O Deleite da Mulher Barbada* and slapstick – also through kinging – are structurally constitutive for this photographic work. Of course, this does not justify the automatic reverse conclusion to slapstick, but it does provide clues for a further investigation of slapstick: the missing of a plot, the staging of the performativity of objects, the relationship between pain and painlessness or liberation of pain, and the productive-creative responses to wounding. All these are elements that are stylistically important for slapstick – as a genre as well as a means of expression or style. The question raised by Folegatti's work is whether and to what extent the application of such strategies has consequences for a socio-cultural, political reading of slapstick: can it be that in and through slapstick a view of vulnerability is made possible that is not only metaphysically interesting, but also touches on the very political dimensions of power and powerlessness? Could it also be that in this respect slapstick offers, at least for the framework of the aesthetic or entertaining moment, a way of dealing with power, powerlessness, and disempowerment that dissolves, subverts or otherwise reverses certain socially constituents?

The answer is: "yes," followed by a "however." Not every slapstick film or every adoption or imitation of the stylistic means of slapstick is likely to open up corresponding structures of subversion and community. This remains a question of individual analysis. But the investigation of *O Deleite da Mulher Barbada* shows that such forms of play must be present in slapstick – after all, for that is where they come from. And it shows that these forms of play can have a highly political character. Two things are decisive here: on the one hand, there is the fact that the audience's gaze is actively shaped by the artwork being viewed. On the other hand, this leads to the fact that highly vulnerable or, in the figurative sense, injured corporeality can be thematized in the work of art by becoming the starting point of the performance that transforms it. Basically, it can be said that slapstick does something comparable, but the question of how this works in detail remains open at this point. The performance of the slapstick persona, which – depending on the production background and the actor – can often appear as a one-dimensional character or a character that cannot be grasped further, is superimposed on the pain of the performing body, which is probable according to physical criteria. The strict non-availability of pain or unrealistic survival in light of the injury is the moment of transformation, perhaps the very moment of slapstick, which determines the view of the audience accordingly: instead of laughing at the character, the option becomes available to enter into a kind of community with the protagonist in the laughter, which eventually is a kind of community with the protagonist. This community should, however, be understood as a political one, because the shared experience or knowledge of the injuries to the body, which is staged as intact in the performance, is clearly related to the instruments and environment involved in the performance. These, in turn, as Folegatti's kinging in *O Deleite da Mulher Barbada* shows, must themselves be understood as performatives that carry identifiable socio-political meanings. Together we can enjoy the slapstick survival, which is the delight of burdened people.

Bibliography

And She Was Like BÄM! Ed. *Fifty-Five Photographers*. 2020.
Butler, Judith. *Gender Trouble: Feminism and the Subversion of Identity*. New York: Routledge, 1990.
Butler, Judith. "Imitation and Gender Insubordination." *The Lesbian and Gay Studies Reader* Eds. Henry Abelove, Michèle Aina Barale, and David M. Halperine. New York: Routledge, 1993. 307–320.
Chaffee, Judith, and Olly Crick. Eds. *The Routledge Companion to Commedia dell'Arte*. New York: Routledge, 2015.
Dale, Alan. *Comedy Is a Man in Trouble. Slapstick in American Movies*. Minneapolis: University of Minnesota Press, 2001.
Folegatti, Luiza. *Sequências / Sequences*. 2012 (Website of Luiza Folegatti: http://cargocollective.com/lfolegatti/Photography-1/Sequencias-Sequences (accessed 2 June 2020)).
Folegatti, Luiza. *King ON, Brasil!* 2017, dir. Luiza Folegatti.
Folegatti, Luiza. *Bearded Talks: Polaroids*. 2018 (Website of Luiza Folegatti: http://cargocollective.com/lfolegatti/Bearded-Talks-Polaroids (accessed 17 May 2020)).
Giunta, Andrea. "The Iconographic Turn. The Denormalization of Bodies and Sensibilities in the Work of Latin American Women Artists." *Radical Women: Latin American Art, 1960–1985*. Eds. Cecilia Fajardo-Hill and Andrea Giunta. Los Angeles: Hammer Museum. Munich: Prestel, 2017. 29–34.

Gunning, Tom. "Mechanisms of Laughter: The Devices of Slapstick." *Slapstick Comedy*. Eds. Tom Paulus and Rob King. New York: Routledge, 2010. 137–151.

Halberstam, Jack. *Female Masculinity*. Durham: Duke University Press, 1998.

Hennefeld, Maggie. *Specters of Slapstick & Silent Film Comediennes*. New York: Columbia University Press, 2018.

Hasten, LW. "Gender Pretenders: A Drag King Ethnography," M.A. Thesis (Columbia University, 1999).

King, Rob. "'Uproarious Inventions': The Keystone Film Company, Modernity, and the Art of the Motor." *Slapstick Comedy*. Eds. Tom Paulus and Rob King. New York: Routledge, 2010. 114–136.

Lyons, Alena. Interview with Luiza Folegatti. Personal Interview. Berlin, November 12, 2019.

McGehee, Scott. "The Pre-Eminence of the Actor in Renaissance Context: Subverting the Social Order." *The Routledge Companion to Commedia dell'Arte*. Eds. Judith Chaffee and Olly Crick. New York: Routledge, 2015.

Peacock, Louise. "Conflict and Slapstick in Commedia dell'Arte: The Double Act of Pantalone and Arlecchino." *Comedy Studies* 4 (2013): 59–69.

Peacock, Louise. *Slapstick and Comic Performance: Comedy and Pain*. New York: Palgrave, 2014.

Preeshl, Artemis. *Shakespeare and Commedia dell'Arte*. New York: Routledge, 2017.

Scott, Andrew. *Comedy*. London: Routledge, 2014.

Trahair. Lisa. *The Comedy of Philosophy: Sense and Nonsense in Early Cinematic Slapstick*. Albany: The State University of New York Press, 2007.

Part III: **Narrative Structures of Slapstick**

Alena E. Lyons & Ervin Malakaj
Introduction

Lisa Trahair opens *The Philosophy of Comedy* by discussing slapstick's peculiar relationship to narrative, a topic that has long preoccupied scholarship on slapstick and that the essays in this part of this volume also explore. First, Tahair remarks that narrative is not integral to the gag's function; it plays a secondary, even nonessential role in producing laughter (2007, 35–57). Put differently, if narrative (and the majority of discourse theorizing it) is first and foremost invested in the production of meaning – within and as a result of certain structures – slapstick's gags could even be said to stand in opposition to it, given that they can operate on their own. Slapstick's opposition to narrative is also to be found in some theories of the comic (e.g., Trahair 2007, 15–20), which posit that a mode such as slapstick produces laughter by suspending meaning. In a similar vein, film theorists such as Tom Gunning have remarked on slapstick's investment in the nonsensical. Gunning notes that the gag in slapstick cinema "produces the collapse of purpose" in favor of "a strong sensual effect" (2020, 141).

The audience's affective response to slapstick gags has been a focal point of scholarly discussions on slapstick's relationship to narrative. As Donald Crafton's work has shown, while the spectacle of the gag "often makes the plots of slapstick comedies distinctively incoherent," thereby suggesting an antithetical relation to narrative, it does so "delightfully" (1995, 108). For Crafton, the structures of delight are, however, connected to narrative, which Crafton understands as a "system for providing the spectator with sufficient knowledge to make causal links between represented links" (119). The gag is "irreconcilable" (119) with meaning-making and causality. It is not interested in "providing knowledge," but rather in what Crafton calls "misdirecting" (119): as instances that work against "epistemological comprehension," gags operate within, through, and against narrative to delight their viewers. Trahair's work on the tension between gags and narrative in slapstick aligns with such scholarship:

> Although many gags take narrative as the unit of meaning they transgress or destroy narrative in the process of making fun of something else, the comic targets meaning at other levels as well and may even rely on narrative to do so. When this happens – as in the case of articulated gags – whether the comic is subordinate to narrative, in which case the gag's purpose is to propel the narrative forward, or whether narrative form is being subtly deployed in the service of the comic, is unclear. (2007, 57)

Gags, by operating independently from narrative structures to generate an effect in their relation to audiences, at times maintain a mere anarchic relation to narrative: it is not necessary for them to "work." At other times, however, slapstick gags are reintegrated into the narrative arch of a given text. This difference becomes clear within the development of slapstick film. Take, for example, the slapstick shorts in the age of the "cinema of attractions" (Gunning 1990) which are nearly entirely constituted by a linear row of gags that only loosely interact with one another in terms of causality conditioned by a plot. In comparison, the gags in later feature-length slapstick films such as Charlie Chaplin's (1889–1977) *Modern Times* (1936) interact with the overarching plot by contributing to and producing causality within the narrative framework and are thus shaping it.

Such a nuanced perspective, which creates room for us to consider slapstick as both non- or counter-narrative *and* as a feature working within narrative, can lead slapstick research into new directions. Such a perspective helps us read slapstick both as a genre and as a mode of expression, readings which in turn both generate further studies of narrative's relationship to slapstick, and lay the groundwork for interdisciplinary approaches to the latter. The chapters in this section study slapstick's relation to narrative structures by exploring the ordering principles by which the materiality of the body essential for the slapstick moment comes into contact with the materiality of the narrative form used to express it. Apart from the question of how narratives of slapstick, as well as slapstick itself as narrative, work within categories of space, time, and other models of order, this section deals with slapstick as a field with a history and traditions constituted by narrative structures and functions. In doing so, this section underlines the various possible relations between narrative (and the performative act of narrating) and slapstick – even against the usual understanding of slapstick as merely a form of physical comedy. In other words, the section views slapstick as something complex and challenging: understanding it involves systematically conceptualizing the shifting relation between audiences and slapstick gags produced in relation to narrative structure(s).

Alexander Kling opens this section with a contribution examining slapstick in German romanticism. Following a reflection about the problematic relation between human subject and object (see also the section "Instruments of Slapstick" in this volume), as well as a consideration of the special relationship of the nineteenth century as a threshold century situated between the enlightenment and industrialization, Kling turns to things and thingness. The chapter places comic and thing theories of the period in dialogue with each other. Using Heinrich von Kleist's (1777–1811) drama *Der zerbrochne Krug* [*The Broken Jug*, 1808] as an example, the chapter discusses Stephan Schütze's (1771–1839) theory of the comic, which scholarship in literary studies research has viewed as an early precursor to the theory of slapstick. Kling shows how essential philosophical and theoretical components of romanticism provide the theoretical basis for a systematic analysis of narrative structures of slapstick.

Claudia Sassen and Stefan Schroeder elaborate on the concept of seriality through an in-depth analysis of the cinematic styles at the heart of the work by silent film comedian Larry Semon (1889–1928). Semon is well-known in the history of slapstick for reforming the film genre. As outlined above, typical slapstick films of the 1910s consisted primarily of strings of gags that showed no or little dependence to an overarching plot structure. Semon, partly in response to audience dissatisfaction, resolved this narrative absence by developing plots from which the slapstick gags emerged. Sassen and Schroeder show how the entanglements of different serial levels constitute and structure Semon's slapstick style. They thereby expound how seriality becomes a formative element for a narratology of slapstick.

Claudia Sassen examines an advertising cartoon portfolio from 1969 by the German comedian and director Loriot (1923–2011). Sassen focuses on contexts that have so far been disregarded by slapstick research. One is the history of marketing, in which slapstick effects a specific relationship with its audience. The second is the medium of the cartoon. In the example studied in the chapter, cartoons refer to simple caricature-like drawings which were a trademark style for Loriot. The scenes depicted in the portfolio thematize ordinary situations from bourgeois everyday life. This highly ordered life, in turn, is accompanied by short texts that contextualize the rather unspecific scenes and always redefine them through a mode that Sassen describes a chaotic-anarchistic slapstick. Sassen reconstructs this interplay of order and chaos as well as the narrative structure that results from it by studying the text-image relations in these scenes.

Works cited

Crafton, Donald. "Pie and Chase: Gag, Spectacle and Narrative in Slapstick." *Classical Hollywood Comedy*. Eds. Kristine Brunovska Karnick and Henry Jenkins. New York: Routledge, 1995. 106–119.

Gunning, Tom. "Mechanisms of Laughter: The Devices of Slapstick." *Slapstick Comedy*. Eds. Tom Paulus and Rob King. New York: Routledge, 2010. 137–151.

Gunning, Tom. "The Cinema of Attractions: Early Film, Its Spectator and the Avant-Garde." *Early Cinema: Space, Frame, Narrative*. Ed. Thomas Elsaesser. London: BFI, 1990. 56–62.

Trahair, Lisa. *The Comedy of Philosophy: Sense and Nonsense in Early Cinematic Slapstick*. Albany: The State University of New York Press, 2007.

Alexander Kling
Telling and Showing: Slapstick in Stephan Schütze's Comic Theory and Heinrich von Kleist's *Der zerbrochne Krug*

"We seek the absolute everywhere and only ever find things" (Novalis 2008, 390).[1] In its brevity, this opening sentence of Novalis's (1772–1801) *Blütenstaub*-Fragmente [*Pollen-Fragments*, 1798] demonstrates not only the essence of German romanticism; this deceivingly simple sentence also expresses an oppositional structure impressed on Western thought: the absolute (*das Unbedingte*), which represents subjects, ideas, the mind, and imagination, and its opposite, the conditional (things) (*das Bedingte*), which includes material objects that, next to quotidian objects, also include bodies to which humans, as physical beings, belong. Even in their hierarchical arrangement it would not be difficult to connect this relationship between things and non-things with the central concepts of romanticism (see Holm and Oesterle 2011). Longing (*Sehnsucht*), irony, fragment, or progressive universal poetry are motifs, techniques, and forms by which the unconditioned is made visible in the boundaries of the conditioned.

Building on this observation, the first of the following sections will demonstrate how various oppositional pairs central to romanticism are also crucial aspects of slapstick comedy. In order to describe more precisely the relation between romantic comic theory and slapstick, I will initially explore various conjunctions between comic theory and thing theory. The second section will demonstrate that oppositional pairs such as subject/object, mind (spirit)/body, and freedom/necessity are not only of general importance for romantic literature, but also for the comic theories of the romantics. The focus will be on comic theories not for their romantic but for their slapstick characteristics. The central comic theory foregrounded in this chapter is that of Stephan Schütze (1771–1839), who may have been forgotten were it not for Johannes F. Lehmann's (2011, 2012, 2015) recent acknowledgement that Schütze's counts as the "first comic theory of *slapstick*" (2015, 101). According to Lehmann, Schütze's work belongs in the lineage of other more widely known comic theories, such as those by Jean Paul (1763–1825), F. W. J. Schelling (1775–1854), Friedrich Theodor Vischer (1807–1887), and Henri

---

[1] "Wir suchen überall das Unbedingte und finden immer nur die Dinge." Unless otherwise noted, all translations are by Laura Isakov.

Translated by Laura Isakov

Bergson (1859–1941). Finally, the third section shows how considering the comic theories of the romantics can help to describe the slapstick moments in Heinrich von Kleist's (1777–1811) *Der zerbrochne Krug* [*The Broken Jug*, 1808].

1 Slapstick, things, narrative

One of the "most effective forms of the comic," according to Karlheinz Stierle, is the decussation, or crossing over, of a "planned action" through an "anti-action," that is, the moment when the "object [. . .] becomes a quasi-subject which appears to have the power to make use of the acting subject, turning it into a quasi-object" (1976, 242). Stierle understands the comic firstly in terms of plot development, in which two actions, one intended and one unintended, come into conflict with each other. Secondly, Stierle associates this with a reversal of the subject-object relation: human subjects lose control over their own actions as the object takes the position of control and thus transforms the human subject from an acting to a reacting figure. Conversely, the (thing) object proves to be "resistant" (242); it gains its own agency and switches therefore to the position of the acting subject.

It may be a coincidence that only a few years before Michel Serres's (1930–2019) *Le Parasite* (1980, 301–314) Stierle coined the terms 'Quasi-Subject' and 'Quasi-Object,' which Bruno Latour (*1947) subsequently used in his work on the actor-network-theory (1993, 51–55).Beyond studying terminological similarities among these theorists, however, lies the possibility to establish conceptual overlaps between the comic theories on the one hand and the thing theories on the other (see Lehmann 2012; Kling 2018). Both theories are interested in the resistance of non-human entities. The agency of things simultaneously undermines the autonomy of the human subject as well as anthropocentric distributions of action powers, recognizing action instead as a jointly operated process of co-action by human and non-human beings (see Latour 2005, 63–86). This, in turn, is linked to the fact that both comic and thing theories look at culturally relevant oppositional pairs and simultaneously question how these pairs become unstable and fluid. This is already clear in Stierle's distinction between subject and object. Furthermore, it is worth noting the distinction between human action and the material framework of this action. Latour finds it crucial to prove that things are involved in human actions – for this he uses the metaphor of the theater stage, where the stage itself, along with other "actors" such as lighting and props, is as involved in the plot as is the human actor (Latour 2005, 46–47).

That the considerations of affinities between comic and thing theories can be linked to slapstick results from the fact that slapstick already carries the thing in its name – the term goes back to a prop of the *commedia dell'arte*. As a generic term for a specific form of the comic, the term is therefore also younger than the phenomenon it describes: as research repeatedly emphasizes, slapstick is already found in the ancient comedies of Aristophanes. With the development of *commedia dell'arte* in the sixteenth century, a tradition can be traced that reaches from the circus to the silent film and to sound film (McLeish 1980, 13–22; Peacock 2014, 15–39). However, the term slapstick as demarcating a specific type of comicality is only established around 1900 in connection with silent film (Peacock 2014, 19).

Slapstick is often described as a lower form of the comic. One reason for this is that it is episodic and, unlike character or intrigue comedy, slapstick can scarcely carry a narrative arc (for the difference between episodic and narrative-oriented comedy, see Warning 1976, 283–297; for the relevance of this difference with regard to the comic theory of the romantics, see Kraft 2011, 201–240). With regard to the medial specifications of slapstick, it is often discussed in relation to a theatre or a cinema of attractions, in juxtaposition to a theatre or a cinema of narration (McLeish 1980, 18–19; Brandlmeier 1995, 53). A second reason slapstick is described as lower form of the comic is that slapstick is "physical comedy" (Dale 2000, 1): human and non-human bodies interact with each other, often resulting in scenes of violence and pain (see Peacock 2014), whereby the existential involvement of man in the world of things is brought into view (see Dale 2000, 9–11).

Slapstick sits in the shadow of less physical and violent varieties of the comic. To cite just one example: in the comic treatment of the Amphitryon myth, as found in Plautus (c. 254–184 BC), Molière (1622–1673), or Kleist, the comicality of the entire plot structure results from Jupiter's intrigue and the resulting confusion. In this entire plot structure, slapstick scenes are embedded, e.g. when Mercury takes on the appearance of the servant Sosias and beats the actual Sosias out of his own self. This is, admittedly, a rather raw form of slapstick that does not require much artistic skill from the performers. However, the performers – at the very least – have to manage both the stage violence while simultaneously keeping the audience aware of the nature of the game. One means to ensure this is the stick, as used by Mercury in Molière (1734, 43) and later on by Kleist (1987–1997, Vol. 1, 390),[2] whereas the prop is not to be found in Plautus's version, necessitating

---

[2] All subsequent citations of Heinrich von Kleist's works cite this edition with the abbreviation *DKV*, listing the volume and page number.

Mercury to beat up Sosias by administering blows with bare fists (1960, 27). Thus, the optical and acoustic 'special effects' of the *commedia dell'arte* found their way into the comedy of French classicism of the seventeenth century and German romanticism of the first third of the nineteenth century where they contribute to the comic effects.

The aforementioned episodic and physical characteristics raise the question of the possibility of a linguistic and narrative conception of slapstick comedy. Based on these characteristics one could understand slapstick as decidedly anti-linguistic and anti-narrative; slapstick is found where language is silent – in the stuttering, stumbling, and beating of the body or in the artistic simulation of these actions. In contrast to this consideration, however, the historical texts already evidence that slapstick comedy is also found in linguistic and narrative form. One can argue whether or not slapstick scenes in the medium of a linguistic narration manifest to the same effect as a physical realization that draws its comic energy not least from an artistic presentation. But such a concern already shifts the question of the possibility of a linguistic and narrative constitution of slapstick comic from "if at all" to "how." My chapter addresses "how" slapstick comedy unfolds in a narrative: slapstick scenes designed in the medium of a linguistic narration commonly switch to a dramatic mode to generate an intense comic effect. The distinction between a narrative and a dramatic mode has already been established by Plato (c. 427–348 BC) (*Politeia*, 392c–394c). Likewise, Johann Wolfgang Goethe (1749–1832) and Friedrich Schiller (1759–1805) have juxtaposed the epicist who "recites the event completely in the past" ["die Begebenheit als vollkommen vergangen vorträgt"], and the dramatist who depicts the event "completely present" ["vollkommen gegenwärtig darstellt"] (Goethe/Schiller 2004, 126). Finally, in the context of narratology, Norman Friedman coined the terms "telling" and "showing" (1955, 1161). Building from these positions, the unfolding of a dramatic mode in a narrative speech act is thus understood in such a way that the static telling is dynamised by a vivid showing: the narrated event – and this also means the past event – is depicted as if it happens in the present moment. This occurs as the causal process of the event and is not conceived as completed (and therefore closed), but rather is conceptualized as presently developing and therefore as open – for example, by means of narrating in the present tense. In addition, the linguistic representation of the events can be supported by physical sequels, so that the past events are also made scenically present. The next section investigates these considerations on slapstick as they relate to the comic theory of the romantics.

2 Slapstick and comic theory in romanticism

Comicality results from a 'what' and from a 'how,' that is, from a comic event on the one hand, and its representation or perception on the other. Since up until the eighteenth century the reflection on the comic took place above all – but, of course, not only – in books of rhetoric and poetry, it is no surprise that for a long time the focus was on the appropriateness of objects and representations of the comedic (which certainly does not mean that the practice of comedy necessarily adhered to it – one only has to think of the art of improvisation of the *commedia dell'arte*). Given the dwindling normative binding force of rhetoric and so-called rule poetry (*Regelpoetik*), it is only logical that the comic rose to the rank of an aesthetic category. Since 1800, a comic theory develops in its own right and considers the comic alongside the sublime as a variant of beauty. The question is no longer what the object of comedy should be, but what causes comedy and laughter: the comic attains an anthropological foundation. And likewise, it is not so much a question of how the comic is to be designed in terms of a production aesthetics (*Produktionsästhetik*), but rather how viewers or recipients have to position themselves in relation to the object and how they are involved in the generation of the comic effect.

With regard to the theory of perception of comic phenomena formulated around 1800, two important aspects can be emphasized in reference to slapstick: detachment and the reflexive performance of the observer. "In the comedy," Schiller writes, "our state is calm, clear, free, cheerful; we feel neither active nor afflicted; we look at everything, yet everything remains external to us; this is the state of the gods, who are not concerned with anything human, floating freely above everything, untouched by fate, not forced by any law" (2004, 1018).[3] Unlike tragedy, which involves the viewer in the action and leads him to sympathize, for Schiller the comedy viewer is characterized by non-participation. It is in this detachment that a potential reason for slapstick comedy can be recognized; instead of sympathizing with the hero, the viewer enjoys his misadventures in a cheerful, peaceful manner, even when such activity is connected to violence and pain. One hundred years after Schiller, Henri Bergson examined this insensitivity more specifically with regards to slapstick comedy, which he describes as the "anesthesia of the heart" (1911, 5).

---

[3] "Unser Zustand in der Komödie ist ruhig, klar, frei, heiter, wir fühlen uns weder tätig noch leidend, wir schauen an, und alles bleibt außer uns; dies ist der Zustand der Götter, die sich um nichts Menschliches bekümmern, die über allem frei schweben, die kein Schicksal berührt, die kein Gesetz zwingt."

Detachment is apparently opposed to the viewer's involvement in the production of the comic phenomenon that Jean Paul formulated in particular in connection with his theory of "borrowing" [Theorie des 'Leihens']. According to Jean Paul's Sancho Pansa example, the viewer lends his own knowledge to the unaware figure. In this way the action of the character becomes nonsensical; in the interplay of events and observer there emerges an "infinite inconsistency" ["unendliche Ungereimtheit"], which finally leads to Jean Paul's argument that "the comic [. . .] never lives in the object, but in the subject"[4] (1973, 110). According to Jean Paul, only the participation of the viewer brings forth the comic moment. However, this does not contradict detachment, since participation in this case is not to be understood affectively as a form of compassion, but rather from a superior position of observation. Especially for slapstick comedy, viewer participation is, after all, important insofar as it brings knowledge and expectations to the action – it is in the interplay of events and observation that slapstick comedy arises, such as when a character does something that the viewer knows he or she should not do, or when the viewer projects the course of a causal process which is then increased or redirected by unexpected events.

In the next step, it is important to consider the 'what' along with the comic events. Romantic comic theory is striking in that the comic always emerges from oppositional pairs – the absolute (*das Unbedingte*) and the thing, the subject and the object, freedom and necessity. First, we consider Novalis's definition of humor: "Humor is the result of a free intermingling of the conditional and the absolute"[5] (2008, 396). Second, we have Friedrich Schlegel's (1772–1829) determination of romantic irony as the "indissoluble conflict of the absolute and the conditional"[6] (1967, 160). Finally, for Schelling, the comic arises from the fact that the "original" allocation of freedom to the subject and necessity to the object is reversed (1985, 539–540). The positions of Novalis, Schlegel, and Schelling must be more precisely considered, if only because they address different phenomena with humor, irony, and the comic. Nevertheless, these sentences confirm they have in common the reversing and collapsing of oppositional pairs that produce the different kinds of comic effects.

Of all the romantic comic theories, the texts of Stephan Schütze, especially his essay "Üeber das Komische" ["On the Comic," 1810] and *Versuch einer Theorie des Komischen* [*An Attempted Theory of the Comic*, 1817], should be more closely considered. Schütze starts with the abovementioned oppositional pairs:

---

4 "das Komische [. . .] nie im Objekte wohnt, sondern im Subjekte."
5 "ist Resultat einer freien Vermischung des Bedingten und Unbedingten."
6 "unauflöslichen Widerstreit des Unbedingten und des Bedingten."

"The comic always hovers between two natures: between body and mind, the conditional and the absolute, and outward necessity and half-freedom"[7] (1810, 294). Above all, the last oppositional pair, that of freedom and necessity, is important for Schütze's comic theory. He defines the comic as follows:

> The comic is a perception that arouses the momentary dark feeling that while believing to act freely or striving to do so, humans are the objects of the amusing game whereby nature mocks the limited freedom of humans in comparison to a higher freedom.[8] (1817, 23)

Schütze also distinguishes between comic events and their perception. For him, the event results from a tension between humans who believe that they are free in their actions and nature, meaning the world of surrounding things, which limits the freedom of humans and resists their will, thereby unfolding its own agency. Thus, on the one hand observers recognize in the comic event the conditionality of human existence, on the other hand they realize a "higher freedom." This higher freedom is to be understood as an ideal that humans can never fully reach on account of their limitations; it goes beyond humankind and could be interpreted as the sum of all existing agencies, be they of human or nonhuman beings. Therefore, for Schütze, "absolute freedom" ["absolute Freiheit"] only "exists" in the "wholeness of the world" ["Ganzheit der Welt"] (1810, 290).

Like many other comic theorists of the 18th and 19th centuries, Schütze sees a basic requirement for the comic in the constitution of humankind as understood by contemporary anthropology as *homo duplex* – possessing a mind, will, and freedom in addition to a body involved in the causal processes of matter. Therefore, the oppositional pairs that are used time and again to describe the comic are inherent in humans themselves. To determine this particularity of humankind in terms of the comic, Schütze places humans in opposition to other beings. Firstly, for God it is typical that there is "no distance between the will and its fulfillment [. . .] across neither time nor space"[9] (1817, 52). Secondly, inanimate things lack agency as constitutive moments of the comic: "the dead is only as far from the circle of the risible as it can appear to be neither active nor gifted with reason"[10] (37; for

---

7 "Immer schwebt das Komische zwischen zwei Naturen, zwischen Körper und Geist, dem Bedingten und Unbedingten, der äussern Notwendigkeit und der halben Freiheit."
8 "Das Komische ist eine Wahrnehmung, welche nach Augenblicken das dunkele Gefühl erregt, daß die Natur mit dem Menschen, während er frey zu handeln glaubt oder strebt, ein heiteres Spiel treibt, wodurch die beschränkte Freyheit des Menschen in Beziehung auf eine höhere verspottet wird."
9 "zwischen dem Willen und seiner Erfüllung keine Entfernung [. . .] weder durch Zeit noch durch Raum."
10 "Das Todte liegt nur in so fern außer dem Kreise des Lächerlichen, als es nicht handelnd und mit Verstand begabt erscheinen kann."

opposition between the living and the dead see Lehmann 2011, 127–129). Finally, Schütze grants animals a trace of the comic, though the "great restriction of their reasoning and freedom"[11] leads to them "carrying only a glimmer of ridiculousness in themselves"[12] (1817, 42–43).

The qualities that predestine humans to be comic beings become visible as they are delineated by God, things, and animals. For Schütze, humans are free entities of agency, each with an individual will and particular goals. The problem, however, is that individual human will and fulfillment do not coincide; meaning one must traverse time and space to achieve the desired goals and thus become dependent on the external environment: "There must be things that can satisfy him [the individual]; there must be a world; only man's pursuit of things beside themselves can bring one to action, and one's freedom to exert"[13] (51). As already noted, Schütze recognizes that while humans are free and acting beings, they can only exist in the environment of things that in turn limit freedom and action. Schütze therefore ascribes a kind of life to the supposedly "dead objects" ["todten Gegenständen"] from a "higher viewpoint" ["höheren Ansicht"]: There is "no dead state of being; rather, this is regarded as a part of, a means of, and in relation with something living and acting"[14] (37–38). Humans, who have to resort to the world of things for the fulfillment of their will, are forced to act with and against the things. Therefore, things win their moment of agency, making themselves "visible and tangible" ["sichtbar und fühlbar"], whereby they can "obstruct the human plan" ["Plan des Menschen vereiteln"] (55).

Schütze's comic theory is applicable to slapstick, which emanates from man but simultaneously shapes the non-human beings as actors. For Schütze, the comic is decidedly based on the interplay between human and non-human beings. Although things do not act without the human being, neither is any action of the human being imaginable without the world of things. Action is always already interaction resulting from what Schütze calls a "shared power" ["vertheilten Macht"] between the entities (56). This interaction becomes comic when human goals and intentions – expected to be achieved through action – are disrupted and deviated by the agency of things in a surprising way. Two 'readings' of this kind of comicality can be distinguished, which are also relevant for the slapstick comedy. The

---

[11] "große Beschränktheit ihres Verstandes und ihrer Freyheit."
[12] "daß sie nur einen Schimmer von Lächerlichkeit an sich tragen."
[13] "es müssen auch Dinge, die ihn befriedigen können, es muß eine Welt vorhanden seyn; sein Streben nach Dingen außer ihm kann ihn erst zur Thätigkeit, und seine Freyheit zur Ausübung bringen."
[14] "kein todtes Seyn, sondern dieses wird als Theil und Mittel von etwas Lebendigem und Handelnden betrachtet, und kann damit in Verbindung gestellt werden."

first regards the matter of the ridiculousness of the human being, because with the power of things slapstick comedy exposes man's belief in an exclusive autonomy as an anthropocentric, ontologically unjustified hubris. The second 'reading' results from Schütze's consideration that with the limited freedom of man a higher freedom becomes simultaneously visible. Nonhuman beings are limiting human action, but, from a perspective beyond the human, this limitation does not reduce, but rather increases the potential for action. Schütze demonstrates how recognizing this allows the human viewer to laugh at the fact that his own embeddedness in the world of things, the "wholeness of the world," does not constitute a degradation, but is rather a source of pleasure.

The question remains how the co-action of human and non-human beings can be represented artistically and, above all, literarily. According to Schütze, the spectator looks at

> a work of art as a piece of the world, as an example world. [. . .] Viewers watch an incident, an action, as if standing in the full market of life. What fooleries they want to find out about it, be it much or little, depends on the individual viewers, their minds, and their perspective.[15] (194–195)

According to this formulation, for Schütze – as well as for Jean Paul – the comic lies primarily in the viewer, not in the observed. However, Schütze's artistic understanding is even more important: as an "example world," artwork serves as a means of illustration, i.e., from something mundane ["market of life"], which is hardly reflected as such. If in the work of art a person who conflicts with things is shown, then, according to Schütze, this is a thoroughly realistic and epistemological staging of the *conditio humana*, the often-forgotten and therefore painfully experienced intertwining of man and the world.

In this context, Schütze determines the question of genre between an "indirect" narrative and a "direct" dramatic representation of the comic (192). While the narrative is to be understood in the first place as a "means of relief" ["Erleichterungsmittel"] regarding the depiction of comic events, the dramatic staging of these events contributes to a "strong sensualizing" ["starken Versinnlichung"] (192–193) whereby the impression on the observer is intensified. Therefore, unlike the narrative, the drama has an immediacy that supports the comic effect. Thus, Schütze states further that, "even the indirect representation strives towards the dramatic, and thereby it helps itself to a portion of its sensual

---

15 "Ein Kunstwerk wie ein Stück von der Welt, wie eine Beispielswelt. [. . .] Der Zuschauer sieht einem Vorfall, einer Handlung zu, wie wenn er auf dem vollen Markte des Lebens stände, und was er daran Thörigtes finden will, ob viel oder wenig, das kommt auf ihn, auf seinen Geist, und auf seine Ansicht an."

clarity"[16] (1817, 192). Here Schütze precisely describes the transition from telling to showing. His comic theory assumes that slapstick can occur in the medium of a linguistic narration while the form of presentation changes it into a dramatic mode so that the comic effect is established by means of sensualizing, immediacy and, as Friedman states, "vividness" (1955, 1161). In the next step, I will test these theoretical deliberations by applying them to a concrete example: Kleist's *Der zerbrochne Krug*.

3 Heinrich von Kleist's *Der zerbrochne Krug*

In a May 1799 letter to his sister Ulrike, Heinrich von Kleist invokes the autonomy of the "free, thinking human" ["freien, denkenden Menschen"] as the designer of his own "life plan" ["Lebensplan"] and who does not act according to a "game of chance" ["Spiel des Zufalls"] like a "doll on the wire of fate" ["Puppe am Drahte des Schicksals"] (*DKV*, Vol. 4, 38 and 40). Plan and coincidence, intention and fatalism, autonomy and heteronomy oppose each other here. It is well known that Kleist's life will increasingly drift to the latter side in subsequent years. The frustrations of his life plan, in so far as he had ever had one, goes hand in hand with a release of contingency, which Kleist depicts in his literary texts as well. Already in the letters such emblematic scenes are found, and these can also be associated with slapstick.

At the end of 1800, Kleist reflects in a letter to his fiancée Wilhelmine von Zenge about the physical laws of gravity: "Why," asked Kleist at the sight of an archway, "does not the arch collapse, seeing as it has *no support*? It stands, I replied, *because all the stones want to collapse at the same time*"[17] (*DKV*, Vol. 4, 159). For Kleist, this consideration became a metaphor of life; from the sight of the archway he gained the "consolation [. . .] that I too would hold on, even if everything lets me sink"[18] (159). Yet, for my considerations it is not the metaphor, but the literal, that is decisive here. The archway is clearly a demonstration of forces at work within supposedly static things and so long as these forces remain balanced, the state of rest (static condition) remains (for an overview on forces and things in Kleist's texts see Böhme 2015). Slapstick also works with physical

---

[16] "strebt selbst jene indirecte Darstellungsweise zum Dramatischen hinüber, und bedient sich zum Theil der sinnlichen Deutlichkeit desselben."
[17] "Warum, sinkt wohl das Gewölbe nicht ein, da es doch *keine Stütze* hat? Es steht, antwortete ich, *weil alle Steine aufeinmal einstürzen wollen*."
[18] "Trost [. . .], daß auch ich mich halten würde, wenn alles mich sinken läßt."

forces such as gravity, in which the comic emerges as a result of the shift from a static to a dynamic state. In doing so, it can lead to an expansion, with an ever-increasing number of things to be integrated into the dynamic events, so that the first impulse movement is perpetually continued by the release of the forces stored in things (potential energy). From this perspective, slapstick is the dynamic event between two equilibrium states; the longer the dynamic state is maintained, the more the comic is increased.

Kleist's letters of July 1801 also describe a second slapstick event. On their way to Paris, Kleist and his sister remain seated in the coach during a rest stop in Butzbach, when suddenly "a donkey behind us raised a hideous squeal"[19] and so the horses, who had been taken off their reins, were agitated to a frenzy:

> The poor horses [. . .] rose high in the air and spurred us on, reins in full *carrière,* over the stone pavement through the city. I reached for the reins, but they hung suspended over their chests, and before I had time to think of the magnitude of the danger, the carriage was knocked over with us inside, and was overturned – and human life hung on a single donkey cry?[20]
> (*DKV,* Vol. 4, 242–43, for a closer consideration of this episode, see Bohrer 1989, 93–95; Beyer 2019)

The last sentence expresses the contingency of human existence in a nutshell: Kleist und Ulrike do not respond to the donkey's scream unlike the horses, the two are "already so reasonable [. . .], not to be shy over it" ["grade so vernünftig [. . .], dabei nicht scheu zu werden"] (*DKV,* Vol. 4, 242). Yet this self-restraint is unimportant insofar as the donkey's scream sets off a chain reaction that entangles their self-restraint in an event within which they are powerless; the nonhuman entities – the donkey, the horses, the reins, the coach – evade human control and, conversely, involve humans in an action in which they can no longer actively intervene. In the end, it is pure coincidence that parts of the carriage are left lying around "overturned" ["umgestürzt"], "shattered" ["zerschmettert"], "broken" ["zerbrochen"], and "tattered" ["zerrissen"], whereas Kleist and Ulrike were "completely fresh and healthy [. . .] embracing each other" ["ganz frisch u gesund [. . .] umarmten"] (243).

---

[19] "ein Esel hinter uns ein abscheuliches Geschrei erhob."
[20] "Die armen Pferde [. . .] hoben sich hoch in die Höhe und gingen spornstreichs mit uns in vollem Carriere über das Steinpflaster der Stadt durch. Ich griff nach dem Zügel, aber die hingen ihnen, aufgelöst, über der Brust, u ehe ich Zeit hatte, an die Größe der Gefahr zu denken, schlug schon der Wagen mit uns um, u wir stürzten – Und an einem Eselsgeschrei hing ein Menschenleben?"

The epistolary scenes show the supposed autonomy of human action being confronted with a contingency that evolves from the actions of non-human beings. This is emblematic of Kleist's life, as well as of life in the modern age, which is imprinted with a slapstick character. In Kleist's texts the contingency is closely related to the semantics of the *Fall*: be it literally or metaphorically, theologically or juridically, Kleist's texts repeatedly deal with falling, stumbling and toppling, as well as with the incident (*Vorfall*), the Biblical Fall of Man (*Sündenfall*), and the legal case (*Rechtsfall*) (see Neumann 1994; Földenyi 1999, 121–125; Pusse 2004, 31–49; Ott 2012). Scholarship has repeatedly stated that in *Der zerbrochne Krug* the semantics of the *Fall* are the center of attention. There is no need, therefore, to discuss in further detail the stumbling of the language with which Judge Adam falls into the text, and the stuttering of the body, which constantly produces failures.

Another well-known incident of relevance is the theatrical case of *Der zerbrochne Krug*: Goethe's premier in Weimar on March 2, 1808. Even though the eyewitness accounts are unclear and the theme of the complete failure of staging emerges only gradually, the reports contain a few points of interest with regard to slapstick. A review in the *Allgemeine deutsche Theater-Zeitung* from March 11, 1808, states:

> But help me, Heaven help! Now we have to listen to the second and the hour-long third act, which consists completely in a single trial interrogation, all in one sitting. The narrator does a good job, and it is interesting because of him, but the dramatic poet must not remove the discovered truth so infinitely far from the final confession. His ignorance of every dramatic rule proves that the author is not a playwright.[21]   (qtd. in Sembdner 1996, 226)

Here the individual criticisms of the other eyewitness reports are found bundled together: the play is too long and clunky; it lacks both action and a dynamic storyline, so there is nothing to see – everything is just 'listening.' The viewers quickly receive the knowledge about the perpetrator, but the final revelation is "infinitely" postponed. Altogether it shows that Kleist seemingly does not master the rules of drama and that he is capable of telling, but not showing.

It is striking that the criticism denies the piece the crucial characteristic features of slapstick: the missing tempo, the optical uneventfulness, the narrative static lacking every sensuality and liveliness. As the entire plot structure could apparently not sustain the tension required for public entertainment as well, the

---

[21] "Aber hilf Himmel, hilf! Nun müssen wir noch den zweiten und den [. . .] eine Stunde währenden dritten Akt, alles ein einziges Verhör, mit anhören. Dem Erzähler kommt es wohl zu, und wird bei ihm interessant, aber der dramatische Dichter darf die entdeckte Wahrheit nicht so unendlich weit vom endlichen Bekenntnis entfernen. Daß der Verfasser kein Dramatiker ist, beweist seine Unkunde jeder dramatischen Regel."

piece had to fail. However, all critiques of *Der zerbrochne Krug* refer to the staging of Kleist's piece and not to the written text, which was not published until 1811. One could excuse Kleist from wrongdoing in this respect, because reproaches should be directed at Goethe's stage production. Yet, such an assertion should be examined in the text itself and its own attempt at theatricality.

Even a superficial view of the text reveals that all the characters of the piece are involved in slapstick scenes, be it as agents or recipients. Chronologically arranged, this applies to the "hero," the jug (Graham 1955; for additional analyses on things as actors in dramatic texts in general and in Kleist's *Der zerbrochne Krug* in particular, see Klotz 2000 and Klotz et al. 2013, 425–441). In the sense of a "biography of a thing" (Kopytoff 1986), Ms. Marthe reports on its 'life story': the jug is repeatedly involved in struggles, wars and catastrophes, it is captured, falls out the window, ends up in a fire, yet, unlike the people in its environment, the jug survives all these events unscathed (see *DKV*, Vol. 1, 312–314) until it is finally broken by Adam during his night visit to the room of Marthe's daughter Eve. This then invokes the next slapstick scene, which involves the jug, Adam, Eve, and Eve's fiancé Rupprecht. Adam extortionately acquired access to Eve's room, but Rupprecht's arrival forced him to flee, which Rupprecht reports to the court without knowing that the fugitive is the judge himself. Rupprecht describes how upon his entrance the jug falls from the window sill – Adam had put his wig on it and when he grabs it during his escape, the jug falls over (371). Adam jumped out the window but remained hanging on the vine leaves and Rupprecht struck him with a doorknob until Adam threw sand in his eyes and could flee, leaving the wig behind and carrying with him two head wounds (321–323). It is this scene with the destruction of the jug, the loss of the wig, and the wounding of Adam's body from which the rest of the action takes place. Adam is now forced to explain his head wounds and the absence of the wig to the clerk Licht and to the court counselor Walter. In each case, Adam tells fictional slapstick scenes, e.g., from his fall out of bed (287–289) and the setting of the wig on a candle (340), so as to conceal the events that occurred in Eve's bedroom. Furthermore, court counselor Walter's involvement in slapstick scenes extends beyond his role as recipient of Adam's stories. The shaft of his carriage has broken, so Walter has himself experienced a typical slapstick collision with the world of things (293). A final slapstick scene is found at the end of the piece: with Adam's guilt exposed, he escapes from the courthouse and is watched through the window by those who are left behind:

> Licht (*at the window*): Look, like Judge Adam I beseech you,
>   Up hill, down hill, as he flees the wheel and gallows,
>   The ploughed up, wintered field stomped through!

> Walter: What? Is that Judge Adam?
>
> Licht: Indeed!
>
> Several: Now he comes on the street. Look! Look!
> How the wig whips his back!²² (*DKV*, Vol.1, 357)

The fact that the wig punishes Adam as he flees can be understood in the sense of a double body (see Matala de Mazza 2001, 167–170): the wig represents the judicial authority which Adam himself should embody, and renders punishment by whipping the bared body of the offender. Moreover, this scene is connected with a previous one in which Rupprecht hits Adam's coat "for want of a hump" ["[i]n Ermangelung des Buckels"] (*DKV*, Vol. 1, 355). The positions are repeatedly exchanged between subject and object: Rupprecht, the defendant, becomes the persecutor, the judge's coat becomes the punished object. Later on, Adam takes the role of the punished object, while the wig moves up in status to the subject of persecutor.

As these examples demonstrate, slapstick scenes are omnipresent in Kleist's *Der zerbrochne Krug*. The obfuscation and the exposure of the initial crime are grouped around slapstick events which shape the course of events from beginning to end. Given all the action connected with these slapstick scenes, how is it possible that the Weimar public described the piece as entirely lacking dynamism, liveliness, and acrobatics? The answer is obvious: none of the described slapstick scenes is shown on the stage – all of them are either told later on or, in the case of Adam's flight, in the mode of teichoscopy. Kleist's drama thus brings slapstick not in the form of a showing, but as a telling on the stage. The result is the missing of a "strong sensualization" ["starke[] Versinnlichung"], which can be realized, following Schütze, only in a dramatic mode. This perspective seems to confirm the findings of the contemporary eyewitnesses, who attributed the failure of the production to Kleist's text. Conversely, Goethe's directorial work, which was aimed at declamation and a "restraint of movement" ["Gebundenheit der Bewegung"] (Hinck 1959, 99), only furthered the text's preference of the linguistic play over the physical action.

---

22 "Licht (*am Fenster*): Seht, wie der Richter Adam, bitt' ich euch,
Berg auf, Berg ab, als flöh er Rad und Galgen,
Das aufgepflügte Winterfeld durchstampft!
Walter: Was? Ist das Richter Adam?
Licht: Allerdings!
Mehrere: Jetzt kommt er auf die Straße. Seht! seht!
Wie die Perücke ihm den Rücken peitscht!"

The question remains, however, whether or not the claim that in Kleist's play slapstick scenes take place exclusively off stage and are then later brought on the stage by means of telling is actually accurate. In considering *On the Gradual Production of Thoughts Whilst Speaking* [*Über die allmähige Verfertigung der Gedanken beim Reden*, 1805/1806], Kleist's texts are marked by a signature suddenness. They consequently characterize themselves by reality produced through a speech act. To illustrate this, a passage from *Der zerbrochne Krug* should be reconsidered in more detail. In reply to Licht's question of how Adam got his head wounds, Adam answers:

> Adam: [. . .] With the accursed billy-goat,
> I fought at the stove, if you like. Now I know.
> Because I lose my balance, and so to speak,
> Drowning in air, I reach around me,
> Grab those pants that were drenched last night
> And hung on the frame of the oven.
> Now I grab them, you understand, thinking
> To hold fast to my goal, and now tearing
> The band; now, band and pants and I, overturn,
> And my head with the brow leveled
> With the oven, just where a billy-goat
> Thrust out his nose around the corner.
>
> Licht (*laughs*): [. . .]²³ (DKV, Vol. 1, 289)

Researchers have noted that Adam's claim to have fallen on a goat, an animal considered as a symbol of sexuality, exposes exactly what Adam wants to obscure (see Schmidt 2003, 70). While this observation focuses on the symbolism of Adam's speech, another observation arises when analyzed with a stronger consideration of the bodily action. Adam invents a slapstick event to explain the physical marks on

---

23 "Adam: [. . .] Mit dem verfluchten Ziegenbock,
Am Ofen focht' ich, wenn ihr wollt. Jetzt weiß' ich's.
Da ich das Gleichgewicht verlier, und gleichsam
Ertrunken in den Lüften um mich greife,
Faß' ich die Hosen, die ich gestern Abend
Durchnäßt an das Gestell des Ofens hing.
Nun faß ich sie, versteht ihr, denke mich,
Ich Tor, daran zu halten, und nun reißt
Der Bund; Bund jetzt und Hos' und ich, wir stürzen,
Und Häuptings mit dem Stirnblatt schmettr' ich auf
Den Ofen hin, just wo ein Ziegenbock
Die Nase an der Ecke vorstreckt.
Licht (*lacht*): [. . .]"

his body, which resulted from violence sustained in another, real slapstick scene. It is striking that one can watch the invention itself and, in this context, Adam's response changes from telling to showing: Adam begins in the past tense ("I fought" ["focht ich"]) and still seems to be on the search for a suitable incident, which gets caught by his counterpart ("if you like" ["wenn ihr wollt"]). After the fictitious event is conceptually designed in an outline ("Now I know" ["weiß' ich's"]), Adam changes into the present tense: the slapstick experience becomes the current present ("lose" ["verlier"], "reach around me" ["greife"], "Grab" ["Fass ich"], "tearing" ["reißt"], "overturn" ["stürzen"]); he uses the past tense only for actions that took place before the depicted event, such as the hanging of the wet pants. Yet, the temporal change of the verb from the past tense to the present tense is not the only characteristic of the transition from telling to showing. A realization and animation of the scene is accomplished by the simulation of *hic et nunc*: the creation of the present in a temporal sense keeps pace with the tense of the verbs from the accumulation of temporal adverbs, all of which decisively mark the 'now' of the event ["Jetzt," "Nun," "just"]. Although such deictic adverbs are missing for the 'here,' a spatial realization takes place in that Adam's speech brings on the co-playing things so that slapstick becomes present on the stage as an interaction, i.e., a togetherness and opposition between the human being and the world of things.

Adam's time-covering, almost time-stretching style of speech serves primarily to synchronize language and body to create an open horizon for slapstick action. This manner of speaking arises by insertions ("versteht ihr, denke mich, [Ich Tor, daran zu halten"]), allowing the body to reenact the spoken scene. The pauses in Adam's speech are equally notable. As the utterance contains a line jump after the word "tearing" ["reißt"], a pause is established to permit the actor enough time to physically act out the spoken action, briefly bringing attention to that which tears – the (waist)band ["Bund"]. Moreover, in the following verse, the semicolon after "Bund" marks a speech break, making it unclear which consequences arise from the tearing of the waistband. In the second part of the verse this ambiguity is continued by the anadiplosis of "Bund," a word that, in German, can mean both "waistband" and "union." The utterance can be read as an ellipse ("The band now tears" ["Der Bund reißt jetzt"]), whereby the "now" marks the typical slapstick moment, when the entire action is stopped in a 'freeze' and seems to be stretched to the utmost extreme before it collapses. First, the two interconnected entities of the pants and the human self ("the pants and I" ["Hos' und ich"]) are named, combined into a "we," afterwards they are brought together to the fall. Therefore, the linguistic production of the open horizon of action retains the precarious moment when the human subject loses self-control and control over things to the point of becoming the 'game ball' of physical processes, such as the tearing and falling.

When Adam's depiction of his physical interaction with the world of things is understood as implicit stage directions (see Pfister 2001, 37–38), he plays a slapstick scene that has never happened and thereby demonstrates how the staging of slapstick can alternate between a telling and a showing. In this respect, Adam's conjuring up of physical events is meta-slapstick. Licht reacts to this meta-slapstick with something the Weimar public denied the piece – a laugh. This, in turn, draws out a string of other text passages that can also be understood to demonstrate the switch from telling to showing. For example, in Adam's description of the burning of the wig (see *DKV*, Vol. 1, 340), as well as in both Rupprecht's (321–323) and Eve's (371–372) depictions of the nocturnal events, one can observe the shift from the preterite tense to the present tense, the simulation of a *hic et nunc*, and the production of an open horizon of action.

These findings indicate the need to revise the previous observation of a prevalent narrative mode in Kleist's piece. Instead one has to recognize that the narration of former (fictitious) events is effectively transferred to a dramatic mode – the 'told' is visualized, the 'telling' dynamically adjusts the staging as it is physically brought to life. Kleist's text shows how slapstick scenes are produced linguistically and physically. The failure of the Weimar performance therefore was not a result of the presentation of a *Sprechstück* on a stage whose director preferred the linguistic play over the physical. Instead, the corporally-fulfilled language of Kleist's text and Goethe's speech-driven theater were incompatible with one another. On this basis, the performance had to break to "pieces" ["Stücke"], as Goethe writes two years after the premiere (qtd. in Sembdner 1996, 230).

One spectator of the Weimar performance was Stephan Schütze, who wrote in his diary, "in the theater, *Der zerbrochne Krug*, until half-past nine" ["Im Theater der zerbrochene Krug bis halb 10"], referring again to the length of the theater evening, but saying nothing about the quality of the piece or the staging (222). It is important to demarcate that the relationship between Schütze's comic theory and Kleist's comedy is one of timing; the play came before the theory. This can be viewed as a typical constellation – it is not about an effect of theory's influence on comedic practice, but rather about a mutual exchange. Therefore, on the one hand comic texts can be considered by means of contemporary comic theories. Next to the comic theories of the romantics, *Der zerbrochne Krug* contains a connection with Schiller, who wrote that "in the comedy [. . .] everything from the moralistic forum [must] be played on the physical one, because the moralistic allows no indifference"[24] (2004, 1017). Such a projection into the physical

---

[24] "dass in der Komödie [. . .] alles von dem moralischen Forum auf das physische gespielt werden [muss], denn das moralische erlaubt keine Indifferenz."

can be recognized in Kleist's play since the question after vice and crime is represented by means of different things (above all, the jug) and a figure (Adam) driven by bodily desires. In this way the play reaches a "neutralization" ["Neutralisierung"] (1017) of the moralistic and establishes the possibility to turn the case of sexual assault into the comic. On the other hand, if one considers the comic theories on the basis of comic texts, comic theories always fall back on specific examples which are then condensed into more general principles. The impression that comic theories only capture special forms of the comic may be the result of the foundation of theory in individual examples.

Schütze does not mention *Der zerbrochne Krug* in his comic theoretical writings. Nevertheless, one can identify parallels between the play and his theory: the piece deals with the collision of the human being with the world of things. Adam is a character driven by his bodily desires and ruthlessly pursues the fulfillment of these desires against morality and law. However, to fulfill his desires, he must transverse the world of things, constantly coming into conflict with them – with jugs and wigs, vine leaves and traces in the snow, doorknobs and human bodies. Thus, Adam's autonomy is demonstrated in its limitations. The play lets an unconditioned, instinctive will collide with the resistance of things. The fact that Schütze anthropologically substantiates his comic theory is similarly observed within Kleist's play: not only does Adam carry the attributes of his biblical namesake, from Oedipus, the devil and the tomfool (*Hanswurst*) (see Wellbery 1997), in Hebrew the name simply means 'the man.' Therefore, Adam can be understood as an 'example figure' with which the *conditio humana* – that is, the integration of humankind in the world of things – with all their slapstick consequences are brought to view. This is once again represented at the end of Kleist's comedy. While the figures from the window observe how Adam flees on the "plowed winter field" ["aufgepflügte Winterfeld"] and is whipped by the wig, they see – in a theater in the theater – how Adam brings in reductionistic form humankind's position in the world onto the stage. Adam's attempt to save himself from any experience with the painful and treacherous things in the unconditional and open fails because of the fact that the things remain on his heels – if not in the form of *slapstick*, then in the form of *slapwig*.

Bibliography

Bergson, Henri. *Laughter: An Essay on the Meaning of the Comic.* Transl. by Cloudesley Brereton and Fred Rothwell. London: Macmillan, 1911.
Beyer, Marcel. "The Fast and the Furious, Juni 1801." *Unarten: Kleist und das Gesetz der Gattung.* Eds. Andrea Allerkamp, Matthias Preuss, and Sebastian Schönbeck. Bielefeld: Transcript, 2019. 213–229.
Böhme, Hartmut. "'Diese ungeheure Wendung der Dinge': Zur Wirkkraft der Objekte in Kleists Werk." *Kleist Jahrbuch* (2015): 23–46.
Bohrer, Karl Heinz. *Der romantische Brief: Die Entstehung ästhetischer Subjektivität.* Frankfurt am Main: Suhrkamp, 1989.
Brandlmeier, Thomas. "Fin de Siècle Comedy Culture." *Slapstick & Co.: Frühe Filmkomödien – Early Comedies.* Eds. Helga Belach and Wolfgang Jacobsen. Berlin: Argon, 1995. 17–75.
Dale, Alan. *Comedy is a Man in Trouble: Slapstick in American Movies.* Minneapolis: University of Minnesota Press, 2000.
Földényi, László. *Heinrich von Kleist: Im Netz der Wörter.* Transl. by Akos Doma. Munich: Matthes & Seitz, 1999.
Friedman, Norman. "Point of View in Fiction: The Development of a Critical Concept." *PMLA* 70 (1955): 1160–1184.
Goethe, Johann Wolfgang und Friedrich Schiller. "Über epische und dramatische Dichtung." *Johann Wolfgang Goethe: Sämtliche Werke nach Epochen seines Schaffens.* Münchner Ausgabe. Vol. 4.2.: Wirkungen der Französischen Revolution 1791–1797. Eds. Klaus H. Kiefer et al. Munich: btb, 2006. 126–128.
Graham, Ilse. "The Broken Pitcher: Hero of Kleist's Comedy." *Modern Language Quarterly* 16 (1955): 99–113.
Hinck, Walter. "Der Bewegungsstil der Weimarer Bühne: Zum Problem des Allegorischen bei Goethe." *Goethe-Jahrbuch* 13 (1959): 94–106.
Holm, Christine und Günter Oesterle. Eds. *Schläft ein Lied in allen Dingen: Romantische Dingpoetik.* Würzburg: Königshausen und Neumann, 2011.
Jean Paul. "Vorschule der Ästhetik." *Jean Paul: Werke.* Vol. 5: Vorschule der Ästhetik, Levana oder Erziehlehre, Politische Schriften. Munich: Hanser, 1973. 7–514.
Kleist, Heinrich von. *Sämtliche Werke und Briefe in vier Bänden.* Eds. Ilse-Marie Barth, Klaus Müller-Salget, Stefan Ormanns, and Hinrich C. Seeba. Frankfurt am Main: Deutscher Klassiker Verlag, 1987–1997 (=*DKV*).
Kling, Alexander. "Aus dem Rahmen fallen: Dingtheorie, Narratologie und das Komische (Platon, Vischer, Loriot)." *Res und verba: Die Narrative der Dinge.* Eds. Martina Wernli and Alexander Kling. Freiburg i.Br.: Rombach, 2018. 309–332.
Klotz, Volker. *Gegenstand als Gegenspieler: Widersacher auf der Bühne: Dinge, Briefe, aber auch Barbiere.* Vienna: Sonderzahl, 2000.
Klotz, Volker, et al. *Komödie: Etappen ihrer Geschichte von der Antike bis heute.* Frankfurt am Main: Fischer, 2013.
Kopytoff, Igor. "The Cultural Biography of Things: Commoditization as Process." *The Social Life of Things: Commodities in Cultural Perspective.* Ed. Arjun Appadurai. Cambridge: Cambridge University Press, 1986. 64–91.
Kraft, Stephan. *Zum Ende der Komödie: Eine Theoriegeschichte des Happyends.* Göttingen: Wallstein, 2011.

Latour, Bruno. *We Have Never Been Modern*. Transl. by Catherine Porter. Cambridge: Harvard University Press, 1993.
Latour, Bruno. *Reassembling the Social: An Introduction to Actor-Network-Theory*. Oxford: Oxford University Press, 2005.
Lehmann, Johannes F. "'Das Vorhandenseyn einer Körperwelt': Widerständige Dinge zwischen Komik und Zufall in der romantischen Komiktheorie Stephan Schützes und bei E.T.A. Hoffmann." *Schläft ein Lied in allen Dingen: Romantische Dingpoetik*. Eds. Christiane Holm and Günter Oesterle. Würzburg: Königshausen und Neumann, 2011. 121–134.
Lehmann, Johannes F. "Vom Leben und Tod der Dinge: Zur Aktualität der romantischen Komiktheorie Stephan Schützes." *Limbus – Australisches Jahrbuch für germanistische Literatur- und Kulturwissenschaft* 5 (2012): 105–121.
Lehmann, Johannes F. "Stephan Schütze – Dichter, Publizist, Komiktheoretiker." *Magdeburger Literaten von der Frühen Neuzeit bis zur Gegenwart*. Eds. Dagmar Ende and Thorsten Unger. Heidelberg: Winter, 2015. 85–105.
McLeish, Kenneth. *The Theatre of Aristophanes*. London: Thames and Hudson, 1980.
Matala de Mazza, Ethel: "Recht für bare Münze. Institutionen und Gesetzeskraft in Kleists 'Zerbrochenem Krug'." *Kleist Jahrbuch* (2001): 160–177.
Moliere. "Amphitrion. Comédie." *Oeuvres de Moliere*. Nouvelle Édition. Tome Sixiéme. Paris: Michel de l'Ormeraie, 1734. 21–128.
Neumann, Gerhard. Ed. *Heinrich von Kleist: Kriegsfall – Rechtsfall – Sündenfall*. Freiburg i.Br.: Rombach, 1994.
Novalis. "Blütenstaub [Nach dem Erstdruck im Athenaeum 1798]." *Novalis: Gesammelte Werke*. Ed. Hans Jürgen Balmes. Frankfurt am Main: Fischer, 2008. 390–416.
Ott, Michael. "Der Fall ins Drama: Über Kleists Dramenanfänge." *Der Einsatz des Dramas: Dramenanfänge, Wissenschaftspoetik und Gattungspolitik*. Eds. Claude Haas and Andrea Polaschegg. Freiburg i.Br.: Rombach, 2012. 91–113.
Peacock, Louise. *Slapstick and Comic Performance. Comedy and Pain*. New York: Palgrave Macmillan, 2014.
Pfister, Manfred. *Das Drama: Theorie und Analyse*. Munich: Fink, 2001.
Pusse, Tina-Karen. *Von Fall zu Fall: Lektüren zum Lachen. Kleist, Hoffmann, Nietzsche, Kafka & Strauß*. Freiburg i.Br: Rombach, 2004.
Schelling, Friedrich Wilhelm Joseph. "Philosophie der Kunst (1802/1803)." *Ausgewählte Schriften*. Vol. 2: 1801–1803. Frankfurt a.M.: Suhrkamp, 1985. 181–564.
Schiller, Friedrich. "Tragödie und Komödie." *Friedrich Schiller: Sämtliche Werke*. Vol. V: Erzählungen. Theoretische Schriften. Ed. Wolfgang Riedel. Munich: dtv, 2004. 1017–1018.
Schlegel, Friedrich. "Kritische Fragmente." *Kritische Friedrich-Schlegel-Ausgabe*. Vol. 2. Charakteristiken und Kritiken I (1796–1801). Ed. Hans Eichner. Munich: Ferdinand Schöningh, 1967. 147–163.
Schmidt, Jochen. *Heinrich von Kleist: Die Dramen und Erzählungen in ihrer Epoche*. Darmstadt: WBG, 2003.
Schütze, Stephan. "Ueber das Komische." *Stephan Schütze: Gedanken und Einfälle über Leben und Kunst*. Leipzig: J.F. Gleditsch, 1810. 278–296.
Schütze, Stephan. *Versuch einer Theorie des Komischen*. Leipzig: Johann Friedrich Hartknoch, 1817.
Sembdner, Helmut: "Der 'Zerbrochne Krug' in Goethes Inszenierung." *In Sachen Kleist: Beiträge zur Forschung*. Ed. Helmut Sembdner. Munich: Hanser, 1994. 57–67.

Sembdner, Helmut. Ed. *Heinrich von Kleists Lebensspuren: Dokumente und Berichte der Zeitgenossen*. Munich: dtv, 1996.

Sembdner, Helmut. Ed. *Heinrich von Kleists Nachruhm: Eine Wirkungsgeschichte in Dokumenten*. Munich: dtv, 1997.

Serres, Michel. *Le Parasite*. Paris: Grasset, 1980.

Stierle, Karlheinz. "Komik der Handlung, Komik der Sprachhandlung, Komik der Komödie." *Das Komische*. Eds. Wolfgang Preisendanz and Rainer Warning. Munich: Fink, 1976. 237–268.

Warning, Rainer. "Elemente einer Pragmasemiotik der Komödie." *Das Komische*. Eds. Wolfgang Preisendanz and Rainer Warning. Munich: Fink, 1976. 279–333.

Wellbery, David E. "*Der zerbrochne Krug*: Das Spiel der Geschlechterdifferenz." *Kleists Dramen*. Ed. Walter Hinderer. Stuttgart: Reclam, 1997. 11–32.

Claudia Sassen & Stefan Schroeder
A Constraint-Based Approach to the Slapstick Seriality in Larry Semon Comedies, 1918–1920

When early film auteur Lawrence "Larry" Semon (1889–1928) signed a contract for a series of sixteen two-reel farces in 1918 with the Vitagraph Company of America, he found himself on the verge to stardom and at the peak of his creative powers.[1] As discussed in this chapter, Semon developed a distinctive cinematographic slapstick style that can be defined via two types of seriality: 1) A *closed seriality* of production features and 2) a *running-gag based, open seriality* within and between films which we refer to as an a) *inner* and b) *outer seriality*.

1 Seriality

Let us first understand what seriality means when it comes to media. Serial production, structures, and aesthetics are viewed as modern techniques of storytelling. They are closely linked to the cyclic movements of machines and their accompanying serialized industrial production (see Beil et al. 2012, 10) with the potential of continuing infinitely (see Eco 1989, 319). According to Christine Mielke, "seriality" and "series" refer to "an episode that belongs in form and content to a series" defined by a continued sequence of actions, whereas "cycle" alludes to form and manner of the sequence in terms of "closeness" or closure of a narrative arch (Mielke 2006, 45–46; cf. Weixler 2016, 145).[2] In this context, Frank Kelleter discusses an "open" and "closed variant" of seriality, also indicating that recent research prefers not to consider these separately (2013, 22–31). The principle of continuation makes recipients believe that they are enjoying the story as a novelty, yet they simply experience the return of an ever-constant scheme (Eco 1989, 305). It is again the principle of continuation which makes recipients long for every

---

1 The authors would like to thank Patrick Skacel for making available high definition prints of Semon's two reelers, Steve Rydzewski and Sven-Lars Kludig for photographic reproductions and all the publishers that have been providing high definition reproductions of Krazy Kat accessible via the Comic Strip Library (http://www.comicstriplibrary.org/copyright). We would also like to thank Ciné Ressources (http://www.cineressources.net) for granting access to hard to find back issues of cine magazines and other gems.
2 Unless otherwise noted, translations are ours.

new episode and after experiencing it to anticipate the next. The recipients' appreciation of the series is triggered by difference and variation. Likewise difference and variation are responsible for continuation and viability. Hence, a series follows its own rules and is full of paradoxes in that it is ever-finished, but never complete (see Kelleter 2013, 12). The scholarly analysis of seriality has concentrated on film and TV sequels (e.g., Hickethier 1991; Oltean 1993; Mittell 2013), on commercials from an empirical and sociological perspective (e.g., Erbeldinger and Kochhan 1998; Ayaß 2002), comic strips (Oltean 1993), adjacent genres such as photographic series (Ruchatz 1998), and music (Kursell 2012). To our knowledge, the seriality of slapstick comedy has not received sufficient scholarly attention. As Semon's seriality does not apply to film sequels in that a story develops from episode to episode, but rather to the variation of chases within and between films, we have decided to postulate a 1) *closed seriality* of production features and to break down the 2) *open* variant of *seriality* into an a) *inner* and b) *outer seriality*. While *closed seriality* defines all properties that do not undergo changes and *open seriality* encompasses features that experience variation, both types of seriality add to a trademark: for also the way in which something is being varied may occur within a restrictive framework, to which we refer as *constraints*.

The following sections explore the features and the function of these types of seriality and the constraints to which they adhere by examining in detail a common scenario in Semon films and an essential component of slapstick comedy broadly: the chase sequence.

2 A set of basic Semonesque production features

The early Semon comedies from 1918 to 1920 made a tremendous impact on contemporary audiences and critics. It is owed to Semon's high quality standards that his comedies speak even to audiences today. A long list of inventive gags and breath-taking stunts, both flawlessly performed, left his colleagues such as Buster Keaton (1895–1966) in awe: unusual camera angles and occasionally an experimental, yet an ever-harmonious exploitation of the cinematic frame (e.g., *Solid Concrete* 1920, *Passing the Buck* 1919); accurate continuity and timing (e.g., *His Home Sweet Home* 1919); ballet-like choreographed chase sequences (e.g., *Gall and Golf* 1917, *Huns and Hyphens* 1918); and a connected story with gags embedded in the action to advance the story. All these attributes suggest there was some kind of documentation that was accompanying production in the form of an "illustrated scenario" known today as story board. With pictures still on orthochromatic base, Semon's films elaborate the clarity of geometrical foreground and background structures and shape a world that in retrospect might be called a surrealist one, not least because Semon had among his admirers René Clair or Petr Král (see Florey 1923 and Král 1969). Bricks ultimately held together by the wallpaper (e.g., *Hindoos and Hazards*, 1918), bicycles swiftly passing by motorbikes (e.g., *The Suitor*, 1920), people choosing shortcuts through walls or ceilings in order to flee their malefactors (e.g., *Humbugs and Husbands*, 1918) or over roofs in order to dash from rural areas to the big city (e.g., *The Star Boarder*, 1918; *Huns and Hyphens*, 1918) add to an anarchist system in which reality and dreams do not contradict – which are also key features of surrealism (see Burdorf, Fasbender, and Moenninghoff 2007, 742–743).

Ultimately contributing to the set of distinctive production features, Semon's screen persona "Larry" has been resonating with audiences of all generations. Larry, dressed in giant overalls complete with his derby, typically counters his self-afflicted predicaments thanks to frolicking cleverness. His contradictory face, once described by Jean-Jacques Couderc as sporting "suspicious, yet worried eyes, lips shaping a smirk that was more diabolic than charming" (2000, 288), makes Semon one of the most recognizable and conspicuous characters in film history.

3 Contesting customary slapstick comedy

After a series of attempts (see *Moving Picture World* 1917, 1707), Semon eventually had managed to establish a marketing niche for his work: he took advantage of cinemagoers, who had started to complain about customary slapstick comedy, because they felt that the frequent and erratic chase sequence, notoriously collapsing people, and gooey missiles were not engaging at all (see *Picture-Play Magazine* 1920, 77). It is not that Semon spared his audience pie throwing and a fade-out of a comedian kissing the leading lady, for instance. Nor could he do without chases in cars or on motorcycles. The Semon comedy promised audiences a rigorous program that reached beyond mere spectacle of the gag. The storyline leading up to the kiss in a given episode made sense to cinemagoers and chases were equipped with gags worthwhile so that the impression of "darned foolishness" (77) could be dispelled. Semon knew how to rework the erraticness and superficiality of roughhouse in that he enriched it by existential groundedness. Hence, he countered yet did not eliminate the irregularities of roughhouse and made it void of disturbing desemantisation: in the 1910s, many comedians were upsetting the world order to the point that particular gags had no obvious meaning within a scene and did not help to foster the development of the plot. Semon, in his movies from 1918–1920, worked to reconfigure roughhouse by presenting irregularities in the storyline, but only insofar as they would serve as gags and be subsumed in a broader narrative. As contemporary news writer Herbert Howe noted, Semon "put slapstick into artistic backgrounds and unfold[ed] a connected story" (1920, 25) in that his gags developed from the plot. Semon equipped his comedies with patterns through which he gave audiences confidence in "the way the laughs [were] worked up" and guaranteed them that they would experience "some ingenuity in the action" (*New York Dramatic Mirror* 1916, 34).

4 A slapstick world in response to itself and to the patterns of technical constraints

Semon often relied on the impact of industrial constructions such as gas holders (e.g., *Humbugs and Husbands*, 1918) or water tanks (e.g., *His Home Sweet Home*, 1919), concrete factories (e.g, *Solid Concrete*, 1920) and fire escapes (e.g., *Frauds and Frenzies*, 1918; *Humbugs and Husbands*; *Dull Care*, 1919) and used their patterned shapes to an aesthetic effect serving slapstick humor. All actors in these comedies frequently find themselves couched between geometric lines. They live between rows of telegraph poles that effectively represent vanishing points on screen and gas holders constructed of regular diagonals. In *Humbugs and Husbands*, structures are taken to another level when Semon boards a car of rims in spiral design and drives up a building's wall and roof, tracing its rectangular shapes, then glides over the wires of telegraph poles and slides down a pillar only to touch ground again. These recurring patterns of tracing the geometry of the setting do not only provide Semon comedies with recognizability and reliability – a trademark of sorts for the slapstick style he used – but also mirror the conditions of the silent black and white moving image that, although restrictive in some sense, provided Semon access to new technical possibilities. In this light, orthochromatic film prompted make-up artists, cameramen, and actors to experiment in order to achieve solid methods for realizing a cinematic vision. So, despite its missing sound and color/panchromatic base, the limited film technology in the 1910s was made profitable and led to the creation of an abstract and mysterious world that quite often seemed to come close to a sketch.

5 Semon and Herriman: two different approaches with a similar outcome

While Semon made the best of what the medium film offered him, contemporary cartoonist George Herriman (1880–1944) intentionally narrowed down his artistic possibilities with his cartoon series of *Krazy Kat and Ignatz*, which featured both Semon and Herriman and arrived at a production atmosphere and design features quite similar to that of Semon's works (see Figure 1). We will examine Semon's repertory of production features in his comedy by comparing his work to that of Herriman.

Herriman was known for his collaboration with film comedians (Tisserand 2010, 6), had the full gamut of drawing and linguistic facilities at his command, and could bend and distort the newspaper medium as he pleased (see Blackbeard 2002, 118). Most prominently with his three-decade-spanning "funny animal strip" (Weixler 2016, 145) *Krazy Kat and Ignatz*, he intentionally restricted his cartoons, working with strong narrative ellipsis (Bahners 2010, 89) and purposely understylized or flat characters of mere ink outlines that did not even appear in color before the 1930s. Herriman generated a microcosm (*Coconino County*) that essentially mirrors Semon's film world and vice versa. In the fictional world of both Herriman and Semon it never really gets light, as the sun categorically does not reach its functional zenith. Moreover, there is an atmosphere that clings to its fundamental ingredient of looming melancholy and characters that can basically enter and operate every spatial context as they desire. In this vain, Krazy (one of the main characters in the cartoon) is represented in the water by Katfish and in the air by Katbird, alternatively. All transportation means in the comic are available to the characters no matter the cost – at times characters simply occupy a place or get to a place without explanation. Larry, in this regard, holds the record as a cumulative user of multiple transportation means: his hyperactivity makes him come close to a flying amphibian who is aided by modern transportation techniques which in turn are enhanced by his acrobatic abilities to leap, climb, and swim whenever he pleases. This is, for instance, showcased in the final chase of *Pluck and Plotters* (1918) where Larry fights his enemies by ship, bike, and rocket and displays the physical activities of running, diving, and climbing.

The unmotivated, ever-changing background of Coconino County informs Semon's comedies. The vast movement types and the quick transformation of rural to urban settings from scene to scene takes place in the Semon comedies in a similar fashion as it did in the comic. Semon comedies also feature a vast number of different backgrounds, typically when the camera follows Larry and

Figure 1: An episode of Herriman's *Krazy Kat and Ignatz* of 30 April 1916. http://www.comicstriplibrary.org/display/7.

his chasers to a landmark such as a barn whose roof needs to be ascended, since Larry hopes to get rid of his pursuers for good. When the orientation of pursuit changes back towards the starting point of a given chase, the background of the initial route is substituted by a completely different background. This is the case in *Huns and Hyphens*, where Larry and a gang of crooks fight on a dusty street, then head to said barn. Instead of following a straight path, they steer in another direction. In fact, although reason would dictate that the new path would lead them back to their initial path, they in fact do not pass the same dusty street again. Instead they find themselves within a setting of solid high buildings. The actors along with the audience profit from this break with logic, for the new scenery allows for a different kind of chase, in other words for more variation of the same theme.

Another basic pattern to be varied within and between films (inner and outer, or open, seriality) is at stake when Larry uses an umbrella to travel from tremendous heights back to the ground. This sequence is part of *Huns and Hyphens* and undergoes variation in *Passing the Buck*, *The Star Boarder* and *The Fly Cop*. Instead of a horrible fall, Larry glides smoothly through a world of different backgrounds made available through back projection, either solitary or accompanied by the villain he seeks to fight. Evidently, the flying subjects move away from their local origin of chase. They clearly head into the opposite direction only to end up at their starting point by a final vertical drift from the upper rim of the picture, as though out of nowhere (*Huns and Hyphens*, *The Star Boarder*). To this end, nothing can explain this scenery, except that Larry and the occasional accompanying villain could have surrounded the whole world – or at least the whole town.

Even Herriman's bricks, of which Ignatz dedicates at minimum one per episode to Krazy Kat's hindhead, come up in Semon comedies. Here the "bricks" markedly proliferate, namely in chase sequences that lead through walls for reasons of economy of itinerary or in scenes that have the protagonists break through roofs and ceilings, also causing a hazard to their heads. While Larry potentially recovers from impact in a "cartoon-like ability to regenerate" (Marschall 2007, 557) in an ever-different role, Krazy and Ignatz resurrect in a genuine cartoon ability to regenerate. However, Coconino County and Semon's Vitagraph world differ in the way in which they were effected: while Herriman deliberately reduced his design possibilities in order to enrich his spectrum to convey meaning, Semon purposely used the restrictions he was prescribed by the medium film to their best outcome in a most productive, constructive, and creative way. What in fact seemed to limit his creative opportunities, Semon used in perfection to devise his own artistic and aesthetic style. Many examples in the following will further elaborate how restrictions and constraints of the black and white silent screen became adapted by Semon as an artistic language that carries its own meaning and specific effects.

6 *Hindoos and Hazards*: a constraint-based pilot

Hindoos and Hazards could be regarded as pilot movie to the new series of two-reelers in terms of atmosphere, design, and seriality. Two-reelers testify how well Semon (and his alter ego Larry) worked for the constraint-based orthochromatic black and white medium that made every reddish tone appear black, and blues were reformulated as a light grey, causing water-blue eyes to become diaphanous. At the same time, it shows how well Semon knew to employ his cinematic conditions: the film's medium gives Semon's frail body with its spiderlike arms even more a ghostly, sketchy appearance. His whitened, boney, "dismal visage" as of someone "from the undertaking business" (Bartlett and Kelly 1918, 67) that seems to melt with his derby into an inseparable unit (e.g., *Dunces and Dangers* 1918) leads to an even sharper jawline and resonates with the aforementioned geometrical lines of street architecture.

Semon responded to the restricted medium with the construction of an abstract world in which painstakingly crafted make up and costumes echo said restrictions in an artistic manner. His artistic means define the diegesis by giving the Semonesque slapstick world its characteristic shape: as its inhabitants are moving within the boundaries of this fictional world, they seem made for it and, vice versa, this world seems exclusively reserved for them. Their costume and make up save them from visually drowning within the razor-sharp architecture. Likewise, each character of Semon's world would be unable to survive in any other world and costume. Hence, makeup and outfits become life-saving gadgets quite in the vain of biological mimicry: they correspond to an aggressive and most conspicuous design that cannot be ignored. In particular, Semon takes advantage of the circumstances and comes along like a fashion icon: clad in slightly altered – yet always loud – costume with every new comedy, quite frequently only with a modified pattern of his tie.

Larry drew from a basic design pool of grease paint and heavy eyeliner, baggy pants, and shirts of checked and striped patterns that extrapolate the given geometrical structures and culminate in Semon's edgy signature eyebrows (see Figures 2 and 3). In his comedies, Larry frequently reacts with a foolish grin and a frozen stare, amplified by his kohl-rimmed eyes. At the time of his first two-reelers, this make up was often accompanied by eyeshadow that he extended to his eyebrows. His blankness and frozenness could not have contrasted more with the physical havoc of slapstick and might have been an allusion to the so-called "shell shock syndrome." The condition first described psychological trauma of soldiers who had escaped the trenches of WWI, but the term soon became associated with malingering in some contexts (Jones, Fear, and Wessely 2007, 1641). The latter might have been an incentive to integrate shell shock into comedy; however, it

Figure 2: Lobby card from *Traps and Tangles* (1918) that depicts the fashionista-like quality of the Larry Semon persona, his leading lady Madge Kirby and Otto Lederer (from right to left). Authors' collection.

was common for early slapstick movies to not spare any group of people mockery of any kind, notably the solo films of Stan Laurel (see Everson 1980, 21). The fights of the World War might as well have found their mirror in the sequences of slapstick escape.

Whenever Larry flees, the shapes of his costume stand out prominently, their preciseness aiding the pursuit (see Figure 4). The different stages of the chase sequence subsequently follow precise timing. Likewise, exactness and geometry generate anonymity and to a certain degree even immobility, resulting in an industrialization of chase in that only particular forms of exit are allowed (as a form of closed seriality within an open seriality): frequently, Larry's sole choice in the escape is balancing over telegraph wires or leaping from the top floor in order to escape his foes. While pursuers multiply, the opportunities to escape in the actual situation however do not. He cannot take the way out by crossing the road under him (e.g., *Hindoos and Hazards*) or by tiptoe-ing down the stairs next door. While the number of emergency exits per situation usually narrows to one, Larry, in spontaneous response, discovers new options to react to this closed system (as a form of open seriality within a closed seriality). He thereby not only stretches his inventory to handle the challenge of incremental

Figure 3: Publicity shot for *Passing the Buck* (1919) with Semon's signature stare that probably was a nod to the shell-shock syndrome, a term coined in WWI. From Ciné Pour Tous, 22 May 1920, No. 38, back cover, http://www.cineressources.net/consultationPdf/web/o000/373.pdf.

restriction, but also processes the given patterns as they are made available in order to produce new ones.

Yet Larry acts in an intelligent world, which he counters with blissful ignorance. Even the telegraph poles, as being painstakingly placed, register intelligence. His survival is owed more to luck than understanding even if he is shown deliberating his options. In Semon's comedies, danger is towering everywhere. Larry is exposed to a secularized system in which nobody comes to his aid unless he subjects the given technical settings to his purposes, even if by coincidence. In *Hindoos and Hazards*, one idea unfolds through variation (inner seriality) into a complete plot that feels like one big chase, although there is some initial sequence that prepares polarization: tourist Frank Alexander snatches an invaluable necklace from Indian idol Vichnou, which results in a gang of priests pursuing him. He stumbles across Larry and thrusts the necklace into his hand. Larry does not want to part with the necklace, so then a fast and scary pursuit begins. Trying to rid himself of his ever-proliferating persecutors, Larry makes use of every gadget available. Whenever he dares to show traces of feeling at ease, his opponents emerge from the most remote of hideaways.

The appearance of Larry's pursuers, on the one hand, is unmotivated as they seem to materialize from nothing, bare of any information system. On the other hand, all of them strive for one goal: to reclaim the necklace. In one instance, Larry rushes like a bee-stung funambulist on telegraph wires across a road to which he has resorted. As the antagonists creep up the poles from either side, he jumps onto a flatbed truck passing underneath, landing on a load of bricks, and finds himself again eye-to-eye with his adversaries. Turning to an empty streetcar crossing, he takes a seat at its front, facing the recipient with an expression of deepest relief. Within seconds, his enemies surface from the other seats, prophetically expecting him. Larry's movements of escape proliferate in that they are mirrored: whenever he flees, the others follow. Whenever he does not flee, the others remain in their position, waiting. When Larry rises on the tram, his pursuers rise as well, when Larry sits down, then his pursuers sit down as well. Thus, a pursuit multiplies the movement of the pursued.

With regard to production features, Semon's comedies employ a specific formal schematization which leads up to the larger entity of a *closed seriality*: cinematic narration operates according to its own rules. Here these rules have been

Figure 4: The geometrical shapes of Semon's world were extrapolated in his costume design and make up. Illustration based on *The Sawmill* (1921).

established by Semon, who makes them visible and comprehensible as such for his audience – i.e., he reveals to recipients his rules as being very specific ones of formal schematization. In effect, Semon comedies create and define their own closed seriality by creating reoccurring formal and aesthetic means. For instance, *Hindoos and Hazards* creates and amplifies tension from one situation to the next, without regard for precipitation or speed, although in the end the image of pursuers and pursued blur and dissolve. The comedy profits from signature photography and Semon's acting. Only Larry and his stock company populate the screen, emphasizing the atmosphere of utter seclusion. Moments of fear alternate with moments of deceptive safety. Not only is Larry forced to align with these patterns, but also the viewer is required to do so in order to follow and understand the comedies' plotline. Larry flees and escapes his antagonists, yet he does not escape the world of constraints mirrored in the repetitiveness of situations. Indeed, audiences see the patterns of seriality in every new Semon comedy as well as in every single situation into which Larry stumbles. They learn that this world, which is functioning within its own rules and is so different from naturalism, can offer no escape for a person obviously designed for it. This, in turn, is something audiences can enjoy as they witness the emergence of another gag.

Whenever a chase is on, Larry experiences isolation. Partly it manifests in the closed seriality of his pursuers in which it is hard to tell one apart from the other. All of them wear the same make up and the same costume as a realization variant of the requirement to be not spotted by third party chasers and thus to live on. Larry can only move on by standing out (biological mimicry), whereas the chasers and extras are obliged by design to conceal themselves, adjusting to low key features of the backgrounds of their surroundings (biological mimesis).[3] This scheme of mimesis and mimicry may partly have been broken up by the fashion of the times worn by Semon's leading lady and his beauty brigade. Fashion was highly influenced by the dazzle camouflage patterns of WWI warships which, although highly erratic in execution, could be boiled down to the use of alternating dark and light stripes "to disrupt the perception of their range, heading, size, shape and speed" (Scott-Samuel et al. 2011, 1). In the fashion context, the dazzle camouflage, meant as functional mimesis, is turned into a mimicry: fashion imitates particular patterns and makes those who wear them stand out. Isolation is further emphasized by the anonymous faces of extras, a variation of biological mimesis. Among them is a taxi driver who coincidentally supports

---

3 We follow a basic definition of mimicry and mimesis (camouflage). Mimicry means to adapt to background patterns in order to stand out and thereby to survive. Mimesis relates to the adaptation of background patterns in order to become invisible and henceforth to survive; however, invisibility is normally challenged as soon as movement is involved.

Larry's chain of escape activity (e.g., *Hindoos and Hazards*). The taxi driver hardly wears make up and thus appears as if faded. Consequently, he acts as if he was not part of the scene, unaware of the fight in the back of his car. Should Larry make advances to approach him, he would not be able to do so. Despite both of them sharing the same vehicle, there is an impenetrable, invisible wall between them.

In the opening sequence of *Huns & Hyphens,* Larry, complete with his ever-clownish tuxedo, pale face, and eager moves, evidently does not fit the company of the well-dressed high society members. However, he acts amidst them as if born into their circle. Again, the viewer perceives Larry as a clear contrast to a world that consists of its own particular constraints and regulations in which he is nonetheless fully accepted. With every new comedy it becomes obvious that Larry's main attribute is that of the fitting misfit. It makes him the artificial yet adapted subject in a world that to some extent strikes the viewer as familiar. In *Hindoos and Hazards*, Larry rests outside Frank Alexander's house and puffs away on a cigarette, while eight Hindu men are busy setting up a riot inside. Larry is unaware of the situation, as if he was as deaf to the mayhem as the film is silent. As a perfect example of creativity conjoined with a healthy ease of mind, he turns out to be a likeable chap, a character the viewer can identify with, the brilliant hero and living artist whom audiences likewise adore and maybe even envy because he always appears able to rest on the fact that with his happy-go-lucky disposition he can navigate the absurdities he faces. In the sense of comedy director E. Mason Hopper's (1885–1967) concept of slapstick, Semon gave "people a chance to laugh at something they'd cry about at home" (Swanson 1981, 26–27).

7 Constraints meeting traditions: the outcome of a most recognizable subgenre and its "double character"

In an attempt to determine characters that might qualify as Larry's predecessors, *commedia dell'arte*'s harlequin comes to mind. Harlequin's transformation throughout the history of comedy leads to Larry, who, as a child of troupers, had fully been trained in pantomime himself. Moreover, he sits positioned in a tradition of early film comedians such as Marcel Perez (1884–1929). Semon's films show that cinematography brings forth a synthesis of traditions of representation and innovation in production that attributes cinema a "'modern' double character" between Plato's (428/427–348/347 BC) *mimesis* and *diegesis*, between mechanical (optical-chemical) recording and fantastical (electrical) projection (Siegrist 2017, 350).

Taken together, these factors conjoined with Larry's impersonation of the unconventional, witty, and physical type of character, catapult his audience to a meta-level of comedy and hence allow for reflection.

Comedy as a genre features many examples of characters, which seem not quite appropriate to the world surrounding them. A famous example is Mary Chase's (1907–1981) protagonist Elwood P. Dowd, best buddy of invisible Harvey in the theatre play and later movie adaption of the same title. Dowd is a bizarre, though balanced character in yet another strange world. He finds his very own way to cope with the world around him and thereby makes audiences reflect this world on the basis of criteria different from those of everyday life. This corresponds to Larry, who is using a miniature car for transportation and a dog's den as garage (e.g., *Huns and Hyphens*). Since Semon's world puts its specific and grotesque rules forward to an extreme, innocent Larry outdoes himself: in an absurd and preposterous increase of stamina and creativity of one single person against a hostile group (which was expressed in racist terms in *Hindoos and Hazards* in the form of presenting an anonymous mass of cultural strangers), he evolves into an affable and well-tempered relatable figure. His successful escape from enemies is likely because his role is a self-fulfilling one. Accustomed to the serial concept of Semon's comedies, viewers find themselves in the position to anticipate Larry's ever-reconciliatory solution to the current predicament out of which not only he, but also everyone else involved, emerges unharmed.

Larry's secret of success is more than a matter of design style and spontaneity, but of a kind-hearted and good-humored adaptation to the fictional world in which he lives. As his character easily connects with audiences, he and his viewers jointly pass through this world in a safe manner and remain unharmed. Moreover, Larry's chase sequences are the epitome of virtuosity owed to the use and re-use of the simplest props: tables, doors, roofs, flagpoles and umbrellas. So, the concept of constraints is at stake here again. To be more precise, the concept of working with constraints in a creative way is mirrored in the use of simple and reoccurring props. Although in this case it is not a question of technical restrictions, Semon adapts the narration concept of reoccurrence even in the decision for these props. Narration, mise-en-scène, decoration, and acting thereby collectively effect an aesthetic whole.

With the meta-level of comedy and its technical and aesthetic conditions another feature of the restricted structure of silent screen comedy emerges: the asynchronous presentation of image and words of which the latter follow the former, since in early cinema it was common to let title cards clarify the action. The viewer perceives the image, muses about its significance, and only then reads and understands. Likewise known for cartoons and comic strips – wherein the combination of text and action is tied up in one panel – the process of visual perception and graphostylistic disambiguation mirrors the sluggish thinking process in Larry's face, which was once described as a "blank screen visage" of a "lackadaisical exterior" (Gentz 1919, 16). Watching Larry reflect projects the medium's slowness (in Larry's case this slowness registers through his slow processing of ideas) right into the audience. At the same time, audiences may feel related to Larry because his artificially slow way of thinking relates to the viewers' intellectual reception. The presentation and processing of image and text in silent movies has its effect on reception and intellectual processing, which moves forward step by step, one after the other and thus slower than normal. It corresponds to the way in which the thinking process has been staged with Larry: visualized and decelerated. Hence, form and content go hand in hand. At this point, the relation of silent screen's restrictions and its often cited "over-acting" is transparent: in a limited world of the yet many shades of grey between the black and white extremes, clear-cut lines and obvious alienation from the familiar (see Spies 1997, 147), grotesque facial expressions, strange body moves that might result in convulsions and exaggerated reactions, comic mannerisms, and gags of this sort are by no means novel. Semon himself had to point his boss Albert E. Smith (1875–1958) to the fact that there was "not a thing new in the comedy game" (Schallert 1920, 29). Just like his colleagues, he was relying on a bonded stock of old stunts and jokes that had obtained wide circulation, some of them laid down in newspaper cartoons, which in turn were nothing but rehashes of older ideas, ideally "with a new twist" (29).

In its early years and since, film was influenced by the stage. Exaggerated and distorted acting has characterized theater comedy throughout every century (see Ellrich et al. 174). In addition to the *commedia dell'arte* mentioned above, there are William Shakespeare's (1564–1616) comedies (Suerbaum 1989, 436–439) as well as popular comedy before and around 1900: boulevard, vaudeville, music hall theatre, or the German *Schwank* (Klotz 2007, 152–153). Moreover, there is also the art of silent stage performance *par excellence*: the pantomime (brought to perfection by Jean-Baptiste Deburau [1796–1846] in the nineteenth century) from which Semon seems to be inspired for his own make up and antics (see Mast 1979, 194–195).

A particular way of acting influenced early film slapstick: the specific aesthetic conditions in relation to necessary restrictions forced onto silver screen art go hand in hand with the grotesque interpolation of acting and actions mentioned above, for both turn out as a significantly overdrawn and schematic way of citing real-world elements. Certainly, exaggeration is not a distinctive feature of comedies: considering early *chefs-d'œuvre* of German expressionist film, exaggeration is turned into a less comic and ironic, nonetheless grotesquely overdone style to express inner states of suffering and despair. So, comedy and seriousness share the same basis. Nonetheless these two elements also mark the foundation of every credible comic effect (see Weston 1996, 296), which needs to be transferred in a suitable way to the outside, a requirement with which Semon complies. Due to the restrictions pointed out, he gives the genre its characteristic face, something that ingeniously fulfils the requirements of comic acting by serving both: the audiences' entertainment and its distance to the fictitious world, both caused by "eccentricity of characterization" (Gentz 1919, 16) and calculated alienation.

The pool of production features makes the seriality of gags identifiable as those belonging to Semon. Within this pool, there is room for variation without jeopardizing his recognizability. Variation takes place in an inner and an outer context and is responsible for the development of narrative elements, which Semon employs to form an artwork that bears an entirety of its own. The films are formally and thematically closed units whose form is continually repeated and yet varied. As a result, the films refer to themselves and become self-referential and self-fulfilling: these references are constantly generated from the same, already established form, which bears the mark of Semonesque inner closeness.

In spite of the occasional rehash of ideas such as Chaplin's gentle onlooker that Semon used in *Between the Acts* (1919), the seriality in Semon's work does not unequivocally build a chain with another sort of slapstick comedy or aims at imitating it respectively. Quite on the contrary, this subgenre has invented itself from scratch in that the influences mentioned crystallize in the new medium film with its specific constraints – if not creative constraints – and result in a completely novel way of narration. By this, the aesthetic means become a recurring value *per se*. Not only do they form narrative procedures (in terms of "somehow the content needs to be conveyed anyway"), but instead they become part of the content: form and content go together. Strikingly, this is a case of the self-fulfilling self-reference of content and aesthetics: while the restrictions of the monochrome silent screen make specific aesthetic decisions necessary, these forms emancipate completely from their prescribed starting conditions and establish a new subgenre of comedy, which now stands for itself. The genre of silent slapstick with its abstract and artificial conditions does not only make Semon's seriality distinctive, but turns it into a form of creative artistic presentation. In short, the fact that aesthetic characteristics are recognizable becomes a re-occurring value in itself for the Semon comedy, which can be varied within its restrictions again and again. Hence, recursion as a process that applies to its own output is also undeniably a matter of slapstick, at least of silent slapstick.

8 The entanglement of serialities

A feature of Semon's two-reelers is an *inner seriality* that gets complemented by means of an *outer seriality*. This is accomplished as one film connects to another by taking up the former's particular running gags. The recurring alliterations of Semon's film titles also show a sense of outer seriality, a concept that was initiated early in Semon's Vitagraph career (1916) and abandoned after seven titles into his 1918 contract. It marked a general phenomenon in the 1910s. While Larry resurfaces in nearly every new film in a different role, as son-in-law, stage hand, but most frequently as special agent, quite many of these comedies culminate in a hassle staged on the same Los Angeles multi-story building featured in *Dunces and Dangers*, *Huns and Hyphens*, *Passing the Buck*, *The Star Boarder*, and *The Fly Cop* (see Figure 5).

Resuming a gag in a Semon series did not mean its identical projection from the preceding comedy into the current one, but instead relied on the gag's variation. Its variation in turn leads to an inner seriality of the outer seriality, notably through reuse of production gadgets such as ladders, flagpoles, umbrellas, and wires. Although the thought of Semon acting on top of a roof might arouse the audience's expectation of predictable antics, the execution is highly complicated, giving way to precise complementary processes. Contemporary patrons could enjoy his films in a programmatic order at an output of one every four weeks and experience the contiguity of inter-film running gags. This is not the case today, because it is challenging to reconstruct release dates and original prints, which in the end would make a serial view speculative. From one Semon comedy to the next there was no story headline that read "to be continued next week," as was the case for contemporary serials such as Pearl White's (1889–1938) *The Perils of Pauline* (1914). Like Herriman's Krazy Kat, Semon's two-reelers had no "open-ended serial narrative" (Gardner 2013, 244) and thus offered no cliff-hangers, at least no metaphoric ones. Semon's seriality is a running gag within films and a running gag revisited between films. This is mostly culminated in a final or pre-final sequence that always comes to a different closing, mostly returning to the point where the chase started. Every variation represents a closed system; the return to the starting point symbolizes the ability of the protagonist and his foils to regenerate as soon as the next comedy begins.

The final chase of *Passing the Buck* (1919) exemplifies the entanglement of serialities through its presentation of a literal escalation. The plot rises to its culmination point while Larry and a villain crawl up to breath-taking heights. We will read this final chase as representative for Semon chase sequences (e.g., *Huns and Hyphens*, *The Star Boarder* and *The Fly Cop*, and *Dunces and Dangers*) (see Figures 6–9). In *Passing the Buck*, distinguished house detective Larry has

Figure 5: Continuity shot of Semon (right) and two unidentified actors, high and dizzy in *The Fly Cop* (1920). From *Picture Show* 1921, 7.

to take care of antique Hindu crown jewels that have arrived in an everyday bag. Derogatorily scripted and characterized crooked Hindu men exchange the bag for a similar-looking one with a bomb. An endless mix-up ensues, which ends with Larry finally in repossession of the jewels. He climbs a chandelier and resorts to the hotel's roof (see also Figure 6). A Hindu man grabs Larry's legs, follows him to the roof and snatches the bag. The Hindu man takes the lead in the chase by using a ladder to get to the next roof level. Larry tries to tumble the roof. Next, the Hindu man grabs the rope of a flagpole and climbs to its peak. Larry horizontalizes the pole, as it is now located on the same level as the second roof. The Hindu man grabs the rope again and, as a result of the shift in spatial relation, now scrambles down the rope. Initially, the Hindu man scrambles *up* the rope so he can escape Larry. Now the Hindu man scrambles *down* to eliminate Larry as his predator. Although the turning of the pole leads to a redefinition of spatial conditions, the goal to elude remains the same. The altered spatial conditions in turn lead to a change of use of the same gadget. Larry is located almost on the pole's outer corner. Once Larry reaches its peak, he whets his razor blade and threatens to cut the rope, unless the Hindu man throws the bag upwards. The Hindu man gives in to this threat, but Larry cuts the rope just the same. The Hindu man falls, and breaks through a door, which brings him back to the start of the chase sequence. Larry triumphs only to learn that Frank Alexander (another crook) armed with a mallet unexpectedly tampers with the pole's root. It is now Larry's turn to scramble down the rope. He makes the rope swing and lands on a chimney, which he also sets into pendular motion.

Larry and his break through the aforementioned door bring him back to the start. The turning point of the chase is the moment the flagpole is turned over, rendering the framing of the shot symmetrical. Considering the cost-benefit ratio with both of them ending up where they began, the action is a waste of time and energy rendered in slapstick fashion. Semon chases mirror a cybernetic circle: a closed system in which an actual value is measured against a desired value. In this context, even accidental solutions can satisfy the requirement of a desired value.

In *Huns and Hyphens*, released months before *Passing the Buck*, one chase-related focal point is an umbrella. Unlike the flagpole in *Passing the Buck* that is subsequently used by the protagonists, the umbrella is jointly operated. For the villain it signifies escape, for Larry pursuit. A difference in function is attained in the simultaneousness of use, signaling the centrality of temporality to the chase. In comparison, the flagpole's function is defined by linearity (subsequent use) and the change of spatiality.

If the narrative course of tragedy can be represented by a downward slope, the high and dizzy chase sequences of at least *Huns and Hyphens*, *Passing the Buck,* and *The Star Boarder* can be depicted by a left-turning circle. In fact, all of them end up at the same starting point on the left side of the screen. *The Fly Cop* starts left as well, however the chase is not terminated: Larry stands at the end of a ladder, which hovers above Los Angeles. The situation shifts to a metaleptic scene with Lawrence Semon, scenario writer, arguing through double-exposure with his creation Larry, in costume, of whom the latter obviously rejects to perform the resolve of the ladder scene. Fumingly, he leaves and slams the door. Semon loved to recur to this metalepsis and varied it in turn for films such as *The Headwaiter* (1919), *The Agent* (1923) and *Oh, What a Man* (1927), again producing closed circles through the inner seriality of running gags.

Hindoos and Hazards offers insight into the serial character of Semon's slapstick. Larry stands for the individual's fight against the anonymous mass in a closed world, whereby its coincidental and accidental conditions are presented as restricted aesthetics of a silent screen microcosm. The conformity of the chasers jointly wearing turbans, which stereotype the image of cultural strangers as a threat, is now placed against the uniqueness of the innocent protagonist

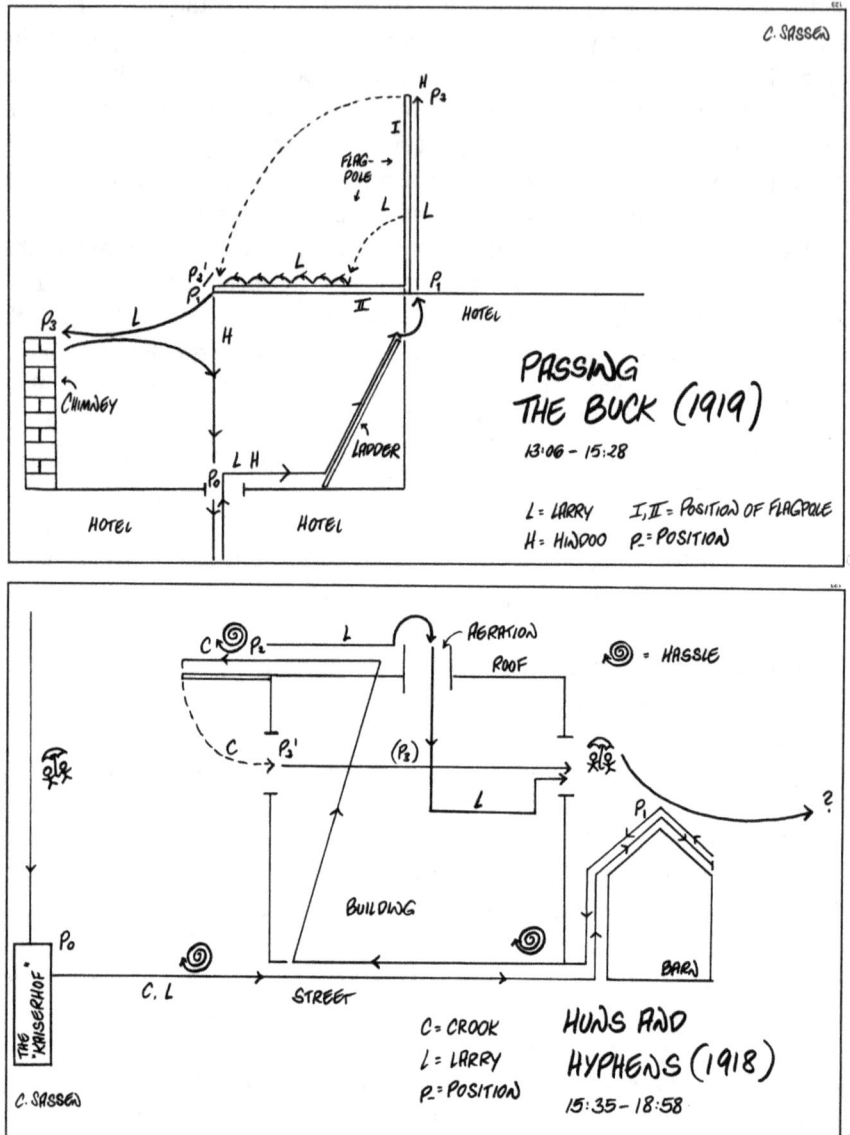

Figures 6–9: Simplified reconstructions of high and dizzy chase itineraries in Semon comedies.

Slapstick Seriality in Larry Semon Comedies — 207

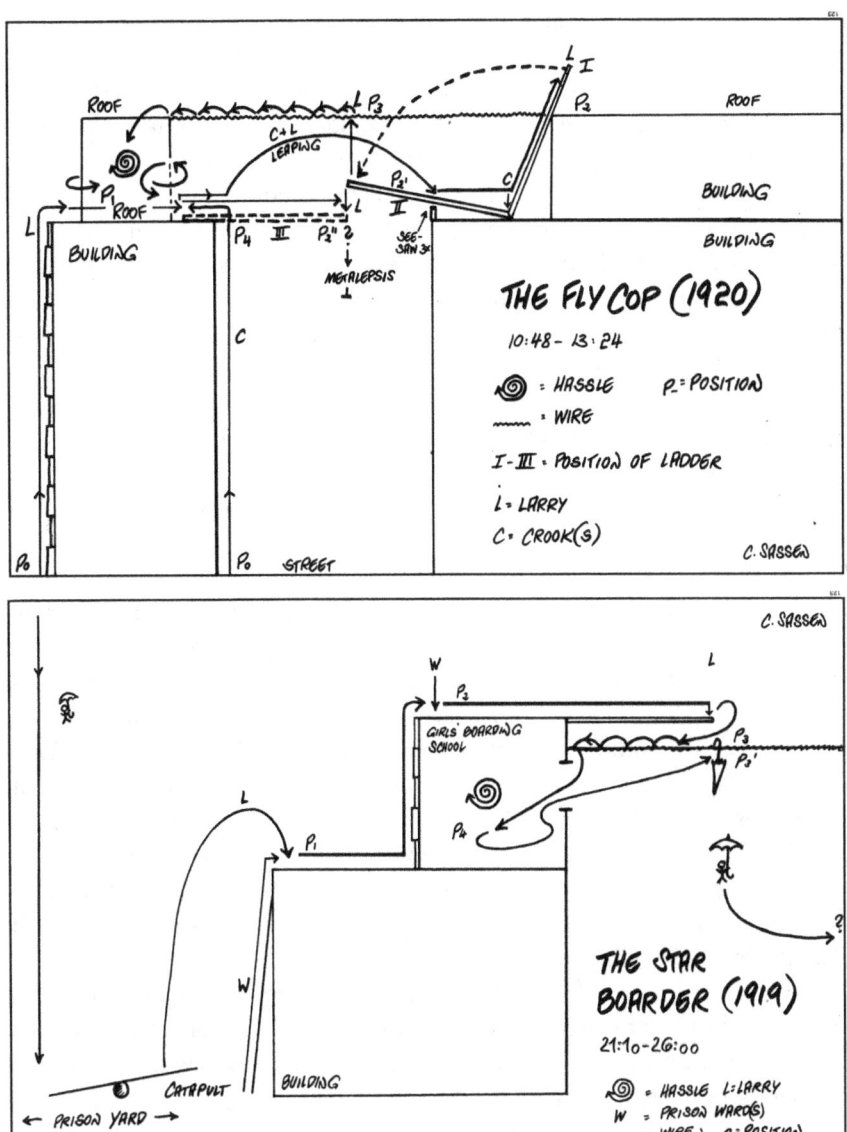

Figures 6–9 (continued)

pursued. This feature becomes even more prevalent as the chasers never turn out to be distinguishable. They mostly act as a group that never fails to display its utter inaptitude. In the beginning of *Hindoos and Hazards*, it takes eight of them to menace one single man, Frank Alexander, in order to take Vichnou's necklace from him. Despite their comparably great number, their endeavor is no success. Should Larry bump into only one of his adversaries, an action that allows for an extended view on one single person, every hope for uniqueness is shattered. This is mostly the case because each one remains interchangeable with the others in their outer appearance, goals, actions, and reactions, as if a reincarnation of the last one Larry escaped. In fact, Larry's antagonists attribute a surrealist eternity to this never-ending pursuit.

The impression of reincarnation assumes another twist: each persecutor that Larry leaves behind resurrects in the next persecutor immediately thereafter. The film's ethnocentric view on the Hindu group makes use of a racist abstract fear of the strange and the foreign, attributing an alleged explicitly dumb behavior to the portrayal of this group. Without any sensitivity for discrimination and racism, the effect on contemporary audiences is obviously intended to be laughter, for the chasers and the whole chase eventually turn out to be harmless. The chasers cannot use the majority to their advantage, for they are part of a rule that mingles them as an anonymous mass, as an immobile giant against the individual. Nevertheless, they believe themselves so strong that they even let Larry escape in situations of extreme distress and highest emergency. Their behavior creates a comic difference between their self-image and the audience's impression (cf. Greiner 1992, 99). The stereotype confirms the audience's ethnocentric perspective and consequently supports Semon's closed seriality: the closed serial connection is a prerequisite for the production rules of Semon's microcosm and so it builds in features well-known to the recipient in order to create a familiar context.

Thus, Larry's world defines a system of grotesque exaggeration typical of comedy, in particular when dealing with an over-fulfilment or under-fulfilment of the commonly expected (cf. Stockinger 2013, 28). The way in which Larry beats his chasers evidences the (accidental) creativity of a character, who knows to hide a burning cigarette on his tongue mouth closed (e.g., *Hindoos and Hazards*), to direct tiny cars without engine and radio (e.g., *Huns and Hyphens*), and to misuse without further ado the vanity of his leading lady to rid himself of precious jewels (e.g., *Hindoos and Hazards*). His persecutors, by contrast, turn out to be short-sighted and without feel for weight as they carry off a box without realizing that it does not contain anybody – first and foremost not Larry. The same applies when the Hindu men get involved with Larry's concept of converting reality into one that fits his objectives. It is tempting to believe that the pursuers force their "prey" into situations of distress; however, at second glance it becomes obvious that the pursued makes the pursuers accord with his rules, causing them distress. When Larry hides in a box, they carry it off without him; when he jumps onto a tram, they follow and copy his gestures; when he scrambles down a bridge, they splash into water. The chasers mimicking Larry's every movement might suggest their control over the person hunted. Yet viewed from an outer perspective, every control-related feature follows its own absurd rules. This is primarily caused by Larry: he turns the group's weakness mirrored in their conformity into a bizarre power that he assumes over the group and productively uses the concept of inner and outer seriality.

Finally, the principle of proliferation in *Hindoos & Hazards* is not only reflected in the chasers multiplying, but also in the abundance of inanimate elements such as holes and concrete pipes, which correspond to the at times even synchronous choreographic actions of the chasers, who frequently duck and creep around. Nevertheless, the comic effect of multiplication is most often shown by the consequent repetition of the situation, which undergoes slight variation. Part of the grotesque effect is the presentation of hunting as an end in itself, which is motivated by one initial event, but then works as the definition of the subgenre in itself. Audiences familiar with the genre will anticipate basic rules (such as the explosion of a water tower, cf. *The Grocery Clerk* 1919) and maybe even a happy ending and laugh about its carefully directed unforeseen variants. In this way, seriality prepares the ground for the concept of originality, which is the deviation from the usual. Deviation could never be perceived without an awareness of what is common, which is defined by the serial character of production features.

9 Seriality, expectations, and learning-effects

The laughter triggered by the totality of slapstick elements ranging from Larry's grotesque pursuers to his geometrically outlined clothes to his white clownish face is conditioned by what Henri Bergson describes as a specific form of inertia or mechanical stiffness stimulating deviations from the normal (1913, 21). If a gag effectively ruptures this inertia, the recipient is willing to follow the storyline of the character affected by this rupture which Bergson postulates as "some kind of cramp of will and distortion of soul" (15). Bergson's description reflects what Semon's characters act out physically. These elements connected to slapstick in general become even more ridiculous through their repetition, reverberated further through seriality.

It is almost inevitable that this *perpetual mobilé* of repetition and variation comes to a logical end only by going back to the beginning. In this light, *Hindoos and Hazards* closes in a now indeed endless row of chasers running after the original necklace thief in exactly the same room where the chase started. In *Huns and Hyphens*, everyone ends up in the same, now destroyed restaurant the recipient encountered close to the beginning. In *The Star Boarder*, Larry involuntarily returns to the prison yard from which he fled, while in *Passing the Buck* Larry and the crook fall through the same door they once intended to employ as starting point for the culminating chase. It seems inevitable that in a small, artificial world like Larry's it is obligatory to always get back to where one started from in order to provide the ground for the proverbial cartoon-like ability to regenerate. In this light, it is reminiscent of the cyclic movement of machines. In this way, the inner and outer seriality, with their concomitant running gag-like variation, also inherit the feature of an automated, closed seriality that stands for industrial design. Here variation on the base of a constant structure and production, so to speak inert features, fall into one.

Seriality positions viewers into a system of expectations within a pool of options. At the same time, they hope for a learning effect of the protagonists, but realize that this effect does not apply as it must not apply. Otherwise there would be no room for seriality and variation – like the everlasting potential for crisis in every sequel without which it could not survive. So, a disavowed learning effect becomes the indispensable requirement for seriality. Seriality perpetuates the comic plot only as long as the protagonist has not learnt to break the seriality. In fact, Larry and Frank Alexander do not stop making mistakes, while the Hindu men do not learn that their attacks result in constant failures. Larry does not learn that the Hindu men do not cease to chase him. A learning effect could at most be attributed to the fact that within the boundaries of seriality the act of resurfacing varies. With actions tested against the rules of reasonability and sense, the complete incongruity between expectation and fulfilment becomes visible (cf. Greiner 1992, 99; Bartl 2009, 14). This is achieved primarily through an increasing deviation from normativity, which is characteristic of the comic effect: the Hindu men follow Larry up the telegraph wires from both sides just as the nameless gang in *Huns and Hyphens* chases him up to the aforementioned barn roof from both sides instead of just waiting for him to come down, something that he would have done sooner or later. Just like many incidents in Semon's two-reelers this might be reminiscent of Aristotle's statement that comedy imitates "worse people" unlike tragedy which imitates "better people" (1987, 33). What exactly makes those people worse than "normal" people seems to be a combination of a lack of goodwill and stupidity in their helpless attempt at outsmarting Larry.

10 Conclusion

Larry Semon's two-reelers raise the awareness for a peculiar world whose structures are exaggerated by the principles of slapstick and made visible through repetition and variation. Where the "farce shows that everything has its price and is deception and fraud, [. . .] assures us that it is the principles of the most cutthroat selfishness and rivalry that count" and "insists insolence leads to happiness" (Brandlmeier 1995, 17–19), repetition and variation make sure that Semon's slapstick never loses its intriguing quality of always presenting the same old story in a new, yet recognizable fashion, as if an amalgamation of its closed, inner, and outer seriality took place. Next to the entertaining quality of his films, Semon invites audiences to reflect structure (as static base) and constraints (relating to the dynamics of a process), stimulus and response, cause and effect, action and reaction, as well as the varieties of the foreseeable and unforeseeable. Even surpassing the phenomenon of a specific interpretation of the world itself, Semon's comedies of this early era seem to be an exercise for audiences to sharpen their perception of structures in general and of how they work and have effects. So Semon's two-reelers are not only amusing, but also a nearly invisible training for experiencing a world from a deliberate and reflective perspective.

Bibliography

Aristotle. *The Poetics of Aristotle*. Chapel Hill: University of North Carolina, 1987.
Ayaß, Ruth. "Zwischen Innovation und Repetition: Der Fernsehwerbespot als mediale Gattung." *Die Gesellschaft der Werbung*. Ed. Herbert Willems. Wiesbaden: Westdeutscher Verlag, 2002. 155–171.
Bahners, Patrick. "Danke für die Extratinte!" *"Eikones": Das Erzählende und das erzählte Bild*. Ed. Alexander Honold and Ralf Simon. Paderborn: Fink, 2010. 86–124.
Bartl, Andrea. *Die deutsche Komödie*. Stuttgart: Reclam, 2009.
Bartlett, Randolph, and Kitty Kelly. "The Shadow Stage." *Photoplay Magazine*, Vol. 13, No. 3, February 1918, 65–69.
Beil, Benjamin, Engell, Lorenz, Schröter, Jens, Schwaab, Herbert, and Daniela Wentz. "Die Serie." Eds. Benjamin Beil, Lorenz Engell, Jens Schröter, Herbert Schwaab, and Daniela Wentz. *Zeitschrift für Medienwissenschaft: Die Serie* 7 (2012): 10–16.
Bergson, Henri. *Le rire: Essai sur la signification du comique*. Paris: Librairies Félix Alcan et Guillaumin Réunies, 1913.
Blackbeard, Bill. "The Ignatz Mouse Debaffler Page." *Krazy & Ignatz 1925–26*. Seattle: Fantagraphics Books, 2002, entry 8/16/25.
Brandlmeier, Thomas. "Fin de siècle comedy culture." *Slapstick & Co*. Eds. Helga Belach and Wolfgang Jacobsen. Berlin: Stiftung Deutsche Kinemathek, 1995. 16–75.

Burdorf, Dieter, Christoph Fasbender, and Burkhard Moenninghoff. Eds. *Metzler Lexikon Literatur*. Stuttgart: Metzler, 2007.
Eco, Umberto. "Serialität im Universum der Kunst und der Massenmedien." *Im Labyrinth der Vernunft*. Ed. Umberto Eco. Leipzig: Reclam, 1989. 301–324.
Ellrich, Lutz, Peter von Möllendorff, Werner Röcke, Bernhard Greiner, and Arne Kapitza "Komik mit theatralen Mitteln." *Komik: Ein interdisziplinäres Handbuch*. Ed. Uwe Wirth. Stuttgart: Metzler, 2017. 174–220.
Erbeldinger, Harald, and Christoph Kochhan. "Humor in der Werbung." *Die umworbene Gesellschaft*. Ed. Michael Jäckel. Opladen: Westdeutscher Verlag, 1998. 141–177.
Everson, William K. *Laurel und Hardy und ihre Filme*. Gütersloh: Bertelsmann, 1980.
Florey, Robert. "Zigoto." *Filmland*. Paris: Editions de cinémagazine, 1923.
Gardner, Jared. "A History of the Narrative Comic Strip." *From Comic Strips to Graphic Novels*. Eds. Daniel Stein and Jan-Noël Thon. Berlin: De Gruyter, 2013. 241–253.
Gentz, Will T. "A Cartoonist Turned Comedian." *The Photo-Play World*, Vol. 2, No. 8, June 1919, 16.
Greiner, Bernhard. *Die Komödie*, Tübingen: utb, 1992.
Hickethier, Knut. *Die Fernsehserie und das Serielle des Fernsehens*. Lüneburg: Kultur-Medien-Kommunikation, 1991.
Howe, Herbert. "Cartooned into the Cinema." *Photoplay*, October 1920, 25.
Jones, Edgar, Nicola T. Fear, and Simon Wessely. "Shell Shock and Mild Traumatic Brain Injury." *American Journal of Psychiatry* 164 (2007): 1641–1645.
Kelleter, Frank. "Populäre Serialität." *Populäre Serialität: Narration – Evolution – Distinktion*. Ed. Frank Kelleter. Bielefeld: transcript, 2013. 11–48.
Klotz, Volker. *Bürgerliches Lachtheater*. Heidelberg: Winter, 2007.
Král, Petr. "Le Message de Larry Semon." *Positif*, 106 (1969): 28–33.
Kursell, Julia. "Presque une image matérielle." Eds. Benjamin Beil, Lorenz Engell, Jens Schröter, Herbert Schwaab, and Daniela Wentz. *Zeitschrift für Medienwissenschaft: Die Serie* 7 (2012): 57–69.
Marschall, Susanne. "Slapstick." *Reclams Sachlexikon des Films*. Ed. Thomas Koebner. Stuttgart: Reclam, 2007. 557.
Mast, Gerald. *The Comic Mind*. Chicago: University of Chicago Press, 1979.
Mielke, Christine. *Zyklisch-serielle Narration: Erzähltes Erzählen von 1001 Nacht bis zur TV-Serie*. Berlin: De Gruyter, 2006.
Moving Picture World. "Gall and Golf." September 15, 1917, 1707.
Mittell, Jason. "Narrative Komplexität im amerikanischen Gegenwartsfernsehen." *Populäre Serialität: Narration – Evolution – Distinktion*. Ed. Frank Kelleter. Bielefeld: transcript, 2013. 97–122.
New York Dramatic Mirror. "Help! Help! Help!" November 4, 1916, 34.
Oltean, Tudor. "Series and Seriality in Media Culture." *European Journal of Communication* 8 (1993): 5–31.
Picture-Play Magazine. "What the Fans Think." April 1920, 77.
Picture Show. "Larry Semon – The Vitagraph Fun Maker." No. 124, Vol. 5, September 10, 1921, 7.
Ruchatz, Jens. "Ein Foto kommt selten allein." *Fotogeschichte*, 18, No. 68–69, (1998): 31–46.
Schallert, Edwin. "Exploding the Comedy Plot." *Los Angeles Sunday Times*, Vol. 39, June 6, 1920, 29.
Scott-Samuel, Nicholas E., Roland Baddeley, Chloe E. Palmer, and Innes C. Cuthill. "Dazzle Camouflage Affects Speed Perception." *PLoS ONE* 6(6): 2011, e20233.

Siegrist, Hansmartin. "Komik mit filmischen Mitteln." *Komik: Ein interdisziplinäres Handbuch.* Ed. Uwe Wirth. Stuttgart: Metzler, 2017. 350.

Spies, Bernhard. *Die Komödie in der deutschsprachigen Literatur des Exils.* Würzburg: Königshausen und Neumann, 1997.

Swanson, Gloria. *Swanson on Swanson.* London: Michael Joseph, 1981.

Stockinger, Claudia. Ed. *Schuld, Sühne, Humor: Der Tatort als Spiegel des Religiösen.* Karlsruhe: Evangelische Akademie Baden, 2013.

Suerbaum, Ulrich. *Das Elisabethanische Zeitalter.* Stuttgart: Reclam, 1989.

Tisserand, Michael. "New Orleans to Coconino." *Krazy Kat. A Collection of Sundays.* Eds. Patrick McDonnell and Peter Maresca. Palo Alto: Sunday Press, 2010. 5–6, col. 3.

Weixler, Antonius. "Vom Comicstrip zum comic book." *Comics und Graphic Novels: Eine Einführung.* Eds. Julia Abel and Christian Klein. Berlin: Springer, 2016. 143–155.

Weston, Judith. *Directing Actors.* Studio City: Michael Wiese Productions, 1996.

A playlist of all Semon comedies mentioned in this writing can be accessed here: https://www.youtube.com/playlist?list=PLdLWXlx3qFApKvKbkrHvBnVw6Rmq71KVP (accessed August 1, 2020).

Claudia Sassen
The Anonymized Randomness of Vicco von B.: On Chaos and Order in Loriot's Agfa Advertisements

In the late 1960s, Loriot (the alias of Vicco von Bülow, 1923–2011) designed a commercial advertisement portfolio of seventeen monochrome cartoons for Agfa-Gevaert, which advertised optical devices for the serious amateur.[1] The portfolio contributes to the understanding of the concept of slapstick in two ways. On the one hand, it relates to staged slapstick similar to that on stage and on film, which is mostly (but not necessarily) performed mute and with an emphasis on physical performance in chase sequences, cake fights, flying real estate, and explosions. Slapstick is, in these instances, characterized as not subtle (Frahm 2017, 35) but as dependent on large-scale disruption marked by anarchistic features. On the other hand, the advertisement portfolio relates to a form of involuntary slapstick which, however, can only be recognized in the context of Agfa retrospectively. Slapstick makes people laugh at what they usually find painful, as Essanay comedy director E. Mason "Lightning" Hopper formulated in 1912 (Swanson 1981, 26–27), referring to the staged and particularly physically realized form of the genre he deployed frequently (Thurner 2005, 334). Slapstick is inspired by everyday life and draws on the intricacy of the object, which confronts the target with powerlessness from which there seems to be no escape. In colloquial language, slapstick entails even more. It can refer to an open-minded, chaos-inducing infiltration of experiences that are perceived not by the actors but only by the spectators as slapstick and only so from the distance or retrospectively.

Both forms of slapstick do not cancel one another out in the context of Loriot's Agfa portfolio, but are united through the instantiation of arbitrariness in this work. In the following, the relationship between chaos and order and its destruction and restoration will be considered from a commercial, linguistic, and graphic perspective. In addition to the cartoons, the portfolio contains other elements such as introductory text and product description boards. However, as the seriality and aspect of variation are in the foreground, the focus in this chapter will be on the cartoons and their captions.

---

[1] The author wishes to thank Ludger Hoffmann and his Dienstagskolloquium for discussion and ideas, Ervin Malakaj for translation, Susanne von Bülow, Studio Loriot, Sabine Zeller, Diogenes, and Weinbrennerei Dujardin, Krefeld, for permission to use images in this chapter.

https://doi.org/10.1515/9783110571981-014

1 Randomness of the first order: slapstick through retrospection

1.1 Cross-industry waiver of the unique selling point

The involuntary slapstick associated with Loriot's Agfa advertisement unfolds on a promotional-conceptual level that extends into the arena of variation and seriality (see Section 2.1). Reinhard Siemes notes that the Loriot advertising era spanned from the 1950s to the 1970s and is characterized as a "curiosity" (2009, 60). It counteracted the for the time usual advertising principles, especially the notion of the unique selling proposition, i.e., a focus on the unique selling point of a given marketed object, which was for a long time considered an indispensable component of advertisements (60–61). For none of Loriot's many advertisement campaigns came without the infamous *Knollnasenmännchen* [bubble-nosed little man], which was exposed to the pattern of dignity tolerated disturbance. The multiple layers to his comedy, its hidden, deeper meanings, and the so-called "dry legend style" ("Legendenstil") (see Section 2.2), which Loriot sought to expand and which was important for the artist, were all already well developed at that point (Neumann 2011, 170). Within a few years, Loriot, who was easily persuaded to start a new project, had orders from so many companies that one wonders how they could forego their unique selling proposition given that they all worked with the same artist (Siemes 2009, 60–61). In "modern, instrumentalized advertising," according to Siemes, Loriot's little men would also seek their place in vain, unable to survive the pretest and leave all testers disoriented, yearning for "elevated enjoyment" and "entitlement" (60).

Loriot's situational comedy with its confident fateful figures was prominent for ocean liners (MS Bremen), deodorants (8x4), milk chocolate (auto-cola, see Siemes 2009, 60), tubes (Gemeinschaftswerbung der Lebensmittelindustrie and William Wilkens, see Gass 1958, 207 and Neumann 2011, 425), cough medicine (Optipect), and in the advertising films for pipe tobacco (Stanwell), the Aktion Sorgenkind (see Neumann 2011), and men's outerwear (see Siemes 2009, 60–61). In 1971, Optipect and Lord Extra even advertised with identical Loriot skat card sets. This non-exclusive, promotional monoculture can be explained by technical and media requirements of the time: for most companies, management, often in partnership with the owner of a family business, determined what the product advertising would look like. Agencies were rarely used, but relied on the intuition of individuals who instructed the company's own advertising manager to produce something similar to the work of the competition (see Gass 1958, 70 and 71). According to Gass, comedy was able to establish itself in the advertising culture and each company wanted to "try their own fun in humor" (70). Individual companies thus came to advertise with the brand Loriot for their in-house brand.

1.2 Advertisement sector abandonment of the unique selling point

Loriot's advertising activities within given advertisement sectors as well as across sectors were all characterized by a slapstick mode principally interested in arbitrariness, which in turn came to shape these sectors. In the wake of a special serial creative revolution post-WWII in the use of humor for advertisements, the advertising consultant Achim Aschke initiated such a popular campaign with the spirit industry for the brand Dujardin Weinbrand. The brand, which was known primarily in the Ruhr area of Germany until 1952, became the industry leader (*Der Spiegel* 1968).

To this end, Dujardin enlisted the help of the "dramatist among the German cartoonists," Gerhard Brinkmann (Gass 1958, 68). His visual jokes combined – always in the moment before the catastrophe captured in the image – everyday types with surrealistic situations, all of which converged in the slogan, "let's drink a Dujardin" ["darauf einen Dujardin"]. The trend prompted many other manufacturers to work with less serious and more humorous material, a belief in a one-trick advertisement strategy, which should have ultimately failed many, as the advertisement expert Gass noted in 1958 (68–71). And yet these presumptions were counteracted. Scharlachberg, despite very similar presentation of its ads – and with the help of Loriot – surpassed Dujardin in its success on the spirit market (see *Der Spiegel* 1968). In addition to the brands Schinkenhäger, Hammer, Chantré, and Noris, which all used humorous themes in their distinct advertisements, Scharlachberg engaged with visual jokes, which effectively helped viewers connect to the brand through its slogan (e.g., "Take it easy, take a Scharlachberg!").

From 1959 to 1966, Loriot was under contract with Scharlachberg and produced cartoons for the brand that were clearly reflected in Dujardin's predecessor campaigns; that is, Dujardin's visual jokes sometimes served as model for Scharlachberg down to the point of gag detail (see Figures 1 and 2). This included a scheduled flight: a passenger looks out of the window and sees a witch on a broom. Another scene shows a lady with a shouldered fox fur in which the head of the garment becomes the source of despair for sausage sellers (Brinkmann) and tram passengers (Loriot). Loriot's introduction for the anthology he later published for Scharlachberg proves insightful in this regard: "I have been very careful to describe only those situations that are worthy of account because of the frequency of their appearance" (1962, 8). However, it remains difficult to reconstruct who among the two cartoonists (Loriot or Brinkmann) inspired whom first. Loriot's advertisements for Scharlachberg were published in numerous magazines. In many cases he relied on his own old material from the 1950s, which he reproduced and modified to correspond to the now professionally recognizable Loriot-style (Neumann 2011, 181). The trend of frequent gag reuse among brands continued. For instance, the Paderborn beer company adapted Loriot's cartoons from Scharlachberg for its coasters (e.g., a goalkeeper who is shot by the approaching ball through the net 1965/69). Paderborn beer also hired Brinkmann in the late 1960s for a new edition of his cartoons from the 1950s (Warsteiner 2003).

Figures 1 and 2: Loriot's adapting of advertisement material for Scharlachberg (right, ca. 1963) from a 1955 Dujardin advertisement drawn by an unidentified artist (left).

Apart from the reuse of the graphic corporate design and many new ideas, Loriot also reproduced himself linguistically and stylistically in some of his advertising series (Optipect, auto-cola, and Agfa). This is the case in his recycling of his "legend style" (Neumann 2011, 170), the self-described "official and robotic catalogue language" (278), as well as the "German used in offices" (Isfort 2008), in which he adjusts material to serve the purpose of the advertisement and its audiences with heightened subtlety (see for example Agfa and Optipect).

2 Randomness of the first order: corporate design of the Agfa advertisements

2.1 Structure and entanglement

Loriot's Agfa advertisement portfolio takes a special place in a broader advertisement culture. While standard practice for advertisements is their placement in different places that renders them serendipitously encounterable – i.e., one discovers them in an undirected and playful manner and anticipates follow-up advertisements in unexpected places (Möller 2017, 137–38) – the Agfa advertisement portfolio was available as a booklet. Thus, the medial conditions for the portfolio order the seventeen Loriot cartoons. Despite this ordering, however, one could begin reading and viewing the ads "in the middle" (137). This is especially the case since each cartoon can be perceived and understood like an advertisement in its own right without having to depend on the information presented in the preceding cartoon. A series of cartoons such as this is reminiscent of the recurrent, cyclical movements of machines when considering how their corporate design, i.e., their constant closed or formal features work. The principle of continuation dictating the serial content of the advertisement portfolio, which promises "novelty in the story" it tells but de facto secures only the recurrence of a constant scheme (Eco 1989, 305), operates at the core of Loriot's advertisement portfolio every time one turns the page. Above all, the variation in the material secures the audience's appreciation and generate support for the continual engagement with the work, thereby revitalizing interest in each page. Through each new episode, here each new page of the portfolio, the audience acquires a sense about the pattern and develops expectations about the continuation of the storyline. One can trust a series as long as it does not violate the pattern of these recognizable traits. Here, a reciprocal relationship between producer and audience develops on the premise of reliability: the producer provides recognition and the audience confidence in this recognition, which in turn stimulates the expectation and recognition of subsequent iterations of the story in each given cartoon. The quality of the individual ads must remain the same; each must not get worse or better for the dynamic to work.

Series have their own rules and are highly paradoxical in that they are always complete but never finished (see Kelleter 2013, 12). Loriot's series appears visually complete even as its internal structure could be extended. Apart from the fact that Loriot supplies Agfa with cartoons, which are funny in their own right, the elements of series are on their own already characterized by a typical slapstick-like and humorous *comic or cartoon-like regenerative ability* (Marschall 2007, 557). In this capacity for regeneration lies the key to the potentially endless variation: typically, the advertisements comprised of the product, the headline, the brand name, the logo or its associated figures are presented again and again. The advertisements playfully engage, for example, in minimal fashion with the packaging details of objects as in the case with Lucky Strike, which kaleidoscopically and, at the same time, surprisingly meaningfully are reconfigured again and again in a different way from advertisement to advertisement. If they are destroyed in this process, they are resurrected. The typical advertisement is also a running gag, which is another typical slapstick element. In other words, each advertisement offers a "repeated presentation of a basic situation, whereby each repetition is a new resolution of the problem created in the initial basic situation" (Hembus in Everson 1980, preface). The Agfa advertisement builds up a running gag especially through the variable use of the film camera Agfa Movex. The camera is destroyed and yet not destroyed (as presented in the Agfa proof number three [Beweis 3], Miss Sieglinde N. partially sabotages the beginning of the 100 m run in the European Championship for the gentlemen running in that she shamelessly keeps close to them, see Figure 3). Generally, the use of Agfa products in the cartoons destroys an order which subsequently culminates in physical destruction (Proof 17, see Figure 5).

The total advertisement portfolio, in which Agfa's long tradition met Loriot's recognizable style, evokes a plea in court. The front cover reads like a headline: "Loriot shows you . . .," while the back cover states, ". . . that Agfa presents make for great gifts!" Following a foreword, which refers to Loriot as a "world renowned artist," Loriot proceeds to offer a seventeen-fold argument in support of this claim, which could also be read as seventeen suggestions for how to use the optical equipment advertised. These are framed by fold-out colored boards, which present the Agfa products in a realistic representation against a cadmium yellow background. Each of these one-panel cartoons is accompanied by a caption, which in the broadest sense could be considered as running text, since it addresses the particular product shown in the cartoon. However, there are no headlines or slogans for the individual ads. Typical for an advertisement series is that the ads can be viewed as micro-narratives (Niehaus 2014, 272), which are related to the respective cartoon with text on individual subthemes for dealing with optical devices in everyday life and which tell their own story. The caption is the narrative and the picture itself a snapshot, as if the viewer were to hold the camera to capture and compress the second in which the moment took place.

Beweis 3:

Beim Start zur Europameisterschaft der Herren im 100-Meter-Lauf glückte Fräulein Sieglinde N. mit ihrer AGFA Movex SV eine Schmalfilmstudie von sporthistorischer Bedeutung.

Figure 3: Agfa Proof 3: While other athletes are already in action, Sieglinde N. (center) uses an Agfa film camera to immortalize the starting position of a stranger in a still image, creating for the viewer an unbridgeable connection between the dynamics and statics.

A second level, that of the funny narration within the entire advertisement campaign or individual ads that reference one another, is conceivable, but not realistic. From a marketing point of view, a narration of the second level would be easy to realize, since the audience has all the elements of this series arranged in stable order. In the case of Agfa, a beginning and ending cartoon frame the remaining fifteen cartoons that are serially interchangeable and show no narrative evolution among themselves: the internal order may be random, but the placement of the first and the last cartoon is not – a partial requirement is present.

In Proof 1, Loriot's world resembles a crafted idyll in which "auditor Karl-Heinz L. and his [unnamed] fiancé" each film the other, hovering almost elf-like over a flawlessly maintained flower lawn (see Figure 4). The caption reads, "Auditors Karl-Heinz L. and his fiancé have finally provided passionate content for their engagement period with the acquisition of an Agfa Movex." In the subsequent cartoons, Loriot shows us ways out of this idyll – and also provides again a way back into it. His world is overthrown by the apparently consistent use of the Agfa product that dissolves into slapstick chaos. The corresponding caption immediately sets this chaotic world back – or at least appears to suggest an attempt thereof: while "Official K. from Dortmund" (Proof 2) is exposed down to his long johns during an accident, his "wife" films the event with documentary zeal. The caption reads, "The spouse of Official K. from Dortmund captured with the Movexoom S a nice recording of her husband's downhill skiing in the sublime mountains of the Upper Engadin." The caption aims to present the incident as a progression in a specific ski discipline and thus to recover the situation again to a socially acceptable level. The use of the photographic apparatus, which relies on the temporary standstill of the subject (photograph) or the impartial continuation of an action (film) for a satisfactory result, has at the same time an ordering effect as it serves a slapstick-like function (Siemes 2011, 61).

Proof 1 takes on the role of a control group for an undistracted, friction-free world in which no traffic is sabotaged, family members are snubbed, or criminal work postponed indefinitely. Chaos is superficially not intelligible. However, under the surface it lurks already: namely, it is legible when the auditor Karl-Heinz L. and his fiancé are filming one another's camera lens. In addition, they are probably not floating (despite its appearance) but are stepping hard on the ground, which would make for a difficult viewing on the evening the recording is shown to an audience. The concluding cartoon in its position follows its own logic, too: in comparison to the other cartoons, it represents entropy. The subject here is the irreversible destruction similar to the subject matter captured in Loriot's later short film "Zimmerverwüstung" ["Room Devastation," 1976]. A room decorated for Christmas is extensively devastated by children as the mother documents the action on camera. The caption here remains impotent: despite its attempt to semantically recover the situation (Römer 1974, 81) it cannot undo the damage made. The text focuses less on the actual action than on the "festive splendor in the eyes of the children." The caption reads in its entirety, "The effortless handling of the Agfa Movex S allowed the housewife Helga D. from Bremen to capture the festive splendor in the eyes of her children for years to come."

The cartoons are also characterized by slapstick moments without the text. Slapstick is only reinforced by the fact that the text tries hard to repair and apologize for the foregrounded world order captured in the image: the formulations elicit from the audience thoughts it would never have on its

Beweis 1:

Wirtschaftsprüfer Karl-Heinz L. und seine Verlobte haben mit dem Erwerb je einer AGFA Movex ihrer Brautzeit endlich einen leidenschaftlichen Inhalt gegeben.

Figure 4: Agfa Proof 1, in which the home-like structure captured in the image remains still free from interferences.

own. Here, too, the cartoons have lots to offer: no matter how disruptive a situation is, Loriot's language always finds a way – similar to a chase – to maneuver out of a tricky situation or to escape it; at least as long one has not seen right through what the text wants one to understand from the situation.

2.2 Entanglement of language and cartoon

Loriot's linguistic comedy works on the basis of "emphasized objectivity and distinction," which, as a result of the caption, stands in "vertical contrast" to

Beweis 17:

Die mühelose Handhabung der Agfa Movex S erlaubt der Bremer Hausfrau Helga D., den festlichen Glanz in den Augen ihrer Kinder für spätere Jahre einzufangen.

Figure 5: Agfa Proof 17: the final cartoon in the portfolio: "festive splendor" in children's eyes is preserved, the design of the room decorated for Christmas is not. Its destruction is cemented.

the images (compare here the matching movement of the eyes from the image to the text and vice versa) (Neumann 2011, 172). This comedy operates on the premise that the text's "absurd ideas" are recorded (172) and always endowed with a potential of "talking at cross-purposes" (Karasek 1988, 217) only to find some common ground eventually. But it is not the vertical contrast alone. Loriot works in different ways with interwoven comedy-generating contrasts and uses their variable effects in his favor. In addition to the vertical, Neumann identifies as prominent the horizontal contrast, which operates within the text and/or image plane or between the captions of a series of drawings (2011, 170). This process can be visualized to be at the same height in the layout of the portfolio.

In the case of Loriot, what characterizes this complex pattern is an entanglement of "what is said and meant, what is shown and camouflaged" (op den Platz 2016, 44).

On its own, the caption of the Agfa advertisement is non-sensational, not funny, and not orderly, because its syntactically smooth form and stylistic lexicon do not give reason to order anything. The caption can be read hyperbolically and euphemistically only in conjunction with the cartoon, since the cartoon is indeed "*more or less directly* a transformation of the text" (Neumann 2011, 172; emphasis mine) that disambiguates language and formally reduces the precise style. The language in the cartoons garbles the events depicted in the cartoons since it draws on a repertoire of generally valid yet stereotyped formulations whose cadence is weighted on the right side of the mid-section of a German sentence. Despite this insight and focus on a specific moment of a text, an overall view of the text is necessary. Even though the stereotype is already apparent to the audience as a result of the series format (whose seriality implies dependence on stereotype), the audience is nonetheless unprepared for what is ahead. Take, for instance, Proof 9 (see Figure 6): "The self-recorded color photograph in Agfacolor of their parents' wedding is a beautiful memory of lasting value for Thomas, Berta, and Bubi." The "beautiful memory of lasting value," which the contemporary audience probably already identified as a conventional phrase common in the advertising culture of the time, is part of a disproportionality, because it casts what would for the time have been scandalous material as secondary as it foregrounds the Agfacolor photography. Agfa is, strictly speaking, the main component of this cartoon, but it is abused in order to interject the key component of subject material considered socially taboo, generating a horizontal contrast on the image plane itself.[2] In Proof 9, the bride and groom take the first steps outside of the location in which they got married as their three children, arranged side-by-side according to height, synchronously photograph them, each holding a camera.

The fact that the children in Proof 9 were born prior to the marriage is only apparent from the cartoon. The mere text – "the self-recorded color photograph [. . .] of their parents" – could refer to the discovery of the picture in a photo album. The self-photographed photo thus does not point to who took the photo and does not necessarily include the children as original photographers. Just as in the first step the cartoon foregrounds the Agfa product, once the euphemism is deciphered in a second step the principality of the gag comes to the fore: the surprise captured in the process of disambiguating the puzzle preoccupies the audience.

---

[2] Only as a result of the 1949 German Basic Law was the status of an illegitimate child equated with that of the marital child. The population had to get used to this shift.

Beweis 9:

Für Thomas, Berta und Bubi ist das selbstaufgenommene Farbfoto in Agfacolor von der Hochzeit ihrer Eltern eine schöne Erinnerung von bleibendem Wert.

Figure 6: Agfa Proof 9. The dismantling of social foundations. Three children conceived before marriage stand in front of a church.

Proof 5 is a cartoon, which on the one hand achieves a comical effect through the vertical contrast by means of disproportionality, on the other hand by means of the grammatical structure of the caption (see Figure 7). The head of his department, Albert E., photographs his secretaries as they sunbathe in front of an open window in their office, which they transformed into a beach without consulting their superior. The caption reads, "Head of department Albert E. has an Optima-Rapid and is primarily interested in life-like atmospheric images in his work environment." The phrase "atmospheric images [Stimmungsbilder] in his work environment [Arbeitsatmosphäre]" maintains two meanings: "atmospheric images" and "environment" in the German original also refer to abstractions in the emotional world. This doubling is universal and positive.

On first reading, "life-like" refers to a realistic representation – here, the opposite of unworldly – but, on second read, another representation becomes intelligible. It is also a realistic representation, but one which represents the hedonism, the free movement and the uninhibition of society as a given. While the vertical contrast is not as foregrounded here as it is in other cartoons, something happens verbally. The connection among the personal data, status, first name, abbreviated last name, and the Agfa product is linked through a coordinating conjunction ("and") with the context depicted in the situation. Notably, the caption does *not* read, "Head of department Albert E., *who owns an Optima-Rapid*, is primarily interested in life-like atmospheric images in his work environment." The fact that the Optima-Rapid belongs to Albert is not pushed into an appositive relative clause – i.e., from the main clause into a subordinate clause and thus out of the focus of the discussion – but rather structurally retains its position on the same level as the situational representation ("life-like atmospheric picture"). The main point here, namely that Albert caught his two secretaries in a sticky situation, is linguistically glossed over by the fact that the text only mentions his possession of the Optima-Rapid and not that he is using the camera to voyeuristically court them. Depending on the way one reads the texts, the leveling of relative importance of the information presented in the sentence through the use of the coordinating conjunction either raises or lowers the status of the information mentioned in both phrases. The fact that Albert "is primarily interested in life-like atmospheric images" corresponds again to a shift in the meaning of the cartoon overall: the meaning of "being interested" in the sense of a cognitive affinity toward objects or persons is largely neutrally coded. The fact that he documents these images again is linguistically rendered secondary. The marker "primarily" does not provide enough information for a reliable interpretation.

The phrase may refer to the fact that Albert wants to photograph and, above all, wants to photograph people, or that he values primarily "atmospheric images," meaning not the sound documentation or written depiction outside of that of the photograph. The fact that the first part of the caption is associated with the second part despite its structural weighting leads to a general, mutually reinforcing and substantive trivialization of what is shown. The embedding of the phrase "life-like atmospheric images" attached to the coordinating conjunction mitigates the explosive effect of what is shown: the conversion of the office space in an anarchic act is relativized and overshadowed by the quiet and matter-of-fact photoshoot conducted by the supervisor. Slapstick, here, is intensified.

This is where the catalogue language connects, which conveys an inauthenticity itself euphemistically enigmatic as it can only be revealed through the

Beweis 5:

Abteilungsleiter Albert E. besitzt eine Optima-Rapid und ist in erster Linie an lebensnahen Stimmungsbildern aus seiner Arbeitsatmosphäre interessiert.

Figure 7: Agfa Proof 5: the office after it has been transformed into a leisure and adventure site.

juxtaposition with the cartoon. Although the language seeks to mitigate the severity of the breach of social norms depicted in the cartoon in order to eradicate the chaos through excuses and justifications, it in turn only generates new chaos, because the audience is translating the language from its status as inauthentic. What derails the apprehension of the material – i.e., the act of viewing – is the realization that what is linguistically conveyed is not even the opposite of what is to be expected in the context; instead, the language of the cartoon generates an extension of its meaning and is formulated in such a way that it cannot be categorized as a lie. Because language is right if, for example, the caption reads as it does in Proof 4: "Goalkeeper Claus P. from the 1. Soccer Club Laubenheim photographed with his AGFA Iso-Rapid *the match-winning goal in the 48th minute*" (emphasis mine). The cartoon shows a keeper, who in fact photographs the match-winning goal, but does so *pars pro toto* as the opposing team shoots the goal. The ball has already arrived in his goal, albeit still in the air.

Loriot's language is characterized by his dry legend style famous for the alleged life-coaching scenarios captured in the cartoons. This style is intertextually dependent on the "precise, informative" (Neumann 2011, 170) style derived from nineteenth-century book language that one could find in the self-help literature well into the 1960s and which reflects the society accounted for by the mud pit scenes in slapstick films. This style was combined with the advice columns and behavior guides in the pages of the illustrated press of the 1950s (170). More importantly, this style seems to have its origin in the office culture of the period. Loriot depicts in his cartoons the pathos captured in office culture, which is characterized by efficiently condensed language. The language is not explicit, it bears hints of dilettantism, and something that thematizes quotidian life however in inappropriate fashion. In this way, this language is not interested in the reader and reinforces the process of talking at cross-purposes with one another.

Loriot's characterization of his texts as catalogue language refers significantly to the now well-researched language in tourism in the context of travel catalogues (see Gansel 2009, Bachmann-Stein 2017), which is also a form of advertising. Catalogue language arises because sellers have the obligation to present their products objectively. Notably, they are not obligated to present their offers negatively (see Bachmann-Stein 2017). Loriot, in turn, has no reason to present the advertised Agfa device objectively. Rather, he uses the catalogue language to depict in linguistically objective matter the social conventions broken in individual cartoons (philandering, illegitimate children, public exposure) as well as the unlawful or simply disturbing behavior (partial narrative thwarting through barrage at sport events, failure to help others during a hunt trip, the use of binoculars to enlarge the décolleté from a distance). Catalogue language helps regulate these respective situations engendered by the contact with the Agfa product. The hyperbolic utterances in this language are often "pragmatic euphemisms" with which the writers of such texts try to "gloss over unpleasant truths" (Wanzeck 2010, 84).

From the perspective of pragmatics, this veiling linguistic usage can often hardly be distinguished from irony, sarcasm, or verbal aggression (Bąk 2017, 41), thus also becoming an example of unbridled slapstick potential. This "secret code" (50) is controversial in that it is not clear if it is persuasive enough (cf. Bachmann-Stein 2017, 120), thus it profits from the lack of certainty of the efficiency of conventions, or the "conventionalizing of the specific handling of tourism communication [in a certain register]" (Gansel 2009, 77). The code is easy to miss as certain phrases are prone to being misused in unfortunate situations.

With Loriot we have to assume that the slapstick situations generated by the use of the Agfa devices have been perceived by the audience as a disruption to the dominant habitus of their time. Those engaging with the portfolio must have either immediately recognized the disruptions captured in the cartoon or would have known that the cartoons are interested in this disruption. An audience member must therefore have been able to "provide special understanding if he wants to glean what is going on" (Bachmann-Stein 2017, 126), or, as Wirth has shown, "only the person, who is able to determine the interference of two different languages, can grasp the ambivalence captured in the duplicitous meaning of a word" (2009, 322). After all, the audience has the option to have been trained over the course of being exposed to seventeen cartoons to develop a suspicious disposition with regard to the text's content. The expectation that there will be a continuation of the story (which is stimulated by the seriality of the portfolio) is designed to anticipate the unveiling of the veiled language. The only question that remains for the audience is how Loriot will do it in the next installment. If the implementation surpasses the expectation of the audience, the comedic effect intensifies. If this were not the case, then one would have to speak of disappointment with regard to that which the travel catalogue promises. However, what is at stake here is not a linear exaggeration of a fact but a vertical contrast that shows the audience things it was not anticipating but ones located within an arm's reach of the description and information provided. According to Bachmann-Stein, there are three ways to approach euphemisms: relativization and differentiation of the hyperbolic content, as well as the decoding of veiling linguistic usage (2017, 138), all of which seem present in Loriot's work. Regardless of whether the Agfa advertisement begins with the image or with the texts, the audience discovers a break between the two. This break is generated by a process of mutual deduction of what is taking place in the image and the text, which each time one casts a gaze upon either undergoes another process, namely that of reactivation of another evaluation of what is taking place.

2.3 The Agfa product as social agitator and regulator

Loriot uses the power of the single frame, which provokes further reflection at the same time as it remains grounded in its non-resolution of the problem it poses. Here, arrested development is a constant component, albeit varied in its consistent appearance throughout cartoons. The arrested development is a theme that appears in those characters, who use the Agfa products (Proof 1–17), those captured with them (Proof 3, 11, 12, and 15), the observers (Proof 3, 11, and 13) and the carefully selected audience (Proof 6, 14, and 16). Sometimes this depiction turns into a meaningless crossover between film and photography: while traditionally the subject being filmed is asked to be at ease in order to make the best of the shoot, the cartoons tend to depict the character being filmed as the one who should be at rest. In Loriot's case, the use of film cameras evokes the standard aspects of striking a pose common in photography and filming. It also evokes a rather unfortunate general continuity of this subject matter (Proof 1 and 12). For example, one of the cartoons depicts a lawyer driving back from Naples to Flensburg in his convertible while continually filming his family in focus throughout the ride (see Figure 8). One can here assume that his creative variation in photography lags considerably behind the work of Buster Keaton in his travelogue *The Railrodder* (1965), but maintains a related comedic function.

Beweis 12:

Die Rückfahrt von Neapel nach Kiel im offenen Cabriolet nutzte Rechtsanwalt Hermann Sch. mit Hilfe seiner Agfa Movex SV zur Aufnahme eines abendfüllenden, künstlerischen Kulturfilmes.

Figure 8: Agfa Proof 12: the intuitive striking of a pose as soon as the lens is pointed at the subject.

Except for Proof 14, in which a binocular is used instead of a camera, no other cartoon features a protest or criticism of the event captured. Perhaps one has to dismiss those depicted in the cartoons as sluggish in their skill to perceive what is going on. Nonetheless, no matter what happens and no matter how the Agfa product is used in the cartoon it is treated as a matter of course. If something is matter of course then it is also to a certain extent arbitrary. One does not even have to go so far to call those figures shown in the cartoons as composed or to say that they deliberately take something as a given. They do not even denounce any indignation depicted, but rather give their (unconditional) consent for what is happening and thus intensify what is a characteristic feature of the slow-burn in Laurel and Hardy films. The Agfa product user, in turn, does not need to be legitimized in his actions because the Agfa product itself facilitates them. The person with the camera is, in this context, always the protagonist and has domain over the field of vision: it causes the spectator, similar to the process of linguistic deixis, to understand what is foregrounded in a given cartoon. The cartoons seek to establish a synchronous focalization through the camera holder, which simultaneously generates among viewers a triumphant sensation of being present in a situation not possible without the camera.

As a device serving as a prosthesis for the reaction captured in the cartoon, the Agfa product dispenses with the gestures of the angered and the deceived and instead ensures order. For example, Albert E. does not resort to indignation and triumph when he photographs his secretaries in beach outfit in their office. He was after all reliably documenting the event with his camera. This is also the case in Proof 8, when Mrs. Director F. caught her husband with his typist in his lap, or in Proof 17, when the mother records her destructive children to be filmically preserved for eternity. In this manner, the characters depicted negotiate each event visually (i.e., through the camera) without casting any judgement. In Proof 10, the film camera rejects empathy and assistance when the manufacturer Rupprecht G. prefers to film a friend fleeing from a swarm of hares rather than helping him.

The fact that a second-level narrative, in which one cartoon reacts to the material presented in another, does not apply to the Agfa advertisement series can be explained by taking a closer look at the conceptual differences of the characters, despite the fact that they have identical appearances. They have nothing to do with one another and are at most linked through their use of the Agfa products. There are also ads that can be understood only in relation to the preceding ad, which opens a third metalevel of narration captured in the dossier. It is possible to encounter a component in one cartoon, which shares an affinity with another component as a result of similarities that lie outside of the components foregrounded by the advertisement series – a quality which reaches beyond the meta-level of individual advertisements. Advertising documents are thus part of the social reality that is constituted of norms, values, and ideas and which "ultimately determines the form and language of advertising" (Cölfen 2002, 658). It is not enough for advertisers to articulate textually and visually the wishes of their customers in order to communicate them through the medium of the ad. Instead, that which advertisements are meant to communicate should integrate aspects of the reality governing the experience of the audience and should reflect and contain their "collective consciousness" (Gries, Ilgen, Schindelbeck 1995, 2). It is thus to be expected – although "there is no irrefutable proof for this claim" (Cölfen 2002, 662) – that advertisements contain "ideas of a reality [. . .] which are shared and understood by a large number of members of a given society at any given time" (658).

The Agfa advertisement series seems to contain regular depictions of social norms, which Loriot permits his characters to break through amateur behavior. According to Siemes, "Loriot's contrived mishaps, especially in their condensed form, [stood] [. . .] in a beautiful contradiction to the rigid society of the 1950s" (2009, 60–61). Yet even despite his interest in distortion of society (chaos), Loriot always remained invariably appropriate (order). No matter how extensive the caprices of his Agfa protagonists may have been, they were always socially palatable. The accountant Karl-Heinz L. has a fiancé, Mr. Wilhelm H. has a family, Mrs. Director F. photographs her husband Mr. Director F., Councilor K. from Dortmund is married, Sieglinde N. is a young woman (a "Fräulein"); Anita B., as well as Helga D., holds the status of housewife and is obviously already married; the audience has to be a bit more generous with the storyline of the parents of Thomas, Berta, and Bubi, but at the very least we are witnessing their wedding and the readjustment of the social context through marriage; if secretary Monika Pf. goes out in the company of men then she does so with a friend, which signals that some distance between the two is granted. The other characters are grounded through their profession and maintain a good standing in the world: Claus P. is a goalkeeper, Albert E. is department head, Günther O. works in a factory, Hermann Sch. is lawyer, Rudolf K. is a sergeant in the police force, Hans-Georg O. is member of the student council, and Paul W. was trained as a vault specialist. The female characters, who remain nameless and help shape the compromising situations in cartoons, fit seamlessly into the events and the discourse of a given situation since they sensitively document the hairstyle or the wardrobe of an abused or betrayed wife through the example of their own experiences. The job titles not only ground the characters socially, but they also affirm that the protagonists are decidedly amateur photographers: that is, they are not trained.

2.4 The representation of the actors

Loriot's graphics consist of monochrome, precise ink drawings done with a light brush against a white surface. The protagonists, which also include the Agfa products themselves, are mostly colored black and are almost exclusively depicted from a distance. Similar to techniques common in slapstick films, the bubble-nosed protagonists all appear to stem from the same manageable gene pool. Although binary conceptions of sex are present in the depictions, all characters appear asexual (at most, as is the example in Proof 14, one could find a hint of sexual attraction). And yet, the imagined world of Loriot's cartoons provides evidence that there are some stimuli at work that preserve the genetic reproduction: there are children in the cartoons.

The characters have a flat forehead as well as a pronounced philtrum which leads to a slim upper lip and a slight overbite. They have no lower lip, but do have a slight chin. Broadly speaking, the characters appear to share a relation with the *Homo australopithecus*. They have five fingers, which sometimes appear to be six. The hands take a dominant role in the cartoons while the feet, in concert with other cartoon traditions, almost completely disappear. The thinning hair is not worth styling on the characters, which is why they smooth it over. Despite all this, the female characters appear to have the same hair stylist and wear, almost exclusively, a page boy haircut with curved tip leading to the cheek, shape the frontal fringe over the round brush and surprisingly do not give in to the dominant hairstyle of its time: the B52. The men, if they have not lost most of their hair already, sport a swirl. Eyes appear either as dots or, if drawn in more complex fashion, appear chaste, indignant, or dignified. The overall loveless and demure disposition of the characters give the impression that all male characters were male and that all female characters were men disguised as women. This brings about a tension in the cartoons with regard to gender and sex (cf. op den Platz 2016, 47–50, 73).

That the characters appear to be crossdressing was ensured by the fact that, apart from the main hair on their head, everyone seems to the same body type. Even the partly uncovered leg of the soccer player remains hairless, indicating that the same body is used for all characters and only few discriminating qualities are added. The principle of the disguised figure applies also to Loriot's children characters: as a result, they look prematurely aged, almost senile. The women retain a unique characteristic through the ventral and dorsal prominences and the leg kink. The older woman depicted in the cartoons can be distinguished from the younger woman only by the degree of said protuberance, which are often extended into the hilly landscape in the background. Loriot's contemporary audiences were already outraged by the "ugly depictions," as

Loriot remarked in an interview with Robert Gernhardt: "This man in the cut suit and the bubble nose and the woman in the flowered dress, they did not really exist. They simply represented man and woman par excellence for me" (1993, 50–51). The negative reception of Loriot's image of women at the time can be gleaned from the letters he received from audiences who suggested that he "be institutionalized" (Loriot 1958, 140).

2.5 Chances and risks of the amateur

Similar to the idiocy of which Loriot was accused, his protagonists, in spite of solvable problems, are dealing with unprofessional background noise, disarming naivete, and resulting chaos in their engagement with the Agfa products. As in silent slapstick films, they play both "with the medium as well as the consequences of modernity" (Ellrich 2017, 296). Binoculars are used at close range, non-focusing eyes are closed shut, film cameras are used for still images and continuous subjects, other cameras are used as if autofocus, steady cam, and high resolution were part of the everyday. Moreover, the characters generally and unconditionally insist on their actions while arbitrarily breaking existing rules. The cartoons relish the fact that the errors at the core of the storyline are entirely avoidable. What on the one hand may represent a hopelessly dilettantish mode of behavior, on the other hand facilitates freedom that brings about its own order to the scene and which the amateur can afford and maintain. The Agfa advertisement portfolio thus stands in the tradition of and struggle for processes of self-understanding and self-confidence. For the history of amateur filmmaking and photography is as old as both film and photography. Both forms evolved at an indefinable point into a professional branch, which is a "generally recognized art form" and a non-professional branch, "at best recognized as part of our culture" (Kuball 1980/1, 14). Loriot's characters embody the type of amateur, who is characterized by what the German film pioneer Guido Seeber described as "prerequisite lacking" and the "optimism [. . .] with which one approaches previously foreign matter" (Seeber 1929, cited in Kuball 1980/1, 9). In this sense, Loriot's figure of the amateur occasionally seems to photograph things that are not usually photographed.

As a result of their unrestrained nature and rejection of rules, Loriot's amateurs are not responsible for the choice and realization of their subjects and appear not concerned about values or the precision of the recordings – this is especially the case with regard to consent to photograph or film their subjects. Furthermore, Loriot's amateurs give shape to the grotesqueness of a given situation, which is a component of slapstick. The professional has always emerged from amateur work. Already in 1917 the boundaries between the two statuses are blurred: the American slapstick director Lawrence "Larry" Semon reported innocently to the trade journal *Motography* that he was prevented from completing his films on time. Further research indicates that Semon spontaneously shot chase sequences on major streets in Manhattan and let his protagonists do their work in random front yards without the knowledge let alone the consent of the owners. In the end, he permanently and involuntarily was in dialogue with the police while his performers spent the rest of the day in prison (*Motography* 1917, 1221). This was one component of a self-referentiality that could have been part of his films.

Amateur photographers as well as amateur filmmakers are confronted with the paradox that they are simultaneously never proficient or eager to reach proficiency in their work. Thus, they become a point of attention for professionals because they, as Robert Flaherty noted in 1928, are "the hope of film art" (Flaherty 1928, cited in Kuball 1980/1, 99). In contrast to the commercial film industry, amateurs have the luxury of pursuing artistic experiments.

Amateurs provide insight into concrete details about daily life by showing what is important for the individual. The film amateur subscribes to personal ideas and dreams and captures them for posterity. His images are more authentic, because they are not commercially coded and because they are not expected to be good (Kuball 1980/2, 10). Even Loriot's amateurs are not perfect. However, they believe that they are. For the most part, this relates to the nonchalance with which characters film and project images.

However, the amateurs could have subscribed to the guiding principles of the film and photography handbooks, which appeared around 1900 and were part of the so called "trivial and surprise bag literature" (Herbst 1976, cited in Kuball 1980/1, 15). In this regard, the amateurs could have adapted the usual methods common among the professionals without ever adopting their own personal styles. This is in complete juxtaposition to the type of advice given to amateurs today, which entails setting shutter speed and aperture manually and to distinguish autofocus from the trigger.

Agfa and Loriot provide amateurs with a forum in their advertising dossier. In the context of the advertisement, they permit the amateurs to take up a space similar to that of the professional in the context of the Agfa-Products, while at the same time allowing them to develop their own affective film and photography world even when each of the accompanying texts is apologetic about the content presented in the cartoon. Slapstick lies in the choice and the realization of the subject matter of each cartoon.

While the amateur equipment had largely developed alongside the technology used by the professionals, the production methods developed in different directions throughout the 1920s: the larger apparatuses were part of the domain of the professionals, they used the studio for their work, they perfected the art of lighting as well as that of montage during filming, and made use of sound as well. Even though the sound film was already available to amateur filmmakers in the 1930s thanks to the Draloston self-recording record, the recording remained silent in Loriot's Agfa film advertisements. The amateur worked with practical and affordable equipment, typically with small spring-driven cameras (battery-powered at Agfa) and narrow film cartages (the Agfa version was no longer 9.5 mm, but came in Normal and Super versions at 8 mm). As a result of the affordability of the narrow film strip material, home video practice was no longer only reserved for the upper middle and upper classes, but was now also available to the "prestige seeking middle class" comprised of employees, merchants, academics, and technicians (Kuball 1980/2, 9–10). The latter are literally bustling in Loriot's advertisements. From the auditor to the lawyer, department head to goalkeeper, the housewife and dayworkers to the privy councilor: all are present. However, sometimes there are also directors (e.g., Proof 8) and manufacturers (e.g., Proof 10), which emphasizes the effect of the Agfa product across all layers of society.

3 Randomness of the third order: linguistically variable interior design of cartoons

Amateur cinema is typically not public and, besides of famous examples including Julius Neubronner (1852–1932), Fritz Boden, and Leopold zur Lippe, the names of the amateurs remain largely anonymous (see Kuball 1980/1, 14). Even when the TV channel Westdeutscher Rundfunk launched a documentaries series on amateur filmmaking in 1980, it proclaimed that "existing material is to be used to understand the history of amateur film technology and praxis. [. . .] little is known about the people standing in front of and behind the camera" (14). It is at this point that Agfa and Loriot take center stage only to create fresh chaos and confusion: the advertisement dossier thematizes technical details of amateur filmmaking and indeed gives the amateurs a face – albeit an interchangeable face which defies individuation. The accompanying text, which appears as a corrective to the euphemisms generated in the cartoon, creates a pseudo-individualization by giving its protagonists names and assigns them occupations, places of residence and marital status. At the same time the text exposes characters to arbitrariness, because all surnames never appear completely but in abbreviated form. In contrast to the characters, the cartoons meticulously name and thus provide an especially explicit set of details about all the Agfa products referenced, which range from the Agfa Movex to the Movexoom S, the Iso-Rapid, Optima-Rapid 500 V, the Diamator 100 (a projector), the Movex SV, down to the Movector S. This exaggerated individuation – in its excessive detail – bears comedic effects.

It seems contradictory that Loriot tends to censor his characters linguistically by not giving them many lines while rendering them clearly visible in the cartoons and thus principally identifiable. But this in turn is also not the case, because all figures correspond to the principles of corporate design, which also renders them anonymous as a result of the visual arbitrariness required of advertisements. At times, however, the narrator provides the audience with valuable information about the cartoon setting, which gently lifts the veil of anonymity that hovers above each frame. This takes place through Loriot's particular mode of anonymization. Proof 11 depicts a Monika Pf. and not a Monika P.; Proof 12 depicts Hermann Sch. and not Hermann S.; Proof 4 has a Claus P. and not Klaus P.; and Proof 1 concerns the auditor Karl-Heinz L. and not the auditor Karl Heinz L. (with a hyphen in the name). There is some variation in the system of abbreviation: none of the initials occur more than once and almost all are consonants. With each addition of job titles and/or city names Loriot lowers the non-specificity of character identification but at the same time leaves enough room to speculate and provides an illusion that more information is within grasp. As Alfred Lichtwark notes, the poor cinema of amateurs can afford the luxury of representing all the characteristics of personal distinctiveness (1897: 92). Personal uniqueness applies to the activities of Loriot's characters; but taken individually, they are interchangeable and their markers arbitrary and are further anonymized through this arbitrariness.

The abbreviations within the picture captions, which aim to generate some order to what is depicted, in turn create their own internal order. By having only the initials of surnames, they give the option of categorizing characters into a register. The practice with which Loriot erases his female protagonists linguistically also absurdly appears to provide a sense of order. The nameless designation in "Auditor Karl-Heinz L. and his fiancé" (Proof 1) or the subsumption of the wife into the last name of her husband ("Mrs. Director F." in Proof 8) is outdone through the caption in Proof 2: "*The spouse of Official K. from Dortmund* captured with the Movexoom S a nice recording of the progress of her husband in downhill skiing in the sublime mountains of the Upper Engadin." It does not say, "The wife of Official K. from Dortmund captured . . . HIS progress." Instead, the caption recurs through the accusative object to "nice recording of the progress of her husband" to a genitive attribute ("of her husband" [ihres Gatten]) and does not use the anaphoric refence, thereby double-broaching and thus emphasizing said husband. Under certain circumstances this is a reference to the then prevailing social convention to "identify" wives through their husband's names and surnames (e.g., Empress Friedrich, Mrs. Councilor). In any case, the anonymity of Loriot's female characters in the Agfa dossier is therefore higher than that of his male ones.

4 Conclusion

Loriot's Agfa advertisement dossier presents a multi-layered engagement with slapstick. Accordingly, the type of slapstick prevalent throughout the dossier does not only insist on using the Agfa product to change the course of action depicted in a given cartoon. It is also not only limited to situating Loriot's advertisement campaign in the tradition of marketing and advertisement, which renounces its unique selling proposition in corporate design only to counteract the arbitrariness of its content through a seamless merger between cartoon plot and language use. Above all it is the interaction of text and image that keeps the intellect and the eye of the beholder readily engaged. As soon as the audience discovers the tension between the two, it searches for causalities and possibilities to remedy this tension, possibly also to suit itself, so that it does not have to be persuaded of the hyperbolic expressions at the core of the cartoons.

Finally, the question arises as to whether the text is now a regularity framework for social misdeeds or if it has nothing to do with the image. Just as the language is arbitrary and not dependent on just one structure, so too do audiences never escape the loop between language and text, no matter what decision they make about which order they should follow. The iterative engagement with the material leads to the wish to renew engagement and thereby to determine the meaning. After all, is it not also arbitrary how text and image are to be interpreted in their interaction? That may be, but the tension between text and image in the cartoon does not leave audiences be. This is how the cartoons stage a long running chase scene and thus lead to a slapstick scenario: the audience attempts to determine the order in both text and image, while Loriot – knowing that the audience is insecure about its attempt to understand both text and image individually – sneaks away and absolves himself of any responsibility in the matter.

Bibliography

Bachmann-Stein, Andrea. "Verschleierungsstrategien in Reisekatalogen." *Verhüllender Sprachgebrauch: Textsorten- und diskurstypische Euphemismen*. Eds. Enrico Garavelli and Hartmut Lenk. Berlin: Frank & Timme, 2017. 119–139.
Bąk, Pawel. "Euphemismus als Charakteristikum von Textsorten und Diskursen am Beispiel der Arbeitszeugnisse." *Verhüllender Sprachgebrauch: Textsorten- und diskurstypische Euphemismen*. Eds. Enrico Garavelli and Hartmut Lenk. Berlin: Frank & Timme, 2017. 39–59.
Cölfen, Hermann. "Semper idem oder Jeden Tag wie neu?" *Die Gesellschaft der Werbung*. Ed. Herbert Willems. Wiesbaden: Westdeutscher Verlag, 2002. 657–674.
Ellrich, Lutz. "Komik mit medialen und künstlerischen Mitteln." *Komik*. Ed. Uwe Wirth. Stuttgart: Metzler, 2017. 295–299.
Everson, William K. *Laurel und Hardy und ihre Filme*. Gütersloh: Bertelsmann, 1980.
Frahm, Ole. "Comics." *Komik*. Ed. Uwe Wirth. Stuttgart: Metzler, 2017. 339–350.
Gansel, Christina. "Textsorten in Reisekatalogen: Wirklichkeitskonstruktion oder realitätsnahe Beschreibung." *Perspektiven auf Wort, Satz und Text: Semantisierungsprozesse auf unterschiedlichen Ebenen des Sprachsystems*. Eds. Andrea Bachmann-Stein, Stephan Merten, and Christine Roth. Trier: Wissenschaftlicher Verlag, 2009. 67–78.
Gass, Franz Ulrich. *Besser werben mit Humor*. Stuttgart: Seewald, 1957.
Gernhardt, Robert. "Ein Herr mit Hintersinn." *Stern*, No. 45 (1993): 50–51.
Gries, Rainer, Volker Ilgen, and Dirk Schindelbeck. *Ins Gehirn der Masse kriechen!* Darmstadt: Wissenschaftliche Buchgesellschaft, 1995.
Isfort, Volker. "Von Hunden und Herren." *Abendzeitung*. Munich, 12 November 2008.
Karasek, Hellmuth. "Der Faun und sein Wunschtraum." *Der Spiegel*, No. 10 (1988): 216–222.
Kelleter, Frank. "Populäre Serialität." *Populäre Serialität: Narration – Evolution – Distinktion*. Ed. Frank Kelleter. Bielefeld: transcript, 2013. 11–48.
Kuball, Michael. *Familienkino*. Reinbek: Rowohlt, 1980.
Lichtwark, Alfred. *Vom Arbeitsfeld des Dilettantismus*. Dresden: Gerhard Kühtmann, 1897.
Loriot. *Loriot beweist Ihnen . . . daß Sie mit Agfa Geschenken jedem eine große Freude machen können*. Wiesbaden: Agfa-Gevaert, 1969.
Loriot. *Nimm's leicht!* Zurich: Diogenes, 1962.
Loriot. *Möpse und Menschen*. Zurich: Diogenes, 1958.
Marschall, Susanne. "Slapstick." *Reclams Sachlexikon des Films*. Ed. Thomas Koebner. Stuttgart: Reclam. 2007. 557.
Möller, Reinhard M. "Serendipity." *Poetik und Poesie der Werbung*. Eds. Martina Allen and Ruth Knepel. Bielefeld: transcript, 2017. 137–156.
Motography. "Director Gets Too Much Attention." Vol. XVII, No. 23, 9 June 1917, 1221.
Neumann, Stefan. *Loriot und die Hochkomik*. Trier: WVT, 2011.
Niehaus, Michael. "Stehende Figur." *Kulturen des Kleinen*. Eds. Sabiene Autsch, Claudia Öhlschläger, and Leonie Süwolto. Paderborn: Fink, 2014. 265–281.
op den Platz, Michel. *Männer sind . . . Und Frauen auch . . . Überleg dir das mal!* Würzburg: Königshausen & Neumann, 2016.
Römer, Ruth. *Die Sprache der Anzeigenwerbung*. Düsseldorf: Schwann, 1974.

Scheffran-Pieper, Barbara. *250 Jahre das einzig wahre Warsteiner. Tradition und Innovation. 1753–2003*. Warstein: Warsteiner Brauerei, 2003. 62–63.
Siemes, Reinhard. "Alles in Unordnung." *Loriot – Ach was!* Eds. Peter Paul Kubitz and Gerlinde Waz. Ostfildern: Hatje Cantz, 2009. 60–69.
Der Spiegel. "Werbung/Aschke – Darauf einen." 44, 28 October 1968.
Swanson, Gloria. *Swanson on Swanson*. London: Michael Joseph, 1981.
Thurner, Christina. "Komische Melancholie: Slapstick-Zitate bei Meg Stuart und Joachim Schlömer." *Maske und Kothurn: Internationale Beiträge zur Theater-, Film- und Medienwissenschaft* 51.1 (2005): 331–338.
Wanzeck, Christiane. *Lexikologie. Beschreibung von Wort und Wortschatz im Deutschen*. Göttingen: Vandenhoeck & Ruprecht, 2010. 82–86.
Wirth, Uwe. "Ambiguität im Kontext von Witz und Komik." *Amphibolie – Ambiguität – Ambivalenz: Die Struktur antagonistisch-gleichzeitiger Zweiwertigkeit*. Eds. Frauke Berndt and Stephan Kammer. Würzburg: Königshausen und Neumann, 2009. 321–332.

Part IV: **Bodies of Slapstick**

Ervin Malakaj & Alena E. Lyons
Introduction

As scholars have examined at length, slapstick is immediately invested in materiality. For Alan Dale, slapstick provides "a response to the frustrations of physical existence" (2000, 28). It hinges on the seemingly limitless agility of the material body as it faces force. In other words, although the classic slapstick protagonist chronically falls or suffers blows, the material body attached to this character miraculously persists. As Muriel Andrin notes, "the slapstick body remains unaffected by the kind of violence that, in reality, would cause death and suffering" (2010, 232; see also Clayton 2007, 168–182). Instead, slapstick rehearses for audiences real dangers of modern life without sustained harm or casualty. Ultimately, though, the physical comedy at the heart of slapstick "liberates us," as Andrew Scott's work has shown (2014, 73). Scott argues that the "hapless bodies" of slapstick characters "endure every indignity and hardship so that we do not have to" (73). Moreover, he notes, "by watching the[se bodies] court death, or be repeatedly assaulted and still get back up for more, we are freed from the need to sympathize, and our laughter can be pleasurably sadistic" (73).

The seemingly infinite endurance of the slapstick body stands at odds with the body as it figures in the discourse on biopolitics. As Michel Foucault famously established, the eighteenth century "discovered the body as object and target of power" (1995, 136). The disciplinary methods that emerged or were streamlined at the time rendered the body into a site at which power could be exhibited, harnessed, extracted, and produced. By being the recipient of disciplinary force, "the human body was entering a machinery of power that explores it, breaks it down and rearranges it" (138). In this context, the disciplined body became a prime instrument of population control – a discursive and material instantiation of power concentrated to serve the means of the state. By contrast, the slapstick body interrupts the seamless pressures of disciplinary force. Instead of yielding to power, the slapstick body resists it on the basis of its agility. Such endurance reaches beyond the confines of the text itself. Even the happy ending of a classic slapstick comedy only offers the body momentary repose from the dangers that plague it. The cycle of violence in which the characters of slapstick are caught implicitly spirals on beyond the film's ending (see Hansen 2012, 264; Peacock 2014, 40–41). The characters of slapstick cannot escape physical harm, but they can, and do, bounce back from it. In this light, the body, with the capacity to resist disciplinary force, is not always only a repository for suffering, but also a threat to a system of power futilely trying to discipline it.

https://doi.org/10.1515/9783110571981-015

Scholars have shown how slapstick's physical comedy also offered early twentieth-century audiences a vision of resistance to modern technology. Lauren Rabinovitz notes that slapstick "helped to displace traditional conceptions of the machine as an instrument of productive labor with a modern conception of the machine as a site of bodily pleasure" (2012, 140). Here, Rabinovitz draws on the work of Rob King, who noted that the Keystone Film Company, which produced some of the most prominent slapstick comedies in the 1910s, was not only preoccupied with machines and industrialization, but through its films also "mediated the meanings of mechanization for a public whose own encounters with technology often betrayed startling uncertainties and ambiguities" (King 2008, 181; see also King 2010, 116 and Solomon 2016, 7–8). The slapstick body that fails to operate machinery safely or as instructed stimulates laughter, and by doing so demystifies and degrades the claim of machinery on modern life.

While recognizing the power-defying bodily agility of the slapstick body or its resistance (by succumbing) to the perils of modernization, we must be wary of overdetermining it, and of readily affirming its implications. Writing about slapstick comediennes, Maggie Hennefeld has shown that the power-resistant qualities of the slapstick body "reveal the slippery middle ground between disciplinary and revolutionary accounts of comedy's social effects" (2018, 15). She continues: "As much as female slapstick corporeality offers an alternative to the strictures of traditional femininity, it also represents an inescapable response to industrial mechanization: an entrapment of the living body in the ceaseless production of revolutionary novelty" (15–16). Mystifyingly vulnerable yet at the same time recalcitrant in the face of the modern world, the slapstick body provides a rich resource with which to theorize the relationship between the body and its environment.

The contributions to this section take the considerations about the slapstick body as point of departure. Each considers the slapstick body as a means of analyzing cultural texts. Moreover, each contributes to the scholarship on slapstick by advancing new approaches to the materiality of the slapstick body in its relation to the genres and media in which it is presented. For Caroline Frank, the slapstick body is central in the tragicomedies she discusses, all of which were written for the stage. In fact, her close analysis of the physical humor in isolated scenes shows how these narrative moments – and in particular the body at their core – are a means of highlighting the unity of the tragic and the comic elements in these texts. To this end, Frank examines dramatic texts from around 1800, 1900, the 1960s, as well as recent dramatizations of them in order to trace the long history of the centrality of the slapstick body in fusing the tragic and the comic.

Irina Hron's chapter, in turn, considers the limitations of materiality by attending to slapstick in postmodern drama. In her analysis of Wolfgang Hildesheimer's (1916–1991) early plays, Hron notes that slapstick moments in postmodern writing relate to the body but also instantiate an antimetaphysics (i.e., an investment in knowledge located beyond the limits of bodies) at the core of such texts. Her work points to dramatic works that quote slapstick's investment in physicality only to subvert it and deploy it for their own purposes.

Valerie Weinstein's contribution concerns the early slapstick comedies of Ernst Lubitsch (1892–1947). In her piece, Weinstein examines the political import of Lubitsch's physical comedy, probing the extent to which its key physical components are part and parcel of the director's commitment to articulating Jewish difference in the 1910s. In effect, Lubitsch mobilized slapstick's investment in physicality in vital ways to forge narratives espousing a particular type of Jewish humor. Collectively, these three chapters offer different approaches to study embodiment in slapstick performance.

Works cited

Andrin, Muriel. "Back to the 'Slap': Slapstick's Hyperbolic Gesture and the Rhetoric of Violence." *Slapstick Comedy*. Eds. Tom Paulus and Rob King. New York: Routledge, 2010. 226–236.

Clayton, Alex. *The Body in Hollywood Slapstick*. Jefferson: McFarland & Co., 2007.

Foucault, Michel. *Discipline & Punish: The Birth of the Prison*. New York: Vintage, 1995.

Hansen, Miriam. *Cinema and Experience: Siegfried Kracauer, Walter Benjamin, and Theodor Adorno*. Berkeley: University of California Press, 2012.

Hennefeld, Maggie. *Specters of Slapstick and Silent Film Comediennes*. New York: Columbia University Press, 2018.

King, Rob. *The Fun Factory: The Keystone Film Company and the Emergence of Mass Culture*. Berkeley: University of California Press, 2008.

King, Rob. "'Uproarious Inventions': The Keystone Film Company, Modernity, and the Art of the Motor." *Slapstick Comedy*. Eds. Tom Paulus and Rob King. New York: Routledge, 2010. 114–136.

Peacock, Louis. *Slapstick and Comic Performance: Comedy and Pain*. New York: Palgrave, 2014.

Rabinovitz, Lauren. *Electric Dreamland: Amusement Parks, Movies, and American Modernity*. New York: Columbia University Press, 2012.

Scott, Andrew. *Comedy*. New York: Routledge, 2014.

Solomon, William. *Slapstick Modernism: Chaplin to Kerouac to Iggy Pop*. Springfield: University of Illinois Press, 2016.

Caroline Frank
The Tragicomic Body: On the Relation between Tragicomedies and Slapstick

This chapter seeks to apply the concept of slapstick describing a cinematic form of physical comedy to an analysis of dramatic texts and their stage productions. Although this application seems incompatible at first sight, this intermedial transfer can be justified by the fact that filmic slapstick borrows some of its essential elements from comedy theater. In the *commedia dell'arte*, the 'slap stick' (the 'bataccio') was originally a device with which the comic characters hit each other on stage. Moreover, the ribald comedy and its often grotesque situations typical of slapstick can be traced back to the genre of the burlesque in theater (see von Ahnen 2006, 179). Thus, in this article I recover slapstick for the analysis of dramatic texts and their stage productions in order to be able to define the dramatic genre of tragicomedy in a more differentiated way than literary studies has done so far. I will demonstrate the centrality of slapstick, particularly as it relates to the description, interpretation, and typologisation of body-related comedy (amongst other things between the poles of [corporeal] identity and the grotesque).[1] In doing so, the chapter approaches dramatically staged slapstick in terms of both literary history and genre theory.

I will begin with the examination of two examples in literary history from the end of the eighteenth and from the beginning of the nineteenth century, namely Jakob Michael Reinhold Lenz's (1751–1792) *Der Hofmeister oder Vortheile der Privaterziehung* [*The Tutor, or The Advantages of Private Education*, 1774] and Heinrich von Kleist's (1777–1811) *Amphitryon* (1807). My reading of both texts focusses on the specific Shakespeare reception in this era, which fostered the intense theoretical engagement with tragicomedy. Because of its open form, this genre was regarded as a literary form adequate to modern consciousness. Next, I will examine two tragicomedies from the twentieth century by way of comparison, Gerhart Hauptmann's (1862–1942) *Die Ratten* [*The Rats*, 1911] and Friedrich Dürrenmatt's (1921–1990) *Die Physiker* [*The Physicists*, 1961], which exemplify the renewed interest in the genre after 1900. The question regarding the function of slapstick – not only for the tragicomic plot and the character constellation but also for the emotional impact of tragicomedy on the spectators – is of central importance for my analysis and comparison of the dramatic texts and of selected

---

[1] My study contrasts the work of Guthke (1968) and Zipfel (2017) in this regard.

https://doi.org/10.1515/9783110571981-016

stage productions from approximately the last thirty years. In the final section, I will assess to what extent tragicomedies, written in different epochs of literary history, show different qualities of slapstick as well.

1 Tragicomedy as a much-discussed genre and its relation to slapstick

The rather low number of comprehensive scholarly publications on tragicomedy indicates an academic uneasiness with examining the genre. An explanation for this can be found in literary history. Since Plautus's (approx. 254–184 B.C.) *Amphitruo* (no exact date), the first known text that was called a tragicomedy by its author, there have always been authors who deliberately marked their dramatic texts as tragicomedies. Far more often, though, there have been polemics against the genre especially from a poetological perspective, which denied tragicomedy any kind of literary quality. In the German-speaking world, Martin Opitz (1597–1639) and Johann Christoph Gottsched (1700–1766) provide examples in this regard. For instance, in his enlightenment-oriented, rule-governed poetics, Gottsched refers to Plautus's genre designation only to declare it unworthy of discussion in just a few sentences: "Plautus called his *Amphitryon* a tragicomedy, because he thought that only royal characters are allowed in tragedy. But tragicomedy is such an inappropriate term, as if I were to say funny lament. It is a monster" (1973, 351–352).[2] In order to limit the rule violation, Plautus had to invent a genre that would unite tragedy and comedy. However, in Gottsched's poetics such a genre cannot exist: the happy ending of the play automatically makes it a comedy, even though it violates the estates-clause.[3]

This restrictive perspective on the genre of the tragicomedy in the German-speaking world slowly becomes more relaxed in the course of the intense Shakespeare reception during the eighteenth century. Following the Spanish author Felix Lope de Vega (1562–1635), Gotthold Ephraim Lessing (1729–1781) becomes

---

2 "Plautus hat seinen *Amphitryon* eine Tragicomödie genennt; weil er glaubte, daß königliche Personen allein für die Tragödie gehöreten. Allein eine Tragikomödie giebt einen so ungereimten Begriff, als wenn ich sagte, ein lustiges Klagelied. Es ist ein Ungeheuer." All translation, unless otherwise noted, are mine.

3 The *Ständeklausel* (*estates-clause*) was a principle in poetic theatre by which attempts were made to transfer the principles of Classicist French drama into German theatre. It stated that only kings, princes, and other people of high rank were to be shown in tragedies and that those of the middle classes could only be shown onstage in comedies.

one of the first dramaturgs to connect tragicomedy to the mimesis argument. For Lessing, tragicomedy's combination of the tragic and the comic could be seen as an imitation of nature's diversity. However, and this is one of Lessing's central points of criticism in his comments about tragicomedy in the seventieth part of his *Hamburgische Dramaturgie* [*Hamburg Dramaturgy*, 1767–1769], it is only an imitation of nature's phenomena that fails to consider the nature of human perception. According to Lessing, it is an elementary human faculty to perceive and experience the diversity of nature by 'isolation' and 'selection' in the first place. Thus, it is a central task of art "to relieve us in the domain of beauty of this isolation and to help us focus our attention" (Lessing 1981, 361).[4] Lessing uses this as an argument to justify why playwrights should avoid writing tragicomedies, if possible. However, in some special cases it is permitted and even necessary if "seriousness creates laughter, sadness creates joy or vice versa so immediately that the abstraction of the one or the other becomes impossible for us" (361–362).[5]

The dramatic texts examined in the following all have in common that they merge the tragic and the comic in the way described by Lessing; however, none of the texts exhibit a clear inclination toward either genre, at least not from the perspective of the reader.[6] Dramatic texts that combine tragic and comic elements have an affinity to slapstick-like physical comedy in the tradition of Charlie Chaplin (1889–1977). In this sense, slapstick-like physical comedy can be considered as a *pars pro toto* of the tragicomic. The very early slapstick films focused on aggressive forms of comedy like the struggle between human beings

---

[4] "uns in dem Reiche des Schönen dieser Absonderung zu überheben, uns die Fixierung unserer Aufmerksamkeit zu erleichtern."

[5] "der Ernst das Lachen, die Traurigkeit die Freude, oder umgekehrt, so unmittelbar erzeugt, daß uns die Abstraktion des einen oder des andern unmöglich fällt."

[6] Unlike *Amphitryon* with its intertextual reference structure or *The Rats* with its explanatory subtitle, *Der Hofmeister* and *Die Physiker* are not explicitly marked as tragicomedies. Their attribution to the genre can be made plausible, however, by poetological statements. See especially Lenz's remarks about comedy in the *Rezension des Neuen Menoza*: "Comedy is a painting of human society, and when it gets serious, the painting cannot be laughable. [. . .] Therefore, our German comedy writers must write comic and tragic at once" ["Komödie ist Gemälde der menschlichen Gesellschaft, und wenn die ernsthaft wird, kann das Gemälde nicht lachend werden. [. . .] Daher müssen unsere deutschen Komödienschreiber komisch und tragisch zugleich schreiben."] (1966, 419). Similarly, Dürrenmatt writes in *Theaterprobleme* that tragedies in the classical sense cannot exist anymore because of society's collective guilt which can no longer be expressed as the guilt of individual tragic heroes in the theatre. Nevertheless, the tragic is "still possible, even if the pure tragedy is no longer possible. We can achieve the tragic from within the comedy, bringing it forth as a terrible moment" ["immer noch möglich, auch wenn die reine Tragödie nicht mehr möglich ist. Wir können das Tragische aus der Komödie heraus erzielen, hervorbringen als einen schrecklichen Moment"] (Dürrenmatt 1955, 37).

and things, custard-pie battles, chases or beatings in which the bodies of the actors possess, as Susanne Marschall has shown, a "cartoonish ability for regeneration" (Marschall 2011, 657; Andrin 2010, 231). With the tramp, however, Chaplin establishes a central symbolic character that can be read as genuinely tragicomic and that had a lasting effect on filmic slapstick. The tramp navigates highly diverse social roles while remaining a "likeable, graceful loser of modernity" (Marschall 2011, 657). This navigation confers sociopolitical dimensions to Chaplin's films, which present social differences in a humorous, comic manner.

In order to outline some similarities, I examine tragicomedies with respect to their use of specific forms of slapstick-like physical comedy. In doing so, it is necessary to develop a working concept of slapstick, which is broad enough to contain both filmic and theatrical forms of physical comedy, but which also considers the specific character of dramatic texts. Whereas filmic slapstick unfolds its tragicomic character mainly visually and acoustically, dramatic texts are limited to the semiotic system of language. Early slapstick films, strongly influenced by the cinema of attractions (see Gunning 1986), employ specific cinematographic techniques like stop motion, reverse motion, time lapse or incongruence between image and sound in order to cinematically create scenes of physical comedy.[7] Furthermore, the classic slapstick film consists of a succession of comic situations rather than of a coherent plot (cf. Seeßlen 1982, 31) whereas slapstick-like comedy in dramatic texts may be functional for the plot but is normally only used in certain situations. That is why slapstick-like situation comedy is often only hinted at in the dramatic text, for instance by means of information given in the stage directions or in combination with forms of verbal comedy, comedy of disguises, or comedy of mistaken identities. Because a stage production also offers theatrical possibilities for staging slapstick, in the following every text will also be compared with a recording of a stage performance.

Slapstick in dramatic texts may well contain paradigmatic elements of filmic slapstick like the struggle between human beings and things, chases, bodily mishaps, falls and other acrobatic forms of physical comedy. However, far more often dramatic forms of slapstick are subtler and only implied, for instance in the conflict between ego identity and corporeal identity, in forms of travesty or role refusal, in the (physical) resistance against (supposed) social constraints or in the unleashing of sexual drives (see Marschall 2001, 660). In the following, I will especially focus on such text passages and will examine them with regard to

---

[7] For different cinematic techniques of creating slapstick, see Brandlmeier (1995, 52). About the importance of the relation between image and sound for filmic physical comedy, see Seeßlen (1982, 27).

tragicomic slapstick inherent in physical situation comedy. However, as is typical for filmic slapstick, the physical or emotional pain caused is semantically overcoded and can be read as a symbolic condensation of the individual's subjection to social or other forces beyond its control.[8]

2 *Der Hofmeister* and *Amphitryon*: slapstick and the search for identity

Although the historiography of German literature classifies Lenz's *Der Hofmeister* as a *Sturm und Drang* (*Storm and Stress*) drama and Kleist's *Amphitryon* as a romantic drama, a comparative analysis of both tragicomedies with regard to their slapstick-like elements seems useful nevertheless. Both texts were written at a time when the combination of tragic and comic elements was encouraged by the influence of William Shakespeare's plays on German theater and their effective erosion of boundaries between genres (see Patterson 2003). At least implicitly the two plays are disassociated from classical enlightenment texts that banned physical comedy as conveyed by characters like Hanswurst or Harlequin from the stage (see von Ahnen 2005, 182).

Lenz calls *Der Hofmeister* a comedy but regards comedies as "pictures of human society" ["Gemälde der menschlichen Gesellschaft"] which usually are also serious and oblige the writer of comedies to write "comically and tragically at the same time" ["komisch und tragisch zugleich"] (Lenz 1966, 419). Tragic elements are mainly found in the central plot around the tutor Läuffer and his (imagined) love for his pupil Gustchen. Latent tragedy can be found in the description of the precarious situation of private teachers in aristocratic or bourgeois houses, who are treated, as the text says, like "servants" ["Domestiken"] (Lenz 1987, 46). Furthermore, tragedy – in the sense of painful occurrences which, at least from the situational perspective of the characters, cannot be averted – develops in the main plot by Gustchen's unwanted pregnancy, by her and the tutor's escape, by the Major's attempt to kill Läuffer and take revenge for the dishonoring of his daughter, by Läuffer's self-castration by which he wants to get rid of his uncontrollable drives, and by Gustchen's suicide attempt which only at the last minute is foiled by her father (cf. Wiessmeyer 1996, 331).

---

[8] Following Alan Dale, I use the term "slapstick" as synonymous with "physical comedy" in order to apply it beyond filmic usage. Dale justifies this by the fact that most early slapstick entertainers came from vaudeville or the music hall traditions (2000, 30). For the possible origins of American slapstick in the comedy of the British music hall see Dixon (2010).

However, the comedic denouement at the end of the play fulfills a special function for the play. Here physical comedy, hitherto mainly restricted to the subplot around the character of Pätus, now also spreads to the main plot. The happy ending, which is (seemingly) satisfactory for all characters, is introduced by a string of rather unlikely coincidences: a sudden lottery win reunites Pätus and Fritz with their fathers. Just at the moment when grief-stricken Gustchen wants to take her life her father appears and rescues her. In spite of the self-castration, Läuffer finds a new girl for whom physical love is not important, and so on. The final scene surpasses these coincidences with further unlikely occurrences: slapstick-like moments of physical comedy develop from the increasingly fast-paced plot, as several couples and family members get together in quick succession. Different from the preceding scenes, the stage directions here include several hints at the characters' spatial distribution and at their abrupt and thus comedic body movements. First Gustchen and the maid Rehaar hide in the adjoining room, then Fritz falls on his knees before his father, the Privy Councilor. The father, however, quickly lifts Fritz up again (Lenz 1987, 118) and embraces him, which concludes the first reconciliation. Directly afterwards, the Privy Councilor becomes the (spatial) organizer of the other pairings (119):

> PRIVY COUNCILOR: I see – Don't you want to step into that chamber for a moment? *(Leads him to the door.)*
>
> PÄTUS *(opens and shrieks back, holding his head with both his hands)*: Jungfer Rehaar – At your feet – *(Behind the scene.).* Am I so fortunate? Or is it just a dream? A Delirium? – An enchantment? –
>
> PRIVY COUNCILOR: Let's leave him. – *(Turns to Fritz.) And you are still thinking of Gustchen?* [. . .] Here! *(Leads him into the chamber.)*
>
> FRITZ *(off stage, screaming loudly)*: Gustchen! – Do I see a shadow image? (Lenz 2019, 86–87)[9]

---

9 "GEHEIMER RAT: Ich merke – Wollen Sie [Pätus] nicht auf einen Augenblick in die Kammer spazieren? *Führt ihn an die Tür.*
PÄTUS *macht auf und fährt zurück, sich mit beiden Händen an den Kopf greifend*: Jungfer Rehaar – Zu Ihren Füßen – *Hinter der Szene.* Bin ich so glücklich? oder ist's nur ein Traum? Ein Rausch? – Eine Bezauberung? –
GEHEIMER RAT: Lassen wir ihn! – *Kehrt zu Fritz.* Und du denkst noch an Gustchen? [. . .] Hier! *Führt ihn in die Kammer.*
FRITZ *hinter der Szene mit lautem Geschrei*: Gustchen! – Seh ich ein Schattenbild?"

Here comedy is created by the repetition and by the euphoria of the characters about the new pairings which is not directly correlated to their former behavior. It is further enhanced when, in the same scene, the old Pätus becomes reconciled with his mother and both the Major and the old Pätus are reunited with their children. Everyone is in each other's arms in no time, which creates an effect of physical comedy which can be described as decidedly slapstick-like since it has the function of implicit social criticism and shows that the search for identity and happiness is only superficially successful. All characters find a partner: the female characters are handed over like marionettes (see Lappe 1980, 16) to the male ones who, however, in spite of their comical physical movements, remain passive themselves in this orgy of reconciliation. They are pawns in the hands of the Privy Councilor, who, in turn, is merely a victim of the ironic coincidences at the end of the drama.

The play's final scenes almost demand an exaggerated staging that makes use of physical comedy. Hence it may at first be surprising that the theatre film *Der Hofmeister* (1975/1976), based on Bertolt Brecht's (1898–1956) version and directed by Harry Buckwitz (1904–1987), makes no use of slapstick. Compared to Lenz's drama, the lack of slapstick is particularly apparent in the final sequences: they only deal with the union of Fritz and Gustchen, which, unlike in the play, is not organized by the Privy Councilor and which centers on Fritz's decision to accept Gustchen's child as his own. The film evokes comedy only through the staged mawkishness, which culminates in the Majoress's singing of a schmaltzy Christmas minuet in celebration of the happiness of the new family.[10] The adaptation in the form of a theatre film, which makes recourse to Brecht's reworking of Lenz's drama conveys social criticism directly by the characters' discourse; however, by not using physical comedy, *Der Hofmeister* deprives itself of a subtler way of provoking in the viewer a critical reflection about the action and the deplorable state of social affairs by means of tragicomic proxemics.[11]

By contrast, different forms of social criticism complement each other in Lenz's dramatic text. First, the conflicts of social position and identity that are addressed in the play are solved only superficially: Läuffer's deep identity

---

10 See 1:48:23–1:49:24. Different than in Lenz's drama this is not the last, but the next-to-last scene of the theatre film. The last scene unites the tutor and Lise, and Wenzeslaus has to admit that he was wrong about Läuffer. With this change in the temporal chronology of the scenes the film focusses on Läuffer's fate and, unlike the dramatic text, does not let it merge into a fatalistic and at the same time highly questionable comedic finale which concerns all the characters.

11 Erika Fischer-Lichte defines the proxemic signs of the theatre as gestural signs, which however can only be attributed with a meaning if they are related to the surrounding space at the same time (1983, 87).

crisis, which leads to castration, is marginalized by his finding a future wife, Lise, who does not seem to care about his emasculation. Furthermore, the solution of the tutor problem, so central to the play, appears ridiculous: in the last scenes, the critical depiction of the profession of the tutor goes up into comedic smoke, not least because of the slapstick. This is carried to extremes by Fritz von Berg when he accepts the child fathered by Läuffer as his own and ends the play with the sardonic sentence: "At least, my sweet boy, I shall never have you educated by tutors" (Lenz 2019, 89).[12] The exaggeration of the comedic ending articulates that the problems of the contemporary educational system, which the text addresses and which are based on social hierarchies, cannot be solved in this manner.

In all his plays, Lenz shows the "ridiculous contrast between the bourgeois individual's demand for self-realization and the constraints of society" (Winter 2000, 58).[13] In *Der Hofmeister*, Lenz succeeds in expressing this very specifically by using slapstick-like physical comedy, which becomes a *pars pro toto* for the tragicomedy constitutive for the play. At first glance, the slapstick of the ending is only amusing; but it is in fact a text-immanent embodiment of the "ridiculous" ["lächerlich[e]"] (Winter 2000, 58) and tragicomic failure of the (bourgeois) individual due to social constraints.

In *Der Hofmeister*, the search of the bourgeois individual for an identity fails because of the unalterable social structures or it is declared obsolete by a chain of unlikely coincidences. Kleist's *Amphitryon* also deals with the question of ego identity, though not in the sense of expounding problems of social constraints – the drama maintains a broader ontological scope. The gods Zeus and Mercury assume the form of the Theban commander Amphitryon and his servant Sosias; Zeus desires Alkmene, Amphitryon's wife. Neither their wives nor the Thebans recognize Amphitryon and Sosias as themselves because their other, false selves played by the Gods, who represent them more convincingly than they themselves do. For Amphitryon and Alkmene in particular this series of mistaken identities becomes tragic: Alkmene betrays her husband without knowing it. Consequently, she suffers when she realizes that she has mistaken another man for her husband and feels the mistake is irreconcilable. Even when she finds out that it has been Zeus, the Father of the Gods, who has lain with her, her fainting in the last scene leaves open whether she can absolve herself of her guilt. Amphitryon, by contrast, at first suffers so much from the suspicion of Alkmene's infidelity and the

---

12 "Wenigstens, mein süßer Junge! werd ich dich nie durch Hofmeister erziehen lassen" (Lenz 1987, 123).
13 "Lächerlichen Kontrast zwischen dem Selbstentfaltungsanspruch des bürgerlichen Menschen und den Zwängen der Umwelt."

The Tragicomic Body: On the Relation between Tragicomedies and Slapstick — 257

loss of his ego identity that he contemplates suicide. However, his suffering and the tragedy related to him only last until he learns that Zeus had taken possession of his identity. When, furthermore, his wish for a demi-god as a son is fulfilled and his honor is restored, he willingly accepts the now untragic role of the cuckold. Thus, at the end of the play it is possible for him to take the perspective of the readers who, because of their informational advantage, see Amphitryon right from the beginning as part of a "playfully arranged" ["spielerisch aufgestellten"] (Zipfel 2017, 144) character constellation.

While the plot around the characters of Amphitryon and Alkmene has features of tragedy, the subplot around Sosias and his divine alter ego, Mercury, is comic. Here the dominant verbal comedy, ranging from wordplay and witty phrasing to stichomythia, is complemented by various forms of situation comedy: apart from the comedy of mistaken identities and the comedy of disguises[14] there are also physical stage actions containing motion comedy. This is even augmented by the repetition of the course of action in the encounters of Sosias and his doppelgänger Mercury. The events surrounding the servant character Sosias and thus also the scenes of physical comedy carry special importance for the play in spite of being classified as parts of the sub-plot. For instance, the first scene starts with a monologue of Sosias; in the whole play he speaks more verses than any other character (see Zeiringer 1996, 555). This is also important in so far as Sosias defines himself basically via his material corporeality and his bodily needs, and is also defined by other characters this way. Hence, with the character Sosias, Kleist manages to reinstate corporeality as a dramatic topic, which had been frowned upon in the German theater since Gottsched.

The first scene of Act I begins in medias res: by means of a (role) play within the play Sosias practices how he could, at the behest of Amphitryon, deliver the good news of the victory over the Athenians to Alkmene. In doing so, he not only assumes his role as a messenger but also plays the role of Alkmene, imagined by him and represented by a lantern as a placeholder. He also takes the role of a "stage director" when he again and again gives himself laudatory instructions. In this way, he anticipates the central topic of the play – the question of the stability of identity. Even if Kleist's stage directions do not contain any information about how Sosias positions himself on stage during this enacted dialogue, the adoption of both speaking parts including the directorial instructions is a clear indication that this scene may or even must be played using physical comedy. Furthermore,

---

14 Unlike Harald Fricke and Angela Salvisberg, I consider the comedy of disguises and the comedy of mistaken identities as belonging to the supercategory of situation comedy, as disguises and mistaken identities are usually bound to specific situations (see Fricke and Salvisberg 1997, 279).

Sosias's body becomes an object of the action quite directly when he uses the palm of his hand as a prop for showing the imagined Alkmene the course of the battle on a map: "My gracious lady, I am at your service. About this victory I can, I flatter / myself, provide you with a full report. / Imagine, then, if you will be so kind, / Pharissa standing over on this side – / *(He indicates the places on his hand.)*" (Kleist 2002, 95; emphasis in original).[15]

The incorporation of objects into the role play also has a slapstick-like effect, even though at this point of the play one cannot yet speak about a "cussedness of things" [Tücke der Objekte] (Zeyringer 1996, 560), as Klaus Zeyringer calls it in anticipation of the diadem which is evidence of the adultery.

The potential for slapstick inherent in the first scene's monologue was fully exploited in the production of *Amphitryon* at the Münchner Kammerspiele in 1999. Sosias, played by Lambert Hanel, changes his position on stage in quick alternation: when he plays Sosias, the herald of the victorious battle, he stands at the entrance of Amphitryon's palace; when he represents Alkmene, he runs down several steps on the staircase each time. Physical comedy is created not just by the fast movements of the actor, but also by his theatrical acting, rich in gesture and therefore hyperbolical,[16] and by altering his voice.

Even more conspicuous physical comedy is evoked in the dramatic text in the following scene, the second scene of Act I. Mercury, in the guise of Sosias, denies Sosias access to the palace. The verbal duel in which the two characters

Figure 1–3: Sosias in quick alternation plays Alkmene (right, 05:43) and himself (left, 03:42).

---

15 "Ich bin zu euern Diensten, gnäd'ge Frau. / Denn in der Tat kann ich von diesem Siege / Vollständ'ge Auskunft, schmeichl' ich mir, erteilen: / Stellt Euch, wenn ihr die Güte haben wollt, / Auf dieser Seite hier – / *Er bezeichnet die Örter auf seiner Hand.* / Pharissa vor" (Kleist 1991, 385; emphasis in original).

16 Muriel Andrin points out that slapstick often also appears in hyperbolic gestures: slapstick "shares with melodrama one of its constitutive rhetorical figures, the expression or representation of actions, characters, and gestures in excessive or exaggerated ways" (2010, 227).

speak quietly to themselves in rapid alternation and loudly to one another climaxes in a scene of physical violence: Sosias approaches the entrance of the palace and Mercury stops him from entering by giving him a thrashing. Although Sosias complains of back pain afterwards, his ironic comment about this incident ("Some glorious embassy I've made of it!" [Kleist 2002, 105; "Das war mir eine rühmliche Gesellschaft" (Kleist 1991, 395)]) indicates that his body, as is known from characters in slapstick films, has a "cartoonish ability for regeneration" (Marschall 2011, 657).

The physical comedy transported in the first two scenes by Sosias's double role as himself and Alkmene and by Mercury in the role of Sosias can be read as a key to an understanding of the entire text. The central issue is already addressed here with slapstick-like defamiliarization strategies: the fragility of ego identity and its dependence on attestation by a counterpart. The explicit physical comedy, which tones down the tragedy of the instability of identity, is not without effect on the more tragic main plot. With Sosias, Kleist develops a character who sets Amphitryon and Alkmene an example of a different behavior variant. In the course of the play, the focus on material corporeality and on his bodily needs seems to relieve Sosias of the problem that his ego identity has become fragile. Instead of insisting on his uniqueness and its attestation by others, Sosias accepts that he was "de-sosiatised" ["entsosiatisiert"] (Kleist 1991, 454). And while the quarrel between Zeus and Amphitryon for the position as legitimate husband of Alkmene comes to a head, Sosias increasingly refers to his body and its needs, for example for food consumption (see Jauß 1979, 237). By defining his body more and more from a material and less from an ideational perspective, he succeeds in toning down the tragedy of identity loss. He experiences it not solely as tragic, but also as (physically) comic. Kleist's *Amphitryon* therefore offers a more explicit solution for the modern individual's increasingly problematic search for identity than Lenz's *Der Hofmeister*. In the play, the slapstick-like physical comedy can be interpreted as a different way of dealing with the imminent identity loss, one that protects the individual from existential uncertainty.[17]

---

[17] This text-immanent interpretation of the slapstick-variant chosen by Lenz correlates with Miriam Hansen's proposition concerning slapstick-films, which assumes that slapstick opens an aesthetic horizon in which "the traumatic effects of modernity were reflected" (1999, 69).

3 *Die Ratten* and *Die Physiker*: slapstick and the grotesque

Since the middle of the nineteenth century and especially after 1871, nationalist currents promoting a "national unification" take ground in Imperial Germany, leading to an officially supported "affirmative art production" in the form of, for example, patriotic dramas (Sandig 1980, 131). With ongoing industrialization and the multiple problems resulting from it for a newly developing industrial proletariat, especially naturalist authors turn to the literarisation of social injustices. Often, social injustices are no longer shown in the texts as purely tragic and therefore unavoidable, but they are combined with comic elements that sometimes even reach the grotesque and which often only serve to enhance tragedy.[18]

Gerhart Hauptmann explicitly called his drama *Die Ratten*, which premiered in 1911, a "Berlin tragicomedy." With this subtitle, Hauptmann not only referred to the combination of the tragic and the comic but also to the metropolitan setting: in a multi-level tenement building in Berlin two social groups encounter each other. Hassenreuter, a former theatre director with a bourgeois background, stores his costume stock in the tenement's attic and gives lessons to drama students. One floor below lives Frau John, a cleaning woman who takes care of the attic. She kidnaps a new-born child in order to save her marriage and to cope with the death of her son who died from diphtheria. The plot around Frau John and the other characters from the Berlin proletariat is tragic at its core: some characters cannot, others do not want to escape from their milieu and its determinations. By contrast, the plot around Director Hassenreuter is dominated by comic situations, which at times tend towards slapstick-like physical comedy.

In the first act already, the tragic and the comic meet right away in the space of the attic. The detailed description of the spatial circumstances in the stage directions anticipate the eerie atmosphere of the action. In the attic, there is only "uncertain light" ["ungewisses Licht"], the room has no windows, and is full of costumes which have a mysterious quality in the half-light (Hauptmann 1965, 735). This oppressive atmosphere is reflected in the dramatic plot through the talk between Henriette John and Pauline Pieperkarcka. With a vested interest

---

[18] For the development of the tragicomic genre since the turn of the century see Guthke (1968, 141–144). Apart from Hauptmann, Peter Sprengel categorizes Frank Wedekind (1864–1918), Carl Sternheim (1878–1942), and Arthur Schnitzler (1862–1931) among the group of authors who at the turn of the century develop a preference for tragicomic modes of writing (Sprengel 1994, 265).

Henriette tries to convince the apparently suicidal and pregnant Pauline to hand over the baby, the result of an affair, to her after giving birth. However, after an "uncanny interlude" ["unheimlichen Zwischenspiel"] (Zipfel 2017, 185) with Henriette's brother, who will later become the murderer of Pauline, a comedic part follows. Hassenreuter meets his lover in the attic; earlier, his daughter Walburga, who has a date with her secret boyfriend Spitta, hid from her father in an adjacent chamber. Into the same chamber, from which the characters can follow the events in the attic at least acoustically, Frau John has fled with Pauline, who is in labor and in the course of the scene secretly gives birth to her child. Soon thereafter, Hassenreuter's lover hides in another room of the attic when Spitta meets Hassenreuter. As in *Der Hofmeister*, in this scene of *Die Ratten* slapstick comedy is created by the various room changes in quick succession, with the comic effect being increased by dialogue comedy and comedy of disguises.

In the 2008 Michael Thalheimer (*1965) production of *Die Ratten* at the Deutsches Theater in Berlin, the oppressive atmosphere of the room is reflected by Olaf Altmann's stage design: an overhanging wooden construction reaching to the edge of the stage represents the attic and forces the actors to perform the entire play in stooped posture. The stage lighting underlines the glum mood of scenes, as the rear of the stage is entirely in the dark and only the front is lit harshly, so that in the first act the characters in their "hiding place" can only be seen up to their hips. The slapstick created by the actors fleeing to the rear of the stage in quick succession intensifies in this stage production by the grotesque corporeality of Hassenreuter – played by Horst Lebinsky – who undresses rapidly and approaches his lover in a boorish and lecherous manner, only to be kept from having sex by Spitta's arrival.

At the end of *Die Ratten*, similar to *Der Hofmeister* and *Amphitryon*, tragedy and comedy meet directly, with physical comedy being of central importance. Frau John can no longer conceal that she kidnapped a child; her previously unsuspecting husband, as well as the accidentally visiting Hassenreuters, have learned the truth in

Figure 2: Left: "Hide and seek" (10:11). Right: Hassenreuter in lecherous action (12:40).

the meantime. She sees no other way out than to kill herself along with the child. In this extremely dramatic scene, the ensuing slapstick has a grotesque effect, as it evokes dread and laughter at the same time (see Meyer 2007, 297). Hassenreuter and Spitta "throw themselves in the way of the desperate woman" ["werfen sich der Verzweifelten entgegen"] and Hassenreuter begins a comic, elliptic monologue, in which he turns himself into the director of this scene of situation comedy:

> Stop! I intervene at this point! Here I am responsible! Whom the boy may belong – [. . .] Forward march, Spitta! Fight, Spitta! Here your characteristics are well in place! Come on! That's the way! Bravo! As if it were the baby Jesus! Bravo![19]   (Hauptmann 1969, 830)

Hassenreuter and Spitta intentionally do not stop Frau John, who then takes her life by defenestration. While in this way the plot around Frau John has the most tragic outcome imaginable, the plot around Hassenreuter has all the features of the ending of a comedy: Walburga and Spitta get together and Hassenreuter becomes a theater director again. Different from *Der Hofmeister* and *Amphitryon*, the comic is not preferred over the tragic at the end of the drama. The slapstick-like comedy in the last scene rather functions as a *pars pro toto* for the sobering message of the play: the social differences clash mercilessly, and the bourgeoisie cannot or does not want to see the multiple material and psychical problems of the lower class, not to mention solving them.[20] The slapstick exposes Hassenreuter to ridicule as a representative of this ignorant educated bourgeoisie. By its immediate combination of tragedy and comedy, slapstick explicitly asks the reader to reflect on the action. Therefore, in *Die Ratten*, too, the few slapstick elements are of special importance as they convey in nuce the intended effect on the reader, who has to tolerate the grotesque contradictions.

The grotesque has an even more central role in *Die Physiker*. In *Theaterprobleme* [Theater Problems] (1955), Dürrenmatt explicitly states that the grotesque comedy in his plays, which often also manifests physically, is supposed to have an effect on the reader. Especially because his plays mostly end in disillusionment, comedy – regarded by Dürrenmatt as a combination of the tragic and the comic – functions as "a mousetrap into which the audience falls again and again" ["eine Mausfalle, in die das Publikum immer wieder gerät"] and by hich they "can get attacked, seduced, cheated" ["angegriffen, verführt, überlistet werden kann"]

---

[19] "Halt! Hier greife ich ein! Hier bin ich zuständig! Wem das Knäblein hier auch immer gehören mag – [. . .] Vorwärts, Spitta! Kämpfen Sie, Spitta! Hier sind Ihre Eigenschaften am Platz! Vorwärts! Vorsicht! So! Bravo! Als wär' es das Jesuskind! Bravo!"
[20] For the tragicomic "blindness" of the characters around Hassenreuter, see Sprengel (1994, 265; 1984, 146).

The Tragicomic Body: On the Relation between Tragicomedies and Slapstick — 263

(1955, 39). While physical comedy is foremost entertaining, it is nevertheless meant to make the reader reflect on the sociocritical message of the texts without even noticing.

On the one hand, *Die Physiker* is a fictionalized criticism of the nuclear development, on the other hand it is also a devastating survey of the present times: "In the face of coincidence reducing the freedom of action to absurdity, the question of the responsibility of the individual scientist becomes irrelevant"[21] (Grimm 2013, 113). The plot is highly tragic in a nihilist sense, as Möbius cannot revoke the world formula that he has thought up. His knowledge is in the world and can thus be misused by Frau von Zahnd. The plot around three patients of a mental institution, who are finally revealed to be a physicist in the possession of the world formula and two physicists acting as secret agents, contains a variety of grotesque scenes. Not all of these have slapstick-like character, however. A grotesque and entertaining impression is often rather created by a series of apparently absurd coincidences such as the murder of the three nurses. Physical comedy is mostly used by supporting characters, whose movements are reminiscent of slapstick, for example the "giant-like" ["riesenhaft"] male nurses who lay the table for the three physicists in a sort of rehearsed spatial choreography and who behave as nimble and agile servants of the physicists in spite of their physiognomy (Dürrenmatt 1963, 326–327). Likewise, mention must be made of the scene in which Möbius plays the madman in front of his family after a whimsical musical interlude by his sons. There he positions himself with fast and apparently uncontrollable movements in different places of the room (304–305). Physical comedy underlines the grotesque situation comedy, comedy of disguises, and dialogue comedy of the play. It is one comic element among various others in the play.

The relative importance of comic elements is quite different in the stage production of *Die Physiker* at the Schauspielhaus Zürich, which after 2013 was revived in February 2018. In this production, almost every movement is grotesquely exaggerated and slapstick-like. The stage, which represents a neon-green psychiatric cell, contains hidden trampolines by which the actors jump onto and behind the stage sets in acrobatic stunts. Over and over they catch their fingers in the door or trip over the too long sleeves of their straitjackets.[22] Similar to filmic slapstick, they do not show any physical reactions and behave like mechanically controlled rubber dolls, who can only move their bodies with

---

[21] "Angesichts der vom Zufall ad absurdum geführten Handlungsfreiheit wird die Frage nach der Verantwortung des einzelnen Naturwissenschaftlers irrelevant."
[22] For a description of the acrobatic stunts, see Fellmann (2013).

Figure 3: Inspector after falling, Möbius and Zahnd climbing (122:50).

grotesque distortions and theatricality. The stage sets, as well as the actors' bodies, turn out to be obstacles that, in the end, cannot be overcome.

Different from the dramatic text, the originally intended effect of a sparing use of slapstick is lost. The audience gets to see a very physical and extremely entertaining stage production, but the slapstick gags in their grotesque exaggeration can only insufficiently convey the tragedy of the play.

4 Conclusion: slapstick as a *pars pro toto* of the tragicomic

Of course, it was not the aim of this chapter to conclusively answer the question of the role of slapstick in modern German language tragicomedies. The selected examples of texts and stage productions only allow to outline some tendencies: all four tragicomic texts contain various scenes with implicit or explicit slapstick comedy. In all cases, the slapstick scenes can also be interpreted as a *pars pro toto* of the tragicomic plot, as they bring together – with different emphasis – the tragic and the comic. A comparison of the texts, however, makes substantial differences in quality evident: in *Der Hofmeister* and *Amphitryon*, the slapstick-like scenes revolve around the central identity problem. The character Läuffer in *Der Hofmeister* fails in his search for a (bourgeois) identity; however, this search is declared obsolete by the accumulation of coincidences and the happy pairings in the last scene. In spite of the happy, comedy-like ending, the slapstick quality of the reunion scene is latently tragic as it can only superficially camouflage but not overcome the social injustices addressed in the course of the play. In *Amphitryon*, the slapstick embodied by the (supporting) character Sosias is a text-internal solution variant of the ontic identity dilemma. This variant is only tragic because it represents an adaptation to an imposed identity loss.

In the end, though, both tragicomedies are resolved into a comedy-like ending whose slapstick can only indirectly be read as a sociocritical drama element.

This makes for an important difference to the two plays written after 1900. In spite of some comic elements in these dramas, they end tragically, and they can more obviously be seen as expressions of the social injustices diagnosed by Hauptmann and Dürrenmatt and of the major social issues of modernity. In both texts, slapstick can be read as a *pars pro toto* of the grotesque quality of the plays: the tragic and the comic clash unchecked, but in the end the laughter sticks in the readers' throats in the face of the inexorable tragic developments.

Disregarding these differences in the quality of the slapstick, all four tragicomedies have in common that, unlike classic slapstick films, they contain only a few slapstick scenes. However, these scenes carry special importance for an understanding of the texts: by means of situation comedy they condense the raised issues of the individual's position in and its responsibility for society, and they make them visually tangible in a stage production. If, however, as in Harry Buckwitz's *Hofmeister* production, slapstick is entirely renounced or if, as in Fritsch's *Physiker* production, there is too much slapstick, the subtle overdetermination of slapstick implied in the texts is lost.

Bibliography

Amphitryon (D 1999, Münchner Kammerspiele). Director: Dieter Dorn. Stage and Costumes: Jürgen Rose. Actors: Michael Maertens (Jupiter), Oliver Näele (Merku), Jens Harzer (Amphitryon), Lambert Hamel (Sosias), Sibylle Canonica (Alkmene). 3Sat. Television Recording 2000. 150 mins.

Andrin, Muriel. "Back to the 'Slap.' Slapstick's Hyperbolic Gesture and the Rhetoric of Violence." *Slapstick Comedy*. Ed. Tom Paulus and Rob King. New York: Routledge, 2010. 226–235.

Ahnen, Helmut von. *Das Komische auf der Bühne: Versuch einer Systematik*. Munich: Herbert Utz Verlag, 2006.

Becker-Cantarino, Barbara. "Jakob Michael Reinhold Lenz: *Der Hofmeister*." *Interpretationen: Dramen des Sturm und Drang*. Stuttgart: Reclam, 1986. 33–56.

Brandlmeier, Thomas. "Lachkultur des Fin de siècle." *Slapstick & Co: Frühe Filmkomödien. Early Comedies*. Ed. Helga Belach and Wolfgang Jacobsen. Berlin: Argon Verlag, 1995. 16–75.

Dale, Alan. *Comedy is a Man in Trouble: Slapstick in American Movies*. Minneapolis: University of Minnesota Press, 2000.

Der Hofmeister (D 1975/1976). Director: Harry Buckwitz. Camera: Werner Rosemann. Actors: Anita Lochner (Gustchen), Hans Helmut Dickow (Major von Berg), Ernst Jacobi (Läuffer/Hofmeister). Hessischer Rundfunk. Television Recording. 117 mins.

Die Ratten (D 2008, Deutsches Theater Berlin). Director: Michael Thalheimer. Stage: Olaf Altmann. Costumes: Michaela Barth. Music: Bert Wrede. Actors: Constanze Becker (Frau John), Regine Zimmermann (Pauline Piperkarcka), Horst Lebinsky (Harro Hassenreuther). ZDF-Theater-Edition. Belvedere: 99 mins.

Die Physiker (D 2013). Director: Herbert Fritsch. Stage: Herbert Fritsch. Actors: Mathilde von Zahnd (Corinna Harfouch), Milian Zerzawy (Möbius), Gottfried Breitfuß (Einstein), Jean Pierre Cornus (Kommissar). ZDFkultur: 105 mins.

Dixon, Bryony. "The Good Thieves. On the Origins of Situation Comedy in the British Music Hall." *Slapstick Comedy*. Ed. Tom Paulus and Rob King. New York: Routledge, 2010. 21–36.

Dürrenmatt, Friedrich. "Die Physiker." *Komödien II und frühe Stücke*. Zurich: Arche, 1963. 283–355.

Dürrenmatt, Friedrich *Theaterprobleme*. Zurich: Arche, 1955.

Fellmann, Christoph. "Die Slapstickformel." https://www.nachtkritik.de/index.php?option=com_content&view=article&id=8647:die-physiker-herbert-fritsch-teilchenbeschleunigt-friedrich-duerrenmatts-apokalyptische-komoedie-am-urauffuehrungsort-in-zuerich&catid=38:die-nachtkritik&Itemid=40 (accessed 5 March 2019).

Fischer-Lichte, Erika. *Semiotik des Theaters: Eine Einführung. Vol.1: Das System der theatralischen Zeichen*. Tübingen: Narr, 1983.

Fricke, Harald, and Angelika Salvisberg. "Bühnenrede." *Reallexikon der deutschen Literaturwissenschaft. Vol. I: A–G*. Ed. Klaus Weimar. Berlin: De Gruyter, 1997. 279–282.

Gottsched, Johann Christoph. *Ausgewählte Werke. Vol. 6, Part 2: Versuch einer critischen Dichtkunst: Anderer besonderer Theil [1730]*. Ed. Joachim Birke and Brigitte Birke. Berlin: De Gruyter, 1973.

Grimm, Gunter E. *Friedrich Dürrenmatt*. Marburg: Tectum, 2013.

Guthke, Siegfried. *Die moderne Tragikomödie: Theorie und Gestalt*. Göttingen: Vandenhoek & Ruprecht, 1968.

Gunning, Tom. "The Cinema of Attractions: Early Film, Its Spectator and the Avantgarde." *Wide Angle* 8, 3–4 (1986): 63–70.

Hansen, Miriam. "The Mass Production of the Senses. Classical Cinema as Vernacular Modernism." *Modernism/Modernity* 6.2 (1999): 59–77.

Hauptmann, Gerhart. "Die Ratten." *Sämtliche Werke*. Ed. Hans-Egon Hass. Darmstadt: Wissenschaftliche Buchgesellschaft, 1965. 731–831.

Jauß, Hans Robert. "Poetik und Problematik von Identität und Rolle in der Geschichte des Amphitryon." *Identität*. Ed. Odo Marquard and Karlheinz Stierle. Munich: Fink, 1979. 213–253.

Kleist, Heinrich von. "Amphitryon. Ein Lustspiel nach Molière." *Sämtliche Werke und Briefe. Vol. 1: Dramen 1802–1807*. Ed. Ilse-Marie Barth and Hinrich C. Seeba. Frankfurt am Main: Deutscher Klassiker Verlag, 1991. 377–461.

Kleist, Heinrich von. *Heinrich von Kleist: Plays*. Ed. Walter Hinderer. New York: Continuum, 2002.

Lappe, Claus O. "Wer hat Gustchens Kind gezeugt? Zeitstruktur und Rollenspiel in Lenz' Hofmeister." *Deutsche Vierteljahresschrift für Literaturwissenschaft und Geistesgeschichte* 54 (1980): 14–46.

Lenz, Jakob Michael Reinhold. "Der Hofmeister. Oder Vorteile der Privaterziehung." *Werke und Briefe in drei Bänden*. Ed. Sigrid Damm. Vol. 1. Munich: Carl Hanser, 1987. 41–124.

Lenz, Jakob Michael Reinhold. *Selected Works by J. M. R. Lenz: Plays, Stories, Essays, and Poems*. Ed. Martin Wagner and Ellwood Wiggins. Rochester: Camden House, 2019.

Lenz, Jakob Michael Reinhold. "Rezension des Neuen Menoza [1774]. Von dem Verfasser selbst aufgesetzt." *Werke und Schriften I*. Ed. Britta Titel and Hellmut Haug. Stuttgart: Goverts, 1966. 414–420.

Lessing, Gotthold Ephraim. *Hamburgische Dramaturgie* [1767]. Ed. Klaus L. Berghahn. Stuttgart: Reclam, 1981.

Marschall, Susanne. "Slapstick." *Reclams Sachlexikon des Films*. Ed. Thomas Koebner. Stuttgart: Reclam, 2011. 657–661.

Meyer, Urs. "Groteske." *Metzler Lexikon Literatur*. Ed. Dieter Burdorf, Christoph Fasbender, and Burkhard Moenninghoff. Stuttgart: Metzler, 2007. 297–198.

Patterson, Michael. "The Theater Practice of the *Sturm und Drang*." *Literature of the Sturm und Drang*. Ed. David Hill. Rochester: Camden House, 2003. 141–157.

Sandig, Holger. *Deutsche Dramaturgie des Grotesken um die Jahrhundertwende*. Munich: Fink, 1980.

Seeßlen, Georg. *Klassiker der Filmkomik. Geschichte und Mythologie des komischen Films*. Mit einer Filmografie von Peter Horn und einer Bibliographie von Jürgen Berger. Reinbek: Rowohlt, 1982.

Sprengel, Peter. *Gerhart Hauptmann. Epoche – Werk – Wirkung*. Munich: Beck, 1984.

Sprengel, Peter. "Gerhart Hauptmann: *Die Ratten* (1911)." *Interpretationen. Dramen des Naturalismus*. Stuttgart: Reclam, 1994. 243–282.

Wiessmeyer, Monika. "Gesellschaftskritik in der Tragikomödie: *Der Hofmeister* (1774) und *Die Soldaten* (1776) von J.M.R. Lenz." *Jakob Michael Reinhold Lenz im Spiegel der Forschung*. Ed. Matthias Luserke. Hildesheim: Georg Olms Verlag, 1995. 368–380.

Winter, Hans-Gerd. *Jakob Michael Reinhold Lenz*. Stuttgart: Metzler 2000.

Zipfel, Frank. *Tragikomödien. Kombinationsformen von Tragik und Komik im europäischen Drama des 19. und 20. Jahrhunderts*. Stuttgart: Metzler, 2017.

Zeyringer, Klaus. "'Wo kömmt der Witz mir her?' Eine 'Lustspielfigur par excellence.' Zu den Sosias-Szenen in Kleists *Amphitryon*." *Deutsche Vierteljahresschrift für Literaturwissenschaft und Geistesgeschichte* 70 (1996): 552–568.

Irina Hron
'Or Words to That Effect':
The Antimetaphysics of Slapstick

Antimetaphysical slapstick – as a figure of thought – draws on the traditions of the theatric and cinematic slapstick as well as on the postulates and thought structures of a 'philosophy of difference' dating back to the formation of postmodern or poststructuralist theory. The antimetaphysical variety of slapstick, outlined in this chapter, develops first from within the traditional concept of body-related comedy and subsequently intersects with a number of other forms of comedy and the comedic. Notably, subtleties of distinction between comedy genres such as satire, parody, farce, or travesty do not play a role here, as the focus is on the use of specific operations and techniques that are traditionally attributed to slapstick and can even be found in the discourses of poststructuralism and postmodernism (sense, nonsense, repetition, seriality). Drawing particularly on Gilles Deleuze's treatise *Logique du sens* [*The Logic of Sense*, 1969], this chapter examines to what extent these techniques yield the construct of an antimetaphysical variant of slapstick which is no longer driven by a metaphysical desire to get to the bottom of things, and which is fundamentally independent from genre. Instead, the question of how the comedic is *produced*, i.e., constructed through comic operations is discussed in detail using the example of German dramatist Wolfgang Hildesheimer's comic plays. On the one hand, this leads to a novel reading of Hildesheimer's early theater that outlines the structure and special features of antimetaphysical slapstick. On the other hand, it results in an original contribution that refines the overall definition of slapstick.

1 (Anti-)Metaphysical constructs of slapstick (Deleuze, Hildesheimer)

Basic principles of 1920s film theory draw on a definition of the term slapstick as a "deeply embedded cinematic form," as noted in the *Dictionary of Film Studies* (2012). These principles influence our understanding of slapstick as much as the tradition dating back to the *commedia dell'arte*, in which the slap stick comes

---

Translated by Laura Isakov

from Arlecchino's *batocchio* and Harlequin's *batte* (cf. Peacock 2013, 61–66; Trahair 2007, 47; Esslin 1983). In his influential study *The Theatre of the Absurd* (1961) Martin Esslin vividly describes how "the line from the *mimus* of antiquity, through the clowns and jesters of Middle Ages and the Zanni and Arlecchini of the *commedia dell'arte*" (335) emerged, from which, in turn, the twentieth century derived the silent film comedy. Thus, this chapter references a whole range of traditions, reaching from the "rich theatrical tradition of slapstick (in *commedia dell'arte*, in 18th and 19th century pantomimes, in circus clowning to name but a few)" (Peacock 2010, 94) to the silent cinema and to postmodern slapstick (cf. Gilotta 2008). The decisive turn of the antimetaphysical variant, however, lies in its reference to the body or to the comic corporeality. It centers on a corporeality which initially ensures the recognizability of the prototypical characters of both theatric and cinematic slapstick – from Arlecchino to the clown to Charlie Chaplin; this, as it turns out, is a corporeality which has "shaped the way that many contemporary artists represent the body in their works" (Gillota 2008, 3). But what role can the body still play in a postmodern understanding of slapstick where "bodies have lost their measure and are only illusions"[1] [205]?

The link between slapstick and poststructuralism has been drawn several times, albeit never before in the constellation at the center of this article. In his thesis, David Gillota notes that slapstick "explores many of the same issues that postmodern artists typically interrogate" (Gillota 2008, 6; cf. also Hutcheon 1988 and 1989). Likewise, in *The Comedy of Philosophy: Sense and Nonsense in Early Cinematic Slapstick* (2007), Lisa Trahair explores Bataille, Deleuze, Derrida, Freud, and Lyotard; she argues that a number of disciplines and theories of the last few years have prominently featured research dealing with comic techniques, "most significantly in the discourses of poststructuralism and postmodernism" (1). This applies in particular to aspects such as the ludic, the joke play, and laughter (5). On this basis, Trahair supports the thesis that "aspects of both postmodernism and poststructuralism have a largely unperceived debt to the tenets of the comic" (5). The consideration that theoretical approaches attributed to postmodernism or poststructuralism "theorize the specificity of the comic's formations" (1) in an original way, also inform the starting point for further argumentation undertaken here.

*

Gilles Deleuze's intriguing treatise on the logic of sense as well as his intensive study of the processes of sense- and nonsense-formation is certainly one

---

[1] All citations from the 2001 English translation of Deleuze's *Logique du sens* will be identified by page numbers in squared brackets.

of the most complex examinations of a specifically postmodern comic style. His work is particularly suitable for literary study, as Deleuze develops his argument for the most part on the basis of literary texts, including works by James Joyce (1882–1941), Antonin Artaud (1896–1948), and particularly Lewis Carroll's nonsense-books (*Alice's Adventures in Wonderland* [1865], *Through the Looking-Glass, and What Alice Found There* [1871], and *Sylvie and Bruno* [1889]). Consequently, in his *Logic of Sense*, the concept of sense no longer references a profound or even metaphysical content of language or of things. Rather, it is shifted to a flat surface without any depth or substance of its own. On this surface, sense is presented as an *effect*:

> In short, sense is always an *effect*. It is not an effect merely in the causal sense; it is also an effect in the sense of an "optical effect" or a "sound effect," or, even better, a surface effect, a position effect, and a language effect. [70]

Accordingly, Deleuze's conception of sense is shown as an *outcome*. The category of sense is thus detached from the category of meaning, and sense and nonsense are no longer reproduced in the binary relationship of true and false. Sentences and texts that, at first glance, appear senseless, as they are rendered either irrelevant or are simply false according to the laws of occidental logic, nevertheless *have* a sense: "That which has a sense has also a meaning, but for reasons which are different from its having a sense" [70]. Instead, they are directly related to nonsense, which "has no sense, and that which, as such and as it enacts the donation of sense, is opposed to the absence of sense" [71]. Thus, sense is no longer regarded as a fundamental metaphysical principle, but as a construct: "It is thus pleasing that there resounds today the news that sense is never a principle or an origin, but that it is *produced*. It is not something to discover, to restore, and to re-employ; it is something to *produce* by a new machinery" [72; emphasis mine].

Lisa Trahair illuminates those aspects of sense vs. meaning in the context of her groundbreaking research on slapstick, where she identifies a series of specific "comic processes and operations, along with their relation to meaning" (2007, 7). Trahair's study on "the imbrication of the comic and meaning, of sense and nonsense" (7) builds on the comic theories of Sigmund Freud (1856–1939) and Georges Bataille (1897–1962), with a focus on the slapstick cinema of the 1920s. Likewise, the following chapter will explore the connection between slapstick, sense, and meaning, although the object of study is German-language drama from the post-war period which feature vital parallels to basic premises of slapstick comedy. Thus, the chapter revisits the issue of body/language-duality, which constitutes a foundation of slapstick as it is usually defined as *body* comedy. It does so in examining those corporealities that are no longer bound to a metaphysical understanding of person and body, but instead operate on surfaces and as sense-figures in relationship to nonsense figures. Crucially, this chapter investigates the consequences of the poststructuralist "discovery of incorporeal events, meanings, or effects, which are irreducible to 'deep' bodies and to 'lofty' ideas" [132] for a theory of postmodern or 'antimetaphysical' slapstick. This is pursued further by a series of literary case studies of Wolfgang Hildesheimer (1916–1991), a post-war German-speaking writer whose plays concern questions of interpretation and meaning as well as sense and nonsense: "He who waits for an interpretation waits in vain. He will not receive it until the meaning [*Sinn*] of creation is explained to him by a competent party, thus never" (Hildesheimer 1988, 14; translation[2]). Most notably, however, is the fact that Hildesheimer's dramatis personae are no longer driven by a metaphysical desire to get to the bottom of things or explore their depth. Rather, they appear – with reference to Arthur Schopenhauer's famous dictum – as *animalia postmetaphysici* (see Section 4 of this chapter).

In fact, in Hildesheimer's early plays, one constantly stumbles over paradoxical sense and nonsense effects that cause involuntary laughter. Never-ending series of bizarre to grotesque constellations refer directly to the staging of humor and comic absurdity, which will be examined here for their parallels to basic premises of slapstick. Past research usually attributed the literary strategies and operations in these plays to absurdist literature (cf. Hildesheimer 1988; Weinhold 1983; Blamberger 1986; Lorenz 1986). However, these plays are far less known than the author's later work and have, as of yet, not been read with regard to the comedic strategies of slapstick (cf. Lorenz 1986). Previous approaches have undertaken a refining of an occasionally imprecise concept of the Absurd and have imposed this concept onto Hildesheimer's plays, usually with recourse to his Erlangen speech "Über das absurde Theater" ("On the Absurd Theater," 1989). However, a side glance at the work of Henri Bergson (1859–1941) already reveals that, conceptually speaking, the absurd recedes into the background as a category subordinate to the comedic: "It [the absurdity] does not create the comedic, but rather derives from it" ([1900], 474; translation). Eventually, the categories of sense and nonsense come to the foreground and form the beginning of the framework of a slapstick comedy that no longer rests on the foundation of metaphysics or profundity.

Even the historical context of the literary examples, situated as they are in the post-war period, is quite revealing, since the slapstick phenomenon is often

---

[2] All citations marked as "translation" in the parenthetical reference the original but are reproduced in English translation.

described as reaction to a crisis. This is further emphasized through the "feeling of nostalgia that marked the rediscovery and recycling of slapstick comedy after World War II" (Jacobs and D'Haeyere 2017, 32), suggesting that the connection between slapstick and crisis is not a coincidence (cf. Hildesheimer 1988; Flaig 2013; Saunders 1987; Jacobs and D'Haeyere 2017). The struggle for an unencumbered language as well as the rejection of old (or the search for new) descriptive categories – as happened in poststructuralism with regard to both the duality of body and language and to postulations of identity and unity – unfold against this background. The experience of the world wars "does not tolerate the subsistence of God as an original individuality, nor the self as a Person, nor the world as an element of the self and as God's product" [176]. Consequently, the definition of slapstick as, first and foremost, '*body* comedy' has to be reconsidered in the context of the postmodern era and poststructuralism and then examined in terms of, firstly, how it stands in relation to an antimetaphysical variant of slapstick emerging from the comic body and, secondly, what role sense and nonsense play. The following close readings of Hildesheimer's 'plays, in which it gets dark' ['Stücke, in denen es dunkel wird'], as his early plays are called, reveal that the marker of absurdity is only *one* component of the idiosyncratic aesthetic that crystallizes in the course of the readings. Rather, it makes sense to work with a more encompassing definition of slapstick comedy that absorbs the absurd elements, for it was "[t]he slapstick tradition" which "brought an *absurd reality* to the fore, in which the laws of gravity, inertia, logic, and commerce were suspended and everyday objects mysteriously came to life, shifted shapes, and were transformed" (Jacobs and D'Haeyere 2017, 30; emphasis mine).

Since the antimetaphysical variety of slapstick no longer operates within the limits of a metaphysical world edifice, speech or discourse now comes to the fore instead of the body. While the silent comedians "had to be as funny as possibly physically, *without the help or hindrance of words*" (Gillota 2008, 1; emphasis in original), Hildesheimer's *animalia postmetaphysici* produce comic actions primarily *with* and *out of* the word. They emerge as 'speech generators' akin to poststructuralist figures whose bodies seem to be bracketed off. It is true that their physicality is still present in the stage directions, such as when the figures are described as being "*expansive*" [LF, 207[3]], "petite" (SP,

---

[3] In this article all citations from Hildesheimer's texts reference the German original but are reproduced here in English translation. The page numbers from the German original of "Landschaft mit Figuren" ["Landscape with Figures"] are taken from Hildesheimer [1958] 1989. References to this edition will be identified in parentheses by LF followed by page numbers.

315[4]) or as "steely and yet flexible" (LF, 216). But it is precisely at these interfaces that the shift from the body to the incorporeal or to discourse can be most clearly demonstrated. Particularly noteworthy here is the shifting of the specific physicality of slapstick, described by Steven Jacobs as the "succession of staccato bits of movements" (2018, 226), i.e., the mechanization of the body. Once again, in antimetaphysical slapstick, the mechanical is suddenly no longer located on the level of the body but on the level of speech and speaking. Paradigmatically, the figure of the '*Hausknecht*' [man servant] Philip from "Pastorale oder die Zeit für Kakao" ["Pastorale or the Time for Cocoa," 1958][5] is a symptom of this: he continually completes the sentences of the figures surrounding him in a highly mechanical manner while, at the same time, complementing their physical movements. He repeatedly uses common phrases: "PHILIP *again automatically, monotonously*: He was on horseback, was an exemplary rider!" (LF, 190). It is that interface between corporeality and language at which the comic movements of the body are transformed into comical speech movements that harken back to Deleuze's definition of speaking as "the movement of the surface" [23]. The boundary on which the difference between language and body is articulated turns out to be a critical joint, where common and often reductionist definitions of slapstick as pure body comedy differ from a post- or rather antimetaphysical understanding of slapstick.

All of the aspects discussed thus far are closely examined in the following sections using literary examples from Hildesheimer's early plays. What emerges over the course of the analysis is a compilation of the components comprising an antimetaphysical variety of slapstick, which now, instead of generating metaphysical systems, constructs a world that rests on the principles of sense, nonsense, surface, and seriality.

---

4 All page numbers from the German original of "Der schiefe Turm von Pisa" ["The Leaning Tower of Pisa"] are taken from Hildesheimer [1959] 1989. References to this edition will be identified in parentheses by SP followed by page numbers.
5 All page numbers from the German original of "Pastorale or The Time for Cocoa" are taken from Hildesheimer [1958] 1989. References to this edition will be identified in parentheses by PS followed by page numbers.

2 Postmodern wonderlands: a matter of pain and death

The first matter in dealing with a postmodernist or poststructuralist style of slapstick concerns the setup of the comic world as well as the peculiarities of its inhabitants whose "identity is essentially fortuitous" [178]. A world in which "a series of individualities must be traversed by each" [178] necessarily differs from a world setup bound to comic theories that are fundamentally indebted to metaphysics. It quickly becomes apparent that the slapstick world is, in many ways, closer to the poststructuralist cosmology, which is strongly influenced by chance, than to a sphere oriented around a metaphysical world edifice. This partly has to do with the changing status of the great metaphysical postulates. The basic occidental postulates of sense, unity, and identity are shaken to their foundations in Deleuze's book on logic, as in poststructuralism in general. The reality that this creates is reminiscent, at times, of the wonderland in which Alice gets lost, and which also unveils crucial parallels to the reality of slapstick "in which the laws of gravity, inertia, logic, and commerce were suspended and everyday objects mysteriously came to life, shifted shapes, and were transformed" (Jacobs and D'Haeyere 2017, 30). The example of cinematic slapstick, in particular, shows how the laws of logic and gravity are continually over-used or even lifted. This often becomes apparent in the fact that the comedians of the early silent films stumble from one precarious situation to the next. Prominent examples of this include Harold Lloyd (1893–1971), who dangles from a clock high over the streets of Los Angeles in *Safety Last* (1924) and Buster Keaton (1895–1966), who, in the film *One Week* (1921), is buried under a piano. It is crucial that, as a rule, nothing of particular concern befalls the usually clumsy comedians so that their actions are "painful [. . .] only for comic purposes and never truly life-threatening" (Peacock 2010, 93). The same is true of the order of things in Deleuze's logic book, albeit for entirely different reasons, since "[t]here is no circle of birth and death to escape from" [137]. This is directly reflected in Hildesheimer's works, in which the death of a character often does nothing more than cause a shrug of the shoulders. Does such indifference in Hildesheimer's *Die Uhren* ("The Clocks," 1958)[6] – given that "the entire cabinet died from mushroom poisoning" (UR, 274) – hinge on the fact that in the world of nonsense-plays death no longer has any weight since "no one ever dies, but has always just died or is always going to die" [63]? Moreover, the

---

[6] All page numbers from the German original of "The Clocks" ("Die Uhren") are taken from Hildesheimer [1958] 1989. References to this edition will be identified in parentheses by UR followed by page numbers.

postmodern body is no longer seen as a sacred or self-identical vessel open to the experience of transcendence. Rather, the human body transforms to the surface, so that everything that happens to the body only scratches on that surface: "But what we mean by [. . .] 'to cut,' and 'to be cut,' etc., is something entirely different. These are no longer states of affairs – mixtures deep inside bodies – but incorporeal events at the surface" [6]. Consequently, pain and the sensation of pain also transform from a highly existential "state anterior to language," which "has no referential context" (Scarry 1985, 4), to expressive and effective comic pain. This demands that the characters, despite all apparent robustness, are always poised to be "risking life and limb in order to generate laughter" (Peacock 2010, 93). In the antimetaphysical variety of comic pain and death, the categories of sense and meaning, and in particular surface-sense as an antithesis to the deep sense, come into play to a much greater extent. An example of this is Hildesheimer's "Pastorale," in which one of the characters actually *dies*:

PHILIP	One of the pupils is dead
	[. . .]
PHILIP	Just one.
SELMA	*curiously*: Which one is it?
PHILIP	Dietrich. *He points to the corpse:* Here he lies.
SELMA	*looks at the corpse*: That is Abel.
PHILIP	Is that not indifferent?
SELMA	Sure. (PT, 197)

Death, however, is merely noted and is transformed into an occasion for speech, a structural feature generating sense that has no meaning anymore.

3 Gag machines: Báthos – gag – paradox

In his *Ästhetische Theorie* [*Aesthetic Theory*, 1967], Theodor W. Adorno (1903–1969) notes that "Beckett's anti-heroes, as is well known, were modelled on circus clowns and the slapstick comedy of the early cinema" (1984, 121). Something similar could also be said for the figures of Hildesheimer's 'plays, in which it gets dark.' And indeed, what allies Hildesheimer to Beckett is that, following Adorno, both are not content with "the old metaphysical subject, which seems to rebel emphatically against instrumental reason, but in reality only represents identity disguised as subject" (Benne 2019, 13; translation). Moreover, an element, which sets the figures in Hildesheimer's literary world apart in a highly characteristic manner from the slapstick comedians, can be described by referring to the term *Báthos* in the work of the English poet Alexander Pope (1688–1744). Here, "the transition from the mode of wonder and convulsion [. . .] to the mode of laughter happens in a brief moment" (Schulzki 2015, 413). Although βάθος [*bathous*] means depth or abyss in ancient Greek, it does not at all reference a mode of emotion or profoundness; on the contrary, it concerns an abrupt fall into the ridiculous or even the trivial, far from any notion of the sublime. The title of Pope's treatise on the *Art of Sinking in Poetry* (1727) already makes this downward movement clear. And it enables a rather productive connection to Deleuze's theory of sense, for here as there the surface replaces depth: "'Depth' is no longer a compliment" [9]. But at what point does the bathetical dimension of the ridiculous come to bear? A look at Hildesheimer's figures offers, indeed, a 'deep' look at them as they consistently turn out to be not deep or profound, but rather "flat animals" [9]; they are discursive catalysts which constantly emit hollow and empty phrases. Instead of original speeches, they produce only incomplete and often incorrect quotes, such as in the following example: "*[THE PRESIDENT] pulls out a booklet, opens it, looks into it:* 'Man is human', – to speak with the poets! *Sticks the booklet back again*" (PT, 181). What is noteworthy here is the fact that the matter of the shallow depths is taken up by the figures in the plays and is blatantly made into the subject of discourse. In "Pastorale," the figures communicate in this way about the emotional content of a particular passage of a piece of music: "PRESIDENT It [the place] has it all. / FRL. DR. Open depths, – *sighs:* Depths. Let's sing! *Clears throat*" (LF, 171). All speech remains consistently on the surface; even those sentences that present themselves as profound at first turn out to be 'flat.' The characters are not driven by a metaphysical desire to get to the bottom of things or explore their depth. Instead, the galloping exchange of words produces an incessant comical flipping of the positions, as Wolfgang Iser has famously described: "[E]ach position causes the other to flip. This initially results in the instability of comical conditions" (1976, 399; translation). In the case of Hildesheimer's plays, this generates the continuous gag structure that is so characteristic of slapstick (cf. Trahair 2007, 44; Lorenz 1986); this is a structure which thrives on the basis of the abrupt flipping, as demonstrated in the following example: "PHILIP Are you an honorable man? / ABEL Since I was twenty-one" (PT, 192). The dialogues in "Landscape with Figures" (1958, "Landschaft mit Figuren") also follow this pattern: "MRS. S. [. . .] How long has it been since we last saw each other? / ADRIAN We've never seen each other before! / MRS. S. *astonished*: That long!" (LF, 208). What at this point is added to the elements of the bathetic and the gag is a central figure of thought, also for Deleuze, namely, that of the paradox: "It is here, however, that the gift of meaning occurs, in this region which precedes all good sense and all common sense. For here, with the passion of the paradox, language attains its highest power" [79]. The preceding example demonstrates how paradoxes "allow us to be present at the genesis of the contradiction" [74].

In fact, abrupt and paradoxical tipping from one pole to another is the basis for a series of comic and comical theories, including, for example, Henri Bergson's *Le rire* (*Laughter*, 1900), as well as in Jean Paul's *Vorschule der Ästhetik* [*Introduction to Aesthetics*, 1804]: "In short, the hereditary enemy of the sublime is the ridiculous" (105; translation). However, a poststructuralist or antimetaphysical variety of this tipping is no longer based on the metaphysical idea of a "living being" (414) or even on one of the sublime, but instead decidedly prefers the surface and thus the comedy that arises from this surface. Deleuze describes this paradigm shift on the basis of a concept of humor without any depth: "Humor is the art of the surface, which is opposed to the old irony, the art of depths and heights" [9]. It thus comes to no surprise that all speech acts in Hildesheimer's plays remain on the surface; they lack any depth and thus prove to be *bathetic*. Even the element of bathos creeps into the word exchanges among the figures on a meta-level. Over and over again, it is the president in "Pastorale" who comes to instantiate the figure of Pope's bathos, that is, the tipping into ridiculousness with astonishing precision: "From the sublime to the ridiculous, *it is only one step*" (PT, 185; emphasis mine). But the literary text does not stop at a mere statement; instead, it spins the sentence into the aforementioned gag-structure by letting the Fräulein Dr. immediately counter it: "But even so, a step" (185). The gag, that indispensable component of slapstick, which "stems directly from the clowning and acrobatic dancing of music hall and vaudeville" (Esslin 1983, 335), contributes significantly to the emergence of an antimetaphysical aesthetic derived from surfaces. But unlike common definitions, which ascertain that the gag has a "tendency to disrupt the aims and operations of the narrative" (Trahair 2007, 45), the approximated gag structure seen here essentially transforms into a powerful engine that generates and guarantees the action. The characters no longer speak portentously, but they add one phrase to the other, which inevitably leads to a series of gags. As a result, they solidify into comedic speech-machines, as Hildesheimer's "Pastorale" already demonstrated in exemplary fashion. The protagonists (male and female) merely repeat shreds of *Kunstlieder* and everyday phrases, endowing them with highly mechanical qualities; they crystalize into speech- or gag-machines, which in a Deleuzian manner are "speaking, without speaking" [173]:

PHILIP	*counting:* One, two, three, four, one, two, three, four . . . *measures the beats.*
PRESIDENT	*sings:* O holde Kunst! Du reichst vom Morgenrot Zur Renaissance, und weiter. Alles ist Gefühl . . . [7]
PHILIP	*points to the notes:* Gis!
PRESIDENT	Pardon?
PHILIP	The Ge in *Gefühl* is not sung as Ge, but as Gis. *Sings:* Gis*fühl*, Gis*fühl*!
PRESIDENT	You have an ear for music?
PHILIP	Like many other things, I owe it to evening classes. (PT, 168)

What is presented on the surface is an ensemble of art lovers who meet to sing German *Kunstlieder* together. Of significance is that the verse line "O holde Kunst" ["O blessed art"] refers to the opening verse from Franz Schubert's (1797–1828) song *An die Musik* [*To the Music*, 1817], which, even before Hildesheimer, had been considered a common phrase. As expected, however, the moment of recognition instantly flips into the mode of laughter and sinks – in manner of Pope's *bathous* – into triviality and ridiculousness. In this way, the gag structure undermines and subverts the "restricted economy of narrative" (Trahair 2007, 44) analogous to the classic slapstick method. However, in the antimetaphysical variety of slapstick, this gag structure merges with bathos and transforms into a surface comedy. The surface becomes the "locus of sense and expression" [125], which, in turn, implies that "[s]ense is that which is formed and deployed at the surface" [125]. However, it by no means coincides with *the* or *a* meaning. For the above-quoted passage this means that the song is recognizable as a discrete unit of sense; however, on its own remains without any (deeper) meaning. Even feeling or empathy themselves turn into a 'Gis-fühl' (instead of *Gefühl* [feeling]) and thus take the form of a punchline for a corny joke, while Philip's dubious knowledge of music theory, acquired from evening classes, is also part of that flat surface comedy. The characters no longer speak seriously, they do not speak profoundly, they do not speak ironically – they simply *speak*. The corporeality that is so prominent in classical slapstick must now give way to structure, the "machine for the production of incorporeal sense (*skindapsos*)" [71].

---

[7] "O blessed art! You reach from the dawn/to the Renaissance, und onwards. Everything is feeling . . . ."

4 *Animal postmetaphysicum*: articulations of difference

At the center of nearly all (pre-)modern theories of laughter and comedy – and this is especially true of slapstick – is the body, or comic body, which is arranged, staged, and adapted to create a laugh. While Helmuth Plessner (1892–1985) understands laughter as the body's distressed answer to the "simultaneity of oppositional senses" (Wirth 1999, 11), Mikhail M. Bakhtin (1895–1975) considers the highly prolific phantasms of a cosmic-universal corporeity and the rebirth of the grotesque body (cf. 1996, 15). Bergson, in turn, presents the mechanized corporeality outlined above, together with its mechanical stiffness, which is crucial for the body image of slapstick. Finally, with the unbridled desire to evoke laughter, the classic slapstick of silent cinema is accompanied by a very specific corporeality that can be described as the "succession of staccato bits of movements" (Jacobs 2018, 226). It was Charlie Chaplin who – with his "dissected 'expressive movements'" (225) – carried such body staccato to extremes as captured in the so-called 'chaplinades.' Underlying this is the idea of a mechanization of the body, which can already be detected in the *commedia dell'arte*, where it is clearly socially encoded (cf. Peacock 2013). The "fascination for the conflation of bodies and machines, animated ready-made objects" (225) is thus unsurprising. This applies all the more to the development of an antimetaphysical slapstick, since the body is deprived of its metaphysical image of God through its fusion with the machine and thus transforms into the *animal postmetaphysicum*.

The term *animal postmetaphysicum* draws on Arthur Schopenhauer's (1788–1860) famous dictum of man as *animal metaphysicum*, that is, as a creature seeking out the metaphysical, outlined in the philosopher's *Die Welt als Wille und Vorstellung* [*The World as Will and Representation*, 1819]: "With this reflection and astonishment man's very own *need for metaphysics* emerges: he is therefore an 'animal metaphysicum'" (1986, 207; translation). Wolfgang Hildesheimer's figures are no longer beings seeking out the metaphysical, although they are at first glance dramatis personae endowed with the essential context and identity markers: name, gender, occupation. They are called Selma, Abel, Herr von Ruhr, and Elsa Renate. By profession they are mountain assessors, hairdressers, consuls, and shepherds. But right from the start, after the first stage directions or verbal exchanges, the figures turn out to be already broken, often mechanical and doll-like, and often not even identical to themselves.

An essential trait that connects Hildesheimer's protagonists with the figures of the classic slapstick is, first of all, the reduction of their corporeality to a few, mostly external traits based on the model of the clown or the *mimus* of antiquity, thus displaying a close relationship to "the performers of wordless skills – jugglers, acrobats, tightrope walkers, aerialists, and animal trainers" (Esslin 1983, 329–330). Initially, the individual and unique body is made to disappear in this way. A striking example of such a clownish insert is, once again, provided by the character Philip who, in "Landscape with Figures," not only repeats individual phrases or the phrases of others; his body is additionally converted to function as a music stand and is thus mechanized *in extremo*:

> PHILIP I stand on my left foot. *Stands on his left foot and takes a small stick out of the pocket.* The right leg, *points with the stick to the right leg* by tucking it up to the trunk *he tucks the right leg up* I will position it in such manner, that I, with the lower calf of said limb, *he points with the stick to his right calf* will defend the scores of our president against the wind. *He puts the right lower leg over the president's music stand.* (PT, 176–177)

The mechanization presented here down to the smallest detail implies the deindividualization mentioned earlier, whereby the comic, as Bergson describes it, already sticks to the surface of the person and thus cannot develop a profound effect.

The transition "from bodies to the incorporeal" [10] increasingly comes to the fore in Hildesheimer's plays. The mechanized slapstick body transforms into an antimetaphysical figure of fading, and the comic body is replaced by comical and highly mechanized speech, which seems to come from mechanized 'speech dolls': "BETTINA turns the music box. It plays a childish, old-fashioned tune. / Mr. von Ruhr, Mrs. Satorius and Colin are beginning to revive" (LF, 253). The corporeality ranging from 'obese' (LF, 230) to 'petite' (TP, 315) is completely obscured by discursive speech; and the figures appear increasingly as 'surface beings' constantly forced to speak, since "[t]o speak, though, is the movement of the surface, and of ideational attributes or incorporeal events" [23]. The thesis of this chapter is precisely this: that antimetaphysical slapstick is undoing the basic premises of a "comedy based on movements, gestures, and facial expressions" or any form of pure body humor. Antimetaphysical slapstick figures, instead, turn out to be silly actors, who continue to slip on a (linguistic) surface, "where there is no longer anything to denote or even to signify, but where pure sense is produced" [136].

This is accompanied by an epochal decentralization of the once self-identical subject, which implies a fundamental transformation of formerly metaphysical beings. This turns into "figures as props, for example, or grotesque figures or figures that embody multiple types in rapid succession or simultaneously" (Hildesheimer 1988, 24). In antimetaphysical slapstick, the identity, which was once authenticated by the flesh or the body, shifts into the language or the discourse: "[e]verything that takes place occurs in and by means of language" [22]. This does not mean, however, that certain aspects of physicality cannot continue to play a role; nonetheless, they are usually closely connected with the level of discourse. A change of appearance thus directly implies a change in the manner of speaking by the speech machines. This can happen quite actively: "COLLECTOR *business-like:* If you please. *He sits down slowly, puts down his old glasses, puts on new glasses with a dark horn edge, takes off his hair – he has a bald head – speaks from now on in a high croaking voice*" (LF, 263; emphasis mine). This changed physicality ushers in a new way of speaking. It can go so far that the figures completely change their character: "MS. DR. *completely changed, ordinary, opens her bag and starts to put on make-up and powder:* You old cracker!" (PT, 194). The woman who previously presented herself as distinguished and was characterized as "wide-eyed, naïve" (191) becomes an ordinary cocotte – by speaking like one. Speaking and being are thus intimately intertwined.

The transformation of the dramatis personae into qualities decidedly *not* driving metaphysics is brought to extremes in "Landscape with Figures", wherein the comedic figures are literally staged as aesthetic 'group pictures with a lady': The ensemble comprising the artist, collector, and specialist visibly delights in the clientele of the portrait painter Adrian, who, in the course of the ongoing events, brings or 'gathers' them together, degrading them to characters of a play or figures of art. Frau Sartorius, Herr von Ruhr, and Colin appear one after the other in his studio to have the painter paint their portrait. By arranging them into a lifelike work of art, namely the eponymous 'Landscape with Figures,' he declares all of them to be play dolls. The collector, who finally buys the work, looks at the characters, who were talking non-stop at the beginning of the play but who are now silent, with an expert eye:

> COLLECTOR [. . .] *He continues with the contemplation, close, then far again. Finally, he takes out a huge magnifying glass from the bag and looks at details such as Mrs. Satorius' nose or Mr. von Ruhr's hand. He also goes into the cage to closely study Colin. He nods his head appreciatively several times:* Great, great! (LF, 252)

The body suddenly and once again becomes the focus of attention the moment the speaking subsides, albeit it is a henceforth completely still body, robbed of any (sense of) humor.

5 *Ad nauseam*: from double acts to multiple series of acts

Finally, the development of an antimetaphysical slapstick requires a look at the correlation of comical event structures. The moment of repetition plays a major role for a series of comic theories, for instance those of Bergson, but also of Freud: "Where situational comedy works through repetition, it is based on the child's peculiar desire for continued repetition (questions, telling stories) through which it comes to plague the adult" (Freud 2000, 210; translation). Karlheinz Stierle even speaks of a "repetition compulsion" (1976, 239; translation), and in fact, repetition can be described as "the temporal mode of comedy" (Erdmann 2003, 13; translation). This applies to the methods of cinematic slapstick: "[u]ninterested in traditional storytelling with its narrative arc, slapstick cinema utilizes a succession of routines with repetitions and variations" (Jacobs and D'Haeyere 2017, 33). The sequence of (regulated) processes that are characterized by repetitions or variations also has a firm place in the thinking of poststructuralism, especially in the work of Deleuze. Although repetition takes an important place in Deleuze's work (e.g., his book *Différence et repetition* [*Difference and Repetition*, 1968]), it is notably overpowered in *The Logic of Sense* by another principle: the principle of seriality, which is "*necessarily realized in the simultaneity of at least two series*" [36; emphasis in original]. Clearly, seriality plays a crucial role in Deleuze's theory of logic, since "[e]verything happens through the resonance of disparates, [. . .] displacement of perspective, differentiation of difference, and not through the identity of contraries" [175]. In this fashion, seriality refers directly to the context of the 'philosophy of difference': the series does not aim at identity, nor at the reducibility of what is different to what is the same, but dedicates itself entirely to chance, since every "identity is essentially fortuitous" [178]. This results in another link to slapstick, in which an often actionless narration "string[s] together a *series* of gags, pratfalls, chases, [and] escapades" (Kuhn and Westwell 2012, 378; emphasis mine), which is either random or contingent from beginning to end. The connection between the individual elements is established only through their affiliation to those series and not based on a compelling narration. Consequently, the context of seriality requires the resolution of a coherent, linear narrative familiar to slapstick and tends instead "toward digressive and destructive ends rather than the resolution that gives narrative its distinctive form" (Trahair 2007, 44). Unlike repetition, the series or seriality is based on a continual shift of the components of the initial series, which refers to subsequent series, and so on. Unsurprisingly, both repetition and seriality belong to the realm of slapstick. Peacock describes this pointedly by showing that the central techniques of slapstick, such as tripping, falling, hitting, and throwing "occur in patterns of repetition and escalation" (2013, 68).

The elements of repetition as well as seriality take a generative role in the works of Hildesheimer. One of the most prominent examples of this are the endless (musical) variations in "Pastorale," which are presented as an incomplete series. In fact, the entire play is framed by variation:

> VOICE OF THE SHEPHERD *stronger*:
> How was the farewell so lukewarm,
> How were the pears so blue!
> Thusly spoke the rose at the lake:
> How does the summer hurt so much! (PT, 165)

This quatrain is picked up again at the very end of the play, where it is repeated with a slight yet recognizable variation:

> VOICE OF THE SHEPHERD *behind the stage*:
> How does the summer hurt so much!
> Thusly spoke the rose at the lake.
> How was the farewell so lukewarm,
> How were the pears so blue! (PT, 200)

The hodgepodge of conversational phrases and commonplace sayings that reveal themselves as decodable fragments of romantic lyricism thus lack any profundity, which is to be understood quite programmatically: "All the linguistic clichés of which German poetry is capable are parodied here in a devastating way" (Lorenz 1986, 99; translation).

The principle of seriality, as well as the characteristic shift of the components of a series, feeds, once more, on a 'philosophy of difference' – in contrast to a metaphysics oriented around identity. Deleuze explicates this in the discussion of one's own name, which will be examined in concert with a series of passages from Hildesheimer's plays. The loss of one's own name marks a loss of identity and thus the 'fall' of the "transcendental subject which retains the form of the person, of personal consciousness, and of subjective identity" [98], whose identity guarantor is lost in the tradition of the Western philosophy of identity: "All these reversals as they appear in infinite identity have one consequence: the contesting of [one's] personal identity and the loss of [one's] proper name" [3]. So, it is only 'logical' that Deleuze grounds his explication of sense and nonsense as well as those relating to seriality with the example of the name: "[E]ach denoting name has a sense which must be denoted by another name: $n_1 \rightarrow n_2 \rightarrow n_3 \rightarrow n_4 \ldots$ " [36]. Following the principles of the philosophy of difference, this goes hand in hand with the a-normality of names that say exactly what they are, since the gesture of *différance*, or the endless poststructuralist postponement, does not permit for such an identity in terms of expression and designation (cf. Derrida 1988, 51). Deleuze calls these words "white words" or esoteric words [64–70]. Due to the structure of $N_1 \rightarrow N_2 \rightarrow N_3 \ldots$ "[t]he name saying its own sense can only be *nonsense*" [67]. In this way, a chain of comical deferrals is created, which negates the nominal unit of the name and creates a theoretically endless chain of reference. There is a gap between the name and the bearer of the name in Hildesheimer's descriptions of the person as illustrated by the following example, in which the woman comments on an approaching figure: "and looks like he's called Kaspar" (UR, 276). It follows that the one named *is* not Kaspar, he is not even *called* Kaspar; he just looks *as though his name were* Kaspar.

The structure of concatenative references, which results in a series of proper names shifted toward one another, is by no means an isolated case with Hildesheimer. Expression and designation regularly diverge and the apparent arbitrariness of the names takes on features of a peculiar serial logic, for example, in "Landscape with Figures":

COLIN	[. . .] A room like a picture, – by Schumann, – or is he differently named?
ADRIAN	Who?
COLIN	Schumann.
ADRIAN	The name is different. (LF, 216)

The sense in all of these examples is always already presupposed as soon as speaking begins, because without this assumption, it would not be possible to begin at all. Deleuze articulates this as such: "I never state the sense of what I am saying. But on the other hand, I can always take the sense of what I say as the object of another proposition whose sense, in turn, I cannot state. I thus enter into the infinite regress of that which is presupposed" [28]. The above-mentioned passage depicts exactly that logic in which the name Schumann references someone who is actually named something else. Nevertheless, Colin knows exactly who is meant, because Schuman points as N_1 to N_2. It therefore follows that even if N2 remains a gap in this passage, the name Schuman unmistakably refers to N2 as a prerequisite.

Another example of the loss of the proper name and thus of the dissolution of the personal identity, which is now accompanied by a completely arbitrary assignment of proper names, is found in "Landscape with Figures." The scene features the addition of another series alongside the above-mentioned example:

MRS. S.	*meekly:* Forgive me, Oskar!
RUHR	*as above:* And do not call me Oskar!
MRS. S.	Helmuth! (LF, 254)

Deleuze describes this serial arbitrariness of the proper name as the "lost name" [75] and ties this to the impossibility of a personal ego, which can take the role of a synthetic unity of apperception or consciousness. Instead, one finds just an empty space: "An empty square for neither man nor God; singularities which are neither general nor individual, neither personal nor universal" [72]. The same is true for "The Clocks," in which the two protagonists are at first identified solely by gender, until the moment where names come up in the text: Horst Dieter and Elsa Renate. However, it remains indeterminable throughout the play whether these are actually the names of the two protagonists. And above all, it is completely irrelevant.

Hildesheimer's plays present the dissolution of the identity guaranteed by a name throughout. In "The Leaning Tower of Pisa," the name appears almost as an arbitrary and freely selectable unit:

> VERENA   And what's your name?
> SERVER   I have a few names, Signora. Which one do you like?
> VERENA   *ambiguous*: I love Paolo.
> SERVER   That's also my name.
> VERENA   And me?
> SERVER   What about Francesca?
> VERENA   That would be great. (SP, 318)

This gesture of a free floating of the names is driven to the extreme once suddenly only a single common name exists, which can be arbitrarily applied to *all* figures:

> VERENA   Are all women named Lucia here?
> RALF   The majority.
> VERENA   And the men?
> RALF   Luigi.
> VERENA   The majority?
> RALF   All of them. (SP, 312)

The basis for this free floating of the names is the eradication of common sense that underlies Deleuzian logic, and which again connects to antimetaphysical slapstick. In doing so, it references again a difference beyond a homogenous identity: "[G]ood sense is said of one direction only: it is the unique sense and expresses the demand of an order according to which a direction is necessary to choose one direction and to hold on to it" [75]. However, the paradoxes of sense, which arise as a result of the elimination of the mind to which the various name-chains belong, are characterized in that "[t]hey always have the characteristics of going in both directions at once, and of rendering identification impossible" [75]. This directional duality is accompanied by a duality or doubling of the figures – a process which Deleuze articulates as "one is always mad *in tandem*" [79]. Every 'I' turns in a different direction, but the two directions are inseparable and thereby indeterminable. The figures are therefore always mad as (at least) a pair, for "[t]wo are necessary for being mad" [79]. In Hildesheimer's plays this is much more frequently the case and even in much larger constellations.

The remainder of this chapter will examine Deleuze's decisive antimetaphysical concept of the mad duality with a focus on the slapstick double act, which is a standard feature of slapstick equally important for Beckett who, in turn, influenced Hildesheimer. The double act is also based on the idea that one is mad as a pair, but, as a rule, takes place within the framework of a functioning metaphysical system. Peacock notes that, for example, "Pantalone and Arlecchino constitute an archetypal slapstick double act" (2013, 59). In referring to the tradition of *commedia dell'arte*, to which Pantalone and Arlecchino belong, the fundamental conflict arises as a result of "a series of social, physical and intellectual binary oppositions: wealth versus poverty; high status versus low status; intelligence versus stupidity and age versus youth" (59), i.e., as a result of clear opposition. The clearly delineated scenario of the double act therefore allows an additional detailed consideration of the parallels and differences between the classic slapstick and its postmodern style. In fact, Hildesheimer also takes on the construct of the double act, albeit in a broken form. In the sense of the postmodern theorems, there are, or there can be, no clear oppositions, as these would ultimately lead back to a process of identity formation or could have the effect of unification. Therefore, to give just one example, no clearly clever or stupid part can be isolated, and even the seemingly intelligent or profound figures usually give only "banalities in the form of clichéd speech" (Hildesheimer 1988, 16).

The most expressive example of this are the twins Abel and Dietrich Asbach from "Pastorale," who are, indeed, inseparable and therefore are "always crazy for two" [107]. At first glance, they actually seem to conform to the schema of contrarian double acts: one of the twins, Dietrich, is "about sixty, tall and thin, wearing a top hat, stand-up collar, black tie, white waistcoat, with a huge gold watch chain, gray trousers and black jacket, horn-rimmed glasses, bald head" (174). He has a botany drum with him, while the second, Abel, naturally the same age as his brother, runs around with a butterfly net and is characterized as "small and fat" and "dressed exactly the same" (174). The fact that the two are twins is at first exclusively demarked visually through their outermost surface, namely, their clothing. Their physicality, on the other hand, is fully in keeping with the binary opposition of slapstick, as exemplified by Laurel and Hardy or Don Quixote and Sancho Panza. But this is the point at which all similarities end, because in the course of the action the twins prove to be quite the *animalia postmetaphysici* who can no longer maintain a claim to a homogeneous identity. They are both in their sixties and are addressed with titles such as consul and mountain assessor. But their behavior is that of two rascals chasing the fields and begging their governess, Miss Selma, for "cocoa at four" (174). The young woman, who takes on the role of a nanny, in turn talks about "irregularities in the developmental process of her two pupils" (174). Thus, in the case of the two "kind boys" (197), the descriptors relating to childishness and being grown-up are confused, which renders them a paradoxical constellation in several aspects: "On one hand, it [the paradox] appears in the guise of the two simultaneous senses or directions of the becoming-mad and the unforeseeable; on the other hand, it appears as the nonsense of the lost identity and the unrecognizable" [78]. In addition, the two twins are noticeably introduced in the moment of the "acrobatic chase" characteristic of slapstick (cf. Peacock 2013):

PHILIP	There are two gentlemen skittering across the fields.
MISS DR.	The two Messrs. Asbach!
PRESIDENT	*looks through the field glasses:* Where? I see nothing?
MISS DR.	There. [. . .]
PRESIDENT	Now I see them. *Laughs:* How they run, what?
PHILIP	They fell down.
MISS DR .	*laughs:* Charming!
PHILIP	It is difficult running over stubble. Swampland. [. . .]
PRESIDENT	Now they have nearly reached the fence!
MISS DR.	*exuberantly:* Will they climb over it?
PRESIDENT	*amused:* Will they slip under it? (PT, 173)

Yet the differences are as striking as the parallels to classic slapstick. The acrobatic chase is not physically performed on stage, as is particularly the case in the silent film comedies, for instance in Charley Chase's *Mighty Like a Moose* (1926). Instead, the hunt is described – using teichoscopy – through the gaze of the other figures watching them through binoculars and then *speaking* about them. The transition from the bodied to the incorporeal inevitably takes its toll. The major event of the acrobatic chase, which is defined by the "use of stunts and acrobatics as a central performance trope of slapstick" (Peacock 2013, 62), simultaneously 'sinks' and is bathetically reduced to triviality and ridiculousness. The breakneck actions, such as balancing on dizzyingly high scaffolding and skyscrapers as performed by Laurel & Hardy in *Liberty* (1929), turn into a silly prank, which culminates in an escape through the servant's door:

ABEL	. . .our wife wouldn't let us go!
BOTH	We escaped her! *They giggle:* Escaped! Through the servant's door!
DIETRICH	Between the legs of the. . .
ABEL	*pulls him back:* . . .through the legs of the cook and out. . .
BOTH	To freedom! *Looking around:* To freedom! (PT, 174)

In the end, even the doubleness of the twins, as established in the double act by means of binary opposition, leaves much to be desired. The two figures, who hunt each other over the fields, turn out to be one and the same figure which, in the Deleuzian sense, simultaneously diverge in two directions: "PHILIP One was like the other. / SELMA One *was* the other" (PT, 197; emphasis in original). Programmatically, this exchange of words is driven by a gag to a sensible yet meaningless apex: "PHILIP Not entirely. One was a tenor, the other a baritone" (PT, 197).

In summary, the antimetaphysical operations of the comic, which Trahair labels as a "neglected figure in contemporary thought" (2007, 2), are essentially based on the traditions of both the theatric and cinematic slapstick. However, as is the conclusion of this chapter, these are extended in their postmodern or poststructuralist variant into the dimensions of bathos, surface, nonsense, and especially of *sense* – that "thin membrane at the limit of things and words" [31].

Bibliography

Adorno, Theodor W. *Aesthetic Theory*. Eds. Gretel Adorno and Rolf Tiedemann. Trans. C. Lenhadt. London and New York: Routledge & Kegan Paul, 1984.
Bakhtin [Bachtin], Michael M. *Literatur und Karneval: Zur Romantheorie und Lachkultur*. Frankfurt am Main: S. Fischer, 1996.
Bergson, Henri [1900]. "Le rire. Essai sur la signification du comique." *Œuvres*. Ed. André Robinet. Paris: Presses Universitaires de France, 1959. 381–485.
Benne, Christian. "Aesthetica in nuce: Adornos Beckett." *Eros und Erkenntnis. 50 Jahre "Ästhetische Theorie"*. Eds. Martin Endres, Axel Pichler, and Claus Zittel. Berlin and Boston: De Gruyter, 2019. 11–21.
Blamberger, Günter: "Der Rest ist Schweigen. Hildesheimers Literatur des Absurden." *Text + Kritik: Zeitschrift für Literatur* 89/90 (1986): 33–44.
Deleuze, Gilles. *Logique du sens*. Paris: Les Éditions de Minuit, 1969.
Deleuze, Gilles. *Logic of sense*, transl. Constantin V. Boundas, Marl Lester, and Charles J. Stivale. New York: Columbia University Press, 1990.

Derrida, Jacques. "Die différance." *Randgänge der Philosophie*. Vienna: Passagen, 1988.
Derrida, Jacques. *Grammatologie*. Frankfurt am Main: Suhrkamp, 1983.
Erdmann, Eva. Ed. *Der komische Körper: Szenen – Figuren – Formen*. Bielefeld: transcript, 2003.
Esslin, Martin. *The Theatre of the Absurd*. New York: Penguin, 1983.
Flaig, Paul Frederick. *Weimar Slapstick: American Eccentrics, German Grotesques*. 2013. Cornell U, PhD Dissertation.
Freud, Sigmund: "Der Witz und seine Beziehung zum Unbewußten." *Studienausgabe*. Frankfurt am Main: S. Fischer, 2000. 9–219.
Gillota, David. *Belly Laughs: Body Humor in Contemporary American Literature and Film*. 2008. U Florida, PhD Dissertation.
Hildesheimer, Wolfgang. *Die Theaterstücke*. Ed. Volker Jehle. Frankfurt am Main: Suhrkamp, 1989.
Hildesheimer, Wolfgang [1960]. "Über das absurde Theater." *Das Ende der Fiktionen. Reden aus fünfundzwanzig Jahren*. Suhrkamp: Frankfurt am Main, 1988. 9–26.
Iser, Wolfgang. "Das Komische: ein Kipp-Phänomen." *Das Komische*. Eds. Wolfgang Preisendanz and Rainer Warning. Munich: Fink, 1976. 399–402.
Jacobs, Steven. "Slapstick Homes: Architecture in Slapstick Cinema and the *Avant-Garde*." *The Journal of Architecture* 23.2 (2018): 225–248.
Jacobs, Steven, and Hilde D'Haeyere. "Frankfurter Slapstick: Benjamin, Kracauer, and Adorno on American Screen Comedy." *October* 116 (2017): 30–50.
Kuhn, Annette, and Guy Westwell. Eds. *A Dictionary of Film Studies*. Oxford: Oxford University Press, 2012.
Lorenz, Christoph F. "Das fragende Theater des Wolfgang Hildesheimer." *Text + Kritik. Zeitschrift für Literatur* 89/90 (1986): 90–102.
Paul, Jean. *Vorschule der Ästhetik*. Ed. Norbert Miller. Hamburg: Meiner, 1990.
Peacock, Louise. "No Pain: No Gain – the provocation of laughter in slapstick comedy." *Popular Entertainment Studies* 1.2 (2010): 93–106.
Peacock, Louise. "Conflict and slapstick in Commedia dell'Arte – The double act of Pantalone and Arlecchino." *Comedy Studies* 4.1 (2013): 59–69.
Pope, Alexander. "*Peri Bathous*: or, Martin Scriblerus. His Treatise of the Art of Sinking in Poetry." *The Prose Works of Alexander Pope*. Vol. 2: *The Major Works, 1725–144*. Ed. Rosemary Cowler. Oxford: Basil Blackwell, 1986. 171–276.
Saunders, Thomas J. "Comedy as Redemption: American Slapstick in Weimar Culture." *Journal of European Studies* 17.4 (1987): 253–277.
Scarry, Elaine. *The Body in Pain: The Making and Unmaking of the World*. Oxford: Oxford University Press, 1985.
Schopenhauer, Arthur. *Sämtliche Werke*. Ed. Wolfgang Frhr. von Löhneysen. Suhrkamp: Frankfurt am Main, 1986.
Schulzki, Irina. "Vom Bathos: Woody Allens Film *Love and Death*." *Das Komische in der Kultur: Dynamiken der Vermittlung*. Eds. Hajo Diekmanshenke, Stefan Neuhaus, and Uta Schaffers. Marburg: Tectum, 2015. 413–429.
Stierle, Karlheinz. "Komik der Handlung, Komik der Sprachhandlung, Komik der Komödie." *Das Komische*. Eds. Wolfgang Preisendanz and Rainer Warning. Munich: Fink, 1976. 237–268.

Trahair, Lisa. *Comedy of Philosophy: Sense and Nonsense in Early Cinematic Slapstick.*
    New York: University Press of New York, 2007.
Weinhold, Ulrike. "Die Absurdität Wolfgang Hildesheimers." *Amsterdamer Beiträge zur
    Neueren Germanistik* 16 (1983): 329–362.
Wirth, Uwe. *Diskursive Dummheit: Abduktion und Komik als Grenzphänomene des Verstehens.*
    Heidelberg: Winter, 1999.

Valerie Weinstein
Gender and Jewish Difference in Early German Slapstick

Ernst Lubitsch's (1892–1947) performances as the crafty apprentice and Ressel Orla's (1889–1931) as the boss's daughter in *Der Stolz der Firma* [*The Pride of the Firm*] (Carl Wilhelm, 1914) and *Der Blusenkönig* [*The Blouse King*] (Lubitsch, 1917) illustrate how physical humor, hyperbole, violence, and resilience – integral devices of slapstick – create models of Jewish masculinity and femininity in early German film comedy. After providing some background about these films and their engagement with Jewish difference, this chapter advocates for more scholarly attention to gender in German-Jewish film comedy. Then, following an explanation of how slapstick's stylistic features both exaggerate ethnic stereotypes and depict performers as resilient to them, close readings reveal slapstick's central function in Lubitsch's and Orla's gendered performances of Jewishness.

1 Fashion farces and Jewish difference

Pride of the Firm and *Blouse King* are typical late-Wilhelmine fashion farces, silent comedies characterized by "slapstick humor and subversive laughter" and set in the fashion industry (Ganeva 2008, 123). In these films, a male, stereotypically Jewish protagonist claws his way up the ladder of the fashion business, seducing women and playing pranks. Set in the heavily Jewish milieu of the Berlin garment district, and thus sometimes called milieu comedies, fashion farces starring Lubitsch, like *Pride of the Firm* and *Blouse King*, humorously address the challenges and contradictions of German-Jewish attempts at assimilation in the early twentieth century (Weinstein 2006a; Ashkenazi 2012, 21–32; McCormick 2020).

In *Pride of the Firm*, a mischievous Jewish boy migrates to the city and uses his pluck and wit to get rich. After chaotically breaking a display window and getting fired, Siegmund Lachmann (Lubitsch) runs away to Berlin and secures a position at a department store. The head saleslady, Lilly Maass (Martha Kriwitz), advises Siegmund to take out an advance on his wages to get a makeover and new wardrobe. After doing so, Siegmund rises in the firm, but fails to convince his boss, Herr Berg (Victor Arnold), to let him marry his daughter Isolde (Orla). Siegmund places a classified ad, looking to marry into a successful fashion concern. Ironically, Herr Berg answers the ad. Berg invites Siegmund to

Isolde's birthday party. The two fall in love, marry, and produce an heir, "the pride of the firm."

Reviews of *Blouse King* indicate that it follows a similarly roguish protagonist named Sally Katz (Lubitsch) from rags to riches (*Der Kinematograph*, 7 November, 1917). Yet many plot details are lost and only a portion of act three is known still to exist. In the surviving footage, Sally courts Brünhilde Rosenthal (Orla), the boss's daughter, whom he finds unattractive, in order to further his own career. Brünhilde is eager to marry Sally, but her father (Guido Herzfeld) wants her to marry a doctor instead. Herr Rosenthal makes Sally a partner in his firm, on the condition that he *not* marry Brünhilde. The fragment ends with Sally calling on Lissy Maas (Käthe Dorsch), a tall, fair-haired saleslady, who was jealous when she saw him with Brünhilde. Lissy has her maid tell Sally she is not at home. Although incomplete, the *Blouse King* fragment enriches our knowledge of fashion farces and their stock characters because of its extended scenes of the boss's daughter.

Slapstick performances of Jewish difference, such as those in *Pride of the Firm* and *Blouse King*, helped construct modern, secular Jewish identities. In traditional religious communities, Jewish identity is reaffirmed through performance of ritual; in secular communities, ethnic identity needs to be rediscovered and recreated beyond religious practice, through other forms of performance (Bial 2005, 13). A dialectic between actors' performing and spectators' recognizing Jewish difference facilitates such ethnic self-definition. The content of the performers' codes and the audience's ability to recognize and interpret them helps spectators create their own ethnic identities and their own understandings of those identities (Bial 2005). Stage and screen performances functioned in this way for Jews in early twentieth-century Germany (Otte 2006; Ashkenazi 2012). This chapter emphasizes the role of slapstick in such performances and the importance of studying how such performances of Jewishness were gendered.

2 Gendering Jewish difference in German film comedy

Because Lubitsch became a major figure in Hollywood, scholarship on Jewish difference in silent German film comedy has concentrated on his performances, with occasional focus on other male comedians, such as Siegfried Arno (1895–1975), Curt Bois (1901–1991), Reinhold Schünzel (1888–1954) and Fritz Grünbaum (1880–1941) (Kasten 1998; Distelmeyer 2006; Ashkenazi 2012; Stalzer 2015). Jewishness and class mobility have played a significant role in scholarly analyses of Lubitsch's Jewish milieu films (Kasten 1998; Distelmeyer 2006; Weinstein 2006a; Ashkenazi 2012, McCormick 2020). Gender, however, has not been a dominant analytical category, with Lubitsch's performances of Jewish masculinity standing in for Jewishness in general. In an important scholarly intervention, which offers the most sustained analysis of gender in these films to date, Mila Ganeva emphasizes fashion farces' function as fashion shows for non-elite audiences, particularly women (2008, 122–130). Ganeva's interpretation, however, explores the nexus of fashion and femininity rather than the intersection of femininity and Jewish difference.

Other work on gender in early Lubitsch films highlights what Rick McCormick calls the "bad girl" films, the comedies Lubitsch directed starring Ossi Oswalda (1897–1947) and Pola Negri (1897–1987), *Ich möchte kein Mann sein* [*I Don't Want to be a Man*, 1918], *Die Puppe* [*The Doll*, 1919], *Die Austernprinzessin* [*The Oyster Princess*, 1919], and *Die Bergkatze* [*The Mountain Cat*, 1921] (Hake 1992, 81–113; Schlüpmann 1993; Kuzniar 2000, 34–39; McCabe 2003; Weinstein 2006b; McCormick 2020; Malakaj 2021). The "bad girls," however, were not Jewish. Negri was sometimes mistaken for Jewish (Wallach 2017, 48). Yet, Rischka, her character in *The Mountain Cat*, resonates with the star's stereotypical (and problematic) performances of "gypsies" in *Carmen* (Lubitsch, 1919) and *Sumurun* (Lubitsch, 1920) and with her sporadic claims to Romani lineage (Thackrey and Faris 1987). The bad girl comedies' engagement with Jewish difference is indirect. Scholarship on Jewishness and gender in these films interprets femininity as a surrogate for or successor to Jewish difference, rather than something that intersects with it (Ashkenazi 2012, 21–32; McCormick 2020).

The absence of Jewish women from analyses of German silent film comedy is analogous to scholarly trends regarding Hollywood slapstick. On the one hand, women may have been underrepresented in slapstick because of normative femininity, patriarchal constraints on female bodies, and limited opportunities in the film industry (Clayton 2007, 146). On the other hand, film scholarship has marginalized women's slapstick performances further. As Maggie Hennefeld describes, "silent film comedy has been largely historicized as a male affair. Our impressions of silent slapstick are colored more by a bowler hat and cane [of Charlie Chaplin] than by the naughty wink of Cissy Fitzgerald or the oversized taxidermic swan chapeau of Marie Dressler," citing slapstick women comedians who have faded from public memory (2014, 87). Scholarship on Jewish difference in American comedy likewise emphasizes male comedians. Joyce Antler notes, that "while the predominance of Jews in American comedy is well-known [. . .], Jewish *women's* comedy has largely gone unnoticed" (2010, 123; emphasis in the original). Scholarship on silent German-Jewish film humor shows the same gender imbalance.

In order to address the gender imbalance in the scholarship and analyze the construction of gendered Jewish difference in Wilhelmine slapstick, this essay pairs Lubitsch's starring roles with Orla's supporting roles in *Pride of the Firm* and *Blouse King*. To better explain how slapstick is an essential component of this gendered ethnic construction, the next section of this essay theorizes ethnic humor as symbolic violence and the importance of both hyperbole and resilience in Lubitsch's and Orla's slapstick performances.

3 Slapstick violence and gendered Jewish difference

Slapstick's often-violent physical gags exceed and disrupt the narrative economy (Crafton 1995). Muriel Andrin argues that the hyperbolic staging of such violence severs the link between cause and expected effect, making comedians appear invulnerable or immune to the violence represented (2010, 230–233). Alongside typical gags, Lubitsch's and Orla's slapstick performances in *Pride of the Firm* and *Blouse King* integrate physical humor, hyperbole, and violence in additional ways that produce gendered Jewish difference and resilience.

The fashion farces' exaggeration, repetition, and distortion of ethnic stereotypes is a type of slapstick violence. Illustrating how ethnic humor in American slapstick from the 1910s functions as "violence of a different form" from "traditional slapstick violence," Jake Romm cites *Oh, Sammy!* (Edward Dillon, 1913), a comedy in which a Jewish sweatshop worker's boss pressures him to marry his "more homely daughter" rather than the woman he loves. A garment industry comedy with a plot and setting similar to German fashion farces, *Oh, Sammy!* lacks the zany violence of conventional slapstick. Instead, it exercises violence on the Jewish body symbolically rather than literally, through grotesque representations and prosthetic noses (Romm 2017).

Romm attributes the symbolic violence inherent in *Oh, Sammy!*'s exaggerated, comic performances of Jewish difference not only to caricatured ethnic performances, but also to what Katrin Sieg has called "ethnic drag," the performance of a character of one ethnicity by a member of another ethnic group (Sieg 2002). The ethnic drag in *Oh, Sammy!* offends Romm's twenty-first century sensibilities as much as do blackface and yellowface performances in other films he criticizes (2017). Both Lubitsch and Orla had Jewish backgrounds. In this, their performances of Jewish difference differ from those of the non-Jewish actors in *Oh, Sammy!* However, Lubitsch's and Orla's performances are similarly exaggerated for comic effect and highlight grotesque behaviors and physical features coded as Jewish.

It is useful to combine Romm's understanding of the physical exaggeration of ethnic stereotypes as slapstick violence with Andrin's assertion that both hyperbolic violence *and* resilience to it are central features of slapstick. Lubitsch's and Orla's performative hyperbole, like the violent physical gags of the same era, construe these comedians not simply as struck by, but, more productively, as resilient to the symbolic violence of the gendered ethnic stereotypes that they perform. Just as the physical blow does not seriously injure the slapstick comedian, the exaggerated performances of Jewish difference in *Pride of the Firm* do not hurt the characters marked as Jewish. Instead the performers' exaggerated Jewishness led to the film's success with audiences and to the characters' successes in the fictional narrative. Whether or not this was entirely true for the *Blouse King* has been lost with the film's ending.

By staging Jewish-coded characters not only as immune to the violence of ethnic stereotypes but also as exaggerating and benefiting from them, Lubitsch and Orla's performances resemble performances by woman comics whom Kathleen Rowe has theorized as "unruly" (1995). The unruly woman comic embraces her own position as spectacle in order to become subject rather than the object of laughter, disrupting the social and symbolic order (Rowe 1995, 3–4). Central characteristics of unruliness include parody or masquerade, transgression, inversion, and the grotesque (5–9). These characteristics echo key features both of slapstick and of Lubitsch's performances, which I have identified and theorized elsewhere as "Jewish camp" (Weinstein 2006a). Rowe focuses on unruliness as a feminist comic strategy, but unruliness has critical potential to challenge other hierarchical social constructs as well. Lubitsch's and Orla's hyperbolic performances of gendered Jewish difference and of unruly Jewish bodies make them subjects and objects of their own jokes and use slapstick forms to render the performers resilient to the symbolic violence of ethnic humor.

Lubitsch's and Orla's physical comedy in *Pride of the Firm* and *Blouse King* relies on the exaggeration and repetition of physical traits and gestures coded as Jewish, which are performed and framed differently, according to the character's gender. The performers' exaggerations and repetitions exemplify the "pantomimic" acting style characteristic of slapstick and of German film more broadly in this period, which relied on large physical gestures and "somewhat exaggerated facial expressions to be visible in medium-long or long-shot framings" (Thompson 2001, 391). The physicality of Lubitsch's and Orla's performances and their hyperbolic staging of unruly bodies – of the excessive desires, movements, and ethnically coded physical features of Jewish bodies – is a type of slapstick that participated in the construction of gendered Jewish difference. Through hyperbole, unruliness, humor, and happy endings, *Pride of the Firm*'s and *Blouse King*'s slapstick constructs gendered Jewish difference and emphasizes the performers' resilience to the symbolic violence of grotesque ethnic stereotypes.

4 Unruly Jewish bodies I: Lubitsch's performances of Jewish masculinity

As Siegmund Lachmann and Sally Katz, Lubitsch performs unruly excesses of the Jewish male body. The characters' class mobility depends on containing and productively channeling their Jewish-coded excesses. The final shot from *Pride of the Firm*, captioned "before and after," encapsulates this narrative. (See Figure 1.) On the left, Lubitsch appears as the boorish troublemaker from the provinces from the start of the film. On the right, stands the prosperous urbanite that he ultimately becomes.

Figure 1: Siegmund Lachmann (Ernst Lubitsch), before and after. *Pride of the Firm* (Carl Wilhelm, 1914).

Part of the protagonist's journey, condensed in this shot, is changing his costume and grooming to look richer and more assimilated. These changes are construed as ironic because they cannot disguise Lubitsch's ethnically coded body and physiognomy – short and dark with a large nose and exaggerated facial features – a Jewish-coded, humorous appearance for which Wilhelm cast him in the first place (Kasten 1998, 305). Siegmund borrows money for a new outfit and a makeover, which help his career. As he earns more money, he upgrades his wardrobe further, which improves his social status, and so on. The bath, makeover, and new outfit, however, do not hide Lubitsch's own stereotypical appearance, highlighted humorously throughout the film with lighting, makeup, cinematography, jokes about his large nose, and sight gags about his diminutive height. The symmetry and doubling in this closing shot emphasize the performer's bodily sameness, and his unchanged ethnic coding, even as the costume change signals his improved financial circumstances and class position.

The closing shot from *Pride of the Firm* also emphasizes how much the protagonist's change in appearance and status depend on disciplining a body and desires that are out of control. Lubitsch's exaggerated movements are ethnically coded and recognizable as such. Jeannette R. Malkin describes Lubitsch's body language as "the physical translation of a Yiddish idiom," noting that that his "body language – restless, inventive, relentlessly 'Jewish' – had made him a star" (Malkin 2008, 202, 197; see also Eyman 2004, 169). In *Pride of the Firm* Siegmund's unruly body language must be domesticated. This process is hinted at in the contrast between the image on the left, in which Lubitsch is gesticulating and nodding, and his more disciplined and symmetrical body on the right, standing upright, hands bound to a walking stick.

The excess of the unassimilated Jewish male body is a major source of humor in these films. The Lubitsch characters' actions and desires rebel against the norms of bourgeois society in myriad ways. In *Blouse King*, Sally showcases his social impropriety and unruly body when he sits down in his boss's office, straddling the upholstered back of an armchair instead of lowering himself to its seat. By doing so, Sally positions himself higher, closer to his boss, and less formally than etiquette demands. His inappropriate behavior here signals his unsuitability for the office environment and makes a spectacle of his unconventional and willful dominance over it. Large, clumsy, and uncouth social gestures like Sally's characterize Lubitsch's performances of Jewish masculinity.

Typical slapstick gags that interrupt the narrative and exploit the tension between destruction and resilience are also central to Lubitsch's performances of Jewish masculinity. Early on in *Pride of the Firm*, Siegmund falls catastrophically from a ladder through a picture window. In another scene, he spills an unbalanced pyramid of heavy boxes over a balcony onto a rival salesperson's head. Neither these gags nor other similarly destructive ones result in lasting injury but rather in comic outcomes and audience laughter, as is characteristic of the genre (Andrin 2010). They also motivate choices leading to Siegmund's social and economic success. Both violence and an ability to roll with the punches were considered masculine traits in early twentieth century Germany. Thus Lubitsch's use of this type of physical gag conforms to the era's dominant gender norms in some ways. Yet, by emphasizing his characters' lack of physical aptitude, Lubitsch's gags also distinguish Jewish masculinity from normative masculinity by emphasizing wit and resistance to injury rather than size, strength, dexterity, or bravery.

In *Pride of the Firm* Siegmund's Jewish, male body moves humorously from unproductive excess to productive efficiency, playing into German discourses dating back to the nineteenth century that Jewish people lacked a productive work ethic (Campbell 1989). Siegmund transforms from a clumsy rascal to a successful businessman despite being lazy – or, indeed, *because* he is lazy. Siegmund has lack of aptitude for and horror of physical effort. To avoid physical labor that he neither wants to do nor is particularly good at, he tries to find clever and unexpected ways of approaching obstacles. When asked to nail a crate shut, instead of actually doing so, he exhausts a series of alternatives – demonstrating incompetence, provoking his supervisor into hitting him, creating a hubbub, and, finally, making one ineffective attempt at pounding the nail, hitting his own thumb, and retreating to write a letter to his parents. In *Schuhpalast Pinkus* [*Shoe Palace Pinkus*] (Lubitsch, 1916), the Lubitsch protagonist scoots under the pommel horse when his physical education instructor isn't looking, rather than jumping over it as intended, turning failure into success through dishonesty and wit. In *Blouse King* as well, Sally profits from wit and trickery, making social connections by giving away candy and cigars that he bought with his boss's money. The protagonists' reliance on wit rather than work defines Jewish ethnic identity as one that privileges mind over body, cleverness over physical labor.

Lubitsch's slapstick performances repeatedly exaggerate Jewish men's bravado and libido. Hyperbolic, repetitive flirtations and lewd comments celebrate the protagonists' lechery and uncontrolled desires. Lubitsch's protagonists make insistent and repeated inappropriate sexual advances on all kinds of women: upper class customers, co-workers, domestic help, and his boss's daughters. In the films in which the main character is married, such as *Als ich tot war* [*When I was Dead*, 1915] and *Meyer aus Berlin* [*Meyer from Berlin*, 1918], he balks at the constraints posed by marriage. The Lubitsch characters' sexual confidence and the success of their exploits are disproportionate to their social stature and physical appearance, which contemporaries considered comic rather than handsome. In apprentice or lower sales positions, Lubitsch's protagonists make suggestive comments to customers and boss's daughters. The protagonists' sexual desires, confidence, and assertiveness are transgressive, grotesque, and improbable, and as such resist stereotypes of Jewish men as sexual predators in an unruly, slapstick form.

Lubitsch's performances create a modern, secular male Jewish identity with unruly desires, behaviors, and bodies that, even when clothed and groomed like others', never quite fits in. As performed by Lubitsch, these Jewish men compensate for both physical excess and lack of control with a sharp mind, which is good for capitalism and upward social mobility. Lubitsch performs the

Jewish male body as both frenetic and lazy, too large in facial features and too small in stature, too motivated by sexual impulses and too lacking in inhibition. This body requires discipline to assimilate to German culture, to the German-Jewish upper class, and to sexual norms. The narratives in the surviving films corral the protagonist and his desires into a socially sanctioned marriage or repair his broken marriage. In *Pride of the Firm*, the main vehicle of this discipline is a woman coded as Siegmund's Jewish female counterpart: Isolde Berg (Orla), who marries Siegmund and produces the firm's pride and heir.

5 Unruly Jewish bodies II: Orla's performances of Jewish femininity

Orla's performances of the boss's daughters in *Pride of the Firm* and *Blouse King* are unruly iterations of upper class German-Jewish femininity, which complement Lubitsch's repetitive, hyperbolic slapstick performances of upwardly mobile Jewish apprentices. Isolde and Brünhilde look and behave in caricatured, exaggerated ways, coded for spectators of the 1910s as Jewish. The upper class Jewish femininity Orla performs in these roles partially overlaps with Lubitsch's Jewish masculinity and partially with the femininity of the middle class women his characters pursue romantically. Yet they also differ. Orla's unruly slapstick performances in *Pride of the Firm* and *Blouse King* create distinct versions of upper-class Jewish femininity. Before delving into Orla's performances of Jewish femininity and the slapstick techniques she uses, I first introduce readers to this forgotten actor's biography and star persona.

Orla had a brief, bright career before her untimely death in 1931. Like Lubitsch, she made her screen breakthrough in *Die Firma heiratet* [*The Firm Marries*] (Carl Wilhelm, 1913), a fashion farce, of which no known copies exist. Orla claimed Walter Turszinski (1874–1915) wrote the script for her after seeing her perform on stage (Orla 1919). She acted alongside Lubitsch again in *Pride of the Firm*, both of their earliest surviving screen appearances, and in a lost film called *Blindekuh* [*Blind Cow*] (Lubitsch, 1915), by all accounts a milieu comedy. Orla is known to have performed in more than a dozen comedies between 1913 and 1918. It is possible she performed in more. Documentation about German film from this period is notoriously incomplete (Kasten 1998, 301).

Orla had several prolific years as a "comic diva" and then made a successful transition to dramatic roles in 1918 (C.B. 1918). Her career trajectory was typical and consistent with cultural pressures on women actors at the time, which treated comedy as both unfeminine and unserious (Wagner 2011, 41–43).

Similar biases seem to have affected the marketing and memory of Orla as a star. Publicity shots depicted her as a serious beauty rather than as a comedian.

Across genres, Orla performed gender, ethnic, and racial difference in Jewish, redface, yellowface, and vamp roles in major releases. A brief synopsis tellingly describes her as "[a]n exciting brunette, who specialized in roles as antagonist of wicked women [sic] or *femmes fatales*, with her southern face always conflicting with the blonde protagonist" (*Griffithiana* 1990). Orla played Juanita, the eponymous *Halbblut* [*Halfblood*] in Fritz Lang's 1919 film of that name, and Lio Sha, the ethnically ambiguous criminal mastermind in his *Die Spinnen* [*Spiders*] films (Lang 1919, 1920). Orla's casting in exotic and sexually dangerous roles embodying racial difference is consistent with slippages in stereotypes and discourses in Germany of dark haired women as ethnically "other," and with public perception and casting of other dark-haired Jewish women at the time (Wallach 2017, 26–47).

As Orla's star persona developed, she cultivated her image as a serious actor and an exotic femme fatale, leaving the "comic diva" behind, and, along with her, the career baggage and cultural memories of her comic performances. Star culture was just beginning to develop in Germany in the mid 1910s and film critics still disparaged credits as a boring "name cult," which makes confirming performers' identities difficult (*Lichtbild Bühne*, 24 January, 1914). Although Orla is not included in *Pride of the Firm*'s opening credits, which, as is typical for the era, do not include the full cast, secondary sources consistently list her as having been in that film. A process of elimination suggests Orla probably played Isolde, the boss's daughter. It is obvious that the same actor played both Isolde and the boss's daughter in *Blouse King*. I have not found credits for that role either. The actor's face resembles photographs of Orla – possibly wearing a prosthetic nose or putty to make her nose bridge higher, more arched, and more stereotypically "Jewish." I therefore treat *Pride of the Firm* and the *Blouse King* fragment as rare examples of Orla's comedic performances, with the caveat that new or contradictory evidence may unexpectedly surface someday, as did the *Blouse King* fragment (Kasten 1998, 322). By analyzing Orla's slapstick performances in *Pride of the Firm* and *Blouse King*, I begin to excavate this lost phase of Orla's career and to add this Jewish "comic diva" to our scholarly archive. I also broaden the scholarly scrutiny of Jewish difference in German slapstick to include the analysis of Jewish femininity.

Slapstick in the fashion farces juxtaposes Orla's upper class Jewish femininity to the femininity of middle class fashion salon workers. Siegmund and Sally spend a substantial amount of time in the fashion salon flirting with the women who work there. As their jobs demand, these women are attractive and well dressed. Most of them are also taller and fairer haired than Lubitsch and Orla. They know social conventions and how to make themselves and others look stylish and respectable in public. In *Pride of the Firm*, Lilly advises customers and co-workers, coaches Siegmund through his makeover and social transformations, and controls her own appearance and propriety. In private, however – behind curtains at the fashion salon, or in her apartment when Siegmund comes calling – she responds flirtatiously to the apprentice's advances. She, like other white-collar women fashion workers in these films (which do not show sweatshop workers or pieceworkers), treads a cautious line between respectability and romantic agency. Situating these characters in historical context, Ganeva describes the models and salesladies in fashion farces as transgressive and assertive, as "female doubles of sorts to the ambitious Jewish apprentices," similarly seeking to improve their class status through the fashion business (2008, 127).

In describing fashion salon employees as "female doubles" of "Jewish apprentices," Ganeva emphasizes the models' and apprentices' shared class ambitions, pluck, and romantic/sexual agency. Ganeva's word choice, which posits the female as the double of the Jewish, implicitly offers additional insights into the differing ethnic coding in these films. Lubitsch's male protagonists are heavily coded as Jewish. The models and sales personnel, however, lack explicit ethnic coding. The casting of lighter haired women with more delicate and conventionally pretty facial features and the contrast between their appearance and both Lubitsch's and the boss's daughters' emphasize their relative lack of what contemporaries understood as bodily markers of Jewish visibility (see Wallach 2017, 27–51). As with other binary and hierarchical forms of difference (white/Black; straight/queer; masculine/feminine etc.), audiences tend to assume that unmarked characters belong to the dominant position (in this case non-Jewish) and that othered identities are marked (Jewish). As I will expand below, Orla's slapstick style and corporeality in her performances as the bosses' daughters, differs substantially from the actors playing the unmarked and thus not-necessarily-Jewish women in the fashion salon. The Jewish boss's daughter represents a different kind of potential double or partner for the protagonist – not one seeking upward class mobility, as do the protagonist and the fashion workers, but rather one pursuing ethnic endogamy.

Whereas casting, costuming, and makeup exaggerate the physical differences between the fashion-salon women and Lubitsch, cinematic techniques emphasize Orla's "Jewish" features and her physical similarities to him. The composition of medium and full shots in both *Pride of the Firm* and *Blouse King* position Lubitsch so that he looks shorter than the people around him. Once Orla enters the picture, she is framed to look tinier still, dwarfed by the people around her, or by standing far back in a mise-en-scène dominated by impressive décor and either overcrowded or empty space. Isolde's dark hair is frizzy. (Brünhilde's is covered by an oversized black cloche hat.) Her mother pats it down before she meets Siegmund at her birthday party, and after marriage, he pats it down for her. These affectionate gestures call attention to the unruliness of Isolde's frizzy, Jewish hair. Makeup and lighting exaggerate the similarity between Lubitsch's and her facial features and their stereotypical Jewishness. Close-ups of the pair turning toward one another – and, potentially, prosthetics, putty, or make-up – make their noses look like they are the same shape and size, large and with a high bridge, the stereotypical Jewish nose. Heavy eyebrows and dark makeup circles under Orla's eyes also exaggerate her features, as do her pantomimic, comically grotesque facial expressions. Orla's heavy character makeup and facial expressivity are very different from the look created by the glamorous makeup in her headshots and femme fatales roles later in her career and from the more restrained and conventional makeup and facial vocabulary of the women in the fashion salon. A number of symmetrical two shots in both films also emphasize how Isolde/Brünhilde and Siegmund/Sally mirror one another. (See Figure 2.) Orla's makeup, mime-like expressions, staging, and framing all code the bosses' daughters as Jewish and as a physical match for the upwardly mobile Jewish protagonist.

Figure 2: Two shots in *The Blouse King* (Lubitsch, 1917) emphasize the similarities between Brünnhilde (Ressel Orla) and Sally (Ernst Lubitsch).

Orla's costuming and makeup code her as Jewish. Performing as Isolde, she combines this Jewish coded appearance with an exaggerated upper class femininity and immaturity. Where Siegmund is excessively brash, Isolde is excessively demure. Orla's performance exaggerates the docile behavior of a good Jewish girl. In addition to appearing childishly small, she often wears white, takes a background position in shots, and restrains her body movements. She opens her eyes wide in innocence, smiling and cocking her head, or looks down bashfully. She attends a fashion show at Berg's, well dressed and admiring the finery on display, but sits in the background (from the viewers' perspective), hidden by other ladies at the show. Escorted by her mother to meet the bridegroom her father found for her in the newspaper, Isolde looks at him devotedly and gets engaged. In contrast to the fashion workers' assertiveness, flirtation, and pleasure in being on display, Isolde's sexuality submits to parental and social expectations and hides from the viewer's gaze – as when she and her new husband bashfully kiss behind bushes.

In *Pride of the Firm*, ethnic endogamy fulfills parental wishes and the protagonist's class ambitions and lays the foundation for love. The bride's upper class femininity calms the groom's unruly and excessive movements and desires. The repeated calm and intimately framed two shots in the epilogue, the characters' loving looks at one another, their shy embraces on their honeymoon, and the production and celebration of "the pride of the firm" construe them as a well-matched pair. It is this combination of ethnic similarity and class and gender difference that produce Siegmund's final before and after shot.

In *Blouse King*, Orla performs a different slapstick iteration of Jewish femininity. Not only Brünhilde's appearance but also her behavior mirrors Sally's. In her desperation to marry him, despite her father's objections, she transgresses and reverses several social norms. At a time when men were expected to court women, Brünhilde engineers chance meetings, bats her eyes, and moves too close to Sally in unruly performances of sexual assertiveness and class transgression. Brünhilde invites Sally to visit her, calls him on the phone while he is bathing, and announces to her father that they plan to marry. Like Sally, she uses wit and trickery to get what she wants. Having maneuvered herself alone in a room with her father's employee, Brünhilde tries to encourage sexual contact. She unties her own shoe in order to ask Sally to kneel before her and tie it, requiring him to handle her foot and see her ankle. When he does so, Orla's face mimes an exaggerated, open-eyed, eye-rolling expression of bliss, and she proclaims in the intertitles that he should not be so "wild" ["stürmisch"] (0:04:27), projecting the passion she feels onto his less than enthusiastic actions, and highlighting a slapstick reversal of sexual desire: Sally is a sexual predator elsewhere in the film, but Brünhilde becomes the predator here.

Whereas Isolde domesticated Siegmund in *Pride of the Firm*, in *Blouse King* Sally is repulsed by Brünhilde. Being alone with her makes him feel "wretched" ["mies"] (0:04:46). In a woman he finds his own appearance and behavior appalling, indicating that such appearance and behavior should be reserved for men. Sally's and other characters' reactions suggest that to be desirable, women should look and act more like Lissy Maas, the head saleswoman, who is tall and fair haired and resistant to Sally's advances – thus coded as more feminine, more respectable, and less Jewish. Sally's preference for Lissy and disregard for Brünhilde aligns with the era's sexual expectations for upper-class women as well as pressures on Jewish women to be only "subtly or barely visible" (Wallach

2017, 7). It also is tied to the differing cultural associations between men, women, and comedy. In the early twentieth century, comedy was widely seen as unfeminine. Kristen Anderson Wagner argues that women slapstick performers challenged traditional gender roles with their ribald physical comedy and by showing that women could be funny. "If simply having a sense of humor raised doubts about a woman's femininity, then actively engaging in comic performances could be seen as an affront to and unraveling of traditional gender roles" (Wagner 2011, 44).

Orla's performance of Brünhilde's unruly, desiring body is both too Jewish and not feminine enough for Sally. Yet, her performance mimics Lubitsch's, pressing viewers to question why Sally does not like it. Sally's negative reaction to Brünhilde creates an ironic point of view vis-à-vis the protagonist that makes him look like a hypocrite: Sally fails to realize how similar he and Brünhilde are and thus fails to realize how offensive and unattractive he himself is. Sally does not want Brünhilde as a bride any more than Herr Rosenthal wants Sally for a son-in-law. By mirroring Lubitsch's performances of Jewish masculinity in her unruly slapstick performance of Jewish femininity, Orla calls attention to the differing social expectations of Jewish men and Jewish women in realms including appearance, behavior, humor, and sexuality. In this, Orla's performance is consistent with the performances by American-Jewish comediennes analyzed by Antler, which challenge social conventions, male-dominated comic traditions, and gender roles (Antler 2010, 126).

As a fragment, the challenge mounted by Orla's performance in *Blouse King* lacks a large part of its contextual frame. It is impossible to assess the nature and degree of narrative closure on Brünhilde's comic social and sexual transgressions. Different endings would, of course, frame Orla's slapstick performance of Jewish femininity differently, affect the balance between symbolic violence and resilience, and the dynamic between Jewish femininity and Jewish masculinity in that film.

Bibliography

Andrin, Muriel. "Back to the 'Slap': Slapstick's Hyperbolic Gesture." *Slapstick Comedy*. Ed. Tom Paulus and Rob King. New York: Routledge, 2010. 226–235.
Antler, Joyce. "One Clove Away From a Pomander Ball: The Subversive Tradition of Jewish Female Comedians." *Studies in American Jewish Literature* 29 (2010): 123–138.
Ashkenazi, Ofer. *Weimar Film and Modern Jewish Identity*. New York: Palgrave Macmillan, 2012.

Bial, Henry. *Acting Jewish: Negotiating Ethnicity on the American Stage and Screen*. Ann Arbor: University of Michigan Press, 2005.
Campbell, Joan. *Joy in Work, German Work: The National Debate, 1800–1945*. Princeton: Princeton University Press, 1989.
C.B. "Ressel Orla." *Der Film*. http://www.filmhistoriker.de/people/orla.htm. 12 January 1918 (accessed 7 March, 2018).
Clayton, Alex. *The Body in American Slapstick*. Jefferson, NC: McFarland and Company, 2007.
Crafton, Donald. "Pie and Chase: Gag, Spectacle and Narrative in Slapstick Comedy." *Classical Hollywood Comedy*. Ed. Kristine Brunovska Karnick and Henry Jenkins. New York: Routledge, 1995. 106–119.
Der Blusenkönig. Dir. Ernst Lubitsch. Projektions-AG Union, 1917.
Der Stolz der Firma. Dir. Carl Wilhelm. Projektions-AG Union, 1914.
Distelmeyer, Jan. Ed. *Spaß beiseite, Film ab. Jüdischer Humor und verdrängendes Lachen in der Filmkomödie bis 1945*. Munich: Edition Text + Kritik, 2006.
Eyman, Scott. "Ernst Lubitsch 1892–1947: Schauspieler und Regisseur." *Pionere in Celluloid: Juden in der frühen Filmwelt*. Ed. Irene Stratenwerth and Hermann Simon. Berlin: Henschel, 2004. 167–171.
Ganeva, Mila. *Women in Weimar Fashion: Discourses and Displays in German Culture, 1918–1933*. Rochester: Camden House, 2008.
Hake, Sabine. *Passions and Deceptions: The Early Films of Ernst Lubitsch*. Princeton: Princeton University Press, 1992.
Hennefeld, Maggie. "Slapstick Comediennes in Transitional Cinema: Between Body and Medium." *Camera Obscura* 86, Vol. 29, No. 2 (2014): 84–117.
Kasten, Jürgen. "Der Stolz der deutschen Filmkomödie: Die frühen Filme von Ernst Lubitsch 1914–1918." *Mediengeschichte des Films Band 2: Die Modellierung des Kinofilms: Zur Geschichte des Kinoprogramms zwischen Kurzfilm und Langfilm (1905/6–1918)*. Ed. Corinna Müller and Harro Segeberg. Munich: Fink, 1998. 301–332.
Kuzniar, Alice. *The Queer German Cinema*. Stanford: Stanford University Press, 2000.
Malakaj, Ervin. "Lubitsch's Queer Slapstick Aesthetics." *Slapstick: An Interdisciplinary Companion*. Eds. Ervin Malakaj and Alena E. Lyons. Berlin and Boston: De Gruyter, 2021. 333–349.
Malkin, Jeannette R. "The Cinematic Shoe: Ernst Lubitsch's East European 'Tough' in *Pinkus's Shoe Palace*." *Jews and Shoes*. Ed. Edna Nashon. Oxford: Berg, 2008. 195–208.
McCabe, Janet. "Regulating Hidden Pleasures and 'Modern' Identities: Imagined Female Spectators, Early German Popular Cinema, and *The Oyster Princess* (1919)." *Light Motives: German Popular Film in Perspective*. Ed. Randall Halle and Margaret McCarthy. Detroit: Wayne State University Press, 2003. 24–40.
McCormick, Rick. *Sex, Politics, and Comedy: The Transnational Cinema of Ernst Lubitsch – From Berlin to Hollywood*. Bloomington: Indiana University Press, 2020.
Orla, Ressel. "Wie ich zum Film kam." *Film-Kurier*. http://www.filmhistoriker.de/people/orla.htm. 25 June 1919 (accessed 7 March 2018).
Otte, Marline. *Jewish Identities in German Popular Entertainment, 1890–1933*. New York: Cambridge University Press, 2006.
"Ressel Orla." *Griffithiana* 38/39 (October 1990): 25.
Review of *Der Blusenkönig*. *Der Kinematograph*. http://www.filmportal.de/node/11519/material/670343. 7 November 1917 (accessed 28 January 2018).

Review of *Die Firma Heiratet. Lichtbild-Bühne*. https://www.filmportal.de/node/36855/material/622330. 24 January 1914 (accessed 25 April 2018).

Romm, Jake. "Vintage Slapstick Movies Show Just How Much, and How Little, Racism Has Changed." *Forward*. https://forward.com/culture/361155/vintage-slapstick-movies-show-just-how-much-and-how-little-racism-has-chang/. 25 January 2017 (accessed 28 January 2018).

Rowe, Kathleen. *The Unruly Woman: Gender and the Genres of Laughter*. Austin: University of Texas Press, 1995.

Schlüpmann, Heide. "'Ich möchte kein Mann sein' Ernst Lubitsch, Sigmund Freud und die frühe deutsche Komödie." *KINtop 1: Jahrbuch zur Erforschung des frühen Films*. Basel: Stroemfeld/Roter Stern, 1993. 75–92.

Schuhpalast Pinkus. Dir. Ernst Lubitsch. Projektions-AG Union, 1916.

Sieg, Katrin. *Ethnic Drag: Performing Race, Nation, Sexuality in West Germany*. Ann Arbor: University of Michigan Press, 2002.

Stalzer, Alfred. "Jüdische Bühnenkünstler im deutschen und österreichischen Film." *Der jüdische Witz: Zur unabgegoltenen Problematik einer alten Kategorie*. Ed. Burkhard Meyer-Sickendiek and Gunnar Och. Paderborn: Wilhelm Fink, 2015. 225–233.

Thackrey, Ted Jr., and Gerald Faris. "Pola Negri, 'Vamp' of Silent Film, Dies." *Los Angeles Times*. http://articles.latimes.com/1987-08-03/news/mn-546_1_pola-negri. 3 August 1987 (accessed 1 April, 2018).

Thompson, Kristin. "Lubitsch, Acting and the Silent Romantic Comedy." *Film History* 13.4 (2001): 390–408.

Wagner, Kristen Anderson. "'Have Women a Sense of Humor?' Comedy and Femininity in Early Twentieth-Century Film." *The Velvet Light Trap* 68 (Fall 2011): 35–46.

Wallach, Kerry. *Passing Illusions: Jewish Visibility in Weimar Cinema*. Ann Arbor: University of Michigan Press, 2017.

Weinstein, Valerie. "Anti-Semitism or Jewish 'Camp'? Ernst Lubitsch's *Shoe Palace Pinkus* (1916) and *Meyer from Berlin* (1918)." *German Life and Letters* 59.1 (January 2006a): 101–121.

Weinstein, Valerie. "(Un)Fashioning Identities: Ernst Lubitsch's Early Comedies of Mistaken Identity." *Visual Culture in Twentieth-Century Germany: Text as Spectacle*. Ed. Gail Finney. Bloomington: Indiana University Press, 2006b. 120–133.

Part V: **Politics of Slapstick**

Ervin Malakaj & Alena E. Lyons
Introduction

Comedy is always controversial. Alenka Zupančič notes that enjoyment "only exists at the very intersection between the subject and the other/Other" and that "in comedy this intersection itself becomes the scene, the place, the room of action" (2019, 142). However, even if "enjoyment gets a room of its own," it "can only be a common room, or else it is not" (142). That is, the common room of comedy is a fragile construct. Its vulnerability derives from the fact that it is not universally welcoming: some experience this room as a commons, while others view it as threatening and violent. Slapstick, as a comedy genre, operates along similar lines of address. Its politics are shaped by the parameters of inclusion – by the questions of who is hailed as part of the commons, who is pushed out of it, and for whom this space does not exist at all. Slapstick's gags are thus shaped and give rise to complex politics of belonging, rendering any resulting laughter a contentious matter.

Suffering, as a feature of slapstick, is deeply entangled with the messy politics conditioning the enjoyment of comedy. As Louise Peacock has shown, "the performance of slapstick pain is ubiquitous" (2014, 173). From the slips to the falls to the hits and beyond, slapstick gags derive their comedic power from the slapstick protagonist's violent encounter with the material world discussed in the previous section (see, "Bodies of Slapstick"). In fact, slapstick comedians frequently court the extreme in their performances of pain and suffering. As Muriel Andrin has shown, some Buster Keaton (1895–1966) comedies went beyond the pain and suffering in that they were characterized by "an obsession with the threat of death" (2010, 233; see also Clayton 2007, 168–182). At times, this obsession crossed the line of the acceptable for audiences. This was the case with *The General* (1927), in which the gag consists in Keaton accidentally killing another character in the film. As Andrin has shown, this death garnered negative reviews by critics who accused Keaton of betraying the genre (233). The very premise of slapstick is the extreme malleability of the body, which is resistant to the laws of physics or cause and effect (Scott 2014, 73). Audiences in on the joke that the slapstick body can be the recipient of extreme force that it survives unscathed relished in the fantasy of consequence-less pain. Keaton transformed the genre by breaching its very premise — to the detriment of audience support. In fact, the harsh contemporary criticism against Keaton highlights that the act of pushing slapstick's obsession with suffering to the extreme takes on a politics of its own. Even if, as Noël Carroll has shown, the plot of *The General* "does not appear to be the main vehicle for Keaton's vision" (2009, 158) and merely serves as means to arrange and perform the gags themselves, its constellation in the film generated too much discomfort in audiences, jolting viewers out of the fantasy of the genre.

It is worth noting that Keaton's preoccupation with death is part and parcel of the aesthetics of excess that characterize slapstick. To this end, Peacock remarks that "in slapstick we encounter physical excess in the human body and excessive waste and damage in the way sets and props are treated and depicted" (2014, 36). That is, slapstick moments are characterized by an intensity generated from the premise of alternative laws of logic that stand in contrast to life in the real world. As Andrew Scott notes, "typical gags might involve disproportionate sizes, the animation of the inanimate, the slowing down or speeding up of temporality, the personification of objects, and the reversal or rejection of linear cause-and-effect that allows things to be re-contextualized or entirely re-used" (2014, 74). This logic that runs counter to that of the real world is laden with critical potential. Through exaggeration of the (mostly mitigated) effects of the slapstick body's encounter with the material world, slapstick renders bare some of the world's problems. In this vein, Tom Gunning has shown how Charlie Chaplin's (1889–1977) exaggerated performance style (in particular in *Modern Times*, 1936) relies on "the new technological body that promised to be the final step in achieving a modern utopia" (2010, 241). Chaplin's physical features and movements in his films indeed came to be viewed by his contemporary audiences as the most honest expression of technological modernity, its capacities, and its failures.

Moreover, the fragile common space of comedy cited at the opening of this introduction is intensified in slapstick. While all comedy creates precarious audiences who relate differently to it, slapstick's investment in extremity pushes this conceit about comedy itself to the extreme. Slapstick thus often appears crude. Its intentions irritate audiences, which can recognize the component parts of its humor economy acutely based on the extreme performances. The politics of slapstick are thus frequently inscribed on its surface (cf. Hilsabeck 2020, 8–9). That is, the extreme features of slapstick are also extremely legible as such for audiences. Take, for instance, the fragility of the faith in machine technology ridiculed at the core of *Modern Times*. This fragility is enacted scene after scene in which machines fail to interact congruently with humans (09:40–14:00). The scene in which the engineers test out their machine developed to improve the conveyor belt productivity of the workers offers a good example here. This machine would eliminate the time that workers are away from the conveyor belt by feeding workers while they are completing tasks at their stations. Chaplin's character is selected as the test subject. Although clunkily mechanical and visibly confusing for Chaplin's character, the machine successfully feeds him the initial dishes. However, as the machine cycle enters the corn on the cob, the machine's insensitivity to the needs of humans quickly reaches extreme levels. As the cob turns vehemently, Chaplin's character struggles to eat the corn. From here, the machine's mechanized feeding progressively worsens, leaving the engineers scrambling and Chaplin's character grotesquely abused by the extreme failures of this machine experiment. There is no doubt about the prominently legible lesson about humans interacting with machines in this scene.

Politics, as conceived by the contributors to this section, address the relations among slapstick figures and their environment. They consider the mechanisms that govern how figures are positioned into the world, what pressures they face, and what opportunities this world makes available to them. As such, the contributors are less invested in politics as enacted by local, regional, national, and international government structures, but about the vernacular: the effects of social structures on characters and these characters' resistance or submission to power.

In particular, the chapters in this section examine the effects of various kinds of excess and their relationship to suffering as registered in slapstick's surface-level politics. Collectively, they advance new approaches to studying slapstick. In her chapter on slapstick comediennes of the silent era, Maggie Hennefeld examines how the work of early twentieth-century slapstick comediennes is a repository of the era's anxieties surrounding female laughter. The gag-structures and narrative progression of slapstick films featuring comediennes are highly gendered in light of women's ambivalent role in the public sphere. By featuring scenes in which comediennes blow up parts of the household, Hennefeld notes, these films become important artefacts to examine in light of our own, gendered lives today.

In his analysis of Ernst Lubitsch's (1892–1947) early slapstick comedies, Ervin Malakaj considers slapstick's queer potential. Examining the recurring gag structures of failure and disorientation that temper the heterosexual success narratives at the core of the films, Malakaj shows how Lubitsch's protagonists live queer lives and are exemplary subjects for a queer aesthetic. Lubitsch's commitment to abrupt endings that aim to tie together the loose ends of the queer plot structures are, in this reading, not a subjugation of the queer potential enacted in individual gags. Rather, the abruptness of the endings highlights just how incapable they are in containing the queer narrative paths Lubitsch took to get to them.

Ignacio M. Sánchez Prado studies the astonishing transnational success of contemporary Mexican comedian Eugenio Derbez (*1961). For Sánchez Prado, Derbez embodies a long tradition of slapstick performance that spans the entire twentieth and twenty-first centuries, one best described as a form of "binational slapstick" simultaneously capable of reaching Mexican and US audiences. In this consideration, slapstick's politics of address – the genre's capacity to create common ground for audiences to meet and feel hailed by its aesthetics – serve complicated functions as facilitated by the performance style of Derbez.

The section concludes with a chapter by Jiří Hoblík, who considers the interrelationships between scripture and slapstick by reading the humility of slapstick protagonists as both inspired by and commenting on religious history. Humility, as a crucial component of the politics of Christian scripture iconography, informs the characterization and gag structure of the surface politics of slapstick and, thereby, serves as an analytic category for comparative work.

Works cited

Andrin, Muriel. "Back to the 'Slap': Slapstick's Hyperbolic Gesture and the Rhetoric of Violence." *Slapstick Comedy*. Eds. Tom Paulus and Rob King. New York: Routledge, 2010. 226–236.
Carroll, Noël. *Comedy Incarnate: Buster Keaton, Physical Humor, and Bodily Coping*. London: Wiley, 2009.
Clayton, Alex. *The Body in Hollywood Slapstick*. Jefferson: McFarland & Co., 2007.
Gunning, Tom. "Chaplin and the Body of Modernity." *Early Popular Visual Culture* 8.3 (2010): 237–245.
Hilsabeck, Burke. *The Slapstick Camera: Hollywood and the Comedy of Self-Reference*. New York: State University of New York Press, 2020.
Peacock, Louis. *Slapstick and Comic Performance: Comedy and Pain*. New York: Palgrave, 2014.
Scott, Andrew. *Comedy*. New York: Routledge, 2014.
Zupančič, Alenka. "Where does Dirt Come From?" *The Object of Comedy: Philosophies and Performances*. Eds. Jamila M.H. Mascat and Gregor Moder. New York: Palgrave, 2019.

Maggie Hennefeld
Slapstick Comediennes in Silent Cinema: Women's Laughter and the Feminist Politics of Gender in Motion

Perhaps no image caused early film spectators greater discomfort in the 1890s than the public eruption of female laughter: the convulsive explosion of ribs heaving in their tight corsets, loud ripples of vocal mirth issuing from the oral cavities, and, worst of all, the implication that inappropriate innuendos were not lost on female viewers. While many of these tense and uncomfortable visions of female laughter have been long since forgotten, they pose crucial historiographic challenges for feminist film scholars today, and remain broadly resonant and provocative reminders of the very deep-seated social anxieties about women's relationship to laughter and comedy. As this chapter will explore, slapstick comediennes in early cinema both enacted and reflected heated cultural debates about the relationship between gender, comedic pleasure, and feminist social politics. From early 1900s trick films about exploding housemaids, to 19-teens knockabout comedies depicting domestic assault, to 1920s flapper films about commodity capitalism, silent movies featuring slapstick comediennes represent archival traces that reveal crucial formations of modern feminism and popular screen culture.

During the years while moving pictures were emerging as a mass medium and commercial institution, there was an explosion of discourse attempting to regulate and constrain female laughter in public. In 1898, *The New York Herald* advised women to adopt something called "The New Laugh": "It is a laugh, all but the sound, all but the opening of the mouth and the showing of the teeth. It is fun and amusement personified, but all silence" (10). At the same time as the *Herald* coaxed women to pursue an ethereal experience of laughter that would efface the role of the body, *The Woman's Home Companion* leveled its censorship at "the funny woman" ad hominem: "We know you are very funny, but one's face aches with continual smiling, and an exclusively funny diet is about as sustaining as a ration of mere pepper and salt" (21). Whether a site of inappropriate bodily excess or of gastronomical starvation, the female laugh was characterized as corrupt, immoral, and distinctly unfeminine.

Yet, early motion pictures tell a completely different story about women and laughter. It was completely conventional and uncontroversial for women to laugh uproariously onscreen, exemplified by films such as *Rube and Mandy at Coney Island* (Edwin S. Porter, 1903), *Laughing Gas* (Edwin S. Porter, 1907),

Betty and Jane Go to the Theatre (Roméo Bosetti, 1911), *Daisy Doodad's Dial* (Florence Turner, 1914), and *The House of Fifi* (Viggo Larsen, 1914). In *Laughing Gas,* an African-American woman, Mandy (Bertha Regustus), experiences uncontrollable laughter after being given nitrous-oxide (laughing gas) by her dentist, and then proceeds to spread her laughter contagiously throughout the public sphere: to fellow streetcar passengers, gospel churchgoers, white police officers, and even to a justice of the peace. In *Daisy Doodad's Dial*, a bored housewife practices for an amateur face making competition in public, eventually getting herself arrested and then having hysterical visions at night of her own disembodied laughter and spectral facial contortions (see Figure 1). In numerous bourgeois "comedies of manners" throughout the 19-teens and 1920s, women's laughter functioned as a motif that anchored the film's narration.

Figure 1: *Daisy Doodad's Dial*. Source: *Doodad's Dial*, Florence Turner, 1914.

For example, in *House of Fifi* – a German comedy made shortly before the eruption of WWI – a female hat shop proprietor practically causes the downfall of the Prussian Military by enticing high-ranking officers to purchase increasingly expensive ladies' haberdashery. As the gift exchange and marital cuckoldry plots get messy, Fifi (Wanda Treumann) reorients the spectator by halting narrative time, stepping outside of her film character's own body to share an ironic laugh with the spectator. Similarly, in American comedies from this time, such as *Love and Gasoline* (Mabel Normand, 1914), *Are Waitresses Safe?* (Hampton Del Ruth, 1917) with Louise Fazenda, and *The Danger Girl* (Clarence Badger, 1916) with Gloria Swanson, women's extra-diegetic laughter – residing between the fictive world of the film and the living body of the film spectator – provided an image for stabilizing the comic slippage of misidentifications sustained by a film's plot. Female laughter covered over the missing links in comedic film narration.

Beyond the literal image of women laughing, ladies frequently performed outrageous and perverse bodily gestures in order to provoke the convulsive amusement of laughing film spectators. For example, in popular films of what I call the *exploding housemaid genre* (cf. Hennefeld 2014b) – such as *Mary Jane's Mishap* (G.A. Smith, 1903), *A Shocking Incident* (AM&B, 1903), and *How Bridget Made the Fire* (AM&B, 1900) – working-class women accidentally incinerate or electrocute themselves while attempting to perform traditional domestic chores with modern mechanical devices. Using jump cuts adapted from vanishing lady films – "now you see her, now you don't!" – women disappear in puffs of smoke after heaping too much paraffin onto the hearth fire. The instantaneity of the film cut was thereby synchronized with the spontaneous eruption of laughter it provoked for the spectator. Women's calamitous, contortionist, and disappearing bodies somehow had the power to mediate the otherwise very charged relationship between startling screen effects and uproarious spectator embodiment: between onscreen explosions and nervous spectator convulsions.

While audiences delighted in the spectacle of moving pictures throughout the 1890s – at vaudeville variety theaters, traveling shows, garden parties, and community centers – the physical encounter with women's laughing bodies in the public sphere provoked considerable displeasure. Society columnists advised their female readers "to banish the giggles once and for all" ("Here's the New Laugh," 1898, 10), whereas derisive journalists warned all readers against the hazards of female senses of humor: "The funny woman per se is a pestilence in the land. Carelessly and roguishly she seeks only to make the world laugh, sends her merry shot and shells here and there and takes no note of the wounded in the field" ("Without Tact," 1897, 21). Women's humor was here ideologically weaponized– equated with military violence – while female laughter was singled out for public censorship and repression.

Early motion pictures, with their mystifying and slippery relationship to the history and presence of the bodies that they capture, possessed the tremendous capacity to defuse pervasive social anxieties about the eruption of women's laughter in the public sphere. Moreover, the instance of onscreen female comedy provided a curiously potent image for mediating the spectator's own bodily experience of madcap cinematic movement. Like comedy, which hinges on surprise, reversal, and incongruity, filmmaking is all about the spectacle of paradoxes: animating past moments and still photograms as if they had come back to life and were really moving again before our eyes. In late nineteenth- and early twentieth-century American culture, filmmaking and comedic performance represented crucial interlocking sites for women to redefine the norms and constraints of femininity. Meanwhile, the charged image of female humor onscreen gave filmmakers an impetus to experiment with both the aesthetic and formal potentials, and the social and political limits of narrative filmmaking (cf. Hennefeld 2014a).

1 Slapstick comedy and feminist film theory

The intersections between gender and comedic performance have always occupied uncertain places in both feminist film theory (with its polemics of anti-pleasure) and in film histories of slapstick comedy. Traditionally, silent film experts have focused on the genius of the male clowns – Charlie Chaplin, Buster Keaton, Harold Lloyd, Stan Laurel, Oliver Hardy, Fatty Arbuckle, et al. – occasionally mentioning Mabel Normand, Marie Dressler, or Marion Davies as afterthoughts. The ever-evolving spate of "forgotten clowns," including Harry Langdon, Charley Chase, and Raymond Griffiths, builds on the patriarchal canon of comics established in Walter Kerr's *Silent Clowns* (1990), Kevin Brownlow's *The Parade's Gone By* (1976), and William K. Everson's *American Silent Cinema* (1998). Recently, archivists including Mariann Lewinsky, Bryony Dixon, and Elif Rongen-Kaynakçi, as well as feminist historians such as Jennifer Bean (2011), Jane Gaines, Steve Massa (2013), Kristen Anderson Wagner (2011), Jacqueline Stewart (2005), Vicki Callahan (2010) and Joanna Rapf, have helped to unearth and establish the significant presence of slapstick comediennes in silent film historiography. More than a game of archival lost and found, rediscoveries of *forgotten comediennes* – including Cissy Fitzgerald (1873–1941), Valentina Frascaroli (1890–1955), Sarah Duhamel (1873–1926), Gale Henry (1893–1972), Alice Howell (1886–1961), Elfie Fey (1879–1927), and Josie Sadler (1871–1927) – open onto heated debates about the politics of gender and cultural memory, feminist polemics of pleasure and anti-pleasure, and theoretical discourses of gender and sexual performativity through comedy.

The polemical exclusion of comedy from feminist theory has a long history: from Laura Mulvey's famous call for *the radical destruction of visual pleasure* (1975), to Hélène Cixous's puzzling erasure of comedy from her passionate redemption of "The Laugh of the Medusa" (1975), to Linda Williams's pointed exclusion of comedy from her gendered theorization of sexually charged "body genres" (1991), to pervasive tendencies to equate the comedic with the non-serious in recent feminist scholarship and activism. Cultural critics remain as uncertain about the relation between gender politics and comedic laughter now as they have ever been. Rather than *rescue* obscure comediennes from their historical invisibility – itself a desire deriving from a misogynistic fantasy of feminine impotency – it is the gesture of this chapter to put these missing archival links back into circulation. Forgotten slapstick comedienne films raise crucial questions about gendered modernity, comedic ambiguity, and the fluidity of feminist and political identification that speak centrally to our own present day political challenges and cultural anxieties.

2 Early cinema: the public politics of gendered laughter

Early film comedies exploited every imaginable gendered scenario about how women might negotiate the shifting meanings and pervasive instabilities of femininity in modern culture. Films such as *Mary Jane's Mishap*, *Athletic American Girls* (Vitagraph, 1907), and *The Suffragette's Dream* (Pathé, 1909) draw on the unique temporal and spatial capacities of filmmaking to offer up images of outrageous gender and social transformation. Women in these films, as I have mentioned, do extraordinary violence to their own bodies in order to adapt to their shifting conditions of everyday living. They spontaneously combust while doing housework, dismember their own limbs to expedite their labor efficiency, hot wire automobiles to flee from lecherous mashers, or completely overthrow the sexual division of labor in comical visions of gendered modernity. The situations in these films range from suffragette activism, to shoe store foot fetishism, to female mob uprising, to the pornography of walking over a subway grate while wearing an ankle skirt, to licking stamps in a post office. From episodic antics to full-scale revolution, film comedy represented a space for negotiating ruptures and impasses in classical ideals of femininity, as well as projected futures for radical feminist politics.

As Kristen Anderson Wagner has put it, "Comediennes in early twentieth-century entertainments such as vaudeville and silent film were performing at a time when debates about women and comedy were at their most heated and when the very concepts of 'woman' and 'femininity' were undergoing massive transformation" (2011, 35). In film comedies such as *The Sticky Woman* (Alice Guy-Blaché, 1906), *The Consequences of Feminism* (Alice Guy-Blaché, 1906), *Petticoat Camp* (Thanhouser, 1912), *When Women Vote* (Lubin, 1907), and *The Suffragette Sheriff* (Kalem, 1912), the cinematic temporality of comedy provided a testing ground for cultural producers to represent alternative visions of gender identity, filmmaking form, and the politics of cultural pleasure.

For example, *The Consequences of Feminism* satirically exaggerates sexist woes that feminist liberation would be tantamount to rote gender role inversion:

men dressing and acting like women, and women like men (cf. Horak 2015; Stamp 2000). *How Women Got the Vote* (Edison, 1913) literally holds time itself hostage to feminist political progress: traffic halts, bodies freeze in place, and time stands still until women earn voting rights. *Petticoat Camp* humorously depicts a group of outdoorswomen who go on strike from their domestic chores during a co-ed camping trip, and then leave the men's camp in ruins: women use the sexual division of labor as cultural leverage to reveal the instabilities internal to the construction of the very ideal of masculinity.

These archival films flaunt their striking and experimental images of inappropriate reversal and female bodily fluidity: images that thematize the liquidity of gender identity and of feminine social norms. They thereby exhibit the crucial importance of filmmaking for redefining the place of women's bodies in mass culture, as well as the fundamental role of gendered comedy in formative histories of cinema.

In films from the 1890s and 1900s, gendered comedy hinges on the uncertain place of women in the public sphere: the spectator laughs off the shock of tremendous social and civic upheaval. Anca Parvulescu describes early cinema as "a laughing gas party" (2010, 133) in her broadly suggestive book on laughter, gender, and critical theory, and Miriam Hansen links early cinema's *excess of comic appeals* to the potential for early film spectatorship to represent a feminist, alternative public sphere: "a space apart and a space in between [. . .] a site for the imaginative negotiation of gaps" (1994, 118) in one's own lived identity and experience of urban modernity. As Virginia Woolf has put it in her incisive but rarely quoted[1] 1905 essay on gender and humor, "All the hideous excrescences that have overgrown our modern life, the pomps and conventions and dreary solemnities, dread nothing so much as the flash of laughter which, like lightning, shrivels them up and leaves the bones bare" (1986, 60). In other words, laughter hinges on spontaneity – the jolt of surprise erupting into an explosive bodily convulsion – and the temporality of laughter is shot through with gender and social connotations.

For example, in *What Happened in the Tunnel* (Edwin S. Porter, 1903), a white middle-class woman and her African-American maid ride the train unaccompanied by a male authority figure, which makes them vulnerable to assault by a lecherous fellow rider. When the train enters a tunnel and the screen goes dark, the spectator perhaps fears the worst. This tension about sexual vulnerability gets parlayed into uproarious comedy through cinema's capacity for abrupt

---

[1] Many thanks to Jeanne-Mathieu Lessard for finding this rare essay on laughter by Woolf and for generously sharing it with me.

transformation and extreme reversal. The physical location of the tunnel motivates a prolonged jump cut. When visibility returns, the harasser appears in a compromised position embracing not the white lady but her black maid: the effect of a prank by the two women. This comedy of racial and class reversal thereby addresses pervasive anxieties about rape and sexual assault with the racist fantasy of a black woman's sexual unviability (further obfuscating the frequent, traumatic event of black women's rape, abduction, and impregnation by white men, for whom they signified not unviability but free sexual access). The film does not offer a social solution, so much as a temporary resolution forged through laughter. In an incessant chain of displacements, the spectator learns to accept women's increasing presence in risky public spaces by means of the astonishing, spontaneous temporality coordinated through laughter, gender and racial (mis)identifications, and motion picture projection.

As Woolf writes, "Laughter is the expression of the comic spirit within us, and the comic spirit concerns itself with oddities and eccentricities and deviations from the recognised pattern. It makes its comment in the sudden and spontaneous laugh which comes, we hardly know why, and we cannot tell when" (59). Whereas most writers on the comic, such as Freud and Bergson, emphasize the dilution of humor risked by over-explanation – slowing down the joke to the point that it no longer becomes funny – Woolf pointedly asserts that "If we took time to think [. . .] we should find, doubtless, that what is superficially comic is fundamentally tragic, and while the smile was on our lips the water would stand in our eyes" (59). Woolf formulated her views on laughter, gender, and the slippery line between tragedy and comedy in a cultural landscape increasingly influenced by the motion picture technologies. As Laura Mulvey notes in *Death 24x a Second*, "The technological drive towards photography and film had always been animated by the aspiration to preserve the fleeting instability of reality and the passing of time in a fixed image" (2006, 18). However, comedy turns this dynamic on its head. For example, with the trick cut, the jolt of spontaneous transformation stands in for an anxiety about contingency and impermanence. With comedy, to return to Woolf's argument, prolonging the image of rupture risks exposing the basis of comic joy in the burden of tears.

This is precisely the tension driving early gendered film comedies and their push and pull between laughter and pathos – between gleeful social transformation and the utter terror of sexual violence that these films compulsively rehearse. Alice Guy-Blaché's transvestite post office comedy, *A Sticky Woman* (1906), epitomizes the tension between rupture and fixity, between domestic tradition and gender modernity, and between mirthful pleasure and raging anxiety at the heart of this genre. This film depicts the plight of a young housemaid whose bourgeois employer forces her to lick a slew of postage stamps consecutively while standing in line at the post office. Evoking Henri Bergson's definition of the comic as "a growing callousness to social life" (1911, 66), the woman automatically flaps her tongue like a trained seal, or a salivating automaton. However, unable to desexualize her mechanically flapping orifice entirely, she unfortunately attracts the attention of a prurient male bystander. Undiscouraged by her oral rigidity, the man actually calculates the precise interval of her licks, and then rushes in and kisses her just at the very instant when her tongue will flap out of her mouth.

The man takes advantage not of her sexual promiscuity, but of her mechanical precision. Made by one of the most prolific female filmmakers, Alice Guy-Blaché – who directed over 700 films in France and the United States between 1896 and 1920 (cf. McMahan 2013) – *The Sticky Woman* ends by highlighting the abrupt violence of the film cut itself. When the sticky woman and her sketchy assaulter get their faces stuck together due to some postage glue residue accumulated on her lips, an office boy rushes in and snips them apart. What a *difference* a cut makes: half of the gentleman's mustache becomes firmly glued to the sticky woman's face. Again, *The Sticky Woman* performs the rampant fluidity of sexual norms and gender identity through the comic spontaneity necessary to provoke laughter. The temporality of pleasure and amusement becomes a radical site of political opportunity for redefining cultural norms and social traditions.

Although exemplary, *The Sticky Woman* was by no means exceptional. There was a powerful osmosis between women's bodies and emergent film technologies, and comedy presented an irresistible means for exploring the slippery line between these two entities. Other early film comedies make this dynamic more explicit: in *Mary Jane's Mishap*, a British maid explodes out of the chimney while attempting to light her employer's hearth fire with paraffin. A jump cut incinerates her, while a double exposure (the superimposition of multiple photographic exposures) later allows her to return as a specter who haunts mourners at her own gravestone. Women assumed a fantastic range of shapes and textures, places and positions, sexual and racial identities in early filmmaking: transmogrifying themselves into micrographic nicotine fairies (*Princess Nicotine*, 1908), cutting off their own limbs to finish their housework on time (*The Kitchen Maid's Dream*, 1907), razing the public sphere in protest to win voting rights (*Kansas City Saloon Smasher*, 1901), or having spontaneous, female to male sexual reassignment by ingesting magical African seeds (*A Florida Enchantment*, 1914). The collision between comedy and filmmaking represented a crucial horizon for blowing up staid notions of classical femininity, and for exploring and redefining the aesthetics and politics of gender, sexual, and racial identification.

3 Transitional comediennes: polite laughter versus comic anarchy

There were heated debates in late nineteenth and early twentieth centuries about the social meaning or value of laughter and comedy. Typically, the argument goes that we laugh at someone as a form of cruelty in order to correct her/his behavior. Henri Bergson defines laughter as "a social gesture that singles out and represses a special kind of absent-mindedness in men and in events" (1911, 46). Thomas Hobbes (1969), Boris Sidis (1913), James Sully, George Vasey (1877), and many other philosophers and intellectuals all made a version of this argument: that laughter represents a social tool for keeping people in line. It is always premised on *distance* – emotional and psychological distance – between the laughing subject and the object of ridicule. As the poet Charles Baudelaire argues, "Laughter is Satanic" (1956, 411): it is an expression of moral and psychological superiority, as Sully puts it, "to laugh away something in [society's] members which it sees to be unfitting" (411). However, the explanatory power of this *corrective hypothesis* falls short depending on the example at hand. The instance of a woman getting assaulted for licking postage stamps too suggestively, or a suffragette dreaming about freezing traffic and holding time itself hostage to the future of voting rights equality, contrasts sharply with an eccentric walking into a door or a police officer getting hit over the head with a frying pan. The corrective force of laughter is radically diluted by the uncertain and shifting power dynamics that these feminist scenarios provoke.

Indeed, the gender dynamic of slapstick ridicule was always a major point of tension for industry filmmakers working in the comedy genre. Mack Sennett, the director of Keystone Comedies, purportedly lamented that "men don't want to laugh at pretty girls, not convulsively anyway, and so the actresses who specialize in all-out slapstick tend to be women like Marie Dressler, Phyllis Allen, Louise Fazenda, Polly Moran, Dot Farley, Charlotte Greenwood, Martha Raye, and Judy Canova, whom the ordinary male wouldn't think of romantically anyway" (Dale 2002, 105–06). Many Keystone films such as *The Fatal Mallet* (1914), *Teddy at the Throttle* (1917), and *Tillie's Punctured Romance* (1914) – featuring Normand, Swanson, and Dressler respectively – were famous for their repetitive, violent knockabout gags and ingenious choreography of the clown's bodily disintegration (see King 2008). Slapstick violence always teeters between episodic repetition and the risk of irreversible, permanent damage. However, this anxiety about the permanence of bodily abuse becomes especially charged when women's bodies take on the simultaneous hyper-vulnerability and physical invincibility of the slapstick clown.

Sennett's claim that men do not want to laugh convulsively at pretty women (presumably because they would rather be doing other convulsive things to women's bodies, but also because it transgresses classical ideals of femininity as uncorrupted and ethereal) precisely and productively misses the point of why it was so exciting to see women performing in the slapstick genre. Audiences were obsessed with witnessing every possible permutation of women's bodily violation and rescue, and slapstick knockabout was a crucial component of *this perverse, undying fixation with testing the limits of female durability*. The term "slapstick" itself derives from the *commedia dell'arte bataccio*: literally a slap-stick that makes a loud sound effect using two wooden slats while delivering a disproportionately mild blow to the body (cf. Gunning 2010).

The gender dynamics of comic violence drive the plot of many Keystone Comedies. In *Love, Speed, and Thrills* (Walter Wright, 1915), Minta Durfee plays the wife of recurring series character Ambrose (Mack Swain), who has the misfortune of saving an evil villain from hanging himself. After pulling the man off of a cliff by his noose, Ambrose invites this evil villain, Mr. Walrus (Chester Conklin), into his home, where Walrus proceeds to seduce Mrs. Ambrose, spurring a multi-car, extended chase sequence to save Ambrose's wife from abduction and sexual violation. The bodies of everyone involved become completely fantastic and invulnerable to harm. This is the joke of the chase scene: Mrs. Ambrose falls off of a high-speed vehicle at least a dozen times without a scratch. By actualizing and exaggerating the violence that the chase pursuit is meant to defer, this Keystone film lampoons the film industry's Victorian hangovers: the obsession with safeguarding women's bodies from vulnerability and exposure in the public sphere, which had become the plot point in a disproportionate number of film melodramas – epitomized by rescue films such as D.W. Griffith's *The Lonely Villa* (1909) and Lois Weber's *Suspense* (1913), both films about women who telephone for help on the brink of sexual assault by violent intruders (cf. Gunning 1991).

Mabel's Strange Predicament (Mabel Normand, 1914) uses situational comedy instead of high-speed motoring to represent the comic tensions between gendered decorum and bodily anarchism. Like many of the comedies of manners popular in the 19-teens – meant to address an aspirational or bourgeois spectator as opposed to ethnic or working class publics (cf. Keil and Stamps 2004; Field 2015; Bean 2011) – this film centers on the inappropriate place of a woman's body in a fancy hotel and the series of misunderstandings that it triggers. Mabel plays a hotel guest, who is being pursued by a drunken tramp (Chaplin, in his first film appearance as this character[2]). Desperate to evade the

---

[2] Although Chaplin appears as the tramp character in *Kid Auto Races in Venice* (February 7, 1914), which was released before *Mabel's Strange Predicament* (February 9, 1914), the latter was filmed first.

tramp after accidentally locking herself out of her hotel room, Mabel runs through the hallways in her pajamas, sneaks into a strange man's room and hides under his bed, and eventually acts out all of her worst nightmares regarding what might happen to a lone woman residing in a commercial boudoir. This was a key pretext for outrageous female-centric and often feminist comedy in the 19-teens, especially espoused by Keystone: women's excess of vulnerability to public risk and exposure paradoxically drives them into a series of impossibly precarious, comical situations and positions.

Beyond Keystone's all-out slapstick effects, women's physical comedy sprang from a recurring, underlying tension about the viability of its own continued existence, ideologically, physically, and commercially. What would it mean for women's bodies to become funny in relentlessly new, dynamic, and surprising ways against the bourgeois upward mobility and institutional standardization of the American film industry? For example, vaudeville dynamo Eva Tanguay formed her own production company during a brief foray into filmmaking to star in two films: *Energetic Eva* (1916) and *The Wild Girl* (1917) – both of which test the comedienne's explosive bodily excess against the narrative constraints of early Hollywood constructions of femininity. *The Wild Girl* opens with footage of Tanguay's vaudeville act, featuring the comedienne posing in a towering headdress, with her unkempt curly hair poofing out beneath, and sporting glittering jewelry and attire, as a preface to a film about a deprived woman ("Firefly") who is separated from her wealthy parents at birth and then raised among gypsies. Film narratives were often organized around the need to rationalize these contradictory images of femininity as *viscerally unbound*, *politely decorous*, and *commercially resplendent* – all at once!

The codification of film's storytelling grammar was intrinsically bound up with these fraught negotiations of modern femininity. Florence Turner ("The Vitagraph Girl") fled to the United Kingdom to form her own production company and direct herself in a film comedy about a woman who is haunted by the cinematic incongruities of femininity. *Daisy Doodad's Dial* depicts the plight of a homemaker who trains relentlessly to compete in an amateur face-making competition. The plot is especially meta-cinematic in that Daisy Doodad must condense all of the nervous bodily spasms of slapstick clowning into her face – it is really a film about a woman who is preparing for her close-up. After performing some truly horrific facial gestures on a streetcar, Daisy eventually gets herself arrested for public indecency. Mystically, she then transmits her facial gestures over the telephone to her husband in order to instruct him to bail her out of prison. With the emerging syntax of film narrative and character identification – which hinged especially on frequent close-ups of faces – the diffuse bodily anarchism of the clown was often localized to specific body parts and physical gestures.[3] If Daisy can transmit her facial gestures over the telephone, her uncanny ability derives from the broader contradictions internal to comedienne performance: women's aesthetic containment by the emerging conventions of narrative filmmaking, against their persistent, forceful, and inventive means for asserting the anarchic necessity of bodily play fundamental to the slapstick genre.

4 Comediennes blow up the home front

On the cusp of the eruption of WWI in 1914, comediennes portended the traumas of trench warfare by reducing their homes to catastrophic spaces completely uninhabitable for traditional domestic life. European films especially flaunted images of their slapstick comediennes running wild in front of the camera. Film actresses in Britain (such as Alma Taylor and Chrissie White who star in the *Tilly the Tomboy* series), France (Sarah Duhamel, Mistinguett, and Musidora), Italy (Lea Guinchi, Valentina Frascaroli), and Germany (Wanda Treumann, Rosa Porten) continued to indulge in bawdy, demonstrative gags long after moral censorship delimited comedienne physicality in early Hollywood filmmaking. Leading up to and during the War, European comic sensibilities were much darker and more overtly sadistic in depicting the relationship between physical realities of comic violence and the fantastic bodily indestructability of the slapstick clown.

For example, in the French comedienne series, such as *Rosalie* (Pathé, starring Sarah Duhamel, 1911–1912), *Leontine* (Pathé, starring unknown actress, 1910–1911), *Pétronille* (Pathé, starring Sarah Duhamel, 1913–1914), and *Cunégonde* (Luxe, starring unknown actress, 1912–1913),[4] women's gags routinely hinged on turning their domestic spaces into shambles. The trenches on the Marne were probably better fortified against horrific destruction than new Rosalie's new apartment in *Rosalie Moves In* (1911), or Cunégonde's employers' domicile in *Cunégonde Receives Visitors* (1912). The instance of a woman taking a bath or acquiring a toy boat (*Betty's Boat*, 1911) would almost guarantee the erosion of every ceiling or floorboard in her home.

---

[3] The 1920s flapper comedienne Colleen Moore exploits this tendency with the aid of trick photography, performing a series of cross-eyed facial tics in the silent Cinderella farce, *Ella Cinders* (Alfred E. Green, 1926), in a sequence best known as "The Eyes Have It." See Lori Landay's analysis of this film: "The Flapper Film: Comedy, Dance, and Jazz Age Kinaesthetics."
[4] Many of these films and actresses appear on the DVD: *Comic Actresses and Suffragettes: 1910–1914*, curated by Mariann Lewinsky.

There were slews of uproarious female clowns throughout the messy transitional years of the 19-teens, and their performances – in addition to meriting the usual heap of qualifiers such as "ingenious," "virtuosic," and "acrobatic" – are foremost interesting on an existential level: comedy springs from the very legitimacy of its own premise. The comedic tension and nervous anticipation that erupts in convulsive laughter derives from audience and industry discomfort with the fundamental premise of laughing at women's bodily exposure and potential violation. American comediennes including Normand, Turner, Dressler, Swanson, Tanguay, and Durfee, as well as Flora Finch, Alice Howell, Fay Tincher, Polly Moran, Patsy De Forest, Gale Henry, and, *really*, too many other funny ladies to enumerate, provoked every manner of narrative pretense, aesthetic contrivance, or commercial gimmick for motivating the incredible popularity of comedienne slapstick.

Rather than regard this 19-teens period as a linear history of comediennes' increasing physical suppression, closer readings of these transitional comedienne films themselves reveal a very different image of female comedy and physical embodiment. Comediennes wrestled with the contradictions between moral politeness and shocking display, between censorship and transgression – a dynamic tension that often provided the very basis for the comic scenarios that fueled narrative filmmaking as an institution. As Alenka Zupačič argues in *The Odd One In,* comedy is "profoundly materialistic [. . .] not simply [in] that it reminds us of [. . .] the mud, the dirt, dense and coarse reality as our ultimate horizon (which we need to accept) [. . .] [but] because it gives voice and body to the impasses and contradictions of this materiality itself" (2008, 47). Comedy always arises from the gap between *being a body* and *having a body*: between gendered physical experience and its own meta-image.

This contradiction between bodily risk and physical censorship – between unhinged exposure and scrupulous awareness – emerges from the fundamental tensions of modern feminism and gender politics. The conflict or impasse between bodily action and social identification has been of central interest to feminist film theorists, cutting across psychoanalytic writings on language and sexual difference (Mary Ann Doane, Laura Mulvey, Kaja Silverman); Black feminism and critical race theory (bell hooks, Nicole Fleetwood, Jayna Brown); queer theory and activism (Teresa de Lauretis, Jack Halberstam, B. Ruby Rich); and contemporary geopolitics of postcoloniality, nation, and world cinema (Patricia White, Kathleen McHugh, Ella Shohat). Yet, comedy lingers as a largely overlooked terrain and a critical blind spot among these feminist discourses. It still remains largely unrecognized the great extent to which female slapstick comedy speaks centrally to the key concerns and vital debates of feminist film theory. Slapstick comediennes of the silent era tenaciously exploit the gaping chasm between *identification* and *existence* – between the language of sexual difference and the matter of simply existing, a central problematic for feminist media scholars. These eruptive comediennes reveal cinema's formative aesthetic and narrative role in shaping modern feminism. They represent vivid traces of the slippery and mutually constitutive relationship between *female bodily identity* and *visually mediated subjectivity* that feminism has long staked out as a central terrain for its social activism and theoretical analysis.

5 Comic afterimages of the home in ruins

Perhaps no other image provided a more absurd or symbolically potent rejoinder to pervasive social anxieties about suffragette feminism than the utter disaster of slapstick comediennes' household labor. For example, female domestics blow up their own bodies and take their employers' homes along with them in the early comedies (*Mary Jane's Mishap* and *How Bridget Started the Fire*); they turn their homes into amusement parks in awkward negotiations between traditional domestic responsibilities and modern cravings for excitement and adventure (*Betty, Rosalie,* and *Cunégonde* series); and they frequently burlesque staid gender norms, causing a crisis of roles and boundaries even in polite comedies of manners such as *The Patsy* (King Vidor, 1928) and *Mighty Like a Moose* (Leo McCarey, 1926).

In a broadly resonant example, *One Week* (Edward F. Cline, 1920), a bride (Sybil Seely) and groom (Buster Keaton) receive a portable, prefab house as a wedding present. An imaginary resolution to contradictory modern cravings for domestic stability and unprecedented speed and mobility, the house quickly proves to be a completely impossible space to inhabit. In one scene, Seely attempts to take a relaxing bath, despite the constant mayhem and reconstruction erupting around her. Given the inadequate protection of the house, the filmmaker must intervene: she drops the soap and an enormous hand emerges to cover the frame while she lifts her body from the tub to pick it up (see Figure 2). The absurdism of revealing the hand of the censor, indeed a self-reflexive gesture, in a comedy that is all about the hilarious deconstruction of everyday pretenses, raises a far more pointed question: what precisely is being concealed and covered up here, the woman's naked body or her physical status in a slapstick comedy about the very disintegration of traditional domesticity?

Neither radically transgressive nor conservatively pathological, women's laughter and women's comedy reinforced ambivalent structures of spectatorship. Pervasive cultural discomfort about the instance of female laughter made

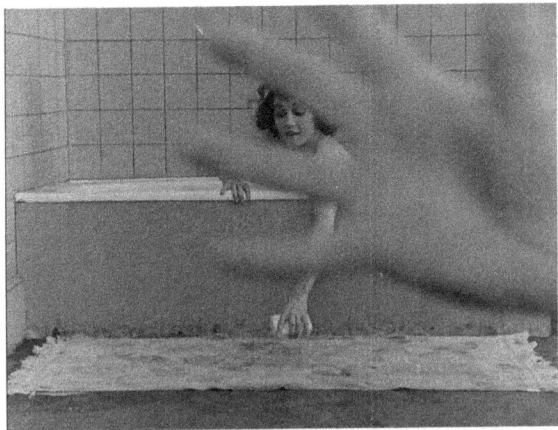

Figure 2: *One Week*. Source: *One Week*, Edward F. Cline, 1920.

the image of comedienne slapstick a ripe format for working through a series of negotiations intrinsic to silent film spectatorship, including the unstable limits between spectator and screen, the dubious social contexts of film exhibition, the collapse between gendered public and private spheres, as well as the uncertain ontological status of capturing and reanimating dead moments. Images of slapstick comediennes in silent cinema blowing up their homes, falling off of motorcycles as if the road were a giant trampoline, or acquiring a mustache in the event of publicly licking postage stamps, remain as resonant now as ever, and continue to speak to our own present day feminist politics, media technologies, and gendered cultural fixations. Slapstick comediennes have haunted the very formations of feminism and modern media culture. It is long past time for their eruptive, unstable, and socially transformative bodies to reclaim their central positions in feminist film theory and women's media activism.

*This chapter was initially published as Chapter 13 of *The Routledge Companion to Cinema and Gender*, edited by Kristin Lené Hole, Dijana Jelača, E. Ann Kaplan, and Patrice Petro (New York: Taylor & Francis, 2016): 141–154.

Bibliography

Baudelaire, Charles. *The Essence of Laughter*. New York: Meridian Books, 1956.
Bean, Jennifer. *Flickers of Desire: Movie Stars of the 1910s*. New Jersey: Rutgers University Press, 2011.

Bergson, Henri. *Laughter: An Essay on the Meaning of the Comic.* New York: MacMillan, 1911.
Callahan, Vicki. *Reclaiming the Archive: Feminism and Film History.* Detroit: Wayne State University Press, 2010.
Cixous, Hélène. "The Laugh of the Medusa." *Signs* 1 (1976): 875–893.
Comic Actresses and Suffragettes: 1910–1914, curated by Mariann Lewinsky. Bologna: Ciniteca di Bologna, 2010.
Dale, Alan. *Comedy Is a Man in Trouble: Slapstick in American Movies.* Minneapolis: University of Minnesota Press, 2002.
Field, Allyson Nadia. *Uplift Cinema: The Emergence of African-American Film and the Possibility of Black Modernity.* Durham: Duke University Press, 2015.
Gunning, Tom. "Heard Over the Phone: *The Lonely Villa* and the de Lorde Tradition of the Terrors of Technology." *Screen* 32.2 (1991): 184–196.
Gunning, Tom. "Mechanisms of Laughter: Devices of Slapstick." *Slapstick Comedy.* Eds. Rob King and Tom Paulus. New York: Routledge, 2010. 137–151.
Hansen, Miriam. *Babel and Babylon.* Cambridge: Harvard University Press, 1994.
Hennefeld, Maggie. "Destructive Metamorphosis: The Comedy of Female Catastrophe and Feminist Film Historiography." *Discourse: Journal for Theoretical Studies in Media and Culture* 36.2 (2014): 176–206.
Hennefeld, Maggie. "Slapstick Comediennes in Transitional Cinema: Between Body and Medium." *Camera Obscura* 29.2 (2014): 84–117.
"HERE's THE NEW LAUGH: Really Not So Much a Laugh as a Vocal Ripple of Merrimen." *Dallas Morning News*, Sept. 11, 1898: 10. Reprinted from *NY Herald*.
Hobbes, Thomas. *Elements of Law, Natural and Politics.* London: Cass, 1969.
Horak, Laura. *Girls Will Be Boys: Cross-Dressed Women, Lesbians, and American Cinema, 1908–1934.* New Jersey: Rutgers University Press, 2015.
Keil, Charlie, and Shelley Stamps. Eds. *American Cinema's Transitional Era: Audiences, Institutions, Practices.* Berkeley: University of California Press, 2004.
King, Robert. *The Fun Factory: The Keystone Film Company and the Emergence of Mass Culture.* Berkeley: University of California Press, 2008.
Landay, Lori. "The Flapper Film: Comedy, Dance, and Jazz Age Kinaesthetics." *A Feminist Reader in Early Cinema.* Eds. Jennifer Bean and Diane Negra. Durham: Duke University Press: 2002. 221–248.
Massa, Steve. *Lame Brains and Lunatics: The Good, the Bad, and the Forgotten of Silent Film Comedy.* Duncan: BearManor Media, 2013.
McMahan, Alison. "Alice Guy Blaché." *Women Film Pioneers Project.* Eds. Jane Gaines, Radha Vatsal, and Monica Dall'Asta. https://wfpp.columbia.edu/pioneer/ccp-alice-guy-blache/ (accessed September 27, 2013).
Mulvey, Laura. *Death 24x a Second: Stillness and the Moving Image.* London: Reaktion Books, 2006.
Mulvey, Laura. "Visual Pleasure and Narrative Cinema." *Screen* 16.3 (1975): 6–18.
Repplier, Agnes. "A Plea for Humor." *The Atlantic Monthly* 63, February 1889, 175–183.
Sidis, Boris. *Psychology of Laugher.* New York: Appleton and Company, 1913.
Stamp, Shelley. *Movie-Struck Girls Women and Motion Picture Culture After the Nickelodeon.* Princeton: Princeton University Press, 2000.
Sully, James. *An Essay on Laughter: Its Forms, Its Causes, Its Development, and Its Value.* London and Bombay: Longmans, Green, and Company, 1902.

Stewart, Jacqueline. *Migrating to the Movies: Cinema and Black Urban Modernity*. Berkeley: University of California Press, 2005.
Vasey, George. *A Philosophy of Laughter and Smiling*. London: J. Burns, 1877.
Williams, Linda. "Film Bodies: Gender, Genre, and Excess." *Film Quarterly* 44.4 (1991): 2–13.
Wagner, Kristen Anderson. "'Have Women a Sense of Humor?': Comedy and Femininity in Early-Twentieth Century Film." *The Velvet Light Trap* 68 (2011): 35–46.
"Without Tact the Humorous Woman Makes More Enemies Than Friends," *The Woman's Home Companion* (republished in *The Cleveland Plain Dealer*), Oct. 10, 1897, 21.
Woolf, Virginia. "The Value of Laughter." *The Essays of Virginia Woolf. Volume I. 1904–1912*. Ed. Andrew McNeillie. London: The Hogarth Press, 1986.
Zupančič, Alenka. *The Odd One In: On Comedy*. Cambridge: MIT Press, 2008.

Ervin Malakaj
Lubitsch's Queer Slapstick Aesthetics

In this chapter, my main aim is to demonstrate in which ways queerness resides within slapstick. More specifically, I draw on scholarship examining queer failure and queer phenomenology in order to unveil the affinity between failure, ambiguity, role reversal, and departures from expectations – i.e., central ideas for queer theory – and slapstick narratives. To demonstrate this link between slapstick and queer aesthetics, I will examine the early slapstick comedies of Ernst Lubitsch (1892–1947). In particular, I will focus on two of Lubitsch's "bad girl" comedies, *Die Puppe* [*The Doll*, 1919] and *Die Bergkatze* [*The Mountain Cat*, 1921] (McCormick 2020; see also Ashkenazi 2012, 21–32). Unlike Lubitsch's *Ich möchte kein Mann sein* [*I Don't Want to be a Man*, 1918], which Richard McCormick has called an emancipatory cross-dressing narrative that captures "hopes about queering, troubling, and overturning" early Weimar "class, ethnic, and gender hierarchies" (2020, 56), or *Schuhpalast Pinkus* [*Shoe Palace Pinkus*, 1916] and *Meyer aus Berlin* [*Meyer from Berlin*, 1918], which Valerie Weinstein has read in terms of their camp aesthetic (2006, 101–121), the queer potentials of Lubitsch's *The Doll* and *The Mountain Cat* have not been examined explicitly. In my reading of *The Doll*, I will show how its depiction of failure is a central means by which a hesitant heterosexuality registers in the film. My approach to *The Mountain Cat*, in turn, will outline how the disorienting desires faced by its lead female character effect a queer genealogy in the film. In both comedies, slapstick drives the articulation of queer moments. More precisely, slapstick establishes the parameters within which a queer aesthetic registers in Lubitsch's films.

1 Hesitant heterosexuality in *The Doll*

Tom Gunning has described the individual components of slapstick that produce laughter in terms of their premise on nonsensicality. For Gunning, slapstick is characterized by an "undermining of sense, logic, or explanation" which favors the "destruction rather than construction" of order (2010, 138). More specifically, "gags and jokes" punctuate the broader narrative in which they are positioned through "an unexpected undermining of an apparent purpose, a detouring, if not derailing, of a rational system of discourse or action" (139). Even if narrative on the whole may eventually subsume individual slapstick devices and attempt to mitigate their absurdity, the effect of the gag or joke is lasting: it "suddenly interrupts, or radically redefines, the apparent predictability of an action or system, leaving its original goals shattered and in tatters" (139). Here, slapstick "plays with ambivalence" (149) in that it regularly posits viewers to encounter what Gunning terms an "illogical legibility" (142). Its offer to viewers of an opportunity to "see how [gags] are put together (or can be taken apart) and [that] they have their own peculiar logic," even in the face of a fundamental momentary indeterminacy, emerges as an integral function of slapstick (142). In essence, slapstick moments are marked by the paradox of engendering a rupture in the narrative world order while concomitantly offering viewers some sense of epistemic stability in apprehending the constructedness of this world. Viewers, in being given a chance to determine the mechanisms animating slapstick based on particular stylistic devices, come to accept slapstick's illogical legibility.

It is precisely at this complex site that one can locate the germination of a queer aesthetic in slapstick. On the one hand, queerness maintains close ties with rupture. Sara Ahmed, in this regard, theorizes a queer subjectivity in terms of its tempered relation to what she terms "lines that direct us" (2006, 13). Drawing on phenomenology, Ahmed posits that the orientations shaping our lives emerge from "lines of thought as well as lines of motion," which "depend on the repetition of norms and conventions, of routes and paths taken" (16). To be queer, then, is to be out of line, to break with linearities. For Ahmed, such "nonalignment produces a queer effect" (83). On the other hand, queerness also maintains ties with the close cousin of rupture, namely, failure. As Jack Halberstam states, failures can become a central mode of resistance "to counter the logics of success that have emerged from the triumphs of global capitalism" (2011, 19). Not succeeding in a matrix governed by the regulatory systems of heteropatriarchal capitalism is thus a queer mode or, as Halberstam states, a "queer form of antidevelopment" ultimately tied with providing access to alternative ways of being (73).

In its capacity to interrupt the orderliness of the status quo and in its drive to capture mishaps, slapstick maintains a strong association with queer tropes. Lubitsch's *The Doll* offers an example of the way that both tropes are deployed in the service of slapstick humor. An adaptation of an adaptation – based on Edmund Audran's operetta *La poupée* (*The Doll*, 1896), which is based on E.T.A. Hoffmann's "Der Sandmann" ["The Sandman," 1816] – Lubitsch considered this film among his best (see Eyman 2000, 66; Dolar 2020). Sabine Hake has already examined the transformative capacity of Lubitsch's slapstick comedies in their generic capability to make available "space for other configurations among narrative, spectacle, and visual pleasure" in which especially "female desire" can register (1992, 81; see also Horak 2020, 42; McBride 2020, 35–90). For Hake, Lubitsch's slapstick comedies "provided an imaginary space in which female desire could find expression and, at the same time, attach itself to the accouterments of modern femininity" (83). In her reading of *The Doll*, Hake sees the titular doll at the center of the narrative as "a metaphor of femininity in the silent cinema" (96). In this regard, "*The Doll* unmasks as artificial what is considered natural. Moreover, by embracing the artificiality of human existence, the film makes possible the playful investigation of sexual difference and, ultimately, of representation itself" (96). Hake here refers to the film's central narrative element: Ossi (Ossi Oswalda), the daughter of the doll maker Hilarius (Victor Janson), takes on the role of a life-sized doll her father fashioned, which Lancelot (Hermann Thimig) purchases as a stand-in for a wife. Lancelot can only inherit the estate of his rich uncle, the Baron of Chanterelle (Max Kronert), if he marries. But, as a result of his anxiety about women and particularly the institution of marriage, Lancelot is driven to the artificial: he purchases what he believes to be an inanimate object which comes alive only upon pressing the correct button – or so he thought. Whereas in Hake's reading Ossi is at the center of the investigation, emerging as the embodiment of the performative nature of gender, in my reading I would like to shift focus to Lancelot. Lancelot's queerness animates the slapstick narrative from the beginning of the film. Drawing on Ahmed's and Halberstam's work, I will examine in which ways Lancelot's inability to conform to the heterosexual dynastic linearieties imagined for him by members of his habitus renders him a failure and thus queer throughout the film in different ways.

At least two ordering principles emerge in the opening sequence of *The Doll*, instantiating what Ahmed calls the processes of "becoming straight," namely, the pressures emanating from our habitus, which place us on a particular path (2006, 79). One such principle relates to the organizing power of the director himself. As Hake states, Lubitsch "draws attention to the film's artificiality" by being present on screen (1992, 99). In the opening of *The Doll*, Lubitsch is shown establishing the mise-en-scène. He unpacks a large box and places its contents next to it. First the lawn, then the house, and then the trees. After placing a small bench in front of the house, he installs a large blank sheet to serve as the background. At this point the camera cuts closer to the setting he just created. Lubitsch places two figurines into this setting. Then he lifts the roof of the house and places the figures inside, at which point another cut signals a transition into the sequence with actors. As the "magician or puppeteer" or perhaps even the master architect, Lubitsch establishes the habitus in which Lancelot regularly falls out of line (Hake 1992, 99). For instance, Lancelot literally falls as he attempts to walk down the curved path (which Lubitsch placed into the scene), rolling down the hill and into a pond. The slapstick moment of the opening captures Lancelot's inability to stay on a fixed route, an idea that will concretize into a trope readily cited throughout the film. Worried that he might catch a cold, Lancelot implores the sun to help him dry. A cluster of clouds presumably fashioned from cardboard or similar material unveil the sun, pointing again to a watchful eye in the sky, which ensures Lancelot gets on his way. The regulatory instance of the sun in the sky is not just an instance of an observant omnipresence, but also serves as a "straightening device," what Ahmed terms a process which foregrounds queer derailment and thereby seeks to remedy it (2006, 23). The sun, thus, "fixes" Lancelot's momentary deviation from the path that directs him.

The second ordering principle is the dynastic line policed by Lancelot's uncle, the Baron of Chanterelle. In order to maintain lineage, the aging patriarch sees it as his duty to secure the passage of the estate to the next of kin. As the closest male family member, Lancelot is designated as the recipient of the estate. The prerequisite for the inheritance, however, is marriage. The baron orchestrates a public search for a bride for his nephew in order to secure the family's dynastic line. That is, the baron arranges a straightening process by which Lancelot could return to the family and fulfill his dynastic obligations. Ahmed describes such type of hereditary inheritance in terms of the centrality of heterosexuality as a binding force between generations:

> Heterosexuality is imagined as the future of the child insofar as heterosexuality is idealized as a social gift and even as the gift of life itself. The gift becomes an inheritance: what is already given or even pregiven. Heterosexuality becomes a social as well as familial inheritance through the endless requirement that the child repay the debt of life with its life. The child who refuses the gift thus becomes seen as a bad debt, as being ungrateful, as the origin of bad feeling. (2006, 86)

In Lubitsch's *The Doll*, lineage expectations befall a character who was not ready for them. That is, the baron had already derailed the lineage by not having offspring of his own. In one scene, the baron's extended family even explicitly accuses him of bad estate planning: the greedy relatives want to lay claim to the estate's capital but see no orderly way to proceed with divvying it up among all the relatives – not abiding by dynastic inheritance here means engendering chaos. In this sense, the baron exhibits a queerness in his own right, the effects of which he hopes to remedy by imposing the pressures of hereditary dynamics on Lancelot.[1] Similar to the intervention of the sun, which embodies a watchful eye keeping Lancelot on his path, the dynasticism imposed on Lancelot by his uncle seeks to remedy the baron's as well as Lancelot's queer

---

[1] An overtly suggestive exchange of glances between the Baron and his servant points to the possibility that the two have a relationship underway, ostensibly implying that the Baron's homosexuality is the reason no offspring was secured to maintain his lineage.

derailment, rendering the figures agents in a system of power reaching beyond their immediate control.

The ordering principles of the world Lancelot inhabits coalesce to form an existential burden for the protagonist. The monastery to which he escapes initially appears a safe haven outside of the reach of the heterosexual system of power depicted in the film; however, and more importantly, the monastery also perpetuates Lancelot's queer departure from familial expectations. More specifically, Lancelot's falling out of line and being led to the monastery is part and parcel of the film's slapstick aesthetics in that the monastery, as a space of shelter, also serves as a queer space. As Lynda L. Coon has remarked, "if 'queerness' is defined as resistance to opposite sex relations, then the early medieval monastery is a very queer space" (2011, 249). That is, away from "women, marriage, and family – markers of normative secular existence" afforded by the seclusion provided by the monastery, Lancelot can maintain the derailed life (Coon 2011, 249). Moreover, his fear of women finds an extreme venue in an exceptionally debauched monastery. The monks, far from being devoted to scripture, enjoy a gluttonous lifestyle (see Wosk 2015, 67; Eyman 2000, 91).[2] This critical depiction of monks preoccupied with nurturing their insatiable hunger instead of devotion heightens the queerness of the site. That is, not only does the monks' marginalized standing serve as magnet for Lancelot, who hopes to escape from the center, but their gluttonous drives intensify Lancelot's queer resistance. The monastery's financial woes are key in this regard. The monks hope to improve their finances through the reward Lancelot's uncle promised to his nephew if he were to return home and marry. The urge to sustain their gluttonous lifestyle drives them to the idea to acquire a mechanical wife for Lancelot. The monks pressure Lancelot toward a fabricated domestic life in which he could maintain a façade presenting a heterosexual union devised to veil his queer way of being in order to appease familial expectations.

Falling out of line means failing for Lancelot. More specifically, failure becomes a way to characterize Lancelot's resistance to accommodate intimidating dynastic expectations. As Ahmed states, "the failure to orient oneself 'toward' the ideal sexual object affects how we live in the world; such a failure is read as a refusal to reproduce and therefore as a threat to the social ordering of life itself" (2006, 91). It is clear from the pressures exerted upon Lancelot that the ideal sexual

---

[2] Scott Eyman (2000) has noted the film's critique of the catholic church through its humor in the monastery scenes. "The film had some good if unstressed fun at the expense of Catholicism; one of the priests gorging himself on a slab of pork notices a hungry man. Ever helpful, he immediately cuts him a piece of dry bread" (2000, 65).

object is a woman and that the future of the estate is linked with his successful heterosexual coupling. By failing to adhere to lineage expectations, Lancelot effectively resists them.

To explain the formation of patterns of queerness in the film as they relate to derailing from paths and thus failing to follow them, I will briefly discuss how childishness becomes a central mode to communicate queer failure in *The Doll*. The film articulates Lancelot's anxiety about marriage through the emasculating effects of child-like behavior. From the opening sequence, in which he bursts out in tears after stumbling down the hill into the pond by his house, to the histrionic crying after his uncle asks him to marry, Lancelot is framed as emotionally undeveloped. Such a depiction likely led some scholars to identify his decided hesitance to marry and have physical contact with women as "absurd" and even "moralistic" (Wosk 2015, 65). In fact, Lancelot insists that even an artificial companion be "respectable," a wish which supports assessments interested in his moralistic leanings. However, I propose queerness as an alternative model to understand Lancelot's peculiar deviations from the norm. That is, even when exhibiting hyper-moralist behavior tied to a general politics of respectability, Lancelot's behavior can be read as a deflection. This is particularly the case when considering that Lancelot's moralism takes place in the scenes in which he bursts out in childish rebellion against the regimenting systems governing his habitus, effecting a calculated queer failure to adhere to the heterosexual matrix of desire. Halberstam articulates the link between children and queer behavior in the following:

> children are not coupled, they are not romantic, they do not have a religious morality, they are not afraid of death or failure, they are collective creatures, they are in a constant state of rebellion against their parents, and they are not the masters of their domain. Children stumble, bumble, fail, fall, hurt; they are mired in difference, not in control of their bodies, not in charge of their lives, and they live according to schedules not of their own making. (2011, 47)

Because of its queer potential, childhood is exposed to extensive policing. Children's bodies and behavior are subjected to extensive control to maintain path-adherence. Lancelot, too, falls victim to the normativizing biopolitics of his habitus, but his embrace of child-like qualities helps queerness prevail in the film in spite of efforts to curtail it. In fact, queerness becomes a mode of resistance for the dominant ordering paradigms in the film.

In this light, the sequence in which Lancelot meets Hilarius further evidences Lancelot's rebelling queerness as rooted in histrionic childishness. The sequence is driven by two sets of parallel actions, one which foregrounds Lancelot's hesitant heterosexual disposition as rooted in childishness as the other highlights the primal virility of Hilarius' boy apprentice, who is significantly younger than

Lancelot. After the apprentice leads Lancelot to a chair at the center of a large waiting area, which later in the sequence serves as showroom for the dolls created in the shop, Hilarius chases the boy away with a slap on the cheek. The apprentice leaves for the workshop. In a medium shot, we see the artificial doll and the apprentice, who smells her sleeve, reacts fondly to the scent, and finally drops on his knees to proclaim, "Dolly, you are the apple of my eye!" He then kisses the arm of the doll. In this moment, music playing outside of the house intrudes and the apprentice winds up the doll for a dance. This scene evokes a wooing game the young boy plays and thereby makes his own sexual drive visible for viewers. His vigorous dancing even leads to the doll breaking and ushers in Ossi's performance in which she takes the place of the artificial doll. Though the apprentice's hyperbolic virility is regularly interrupted by other characters, either by physical violence or happenstance mishap, the film foregrounds it regularly. His figure serves as foil for Lancelot, whose lack of virility takes center stage in the sequence. That is, because of the apprentice's lustful gaze, Lancelot's disinterest (even revulsion!) at the sight of inciting female bodies stands out as non-heterosexual – i.e., queer.

For instance, Lancelot is seated in the showroom among toy-like objects surrounding him as Hilarius prepares to unveil what is behind the curtain. Lancelot's face initially registers excitement. As Hilarius unveils the collection of dolls behind the curtains, Lancelot – similar to the reaction of a child – appears momentarily enthralled by the spectacle. As Hilarius spins a wheel which animates the dolls, devastation begins to register in Lancelot's face as he exclaims, "how rude!," as response to the dolls lifting one of their legs during a dance. In contrast to the apprentice's virility, Lancelot's sheepishness articulates a disgust with the alluded sexual tension captured in the dolls' performance. The appalled Lancelot is then shown in a long shot as the dolls jump down from the two showroom stages and *en masse* inch their way toward a growingly terrified Lancelot, whose childishness registers as he visually blends in into the landscape of toys on the ground that surround him. As two of the dolls sit on his lap, Lancelot is overcome with fright, jumps up from his chair and runs into a corner of the room. This response quotes an earlier scene, in which Lancelot runs away from forty interested single women who respond to his uncle's advertisement and show up to meet their potential spouse.

Viewed against the backdrop of the virility of the much younger apprentice, this scene and a number of similar scenes throughout the film articulate Lancelot's hesitant heterosexuality, which is decidedly queer at its core. Here, queerness is bound up with the slapstick aesthetic of *The Doll*, which draws its energy from ruptures and personal failures in the heterosexual capitalist matrix. In this light, the sudden attempt to reestablish heterosexual order at the end of the film, in which Lancelot and Ossi marry, itself appears derailed. For a film, which predominantly foregrounded its lead character's queer way of being, the ending's insistence on "compulsory heterosexuality" as the chief organizing principle for the world does not mitigate the queer narrative leading up to the ending nor the lingering traces of queerness that presumably will follow both Lancelot and Ossi into their marriage and beyond (Ahmed 2006, 84).[3]

2 Queer orientations and queer kinship in *The Mountain Cat*

Because Lubitsch's *The Mountain Cat* explicitly works with the tropes of regimentation, order, and submission through its depiction of the world of the military, it follows similar paths of queer slapstick failure as *The Doll*. That is, humor emerges in the film as characters chronically fail or derail within the heteropatriarchal capitalist and regimented world of the military. Moreover, the film captures the world of disorder characterizing the habitus of a band of brigands, a marginal social group in comparison to the world of the military which becomes a breeding ground for alternative ways of being in the film. Hake explains that Rischka (Pola Negri), who is the female lead in *The Mountain Cat* and the robber chief's daughter, "prefers the wilderness of the mountains to the trappings of civilization" in a film which ultimately "fails to pacify the woman and ends in a proud affirmation of otherness" (1992, 103).[4] In this section, I will outline in which ways the othering mechanisms for Rischka's character follow racializing paradigms which are intertwined with queer aesthetics. In this reading, Rischka's racialized body and queer subjectivity are legible because Rischka is perpetually out of place in the worlds she inhabits. Though she opts to marry a man from within the world of the brigands despite desiring a union with Alexis (Paul Heidemann), a stand-in for the civilized albeit decadent world of the military, Rischka's decision-making feeds the politics of slapstick as much as it offers fodder for what Ahmed has described as the formation of a queer genealogy – namely, a future based on the effects of "coming into contact with things that reside on different lines, as opening up new kinds of connections" (2006, 154–155). Rischka's

---

[3] Ahmed draws on Adrienne Rich's (1993) work on compulsory heterosexuality (227–255).
[4] For an analysis of Lubitsch's work with star personas such as Oswalda and Negri, see Elsaesser 2000, 209.

impulsive navigation of border-crossing between her familiar habitus and new terrains reveals the germination of a queer kinship model in *The Mountain Cat*.

Rischka maintains a wild and untamable persona throughout the film. From the sequence in which viewers meet her in which she rescues her father from a mutiny through violent force, to her masquerade at the wedding of her love interest Alexis and the commander's daughter Lilli (Edith Meller) during which she wreaks havoc in Lilli's room and plunders the military stronghold, Rischka's body and behavior regularly fall out of line. Even for the carnivalesque world of the brigands, her erratic behavior makes her stand out among her people. As the only woman in the gang, Rischka appears to have been socialized into a setting in which she regularly uses violent force to defend herself from sexual aggression. But her interruption of male advances is painted as failure in that she becomes a fetish object for the brigands. This is most readily visible following her resolute intervention in a mutiny, upon which two of her father's men exhibit a liking to the beating they are getting on their behind and even, in slapstick fashion, seek out ways to persuade her to continue beating them for pleasure.

Rischka's marginalized standing in the world of the brigands brings about a tension between that world, with its status as a presumably nomadic settlement governed by lawless force in which Rischka occupies a position on the margin, and the "civilized" space of the military stronghold. This tension effects a colonial dynamic in *The Mountain Cat*. Most importantly, the colonial dynamic inherent in the dichotomy between the two world orders racializes Rischka upon her contact with Alexis, whose "civilized" world is unreceptive of her difference. Notwithstanding Alexis's vehement advances, which suggest that she could have access to his world, she is rejected by this habitus. However, her racialization stems not only from this rejection, but also from everything that precedes it. Ahmed outlines how "racialization involves the production of 'the racial' body through knowledge, as well as the constitution of both social and bodily space in the everyday encounters we have with others" (2002, 47). In this line of inquiry, a central feature of racialization emerges when considering what happens when a "body-at-home in its world" is no more (2006, 11). That is, a body-at-home in its world, which is "a body that extends into space through how it reaches toward objects that are already 'in place,'" can come to lose its sense of orientation in a world when this world is no longer accommodating of it (2006, 11; See Fanon 1986).[5] For Ahmed, the "white world," which is a "world we know implicitly" and which governs subjects through a presumed familiarity we have to acquire or experience if we want to be at home in that world, disorients non-white bodies

---

[5] Ahmed develops her paradigm in close reading the work of Frantz Fanon (1986).

(2006, 111). The process which stimulates the discourse of the dominance of the "familiarity" and "non-familiarity" with the white world is colonialism, which articulates how a habitus can be "'ready' for certain kinds of bodies" (111). In Ahmed's assessment, "the disorientation affected by racism diminishes capacities for action" (111). When Rischka is rejected from Alexis's world, her scope of action in that world has been diminished and she walks away from it as racialized Other.

Alexis and Rischka first meet in the wilderness of Rischka's domain, which is presumably located somewhere in the Austro-Hungarian empire – "one of those imaginary Balkan countries known from Lubitsch's later Hollywood musicals" (Hake 1992, 104).[6] Alexis passes through the wilderness on his way to the military stronghold when Rischka notices his carriage. When she throws a snowball at the carriage, she calls attention to herself by way of luring the carriage into a trap. This initial segment of the sequence presents her as determined predator whose skills in robbing travelers had previously been proven time and again. The subsequent scenes in the sequence present Rischka navigating the unexpected: Alexis's imperial allure and attraction produced within the vibrant and dangerous venue of what Mary Louise Pratt terms a "contact zone" (2008, 8). Pratt defines the term as "the space of imperial encounters, the space in which peoples geographically and historically separated come into contact with each other and establish ongoing relations, usually involving conditions of coercion, radical inequality, and intractable conflict" (8). Alexis's body bears the signs of imperial wealth and power: not only is he a decorated soldier, but viewers also initially meet him as an object of intensified sexual prowess. In an earlier scene in the film, he is shown departing for the military stronghold as dozens of women and their children, whom he fathered, mourn his departure. In fact, he exhibits this sexual prowess with pride in his first meeting with Rischka. A long shot shows Rischka seated on the ground, sheepishly hiding her gaze behind her hair and behind her knees. Alexis enters the screen from the right, bows, takes out a handkerchief, and places it on the ground. As he takes a seat next to her, a cut shows Rischka shamefacedly look at him through her hair in a medium-close-up. In a long shot, Alexis extends his arm to move her hair and free her gaze. The next shots show him winking at Rischka while she turns her head away in a submissive gesture expressing embarrassment. The turning point in this sequence is Alexis's non-consensual touching: he takes her hand and pets it presumably in a gesture of flirtation. After he kisses her hand, Rischka switches registers. She spits on the spot he kissed, wipes her hand, and visibly upsets Alexis in his self-

---

6 Richard McCormick similarly calls the setting "a mythical Balkan country" (2016, 180).

assured composure, which he maintained throughout his flirtation. As Alexis gets up to leave, Rischka grabs his hand and signals to her fellow brigands that they should approach to complete the robbery.

Even though Rischka is already marked as Other prior to the meeting, it is not until Alexis's arrival and her contact to him that her racializing process commences. Notwithstanding the fact that he meets Rischka in the midst of untamed wilderness, the manner in which Alexis enters the space of Rischka's domain is marked by a confidence metonymically extending the acquired influence he garnered through military success and sexual prowess. He has – as it were – conquered many women previously and has proven himself as decorated soldier, by extension presumably also as socialite. And it is the impetus for conquest, inscribed in his behavior and onto his body as decorated soldier in uniform, that pulsates in the way he "'[takes] up' space" in the scene (Ahmed 2006, 111). In his confidence as he enters this space and interacts with Rischka, Alexis also articulates a familiarity with the world, which follows him no matter the destination. He smiles as he sees Rischka, whose sight should have worried him. Moreover, he interacts with her without hesitating and worrying for his safety. This confidence relates to what Louise Peacock describes as the essence of slapstick, namely, slapstick's capacity to provide an "appearance of the infliction and suffering of pain without the actual anguish" (2014, 16). Alexis's interaction with the predatorial Rischka rests upon the generic contract between the film and its audience that Alexis will not suffer too much in this exchange. Moreover, his familiarity in the sequence is bound up with the privilege system affiliated with whiteness, a process that, according to Ahmed, serves the function of orienting bodies in the way they move through space. In this regard, Ahmed notes that "whiteness becomes what is 'here,' a line from which the world unfolds, which also makes what is 'there' on 'the other side'" (2006, 121). Just by entering the space and disrupting Rischka's chaotic and yet skilled robbery not by willpower but by an allure tied to imperial success, Alexis renders Rischka a subject to his worldly ways, a recipient of the allure who is unable to resist its effects in the moment.

As the scene unfolds, Rischka becomes Alexis's juxtaposition as she resists his advances. That is, she is rendered as his opposite and thus the opposite of whiteness in the colonial sense. What follows is a tension in their power relations to one another, which shift with each interaction. Rischka sternly rejects Alexis's advance and exhibits force in taking him hostage. She momentarily gains the upper hand as Alexis's confusion registers on his face – he appears perplexed that his allure failed to affect Rischka. The shift from Alexis's dominance in the scene to Rischka's is one in a series of similar inversions in power relations between the two that take place throughout the film. Drawing on the work of Henri Bergson (1859–1941), Peacock has demonstrated that such inversion devices are a central mode of slapstick humor (2014, 40; Bergson 1914). Humor ensues in slapstick when "a character, for whatever reason, begins to behave in a way which runs counter to their established character" (Peacock 2014, 40). The inversion dynamic between Alexis and Rischka feeds Rischka's racialization in that it foregrounds her counter imperialist disposition. This is primarily visible when she instructs Alexis to take off his clothes. By undoing his uniform, she dismantles the symbols of imperial dominance. A castration act, as it were, the unclothing gains in currency because it is an activity done in front of Rischka's male brigands. However, yet another inversion takes place: Alexis, in his underwear, quickly recovers his confidence about the world and takes up the space with an understanding of the allure he has on people. Though Rischka remains skeptical, she falls prey to his persistence even in the face of her de-civilizing act. In fact, the robbery fails precisely because of his effective interruption of the way Rischka normally takes up space in such robberies. She lets him go at the cost of drawing critique from her fellow brigands and her father.

Rischka's meeting with Alexis triggers two irreconcilable pressures central in the queer-racializing process in the film: her yearning for a union with Alexis, which signals a possible departure from the life of the brigands, meets the colonial setting of the stronghold, in which she is out of place. First, I would like to discuss how her imagining of a union with Alexis instantiates a queer departure for Rischka. Though tempered by Rischka's rejection of Alexis's advances, she exhibits infatuation with him upon her return to the brigand base following her failed robbery. Rischka rummages through the few clothing items she was able to steal from Alexis and finds a photograph of Alexis among the bounty. Initially shocked at the spectacle of the photograph – presumably the first of its kind she sees – Rischka soon pins it to one wall of her tent and slowly assembles an avatar of Alexis using the rest of his clothes. Her admiration of Alexis in the scene in the tent is an extension of their initial meeting, in which she falls for his allure despite her vigorous resistance. Rischka constructs the avatar as a stand in, an essentialized version of Alexis, in whose presence she can be herself and test out her infatuation openly with only the viewers as witnesses to her admiration. In this light, her imagining of a relationship with Alexis through his clothes and his photograph serves as first part of a fantasy of the good life. (Perhaps even of a queer union with an essentialized, inanimate avatar who comes to life only in her dreams and ultimately resembles the queer union between Lancelot and his doll in *The Doll*.) Notably, this good life comes at the cost accumulated through the departure from the tribal dynamics of the brigands. Her failure to abide by the expectations of the tribe during the robbery already triggers in her father an urgency to marry her off to one of his men by way of curtailing potential future deviations from the dynastic line.

The second part of Rischka's fantasy becomes visible for viewers when they are given access to her dreams in a sequence following the wedding reception between Alexis and Lilli. Heartbroken, Rischka leaves the wedding after intruding the party, passing with the brigands as dinner guests, and rampaging the estate. Alexis kisses Rischka toward the end of this sequence after recognizing her despite her masquerade. The kiss is not a simple turning point for the two, because Alexis expresses his allegiance to the stronghold by proclaiming that he has no choice but to arrest her – in order to forcibly discipline her wild body and behavior. After locking her up in a room, Lilly intervenes and sends her off in anger, accusing her of promiscuity. Back at the brigand outpost, Rischka's dream sequence gives insight into the fantasy she began to craft with the creation of Alexis's avatar. That is, it shows her lovingly interacting with Alexis and even dancing at the very ball at which she was so out of place. Notably, in the fantasy Rischka is in her own clothes and not the clothes in which she masqueraded in order to pass as guest at the military stronghold. In this fantasy, she imagines herself *as she is* interacting with Alexis. The other figures present in the dream are decidedly anthropomorphized snowmen and not real people, supporting the notion that the carnivalesque overtures of the imagined military stronghold are the only way she can take up space in the venue. What the dream sequence highlights is that she can only occupy the space of the military stronghold – the civilized site of imperial wealth – in her dreams.

Rischka realizes the impossibility of a union with Alexis only after once more attempting to enter a relationship with him. Following her own marriage to one of the weakest and clumsiest men among the brigands – this was her father's attempt to curtail her lusting disposition – he lets her go in an impassionate sequence in their tent, in which Rischka breaks out in histrionic desperation about the union. In the shot, she is literally chained to her brigand husband, which is presented as a ritual similar to the ring exchange. Rischka leaves the tent and wanders aimlessly through the landscape. Alexis, likewise upset about his marriage to Lilly, pouts as his servant pressures him to depart for his wedding. Upon entering the carriage, he falls out of it as the carriage departs. Alexis begins to wander into the wilderness. It is in the realm of wilderness, where they initially met, that Alexis and Rischka meet again by chance. This meeting, born out of frustration with the heteropatriarchal demands of the institution of marriage, offers momentary repose. There is even genuine excitement about the prospect of being with one another, which registers in both characters. However, in the moment that Rischka enters Alexis's residence, she loses a sense of comfort that their accidental meeting in the wilderness secured. Ahmed discuses comfort in terms of one's relation to space: "to be comfortable is to be so at ease with one's environment that it is hard to distinguish where one's body ends and the world begins" (2006, 134). Whereas the barren winter landscape is a conduit for comfort in that it seemingly obfuscates the ordering principles from the two worlds in the moment Rischka and Alexis embrace, the regimentation of the residence immediately affects the dynamic between the two negatively. Whereas Alexis's confidence and familiarity yet again thrive, Rischka's racialized body and behavior make her stand out. Still in her wedding gown, a leopard skin which ultimately heightens her status as connected more to the wilderness than the civilized space of the residence, Rischka quarrels with the staff, breaks a chair and sets it on fire, and finally realizes that the residence is not receptive of her body and behavior: it rejects her as a site ultimately not intended to welcome people like her.

Ahmed notes, that "the moments when the body appears 'out of place' are moments of political and personal trouble" (2006, 135). Rischka, in this light, falls into an existential crisis upon recognizing that the very venue in which she hopes to secure Alexis's love is the venue in which she so readily falls out of line. Admittedly, Rischka's realization comes only upon an exchange with Lilly. Lilly rushes to Alexis's residence upon hearing from servants that Rischka is with him. She breaks down in tears in front of Rischka, reminding Rischka that Alexis truly loves her. Rischka, at the realization of the anguish that her illicit (because it is non-sanctioned) union with Alexis causes for Lilly, relinquishes her hold on him. She performs an exaggerated version of herself in an attempt to undo Alexis's infatuation, knowing well in advance that a concentrated version of herself – i.e., she messes with his hair, drinks sparkling wine out of the bottle, and shoots a clock with her gun – would destroy the image he formed of her and would help her reach a high point of feeling out of place in the setting. Rischka's realization that her interference undoes the heterosexual coupling between Alexis and Lilly is part and parcel of her realization that she is out of line, or disoriented in the space she momentarily held to be receptive of her desire. By being disoriented in the space of the colonizer, or, by being made to feel as a body which does not "extend the lines already extended by spaces" of the residence, Rischka occupies a queer subjectivity (Ahmed 2006, 135).

It is indeed Rischka's falling out of line, racialized in the contact zone between colonized and colonizer, that she is brought back to the world of the brigands. Hake has seen in this return an affirmation of otherness. I contend that Rischka's return is, in more concrete terms, an expression of queerness brought about by the disorienting traversing between the two worlds in which she seeks a place. She embarks on a queer path because of a double rejection. Important here is that Rischka does not return to her husband at the brigand outpost with a conviction that this relationship will lead to the fantasy of the good life. On the contrary, Rischka leaves Alexis's house pouting, dissatisfied by the outcome of a situation she hoped would fulfill her fantasy of a life with Alexis. Upon her arrival in their wedding tent, she finds her husband, who appears not to have left the spot since she left. A river of tears flows downhill from the tent in an exaggerated staging in which her husband's hyperbolic devastation manipulates Rischka's disposition: in an abrupt ending similar to *The Doll*, *The Mountain Cat* ends with Rischka giving in and accepting a union with her brigand husband. However, as was the case in *The Doll*, it is important not to see the heterosexual union at the end as a mitigating effect of the queer lines that preceded it. The slapstick effects in *The Mountain Cat* perpetually present Rischka as disoriented, as derailed from the various paths that had been imagined for her. Her queer path thus gives rise to a queer genealogy, which is a line that springs from facing "the impossibility of [the] return, as we face what is behind us" (Ahmed 2006, 155). The heterosexual union at the end of the film does not undo her queer outlook. Rischka's marriage, in fact, is a line that shares close proximity with the queer experience she brings to it.

3 Conclusion: queer slapstick aesthetics and the production of alternative narrative possibilities

Gunning's discussion of an illogical legibility at the core of slapstick, which offers viewers an anchoring point in scenarios decidedly interested in uprooting the status quo, would suggest that Lubitsch's insistence on the heterosexual union at the end of his comedies serves the function of anchoring viewers in some stable reality previously interrupted throughout the film. That is, the broader narrative structure serves the function of mitigating momentary queer ruptures produced by gags or jokes in slapstick narratives. Gunning's work also suggest that studies of slapstick should not just focus on the narrative as a whole, foregrounding the centrality of the momentary disruption to the economies of laughter. In terms of the queer potentials of slapstick comedies, momentary queer ruptures, beyond just being confined to those moments of the narrative in which they take place, in fact linger. Queer moments in slapstick narratives, whether in terms of queer failure or queer derailment, leave a trace not easily erased or forgotten. In my reading of *The Doll* and *The Mountain Cat*, I outline what Alice A. Kuzniar has identified as a pattern in other queer slapstick comedies. Writing about the ending of Lubitsch's cross-dressing comedy *I Don't Want to Be a Man* and Paul Czinner's (1890–1972) *Der Geiger von Florenz* [*The Fiddler of Florence*, 1926], Kuzniar notes that despite the primacy of the "heterosexual pairing" in their ending, both films take "a queer route to" it (2000, 35). Beyond taking a queer path to the ending, Ahmed's work on linearities and queer phenomenology reminds us that a queer path to an ending itself produces alternative lines from which alternative ways of thinking and being can spring and co-exist alongside those foregrounding the status quo. Far from being absent in the ending scenes in which the heterosexual union is foregrounded in *The Doll* and *The Mountain Cat*, queerness, in fact, lingers there, nearly in every sequence leading up to the ending, and reaches well beyond it.

Bibliography

Ahmed, Sara. *Queer Phenomenology: Orientation, Objects, Others*. Durham: Duke University Press, 2006.
Ahmed, Sara. "Racialized Bodies." *Real Bodies: A Sociological Introduction*. Ed. Mary Evans and Ellie Lee. New York: Palgrave, 2002. 46–63.
Ashkenazi, Ofer. *Weimar Film and Modern Jewish Identity*. New York: Palgrave, 2012.
Bergson, Henri. *Laughter: An Essay on the Meaning of the Comic*. New York: Macmillan, 1914.
Coon, Lynda L. *Dark Age Bodies: Gender and Monastic Practice in the Early Medieval West*. Philadelphia: University of Pennsylvania Press, 2011.
Dolar, Mladen. "The Uncanny and the Comic: Freud *avec* Lubitsch." *The Object of Comedy*. Eds. Jamila M.H. Mascat and Gregor Moder. New York: Palgrave, 2020. 15–34.
Elsaesser, Thomas. *Weimar Cinema and After: Germany's Historical Imaginary*. New York: Routledge, 2000.
Eyman, Scott. *Ernst Lubitsch: Laughter in Paradise*. Baltimore: Johns Hopkins University Press, 2000.
Fanon, Frantz. *Black Skin, White Masks*. London: Pluto, 1986.
Gunning, Tom. "Mechanisms of Laughter: The Devices of Slapstick." *Slapstick Comedy*. Ed. Tom Paulus and Rob King. London: Routledge, 2010. 137–152.
Hake, Sabine. *Passions and Deceptions: The Early Films of Ernst Lubitsch*. Princeton: Princeton University Press, 1992.
Halberstam, Judith. *The Queer Art of Failure*. Durham: Duke University Press, 2011.
Horak, Jan-Christopher. "German Film Comedy." *The German Cinema Book*. Eds. Tim Bergfelder, Erica Carter, Deniz Göktürk, and Claudia Sandberg. New York: Bloomsbury, 2020. 39–50.
Kuzniar, Alice A. *The Queer German Cinema*. Stanford: Stanford University Press, 2000.
McBride, Joseph. *How did Lubitsch do it?* New York: Columbia University Press, 2020.
McCormick, Richard. *Sex, Politics, and Comedy: The Transnational Cinema of Ernst Lubitsch*. Indianapolis: Indiana University Press, 2020.
McCormick, Richard. "Transnational Jewish Comedy: Sex and Politics in the Films of Ernst Lubitsch – From Berlin to Hollywood." *Three Way Street: Jews, Germans, and the Transnational*. Ed. Jay Howard Geller and Leslie Morris. Ann Arbor: University of Michigan Press, 2016. 169–197.
Peacock, Louise. *Slapstick and Comic Performance: Comedy and Pain*. London: Palgrave Macmillan, 2014.

Pratt, Mary Louise. *Imperial Eyes: Travel Writing and Transculturation*. New York: Routledge, 2008.
Rich, Adrienne. "Compulsory Heterosexuality and Lesbian Existence." *The Lesbian and Gay Studies Reader*. Ed. Henry Abelove, Michèle Aina Barale, and David M. Halperin. New York: Routledge, 1993. 227–255.
Weinstein, Valerie. "Anti-Semitism or Jewish 'Camp'? Ernst Lubitsch's *Schuhpalast Pinkus* (1916) and *Meyer aus Berlin* (1918)." *German Life and Letters* 59.1 (2006): 101–121.
Wosk, Julie. *My Fair Ladies: Female Robots, Androids and other Artificial Eves*. New Brunswick: Rutgers University Press, 2015.

Ignacio M. Sánchez Prado
The Slapstick of Greater Mexico: The Poetics and Politics of Eugenio Derbez

There are times in cultural history in which remarkable events occur around texts and products that do not appear to have much importance. This is arguably the case with *Overboard* (Rob Greenberg 2018), starring Mexican superstar Eugenio Derbez and U.S. film comedienne Anna Faris. At face value, there is nothing remarkable about *Overboard*. It is a somewhat unimaginative remake of the 1987 Goldie Hawn classic directed by Garry Marshall, a film that was itself unremarkable in its time although it grew to have a cult status of sorts (Pirnia 2017). The original presents Hawn as an obnoxious millionaire who becomes an amnesiac after falling overboard. This allows Russell's character, a carpenter who was left unpaid by Hawn, to pretend to be her husband in payback. It was memorably reviewed by John Updike, who notes the film's debt to 1930s comedies and Hepburn-style performances, and praises the film's message: "*Overboard*, for all its slapstick, takes itself more seriously [. . .] Money is the root of all evil in *Overboard*, and its final overthrow needs a Nineties sequel, in which the money goes overboard" (2012, 48–49). The original's appeal is clearly rooted in Hawn and Russell's screwball chemistry and in Hawn's slapstick bravura, although it is generally considered to be "the domestication of almost anything radical about Hawn" (Lane 2021, 196).

The 2018 version reverts the roles, giving Derbez the comedic weight of the film as the millionaire Leonardo, while Faris's Hawn-influenced performance as Kate brings a subtler version of screwball romance to the film. At face value, the film was a risky proposition for the commercial market. Although Derbez could easily be characterized as the biggest film and television star in Mexico, and even though he fuels the binational media company Pantelion (the producer of *Overboard*, which will be discussed momentarily), his anglophone career up to that point was defined by a secondary role in Rob Schneider's short-lived sitcom *Rob* (2012), stereotypical and minor roles in films directed at the U.S. Latinx audience, like *How to Be a Latin Lover* (Ken Marino 2017), and the occasional appearance on late-night talk shows. Faris, perhaps the most talented slapstick actress of her generation, never quite took off as a movie star and, as explored in a widely circulated *New Yorker* piece, her experience is considered to be representative of the marginalization of female comedians in Hollywood (Friend 2011). Yet, the film is richer and more interesting, partly because of its apparently unremarkable nature. A sharper eye would note, for example, that the

https://doi.org/10.1515/9783110571981-022

gender inversion from the original is performed through a careful staging of the interaction between race and class in the expectations of potential Anglophone viewers.

Portraying Leonardo nonchalantly as a rich Mexican man contravenes the representation of Latinxs in US cinema. Derbez himself is keenly aware of this. In an interview with *USA Today*, Derbez notes:

> When I started coming to the U.S., they were offering me only the typical stereotypical roles: the druggard, the criminal, the gang member, or in the best-case scenario, the gardener or the cook. I was fed up with all these roles that were always the same. And I promised I would try to change the image of Latinos in Hollywood. (Mandell 2018, n.p.)

Given the power of being a co-producer in the film, Derbez was allowed to cast himself in a different role, which in turn he presents as part of a larger politics of representation:

> When we had the years of #OscarsSoWhite, all the African Americans were together and they joined to protest. But right now with this Trump administration, we feel a lot of fear to raise our voices. So we haven't been able to really raise our hands, raise our voices to say we deserve more opportunities. But I think it's important. In my case, it's me producing my own stuff. Right now, I'm my own producer because that's the only way I can have jobs.
> (Mandell 2018, n.p.)

One could certainly add here that Kate, a carpet-cleaner trying to stay afloat as a single mother, represents the white working class that is considered to be in Donald Trump's (*1946) political base, and her screwball romance with a Mexican man is, in itself, a challenge to the politics of segregation and anti-immigration espoused by the U.S. right-wing. The film plays with these stereotypes throughout its development. Leonardo, for instance, is led by Kate to believe that he is a construction worker. She, in turn, dresses him with a Seattle Seahawks jersey, obviously parodying the stereotype of the white working-class male. Mexican viewers will note that the cast includes many well-known actors from Mexican television and cinema, like Omar Chaparro and Jesús Ochoa.

All of this works through a deliberate seamlessness: no one seems to object that Leonardo's purported daughters are blond while he is somewhat dark-skinned. Moreover, Derbez and Faris's physical comedic styles interact without glitches in the context of the family-friendly messaging of the film (which could certainly be read as a "domestication" of Derbez's more risqué brand of humor). Derbez looks quite comfortable with a role written for an all-American actress like Hawn. Notwithstanding the tepid-to-negative reviews and even the skepticism that Derbez and Faris could match Hawn and Russell, the film actually performed quite well. In the United States, it raised fifty million dollars, a remarkable feat if one considers that it opened opposite the second week of a juggernaut, *Avengers: Infinity War* (Anthony and Joe Russo, 2018), and that it handily beat the other midsize film that sought to capture the non-Marvel audience, Jason Reitman's motherhood drama *Tully* (2018), starring Charlize Theron.[1] It was also a phenomenon in Mexico, where it was released as *Hombre al agua*. It raised 546 million pesos (about 29 million dollars) and it actually managed to beat *Avengers* in its opening weekend.[2] It became the biggest first-weekend release for Videocine, Televisa's film arm and Pantelion partner and the dominant company in Mexico's commercial market.

Overboard's commercial success, as well as its ability to casually subvert many of the racial and national divides between Mexico and the United States during the Trump presidency, is part of a larger story of a phenomenon that I call here "binational slapstick." With this, I refer to a tradition of physical comedy that can be traced back to the silent period in cinema, but that, unlike its portrayal in scholarship as an American phenomenon, has always been a site of cultural engagement between Mexico, the United States, and Mexican America. Tom Gunning traces slapstick back to classical stage scenes such as Italian *commedia dell'arte* and understands it to be "the dominant genre of silent comedy," which "acts an archetypal machine of displacement in which an instrument detours from its original purpose into a strong sensual effect" (2010, 140–41). Yet, as Eileen Bowser explored in her classic work on the matter, the significant element of slapstick was the intersection between two factors: the ability of actors to "play directly to the camera," and their drawing "on the cheerfully amoral traditions of pre-1909 film and vaudeville as well as French and Italian comedies," allowing it to mock "the excesses of melodrama" (1994, 183). Still, these accounts firmly located in the silent period of U.S. cinema often miss the close intertwining of slapstick with Mexican performers, as well as Mexico's own film and stage traditions. Charles Ramírez Berg, for instance, reminds us that Lupe Vélez, who rose to fame in the *Mexican Spitfire* films, "had its roots in Mexican vaudeville and was similar to the slapstick pioneered in film by Mack Sennett" (2002, 96). Vélez's performance as a woman in American sound cinema "was continuing the slapstick tradition of silent comedies into sound films" (96). The transnational cultural process takes the center stage in *Mock Classicism*, where Nilo Couret persuasively argues against the study of both Hollywood and the

---

[1] Box-office data for the United States here and below comes from the website Boxofficemojo.com.

[2] Box-office data for Mexico in this instance comes from the 2018 box office report by the Cámara Nacional del Cine (Canacine), the lobby group for film distributors and exhibitors in Mexico: Canacine.org.mx. See also Edgar Apanco (2018).

national film traditions of Latin America as entities of their own and proposes film classicism "as a discourse that mediates and renders the world, looking at the construction of the aesthetic world as diegetic totality and the circulation of the texts and objects in global circuits of economic exchange" (2018, 14–15). His argument rests on the study of Latin American comedians strongly tied to slapstick performance, like Mexican Mario Moreno "Cantinflas" and Argentine Luis Sandrini, and his contribution to this debate is precisely that one should not read these figures as appropriators of a comedic style from the United States or as representatives of some kind of cultural specificity. Instead, Couret proposes to read figures such as Cantinflas and Sandrini as part of a dynamic global (particularly hemispheric and transatlantic) film circuit in which narratives and repertoires were part of a dynamic of exchange.

Eugenio Derbez embodies the latest iteration of a history of slapstick and physical comedy that begins in popular theater traditions of Mexico and the U.S. Southwest, like *carpa* and *teatro de variedades*, which later migrates to cinema via the work of comedians like Cantinflas, Germán Valdés "Tin Tán," or Eulalio González Piporro.[3] In the second part of the twentieth century, this tradition continues through exploitation film stars like Mauricio Garcés, but finds its home in television, thanks particularly to the massive success of Roberto Gómez Bolaños "Chespirito," who commanded a sketch television show that used slapstick to churn beloved characters like "El Chavo del Ocho," a poor child who lived in a barrel in a working class tenement, or "El Chapulín Colorado," a failed superhero dressed like a red grasshopper. The success of Chespirito's slapstick was key to Televisa's dominance of the airwaves in the 1970s and 1980s as well as its internationalization. As John Sinclair and Joseph D. Straubhaar note, "Televisa's Golden Age" was built on differential programming by genre and demographic. In this context, slapstick comedy became central as part of the variety programming that Televisa placed in Channel 2, in which Chespirito's shows became part of a primetime bar that would follow afternoon *telenovelas* (Sinclair and Straubhaar 2013, 40–41). Even as Chespirito's ratings gradually faded in the 1980s, his show remained popular in Central and South America and, more importantly, in the Galavisión network of the United States, the subsidiary of Univision Inc. that broadcasts Televisa's shows in the United States.

Derbez's formational years in the 1980s develop in this comedy bar. Derbez first appeared in the late seasons (1984–1987) of *Cachún Cachún Ra Ra*, a teen

---

[3] I will not trace the history of Mexican film comedy for reasons of space. Unfortunately, there is not much comprehensive scholarly research on the matter, but Rafael Barajas (2016) provides a fairly good history of the genre.

comedy show that took some elements from the variety shows but also developed plot lines in the form of a sitcom, something that was unusually innovative in Mexico, and would later play into Derbez's own shows. He also rose to fame as part of the cast of *Anabel* (1988–1995), a popular sketch comedy series, with strong slapstick overtones, helmed by comedian Anabel Ferreira. Although Ferreira starred in the most popular comedy show of her years, and her show was produced by Enrique Segoviano, of Chespirito fame, becoming the first female comedian to be the central figure in a broadcast of this genre, she faced the same gender challenges as her peers and never quite reached the iconic status of male comedians like Chespirito or Jorge Ortiz de Pinedo. Even as a secondary figure, it was clear that Derbez could steal the scene in roles such as a vegetarian vampire that seeks to fight a superhero (a lizard wrestler) played by Ferreira or Super Rorro, a pretentious actor in casting sessions with a superstar named Yadira, also played by Ferreira.

As *Anabel*'s ratings began to fade, Derbez's star began to rise. After a couple of minor roles in *sexicomedias* like *Más vale amada que quemada* (Jorge Manrique, 1990), Derbez played the role of a man who must disguise as a woman to avoid arrest in *Soy hombre y qué* (Jorge Manrique, 1993).[4] Nonetheless, given the state of crisis in Mexican cinema in the mid-1990s, Derbez developed finally in television, with his immensely popular sketch show *Al derecho y al Derbez* (1993–1995). *Al derecho y al Derbez* grew based on the two key talents in Derbez's performance: versatile physical work that allowed him to play characters with diverse types, and a virtuoso linguistic performance that threw back to Cantinflas's slapstick, in a more risqué and contemporary version. One of the most famous characters is Armando Hoyos, an intellectual wearing magnifying lenses, jersey, and blazer. The sketch is typically foregrounded as an interview for the cultural television, in which an admiring journalist asks questions to the disdainful thinker, who often silences the interviewer and tells him not to interrupt. Fully in character, Derbez would answer the questions with double-entendre aphorisms in which the supposedly deep thoughts were laden with sexual second

---

4 *Sexicomedia* refers to a Mexican film genre which flourished in the 1980s. As television comedy was family oriented, some of the same comedians would develop parallel careers in exploitation films, often also produced or distributed by Televisa. The films were often comedies in which nearly nude and voluptuous women would lust for older, typically working-class men. The genre was very popular in neighborhood theaters prior to the emergence of the cineplex of the 1980s and remain a fixture in television stations both in Mexico and the United States. Many Mexican comedians, like Alfonso Zayas and Luis de Alba, developed their careers in the genre. Derbez came a bit too late to have a defining trajectory in it, but Jorge Manrique, the director of his first starring role, was known for that kind of film.

meanings. In this, Derbez once again traces back to the tradition of Mexican vaudeville and slapstick by deploying a vulgarity aimed at adults without breaking the apparent innocence of the family show. Another example of this was a recurring skit in which he mocked the joint Televisa-QVC home shopping venture CVC. The sketch, in its surface, was an intelligent mockery of the hosts' efforts in selling merchandise (in one episode, for instance, he sells a brick), but the sketch introduced the double-entendre from the get-go. Instead of CVC (or ce-ve-cé in Spanish), the channel was called CTVS (or ce-te-ve-ése), which can also be understood by a Spanish speaker as "your thing is visible." This threading between family entertainment and vulgarity allowed the show to keep Televisa's core conservative audiences while expanding into more adult demographics who were fleeing broadcast television due to the availability of cable.[5]

At this point in time, Derbez's career was very much anchored in Mexico, and thrived through a very intelligent engagement with the status of television comedy at the time. Beyond gender considerations, *Anabel* was also an outdated show in terms of the comedic preferences of Mexican audiences. Chespirito was part of a tradition known as "humorismo blanco" or "white humor," which was proudly featured by Televisa as part of its family-friendly image, and also in response to the State's soft but effective censorship mechanisms (at the time the Direction of Radio, Television and Cinematography, which monitored contents, was part of the Ministry of Government, and kept tabs both on morality and political dissent). This tradition became challenged not only by the loosening of censorship standards, but also by the breakup of Televisa's near monopoly in the 1980s by the emergence of TV Azteca, as well as by the expansion of the media ecosystem through cable and satellite television (Sinclair and Straubhaar 2013, 52). Yet, even before the emergence of TV Azteca in 1993, its publicly-owned predecessor Imevisión aggressively went for the comedy market with *La Caravana* (1988–1992), featuring Ausencio Cruz and Víctor Trujillo, and the various shows of Andrés Bustamante "El Güiri Güiri," which often out-rated *Anabel* and yielded successful characters, some of which, like Trujillo's street clown *Brozo*, remain fixtures of Mexican media until today.

In a previously-cited passage, we saw that Eileen Bowser attributes the success of slapstick to actor-centric approaches to film as well as the deployment of stage traditions of popular humor often seen as vulgar. Derbez's rise is predicated on a slapstick style that very much performs the same operations. Derbez clearly was reviving the sketch show based on the development of a repertoire

---

[5] On the cinematic crisis and the rise of cable see Ignacio M. Sánchez Prado (2014), chapters 1 and 2.

of characters, a style that remained strong from *Chespirito* to *Anabel* and *La Caravana*, and which probably found its peak in Bustamante's work. Bustamante is a very accomplished comic thespian who has created over 200 characters. In some cases the character erases the actor: while Trujillo has other memorable characters (like La Beba Galván or Estetoscopio Medina), he has unquestionably found his strongest success erasing himself and playing Brozo, in whose disguise he has hosted news shows for radio, television, and the internet for decades. In contrast, Derbez is always Derbez and his physical performance often emphasizes his own actoral tics, from a recognizable tone of voice that he varies little among various characters, to the consistent repetition of gags, something that places him closer to Cantinflas and Chespirito than to Bustamante or Trujillo. Yet, the calculated vulgarity of his work in the 1990s avoided the social commentary of Trujillo and Cruz and the whiff of intellectuality present in Bustamante's humor, whose style clearly has marks of his trajectory in cultural and public television.

Derbez's most popular characters are based on the constant repetition of physical and verbal jokes, rather than the discursive deployment of someone like Brozo, whose foundational skits were based on the full narration of a story. Conversely, Derbez has a character, "El lonje moco" (a parody of a radio and cinema horror serial called "El monje loco") that also tells stories, but whose humor really stands in Derbez's over-the-top characterization and his dirty jokes. Another character is "Eloy Gamenó," a frustrated bureaucrat that talks in circles and never says much, ultimately frustrating his interlocutors into grabbing him by the neck and choking him. After this happened, the character would repeat "Óigame no" [roughly: "Listen to me, no"] and recriminate the person for choking him. Derbez's characters thrive on familiarity and verbal performance: they would look the same and sound the same, their gag was often part of their name.

Derbez is also notable as a self-referential comedian who is well aware of television-watching practices. The CTVS sketches certainly mirror the absurdity of a Home Shopping Network in a country where the use of credit cards was very limited. Yet the best example is "El Super Portero" (Super Goalkeeper). This recurring character mocked Televisa's practice of banning mentions of commercial brands in the air: a "goal" in popular parlance meant doing just that, providing on-air, free publicity to a commercial brand. Thusly, "El Super Portero" would be in television shootings stopping the flow of the show when the speaker said a word that would be a commercial brand. For example, in one of the sketches, a sportscaster reports on an avalanche in "el norte de Montana." Given that "El Norte" is also a newspaper, and "Montana" is a cigarette brand, the sportscaster has to say instead: "Newspaper cigarettes." This sketch played with both linguistic slapstick (some of the jokes involved double-entendres) and physical performance, as the goalkeeper would jump into the screen as if he was actually catching a ball. In both "El Super Portero" and CTVS, Derbez draw his humor from the strange practices that came from the erosion of Televisa's economic dominance. In doing this, he skyrocketed to the top of Mexico's ratings.

The mid-1990s are the key point in which Derbez begins to become a binational star. The success of *Al derecho y al Derbez* came at just the right moment. As Imevisión became privatized and turned into TV Azteca, *La caravana* and Andrés Bustamante went off-air and never recovered their popularity in the primetime comedy bar. TV Azteca replaced them with significant success with dubbed versions of U.S. sitcoms, which included *The Fresh Prince of Bel-Air*, *The Nanny*, *Saved by the Bell*, and *The Simpsons*. Yet, Derbez's referential humor and cultural attunement to Mexican culture allowed him to have an edge. In Televisa, competing with shows like *Anabel*, long-running sitcoms like *Papá soltero* (1987–1994) and *Dr. Cándido Pérez* (1987–1993) were coming at the end or their runs and replacements like *La vida en risa* (1994) fail to generate an audience. Televisa copied the model pioneered by Imevisión in 1990 and signed Derbez and other comedians on to be part of the coverage of the 1994 World Cup of Soccer in the United States. His characters would, again, reach a wider audience.

The most important development, though, is the one that allows Derbez to capitalize this success into a binational market. In 1993, Televisa established an alliance with Univisión and Venevisión, which allowed for Televisa's cable channel Galavisión to obtain wider distribution (Sinclair and Straubhaar 2013, 120–21). This brought to Mexico forms of Miami-based Latino media that were received with great success, particularly the variety show *Sábado Gigante*, which was more dynamic than Televisa's long-running equivalent *Siempre en Domingo*, and *Cristina*, a talk-show helmed by Cuban American host Cristina Saralegui. This exposure to television in Spanish not produced in Mexico was happening elsewhere too, as Televisión Azteca began to import telenovelas from Colombia and Brazil, most notably, *Café con aroma de mujer*, which reached such success that it would contend with Mexican telenovelas and would be ultimately the subject of a Mexican remake. Yet, the notable thing is that comedy at large, and sketch comedy in particular, were very much absent from this new programming. Derbez did misfire by trying to have a comedic telenovela, *No tengo madre/ Ya tengo madre/ Ya valió madre* (1997). The title evolved with the plot and it has double meanings. "No tengo madre" means "I have no mother" and "I have no shame," which "Ya valió madre" means "it's over" or "it's ruined." The telenovela never quite worked in tone, as its slapstick comedy and its resource to melodrama were completely at odds with each other.

In any case, the exchange was binational and Derbez managed to become a mainstay of Galavisión's programming with little challenge from the United States. It is worth remembering that U.S.-produced Latino comedies in the 1990s were very short-lived: *House of Buggin'* (1995), featuring John Leguizamo, lasted a month, sandwiched in-between *In Living Color* and *MADtv*, while John Mendoza's sitcom *The Second Half* (1993–1994) barely lasted a season. When Derbez hit Galavisión's airwaves, Televisa was the sole major provider of Mexican-led comedy in the United States. It is worth noting at this point that to understand Derbez as a binational media phenomenon one has to consider that "Latino media" does not refer to a unified ecosystem. Rather, the 1990s were giving birth to a paradigm of media in which speaking English or Spanish makes a significant difference (the first kind of media appealed to second and third generations, while the second one is more popular among first-generation migrants), and so does national origin. Even in Univisión, the Miami-produced shows, led by the Cuban American producers, and the Texas and California shows, focused on the Mexican audience, are distinct. The study of Derbez in the 1990s and the early 2000s is often caught in the middle, as scholars focusing on Latin America, such as Sinclair and Straubhaar, mostly highlight Spanish language television of regional impact, while scholars interested in the U.S. Latino market, such as Christopher Chávez, put significant emphasis on English-language TV or in Univisión. Yet, as Chávez himself notes, the 1990s were a serious period of experimentation in media: Galavisión itself attempted to reach English-language audiences through the Sí TV project and talent like Honduran American comedian Carlos Mencia, who, a decade later, would have his own sketch show in *Comedy Central* (2015, 103). Although Latino television in English would eventually become more predominant, it is also true that Spanish-language television remains crucial in the market and Eugenio Derbez emerged in this period as one of the kings. Yet, it is also clear that Derbez's primary influence is in Mexican and Mexican American media (in Galavisión, for example, but not necessarily in Univisión itself), and even with *Overboard*, his crossovers into English are rare.

Within this landscape, Derbez continued to develop his well-known characters in a second show, *Derbez en cuando* (1998–1999), as well as a rerun version, called *Va de nuez en cuando* (1999–2000), which basically retooled his existing character. However, a new landmark point came with his next television project, *XHDrbz* (2002–2004, with reach in other years). With a firm base both in Televisa's comedy bar and in Galavisión, Derbez introduces major innovations to the genre and to his comedy by pretending that the show is in fact a television network and the sketches constitute individual television shows. In every broadcast, audiences were told that the network granted the new channel its airspace and at the end of the show they would give control back to Televisa or Galavisión. Each sketch was shown with a credit sequence at the end and fully constructed as an autonomous show. While Derbez continued to reprise his beloved characters, *XHDrbz* harnessed a function of slapstick that is not discussed as often: the representation of mediamaking and the demythification of film. As Hilde D'Haeyere discusses in relation to Mack Sennett Comedies on filmmaking, "slapstick cinema frequently revisits the subject of making movies" and the long tradition of Hollywood-on-Hollywood films traces back to slapstick genres (2014, 83).[6] Derbez's comedy carries this line of performance and media engagement from its origins. Besides "El Super Portero," which renders visible the production of a television show and the absurdities of its commercial commitments, one can bring to the fore "El Diablito" ("The Little Devil"), one of his longest-running characters. In these sketches, Derbez uses candid camera videos and gag reels, presented as the works of "El diablito": right before the video's gag, he presses a button so that it looks like his doing. This is slapstick at its core: found videos of physical humor, often violent or painful, presented in a metarreferential way by the show.

HXDrbz became the most radical version of Derbez's meta humor. Bringing back some of his classic repertoire, the show also added parodic telenovelas and satires of children stories like Snow White or Cinderella, fake educational and longform journalism shows, as well as a newscast. A notable show/sketch revolved around "Marilyn Menson," a parody of rock singer Marilyn Manson ("menso" means stupid or dumb in Spanish), who often sang parodies of songs, very much making fun of MTV. There were parodies of film review shows (which included lampoons of actual recently released films) and even a pseudo-cartoon show in which actors showed up with a drawn body and a photograph in lieu of their head. The number of different skits and characters created in over two years is astonishing. Perhaps the most famous skit was *La Familia P. Luche* (The Fur Family), originally introduced in *Derbez en Cuando*, in which Derbez and Consuelo Duval play a family in an over-the-top sitcom in which all characters are dressed in bright-colored fur outfits. This sketch became so popular that it spun off and ran two seasons as a stand-alone, in 2007 and 2012. Metarreferentiality in *XHDrbz* went very far. The very last episode in 2004, for example, featured Derbez playing himself as a producer seeking to save the channel from closure, while uselessly pleading with an executive, who urged him to take a break and to refresh his image. This no doubt echoed the very conversation Derbez had with

---

6 Burke Hilsabeck's (2020) forthcoming book is dedicated to the phenomenon of slapstick and self-reference.

Televisa when the show was cancelled. The show also had a revival in 2012, for Derbez's actual wedding to singer Alessandra Rosaldo, through a whole alternative wedding with characters from La Familia P. Luche.

HXDrbz, in its complexity, was one of the last strands of Televisa's Golden Age paradigm of comedy, stretching Derbez to the very edges of the format. Far from the "humorismo blanco" of the twentieth century, Derbez's vulgar yet controlled humor and his constant reflection on changes in television habits were the perfect fit for the paradigm changes in television media at the time. The unfocused nature of *XHDrbz* replicated the increasingly complex set of options in media for both Mexican – where cable penetration skyrocketed around this time – and Mexican American audiences, faced with a growing set of Spanish-language and Latino-geared networks. As networks in the mid-2000s proliferated, Derbez provided Televisa with its last veritable triumph in ratings and relevance in the old comedy-bar paradigm. His departure would mean the last strand of the comedy bar, which gradually but surely lost its centrality in Televisa's schemes. In any case, the most important legacy for the show in terms of Derbez's construction of binational slapstick is that *XNDrbz* is the moment in which institutional and aesthetic factors align for his comedy to become the continuator of Mexican forms of comedy from both sides of the border. This allows him to enter the final stage of his work, which would surprisingly focus on cinema.

While Derbez's reign in Spanish language television was fully consolidated in by 2005, the medium itself was no longer a place in which to build the type of stardom he harnessed. In the mid-2000s, Televisa and Univisión had a brief fallout regarding distribution rights, which ended later on in the decade with Televisa, furthering its interests in Univisión and expanding distributions to competing networks like Telemundo. From that moment, Mexican programming continued to play a leading role in U.S. Hispanic markets, but the type of comedy embodied by Derbez mostly shows in secondary networks, and often in reruns.[7] At the same time, the Mexican film market underwent a significant reinvention. The privatization of exhibitors and the new schemes of funding that came in the 1990s erased the exploitation films that Televisa stars like Derbez shot in the past, and brought a new economy of middle-class addressed films that raised not only directors of transnational renown, like Alfonso Cuarón, but also a domestic industry firmly grounded in the romantic comedy, a genre that itself fosters a star system.[8] This kind of romantic comedy became successful as

---

[7] A discussion of the reconfigurations of Mexican media in the United States after 2005 can be found in Rodrigo Gómez, Toby Miller and André Dorcé (2014), 44–61.
[8] For a study of these industrial changes, see Ignacio M. Sánchez Prado (2014).

part of a larger middle-class backlash against the Televisa model of comedy, which was increasingly seen in Mexico as too vulgar and lower-class. Thus, as rising costs brought by pay-TV and the opening of cineplexes allowed the segregation and fragmentation of audiences by class, Derbez's model of television began to lose its wide appeal in its core market.[9]

At this point, Televisa in general, and Derbez in particular, regeared part of their traditional media genres. The first salvo in this was an independent movie, *Under the Same Moon* (Patricia Riggen, 2007). Written and directed by an emerging Mexican director with connections to the United States, the film is a melodrama focused on family separation and undocumented migration.[10] The film featured a major Televisa star, Kate del Castillo, as the headliner, and Derbez played a secondary role as an undocumented worker, who escapes a detention center with the protagonist's child. Beyond plot details, what matters here is that there was a new form of structuring binational Mexican media in the film, into which Derbez could reinvent himself. The film garners stars from Mexican television (Del Castillo and Derbez) and music (the popular band Los Tigres del Norte), along with recognizable actors from the Mexican American community (like América Ferrera fresh off her success with *Ugly Betty*). Riggen film found a new formula of profitability, which put together into the same package the strengths of Mexican media that had co-existed but that had not usually been combined. And the results showed: the film had a strong twelve million dollars take in the United States and nearly ten million dollars in Mexico, which made it one of the top-ten Spanish-language films in the United States and one of the top-ten Mexican films in Mexico, in history. Even though Televisa did not have a hand in this particular production, this type of film would eventually become institutionalized when Televisa and Lionsgate Enterntainment created Pantelion, a specialty studio for mostly Mexican centered releases for the U.S.-Latino market.

I will not describe Pantelion's history as I have done it elsewhere in detail.[11] For the purposes of the present chapter, what matters is that Derbez accompanied the project from its early years. The first notable stop was the romantic comedy *No eres tú, soy yo* (*It's Not You, It's Me*, Alejandro Springall, 2010), a remake of an Argentine film. In the film, Derbez plays a doctor who is left by his new bride, and tries to move on by dating other women. Derbez's performance is unusually controlled in comparison to his television work and the film clearly falls into the theatrical aesthetic of the Mexican romantic comedy of the 2000s. The

---

9 On the institutional factors of this change, see Cuauhtémoc Ochoa and Ana Rosas Mantecón (2007).
10 For a discussion on the content and narrative of the film, see Caryn C. Connelly (2012).
11 See Ignacio M. Sánchez Prado (2018).

film had a surprising run, becoming the most popular Mexican film of the year (although it was produced by Warner Brothers Mexico and not Televisa), and a limited release by Pantelion in the United States which yielded 1.3 million dollars. Derbez also crossed over into English with his slapstick style of comedy, most infamously in the Adam Sandler vehicle *Jack and Jill* (Dennis Duggan, 2011), in which Sandler plays a pair of twins, man and woman, and Derbez plays a gardener as well as the character's grandmother. At the same time, he landed a job in the aforementioned *Rob*, in which the white protagonist marries into a Mexican-American family, where Derbez shares credits with Chicano legends like Cheech Marín and Lupe Ontiveros. In these works, Derbez's comedy seems unfocused. In Spanish, the success of *No eres tú, soy yo* clearly relied both on his name and the popularity of the genre, but its contained nature was a clear underutilization of his slapstick talent: the film barely features his physical or verbal trademarks. In *Jack and Jill*, a film that was critically panned but very well received by audiences, Derbez is clearly uncomfortable playing Mexican stereotypes for an Anglo-American audience (his character, for example, hosts a "fiesta" in which Sandler's Jill gets sick with the food). And even though he sometimes steals the show in Rob as the title character's brother in law, his verbal grace is absent and his characterization as a Mexican American feels a bit out of place.

In these discomforts one can begin to see how Derbez is able to move his Mexican slapstick into binational territory. The fragmentation of binational Mexican audiences remains a problem and it is extremely difficult to create media that appeals to both. This was obvious in Pantelion's early years, which yielded films like *Girl in Progress* (Patricia Riggen, 2012) that repeats formulas from *Under the Same Moon* (same director, binational casting, warmhearted family immigration story), and has limited success in the United States while missing the mark in Mexico. Derbez plays a secondary character, "Misión imposible," one of the love interests of the protagonist, played by Eva Mendes. Clearly more comfortable under Riggen's direction, Derbez still feels constrained by a role that corresponds more to the image Americans have of Mexicans in the United States than his own comedic tradition. In this period it is notable that Derbez's difficulties in acting stemmed not only from departing away from the comfort zone and the massive success provided by the Televisa, but also because the United States media environments typecast and marginalize Mexicans in various ways. Having reached the pinnacle of a national medium, Derbez's search for crossover was brave because it meant renouncing his superstar status to become a secondary player in second-rate films and television shows. But it was also telling that not even an actor of his proven success and stature could really go around the casting of Latinos into roles of menial workers and drug dealers. Yet, the hits and misses of this period also showed the elements of a formula that Derbez was well-positioned to embody: a characterization of Mexicans that did not overtly privilege one side of the border over the other (which mean in part, and controversially, sidestepping the long history of Mexican American and Chicano-oriented media), familiar presence in Latino media, resistance to typecasting while deploying stereotypes, and attention to the diversity of Mexican media consumers on both sides of the border. When Derbez achieved creative control as writer, producer, and director, he spawned one of the most unexpected successes of the twenty-first century: *Instructions not Included* (2013).

Instructions not Included is a media phenomenon whose success can only be attributed to the gradual construction of Derbez's slapstick style and media savvy. The film follows the adventures of Valentín, an Acapulco playboy who is forced to take care of his daughter Maggie (Loreto Peralta, a blond girl and the scion of a major corporate family from Mexico) when his one-night stand Julie (an American woman played by Jessica Lindsey) drops her off as an infant in his house. Given that his Acapulco lifestyle was not conducive to raising a child, he crosses the border illegally with Maggie (in a comedic sequence) with the purpose of tracking Julie. Ultimately, he fails, and he is drafted to work as a stunt double for films when he falls off a window and into a pool trying to save the little girl. The film's main plot develops when Julie comes back many years later to challenge Valentín and get custody of the girl. In the end, after losing the trial, Valentín smuggles Maggie back into Mexico. In the end, we learn Maggie has a terminal illness and he and Julie spend the last days of Maggie's life caring for her together. The narrative formula is certainly grounded in melodrama, but the film is fully carried by Derbez's slapstick. Spoken by and large in Spanish (in fact a gag of the film is that Maggie acts as Valentín's translator, excusing Derbez from speaking English), Valentín embodies a sense of humor that looks like a mature version of his XHDrbz years. The verbal performance is there, including some double entendres here and there, and the role of a stunt double plays perfectly to his slapstick humor skills. More importantly, in embodying his slapstick legacy in a binational film, Derbez very clearly goes around the limitation of his previous work in the United States: the stereotypes. While there is a stark separation between Anglos and Mexicans in the film, Mexicans come out on top. There are no menial jobs to be had, the immigration authorities are not a major presence even as Valentín is going through family court proceedings, and Julie is thoroughly the villain of the story. Moreover, instead of having U.S. actors interpreting Mexicans, we actually have some Mexican actors playing Americans (Karla Souza, who had a simultaneous box-office hit with *Nosotros los nobles* plays Renee, Julie's lawyer and girlfriend). In this story, Derbez's physical and linguistic comedy, as well as his metacinematic work (in the stunt double sequences), finds its mature tone, and with it creates the standard of binational Mexican cinema.

As a conclusion, the success of *Instructions not included* is perhaps the best argument to bring into the fore to understand how the Mexican line of slapstick, which has been binational in its origins and is binational now, stands in the core of binational Mexican media and entertainment. The film stands as the highest-grossing Mexican film in Mexico ever, with roughly 50 million dollars, and as the highest-grossing Spanish-language film (and fourth-ever in any foreign language) in the United States, with 45 million. The astonishing thing about this success is that, unlike the previous record holder, Guillermo del Toro's *Pan's Labyrinth* (2006), the US figures were reached without any sign of major crossover into English-language audiences (Stewart 2013). The answer is that it harnessed all of the power Derbez built in the Televisa comedy bar, exported into the Univisión/ Galavisión world (where his shows still run in regular rerun) and invested himself into addressing an underserved binational audience. In doing so, he made slapstick, in body and language performance and in his self-reflective understanding of media, the language of a binational media to come. While *Overboard* did not deliver as big a success, it did succeed in the English-language market, beyond expectations. As Derbez and Pantelion move forward, slapstick may hold the key to their future.

Bibliography

Apanco, Edgar. "Taquilla México: Derbez le gana a los *Avengers*." *Cine Premiere*, 15 May 2018. https://www.cinepremiere.com.mx/taquilla-mexico-hombre-al-agua-derbez.html (accessed 15 September 2019).

Barajas, Rafael, "El Fisgón," and José Antonio Valdés Peña. *¿Actuamos como caballeros como lo que somos? El humor en el cine mexicano*. Mexico: Cineteca Nacional, 2016.

Berg, Charles Ramírez. *Latino Images in Film: Stereotypes, Subversion, Resistance*. Austin: University of Texas Press, 2002.

Bowser, Eileen. *The Transformation of Cinema 1907–1915*. Berkeley: University of California Press, 1994.

Chávez, Christopher. *Reinventing the Latino Television Viewer: Language, Ideology and Practice*. Lanham: Lexington Books, 2015.

Connelly, Caryn. "Illegal Immigration through the Eyes of Child: Patricia Riggen's *La misma luna*." *Studies in Latin American Popular Culture* 30 (2012): 94–109.

Couret, Nilo. *Mock Classicism: Latin American Film Comedy 1930–1960*. Berkeley: University of California Press, 2018.

D'Haeyere, Hilde. "Slapstick on Slapstick: Mack Sennett's Metamovies Revisit the Keystone Film Company." *Film History* 26, No. 2 (2014): 82–111.

Friend, Tad. "Funny like a Guy." *The New Yorker*, April 4, 2011, https://www.newyorker.com/magazine/2011/04/11/funny-like-a-guy (accessed 15 September 2019).

Gómez, Rodrigo, Toby Miller, and André Dorcé. "Converging from the South: Mexican Television in the United States." *Contemporary Latina/o Media: Production, Circulation, Politics*. Eds. Arlene Dávila and Yeidy M. Rivero. New York: New York University Press, 2014. 44–61.

Gunning, Tom. "Mechanisms of Laughter: The Devices of Slapstick." *Slapstick Comedy*. Eds. Tom Paulus and Rob King. London: Routledge, 2010. 137–150.

Hilsabeck, Burke. *The Slapstick Camera: Hollywood and the Comedy of Self-Reference*. Albany: SUNY Press, 2020.

Lane, Christina. "Sally Field and Goldie Hawn: Feminist, Post-Feminist and Cactus Flower Politics." *Acting for America: Move Stars of the 1980s*. Ed. Robert Eberwein. New Brunswick: Rutgers University Press, 2010, 180–200.

Mandell, Andrea. "Q&A: 'Overboard' Star Eugenio Derbez on Trump, Conquering Hollywood and Latin Stereotypes." *USA Today*. March 3, 2018, https://www.usatoday.com/story/life/movies/2018/05/03/overboard-eugenio-derbez-talks-trump-hollywood-and-latin-stereotypes/575276002/ (accessed 30 September 2019).

Ochoa, Cuauhtémoc, and Ana Rosas Mantecón. "Cines y ciudad: inclusión, segregación y fragmentación urbana." *Espacios públicos y prácticas metropolitanas*. Ed. María Ana Portal. Mexico: Consejo Nacional de Ciencia y Tecnología/UAM-Iztapalapa, 2007. 201–252.

Pirnia, Garin. "30 Years Later. Why *Overboard* needed Goldie Hawn and Kurt Russell." *Vanity Fair*, December 15, 2017, https://www.vanityfair.com/hollywood/2017/12/overboard-goldie-hawn-kurt-russell-30th-anniversary (accessed 15 September 2019).

Sánchez Prado, Ignacio M. *Screening Neoliberalism: Transforming Mexican Cinema (1988–2012)*. Nashville: Vanderbilt University Press, 2014.

Sánchez Prado, Ignacio M. "Pantelion: Neoliberalism and Media in the Age of Precarization." *The Precarious Cinemas of the Americas*. Eds. Constanza Burucúa and Carolina Sinitsky. New York: Palgrave, 2018. 267–288.

Sinclair, John, and Joseph D. Straubhaar. *Latin American Television Industries*. London: British Film Institute, 2013.

Stewart, Andrew. "Hollywood Gets 'Instructions' from Latino Audiences." *Variety*. 24 September 2013, https://variety.com/2013/film/box-office/hollywood-gets-instructions-from-latino-audiences-1200665085/ (accessed 25 September 2019).

Updike, John. *Odd Jobs: Essays and Criticism*. New York: Random House Trade Paperbacks, 2012.

Jiří Hoblík
Interpersonal and Social Sensibility in Slapstick from the Perspective of Religious History

When one watches slapstick films, the action, the ridicule, the anarchist, and even the brutal components easily overshadow, or at least detract value from, the ethically positive moments. Nonetheless, these positive moments appear to be of particular importance to viewers, as evidenced by the reflections on slapstick film by Petr Král (1941*): "Where the most 'serious' silent films prize strong individuals, [. . .] from the beginning, slapstick aligns itself with the weak" (1998, 59).[1] Král's thesis necessitates further investigation. Where does this characteristic inclination toward the weak and its inherent ethical dimension register in slapstick film? To pursue this question in its relation to the religious aspects of slapstick, this paper will analyze Charlie Chaplin's (1889–1977) late silent movie *Modern Times* (1936) and David Greene's film *Godspell* (1973), a musical with slapstick moments. In order to interpret both films, analogies will be drawn from the slapstick of Judeo-Christian religious history. These films evidence the aforementioned characteristic inclination toward the weak, which is regarded as a standard feature of Christian religious doctrine. In short, the goal of this investigation will be to explain the connections among slapstick, religion, and interpersonal and social sensibilities, validating the hypothesis that sensibility and laughter exist in a reciprocal relationship in the context of slapstick cinema.

1 Slapstick in religious history

This section uses insights from religious history to evidence the connection between religion and the *slapstickesque*[2] and concretely establish the connection

---

[1] "Kde většina "vážných" němých filmů oslavuje silné jedince, groteska se [. . .] staví od počátku na stranu slabých [. . .]." Unless otherwise noted, all translations into English are by Laura Isakov.
[2] Here, the term slapstickesque references the formal analogies to slapstick comedy, regardless of their cultural context.

Translated by Laura Isakov

https://doi.org/10.1515/9783110571981-023

of comic elements[3] at the core of specific biblical passages and certain medieval spiritual plays. In addition, this section outlines how interpersonal and social sensibility – as a disposition to ethical action – has a foundation in the New Testament. This analysis will outline how religion and the comic need not be viewed as mutually exclusive. However, the ambivalence of this relationship is not easy to grasp given the origins of Christianity and its later developments. The starting point of Christianity is represented in the Gospels, the heart of which is found in the Passion story. This is marked by the themes of the suffering and execution of Christ, which are difficult to associate with the comic. Therefore, there is relatively little room for laughter in the New Testament. Rather, one reads about the ridicule Jesus experiences, especially in the story of Easter (Mt 27:29.31.41; Mk 15:20.31, Lk 22:63; 23,11; 23,36). Nevertheless, there are also motives of joy as a positive state of mind, for example that which is linked to the "Good News" of Jesus (cf. Lk 8:1; 9:6), as well as some of his sayings that convey a sense of humor when read aloud (Mt 15:14 or 23:24).[4] Overall, one cannot say that the New Testament is emotionally cold or entirely sad; nonetheless, there is nothing slapstickesque to be found therein.

Such a search for slapstickesque moments is much more successful in Old Testament literature. Biblical scholarship has understood and undertaken a *comic reading* of the Bible (especially from the 1990s on) and has thereby revealed the presence of humor and the comic in the Old Testament, striving to rehabilitate this presence against various resistances. Here, it is important to note that an explanation regarding the particular linguistically and culturally conditioned peculiarities, which make the humor and the comic "not recognizable" for today's reader. As Robert Carroll has noted, "Humor as we know it today is not a feature of the Bible" (Carroll 1990, 169).[5] However, the legitimate undertaking of excavating the humorous in religious scripture can also lead to an exaggerated optimism, whereby scholars have viewed for example the comic as foundational to the story of Genesis (see Whedbee 1998, 15). The biblical analogies to slapstick (i.e., literary representations of a comical plot that uses the body and props for its expression) are found above all in some of the prophetic symbolic actions with which the Old Testament

---

[3] On the term "comic elements," see Kindt (2017, 2–6): "The comical is a trait attributed to objects (utterances, persons, situations, artifacts, etc.) when they have an amusing effect" (2).

[4] In this context, the otherwise multi-layered concept of joy in the New Testament is particularly important in the sense of a pleasant or positive state of mind, which can at times be noticeably influenced by an emotive force (see Kehrein 2012, 270). Laughter can be understood as a pronounced form of joy (Scott 2014, 171).

[5] "Humor as we know it today is not a feature of the Bible" (Carroll 1990, 169).

prophets give their respective message a visual form, especially as satire.[6] This is clearly demonstrated in the competition that Elijah stages with the Baal prophets (1 Kings 18:24–38). The next analogy is found in the episode of the paraliturgical action of King David dancing in front of the Ark of the Covenant, an extremely precious sacred object, in the context of its transportation to Jerusalem (1 Sam 6: 12–23). His behavior is perceived as crazy, as shown, for example, by his wife Michal's outrage over what she considers to be his un-kingly choice of clothing (Bar-Efrat 1996, 64–65). Therefore, through his appearance and demeanor, King David has inverted his role as king (Hertzberg 1986, 230). Indeed, this results in a comic effect, but it conveys a clear political and religious message: he *rules* as king, but at the same time *subordinates himself* to Yahweh, whose presence is symbolized by the ark, which has been won back from the Philistines.

There is uncertainty whether the entry of Jesus on a donkey in Jerusalem (Mk 11:1–11) can be compared with this, or whether it is a parody of the triumphant entry of Pontius Pilate into the city, as was customary to demonstrate Roman imperial power on the great Jewish holidays (Borg and Crossan 2008, 1–30; Harris 2017, 326–327). What is important, however, is that Jesus of Nazareth is prevalently understood as an embodied example of interpersonal and social sensibility.[7] For example, in the healing stories (i.e., Mk 2:1–12), in which Jesus frequently, and with striking detail, devotes himself to the needy, or in the parable of the good shepherd, who defines his life as for "his sheep" (i.e., for the Other), responding to their need (John 10:11.14). It actually does not matter that these traditions have nothing comic, because the moment of that sensibility must be understood as belonging to the New Testament tradition and even more so to its core. Only much later in the course of the Christian religious tradition do religious components become associated with slapstick.

The mentioned "core" component of sensibility is found partly in the tradition of the Last Supper (1 Cor 11:23b–25; Mk 14:22–25), which is also a key passage for the body theme in the New Testament. Three gestures point to this theme: Jesus takes, breaks, and distributes the bread to his disciples – as a symbol of his

---

6 As far as implementation is concerned, the slapstickesque can be specified by persiflage, a stylistic device affiliated with the comic. For example, when Jeremiah places wooden yokes on his neck and ties him up with rope, he uses his body and chosen props to satirize the foreign kings (Jer. 27:2). Or, when Ezekiel's shorn hair and beard are dramatically burned, chopped and scattered, it is an anticipation of the fall of Jerusalem and therefore seems tragicomic (Fleming Drane 2015, 302).

7 According to David Flusser, Jesus appeared in a time of "new sensitivity" which he revealed, for example, in the commandment of charity with its Jewish roots and prepared an audience among his contemporaries for the acceptance of his teaching (1968, 166).

own body, of those who will suffer, and of those who are also there for the Other (parallel to this, see his ceremonial handling of the chalice) (Schnabel 2006, 653). In this way, Jesus is seen as the one savior who wants to show his solidarity with the suffering, whereby Jesus's words of administration to the chalice (1 K 11:25; Mk 14:24–25) anticipate the eschatological salvation which, among other things, references the resurrection of the dead and thus also implies the definitive abolishment of pain. It should be emphasized that this sensitivity to the suffering of others is given its paradigmatic expression in the small circle of apostles, which should serve as a model for Christian communities. Consequently, the history of Christianity can, without wanting to follow or judge its historical reality, also be understood as the developmental history of a potential sense for and engagement with the suffering of others.

For the reasons detailed above, it is often difficult to associate the religious figure of Jesus with the comic. Besides, slapstick in particular tends toward visual expression, whereas Early Christianity, like Early Judaism, is characterized by a "culture of the word" (i.e., verbal religious communication and written tradition). This changes only partly in the course of the history of the Christian liturgical drama. Religious authorities have striven in every age to guard the sanctity and seriousness of religious practice. Nevertheless, the Middle Ages saw the development of fool festivals with their famous role inversions, such as fool-kings, fool-popes, etc., and some other dramatic elements (Harris 2011: 65–127). Until the early modern period, spiritual plays, which originated in the liturgy of the tenth century, found particularly at Easter and later, with Passion plays, were widely cultivated with great imagination. Here too, the comical and slapstickesque find their place and begin to fuse with religious tradition.

An example is the oldest known, only partially preserved Czech passion play *Mastičkář* [*Ointment Merchant*] from the mid-fourteenth century. In this play, the healer Severín, a well-known comic figure (Camille 1998, 68), wants to prove his healing arts; he therefore raises Abraham's son Isaac from the dead after pouring excrement on Isaac's behind (*Mastičkář*, V. 308–309).[8] Here, the comic plot clearly exceeds the standard conventions. The "remedy" is not poured on the head, but rather on the buttocks. This is most likely an inversive symbolism, inasmuch as for the Middle Ages the hierarchization of the body corresponded to social hierarchization (Veltruská 2006, 14), which also extends to Mikhail Bakhtin's discussion of the grotesque body in the carnival (Bakhtin 1984, 303–436). Moreover, the excrement itself did not necessitate a derogatory meaning, according to

---

8 There are two manuscript fragments, of which the so-called museum manuscript is relied on here. For the text, see *Mastičkář, rukopis muzejní*.

Bakhtin, because in the Middle Ages excrement also symbolized witnessing, giving birth, renewal, and prosperity (148–149). Therefore, the ointment merchant plays an ambivalent rather than a negative role vis-à-vis religious praxis. This scene does not reference a single moment explicitly reminiscent of *physical comedy*, because also the preparation of ointment remedy from human excrement (i.e., from the body) is presented as an extremely comic act. Moreover, during the performance, several of the servant's gags are incursions on the audience that have a funny, even slapstickesque character. For example, a statement by the servant Rubin indicates that his sack full of remedy jars is torn to shreds in the midst of the crowd (*Mastičkář* V. 84–84), which had to evoke a terrible stench. Thus, because of their sporadic occurrence in the text, the slapstickesque moments cannot be reconstructed systematically; however, that does not preclude their existence.[9]

Furthermore, something remarkable happens in the *Ointment Merchant*: next to the healer, who became a comic figure only at the beginning of the fourteenth century and was developed into a comic counterpart to Christ, Isaac emerges as another comical figure in passion plays (Veltruská 2006, 75–84). Is this a parody-like folk form of Christ worship as suggested by Jarmila Veltruská (2006, 84)? Her thesis is not explained in detail, but it suggests that it relates to a lifting up of the tension between the profane and the divine. If the profane, in this context, successfully establishes itself as the main component of the play (see Dauven-van Knippenberg 2009, 360), it points to a new way of conceptualizing the difference between the sacred and the profane. A thorough examination of the social dimension of the play is incomplete without considering the observations of Alfred Thomas. Thomas does not completely exclude Veltruská's thesis. Rather, he interprets the obscene humor in the *Ointment Merchant* as follows: "objects of the play's humor are those who speak a different language and represent a different ethnic group" (1998, 64). Except for Isaac and his father Abraham, Severín's disloyal servant Rubín is most likely coded and for contemporary audiences recognizable as a Jewish figure (68–72). However, although problematic in its reliance on stereotypes as foundation for satire, the depicted Christians have to confront the Jewish perspective, which results in a positive relationship (57). Notably, a straightforward interpretation of the function of humor and sentimentality structures is challenging given the text's origin, and thus it may be assumed that the play served to demonstrate as well as manage the religiously constructed multi-layered tensions and antagonisms between and among social groups. This claim is supported by considering English mystery plays, which frequently captured conflicts with authorities (Eming 2005, 12–13).

---

9 Regarding the slapstickesque in the Passion Plays, see Kuiper (2010, 163) and Walker (2014, 20).

The relation between the comical and the Christian religion, which is a component of mystery plays, is in no way unilaterally negative, but is rather always ambiguous and co-evolving, particularly as it affects the sacred space, liturgy, as well as theology.[10] But, admittedly, it becomes veiled over the course of the long history of religion and culture. In particular, this is true from the moment in history in which the early modern drama emancipated itself from religion and its concerns for the sacred and serious. Consequently, the mystery play in Europe lost its central place in drama culture (see Kenrick 2008, 44; Heers 1986, 50; Brockett and Hildy 2003, 101–103; Kühnel 2001, 316; Müller 2008, 28; Wickham 1994, 112; and Kenrick 2008, 96). In some moments the mutual distance between the comical and the religious is unbridgeable: religious thought, especially that of Christianity, casts the purely spiritual meaning with regards to God, God's Kingship, the resurrection as *indiscernible* in principle, while slapstick mainly offers action to *be observed*. Slapstick demands permanent and intensive hold on the emotions of the spectators, which is already attributed to the pantomime in Roman Antiquity with its slapstickesque elements (Webb 2008, 95). But it can also send an ethical message, as was the case, for example, in Chaplin's *Modern Times*, but also in other slapstick films, such as, for example, the well-known comedy about war and love, *The General* (1926) by Buster Keaton (1895–1966).

In recent decades, attention has been drawn to the relationship between religion and film from a scholarly perspective, with a specific focus on the relationship between religion and slapstick[11]; however, this link requires deeper analysis, which this investigation pursues in terms of ethical motivation in the context of religious history. To this end, a religious studies perspective lends itself well to examine the influence of the religious on slapstick as a part of the secular sphere, including consideration of some of the mutual historical points of contact between drama and religion. This approach relates to the scholarship on the coexistence of the secular and religious in the largely secularized Western society (Habermas 2003, 109).

---

10 For a summary of the Middle Ages, see Szerb (2016, 221–222); regarding the twentieth century, see Lindvall (2016, 3–5). In this regard, Ingvild Saelid Gilhus discusses the contrast between the "normative views on laughter and the laughter of the faithful" (Gilhus 1999, 309).
11 For example, it has been noted in some of Chaplin's films (especially *The Pilgrim*, *The Kid*, and *The Circus*) that "the film comically but kindly portrays the social gospel movement in action" (Lindvall et. al. 2016, 18).

2 Sensibility in *Modern Times*

Charlie Chaplin mastered the tensions and antagonisms of his time and provides an excellent base for the question what the secular film has to do with the Western history of religion. Although a direct link between the New Testament and slapstick cannot be determined, the quintessential slapstick artist Charlie Chaplin is known to have drawn some inspiration from the figure of Jesus. During his childhood, Chaplin received a religious education without developing a close relationship with Christianity. While he then pursued no pronounced religious interest in the course of his life, Chaplin did not want to be called an atheist (Chaplin, Jr. 1960, 239–240). Yet the person of Jesus interested him as being "a lonely man who has been the most misunderstood of all time" (Chaplin 1964, 134). Such statements by Chaplin himself evidence a certain influence of the biblical and Christian Jesus-tradition on the sensitivity and ethos encountered in Chaplin's films, particularly when speaking of a correspondence between religious tradition and the articulation of sensitivity structures in *Modern Times* (see Molyneaux 1991, 111).

Right from the beginning, *Modern Times* reflects the conflicts between the individual, the industrial, and the urban social system (111). On the whole, Chaplin's character moves in a realistic filmic world, with stylized and exaggerated moments in a contrasting tension. Certainly, Chaplin intended his portrayal to exaggerate aesthetically the already exaggerated, that is, the human bondage of industry or high work demands, to indicate certain irrational aspects of man (Král 1998, 187) and other absurdities related to civilized life (Tavernier-Courbin 1991, 129). That said, one must also take into account that the Tramp has a childish, playful, and not only critical relationship to the technical devices. The audience already expects the Tramp to behave strangely. The art of making fun of oneself was one of Chaplin's strong points. When Chaplin attracts the attention of viewers, he also brings them closer to his intention of highlighting the contemporary afflictions tormenting people, while simultaneously freeing the viewers from their own anxiety over how to deal with such worries (Mangold and Bartsch 2012, 89–93). In fact, the reception of this filmic world is unique for each viewer, considering that laughter leads people in unexpected directions whether or not each viewer has also recognized the message of the film (Tavernier-Courbin 1991, 130).

Chaplin's characterization of the Tramp also directly helps him to provide the on-screen images and expressions of sensibility, such as the Tramp's compassion with his fellow mechanic, who got stuck in the wheelwork. While he is not able to free the co-worker during his break, he can at least nourish him from above by using a funnel to pour coffee into his mouth, followed by roast chicken. Here compassion and comedy are very close, operating in contrast to what Henri Bergson (1859–1941) has described as a callousness that accompanies laughter (1924, 11–12; 1914, 4). In this case, the mechanic simultaneously represents the industrial system and its victims, to whom he also belongs. He is the object of laughter and of compassion, a living unity of opposites. A later scene compounds this unity when the Tramp takes responsibility for a poor girl's theft of bread in order to save her from being arrested; he almost acts according to the biblical instruction to fulfill the law of Christ by carrying the burdens of others (cf. Gal. 6:2). The interpersonal and social sensibility are not only observed in the individual scenes, but as the structural features for the entire film. This is also the case in other Chaplin films, especially *Kid* (1921), where the Tramp defies poverty by nurturing and educating a small abandoned boy. Yet another example is found in *City Lights* (1931), where he provides the money for a blind florist's eye surgery, seemingly reflecting Biblical Messianism (see Hurley 1982, 162; Lindvall 2016, 18).

3 The comic and the secular gospel

This section aims to illustrate that the allusions to New Testament ethical demands in connection with slapstick as a genre of comedic film that are implicit present in *Modern Times* reappears long after the end of the silent film era, namely in David Greene's film-musical *Godspell*, in which the main character Jesus takes the form of a clown. This "Christ-Clown" is very different from the classic circus clown, i.e., visually, or to the extent that he often speaks and sometimes sings. What is new here is that the gospel and, in a rather broad understanding, the comic are explicitly united. Above all, the analytical approach for these moments should fall under the question of how the slapstickesque moments in the film affect what was originally a religious message. These appear throughout the first act, alongside other – dialogical, clownish (in the broadest sense), pantomime, or other choreographic (Giere 2014, 86) – moments of the comic or vaudeville theater (a predecessor of the slapstick film) (Baugh 1997, 42; Gunning 1986, 64). Through these various forms, moreover also in relation to the costumes and the interest of the protagonists in their colors, a dynamic and colorful micro-world is formed in which the first act takes place and the second act follows in strong resemblance to the Passion story.

What I refer to as the figure of the Christ-Clown is particularly reminiscent of the dramatic scenes of the short film *Parable* (1964) by Rolf Forsberg (1925–2017), in which a circus clown, after helping others and staging some comical sketches, is murdered in the chapiteau. Here the tent roof acts as a symbol of the vault of heaven (Lindvall and Quicke 2011, 69; Lindvall 2011, 69–71). *Parable* is cited by American theologian Harvey Cox in his famous essay collection *The Feast of Fools: A Theological Essay on Festivity and Fantasy* (1969) in the chapter "Christ the Harlequin" as a testimony to the allegedly inevitable return of the clowns as religious figures in the sixties (1969, 140–141). I mention it here to illustrate that the image of the "Christ-Clown," meaning the embodiment of the comic and at the same time the interpretation of the history and teachings of Jesus, was a postwar phenomenon. If one considers the clown in the sense of a theater, circus, and film artist (Hoche et. al. 1982, 18) who always plays *a role* as a joker, and above all works within a physical medium and with props, then such forms of his performance can be compared to slapstick. Though the Christ-Clown is so specific a character that the demarcating importance is his personality, as opposed to the demarcating qualities of the classical clown, who relies on his appearance and his deeds. This is reminiscent of the biblical Jesus, who is in no way caricatured, but who is in his connection to laughter rehabilitated and newly registered as someone who embodies something human – namely the contrasting emotional polarity of grief and laughter.

What works in conjunction with the film's reference of the Passion story is its intertextual relation to the artistic tradition of the "sad (or even tragic) clown" (Plax 2006, 36). Most importantly, this includes the iconography of "Pierrot" (ca. 1718–1719), a painting by the French rococo painter Jean-Antoine Watteau (1684–1721) which, according to some interpretations, recalls the pictorial representations of Christ (Haskell 1971, 19–15). The sujet of "Pierrot" underwent a transformation and renewed interest in French painting from 1850 onward (Ritter 1989, 181), about the same time as the pantomime and circus-clowning took a noticeable place in culture (Haskell 1971, 6). The work of Georges Rouault (1871–1958) offers another example in his "Tête de clown tragique" ["Head of a Tragic Clown," 1904], which shows a clown face that features the historical artistic elements traditionally used to represent the suffering Christ (Stewart 1999, 10). This cultural history prefigured the comic and the religious iconography in *Godspell*.

John-Michael Tebelak (1949–1985), who wrote the musical that served as foundation for Greene's film, created scenarios in which joy, liveliness, and comprehensibility of the imagery stand in contrast to the rigid official depiction of Jesus in established iconography, ritual and thought of various church traditions. The scenarios were first and foremost a response to his personal experience of alienation during an Easter service at the Pittsburgh Anglican Cathedral in 1970, which Tabelak described in interviews (Laird 2014, 15; Swain 2002, 295–297). After the success of this public performance, Tebelak's former classmate, the composer Stephen Schwartz, made it a musical in the same year (Brunn 2004,

15; Laird 2014, 15–24). This piece is still staged today in middle schools and churches, especially in the United States (Oppenheimer 2011). In 2011 it was performed as an Off-Broadway production (Laird 2014, 42). November 2018 the original cast members joined the Broadway crew for a special *Godspell* performance (de Giere 2018).

Greene's film version of *Godspell*, which was written two years after the musical's premiere, has thus far received sparse scholarly attention next to being sporadically mentioned in non-fiction books (Swain 2002, 292–314; Laird 2014, 15–44; de Giere 2008, 42–69). I will discuss the film with regard to its engagement with the message of Jesus and the slapstickesque in the context of religious history. In particular, what is relevant for the discussion that follows is that when Jesus embodies his teaching, he embodies in particular the call to charity, the fulfillment of which requires activating the sensitivity of others. It is at this moment that the slapstickesque in the film connects to the religious in critical ways. Unlike the theater version, which has as setting the playground, the Jesus figure is moved to the wider area of a city center. As such, the film introduces a new layer of criticism of life in the modern metropolis New York, crowded with people and alienated from life. Jesus, with his four men and five women apostles, strongly evokes the flower people of the hippie movement, contextually also associated with the American Jesus movement of the 1960s. The film loosely follows the story of Jesus. It is primarily composed of individual scenes linked by the stories affiliated with different characters quoting the Gospel of Matthew. In dramatizing the parables through slapstickesque means, these vignettes consequently take on an unusual meaning. For example, the scene thematizing "Love your neighbor" (Mt 22:39) (*Godspell*. Dir. David Greene. Columbia Pictures, 1973. TC: 50:42–52:37) begins with a brawl parodying enmity reminiscent of the old slapstick films. After Jesus courageously intervenes, the kicks and shuffling result in an almost kitschy scene depicting characters mutually hugging and kissing.

As the film progresses, the creative reimagining and reinterpretation of religious iconography for modern audiences leads to a transfiguration of this iconography. Take, for instance, the second act, which presents the Passion story. Jesus is crucified on the wire mesh (1:32:21–1:36:1) in contrast to the traditional iconography depicting the biblical crucifixion of Jesus behind Jerusalem. Consider also that the apostles (both male and female) do not flee; rather, they stay with Jesus and support themselves on the wire mesh as they express their compassion through their gestures, facial expressions, and singing. Moreover, Pamela Grace, examining the lack of the resurrection motif in *Godspell*, has argued that "the ending does not indicate that the film chooses to avoid the miraculous or traditional notions of the afterlife, since there are numerous references to

Jesus' father in heaven, who will reward the good with eternal happiness" (2009, 91). The film is predominantly a story about a master's being in communion with his apostles.

Nevertheless, *Godspell* acts as an analogy to the Christian initiation ritual, which consists of three phases as a kind of rite of passage: the initiates are first called from their everyday lives and are invited for a limited time into a new sperate community, which, in the opinion of Victor Turner (1920–1983) corresponds to what he termed communitas: a relational category rendering "[. . .] society as an unstructured or rudimentarily structured and relatively undeferential comitatus, community, or even communion of equal individuals who submit together to the general authority of the ritual elders" (1969, 95). Jesus instructs the apostles (*Godspell*, TC: 14:26) and thereafter they can witness the story of their "master" (1:07:58–1:36:1), which can also be interpreted as a kind of initiation into the questions of life and death and the sense of community such acquisition of knowledge brings about (1:36:2–1:41:18). When Turner relates the communitas to the social structure, he also offers an interpretative stimulus for the ending of *Godspell*: "There is a dialectic here, for the immediacy of communitas gives way to the mediacy of structure, while, in *rites de passage*, men are released from structure into communitas only to return to structure revitalized by their experience of communitas" (1969, 129).

The initiation experienced by the apostles could thus serve as a religiously motivated and renewed confrontation with everyday dangers and needs for which the film's opening images of the alienation of life in the city speak as *pars pro toto*. Given the means of expression and scenography used to transform the religious material into secular (meaning, especially, the non-sacred and non-ecclesiastical) and given the depicted community a modern form, *Godspell* serves as a secular gospel interpretation simultaneously relativizing the sharp dividing lines between the religious and the profane. Moreover, the film foregrounds not only the audial (through listening), but also the visual (through seeing) dimension of Jesus's doctrine, which originally was primarily characterized as part of a "culture of the word," but in this modern adaptation also works visually. An example of this is the scene featuring a video projection of classic slapstick movie scenes by way of illustrating the Parable of the Prodigal Son (Luke 15:11–32) (*Godspell*, TC: 58: 44–1:05:01).

The union of the serious and the comic as characteristic of Chaplin's films as it is characteristic of *Godspell* can also be interpreted through Bakhtin's discussion of medieval laughter culture, which demonstrated that everything could be the target of parody and that laughter reveals another side of the truth about the world (1984, 91–92). Although the world of slapstick can no longer be seen in the light of a polarity between the divine and the profane, Bakhtin's theory serves as a point of orientation that legitimizes the search for historical precursors as anticipatory variations. Therefore, the musical *Godspell* characterizes the portrayal of Jesus and aspects of his teaching, even though Jesus himself was not a clown figure in the Bible. This discrepancy points, however, to some deeper connections: one cannot expect an historical or dogmatic image from *Godspell*, because it opens up a different approach to the truth about the biblical Jesus – namely, about Jesus as a human, as emotionality and the disposition to laugh belong to humanity in the first place. At the same time, his above-mentioned relationship to laughter is rehabilitated in the New Testament without the Passion story being devalued. Lastly, the Christ Clown in his attitude is necessarily one with the biblical Jesus, whose doctrine he imparts, and who himself, with a good punchline has often relativized all sorts of fixed ideas to the detriment of others, such as, for example, the ideas about the dependence on one's own assets (Mt 6:19–21), on one's own dietary worries (Mt 6:25–34), on legalism that hinders one's own ethical claims (Mt 5:21–48; see Theißen and Merz 2011), and also about blindness towards the weak and socially disadvantaged (Mt 25:31–46). These issues express his sensitivity to other people. Therefore, comic forms seem to represent a potential means to relativize these fetters without denying the serious.

4 On the ambivalence of sensibility

As David Bordwell has noted, "The artwork is necessarily incomplete, needing to be unified and fleshed out by the active participation of the perceiver" (1985, 32). Thus, spectators actively participate in the shaping of meaning in the process of viewing a film. In the case of Chaplin's *Modern Times* and Greene's *Godspell*, matters are a bit complicated in this regard, because the extent to which these films aestheticize ambiguity demands quite a lot of cognitive commitment from spectators.

In line with the writing of John Fiske, one can consider slapstick a pop culture genre in which cultural hegemony and resistance struggle with one another (1989, 29). In both *Modern Times* and *Godspell*, a differently constituted ambivalence is inherent in the way the films use technology and machines by way of critiquing the mechanized civilization, thereby performing the struggle between hegemony and resistance outlined by Fiske (cf. Bergson 1914, 15). According to Barbara Strauß, when laughter teaches people the social, political, economic, or similar pressures, it eases social adjustment, which is also perceived as pressure: in this context, Strauß discusses Chaplin's *Modern Times* as an example of the tragicomic film, in which contradictions, especially between humans and the depersonalizing demands of mechanized modern industry and modern city life, are not decided, but rather, demonstrated and translated into a liberating laugh (2001, 61). The comic satisfies both sides (the hegemonic and the resistance) as well as their ambiguities in relation to the subject. Laughter, therefore, protects humanity from rigidity, from conflict harmonization, and from internal destruction if – in reference to the work of Helmuth Plessner (1970, 42) – it serves as a function of the bodily response to a situation "which is otherwise no longer answerable" (Strauß 2001, 61). Both films attempt, by means of their critique of human relations and sociality under the conditions of technical civilization, to show how, in particular, personal sensitivity clashes with the cold calculus of technology.

To represent such a tension comically is to undertake an inversive operation. This follows the tradition of cultural history, beginning with story of King David in the Old Testament. Inversion stimulates a reevaluation of the current status of human values and, among those who share them, creates their new legitimacy for social life (see Bohrmann 2018, 39). One example are the solidarity structures characterizing the already fictitious fools festivals, which have created empathy for the week and needy in a longing to praise the weak (the child, donkey, and the fool) and to humiliate the powerful (see Heers 1986, 159). Such was the intention that Chaplin, who was once a poor boy, identified with when, as one of the prominent filmmakers, he portrayed the Tramp. Comedy is a possible and proven way to reach revaluation.

In contrast to previous episodes, in the closing scene of *Modern Times* the Tramp returns to his former way of life as though he alone wants to follow the wandering preacher Jesus of Nazareth, who also referenced his chosen lifestyle, including above all else that he had "nowhere to lay his head" (Mt 8:20). At the very least, he wanted to make a claim that would make the spectators follow him literally. Similarly, one can say that, after their "initiation," the apostles in *Godspell* perceive their own lives differently and draw practical consequences from this even though they do not necessarily have to follow their master's fate.

The Czech writer Karel Čapek (1890–1938), who shared the cultural context in which Chaplin's slapstick was widely lauded by its contemporaries, used this background in his feuilleton article titled "Chaplin, or, On Realism" (1925) to draw attention to a shift in the handling of things, which also point to a religious moment in a given scene of his films: "In the hands of Chaplin [objects] lose their symbolic, distanced, or customary meaning and return to the original state of Paradise; they become a naked and surprising reality. It is a realistic discovering; his jokes uncover the paradox of things" (1957, 229).[12] For instance, the Tramp examines a hat based on what it can and cannot be. By explaining one thing, he indeed speaks about another, namely, the world as it operates, and thus articulates the hidden possibilities within random objects (Král 1998, 178–179). Through such an investigation of objects, spectators themselves undergo a transformation. In general, slapstick is about the potential revision of personal sensibility (see Gunning 2010, 238–243) due to its relationship to body language (see Ghalian 2017, 191) and the intense impulses that emerge from the very dynamic images of the extraordinary dealings with ordinary things. Spectators can observe how the Tramp deals with things as a simple human being and, in this respect, "ignores" conventions, faces many misunderstandings, and thus, not only anticipates a comic effect, but also offers a new perspective and enriches the play of meanings inscribed in the film. Therefore, the extent to which the film causes spectators to process their experience with multiple levels of meaning leads to their inability to land on one single interpretation of slapstick's function in the film. This is how in *Godspell* the New Testament traditions are newly articulated through the slapstickesque, or how the mechanic in *Modern Times* stays hidden in the machine despite the sheer impossibility of the context: one does not have to think about whether or not such narrative moves are possible, but rather can relish in the general question of how the naïve complacency of the machine endures in the face of civilizational contradictions. This question must not only be understood in abstract terms, but also as a concrete reflection of the Other, which stands in conflict with the industrial system.

5 Conclusion

This chapter demonstrated that slapstick has a liberating function and can lead to the revision of the mind in terms of respective meanings and motivations. The effect of slapstick, however, is often ambivalent. The slapstickesque conceals the same danger that the meaning will remain unnoticed or misunderstood by the audience. *Godspell* directly attempts to avoid this danger while employing the slapstickesque to develop meaning. In some ways this musical not only confirms the vitality of the slapstick form, but also recalls the history

---

[12] "V rukou Chaplinových pozbývají věci svého symbolického, odtažitého nebo zvykového významu a vracejí se v prvotní rajský stav; stávají se nahou a překvapující skutečností. Je to realistické objevitelství; jeho šprýmy odhalují paradoxii věcí."

of the relationship between the religious and the comical. Additionally, the embodiment processes of the Christ-Clown demonstrate that the doctrine of bearing the burdens of others is an invitation that transcends the border between the religious and the profane, and that it can – and should be – articulated in a new cultural context. Thus, its reinterpretation, de-dogmatization, and dynamics are best supported in the form of slapstick.

The biblical instruction to carry the burdens of others is an ethical demand, one that was vocalized by the Christian authority of Paul of Tarsus and became a well-known component of the Christian religious tradition. While this particular instruction was meant to be just one of many, it expresses the essential basic intentions of Jesus's ethics in that it requires that the interests and needs of others should be prioritized over one's own. This ethical demand also has its counterparts outside the Christian religion in the secular context. In any case, it articulates a cultured human disposition whose development is conditioned by religious history but one that is not restricted to the religious sphere.

The ethical demand (of placing the interests and needs of others first) appears in the films discussed in this chapter. Through their unique variations of the coexistence of the secular and the religious, these films anticipate the post-secular age. This is most specifically the case in *Modern Times*, where it is possible to trace a peculiar cultural influence of religion to Chaplin's biography. *Godspell*, however, transmits widely known religious material into a distinctly original secular context and presents it through secular means. In contrast, *Parable* purposely gives the religious material a completely non-religious form and varies its contents.

This comparison of a classic slapstick film and reception of the slapstickesque demonstrates analogies in terms of content in addition to their formal connection. An element all three films share is the aforementioned representation of the ethical demand issued by the main character. However, this embodiment remains implicit inasmuch as *Modern Times* is far removed from religious explication and *Godspell* and *Parable* are merely gospel-inspired. This confirms that there is a common point of reference that links the long-standing tradition of charity and its secular counterparts. These films always portray a main character's reaction to someone's pain or distress. As an emotive-cognitive schema, this corresponds to a disposition that requires constant remembrance and care, even under the designations such as "compassion" or "empathy." Using an as not yet established (religious-)anthropological term, this analysis denoted this disposition as interpersonal and social sensibility. Analyzing this disposition within an ethical moment served to demonstrate its relation to the selected cinematographic works and the overarching connections to the form of slapstick.

Bibliography

Bakhtin, Mikhail Mikhailovich. *Rabelais and His World*. Transl. Hélène Iswolsky. Bloomington: Indiana University Press, 1984.
Bar-Efrat, Shimon. *Das Zweite Buch Samuel: Ein narratologisch-philologischer Kommentar*. Transl. Johannes Klein. Stuttgart: Kohlhammer, 1996.
Baugh, Lloyd. *Jesus and Christ-Figures in Film*. Kansas City: Sheed & Ward, 1997.
Benjamin, Walter. "Das Kunstwerk im Zeitalter seiner technischen Reproduzierbarkeit (Erste Fassung)." *Gesammelte Schriften*, 1–2. Ed. Rolf Tiedemann and Hermann Schweppenhäuser. Frankfurt am Main: Suhrkamp, 1991. 435–690.
Bergson, Henri. *Laughter: An Essay on the Meaning of the Comic*. Transl. Cloudesley Brereton and Fred Rothwell. New York: Macmillan, 1914.
Bergson, Henri. *Le rire: Essai sur la signification du comique*. Paris: ÉditionsAlcan, 1924.
Biblia hebraica Stuttgartensia. Ed. Karl Elliger. Stuttgart: Deutsche Bibelgesellschaft 2013.
Borg, Marcus J., and John Dominic Crossan. *The Last Week: What the Gospels Really Teach About Jesus's Final Days in Jerusalem*. New York: Harper One, 2007.
Brockett, Oscar G., and Franklin J. Hildy. *History of the Theatre*. New York: Allyn and Bacon, 2003.
Burkert, Walter. *Antike Mysterien: Funktionen und Gehalt*. München: Beck, 2003.
Bohrmann, Thomas. "Einführung in die ethische Filmanalyse." *Angewandte Ethik und Film*. Eds. Thomas Bohrmann, Matthias Reichelt, and Werner Veith. Wiesbaden: Springer, 2018. 37–57.
Brockett, Oscar G., and Franklin J. Hildy. *History of the Theatre*. New York: Allyn and Bacon, 2003.
Brunn, Siglind. Christus als Opernheld im späten 20. Jahrhundert. Waldkirch: Edition Gorz, 2004.
Camille, Michael. "The Image and the Self: Unwriting Late Medieval Bodies." *Framing Medieval Bodies*. Eds. Sarah Kay and Miri Rubin. Manchester: Manchester University Press, 1998. 62–99.
Carroll, Robert P. "Is Humour Also Among the Prophets?" *On Humour and the Comic in the Hebrew Bible*. Eds. Yehuda T. Radday and Athalya Brenner. Sheffield: Almond Press, 1990. 169–189.
Chaplin, Charles. *My Autobiography*. London: Penguin Classics, 1964.
Chaplin, Charles, Jr. *My Father, Charlie Chaplin*. New York: Random House, 1960.
City Lights. Dir. Charles Chaplin. Narr. Charles Chaplin. United Artists, 1931.
Cox, Harvey. *The Feast of Fools: A Theological Essay on Festivity and Fantasy*. Cambridge: Harvard University Press, 1969.
Čapek, Karel. "Chaplin čili O realismu." *Sloupkový gambit*. Prague: Československý spisovatel, 1957. 227–229.
Dahlmanns, Claus. *Die Geschichte des modernen Subjekts: Michel Foucault und Norbert Elias im Vergleich*. Münster: Waxmann, 2008.
Dauven-van Knippenberg, Carla. "mit fröhlicher Berg: Über das Miteinander von Komik und Passion." *Fastnachtsspiele: Weltliches Schauspiel in literarischen und kulturellen Kontexten*. Ed. Klaus Ridder. Tübingen: Niemeyer, 2009. 345–360.
de Giere, Carol. *The Godspell Experience: Inside a Transformative Musical*. Bethel, CT: Scene 1 Publishing, 2014.
de Giere, Carol. *Defying Gravity: The Creative Career of Stephen Schwarz from "Gospell" to "Wicked"*. New York: Applause Theatre & Cinema Books, 2008.
de Giere, Carol. *Godspell Orphaned Songs Concert with Stephen Schwartz Remembered*. https://www.theschwartzscene.com/2018/12/05/orphaned-songs-concert-with-stephen-

schwartz-remembered/. The Schwartz Scene Newsletter, 5 December 2018 (accessed 19 September 2019).
Dingeldei, Dianen. *Das Bensheimer Passionsspiel: Studien zu einem italienisch-deutschen Kulturtransfer*. Münster: Waxmann, 2013.
Eming, Jutta. "Gewalt im Geistlichen Spiel: Das *Donaueschinger* und das *Frankfurter Passionsspiel*." *The German Quarterly* 78.1 (2005): 1–22.
Farnham, Willard. *The Shakespearean Grotesque: Its Genesis and Transformations*. Oxford: Clarendon Press, 1971.
Fietz, Lothar. "Möglichkeiten und Grenzen einer Semiotik des Lachens." *Semiotik, Rhetorik und Soziologie: Vergleichende Studien zum Funktionswandel des Lachens vom Mittelalter zur Gegenwart*. Ed. Lothar Fietz et al. Tübingen: Niemeyer, 1996. 7–20.
Fiske, John. *Understanding Popular Culture*. New York: Routledge, 1989.
Fleming Drane, Olive. "Clowning/Clown Ministry." *Encyclopedia of Christian Education*, 3. Eds. G. Th. Kurian and M. A. Lampor. Lanham: Rowman & Littlefield, 2015. 302–303.
Flusser, David. "A New Sensitivity in Judaism and the Christian Message." *Harvard Theological Review* 68.2 (1961): 107–127.
The General. Dir. Buster Keaton and Clyde Bruckman. Narr. Buster Keaton and Clyde Bruckman. Buster Keaton Productions and Joseph M. Schenck Productions, 1926.
Ghalian, Sonia. "Tramping it out: Charlie Chaplin and the Modern." *Rupkatha Journal on Interdisciplinary Studies in Humanities* 9.2 (2017): 186–194.
Gilhus, Ingvid Saelid. "Lachen/Gelächter." *Metzler Lexikon Religion, 2: Gegenwart – Alltag – Medien*. Eds. Christoph Auffarth et al. Stuttgart: Metzler, 1999. 308–311.
Godspell: A Musical Based on the Gospel According to Matthew. Dir. David Greene. Narr. David Greene and Michael Tebelak. Columbia Pictures, 1973.
Grace, Pamela. *The Religious Film: The Christianity and the Hagiopic*. Malden: Wiley-Blackwell, 2009.
Green. John Richard. *Theatre in Ancient Greek Society*. London: Routledge, 1996.
Gunning, Tom. "Chaplin and the body of modernity." *Early Popular Visual Culture*. 8.3 (2010): 237–245.
Gunning, Tom. "The Cinema of Attraction: Early Cinema, Its Spectator, and the Avant-Garde." *Wide Angle* 8.3–4 (1986): 63–70.
Gunning, Tom. "Crazy Machines in the Garden of Forking Paths: Mischief Gags and the Origins of American Film Comedy." *Classical Hollywood Comedy*. Eds. Kristine Brunovska Karnick and Henry Jenkins. New York: Routledge, 1995. 87–105.
Gunning, Tom. "Mechanisms of Laughter: The Devices of Slapstick." *Slapstick Comedy*. Eds. Rob King and Tom Paulus. New York: Routledge 2010.
Habermas, Jürgen. *The Future of Human Nature*. Cambridge: Polity, 2003.
Harris, Max. "Processional Theatre of Palm Sunday." *The Routledge Research Companion to Early Drama and Performance*. Ed. Pamela King. London: Routledge 2017. 316–331.
Harris, Max. *Sacred Folly: A New History of the Feast of Fools*. Ithaca: Cornell University Press, 2011.
Haskell, Francis. "The Sad Clown: Some Notes on a 19th Century Myth." *French 19th Century Painting and Literature: with Special Reference to the Relevance of Literary Subject Matter to French Painting*. Ed. Ulrich Finke. Manchester: Manchester University Press, 1972. 2–16.
Heers, Jacques. *Vom Mummenschanz zum Machttheater: Europäische Festkultur im Mittelalter*. Transl. Grete Osterwald. Frankfurt am Main: Fischer, 1986.
Hertzberg, Hans Wilhelm. *Die Samuelbücher*. Göttingen: Vandenhoeck & Ruprecht, 1986.

Hoche, Karl et al. *Die großen Clowns*. Königsstein: Taunus, 1982.
Hurley, N. P. "Charles Chaplin." *Religion in Film*. Eds. John R. May and Michael Bird. Knoxville: University of Tennessee Press, 1982, 157–162.
Kehrein, Roland. *Prosodie und Emotionen*. Tübingen: Max Niemeyer, 2012.
Keller, Hildegard Elisabeth. "Lachen und Lachresistenz: Noahs Söhne in der Genesisepik, der Biblia Pauperum und dem Donaueschinger Passionspiel." *Lachgemeinschaften: Kulturelle Inszenierungen und soziale Wirkungen von Gelächter im Mittelalter und in der Frühen Neuzeit*. Eds. Werner Röcke and Hans Rudolf Velten. Berlin: de Gruyter, 2005. 33–59.
Kenrick, John. *Musical Theatre: A History*. New York: Continuum, 2008.
Kierkegaard, Søren. "Enten – Eller. Et livs-fragment", 1. *Søren Kierkegaards samlede værker*. Eds. Anders Björn Drachmann et al. Kopenhagen: Reitzel, 1843.
Kierkegaard, Søren. *Kierkegaard's Writing*, III, Part I: *Either/Or*. Eds. and transl. Howard V. Hong and Edna H. Hong. Princeton: Princeton University Press, 1987.
Kindt, Tom. "Komik." *Komik: Ein interdisziplinäres Handbuch*. Ed. Uwe Wirth. Stuttgart: Metzler, 2017. 2–6.
Kathleen, Kuiper. Ed. *Poetry and Drama: Literary Terms and Concepts*. New York: Britannica Educational Publishing, 2010.
Kid. Dir. Charles Chaplin. Narr. Charles Chaplin. First National, 1921.
Král, Petr. *Groteska čili Morálka šlehačkového dortu*. Prague: Národní filmový archiv, 1998.
Kühnel, Jürgen. "Mediengeschichte des Theaters." *Handbuch der Mediengeschichte*. Ed. Helmut Schanze. Stuttgart: Kröner, 2001. 316–346.
Laird, Paul R. *The Musical Theater of Stephen Schwartz: From Godspell to Wicked and Beyond*. Lanham: Rowman & Littlefield, 2014.
Lampe, Peter. "Das korinthische Herrenmahl im Schnittpunkt hellenistisch-römischer Mahlpraxis und paulinischer Theologia Crucis (1Kor 11, 17–34)." *Zeitschrift für die neutestamentliche Wissenschaft* 82.3–4 (1991): 183–213.
Lindvall, Terry, and Andrew Quicke. *Celluloid Sermons: The Emergence of the Christian Film Industry, 1930–1986*. New York and London: New York University Press, 2011.
Lindvall, Terry. "Silent cinema and religion: An overview (1895–1930)." *The Routledge Companion to Religion and Film*. Ed. John Lyden. New York: Routledge, 2009: 13–31.
Lindvall, Terry et al. *Divine Film Comedies: Biblical Narratives, Film Sub-Genres, and the Comic Spirit*. New York: Routledge, 2016.
Lohse, Eduard, and Annette Merz. *Der historische Jesus: Ein Lehrbuch*. Göttingen: Vandenhoeck & Ruprecht, 2011.
Mangold, Roland, and Anne Bartsch. "Mediale und reale Emotionen – der feine Unterschied." *Emotionen in Literatur und Film*. Ed. Sandra Poppe. Würzburg: Königshausen & Neumann, 2012.
Mastičkář, rukopis muzejní. Ed. Martin Stluka. Prague: Ústav pro jazyk český AV ČR, 2018. http://vokabular.ujc.cas.cz/moduly/edicni/edice/79b5724d-6211-470a-9d0b-50c724a675f5/plny-text/s-aparatem/folio/1r. (Manuscript: Praha: Knihovna Národního muzea. Sign. 1 Ac 55, 3 Fol.; 1r–6v) (accessed 3 February 2018).
Modern Times. Dir. Charles Chaplin. Narr. Charles Chaplin. United Artist, 1936.
Molyneaux, Gerard. "Modern Times and the American culture of the 1930s." *Charlie Chaplin: His Reflection in Modern Times*. Ed. Adolphe Nysenholc. Berlin: de Gruyter 1991. 103–118.

Müller, Jan-Dirk. "Mittelalterliches Theater: Geistliches Spiel." *Theater im Aufbruch: Das europäische Theater der Frühen Neuzeit*. Eds. Roger Lüdeke and Virginia Richter. Tübingen: Niemeyer 2008, 19–30.
Neubauer, Aljoscha C., and Harald Freudenthaler. "Models of Emotional Intelligence." *Emotional Intelligence: An International Handbook*. Eds. Ralf Schulze and Richard D Roberts. Cambridge, MA and Göttingen: Hogrefe & Huber, 2005. 31–50.
Novum Testamentum Graece: Nestle-Aland 28th Edition. Stuttgart: Deutsche Bibelgesellschaft 2013.
Oppenheimer, Mark. *Welcome to the Church of 'Godspell'*. https://www.nytimes.com/2011/11/06/theater/broadway-revival-of-godspell.html. The New York Times, 4.11.2011 (accessed 12 October 2018).
Parable. Dir. Rolf Forsberg and Tom Rook. Narr. Rolf Forsberg. Council of Churches of the City of New York, 1964.
Plax, Julie-Anne. "Interpreting Watteau across the Centuries." *Perspectives on the Artist and the Culture of His Time*. Ed. Antoine Watteau. Newark: University of Delaware Press, 2006, 27–39.
Plessner, Helmuth. *Philosophische Anthropologie. Lachen und Weinen, Das Lächeln, Das Lächeln, Anthropologie der Sinne*. Frankfurt am Main: S. Fischer, 1970.
Ritter, Naomi. *Art as Spectacle: Images of the Entertainer Since Romanticism*. Columbia: University of Missouri Press, 1989.
Schnabel, Eckhard J. *Der erste Brief des Paulus an die Korinther: Historisch Theologische Auslegung*. Wuppertal: Brockhaus, 2006.
Scott, Andrew. *Comedy (The New Critical Idiom)*. New York: Routledge, 2015.
Stewart, Elizabeth-Anne. *Jesus the Holy Fool*. Franklin: Sheed & Ward, 1999.
Strauß, Barbara. "Komik im Zwiespalt: Komik als Konflikt- und Krisenphänomen." *Göttliche Komödien: Religiöse Dimensionen des Komischen im Kino*. Eds. Stephan Orth et al. Köln: KIM, 2001. 55–67.
Swain, Joseph P. *The Broadway Musical: A Critical and Musical Survey, revised and expanded*. Lanham: Scarecrow Press, 2002.
Szerb, Antal. *Geschichte der Weltliteratur*. Transl. András Horn. Basel: Schwabe, 2016.
Tavernier-Courbin, Jacqueline. "The social function of humor in Charles Chaplin's movies." *Charlie Chaplin: His Reflection in Modern Times*. Ed. Adolphe Nysenholc. Berlin: de Gruyter, 1991. 125–130.
Theißen, Gerd, and Merz, Annette. *Der historische Jesus: Ein Lehrbuch*. Göttingen: Vandenhoeck & Ruprecht, 2011.
Thomas, Alfred. *Anne's Bohemia: Czech Literature and Society, 1310–1420*. Minneapolis: University of Minnesota Press, 1998.
Thomas, Alfred. *Reading Women in Late Medieval Europe: Anne of Bohemia and Chaucer's Female*. New York: Palgrave Macmillan, 2010.
Veltruská (Veltrusky), Jarmila. *Posvátné a světské: Osm studií o starém českém divadle*. Prague: Divadelní ústav, 2006.
Walker, Greg. "Croxton, The Play of the Sacrament (1470–1530?)." *The Oxford Anthology of Tudor Drama*. Ed. Greg Walker. Oxford: Oxford University Press, 2014. 20–56.
Webb, Ruth. *Demons and Dancers: Performance in Late Antiquity*. Cambridge: Harvard University Press, 2008.
Whedbee, J. William. *The Bible and the Comic Vision*. Cambridge: Cambridge University Press, 1998.
Wickham, Glynne. *A History of the Theatre (Performing Arts)*. London: Phaidon Press, 1994.

Part VI: **Sticking to the Slap: The Contact Points of Slapstick**

Alena E. Lyons & Ervin Malakaj
Closing Remarks: Creating Openings

The diversity of perspectives and approaches introduced in this volume suggest that slapstick, as an object of study, has a wide terrain. The multiplicity of the interdisciplinary approaches gathered here has shown how slapstick is a theme, a concept, a stylistic device, an aesthetic experience, a pleasure, and a provocation that appears in the most diverse contexts. Wherever we encounter slapstick across media and across time, through interdisciplinary approaches we can activate new knowledge about the object in question. Depending what scholarly approach we undertake, slapstick can look differently in different contexts.

The aim of this volume was to conceptualize slapstick as an interdisciplinary analytical category that could usher in further scholarship on slapstick. Through models of novel methodological approaches that bring together insights from multiple fields of inquiry into dialogue with slapstick and through studies of slapstick in various socio-cultural contexts, we believe that this work will engender various new lines of inquiry about slapstick. The readings in this volume showcase the many lives that slapstick lives in film, literature, music, theatre, and photography. They demonstrate that these cultural products have also developed their own knowledge of slapstick as well as the means to articulate it. Thus, in the final chapter of this volume we would like to present a *transdisciplinary* approach to slapstick. By this we mean a collaborative approach, which for most of us probably differs significantly from the usual scholarly modes of expression. At the center of this approach is the attempt to tackle a research topic through the artistic process. To this end, Anne Brannys enters into a fictional dialogue with the late Dutch photo and video artist Bas Jan Ader (1942–1975) and thereby weaves a web of reflections on slapstick and the manifold encounters with it. In so doing, Brannys takes several themes and ideas from the contributions in this volume and reconnects, rearranges, and transfers them into an artistic as well as literary work.

Anne Brannys
Each One, Who Falls –[1]
A Conversation

Translated by Alena E. Lyons

[1] "Jeder, der fällt –" (Bachmann 1961, 8). Unless otherwise noted, all translations by Alena E. Lyons.

– You [in French: "tu"], and either you [in French: "vous"], will never know all the stories that I still could have told myself in looking at these pictures.[2]

AB: I have seen you fall a few times[3] before, in some cases even several times in a row.[4] Is it relevant for you that you can be watched?[5]

BA:

[2] " – Tu ne sauras jamais, vous non plus, toutes les histoires que j'ai pu encore me raconter en regardant ces images" (Derrida 1985, I).

[3] In the early 1970s, Dutch artist Bas Jan Ader (1942–1975) carried through a series of artistic actions in which he exposed his body to gravity and fell. He usually recorded those projects of "falling" on video so that the processes of these falls can be reconstructed up to today through this documentation.

[4]/[1] In most of the exhibition situations these videos[2] are presented as loops[18]. This means we see the artist in the situation of the set-up, preserving in it until the falling begins, only to see him afterwards – fully sound – again within the experimental set-up etc. This procedure conjures up the figure of the cunning Sisyphus. He is divinely punished for his hubris by pushing a heavy stone up a mountain under greatest torments, just for it to roll down again shortly before reaching the summit and forcing him to start all over again, with no prospect of either of both – the toils of the ascent, the cruel lightness of the descent – ending some day.

In his essay "Le Mythe de Sisyphe" ["The Myth of Sisyphus", 1942] Albert Camus (1913–1960) sketches the title figure as hero of the absurd, who develops acceptance within the profound rift between the longing for sense and the coinciding experience of senselessness in the world (see Camus 2000).

Maike Aden-Schraenen refers to Camus by describing Ader as an "'absurd artist,' who lives his rebellion, his freedom and his passion [. . .], who creates art to not perish in the absurdity of the world" (Aden-Schraenen 2013, 183).

4/2 A second figure comes to my mind: A child's toy of mine, a fool with a colorful face and a belly as round as a ball where its body ended. Whenever it was knocked over or pushed to the ground, it drew himself up again, laughing. This is the resilience we mean when we say in German somebody is a 'Stehaufmännchen' ['tumbler']. But if the constant rising equalizes the falling, what is the point of falling? Do not these two offset each other until the score is zero?[16]

I always felt a bit sorry for my tumbler because it never could lie down and rest. Nonetheless, I did not like it very much.[20]

5 As Maike Aden-Schraenen convincingly argues, the assumption of narcissistic introspection and the need for control of the image carried to the outside world, which characterizes other video works of the same generation, can be contradicted in Ader's case: "The temporal and spatial distance to the original self-staging not only has an objectifying and anonymizing function in relation to the introspection, but also in relation to the external perception. [. . .] The special features of 16mm film are another means of distance[20]. Not only its specific aesthetic in black and white, but also the rattling of the film apparatus when viewed, give the impression that there is a considerable distance between the original self-portrayals and the film images on the screen. A junction of person and image is made more difficult" (Aden-Schraenen 2013, 166).

AB: Your falls have evoked a lot of reactions later.[6] Although you yourself once said that you just fall because of gravity,[7] those, who watch you falling, do see more. How do you cope with such ascriptions[8] to you?

BA:

[6] The main reception of Ader's works only began several decades after his death. Since the 1990s until today there have been and still are numerous exhibitions of his works, which have received much attention, as well as numerous publications. Also, fellow artists dealt with his work in a variety of ways.[8/1, 25]

[7] "When I fell off the roof of my house, or into a canal, it was because gravity made itself master over me" (Ader, qtd. in Sharp 1971, 3).

[8/1] The principally sober experience of gravity[7], which according to the artist, is the primary concern in his "Falling" projects, is filled with a meaning that enhances this experience with aspects such as gloom and melancholy.

A self-endangerment which is not difficult to identify may encourage this interpretation: In his films, concerning the falling, Ader exposes himself to a certain risk of physical injury that cannot be disregarded, so that the banal, everyday experience of gravity in his studies can easily obtain the appearance of an unavoidable befalling, of inescapability and fatefulness[25].

Alexander Dumbadze sees this self-endangerment eventually resulting in an untimely death. And in this inevitability he founds his endeavor to investigate the person Ader and his artistic work as intertwined:

"His death – so sudden, so dramatic, without art historical precedent – necessitates talking about his life alongside his art. This is a historiographic operation that coincides with the particular conditions of Ader's art, which increasingly foregrounded his life and placed it in a dialectical relation with his practice.

To think historically about Ader's life and art is not to compose a biography or to suggest that artistic meanings rests in biography. Rather, it is to see these entities as equally open to interpretation, and to look to their coexistence to explain Ader's relevance today. In his mysterious passing and the unavoidable emphasis on his myth, anachronism and aura becomes one. It is here that Ader remains alive while his death is elsewhere" (Dumbadze 2015, 7).

But there is also a great wit in Ader's work, which has very clearly slapstick-like traits. Humor, lightness, and a certain mischief cannot be overlooked. It is (absolutely) necessary to widen and deepen the rather one-dimensional picture of the melancholic and dramatic hero[20].

In the context of Ader's studies of falling, Christopher Müller additionally refers to Charles Baudelaire's (1821–1867) concept of the comic: "Bas Jan Ader's whirl of movement, and plunge caused by the 'gravity' correspond to the 'absolute comical' in Baudelaire's sense. Ader's refusal to comment explicitly on the act of falling suggests an inevitability that corresponds to the unconsciousness of 'absolute comic' demanded by Baudelaire. Such a relationship between slapstick, Baudelaire's understanding of the absolute comic as well as the actual drastic qualities of the fall forms a peculiar field of tension: In that they must be evaluated as conceptual works on the one hand, but on the other hand differ from classical conceptual approaches through a staged, poetic moment, they can hardly be understood within current art categories" (Müller 2000, 60).

Maike Aden-Schraenen adds: "The laughter may remain oddly strange, but it takes the severity out of Ader's falls – without the protagonist being ridiculed or laughed at. Above all, however, the viewer experiences a certain amount of freedom, even in the broken laughter, in order to relativize for oneself the norming evaluations that taboo failure.

For those who can laugh have attained the diversity of the gaze" (Aden-Schraenen 2013, 87).

The quite one-dimensional concentration of the Ader reception around the turn of the millennium on the more dark, neo-romantic, and fatalistic aspects of his oeuvre probably bespeaks the needs of the recipients rather than sounding out the complexity and ambiguity of it.[16]

AB: In "Broken Fall (organic)" (1971) you hang on the branch[9] of a relatively tall tree[10] until your strength wanes[11], you let go and fall several meters deep into a small water ditch. Does your own yieldingness and fragility reflect your surrounding world[12]?

BA:

8/2 "We have to begin by getting through, and by means of, the *exscription* of our body: its being inscribed-outside, its being placed *outside the text* as the most proper movement of its text; the text *itself* being abandoned, left at its limit. Having no high or low, it's no longer a 'fall'; the body isn't cast out but completely at the limit, at an extreme, outward edge that nothing closes up. I would say: the ring of circumcision is broken, the only thing left is an in-finite line, the tracing of writing, which is itself exscribed, to be followed, infinitely broken, distributed among the multitudes of bodies, a line of separation imparted to all its sites – tangential points, touches, intersections, dislocations" (Nancy 2008, 11; emphasis in original. "L'*exscription* de notre corps, voilà par où il faut d'abord passer. Son inscription-dehors, sa mise *hors-texte* comme le plus *propre* mouvement de son texte: le texte *même* abandonné, laisse sur sa limite. Ce n'est plus une « chute », ça n'a plus ni haut, ni bas, le corps n'est pas déchu, mais tout en limite, en bord externe, extrême, et que rien ne referme. Je dirais: l'anneau des circoncisions est rompu, il n'y a plus qu'une ligne in-finie, le trait de l'écriture elle-même excrite, à suivre infiniment brisé, partagé à travers la multitude des corps, ligne de partage avec tous ses lieux: point de tangence, touches, intersections, dislocations" [Nancy 2000, 14; emphasis in original]).

9 This image evokes the phrase that someone is cutting the bough on which they sit, sabotaging oneself, so to speak. Other idioms that have grown out of physicality, such as the clown who is given the little finger but takes the whole hand, someone who stretches things, etc., can also be associated with and may refer to a basic condition of organic constructions, their vulnerability.

This is also echoed in the title of the work, which on the one side effortlessly integrates itself into the series of "Falling" projects, but on the other side opens up a new dimension.[12]

10 In this first shot, Ader's dangling figure recalls Billie Holiday's (1915–1959) hauntingly conjured, intense and disturbing image of the "Strange Fruit": "Southern trees bear a strange fruit, / blood on the leaves and blood at the root, / black body swinging in the Southern breeze, / strange fruit hanging from the poplar trees. / [...] Here is a fruit for the crows to pluck, / for the rain to gather, for the wind to suck, / for the sun to rot, for the tree to drop, / here is a strange and bitter crop" (Holiday 2017).

When Billie Holiday sang the song, which was connected like no other with the lynching of African Americans in the southern states of the USA, for the first time in 1939, Bas Jan Ader was not yet born.

11 One summer my father lifts me up into the mighty cherry tree of our garden so that I can climb and pick cherries in it. He climbs a high ladder, sets me down on a strong branch and disappears into the garden again. Never would I come up with the idea of my own of climbing on or in trees and mourn after my place in the shade of the tree where I was sitting peacefully before. I fear to fall down and for the sake of safety I do not move at all. The rimous, rough bark of the old tree is pressing painfully against my thighs. I guess the height I am at and notice it's too big to just let me fall. While I am silently waiting to be lifted back down, I hear my grandmother asking for me and I hear my father answering: "She climbs in the cherry tree. I haven't heard from her yet, seems like she doesn't want to come down at all."

12 The title "Broken Fall" bears the addendum: "(organic)." This could refer to the organic material of the tree, whose branch threatens to break under Ader's weight. "If one takes the tree as a typical Romantic motif, it could once again be a critical questioning of the Romantic idealization of nature as stabilizing instance of the human being. Bas Jan Ader would, as it were, explore the idea experimentally, with the result that even the natural-organic [. . .] stabilities that were believed to be solid [. . .] are no longer able to provide any (identificatory) support" (Aden-Schraenen 2013, 85).

But it is Ader himself who, after a while of holding and hanging, finally lets go of the branch so that he *breaks* and *falls* as an organic being. Thus, the reading might also be thinkable that hanging (in the balance) demands of us a strength that cannot be united with our humanity, so that we must fail because of it.

AB: Do you also think that when you turn the fall[13] upside down it is a flight[14]?

BA:

13 Striving for the truth and thoughts that carry weight: Martin Burckhardt describes the philosophical sickness for falling, in which the case/the fall [the German term "Fall" means both] turns into a pitfall [in German: "Falle"], because it assigns the gesture of lightness to unreasonableness and levity, and can no longer integrate it into itself as a necessary countermovement.

"Nevertheless, it seems to me that an unbiased reasoning about what *lightness* could be is almost impossible. For as much as one might be tempted to assign to art that lightness that is taboo in the discourse of balance, so much would one run the risk of placing the weight of the world on it. Rather, it seems sensible to me to assume here a secret, tense, thoroughly incestuous complicity. The light is the counterpart of the weighty, not because it is an opposition, but [. . .] because it is the twin of the *weighty* that reveals its secret in an act of indiscipline. [. . .] In a parodic, ironic way, they could illustrate the Platonic myth of sibling souls seeking each other – only that when they meet, they do not give the image of perfection, but of its division" (Burckhardt 2003, 54–55, emphasis in original).

14 Stories of people who build apparatuses that enable them to rise and take to the air like birds go way back to antiquity. These are characterized by a notion of release not only of the feet being released from the ground, but also of being released from a natural physical limitation. Attempts to fly can therefore by all means be considered as attempts to overcome the human condition.

Numerous artists thematize flying in their works: Starting with the winged gods of the ancient world, through the visionary flying machines of Leonardo Da Vinci (1452–1519), or studies on transcendence within postmodernism as with Yves Klein (1928–1962). The artistic work "Letatlin" (1932) by Wladmir Tatlin (1885–1953) appears particularly touching in this array. This flying apparatus looks convincingly functional and, at the same time, is constructed in such a comprehensible way that it reminds us of the lucidity of flying in our dreams. Tatlin himself has carried out flight attempts in "Letatlin" and failed. But instead of looking for other approaches and solutions, he leaves the work in this very state of suspension between flying high in human dreams and the reality of human limitation, which shimmers behind failure. So, in the end, we do fly when contemplating this work.

AB: The terms "to fall" [in German: "fallen"] and "to fly" [in German: "fliegen"] are ambiguous in German, and, when put together, form the compound "Fliegenfalle" ["fly trap"][15], which points in a completely different direction. Do you think one can fall for the falling or rather for the flying?[16]

BA:

15/1 "This is the day the flies fall awake midsentence and lie stunned on the window-sill shaking with speeches only it isn't speech it is trembling sections of puzzlement which break off suddenly as if the questioner had been shot" (Oswald 2016, 4).[8/2]

15/2 I clearly remember the flypaper my grandmother had hung up in her scullery, where she was preserving fruits and baking the whole summer long. A spiral-shaped, caramel brown ribbon full of black dots, which, always slightly moving, seemed to have no beginning and no end. To be on the safe side, I had tested several times whether small children too would stick to it when they touched it, but then I had trouble getting the glue off. Much later, at the sight of Constantin Brâncuși's (1876–1957) "Coloana fără sfârșit" ["The Endless Column," 1938] I would always sense the gentle scent of fresh jam and smile.

16 In his MFA thesis, Ader explicitly deals with the pair of opposites of "rise and fall" which, according to him, characterizes his artistic intentions. Contrary to later interpretations, it is thus not only gravity that interests him, but also its suspension.

AB: In your video work "I'm too sad to tell you" I see you crying boundlessly, for three minutes and thirty-four seconds[17] and then all over again.[18] I see your face, so massive and close, as if you could lean your head on my shoulder[19] at any moment, but you are further apart than in any other of your works.[20] Is this distance intended?[21]

BA:

For Maike Aden-Schraenen, therefore, the basic theme of his artistic work is already expressed here, in its very beginning: the "ambiguity at the core of the falling movement. In the sense of letting go, it also has a liberating character. Thus, all works that deal with the issue of falling are determined by the ecstatic moments of letting go as well as by the basic human situation of frailty and tragedy" (Aden-Schreanen 2013, 19).

The synthesis of "rise and fall" is what Ader himself describes as "implosion" (which is also the title of his graduate exhibition at the university, a vacuum, the void and the nothingness in which all opposites vanish.[26] "Almost automatically, the question arises as to the nature of nothingness: is this the tragic concept of the abysmal nothing, the so-called 'horror vacui'? Or is the vacuum a potential space of abeyance that promises the gain of new possibilities?" (Aden-Schraenen 2013, 19).

17 There are many statistics circulating on the subject of crying. 40 bathtubs full of tears are shed every year in Germany (Eichinger 2018, n.p.), preferably between 7 and 10 p.m. (Krönig 2015, n.p.). But a single person weeps only 70 liters in the course of their life (Herrmann 2010, n.p.).

Considering the strong emotional connotation of tears, the urge to identify, classify, and order appears to be somewhat odd. Maybe it is also used as a remedy for the helplessness by which we are seized when confronted with grief. There seems to be an empathic transferal within crying in the form of a twofold instability: I am unfathomably sad and I cry because I know no other way. And: I know no remedy for your sadness. So I secretly count your tears, what else shall I do[21, 27]?

18 Like most of Ader's video works, this one is also presented as loop, which as a stylistic device within time-based media in a sense suspends the linear course of time (including the lifetime of everything shown, so that a kind of perpetuity can be perceived within the repetition) (see Bronfen 2009).

At this point the crying, only paused by the fade-in of the title, adds up to an infinite loop of desolation. The viewers are thus almost forced to take a stance, an inner distance, to not fall[8/1, 17].

19/1 The monochrome video shows Ader's portrait, framing only his bust. The weeping face is partly covered by a ghostly cast shadow and temporarily by his own hands. The crying does not appear staged and seems to be of great intensity, it begins immediately after the title picture and ends just as abruptly before the replay repetition starts. There is no sound, so his crying is silent. Not at any point in the film is the reason for the sadness of the portrayed person even hinted at. Through the close-up, the framing and the persuasiveness of the performance, the artist appears close and vulnerable[12].

19/2 Since the dawn of writing, tears have been shed by heroes and heroines. Thus, in the eponymous epic from ancient Babylonian times, Gilgamesh weeps bitterly for the death of his beloved friend (and at the same time for his own mortality, which he thereby becomes aware of) (see Maul, 2014).

The idea of emotional expressiveness being related to gender is a fairly recent view. And yet, for the entire twentieth century, crying seemed to be linked to weakness and could not quite be integrated into the traditional social construction of masculinity (see Lutz, 2000). The crying Bas Jan Ader, who approaches us in a video from 1971, must have taken this prejudice into account and counters it with the strong image of complete dissolution, which addresses our being human and renders any gender issues obsolete in this discourse on mere humanity.

20 More than one irritating moment disturbs the empathic surrendering to the film: As such, the recording of crying for further use as an artistic work and the concomitant awareness of a presentation, of a display of one's own grief, admits a mise-en-scène that is convincingly denied by the actual footage.[19]

The body of works also includes several photographs, supposedly film stills. On closer inspection, the artist's facial expression in the stills appears ambivalent: it could show equally crying and laughing. The fact that similar muscle groups in the face are activated in both mimic expressions makes it difficult to ascribe them unambiguously if the expression appears detached from any context (see Spiekermann 2015, 262). Thus this work, like many others by the artist, balances on the borderline between the comic and the tragic – a tense ambiguity that in this case is transmitted even more directly to the viewer, because it appeals to their empathic ability ("[. . .] mourn with those who mourn," Romans 12:15).

21/22/1 I once knew a little girl who withdrew to the bathroom to cry, to look at herself in the mirror while doing so. I got angry every time I saw this, an unspecific, diffusely directed anger: at her, being one with her reflection? At myself or at the distance between us?

AB: For whom are you crying?[22]

BA:

22/2 Part of the video work was a postcard edition that Bas Jan Ader sent to friends, which had the video's title as text: "I'm too sad to tell you." On the one hand, he announced a sadness, whereupon sympathy, encouragement, solace, or help would have been expected from those close to him. On the other hand, however, the grief is described as so immense that it bears with it an unspeakableness, a surpassing of linguistic means. It is therefore not groundless[13], but unutterable and seemingly resistant against change[18]. It keeps the recipient as much as the close one in the limbo of empathy[22] and uselessness[8/1], it needs the other without letting this other become effective.

AB: Your last artistic work[23] "In Search of the Miraculous"[24] is implicitly also about grief, but not your own.[25] It is also about falling, perhaps even on a larger scale.[26] It is about the sign and about the sign that fails to appear.[27]

BA:

[23] In July 1975, Bas Jan Ader embarks on a sea voyage from Cape Cod, Massachusetts, to Falmouth in the United Kingdom as an artistic performance. He travels alone in a small sailboat, barely four meters in size, which he has named "Ocean Wave."

At the same time, a bulletin was published by the Art & Project gallery in Los Angeles announcing a cooperative exhibition of this work at the gallery and the Groninger Museum in the Netherlands, with a photograph of Ader leaving the harbor and the printed scores of a shanty ("A Life on the Ocean Wave"). Ader had scheduled about two months for the Atlantic crossing; three weeks after his departure, radio contact was lost, and nine months later the sailboat was found unmanned off the coast of Ireland. Since then, there has been no trace of Ader (see Aden-Schraenen 2013, 104–105).

[24] "Now, immortality, you are totally mine! You are streaming toward me with the radiance of a thousand suns through the blindfold on my eyes. Wings are growing on my shoulders, and my spirit is already soaring through the calm ethereal spheres. And like a ship which, borne away by winds, sees the cheerful harbor disappear, so all of life is sinking away from me in twilight. I can still perceive colors and shapes, but everything beneath me is lying in a mist" (Kleist 1978, n.p. "Nun, o Unsterblichkeit, bist du ganz mein! / Du strahlst mir durch die Binde meiner Augen, / Mit Glanz der tausendfachen Sonne zu! Es wachsen Flügel mir auf beiden Schultern, / Durch stille Ätherräume schwingt mein Geist; / Und wie ein Schiff, vom Hauch des Wind entführt, / Die muntre Hafenstadt versinken sieht, / So geht mir dämmernd alles Leben unter: / Jetzt ich Farben noch und Formen, / Und jetzt liegt Nebel alles unter mir" [Kleist 1961, 707].).

[25] The lines of the work's reception go in two directions: On the one hand, a faked disappearance is assumed (especially by colleagues and friends). Other opinions, on the other hand, assume a conscious act of

suicide, which may have already been foreshadowed in previous works⁸/¹.

Mary Sue Ader, the artist's wife, clearly contradicts both interpretations in a telephone interview on May 28, 1976. Countering suicidal intentions, she points, for one thing, to Ader's intensive preparations, research, and training prior to the voyage, for another thing, she points to his experience in sailing (Ader had completed a comparable cruise a few years earlier), and thus emphasizes his intention to actually arrive. When asked what really happened, she answers: "I think the boat was too small and not designed for that kind of a trip and it just couldn't take it. – So you think he's lost? – I'm convinced that he's lost. There's been a lot of speculation about him sailing off and taking a different identity and stuff like that . . . – Do you discount that? – Totally discount it" (Bear 1976, 24–27).[27]

26 Before the tenth century, there was a generally accepted conviction that sailors who ventured too far out into the oceans would fall off the edge of the flat earth into a never-ending void. Ader's disappearance makes him fall far, perhaps out of his own story[1].

27 One of the most sorrowful forms of floating is probably that of the one who waits for an answer at a place where answers once existed. As a zeitgeist phenomenon, the sudden "no-more-answering" bears the very appropriate name "ghosting" and increasingly occurs within volatile communication systems (see Warkentin 2019, n.p.), in which we all float (see Pschera 2013)[2].

Is the non-appearance the absolute form of –[28]

28 "Life indeed is so hard and sad, how can one hope to hold anyone with nothing but written words? To hold is what hands are for." (Kafka 1973, 51. "Es ist mir ein so schlimmes, schweres Leben, wie kann man auch einen Menschen mit bloßen geschriebenen Worten halten wollen, zum Halten sind die Hände da" [Kafka 1999, 247].).

Bibliography

Aden-Schraenen, Maike. *In Search of Bas Jan Ader*. Berlin: Logos, 2013.
Andriesse, Paul. *Bas Jan Ader: kunstenaar/artist*. Amsterdam: Openbaar Kunstbezit, 1988.
Auster, Paul. *Disappearances – Vom Verschwinden: Gedichte – Poems*. Transl. by Werner Schmitz. Berlin and Hamburg: Rowohlt, 2001.
Bachmann, Ingeborg. *Anrufung des Großen Bären*. Munich: R. Piper & Co. Verlag, 1961.
Bear, Liza and Sharp, Willoughby (Interviewers). "Bas Jan Ader. In Search of the Miraculous." *Avalanche* 13 (summer 1976): 24–27.
Bronfen, Elisabeth. "Vergänglichkeit im Blickfeld." *Julia Stoschek Collection: Number Two: Fragile*. Ed. by the Julia Stoschek Foundation e.V. Ostfildern: Hatje Cantz, 2009. 7–14.
Burckhardt, Martin. "Fallsucht: Über die abgründige Leichtigkeit der Philosophie." Leichtigkeit. Ed. Gabriele Brandstetter. *Figuraionen* 1 (2003): 45–57.
Camus, Albert. *Der Mythos des Sisyphos*. Reinbek: Rowohlt, 2000.
Derrida, Jacques. *Droit de regards*. Marie-Françoise Plissart. With a reading by Jacques Derrida. N.p.: Editions de Minuit, 1985. I-XXXVI.
Dumbadze, Alexander. *Bas Jan Ader: Death is Elsewhere*. Chicago: University of Chicago Press, 2015.
Eichinger, Anja Pia. "Heul' doch!" *Der Standard*. 23 June 2018. https://derstandard.at/2000082060754/Heul-doch (accessed May 12, 2019).
Herrmann, Sebastian. "Zehn Dinge über . . . das Weinen." *Süddeutsche Zeitung*. 26 June 2010. https://www.sueddeutsche.de/wissen/zehn-dinge-ueber-das-weinen-1.978940 (accessed 17 June 2019).
Holiday, Billie. "Strange Fruit" (Abel Meeropol), Wagram/Indigo, 2017.
Kafka, Franz. *Briefe 1900–1912. Kritische Ausgabe Vol. 1*. Ed. by Hans-Georg Koch. Frankfurt am Main: S. Fischer Verlag, 1999.
Kafka, Franz. *Letters to Felice*. Ed. Erich Heller and Jürgen Born. Transl. James Stern and Elisabeth Duckworth. New York: Schocken Books, 1973.
Kleist, Heinrich von. *Sämtliche Werke und Briefe*. Ed. Helmut Sembdner. Munich: Deutscher Taschenbuch Verlag, 1961. 629–710.
Kleist, Heinrich von. *Prince Friedrich of Homburg*. Transl. and with a critical introduction by Diana Stone Peters and Federick G. Peters. New York: New Directions Publishing, 1978.
Kröning, Anna. "Warum nur der Mensch das Weinen beherrscht." *Die Welt*. 29 November 2015. https://www.welt.de/gesundheit/psychologie/article149400598/Warum-nur-der-Mensch-das-Weinen-beherrscht.html (accessed 11 June 2019).
Lutz, Tom. *Tränen vergießen: Über die Kunst zu weinen*. Hamburg: Europa-Verlag, 2000.
Das Gilgamesch-Epos. Transl. and comments by Stefan S. Maul. Munich: C.H. Beck, 2014.
Müller, Christopher. Ed. *Bas Jan Ader. Implosion. Filme, Fotografien, Projektionen, Videos und Zeichnungen aus den Jahren 1967–1975*. Cologne: Verlag der Buchhandlung Walther König, 2000.
Nancy, Jean-Luc. *Corpus*. Paris: Éditions Métailié, 2000.
Nancy, Jean-Luc. *Corpus*. Transl. by Richard A. Rand. New York: Fordham University Press, 2008.
Oswald, Alice. *Falling Awake*. London: Jonathan Cape, 2016.
Pschera, Alexander. *Vom Schweben*. Berlin: Matthes und Seitz, 2013.

Simmen, Jeannot. *Schwerelos: Der Traum vom Fliegen in der Kunst der Moderne*. Stuttgart: Edition Cantz, 1991.
Spiekermann, Geraldine. "Auf der Spur der Tränen: Darstellungen des Weinens zwischen Kunst und Wissenschaft." *"So muß ich weinen bitterlich": Zur Kulturgeschichte der Tränen*. Ed. Renate Möhrmann. Stuttgart: Alfred Kröner Verlag, 2015. 233–263.
Warkentin, Natalia. "Wenn der Andere zum Geist wird." *Frankfurter Allgemeine Zeitung*. 19 June 2019. https://www.faz.net/aktuell/stil/leibseele/ich-du-er-sie-es/ghosting-wenn-der-andere-wie-eingeist-verschwindet-16236471.html (accessed 17 June 2019).

Contributors

Courtney J. Andree holds a doctorate in English Literature and Film and Media Studies from Washington University in St. Louis. Her recent work has appeared in *Film History*, *Modern Fiction Studies,* and the *Routledge Handbook of Disability and Sexuality.*

Paul Michael Babiak is a Performance and Cinema Studies scholar specializing in comedy and humor, with a concentration on the history of comedic performance technique. Babiak teaches Film Comedy at Wilfred Laurier University.

Anne Brannys studied fine arts at the Bauhaus University Weimar and philosophy at the Friedrich Schiller University Jena, and received her Ph.D. in fine arts from the Bauhaus University Weimar with the thesis *Eine Enzyklopädie des Zarten* (2017). She has received several awards for her work at the intersection of art and science.

Peter Edwards is Associate Professor in the Department of Musicology at the University of Oslo, and is also composer and musician. In his research he is interested in topics that intersect aesthetics, music analysis, cultural studies, music history, and critical musicology. He is the author of *György Ligeti's Le Grand Macabre: Postmodernism, Musico-Dramatic Form and the Grotesque* (2016).

Caroline Frank is Lecturer of Modern German Literature/Media-Studies at the University of Kassel. Frank's research interests include mental healing in literature and film, quality-TV series, and narratology. Frank is the author of *Raum und Erzählen. Narratologisches Analysemodell und Uwe Tellkamps 'Der Turm'* (2017).

Sebastian Hauck is a theater scholar and Romance philologist who lives in Leipzig. The subject of his master thesis was Gian Lorenzo Bernini and his theater projects. He completed his PhD in 2019 at the University of Leipzig with a thesis entitled *Die Harmonie der Sphären und der Wahnsinn der Isabella. Florentiner Intermedien und Commedia all'improvviso.* He taught at the universities of Leipzig, Bern, Vienna, and Rome. Research Areas: Theater in early modern Italy and France, in Baroque Rome, and *Commedia all'improvviso*.

Maggie Hennefeld is Associate Professor of Cultural Studies & Comparative Literature at the University of Minnesota. She is the author of *Specters of Slapstick and Silent Film Comediennes* (2018), co-editor of the journal *Cultural Critique*, and co-editor of two volumes: *Unwatchable* (2019) and *Abjection Incorporated* (2020).

Jiří Hoblík is lecturer at the Department of Political Science and Philosophy and Humanities of Jan Evangelista Purkyně University in Ústí nad Labem. He is also researcher at the Institute of Philosophy of the Czech Academy of Sciences in Prague. His teaching fields are the history of religious thought, the theory of religion, the aesthetics of religion, and the question of the state and religion. In his research he focusses on early Jewish thought, early Christian literature, and the links between Judaism and early Christianity.

Irina Hron currently holds a position as Lise Meitner Senior Postdoctoral Fellow at the University of Vienna, and she is the Anna Ahrenberg Postdoctoral Fellow at the University of Gothenburg. In 2014, she completed a Ph.D. in Comparative Literature from the LMU Munich and in 2020 received a *venia legendi* from Stockholm University.

Alexander Kling is a research assistant in the department of German and Comparative Literature and Culture at the University Bonn. His work focuses on thing theory and literature, humor and comicality, ecocriticsm and animal studies. His current research project is entitled "Aus dem Rahmen fallen. Zur Literaturgeschichte der Dingkomik (Romantik – Realismus – Moderne)."

Alena E. Lyons is a Ph.D. student in Comparative Literature at Eberhard Karl University of Tübingen, working on a dissertation titled "The Democratization of Political Calculation." She received a Postgraduate Research Grant of Baden-Württemberg and taught at the universities of Tübingen and Hamburg. Her research centers on cultural concepts of the political, the interplay of literature and knowledge, and vulnerability.

Ervin Malakaj is Assistant Professor of German Studies at the University of British Columbia. His research focuses on media studies, queer studies, and critical university studies. He has co-edited the volumes *Market Strategies and German Literature in the Long Nineteenth Century* (2020) and *Diversity and Decolonization in German Studies* (2020).

Ignacio M. Sánchez Prado Ignacio M. Sánchez Prado is Jarvis Thurston and Mona van Duyn Professor in the Humanities at Washington University in St. Louis. His work centers on aesthetics, ideology, and institutions in Mexican literature, cinema, and popular culture.

Claudia Sassen holds a doctorate in computational linguistics. She is a scientific assistant at Technische Universität Dortmund, where she teaches academic writing and researches humor and seriality in advertising. Sassen works as a cartoonist and is the author of *Larry Semon – Daredevil Comedian of the Silent Screen* (2015).

Stefan Schroeder teaches theater, theater practice and creative writing at Technische Universität Dortmund. After studying theater as well as German and English literature at Ruhr University Bochum, he worked as a dramaturg at the municipal theater of Dortmund for nine years. He has published 50 theater plays and works as an author, director, and dramaturg for different theaters.

Carolin Struwe-Rohr is a Research Assistant at LMU Munich in German medieval studies and Principal Investigator of the project "Diabolic Vigilance" (DFG CRC 1369). Her research interests include relations between literature and knowledge, poetology, the short epic, and the courtly epic.

Addie Tsai is a queer, nonbinary writer, artist, and scholar of color. She teaches Creative Writing, Dance, Humanities, and Literature at Houston Community College. The author of the queer Asian young adult novel *Dear Twin*, Tsai is a staff writer at *Spectrum South*, Associate Editor at *Raising Mothers*, and Assistant Fiction Editor at *Anomaly*. Her scholarly work has been published or is forthcoming in *The International Journal of Screendance* and *The Bloomsbury Handbook of Dance and Philosophy*.

Valerie Weinstein is Professor of Women's, Gender, and Sexuality Studies and Niehoff Professor in Film and Media Studies at the University of Cincinnati. Recent publications include *Antisemitism in Film Comedy in Nazi Germany* (2019) and *Rethinking Jewishness in Weimar Cinema* (2021).

Index

Ader, Bas Jan 389, 391–394, 396–404
Adorno, Theodor W. 276
Advertisement 6, 25, 29, 215–221, 223, 225, 227, 229–233, 235–239, 215–239, 339
Agfa 215–216, 218–239, 215–239
Amateur 25, 125, 145, 215, 233, 235–238, 316, 325
Aristophanes 39–40, 167
Aristotle 109, 210

Bakhtin, Mikhail 280, 370–371, 377–378
Bathos 276, 278–279, 289
Bergson, Henri 22, 38–39, 55, 73, 75, 136, 166, 169, 209, 272, 278, 280–281, 283, 321–323, 343–344, 374, 378
Beyoncé 50
Biancolelli, Domenico (Arlequin) 80–81, 87–96
Body 6, 16, 18, 20, 22–23, 26, 31, 54–67, 73, 75–77, 79, 93–94, 101, 105, 107, 109–110, 114, 117, 126–128, 130, 136, 140, 147–148, 150–157, 162, 165, 168, 171, 176–178, 180, 194, 201, 234, 245–247, 249, 254, 258–259, 269–274, 276, 280–282, 296, 298–302, 304, 306, 311–312, 315–316, 318, 324–325, 327–328, 340–343, 345–346, 360, 365, 368–371, 380, 391–392, 395–396, 401
Body genres 110, 318
Borge, Victor 44–46, 51

Catalogue language 218, 227, 229
Causality 54–55, 142, 161–162
Chaos 163, 215, 222, 228, 233, 235, 237, 336
Chaplin, Charlie 11, 17–18, 21, 23, 32–33, 53, 73, 75, 81, 87, 90, 97, 101, 149, 162, 202, 251–252, 270, 280, 295, 312–313, 318, 324, 367, 372–374, 377–379, 381
Clayton, Alex 54–55, 58–59, 67, 245, 295, 311
Coincidence 53–54, 62, 65, 166, 174–175, 196, 254–256, 263–264, 273
Colonial dynamic 341

Comedy 1–4, 6, 12–13, 15–28, 30–33, 37, 39–48, 50–51, 54–55, 73, 75–76, 82, 84, 90, 93, 96, 101–102, 104, 106, 108–110, 114–115, 121, 123–125, 128, 131, 136, 147, 149, 161–162, 165, 167–170, 172–173, 181–182, 188–189, 191, 194, 198–203, 208, 210, 215–216, 223–224, 245–247, 249–265, 269–274, 276, 278–281, 283, 293–297, 301, 306, 311–312, 315–328, 347, 353–356, 358–365, 367, 371–372, 374, 379
Comic routine 80–82, 89
Comic theory 165, 167–172, 174, 181–182
Comicality 167, 169, 172
Commedia all'improvviso 76, 79–81, 89–90, 96
Commedia dell´arte 1, 5, 12, 23, 40, 42, 53, 148, 153, 167–169, 199, 201, 249, 269–270, 280, 287, 324, 353
Constraint 188, 190, 193–194, 198–200, 202, 211, 252, 256, 295, 300, 318, 325
Corporeality 55, 58–59, 66, 155–156, 246, 257, 259, 261, 270, 274, 279–281, 303
Couret, Nilo 353–354
Cross dressing 333, 347

Dale, Alan 60, 62–63, 121, 131–132, 147, 167, 245, 253, 323
Deleuze, Gilles 269–271, 274–275, 277–278, 283–287
Derbez, Eugenio 313–314, 351–365
– *Al Derecho y al Derbez* 355, 358
– *Derbez en Cuando* 359–360
– *How to be a Latin Lover* 351
– *Instructions not Included* 364–365
– *Overboard* 351, 353, 359, 365
– *XHDrbz* 359–361, 364
Disability 2, 4–5, 76, 101, 103, 105, 108–112, 115–117
Disappearance 19, 402–403
Drag king 77, 139–140, 143–149, 151, 153–155
Dürrenmatt, Friedrich 249, 251, 262–263, 265
– *Die Physiker* 249, 251, 262–263

412 — Index

Empathy 108–110, 117, 139, 232, 279, 379, 381, 401
Exploding housemaid genre 317

Falling 2, 16–17, 63, 66, 53–67, 75, 127, 176, 180, 264, 284, 329, 337, 346, 351, 391–395, 397–399, 402
Feminism 41, 315, 319, 327–329
Flapper films 315, 326
Folegatti, Luiza 76–77, 139–157
Formby, George 42–44, 51
Forsberg, Rolf 374
Freud, Sigmund 38, 251, 270, 271, 283, 321

Gag 3–6, 11, 15, 19, 21, 25, 32, 73, 75–76, 82–83, 89, 102, 116–117, 131, 147, 161–163, 187–190, 198, 201–203, 205, 209–210, 217–218, 220, 225, 264, 276–279, 283, 289, 296–297, 299, 311–314, 323, 326, 333–334, 347, 357, 360, 364, 371
Gaze 77, 87, 139–140, 145, 155–156, 230, 288, 305, 339, 342, 394
Greene, David 374–376, 367, 378
– Godspell 367, 374–381
Grotesquerie 24, 33

Halberstam, Jack 145–146, 148, 151, 153, 327, 334–335, 338
Hansen, Miriam 19, 245, 259, 320
Hauptmann, Gerhart 249, 260, 262, 265
– Die Ratten (The Rats) 249, 260–262
Hegemonic masculinity 121–122, 124–126, 128
Hildesheimer, Wolfgang 247, 269, 272–281, 284–287
Histrionic (style) 19, 32, 338, 345
Hoffmann, E.T.A. 334
Hokum stuff 25
Horse-play 17

Illogical legibility 334, 347
Ironic distance 38–39, 42–43, 48, 51

Jesus Christ 66, 262, 368–370, 373–379, 381

Kagel, Mauricio 46–47, 50–51
Keaton, Buster 1–2, 11, 17, 33, 53, 107, 188, 231, 275, 311–312, 318, 328, 372
Keystone 31–32, 246, 323–325
Kinging 77, 139, 143–149, 152–157
Kleist, Heinrich von 162, 166–167, 174–179, 181–182, 249, 253, 256–259, 402
– Amphitryon 167, 249–251, 253, 256–259, 261–262, 264
Knockabout 25–26, 32, 107, 315, 323–324
Krazy Kat 187, 191–193, 203

Lazzo/lazzi 17, 79, 87, 89, 91, 94–96
Lenz, Reinhold 249, 251, 253–256, 259
– Der Hofmeister (The Tutor) 249, 251, 253, 255–256, 259, 261–262, 264
Lessing, Gotthold Ephraim 250–251
– Hamurgische Dramaturgie (Hamburg Dramaturgy) 251
Ligeti, György 47–49
Linder, Max 81, 86–87, 97
Lloyd, Harold 20, 33, 73, 76, 87, 101–107, 109–117, 275, 318
– Welcome Danger 116
Logic 5–6, 21, 38, 46, 54, 56–57, 61, 65, 67, 154, 169, 193, 210, 222, 269–271, 273, 275, 283–286, 312, 333–334
Loriot 2, 163, 215–225, 229–231, 233–239
Lubitsch, Ernst 247, 293–304, 306, 313, 333–336, 340, 342, 347
– Als ich tot war (When I was dead) 300
– Die Bergkatze (The Mountain Cat) 295, 333, 340–341, 347–348
– Der Blusenkönig (The Blouse King) 293–294, 294, 302, 304
– Die Firma heiratet (The Firm Marries) 301
– Die Puppe (The Doll) 295, 333–336, 338–340, 344, 347–348
– Der Stolz der Firma (The Pride of the Firm) 293–294, 305

– *Meyer aus Berlin* (Meyer from Berlin) 300, 333
– *Schuhpalast Pinkus* (Shoe Palace Pinkus) 300, 333

Mask/Maschera 5, 40, 76, 79–81, 90, 93–96, 101, 103, 110, 111, 116
– unmask 146, 153, 335
Masquerade 77, 111, 147, 297, 341, 345
Mastičkář (*Ointment Merchant*) 370–371
Mechanism 63–65, 67, 116, 142, 147, 153, 313, 334, 340, 356
Mexico 351, 353–358, 362–365
Mimesis 198–199, 251
Mockumentary 121, 129
Moltiplicità (di personaggi) 90, 92–93, 95–96
Mozart, Wolfgang Amadeus 37, 40–42, 51
MTV 122–123, 135, 360
Music video 50, 122–123, 135

Narrative mode 27, 54, 181
Negri, Pola 295, 340
Nonperformativity 144, 147

Order 19–20, 28, 65, 67, 83, 144, 162–163, 189, 203, 215–225, 232–233, 235, 238–239, 286, 297, 333–341, 346, 399
Orla, Ressel 293–294, 296–297, 301–306

Pantelion 351, 353, 362–363, 365
Parody 16, 18, 37, 39, 41, 46–48, 50–51, 121, 123–125, 127–129, 132, 145, 269, 297, 352, 357, 360, 369, 371, 376–377
Pascoe, C.J. 132
Pattern 14, 38, 48, 61, 79, 145, 156, 190, 193–194, 196, 198, 216, 219, 225, 277, 284, 321, 338, 347
Phenomenology 333–334, 347
Photography 4–5, 19, 77, 101, 139–140, 145, 149, 155, 198, 225, 231, 235–236, 321, 326, 389
Physical disability 116
Physicality 6, 38, 54–55, 62, 76, 122, 154, 247, 273–274, 282, 287, 297, 326, 395

Porter, Edwin S. 315, 320
Portrait 76, 139–140, 142–144, 149, 151–153, 155, 282, 400

Queer failure 333, 338, 347

Rationalization 18, 21–22, 32
Roughhouse 17, 28, 30–31, 189

Schütze, Stephan 162, 165, 170–174, 178, 181–182
Schwarz, Camillo 81, 84–86, 91, 95–97
Schwarz, Carl 81, 84–86, 91, 95–97
Semon, Larry 33, 163, 187–191, 193–211, 236
– *Hindoos and Hazards* 189, 194–196, 198–200, 205, 208, 210
Sennett, Mack 15–16, 18–19, 22–23, 26, 31–33, 323, 353, 360
Sensibility (interpersonal and social) 367–369, 371, 373–374, 378, 380–381
Seriality 6, 163, 187–188, 193–198, 202–203, 205, 208–211, 215–216, 225, 230, 269, 274, 283–284
Series 6, 27–28, 30, 50, 53, 76, 106, 127, 139–140, 143, 149, 187–189, 191, 194, 203, 218–221, 224–225, 232–233, 237, 256, 263, 271–272, 275, 278, 283–285, 287, 300, 324–326, 328, 343, 355, 391, 395
Shakespeare reception 249–250
Showing 6, 64, 165, 168, 174, 176, 178, 180–181
Solidarity 139, 370, 379

Tebelak, John-Michael 375
Televisa 353–365
Telling 6, 165, 168, 174, 176, 178–181
Text and image 239
The Lonely Island 76, 121–136
The Woman's Home Companion 315
Thing theory 165
Tragicomedy 246, 249–253, 256, 260, 264–265

Trahair, Lisa 54, 131, 139, 161, 270–271, 277–279, 283, 289
Trauma 23, 114, 116–117, 194, 259, 321, 326

Variation 23, 26, 32, 105, 116–117, 140, 142, 154, 188, 193, 196, 198, 202–203, 209–211, 215–216, 219–220, 231, 238, 283–284, 378, 381
Verisimilar (style) 19–21, 32–33
Violence 1, 6, 16, 20–21, 26, 31–33, 39, 46, 48–49, 54, 56, 64, 107–108, 145–146, 152–153, 167, 169, 180, 245, 259, 293, 296–299, 306, 317, 319, 321–324, 326, 339
Vulnerability 26, 77, 109, 128, 139, 147–148, 156, 246, 311, 320, 323–325, 395, 400

Wardrobe malfunction 121, 129–135
Williams, Linda 318
Working-class women 20, 317, 324, 352, 354

Zibaldone 82, 89

www.ingramcontent.com/pod-product-compliance
Lightning Source LLC
Chambersburg PA
CBHW061925220426
43662CB00012B/1812